ROTISSERIE® LEAGUE BASEBALL

ROTISSERIE® LEAGUE BASEBALL

1997 Edition

Edited by
Glen Waggoner

The Rotisserie League
Lee Eisenberg • Rob Fleder • Peter Gethers
Daniel Okrent • Michael Pollet • Cary Schneider
Robert Sklar • Cork Smith • Harry Stein
Glen Waggoner • Steve Wulf

Little, Brown and Company
Boston   New York   Toronto   London

FIRST EDITION

ISBN 0-316-91749-4
International Standard Serial Number 1058-3319

10 9 8 7 6 5 4 3 2 1

HAD

Published simultaneously in Canada by
Little, Brown & Company (Canada) Limited

PRINTED IN THE UNITED STATES OF AMERICA

Contents

ROTISSERIE®
LEAGUE
BASEBALL

Introduction

Three Strikes, You're Out
by Daniel Okrent

My people: It is with hanging head and heavy heart that I address you today. In the years since you first lined up behind my leadership, we have been through a great deal together. We bowed down before Eddie Buddy Joe King Solomon. We envied David Green, wept over Vida Blue, wondered why Jerry White was black and Bud Black was white. We've seen Speyer and we've seen Raines. Oh we happy few, we band of nerds! We've incensed our wives, ignored our children, bored colleagues half to death. And we did it, always, together.

Seventeen years ago this off-season, I invented Rotisserie League Baseball—and now, as I approach the August 23rd or 24th of my years, I leave Rotisserie behind me. Yes, you may have heard about it this past season, read about it in certain major newspapers, discerned it from the pervasive agony you could detect in Bob Costas's eyes. Maybe you, like Frank Torre, tried to rip your heart out when the news came: Daniel Okrent, Beloved Founder and Former Commissioner for Life, was hanging up his Rotissicleats. Why? Well, you might as easily ask Garibaldi why he led that charge up the hill at Gettysburg.

Oh, how I remember how it all began! You probably have bought into the story perpetuated by my apostles, about how we met in a dive on East 52nd Street in Manhattan called La Rôtisserie Française; how we etched the first rules into a slab of granite with the point of Lee Eisenberg's nose; how Glen Waggoner, desperate to belong, agreed to let us have our run of the Columbia University Xerox machines if only we would let him wash our linens and iron our shirts; how Michael Pollet hired someone to take his bar exam for him and, having succeeded at that, paid the kid to go on vacation with his wife, too; how Bruce McCall seduced Valerie Salembier into the first of their many epochal trades—I believe it was Sam Mejias for Harry Spilman—by offering her "a piece of my Canadian bacon." Those were great times—the Rotisserie League in its infancy, a squalling, brawling infant ready to flex its muscles and take on the world.

How long ago was it? Well, let me put it this way: the youngest player in the National League that first Rotisseseason was Wally Backman. Willie

McCovey, who was born the same season that FDR tried to pack the Supreme Court, for God's sake, was the NL's oldest. The Cubs actually had an infielder named Mike Tyson, and Ken Griffey, *Sr.*, hadn't yet turned 30. In fact, of all the players on National League 40-man rosters that season, only one—Tim Raines—was still playing regularly in 1996. The rest—well, listen to some names: Dan Driessen. Ellis Valentine. Jim Rooker. Kurt Bevacqua. Bill North. Remember Dan Morogiello and Herman Segelke? Well, neither do I.

But I'll never forget that first draft, when Rob Fleder of the Mice put together the fabled $100 outfield of Bobby Bonds, Dave Kingman, and Ron LeFlore. It was the season that "Sudden Pete" Gethers (so named because of certain, um, amatory tendencies) hooked up with Glen "Please Call Me Iron Horse" Waggoner to forge the first pennant, and it was the season that Bob Sklar's girlfriend left him (no surprise, that). Records indicate that some guy named Tom Guinzburg was also part of the league that first year, but the only thing that anyone remembers about him is the Urological Duo he had in his bullpen, Kim Seaman and John Urrea.

After that, the seasons flip by like tires in mud: Steve Wulf joins up, wins the pennant in his first try, and disappears from contention for the next decade and a half; Harry Stein and his trusty aide Cary Schneider come soon after, packing some of the most extraordinary gastrointestinal disorders the world has ever known; and, each season, I devotedly encouraged my confreres by conspiring to keep the Okrent Fenokee powerhouse out of first place, just so others might have some fun.

It all happened so fast: one moment we were a buncha crazy, mixed-up kids with stars in our eyes, and then—presto!—we were washed-up hacks who never did figure out a way to make money off the thing. I remember one spring training in St. Pete, when I was approached by a pair of twin gynecologists from French Lick, Indiana, who wanted to thank me "for giving us this wonderful game and not wanting to make any money out of it." Boy, to think people thought we didn't make money out of my baby *on purpose!* If we had known *how* to make money off this thing, would I be wasting my time on this beach in Mustique, dictating a fistful of cheap jokes to my Franco-Polynesian assistant?

Still, in taking my leave of Rotisserie, emotions overwhelm me. To think—never again will I sit in a toilet stall only to have my reverie broken by some dork standing on tiptoes in the crapper next door, leaning into my airspace and telling me, in horrifying, mind-numbing detail, why he didn't trade Dennis Bleeping Lamp for Rowland Office! Never will I try to pass myself off as a responsible figure in the business community, only to have a hugely important client associate my name with a game suited for obsessive-compulsive sociopaths with badly running noses and extreme overbites! That woman from Owings Mill, Maryland, the one who blamed me back in '85 (true story) for destroying her marriage? Well, from this day forward I devote my life to looking for her, determined to make things right, determined to sweep her off her feet and take her to some glorious place beyond the reach of StatPhone, where she and I can drink of the romance in each other's eyes as the sun sets over Love Canal.

And yet, and yet. There is a time to sow and a time to reap, a time to be born and a time to die, a time to ruminate and a time realize that I now have enough to fill the space they've set aside for an Introduction. And so (do) I leave you, with these words:

Keep the wind at your back, an ear to the ground, an eye to the horizon, and an appointment with your chiropractor. Someday we will meet again, and we will smile in quiet acknowledgment of shared memories. Just don't ask me anything, *anything*, about Dennis Bleeping Lamp.

1

The Inner Game

Play Ball!

Call it the Year of the Dinger.

Last season 4,962 home runs sailed out of major league parks, 504 more than the previous mark, set in 1987. Was it the ball? Smaller parks? Bigger hitters? Expansion pitching? Or all of the above?

Doesn't matter.

What does matter is whether it was an aberration—a 1987 for the 1990s—or the beginning of a whole new ballgame.

The 1927 Yankees of Babe Ruth and Lou Gehrig, officially dubbed by hidebound baseball traditionalists as the Greatest Team in Baseball History, hit 158 home runs in the regular season to lead the American League—exactly *102* more homers than the runner-up Philadelphia Athletics. Last season's World Champion Yankees hit 162 round-trippers, but that was the third *fewest* total in the American League.

The single-season record for home runs by one team was 240, set by the Mantle-Maris 1961 New York Yankees. Last season that mark was surpassed by three teams: the Orioles (257), the Mariners (245), and the Athletics (243).

Seven other teams also set franchise records for home runs: Colorado (221), Texas (221), Cleveland (218), Chicago White Sox (195), California (192), Florida (150), and Montreal (148).

Three sluggers—Mark McGwire, Juan Gonzalez, and Ken Griffey—each missed at least 20 games because of injury, yet each managed to set career highs in long balls. How much damage would they have done had they played a full season?

Player	Actual	Projected
McGwire	52	65
Griffey	49	57
Gonzalez	47	57

Remember when Cal Ripken was the only power-hitting shortstop in baseball? Five shortstops went out of the yard at least 24 times in 1996: Alex Rodriguez (36), Barry Larkin (33), Ripken (26), Kevin Elster (24), and Jose Valentin (24).

Two players had 50 or more home runs. That had been done only three times before in baseball history: 1961, 1958, and 1937. Sixteen players had 40-plus homers, twice as many as the previous record (eight in 1961). Forty players swatted 30 or more taters, a dozen more than the twenty-eight who did it in 1987

Care to try to explain Brady Anderson? The guy hits 72 in the first eight years of his career, with a previous high of 21 in 1986, and suddenly he belts 50. *Fifty!* Half that number and he's Rotisserie gold—he's spent most of his career batting leadoff, after all—but 50?

Then there's Kevin Elster. Yeah, sure, you had him back in 1988–91 when he was a Met, and you knew he had some pop then. How much did he go for in your league? Tell us it was more than a buck and we're insisting on a polygraph test. Chances are, Kevin and his 24 round-trippers went undrafted.

Meanwhile, over in the National League, Todd Hundley did something that Roy Campanella, Johnny Bench, and Yogi Berra never did: he hit more than 40 home runs—41, to be exact. Hundley, whose previous career high was 16, had downtowned a grand total of 50 in his six-year career coming into the Year of the Dinger.

How did all this affect Rotisserie baseball? We'll give you just one example. In our own, original Rotisserie League, the team that won—modesty prevents us from mentioning its name, but you can find out for yourself on page 256—bought the three following players at the Auction Draft: Eric Davis ($1), Henry Rodriguez ($1), and Benito Santiago ($3). A couple of fourth/fifth outfielder types and a much-traveled catcher whose best days were clearly behind him. The number of dingers produced by that trio? Ninety-two. 'Nuff said.

Predictably enough, given this unprecedented power explosion, we have decided to devote this chapter—the place where certified deep thinkers traditionally weigh in on the heavy Rotisserie subjects of the moment—to the obvious topic on everybody's mind.

Pitching.

That's right, pitching. Hey, if this home run onslaught continues, the only Rotisserie survivors will be the guys who figure out pitching. Drafting a bunch of guys who can hit 30 and knock in 90 is a snap. Finding a few arms with ERAs lower than the unemployment rate is the tough part.

Mark Batterman and **Ken Kuta** are veteran dabblers in Rotisserie metaphysics. Individually and together, they represent the new age in Rotissethought. They're from Southern California, which explains a lot, and they claim to have had some success in their decade-plus of Rotisserie ownership. Last year, they modestly explained how to create a perfect league from scratch ("Roti-Trek, The Next Generation"). This year, they modestly offer us "Armed and Dangerous: The Ten Commandments of Pitching." Read it carefully and we think you'll agree: they have a lot to be modest about.

What would Rotisserie baseball do without **John Benson?** A veritable one-man research and publishing empire, he studies Rotisserie trends and tests Rotisserie theories while the rest of us sleep. (That's literally true: John is a notorious night worker.) Every year, he gives us a sneak preview of the spring and summer crops down on the farm (see Chapter 4, pages 213–214). Last year, he gave us six can't-miss relief pitching strategies ("How to Spell R-E-L-I-E-F") in these pages. And this year, he provides a revealing historical perspective on starters in "Starting Pitchers: The Return to Normalcy in 1997."

TIME OUT!

Not so fast there, Rookie. (And only you know if you are one.) Before stepping up to the plate in The Inner Game, take a close look at The Rules, Simplified (see pages 19–21). Then memorize the sacred Rotisserie Constitution in Chapter 6 (pages 259–278). Only then, after you have a glimmer of what madness lies ahead, should you proceed. This announcement is brought to you as a public service by the Founding Fathers of Rotisserie League Baseball. Don't come around later saying you weren't warned.

Armed and Dangerous:
The Ten Commandments of Pitching
by Mark Batterman & Ken Kuta
The K-Mark Shoppers

Ryan Klesko swung at the pitch—more accurately, that would be *Ryan Klesko for $15!*—swung at the pitch, uncoiling his bat with the focus and fury of Cecil Fielder and Wade Boggs fighting over the final helping of a postgame chicken dinner. The ball soared into the humid night of Atlanta–Fulton County Stadium, carrying with it on that late September evening the hopes and dreams that make grown men cry.

Not the hopes and dreams of Atlanta fans. Screw the Braves. We are talking the hopes and dreams that matter. Namely, that our team, the K-Mark Shoppers, would edge the hated Fuch Ewes in RBI, gain just one extra point, and slide over the Big Kahunas into the fourth-place money in the hotly contested 1996 California Dreamin' League race.

As we followed the flight of Klesko's big tomahawk chop that fateful autumn eve, we were thinking one thing: the season wouldn't be coming down to one crappy home run if we could ever find a pitching strategy that really worked!

Pitching, smitching. After 12 years of piloting our club through two leagues and the occasional Yoo-Hoo shower, if we know nothing else, we know this: pitching blows.

When it comes to Rotisserie baseball, if hitting is a fresh, jaunty morning in May, then pitching is the butt of August. A dog day, the Bataan Death March, the relentless downward spiral you travel as you watch tired arms fall off and die while your place in the standings drops faster than a pair of Baseball Annie panties.

If hitting is all of the possibilities found in a father's promise to play catch, then pitching is the festering sewer into which you just butterfingered your mitt.

In a word, pitching is where Rotisserie dreams go to die. (Okay, eight words.)

So, if that's the case, right about now you're probably wondering, Why in their infinite wisdom did the forefathers of Rotisserie, the revered disciples of Marse Okrent, the old (but crafty) rulers of Roti-dom, make pitching half the game?

Good question.

Another good question is, What were we thinking when we refused to trade Amaury Telemaco for Larry Walker during the stretch run?!

Clearly, we needed the wisdom and guidance of a higher authority. So we went up onto Mount Chavez Ravine, found a burning bush—we figure it was left over from that Vince Coleman firecracker thing—and came back with two Upper Deck cards inscribed "The Ten Commandments of Pitching."

Being altruistic, selfless fellows—and since the above-mentioned Roti-founders are paying us by the word to write this—we offer those glimmering flashes of revealed wisdom to you, free of charge.

I. THOU SHALT NOT OVERLOOK PITCHING!

Like it or not, if you don't know who's throwing what, where he's doing it, and what his role is, you've got as much of a shot at taking the Yoo-Hoo Plunge as Albert Belle has of escorting Hannah Storm to the next Espie Awards.

Sure, Junior is a four-category ballplayer, Tony Gwynn is money in the bank, and Kenny Lofton runs faster than your mother-in-law at the opening of a Wal-Mart half-off sale, but that still adds up to only 40 points at the most. (Okay, it could add up to 48 if you play in the American League or were crazy enough to expand in the National.) We can't tell you if pitching is really 90% of the game, but it is 50% of *this* game. At some point, you've got to suck it up, go out to the mound, rub up a resin bag, and deal with it!

As the esteemed commissioner of the California Dreamin' League, John Inferrera, likes to say, "There are only two kinds of owners in Rotisserie: Players [teams that finish in the money] and Contributors [teams whose money the Players are finishing in]." It's your choice: pay attention to pitching—or contribute!

II. THOU SHALT PICK A STRATEGY!

For starters—but we're talking relievers, too—you've got to have a plan. It's essential that you march into battle at your high-pressure draft with a strategy as solid as Mo Vaughn's dining-room chair. If you want to be a Player, consider the ones below. With a few breaks (two words: Mark Clark!), they are all good for 30 points or more:

1. **The Just Like the Big Leaguers Strategy.**
   Grab an ace for $25, three starters named Andy for $12 to $15 apiece, and a Big Gun Closer for $35 and try to fill in the rest as you go. Hey, it worked for LaRussa.

2. **The All Middle Reliever Strategy.**
   The Antichrist of strategy number one. Forget the starters. Who needs them? (In the end, they'll just cut your heart out and stomp all over it like Lindy Lincoln did when you were sixteen and just a dweeb with zits all over your face and not making the kind of money you are now.) Grab five or six middle relievers for no money from teams who have weak starting pitching but a lot of big sticks, the above-mentioned Big Gun Closer, and fill in with set-up guys. You'll nail 25 to 30 points in ERA, Ratio, and Saves while picking up 4 or 5 points in slop wins. Valid. Do-able. Maybe even good. But you've got to trade for some

starters later if you play with the Fenokee minimum innings requirement.

3. **The Corner the Closers Strategy.**
   Big-foot everyone at the table by spending balls-to-the-wall to hoard all the available talent, then plunder your fellow owners for a first-class staff when everyone else is panicking for saves. The Michael Milken approach to Rotisserie.

4. **The Draft Greg Maddux Strategy.**
   Feel free to insert your favorite starter here, but be forewarned: unless he *is* Greg Maddux, you won't sleep a wink all summer. A Greg Maddux off year is better than your guy's average year. We offer that as a warning to owners who draft Kevin Brown or Pat Hentgen this season. Sometimes the real thing is the only way to go.

5. **The $9 Pitching Staff Strategy.**
   Spend all your money on offense. Wait until the End Game and take the nine best $1 pitchers available. Yeah, you won't get a great staff, but you won't own Jim Abbott or Frank Castillo either.

III. THOU SHALT DUMP THY STRATEGY!

Remember, Roti-pitching is a flexible miasma of contradiction. All rules about pitching are like a sidewalk of wet cement: perfectly firm, until you try to bounce a 55-foot curveball off it. If your strategy isn't working, find another one. Fast!

IV. THOU SHALT DRAFT BY RATIOS!

We know that this brings back tragic memories of Miss Pennykamp's fifth-period math class, but to borrow from an overused media catch-phrase, "It's the numbers, stupid." At some point, you've got to sit down and analyze some stats. And not just the obvious ones like wins and ERA. Any Contributor can do that. Nope, we're talking deeper. We're talking stat-nerd time.

Forget what the other so-called experts tell you. Hey, did they get *their* info from a burning bush? Who needs them? Even your old frat buddies could find Mussina, Glavine, and Wohlers; but if you want the flag, you've got to dig deeper and uncover those diamonds in the rough. We're talking next year's $3 Cy Young winner and $5 closer.

The key is in two stats. The single best stat by which to analyze any pitcher is hits and walks divided by innings pitched. You know it as Ratio. For rookies, it's K-Ratio, which is strikeouts divided by innings pitched.

Granted, Ratio is an antiquated stat category that seriously flaws the near-perfect game we call Rotisserie. (This, too, can be remedied. See "The K-Factor"—a brilliant, insightful, compelling article about replacing Ratio with Strikeouts, thereby making Rotisserie baseball more fun and challenging while restoring starting pitching to its rightful place of importance—by one M. Batterman in the 1994 edition of this book. We would never suggest that the Roti-gods goofed when they brought the game into being or that they are too damn stubborn to reverse their tragic error, but the article does make for interesting reading.)

But when it comes to analyzing pitching, Ratio is the only way to go.

We sort every pitcher's last year's stats by Ratio and then study the top 25%. First, ignore the obvious studs and throw out the flukes like Tony Fossas, who only pitches to left-handers, and the also-rans like Tim Scott. In 1996, in the National League, you would have discovered that Curt Shilling was back . . . Scott Sanders was a great $1 steal . . . Denny Neagle, Kevin Brown, and Hideo Nomo were for real . . . Doug Drabek, Jim Bullinger, and Starvin' Marvin Freeman were not.

With rookies, we want to know one thing and one thing only. Is this guy striking out at least one per inning? If he ain't, he can be yours, because he's sure not ours. (By the way, the next great breakout pitcher is Chan Ho Park, who posted a 1996 K-Ratio of 1.09—that is, 119 strikeouts in 108.2 innings. No extra charge.)

V. THOU SHALT SPEND THY MONEY WISELY!

There are no hard-and-fast rules. Well, except these:

1. Never bid tall money on a rookie pitcher, any rookie pitcher, unless it's 1981 and his name is Valenzuela.

2. Never bid more than $17 on a starter even—and we believe this with all our hearts—if his name ends in an X (see Commandment II, no. 2). This is just our opinion, but don't forget the laws of supply and demand. At the end of your draft, 25% of the talent—and we use that word advisedly—in the pitching pool will still be available. Spend your money on lumber, lightning, and saves. You can always build a staff later.

3. Plan on spending a buck a save. If you really think John Eriks is going to give you 19 saves—and we respect your right to hold that opinion because that's what makes this a great game, and this great country of ours, great—he really is worth $19.

4. Always make a bid on an established Big Gun Closer when the price is 90% of his value or less, even if you already have one under contract. (Unless, that is, you don't know your butt from a bass fiddle about trading: the last thing you need to do is win the Saves category by 30.)

VI. THOU SHALT CHOOSE YEA OR NAY ON SAVES!

While we're talking Saves, we'll toss this in. Every pitching strategy is "save dependent." At some point, you've got to choose between cornering the save market and getting out. Being manly men, we hang out on the corner. If you subscribe to the theory that you're probably going to have to dump a category and butch up on another one—and we do—saves are the anabolic steroids of Rotisserie. You can't have too many saves when you leave the draft table.

By July, all saves are worth their weight in gold—or, more to the point, SB or HR or BA. You see, during the season, your stats are like boats going up and down in the harbor with the tide. Sometimes some categories will be up, and sometimes some will be down, but your Roti-fortunes will always be riding the ebb and flow. At some point, the tide is going to shift, the DL will make your Frank Thomas disappear and take your lead in HR and RBI along with him. When it does, you'll be happy you listened to old Mark and Ken and have some extra saves to trade. What can we say? Shift happens!

VII. THOU SHALT NOT COVET A HARRIS!

According to James C. and Alan S. Kaufman in the book *The Worst Baseball Pitchers of All Time,* no one named Harris has ever had a really good season in the history of baseball. Never. We haven't done the statistical analysis on this one—we find that sort of thing distasteful—but it's in print, and therefore true.

VIII. THOU SHALT STUDY THE STAFFS!

Are you one of those folks who did their history project at 11 o'clock the night before it was due? That makes us kindred spirits. So, naturally, we had to learn this the hard way. If you're not looking to make a contribution next fall, homework must be done early and often in the Roti-world.

If you're scouting a pitcher, look at the rest of the staff first. If you like the starters, check out the relievers, and vice versa. We know this seems as obvious as Kevin Mitchell trying to steal home, but there is a reason why the Tigers' middle guys get so many wins: their starting pitching sucks! Likewise, there's a reason why the thundering lumber of the Rockies gives their set-up guys so many wins: their middle relief sucks! Likewise, there's a reason why the ERA for the Reds' starting staff was so high . . . you get the point.

IX. THOU SHALT HAVE NO FALSE GODS!

In pitching there are only two sure things: Greg Maddux in the National League and Randy Johnson in the American League. Whoops. There are no sure things.

X. THOU SHALT NEVER DRAFT A GIANTS PITCHER!

Remember the blues classic "If It Weren't for Bad Luck, I'd Have No Luck at All"? It should be the theme song of the M°A°S°H unit formerly known as the Giants pitching staff. We agree that other clubs like the Rockies and the Tigers have staffs that will inflate your ERA faster than the national debt, but when it comes to bad luck, the Giants have an unrivaled streak that's older than Anna Nicole Smith's next husband—and shows no sign of letting up.

Every non-Contributor knows that a jinx is a jinx. Crash Davis said it best: "You gotta respect the streak." Casey Stengel chimed in with "If something bad is going to happen, it'll happen." As Grandma Kuta used to say, "That's life. Have some strudel, Kenny."

You might argue that The Park We Grew Up Calling "The Stick" was fine for Marichal, but we say, Tell that to Roseboro and the bat! Now add these names: Dave Dravecki, Atlee Hammaker, Scott Garrelts, Trevor Wilson, Don Robinson, Kelly Downs, and Bud Black. Gives you the willies doesn't it? And we ain't talking Mays or McCovey. Truth is, Giants pitchers end up spending more time humping the MRI at San Francisco General Hospital than they ever will down at the old ball yard.

When it comes to Giants pitchers—or any pitchers, for that matter—*caveat emptor.*

So, there they are. The Ten Commandments of Pitching. Ten sure-fire, hard-fast-and-tight, can't-miss rules for Rotisserie pitching success. If only they had been delivered to us by the baseball gods sooner. After all, if we had followed these commandments ourselves, we'd probably never have been reduced to rooting for the Klesko dinger that never was to save our sorry Roti-rumps.

But what the hell, if we had followed those other commandments, we probably wouldn't have had as much fun in our twenties.

This year, we've stockpiled Nomo at $16, Mark Clark and Carlos Perez at $1 each, along with Rojas, Tim Worrell, and Terrell Wade at bargain prices. Throw in a couple of great draft picks and the jewel of our minor league system—the next great closer for the Cubs, Steve Rain—and we are ready to play ball!

Because now we've learned that in Rotisserie baseball, commandments, like hearts, should never be broken.

Starting Pitchers:
The Return to Normalcy in 1997
By John Benson

To induce some fingernail-on-blackboard facial expressions in a crowd of veteran Rotisserians, try reciting this litany: Danny Jackson and Frank Viola in 1989; Joel Magrane and Bret Saberhagen in 1990; Orel Hershiser and Dave Stewart in 1991; Ramon Martinez and Chuck Finley in 1992; Bob Tewksbury, Tim Wakefield, and Charles Nagy in 1993 . . . the list goes on.

To impress any particular victim, er, listener, add a few names tailored to the individual's own experience. There is an endless supply to choose from: all those Grade A, Cy Young contender, staff-ace, and ever-so-high-priced starting pitchers who have gone south right after Draft Day and taken their Rotisserie teams down with them.

The steady stream of unhappy outcomes from high-priced, low-value starting pitchers, going back to the beginnings of Rotisserie baseball, early produced early and widespread acceptance of this conventional wisdom: anyone who pays "fair value" for the best starting rotation on paper is courting disaster. Sure, there have always been contrarians, and there was a flurry of Cy Young enthusiasm after Dwight Gooden looked like a world-beater in 1985. But Gooden slipped off the peak of Olympus in 1986, and every smart Rotisserian came to believe in the "Cy Young Jinx" and to be suspicious of all starting pitchers who flirt with greatness.

In the media world, analysts explain the Jinx as an often-understandable collapse following a season in which a pitcher works enough innings to win the award. Among Rotisserians, who would rather find an insight for next year's victory than an excuse for last year's defeat, inconsistent performances by top starters point to an obvious plan of action: to win at Rotisserie baseball, you *must* have good luck with starting pitchers.

If you pay top prices for *last* year's top starters, you cannot be *lucky* enough to win. The best you can do with high-priced starting pitchers is to break even and get what you pay for. Need proof? Look at any first-place roster, and you'll find the names of some very good pitchers who went for tiny prices on Draft Day.

Then in 1994 and 1995, this long-standing conventional wisdom went off the tracks, derailed by an immovable object named Greg Maddux. Maddux had been excellent—a Cy Young winner—in 1992 *and* 1993. The two-year reign was just a mild surprise, no big shock. But then Maddux elevated his surprising performance to a new, higher level, winning two more Cys and keeping his ERA under 1.70 longer than anyone since Walter Johnson's two best years in the dead-ball era, 1912–13.

A new era seemed to have arrived with Maddux. Suddenly there was— or seemed to be—a high (and seemingly predictable) correlation between having Maddux and winning the National League. Even Bobby Cox noted the correlation. And in this new age there was a revival of rites and offerings to those ancient gods of reliable starting pitching. When Maddux was selling for $35 to $40 or more, it seemed to make perfect sense to pay $30 for one of the almost-as-good alternatives. Soon the American League had its own Reliable Ace Starter in Randy Johnson, whose 1995 performance won a Cy Young award and lifted him high above the offensive onslaught that engulfed so many mortal pitchers.

By Draft Day 1996, conventional wisdom and the Cy Young Jinx had been all but forgotten. Bidders went after the best arms with a passion. I would have paid $52 for Maddux myself (having a nice freeze list and a fat spending budget), but someone else bid $53, and I had to build a staff around Ismael Valdes—a happy outcome, inadvertently. The nationwide average price for Maddux had gone from $32 in 1994 to $38 in 1995 to $46 in 1996. (Ask John Wallwork of Roti-Stats; he keeps track of these things.)

Maddux wasn't the only expensive starting pitcher in 1996. Randy Johnson commonly went for $40 or more in Junior Circuit auctions. Mike Mussina, David Cone, Dennis Martinez, and Jack McDowell were not far behind. And guess what the successful bidders for all these top starters had in common by midsummer? Disappointment. In the National League, the second thoughts and regrets came with names like Andy Ashby, Joey Hamilton, John Smiley, Frank Castillo, Jason Isringhausen, and Carlos Perez.

Compared with Maddux owners, Randy Johnson owners in 1996 suffered astonishingly worse. Anyone who shelled out $35 to $40 or more for the Big Unit in 1996 certainly felt the pain in Johnson's back that put him on the disabled list May 12 and then took him out for the year after a brief comeback attempt in August.

Maddux's "off year" in 1996 might have been a career year for any mortal pitcher, but he wasn't supposed to be mortal, not after going for $40 or $50. Maddux had a fine year, but he was arguably just the third-best pitcher in the Atlanta rotation, behind John Smoltz and Tom Glavine. The Cy Young Jinx had reared its ugly head again—finally—and the old gods had again been routed.

Before the 1996 season ended, Rotisserians were getting clues that the top starters would never again sell for such high prices. One Randy Johnson owner who wanted to trade his "bargain-priced" ace ($27) to a noncontender as a great freeze for 1997 was shocked to find no takers. Astute owners had already begun a contemplative activity that I call roster-gazing: staring at first-place rosters and pondering how they came to be in first place. The roster-gazing continued in earnest after the season ended, with predictable results.

In most leagues it was obvious that the recipe for success in 1996 included a healthy measure of good luck (or marvelous insight) in the starting pitcher department—the same recipe that worked in the pre-Maddux era. Names like Kevin Brown, Mark Clark, Jeff Fassero, and Curt Schilling in the National League and Ken Hill, Tim Belcher, Alex Fernandez, and Andy Pettitte in the American League showed that the best pitchers are not always the most expensive pitchers. (Although this year, of course, some of those guys *will* command top dollar.)

Looking at the rosters of also-rans in 1996 races provides a fresh new supply of evidence showing why it's wise to steer clear of the highest-priced starters. The not-so-good rosters were generally burdened with expensive starting pitchers.

Thus, we rediscovered a conventional wisdom and restored our belief in the Cy Young Jinx, with perhaps a footnote added for the next generation of analysts: *with the one notable exception of Greg Maddux during the mid-1990s, Cy Young winners have consistently been bad next-season Rotisserie investments.*

The same curse applies to all starting pitchers who approach greatness: *they are just plain unreliable*.

The point of this rediscovery is that we can now foresee some bidding behavior coming in 1997. A few starting pitchers, including Maddux, will still sell for more than $30, but that barrier is going to be crossed much less often in 1997 than it was in 1996. One obvious question that begs to be answered is, Where did the extra money come from when bidders were putting big money into top starting pitchers in 1996, and where is that money now going to go, if indeed it retreats as predicted? The question is a little complicated.

Surprisingly, the money that inflated the prices of top starting pitchers last year did not come from hitting. Total spending on hitting in all leagues nationwide remained about 65% in 1996, the same level at which it has been for a decade. The extra money for premium starting pitchers came from *other pitchers*. Most notable was a decline in the price of ace relievers—and an overall shortage of ace relievers. After the stunning collapses of Duane Ward and Bryan Harvey in 1994 (90 saves combined in 1993, just six in 1994), bidders were skeptical about putting $40 into any of these "one-category" players in 1995 and 1996. Also in the spring of 1996, fully 13 of the 28 major league teams had serious questions about who was the true ace reliever in their bullpen—and even if there was a true ace. Even for those wanting to shell out big bucks on ace relievers, there weren't many to choose from.

Another phenomenon that became pronounced in 1996—and will very likely vanish in 1997—was the popularity of the $1 starting pitcher. There is no logical explanation for this phenomenon, but I have a good guess about how it happened.

Even before the early days of major league expansion and pitching dilution in 1993–94, there was a general and understandable tendency for bidders to pay $4 or $5 for a known quantity in the starting pitcher department—even a mediocre known quantity—rather than take a risk on a rookie. The desire for halfway reliable starters may have remained in 1996, but it was simply unaffordable for the many teams that spent $60 or $70 on their first three starting pitchers. The $1 leftovers became a product of necessity, and not a very clever invention for those who had to live with them.

Another push toward the cheap starters came from the air of confidence built up by the acquisition of two or three supposedly blue-chip starters. That confidence led to too much optimism about one's ability to choose wisely from the vast supply of newly arrived Steve Wojciechowskis and Esteban Loaizas.

The return to normalcy in 1997 will be no big deal for veteran Rotisserians. The same old reliable methods will work as well as ever, Maddux or no Maddux. A winning team will depend on a solid offense, a fair share of saves, and some carefully chosen and moderately priced starters on the way up in their careers. Buying one All-Star-caliber starter will be OK, especially since this year the price of that ace will be more reasonable than it was in 1996.

Just don't go overboard. Remember: starting pitchers are unreliable. Always have been, always will be.

The Rules, Simplified

1. Rotisserie League teams are made up of real, live major league baseball players who are selected at an auction draft that takes place at the beginning of the season (typically on the first weekend following Opening Day).

2. Each team in a Rotisserie League is composed of 23 players taken from the active rosters of National or American League teams. A Rotisserie League drawn from National League or American League players should have 12 teams. You can, however, have fewer teams.

3. A team consists of five outfielders, two catchers, one second baseman, one shortstop, one middle infielder (either 2B or SS), one first baseman, one third baseman, one corner man (1B or 3B), one utility man (NL) or designated hitter (AL), and nine pitchers.

4. Players are purchased at an open auction. Spending is limited to $260 per team. (If you don't want to use money, call them units or pocorobas or whatever. The point is resource allocation.) Teams may spend less. The first bidder opens the auction with a minimum bid of $1 for any player. The bidding then proceeds around the room (at minimum increments of $1) until only one bidder is left. The process is repeated, with successive owners introducing players to be bid on, until every team has a complement of 23 players.

5. A player is eligible to be drafted for any position at which he appeared in 20 or more games the preceding year. If he did not appear in 20 games at any one position, he is eligible for the position at which he appeared the most times. Once the season starts, a player qualifies for a position by playing it once. Multiple eligibility is okay.

6. Trading is permissible from Auction Draft Day until midnight August 31. After every trade, both teams must be whole—that is, they must have the same number of active players at each position that they had before the trade.

7. If a major league player is put on the disabled list, sent to the minors, traded to the other league, or released, he may be replaced by a player from the free agent pool of unowned talent. Replacement must be made by position. The original player may be either be released or placed on his Rotisserie team's reserve list. A team may not release, reserve, or waive a player without replacing him with another active player.

8. Cumulative team performance is tabulated in four offensive and four pitching categories:

- Composite batting average (BA)
- Total home runs (HR)
- Total runs batted in (RBI)
- Total stolen bases (SB)
- Composite earned run average (ERA)
- Total wins (W)
- Total saves (S)
- Composite ratio: walks (BB) + hits (H) ÷ innings pitched (IP)

9. Teams are ranked from first to last in each of the eight categories. For example, in a 12-team league, the first-place team receives 12 points, the second-place team 11 points, on down to one point for last place. The team with the most points wins the pennant.

10. Prize money is distributed as follows: 50% for first place, 20% for second, 15% for third, 10% for fourth, and 5% for fifth. Even more important, the owner of the winning team receives a bottle of Yoo-Hoo—poured over his/her head. (See Chapter 7, Postgame Shower, pages 293–297.)

● ● ●

"Do I have to play for money?" No. We do, but unlike the big league version, Rotisserie League Baseball can be played for very little money, or none at all. You can play for pennies, Cracker Jack prizes, or nothing at all and still have fun. Just be sure to keep the ratio of "acquisition units" to players at 260:23 for each team on Auction Draft Day.

"What do I do if it's May 15 and I've just gotten around to reading this book? Wait till next year?" Absolutely not! That's second-division thinking! You can start anytime! Put your league together, hold your auction draft, and deduct all stats that accrue prior to that glorious day. Next year, start from scratch.

The rest of your questions are dealt with in the pages that follow. We hope. If not, write us c/o **Rotisserie League Baseball Association, 82 Wall Street, Suite 1105, New York, NY 10005**. Or call at **800-676-7684**. We'll do our best to get you playing what we still modestly call The Greatest Game for Baseball Fans Since Baseball.

2

Scouting Report

1997 Player Ratings

How much will Andruw Jones go for? Will A-Rod overtake Junior as the most expensive American Leaguer? After Matt Williams's third consecutive season shortened by a major injury, will his price fall below $30? Or will playing in that power-packed Indians lineup drive his price to $40? Can Frank Thomas pick up where he left off? Will Randy Johnson come all the way back? What about Greg Maddux—is he done? Has there been a Mark Whiten sighting lately? Will Henry Rodriguez be as overpriced this year as he was underpriced last year? Brady Anderson can't do it again, can he? *Can he?*

So many tough questions. So few certain answers. In Rotisserie, as in life. But in Rotisserie, at least you have an edge—our 1997 Player Ratings.

Wherever you live, February-March-April has to be the best time of the year. Your $24 starter hasn't broken down. Your main speed guy hasn't pulled his hammy yet. Your closer hasn't been relegated to a backup role. The idiot manager who controls the destiny of your hard-hitting bargain third baseman hasn't sat the guy down yet just because he made 14 errors in the first six weeks. You haven't blown a bundle on a phenom who's tearing up the league—the Pacific Coast League. You may not be in first, Bucky, but at least you're not in the cellar.

This is the time of year for lists. Lists ranking, by position and by category, all players in the league(s) you're drafting from. Lists ranking all available players, if yours is a continuing league that permits carryovers from one season to the next. Lists of starting pitchers you want to avoid at all costs (commencing, of course, with a list of all Tigers and Rockies). Lists of the best four-category blue-chippers (very short), long relievers who might give you 5–6 wins for a buck (very long), and backup middle infielders who might actually contribute something (very short). Lists of rookies, farm system players (at least through Double A ball), and really special Little Leaguers in your community. Lists of the worst (in ERA, Ratio, and BA) as well as the best. Lists of fourth and fifth outfielders you can get for a buck or so during the End Game who might, just might, have breakout seasons. Grocery lists, laundry lists, Franz Liszts—you can never have enough lists when preparing for your Auction Draft.

Where should you start? Right here, of course, with our Master List of National League and American League players, listed alphabetically by position, followed by NL and AL starters and relievers, each accompanied by four years of major league stats; a word or two of pithy, insightful, and sometimes even useful analysis; each player's age; and a projected salary based on a start-from-scratch auction draft.

Many people contributed to the 1997 Scouting Report, but only a couple are willing to admit it publicly. Wily veteran John Hassan and brash rookie Brendan O'Connor, who did much of the heavy lifting in the following pages, are known equally for their baseball perspicacity and their willingness to work cheap. All errors of fact or judgment are entirely their fault.

Last season provided a decade's worth of highlights, from Paul Molitor's startling confirmation that life begins at 40 to Kevin Brown's against-the-tide heroics, from reruns of *Home-Run Derby* on the Classic Sports Network to live home-run derbies at your local ballpark, from Jim Leyland's sad farewell to Pittsburgh to Kirby Puckett's infinitely sadder farewell to baseball.

But the most memorable thing about 1996 is that major league baseball managed to give us a full, 162-game season *and* a World Series—just like old times.

As Mel Allen, who died in 1996, would surely have said, *"How about that!"*

STATS NOTES

Want to know who finished strong last season? Who took a nosedive? Uncertain about keeping a veteran player and want to see if he showed signs of slipping? Want to find out whether a certain rookie who started hot and then went cold warmed back up in the second half?

You're in the right place. In addition to the last four years of major league stats, the Scouting Report gives you post All-Star stats for all position players and pitchers evaluated in this chapter—a crucial scouting tool for an owner trying to build a Yoo-Hoo team.

Salary projections are predicated on a start-from-scratch auction draft. In continuing leagues that carry over players from year to year, auction day prices will be skewed by the quality and quantity of available talent.

Players traded from one league to the other during the season appear in the league in which they finished the year. Thus, look for Mark Whiten among AL outfielders (though who knows for how long) and Carlos Baerga among NL middle infielders.

STATS, Inc. is responsible for the numbers in this chapter, for the Rotisserie Stat-Pak in Chapter 3, and for the final 1996 averages at the end of the book. The STATS team, with Steve Moyers leading off and John Dewan batting cleanup, is strictly major league. Check out page 211 for a full list of their publications and services, all of which will help you solve the really important mysteries of life.

HITS. RUNS. NO ERRORS.
ROTI•STATS
CALL 800-676-7684
WWW.ROTISTATS.COM

Behind the Plate

NATIONAL LEAGUE

Catchers
pp. 27–39

Corners
pp. 40–60

Infield
pp. 60–80

Outfield
pp. 80–111

DH
pp. 112–115

Starters
pp. 115–145

Relievers
pp. 146–178

STEVE DECKER
Age 31/R   **$1**

A spare part with a little pop.

Year	Team	Lg.	Pos.	G	AB	R	H	HR	RBI	SB	BA
1993	Florida	NL	C	8	15	0	0	0	1	0	0.000
1995	Florida	NL	C	51	133	12	30	3	13	1	.226
1996	San Francisco	NL	C	57	122	16	28	1	12	0	.230
1996	Colorado	NL	C	10	25	8	8	1	8	1	.320
Post All-Star				27	53	11	12	1	9	1	.226

TONY EUSEBIO
Age 29/R   **$3**

When a washout season follows a breakthrough season, you should always be wary. However, he will get every chance to be the Astros' everyday catcher, and he swings a good enough bat to make him a candidate for Minor Comeback Player of the Year.

Year	Team	Lg.	Pos.	G	AB	R	H	HR	RBI	SB	BA
1994	Houston	NL	C	55	159	18	47	5	30	0	.296
1995	Houston	NL	C	113	368	46	110	6	58	0	.299
1996	Houston	NL	C	58	152	15	41	1	19	0	.270
Post All-Star				39	103	12	30	0	14	0	.291

JOHN FLAHERTY
Age 29/R   **$5**

He keeps putting up solid numbers, and he keeps getting traded. He keeps getting raves for his positive influence on pitching staffs, and he keeps getting traded. He likely has a home in San Diego for the near future—unless he gets traded.

Year	Team	Lg.	Pos.	G	AB	R	H	HR	RBI	SB	BA
1993	Boston	AL	C	13	25	3	3	0	2	0	.120
1994	Detroit	AL	C	34	40	2	6	0	4	0	.150
1995	Detroit	AL	C	112	354	39	86	11	40	0	.243
1996	Detroit	AL	C	47	152	18	38	4	23	1	.250
1996	San Diego	NL	C	72	264	22	80	9	41	2	.303
Post All-Star				56	201	16	60	5	29	1	.299

DARRIN FLETCHER
Age 30/L   **$9**

For four straight years, the word was that the Expos would dump him because he was getting too expensive and they didn't like how he handled pitchers. But when you get past the elite two or three catchers in the league, he starts looking pretty good.

Year	Team	Lg.	Pos.	G	AB	R	H	HR	RBI	SB	BA
1993	Montreal	NL	C	133	396	33	101	9	60	0	.255
1994	Montreal	NL	C	94	285	28	74	10	57	0	.260
1995	Montreal	NL	C	110	350	42	100	11	45	0	.286
1996	Montreal	NL	C	127	394	41	105	12	57	0	.266
Post All-Star				58	168	15	45	4	15	0	.268

TYLER HOUSTON
Age 26/L   **$4**

The Cubs like him because he can play four other positions besides catcher, because he hits left-handed, and because he's young enough to get better. We like him because he was a first-round draft pick who didn't pan out for the very smug Atlanta Braves. You get your kicks where you can find them.

Year	Team	Lg.	Pos.	G	AB	R	H	HR	RBI	SB	BA
1996	Atlanta	NL	1B	33	27	3	6	1	8	0	.222
1996	Chicago	NL	C	46	115	18	39	2	19	3	.339
Post All-Star				41	105	16	32	2	15	3	.305

TODD HUNDLEY
Age 27/B   **$19**

He described his hitting philosophy this way: "They tell me to think about going with pitches and going up the middle and all that, but when push comes to shove, I usually end up going up there trying to get something that I can drive out of the park. It ain't all that scientific when you get right down to it. You lift your weights, you get as strong as you can get, and then you go up there and swing your ass off." Good strategy.

Year	Team	Lg.	Pos.	G	AB	R	H	HR	RBI	SB	BA
1993	New York	NL	C	130	417	40	95	11	53	1	.228
1994	New York	NL	C	91	291	45	69	16	42	2	.237
1995	New York	NL	C	90	275	39	77	15	51	1	.280
1996	New York	NL	C	153	540	85	140	41	112	1	.259
Post All-Star				70	250	41	65	18	46	1	.260

BRIAN JOHNSON
Age 29/R   **$3**

The best ex-Stanford quarterback in the majors. He's also the only one.

Year	Team	Lg.	Pos.	G	AB	R	H	HR	RBI	SB	BA
1994	San Diego	NL	C	36	93	7	23	3	16	0	.247
1995	San Diego	NL	C	68	207	20	52	3	29	0	.251
1996	San Diego	NL	C	82	243	18	66	8	35	0	.272
Post All-Star				33	96	6	21	2	6	0	.219

CHARLES JOHNSON
Age 25/R   **$5**

We know it's tough to be patient as all those 0-fers keep piling up day after day. But the scouts say he has all the ability to still be a 20-homer guy. He'll be playing for a manager used to being patient. He'll likely be surrounded by a much more formidable Marlins lineup. And his defense is so good that he'll get every possible chance to finally learn how to hit. Stay the course. Hold onto your Johnson.

Year	Team	Lg.	Pos.	G	AB	R	H	HR	RBI	SB	BA
1994	Florida	NL	C	4	11	5	5	1	4	0	.455
1995	Florida	NL	C	97	315	40	79	11	39	0	.251
1996	Florida	NL	C	120	386	34	84	13	37	1	.218
Post All-Star				37	112	14	27	4	11	1	.241

JASON KENDALL
Age 22/R   **$7**

Said Jim Leyland late into his final Pirates season, "Kendall is going to hit .300 for a lousy club. He has had to handle a different pitcher every day. He's only just learning how strong he can be. He's going to be at least as good as Sluggo [Don Slaught] was in his good years, and I think he'll end up being a lot better." Good enough for us.

Year	Team	Lg.	Pos.	G	AB	R	H	HR	RBI	SB	BA
1996	Pittsburgh	NL	C	130	414	54	124	3	42	5	.300
Post All-Star				60	186	30	57	2	16	4	.306

Catchers
pp. 27-39

Corners
pp. 40-60

Infield
pp. 60-80

Outfield
pp. 80-111

DH
pp. 112-115

Starters
pp. 115-145

Relievers
pp. 146-178

RANDY KNORR   Age 28/R $1

No thanks.

Year	Team	Lg.	Pos.	G	AB	R	H	HR	RBI	SB	BA
1993	Toronto	AL	C	39	101	11	25	4	20	0	.248
1994	Toronto	AL	C	40	124	20	30	7	19	0	.242
1995	Toronto	AL	C	45	132	18	28	3	16	0	.212
1996	Houston	NL	C	37	87	7	17	1	7	0	.195
Post All-Star				20	38	2	9	1	4	0	.237

TOM LAMPKIN   Age 33/L $1

All you need to know about the Giants' season in 1996 was that once last summer Tom Lampkin was in the starting lineup—and batting cleanup.

Year	Team	Lg.	Pos.	G	AB	R	H	HR	RBI	SB	BA
1993	Milwaukee	AL	C	73	162	22	32	4	25	7	.198
1995	San Francisco	NL	C	65	76	8	21	1	9	2	.276
1996	San Francisco	NL	C	66	177	26	41	6	29	1	.232
Post All-Star				30	78	11	16	3	16	1	.205

MIKE LIEBERTHAL   Age 25/R $4

Phillies general manager Lee Thomas kept insisting all season that this guy would be a quality everyday catcher and should get more playing time. Then-manager Jim Fregosi kept watching Benito Santiago hit home runs while insisting Lieberthal was just a fringe talent. As a result, he refused to sit Santiago. Then Lieberthal blew out his knee and the point became moot until Fregosi was fired. Thomas, who has overseen a franchise with one winning season in a decade, somehow escaped the axe. So his reprieve should bode well for Lieberthal's playing time. However, it might not bode well for either the Phillies or those desperate enough to pick up this guy as their catcher.

Year	Team	Lg.	Pos.	G	AB	R	H	HR	RBI	SB	BA
1994	Philadelphia	NL	C	24	79	6	21	1	5	0	.266
1995	Philadelphia	NL	C	16	47	1	12	0	4	0	.255
1996	Philadelphia	NL	C	50	166	21	42	7	23	0	.253
Post All-Star				17	45	4	7	0	5	0	.156

JAVY LOPEZ   Age 26/R $18

Stop and think for a second. He's two years younger than Piazza with knees about 30 years younger. He'll be kept much fresher into the future than Piazza, who the Dodgers play into the ground. He already has more championship rings than Piazza might ever get. And the Braves think he's poised to be 30-homer player any year now.

Year	Team	Lg.	Pos.	G	AB	R	H	HR	RBI	SB	BA
1993	Atlanta	NL	C	8	16	1	6	1	2	0	.375
1994	Atlanta	NL	C	80	277	27	68	13	35	0	.245
1995	Atlanta	NL	C	100	333	37	105	14	51	0	.315
1996	Atlanta	NL	C	138	489	56	138	23	69	1	.282
Post All-Star				64	220	30	62	11	31	1	.282

KIRT MANWARING   Age 31/R $1

When he was traded, veteran Giants were heard to say how tough it was to say good-bye to a trusted teammate. But you shouldn't find it it too hard to say good-bye to his puny power numbers.

Year	Team	Lg.	Pos.	G	AB	R	H	HR	RBI	SB	BA
1993	San Francisco	NL	C	130	432	48	119	5	49	1	.275
1994	San Francisco	NL	C	97	316	30	79	1	29	1	.250
1995	San Francisco	NL	C	118	379	21	95	4	36	1	.251
1996	San Francisco	NL	C	49	145	9	34	1	14	0	.234
1996	Houston	NL	C	37	82	5	18	0	4	0	.220
Post All-Star				46	108	8	23	0	5	0	.213

BRENT MAYNE   Age 28/L $1

He plays once a week at the most. That might be too much.

Year	Team	Lg.	Pos.	G	AB	R	H	HR	RBI	SB	BA
1993	Kansas City	AL	C	71	205	22	52	2	22	3	.254
1994	Kansas City	AL	C	46	144	19	37	2	20	1	.257
1995	Kansas City	AL	C	110	307	23	77	1	27	0	.251
1996	New York	NL	C	70	99	9	26	1	6	0	.263
Post All-Star				29	45	5	12	0	2	0	.267

JOE OLIVER   Age 31/R $5

Instead of whining about not getting a contract extension, he should count his blessings that he's in the perfect platoon situation. If he's still splitting time in Cincy, he's worth owning. If he talks himself into going somewhere else where he's expected to play every day, stay far away from him.

Year	Team	Lg.	Pos.	G	AB	R	H	HR	RBI	SB	BA
1993	Cincinnati	NL	C	139	482	40	115	14	75	0	.239
1994	Cincinnati	NL	C	6	19	1	4	1	5	0	.211
1995	Milwaukee	AL	C	97	337	43	92	12	51	2	.273
1996	Cincinnati	NL	C	106	289	31	70	11	46	2	.242
Post All-Star				54	152	22	38	7	27	2	.250

JAYHAWK OWENS   Age 28/R $2

Rockies GM Bob Gebhard has been Owens's biggest booster. However, others in the Rockies' organization think he is no more than a backup player. If Owens doesn't swing the bat better early this year, the Jayhawk will become an endangered species.

Year	Team	Lg.	Pos.	G	AB	R	H	HR	RBI	SB	BA
1993	Colorado	NL	C	33	86	12	18	3	6	1	.209
1994	Colorado	NL	C	6	12	4	3	0	1	0	.250
1995	Colorado	NL	C	18	45	7	11	4	12	0	.244
1996	Colorado	NL	C	73	180	31	43	4	17	4	.239
Post All-Star				35	78	16	20	1	6	4	.256

TOM PAGNOZZI   Age 34/R $6

A guy has a career year at 33 in a season where just about everybody is having a career year—what are his chances of doing it again? See where we're heading with this?

Year	Team	Lg.	Pos.	G	AB	R	H	HR	RBI	SB	BA
1993	St. Louis	NL	C	92	330	31	85	7	41	1	.258
1994	St. Louis	NL	C	70	243	21	66	7	40	0	.272
1995	St. Louis	NL	C	62	219	17	47	2	15	0	.215
1996	St. Louis	NL	C	119	407	48	110	13	55	4	.270
Post All-Star				63	214	22	52	7	25	1	.243

EDDIE PEREZ   Age 28/R $3

Spent the year as Greg Maddux's personal catcher, which isn't the worst way to make a living.

Year	Team	Lg.	Pos.	G	AB	R	H	HR	RBI	SB	BA
1995	Atlanta	NL	C	7	13	1	4	1	4	0	.308
1996	Atlanta	NL	C	68	156	19	40	4	17	0	.256
Post All-Star				32	75	8	15	1	6	0	.200

MIKE PIAZZA   Age 28/R $38

Some toppings on your Piazza to ponder: (1) his knees are quickly wearing down and it's not just media bufoonery to suggest that he won't catch forever; (2) he and his daddy Vince are not happy with how Tommy Lasorda was treated by the Dodgers, and when the chance arrives, Piazza will look at his options elsewhere, one being Colorado; (3) Daddy Vince wants to buy a team and has looked into getting a piece of the Phillies, after which he'd love to bring his son home; (4) we're looking at the best offensive player *ever* to play his position; and (5) his production faded down the stretch and the Dodgers must get him more rest during the season or he'll break down, which means the Dodgers need to find a backup catcher better than . . .

Year	Team	Lg.	Pos.	G	AB	R	H	HR	RBI	SB	BA
1993	Los Angeles	NL	C	149	547	81	174	35	112	3	.318
1994	Los Angeles	NL	C	107	405	64	129	24	92	1	.319
1995	Los Angeles	NL	C	112	434	82	150	32	93	1	.346
1996	Los Angeles	NL	C	148	547	87	184	36	105	0	.336
Post All-Star				68	247	40	75	12	42	0	.304

TOM PRINCE   Age 32/R $1

. . . with whom any lineup, including yours, is going to suffer.

Year	Team	Lg.	Pos.	G	AB	R	H	HR	RBI	SB	BA
1993	Pittsburgh	NL	C	66	179	14	35	2	24	1	.196
1994	Los Angeles	NL	C	3	6	2	2	0	1	0	.333
1995	Los Angeles	NL	C	18	40	3	8	1	4	0	.200
1996	Los Angeles	NL	C	40	64	6	19	1	11	0	.297
Post All-Star				16	28	4	10	0	3	0	.357

JEFF REED   Age 34/L $1

He's one of those players always described as being "a good guy to have on your club." Just so long as it's *your* club and not *ours*.

Year	Team	Lg.	Pos.	G	AB	R	H	HR	RBI	SB	BA
1993	San Francisco	NL	C	66	119	10	31	6	12	0	.261
1994	San Francisco	NL	C	50	103	11	18	1	7	0	.175
1995	San Francisco	NL	C	66	113	12	30	0	9	0	.265
1996	Colorado	NL	C	116	341	34	97	8	37	2	.284
Post All-Star				53	152	10	44	1	10	1	.289

Catchers
pp. 27–39

Corners
pp. 40–60

Infield
pp. 60–80

Outfield
pp. 80–111

DH
pp. 112–115

Starters
pp. 115–145

Relievers
pp. 146–178

BENITO SANTIAGO   Age 32/R $14

It might be late July, you're desperate for some runs, and you look at the newspaper for some divine guidance. You see that whomever Benny's playing for is opposed that night by Kevin Foster. A lightbulb immediately goes off above your head. Never mind if Benny is batting .100. You rush to insert him in your lineup. The reason is that you remember from some far-off corner of your twisted mind that Benny is 5 for 5 lifetime against Foster with 4 homers, a double, a walk, and 9 RBI. Don't count on 30 homers again, but Santiago is—and always has been—one of the better offensive catchers in the game. (P.S. Don't look for a repeat year in Toronto.)

Year	Team	Lg.	Pos.	G	AB	R	H	HR	RBI	SB	BA
1993	Florida	NL	C	139	469	49	108	13	50	10	.230
1994	Florida	NL	C	101	337	35	92	11	41	1	.273
1995	Cincinnati	NL	C	81	266	40	76	11	44	2	.286
1996	Philadelphia	NL	C	136	481	71	127	30	85	2	.264
Post All-Star				63	218	34	63	17	42	2	.289

SCOTT SERVAIS   Age 29/R $7

Without much fanfare, he has become a solid player with enough Wrigley Field power to provide Servais with a smile.

Year	Team	Lg.	Pos.	G	AB	R	H	HR	RBI	SB	BA
1993	Houston	NL	C	85	258	24	63	11	32	0	.244
1994	Houston	NL	C	78	251	27	49	9	41	0	.195
1995	Houston	NL	C	28	89	7	20	1	12	0	.225
1995	Chicago	NL	C	52	175	31	50	12	35	2	.286
1996	Chicago	NL	C	129	445	42	118	11	63	0	.265
Post All-Star				57	193	14	51	2	26	0	.264

DANNY SHEAFFER   Age 35/R $1

A body to fill out a roster.

Year	Team	Lg.	Pos.	G	AB	R	H	HR	RBI	SB	BA
1993	Colorado	NL	C	82	216	26	60	4	32	2	.278
1994	Colorado	NL	C	44	110	11	24	1	12	0	.218
1995	St. Louis	NL	C	76	208	24	48	5	30	0	.231
1996	St. Louis	NL	C	79	198	10	45	2	20	3	.227
Post All-Star				30	76	2	12	1	5	1	.158

TIM SPEHR   Age 30/R $1

Pass.

Year	Team	Lg.	Pos.	G	AB	R	H	HR	RBI	SB	BA
1993	Montreal	NL	C	53	87	14	20	2	10	2	.230
1994	Montreal	NL	C	52	36	8	9	0	5	2	.250
1995	Montreal	NL	C	41	35	4	9	1	3	0	.257
1996	Montreal	NL	C	63	44	4	4	1	3	1	.091
Post All-Star				29	17	1	2	0	0	0	.118

EDDIE TAUBENSEE   Age 28/L $8

Now established as a productive major league catcher. Best suited in a platoon role.

Year	Team	Lg.	Pos.	G	AB	R	H	HR	RBI	SB	BA
1993	Houston	NL	C	94	288	26	72	9	42	1	.250
1994	Houston	NL	C	5	10	0	1	0	0	0	.100
1994	Cincinnati	NL	C	61	177	29	52	8	21	2	.294
1995	Cincinnati	NL	C	80	218	32	62	9	44	2	.284
1996	Cincinnati	NL	C	108	327	46	95	12	48	3	.291
Post All-Star				51	143	23	43	7	21	0	.301

LENNY WEBSTER   Age 32/R $1

A nice guy who maintained last summer that one of the biggest thrills of his career was getting booed in Philadelphia while a member of the Phillies. "It felt good to know that at least someone noticed me," said Webster. That also sort of sums up the kind of player you're getting.

Year	Team	Lg.	Pos.	G	AB	R	H	HR	RBI	SB	BA
1993	Minnesota	AL	C	49	106	14	21	1	8	1	.198
1994	Montreal	NL	C	57	143	13	39	5	23	0	.273
1995	Philadelphia	NL	C	49	150	18	40	4	14	0	.267
1996	Montreal	NL	C	78	174	18	40	2	17	0	.230
Post All-Star				31	83	9	19	2	7	0	.229

RICK WILKINS   Age 29/L $7

Houston dumped him after he and then-Astros manager Terry Collins spent too many nights screaming at each other in the dugout. He still could be a 20-homer guy again, which would bring screams of delight from the Giants' dugout. Note we said "could be."

Year	Team	Lg.	Pos.	G	AB	R	H	HR	RBI	SB	BA
1993	Chicago	NL	C	136	446	78	135	30	73	2	.303
1994	Chicago	NL	C	100	313	44	71	7	39	4	.227
1995	Chicago	NL	C	50	162	24	31	6	14	0	.191
1995	Houston	NL	C	15	40	6	10	1	5	0	.250
1996	Houston	NL	C	84	254	34	54	6	23	0	.213
1996	San Francisco	NL	C	52	157	19	46	8	36	0	.293
Post All-Star				65	190	21	50	8	38	0	.263

AMERICAN LEAGUE

SANDY ALOMAR   Age 30/R $9

Lots of people said that Alomar, if healthy, would be one of the top producing catchers in baseball. They were wrong. He finally managed 400 AB last year, and he proved himself only slightly above average.

Year	Team	Lg.	Pos.	G	AB	R	H	HR	RBI	SB	BA
1993	Cleveland	AL	C	64	215	24	58	6	32	3	.270
1994	Cleveland	AL	C	80	292	44	84	14	43	8	.288
1995	Cleveland	AL	C	66	203	32	61	10	35	3	.300
1996	Cleveland	AL	C	127	418	53	110	11	50	1	.263
Post All-Star				55	177	20	41	5	21	0	.232

BRAD AUSMUS   Age 27/R $3

The most promising thing about Ausmus is his speed—any catcher with double-digit SB potential catches our attention. He took a step back in Detroit last year, stealing 13 fewer bases than the year before. Since that was his most appealing aspect (in the warped world of Rotisserie), our interest has ebbed, even with a change of scenery.

Year	Team	Lg.	Pos.	G	AB	R	H	HR	RBI	SB	BA
1993	San Diego	NL	C	49	160	18	41	5	12	2	.256
1994	San Diego	NL	C	101	327	45	82	7	24	5	.251
1995	San Diego	NL	C	103	328	44	96	5	34	16	.293
1996	San Diego	NL	C	50	149	16	27	1	13	1	.181
1996	Detroit	AL	C	75	226	30	56	4	22	3	.248
Post All-Star				61	186	26	46	4	21	3	.247

PAT BORDERS   Age 33/R $5

Saw action in only 50 games, but pitchers like him, and Alomar's not likely to stay healthy again. Take a gamble on a rebirth here.

Year	Team	Lg.	Pos.	G	AB	R	H	HR	RBI	SB	BA
1993	Toronto	AL	C	138	488	38	124	9	55	2	.254
1994	Toronto	AL	C	85	295	24	73	3	26	1	.247
1995	Kansas City	AL	C	52	143	14	33	4	13	0	.231
1995	Houston	NL	C	11	35	1	4	0	0	0	.114
1996	St. Louis	NL	C	26	69	3	22	0	4	0	.319
1996	California	AL	C	19	57	6	13	2	8	0	.228
1996	Chicago	AL	C	31	94	6	26	3	6	0	.277
Post All-Star				39	119	8	32	3	8	0	.269

RAUL CASANOVA   Age 24/B $1

Like Ausmus, a former Padre. But watch what you pay because you'll probably be eating Raul's salary.

Year	Team	Lg.	Pos.	G	AB	R	H	HR	RBI	SB	BA
1996	Detroit	AL	C	25	85	6	16	4	9	0	.188
Post All-Star				10	28	3	8	1	4	0	.286

JORGE FABREGAS   Age 27/L $1

Nice average, but judging from the rest of his stats, you're better off drafting Nanette Fabregas.

Year	Team	Lg.	Pos.	G	AB	R	H	HR	RBI	SB	BA
1994	California	AL	C	43	127	12	36	0	16	2	.283
1995	California	AL	C	73	227	24	56	1	22	0	.247
1996	California	AL	C	90	254	18	73	2	26	0	.287
Post All-Star				48	139	7	43	0	19	0	.309

SAL FASANO   Age 25/R $1

Mike Sweeney has shot past Fasano as the heir apparent. Mike Macfarlane is taking his time going over the hill. Look elsewhere.

Year	Team	Lg.	Pos.	G	AB	R	H	HR	RBI	SB	BA
1996	Kansas City	AL	C	51	143	20	29	6	19	1	.203
Post All-Star				2	3	0	0	0	0	0	0.000

JOE GIRARDI　　　　　　　　　　Age 32/R　　　$10

Girardi was a big part of a big year in the Bronx, and some of what he does can help your team too. No power, but good speed and a surprisingly quick bat set him apart.

Year	Team	Lg.	Pos.	G	AB	R	H	HR	RBI	SB	BA
1993	Colorado	NL	C	86	310	35	90	3	31	6	.290
1994	Colorado	NL	C	93	330	47	91	4	34	3	.276
1995	Colorado	NL	C	125	462	63	121	8	55	3	.262
1996	New York	AL	C	124	422	55	124	2	45	13	.294
Post All-Star				59	197	22	58	2	24	4	.294

TODD GREENE　　　　　　　　　Age 25/R　　　$3

The Angels moved Don Slaught and Pat Borders to make room for this power-hitting phenom, but the full-time job still belongs to Fabregas.

Year	Team	Lg.	Pos.	G	AB	R	H	HR	RBI	SB	BA
1996	California	AL	C	29	79	9	15	2	9	2	.190
Post All-Star				29	79	9	15	2	9	2	.190

BILL HASELMAN　　　　　　　　Age 30/R　　　$2

Solid backup catcher who filled in admirably when Mike Stanley went down in late August.

Year	Team	Lg.	Pos.	G	AB	R	H	HR	RBI	SB	BA
1993	Seattle	AL	C	58	137	21	35	5	16	2	.255
1994	Seattle	AL	C	38	83	11	16	1	8	1	.193
1995	Boston	AL	C	64	152	22	37	5	23	0	.243
1996	Boston	AL	C	77	237	33	65	8	34	4	.274
Post All-Star				42	131	21	39	5	24	3	.298

CHRIS HOILES　　　　　　　　　Age 32/R　　　$18

A bunch of HR, a mess of RBI, and good BA. Too bad he can't catch or throw a lick.

Year	Team	Lg.	Pos.	G	AB	R	H	HR	RBI	SB	BA
1993	Baltimore	AL	C	126	419	80	130	29	82	1	.310
1994	Baltimore	AL	C	99	332	45	82	19	53	2	.247
1995	Baltimore	AL	C	114	352	53	88	19	58	1	.250
1996	Baltimore	AL	C	127	407	64	105	25	73	0	.258
Post All-Star				64	197	29	58	13	43	0	.294

RON KARKOVICE　　　　　　　Age 33/R　　　$3

The knees are shot. The production is way down. A tip of the cap to Karko, who's on his last legs.

Year	Team	Lg.	Pos.	G	AB	R	H	HR	RBI	SB	BA
1993	Chicago	AL	C	128	403	60	92	20	54	2	.228
1994	Chicago	AL	C	77	207	33	44	11	29	0	.213
1995	Chicago	AL	C	113	323	44	70	13	51	2	.217
1996	Chicago	AL	C	111	355	44	78	10	38	0	.220
Post All-Star				40	125	16	29	3	14	0	.232

Catchers
pp. 27-39

Corners
pp. 40-60

Infield
pp. 60-80

Outfield
pp. 80-111

DH
pp. 112-115

Starters
pp. 115-145

Relievers
pp. 146-178

CHAD KREUTER
Age 32/B $1

His season ended with a brutal, shoulder-separating home plate collision with Johnny Damon. His career was heading that way, anyway.

Year	Team	Lg.	Pos.	G	AB	R	H	HR	RBI	SB	BA
1993	Detroit	AL	C	119	374	59	107	15	51	2	.286
1994	Detroit	AL	C	65	170	17	38	1	19	0	.224
1995	Seattle	AL	C	26	75	12	17	1	8	0	.227
1996	Chicago	AL	C	46	114	14	25	3	18	0	.219
Post All-Star				3	9	0	2	0	1	0	.222

JIM LEYRITZ
Age 33/R $2

Excluding the time the Yanks absolutely, positively needed him, the power numbers continued to slip. But with Andy Pettitte as his personal pitcher, he's still a decent number two behind the plate.

Year	Team	Lg.	Pos.	G	AB	R	H	HR	RBI	SB	BA
1993	New York	AL	1B	95	259	43	80	14	53	0	.309
1994	New York	AL	C	75	249	47	66	17	58	0	.265
1995	New York	AL	C	77	264	37	71	7	37	1	.269
1996	New York	AL	C	88	265	23	70	7	40	2	.264
Post All-Star				32	95	9	29	3	16	0	.305

MIKE MACFARLANE
Age 32/R $14

Last year we said the RBI and BA would come up and the homers would stay the same, if he stayed in Boston. We got the important stuff right. More of the same this year. Wherever he plays.

Year	Team	Lg.	Pos.	G	AB	R	H	HR	RBI	SB	BA
1993	Kansas City	AL	C	117	388	55	106	20	67	2	.273
1994	Kansas City	AL	C	92	314	53	80	14	47	1	.255
1995	Boston	AL	C	115	364	45	82	15	51	2	.225
1996	Kansas City	AL	C	112	379	58	104	19	54	3	.274
Post All-Star				55	190	30	52	10	31	1	.274

SANDY MARTINEZ
Age 24/L $2

Just forget about catchers named Sandy.

Year	Team	Lg.	Pos.	G	AB	R	H	HR	RBI	SB	BA
1995	Toronto	AL	C	62	191	12	46	2	25	0	.241
1996	Toronto	AL	C	76	229	17	52	3	18	0	.227
Post All-Star				28	78	5	16	1	4	0	.205

JOHN MARZANO
Age 34/R $1

Remarkably unaccomplished player. Hard to figure why Piniella gave him the third-highest AB total of his career. That's Lou's problem; don't make it yours.

Year	Team	Lg.	Pos.	G	AB	R	H	HR	RBI	SB	BA
1995	Texas	AL	C	2	6	1	2	0	0	0	.333
1996	Seattle	AL	C	41	106	8	26	0	6	0	.245
Post All-Star				21	59	3	14	0	1	0	.237

MIKE MATHENY

Age 26/R　　　**$3**

Nice surge in HR and RBI, but the BA hurts. You could do worse. But let somebody else.

Year	Team	Lg.	Pos.	G	AB	R	H	HR	RBI	SB	BA
1994	Milwaukee	AL	C	28	53	3	12	1	2	0	.226
1995	Milwaukee	AL	C	80	166	13	41	0	21	2	.247
1996	Milwaukee	AL	C	106	313	31	64	8	46	3	.204
Post All-Star				31	83	7	16	4	9	0	.193

GREG MYERS

Age 30/L　　　**$5**

Myers played well enough to keep Matt Walbeck ensconced as a backup. Expect the same this year.

Year	Team	Lg.	Pos.	G	AB	R	H	HR	RBI	SB	BA
1993	California	AL	C	108	290	27	74	7	40	3	.255
1994	California	AL	C	45	126	10	31	2	8	0	.246
1995	California	AL	C	85	273	35	71	9	38	0	.260
1996	Minnesota	AL	C	97	329	37	94	6	47	0	.286
Post All-Star				34	110	10	25	0	7	0	.227

CHARLIE O'BRIEN

Age 35/R　　　**$10**

After two years as Greg Maddux's personal catcher, O'Brien came to Toronto and had his best year ever. Strange reaction, but we'll take it. So should you.

Year	Team	Lg.	Pos.	G	AB	R	H	HR	RBI	SB	BA
1993	New York	NL	C	67	188	15	48	4	23	1	.255
1994	Atlanta	NL	C	51	152	24	37	8	28	0	.243
1995	Atlanta	NL	C	67	198	18	45	9	23	0	.227
1996	Toronto	AL	C	109	324	33	77	13	44	0	.238
Post All-Star				52	167	16	38	7	20	0	.228

MARK PARENT

Age 35/R　　　**$4**

We told you he wouldn't hit 18 homers again. But he still has a very favorable Dinger/Dollar ratio.

Year	Team	Lg.	Pos.	G	AB	R	H	HR	RBI	SB	BA
1993	Baltimore	AL	C	22	54	7	14	4	12	0	.259
1994	Chicago	NL	C	44	99	8	26	3	16	0	.263
1995	Pittsburgh	NL	C	69	233	25	54	15	33	0	.232
1995	Chicago	NL	C	12	32	5	8	3	5	0	.250
1996	Detroit	AL	C	38	104	13	25	7	17	0	.240
1996	Baltimore	AL	C	18	33	4	6	2	6	0	.182
Post All-Star				27	63	7	11	5	10	0	.175

TONY PENA

Age 39/R　　　**$1**

It's pretty much over in real baseball for Tony. It's definitely over in Rotisserie. Adios to one of the good guys.

Year	Team	Lg.	Pos.	G	AB	R	H	HR	RBI	SB	BA
1993	Boston	AL	C	126	304	20	55	4	19	1	.181
1994	Cleveland	AL	C	40	112	18	33	2	10	0	.295
1995	Cleveland	AL	C	91	263	25	69	5	28	1	.262
1996	Cleveland	AL	C	67	174	14	34	1	27	0	.195
Post All-Star				37	91	3	12	0	14	0	.132

IVAN RODRIGUEZ
Age 25/R **$20**

Pudge is the AL's best, and he's only 25. Catch him on the rise.

Year	Team	Lg.	Pos.	G	AB	R	H	HR	RBI	SB	BA
1993	Texas	AL	C	137	473	56	129	10	66	8	.273
1994	Texas	AL	C	99	363	56	108	16	57	6	.298
1995	Texas	AL	C	130	492	56	149	12	67	0	.303
1996	Texas	AL	C	153	639	116	192	19	86	5	.300
Post All-Star				68	297	54	85	9	37	2	.286

DON SLAUGHT
Age 38/R **$2**

Sluggo has another 10, 15 years of line drives left in him.

Year	Team	Lg.	Pos.	G	AB	R	H	HR	RBI	SB	BA
1993	Pittsburgh	NL	C	116	377	34	113	10	55	2	.300
1994	Pittsburgh	NL	C	76	240	21	69	2	21	0	.287
1995	Pittsburgh	NL	C	35	112	13	34	0	13	0	.304
1996	California	AL	C	62	207	23	67	6	32	0	.324
1996	Chicago	AL	C	14	36	2	9	0	4	0	.250
Post All-Star				22	58	3	14	0	4	0	.241

MIKE STANLEY
Age 33/R **$18**

After the plague lifted in Boston, Stanley was right in the thick of the Sox's resurgence. He was heading toward a career year until a herniated disc cut it short. Modern medicine being what it is, Stanley should be fine. Watch him in the spring and bid accordingly.

Year	Team	Lg.	Pos.	G	AB	R	H	HR	RBI	SB	BA
1993	New York	AL	C	130	423	70	129	26	84	1	.305
1994	New York	AL	C	82	290	54	87	17	57	0	.300
1995	New York	AL	C	118	399	63	107	18	83	1	.268
1996	Boston	AL	C	121	397	73	107	24	69	2	.270
Post All-Star				48	155	29	41	12	27	2	.265

TERRY STEINBACH
Age 35/R **$21**

Last year we said, What you see is what you get with Terry Steinbach. Then he goes out and more than doubles his dingers and knocks in 100. So we weren't aware of Al Davis's reconstruction plans, OK? Now he's in Minnesota, and what do we see? Not 35 dingers and 100 ribbies again, that's for sure. We'd settle for 20 and 70. So should you.

Year	Team	Lg.	Pos.	G	AB	R	H	HR	RBI	SB	BA
1993	Oakland	AL	C	104	389	47	111	10	43	3	.285
1994	Oakland	AL	C	103	369	51	105	11	57	2	.285
1995	Oakland	AL	C	114	406	43	113	15	65	1	.278
1996	Oakland	AL	C	145	514	79	140	35	100	0	.272
Post All-Star				69	234	37	64	17	54	0	.274

MIKE SWEENEY
Age 23/R **$6**

Solid prospect but hardly a secret. If he's available, bring him up early when nobody is thinking about catchers.

Year	Team	Lg.	Pos.	G	AB	R	H	HR	RBI	SB	BA
1995	Kansas City	AL	C	4	4	1	1	0	0	0	.250
1996	Kansas City	AL	C	50	165	23	46	4	24	1	.279
Post All-Star				50	165	23	46	4	24	1	.279

DAVE VALLE
Age 36/R **$1**

Somebody has to grab those 200 innings and 90 AB when Rodriguez needs a break from the Texas heat.

Year	Team	Lg.	Pos.	G	AB	R	H	HR	RBI	SB	BA
1993	Seattle	AL	C	135	423	48	109	13	63	1	.258
1994	Boston	AL	C	30	76	6	12	1	5	0	.158
1994	Milwaukee	AL	C	16	36	8	14	1	5	0	.389
1995	Texas	AL	C	36	75	7	18	0	5	1	.240
1996	Texas	AL	C	42	86	14	26	3	17	0	.302
Post All-Star				19	43	5	14	2	9	0	.326

MATT WALBECK
Age 27/B **$1**

Career backup.

Year	Team	Lg.	Pos.	G	AB	R	H	HR	RBI	SB	BA
1993	Chicago	NL	C	11	30	2	6	1	6	0	.200
1994	Minnesota	AL	C	97	338	31	69	5	35	1	.204
1995	Minnesota	AL	C	115	393	40	101	1	44	3	.257
1996	Minnesota	AL	C	63	215	25	48	2	24	3	.223
Post All-Star				49	167	17	37	2	21	3	.222

GEORGE WILLIAMS
Age 27/B **$1**

The most productive thing Williams did last year was prove to the Red Sox that Wil Cordero is not a second baseman. Williams slid hard to break up a double play, and Cordero's "instinctive" reaction led to a broken leg. Steinbach's year keeps Williams in reserve.

Year	Team	Lg.	Pos.	G	AB	R	H	HR	RBI	SB	BA
1995	Oakland	AL	C	29	79	13	23	3	14	0	.291
1996	Oakland	AL	C	56	132	17	20	3	10	0	.152
Post All-Star				15	35	2	4	0	1	0	.114

DAN WILSON
Age 28/R **$15**

Proved himself a capable cog in Seattle's offensive machine. Hit three homers in one game. No matter that he faded some in the second half. Catchers do that.

Year	Team	Lg.	Pos.	G	AB	R	H	HR	RBI	SB	BA
1993	Cincinnati	NL	C	36	76	6	17	0	8	0	.224
1994	Seattle	AL	C	91	282	24	61	3	27	1	.216
1995	Seattle	AL	C	119	399	40	111	9	51	2	.278
1996	Seattle	AL	C	138	491	51	140	18	83	1	.285
Post All-Star				63	218	20	56	6	31	0	.257

Catchers
pp. 27-39

Corners
pp. 40-60

Infield
pp. 60-80

Outfield
pp. 80-111

DH
pp. 112-115

Starters
pp. 115-145

Relievers
pp. 146-178

At the Corners

NATIONAL LEAGUE

SHANE ANDREWS   Age 25/R $14

It's the Expos' way to throw young players to the wolves. One reason is they're cheap. But another reason is that they're usually talented, which is why Andrews was left out there to strike out once every three at bats. He's just scratching the surface of considerable power potential and could emerge this year as a 30-homer guy.

Year	Team	Lg.	Pos.	G	AB	R	H	HR	RBI	SB	BA
1995	Montreal	NL	3B	84	220	27	47	8	31	1	.214
1996	Montreal	NL	3B	127	375	43	85	19	64	3	.227
Post All-Star				61	166	15	30	8	25	0	.181

JEFF BAGWELL   Age 28/R $40

In a normal year, we'd be singing his praises like always. But perhaps we have become jaded, or maybe last season's orgy of numbers just spoiled everyone. All we know is that we were left with the feeling this was not a vintage season for Bagwell. Hey, don't believe us. Ask Bagwell, who said in the final days of the Astros' September collapse, "Let's face it, I stunk for most of the first half and then I stunk over the last three weeks." If only others could stink so much.

Year	Team	Lg.	Pos.	G	AB	R	H	HR	RBI	SB	BA
1993	Houston	NL	1B	142	535	76	171	20	88	13	.320
1994	Houston	NL	1B	110	400	104	147	39	116	15	.368
1995	Houston	NL	1B	114	448	88	130	21	87	12	.290
1996	Houston	NL	1B	162	568	111	179	31	120	21	.315
Post All-Star				73	251	43	80	9	46	6	.319

KIM BATISTE   Age 29/R $1

Don't let the door hit you on the way out.

Year	Team	Lg.	Pos.	G	AB	R	H	HR	RBI	SB	BA
1993	Philadelphia	NL	3B	79	156	14	44	5	29	0	.282
1994	Philadelphia	NL	3B	64	209	17	49	1	13	1	.234
1996	San Francisco	NL	3B	54	130	17	27	3	11	3	.208
Post All-Star				34	94	11	22	2	7	3	.234

DAVID BELL   Age 24/R $1

Nothing more than a spare part.

Year	Team	Lg.	Pos.	G	AB	R	H	HR	RBI	SB	BA
1995	Cleveland	AL	3B	2	2	0	0	0	0	0	0.000
1995	St. Louis	NL	2B	39	144	13	36	2	19	1	.250
1996	St. Louis	NL	3B	62	145	12	31	1	9	1	.214
Post All-Star				5	9	2	2	0	1	1	.222

SEAN BERRY   Age 31/R $18

The tale of the poor man's Caminiti: for much of the year, he had so much debris floating around in his throwing arm that between pitches he'd sometimes rub his shoulder in order to move some pieces so he could throw. Despite that, he produced all season. We see more of the same, especially if he gets the shoulder fixed.

Year	Team	Lg.	Pos.	G	AB	R	H	HR	RBI	SB	BA
1993	Montreal	NL	3B	122	299	50	78	14	49	12	.261
1994	Montreal	NL	3B	103	320	43	89	11	41	14	.278
1995	Montreal	NL	3B	103	314	38	100	14	55	3	.318
1996	Houston	NL	3B	132	431	55	121	17	95	12	.281
Post All-Star				56	162	14	44	6	40	3	.272

MIKE BLOWERS   Age 31/R $10

Pedro Guerrero. German Rivera. Bill Madlock. Jeff Hamilton. Lenny Harris. Tim Wallach. Dave Hansen. Mike Blowers. Since Ron Cey departed, third base in Los Angeles has attracted quite an assortment. Next victim, sign in please.

Year	Team	Lg.	Pos.	G	AB	R	H	HR	RBI	SB	BA
1993	Seattle	AL	3B	127	379	55	106	15	57	1	.280
1994	Seattle	AL	3B	85	270	37	78	9	49	2	.289
1995	Seattle	AL	3B	134	439	59	113	23	96	2	.257
1996	Los Angeles	NL	3B	92	317	31	84	6	38	0	.265
Post All-Star				7	21	4	6	0	2	0	.286

TIM BOGAR   Age 30/R $1

One compelling statistical fact stands out—more strikeouts than total bases. Ouch.

Year	Team	Lg.	Pos.	G	AB	R	H	HR	RBI	SB	BA
1993	New York	NL	SS	78	205	19	50	3	25	0	.244
1994	New York	NL	3B	50	52	5	8	2	5	1	.154
1995	New York	NL	SS	78	145	17	42	1	21	1	.290
1996	New York	NL	1B	91	89	17	19	0	6	1	.213
Post All-Star				53	63	11	14	0	5	1	.222

RICO BROGNA   Age 26/L $14

A veritable mountain of Mets question marks is stacked high in Shea Stadium. It starts at the top with the general manager and manager and continues downward through the outfield, the pitching staff, the infield, and on to first base, where we thought Rico was a fixture. But the Mets traded him to shore up their bullpen. No doubt they had to do the latter, but at the cost of the former? Whatever—he'll *love* the Vet.

Year	Team	Lg.	Pos.	G	AB	R	H	HR	RBI	SB	BA
1994	New York	NL	1B	39	131	16	46	7	20	1	.351
1995	New York	NL	1B	134	495	72	143	22	76	0	.289
1996	New York	NL	1B	55	188	18	48	7	30	0	.255
Post All-Star				0	0	0	0	0	0	0	.000

Catchers
pp. 27-39

Corners
pp. 40-60

Infield
pp. 60-80

Outfield
pp. 80-111

DH
pp. 112-115

Starters
pp. 115-145

Relievers
pp. 146-178

MIKE BUSCH   Age 28/R $1

A "replacement player" who got attention for being shunned by his team-mates, he battled his way to a spot in the majors, where he was shunned for lack of production.

Year	Team	Lg.	Pos.	G	AB	R	H	HR	RBI	SB	BA
1995	Los Angeles	NL	3B	13	17	3	4	3	6	0	.235
1996	Los Angeles	NL	3B	38	83	8	18	4	17	0	.217
Post All-Star				16	55	6	12	3	12	0	.218

KEN CAMINITI   Age 33/B $31

The man who in one Mexican weekend did for Snickers bars what Mickey Tettleton once did for Froot Loops. He played most of the year hurt and became larger than life to his teammates. Said none other than Tony Gwynn, "Heck, it seemed every time we were in a tight spot down the stretch, Cammy would come up, hit a home run, and limp around the bases, and you'd start hearing that music from *The Natural* when Robert Redford hit the lights." Much as we love the guy, though, we don't see a repeat year in Cammy's locker. Look back to 1995 and bid accordingly.

Year	Team	Lg.	Pos.	G	AB	R	H	HR	RBI	SB	BA
1993	Houston	NL	3B	143	543	75	142	13	75	8	.262
1994	Houston	NL	3B	111	406	63	115	18	75	4	.283
1995	San Diego	NL	3B	143	526	74	159	26	94	12	.302
1996	San Diego	NL	3B	146	546	109	178	40	130	11	.326
Post All-Star				73	267	64	96	28	81	9	.360

VINNY CASTILLA   Age 29/R $34

No apologies are needed anymore. Just draft Rockies and have some fun.

Year	Team	Lg.	Pos.	G	AB	R	H	HR	RBI	SB	BA
1993	Colorado	NL	SS	105	337	36	86	9	30	2	.255
1994	Colorado	NL	SS	52	130	16	43	3	18	2	.331
1995	Colorado	NL	3B	139	527	82	163	32	90	2	.309
1996	Colorado	NL	3B	160	629	97	191	40	113	7	.304
Post All-Star				75	291	51	88	23	57	5	.302

ARCHI CIANFROCCO   Age 30/R $1

John Flaherty was still hobbling with a bad ankle when the Padres opened the playoffs. So when asked who might serve as an emergency catcher, manager Bruce Bochy said it would be Archi. When informed, Archi replied, "That would really help those TV ratings."

Year	Team	Lg.	Pos.	G	AB	R	H	HR	RBI	SB	BA
1993	Montreal	NL	1B	12	17	3	4	1	1	0	.235
1993	San Diego	NL	3B	84	279	27	68	11	47	2	.244
1994	San Diego	NL	3B	59	146	9	32	4	13	2	.219
1995	San Diego	NL	1B	51	118	22	31	5	31	0	.263
1996	San Diego	NL	1B	79	192	21	54	2	32	1	.281
Post All-Star				24	50	8	14	1	9	0	.280

GREG COLBRUNN   Age 27/R $12

The Marlins fret that he may be as good as he'll ever be, which is why we shouldn't be surprised to see Jeff Conine at first this year.

Year	Team	Lg.	Pos.	G	AB	R	H	HR	RBI	SB	BA
1993	Montreal	NL	1B	70	153	15	39	4	23	4	.255
1994	Florida	NL	1B	47	155	17	47	6	31	1	.303
1995	Florida	NL	1B	138	528	70	146	23	89	11	.277
1996	Florida	NL	1B	141	511	60	146	16	69	4	.286
Post All-Star				56	190	27	51	8	33	2	.268

ALVARO ESPINOZA   Age 35/R $2

On the whole, we suppose the Trade made sense for the Mets. But why did they want this over-the-hill, fringe player?

Year	Team	Lg.	Pos.	G	AB	R	H	HR	RBI	SB	BA
1993	Cleveland	AL	3B	129	263	34	73	4	27	2	.278
1994	Cleveland	AL	3B	90	231	27	55	1	19	1	.238
1995	Cleveland	AL	2B	66	143	15	36	2	17	0	.252
1996	Cleveland	AL	3B	59	112	12	25	4	11	1	.223
1996	New York	NL	3B	48	134	19	41	4	16	0	.306
Post All-Star				63	171	24	48	6	21	1	.281

GARY GAETTI   Age 38/R $22

We annually make idiots of ourselves by writing him off. So, this time we won't make the same mistake. Instead, we take heed from Tony LaRussa ("The man is a warrior") and say he has at least another productive year left in him.

Year	Team	Lg.	Pos.	G	AB	R	H	HR	RBI	SB	BA
1993	California	AL	3B	20	50	3	9	0	4	1	.180
1993	Kansas City	AL	3B	82	281	37	72	14	46	0	.256
1994	Kansas City	AL	3B	90	327	53	94	12	57	0	.287
1995	Kansas City	AL	3B	137	514	76	134	35	96	3	.261
1996	St. Louis	NL	3B	141	522	71	143	23	80	2	.274
Post All-Star				74	267	36	79	15	45	0	.296

ANDRES GALARRAGA   Age 35/R $42

We feel light-headed, and it's not the Mile High air. It's those amazing numbers put up every year by the Big Cat.

Year	Team	Lg.	Pos.	G	AB	R	H	HR	RBI	SB	BA
1993	Colorado	NL	1B	120	470	71	174	22	98	2	.370
1994	Colorado	NL	1B	103	417	77	133	31	85	8	.319
1995	Colorado	NL	1B	143	554	89	155	31	106	12	.280
1996	Colorado	NL	1B	159	626	119	190	47	150	18	.304
Post All-Star				76	305	64	102	25	75	12	.334

LEO GOMEZ   Age 30/R $9

We didn't even rate him last year, which reflected our firm belief that no one would want him. However, the Cubs stepped up and got some surprising production that will likely not be repeated. Remember these are the Cubs we're talking about. And even an old reliable like . . .

Year	Team	Lg.	Pos.	G	AB	R	H	HR	RBI	SB	BA
1993	Baltimore	AL	3B	71	244	30	48	10	25	0	.197
1994	Baltimore	AL	3B	84	285	46	78	15	56	0	.274
1995	Baltimore	AL	3B	53	127	16	30	4	12	0	.236
1996	Chicago	NL	3B	136	362	44	86	17	56	1	.238
Post All-Star				60	136	12	27	4	20	0	.199

Catchers
pp. 27–39

Corners
pp. 40–60

Infield
pp. 60–80

Outfield
pp. 80–111

DH
pp. 112–115

Starters
pp. 115–145

Relievers
pp. 146–178

MARK GRACE
Age 32/L   **$14**

. . . is finally having questions about staying forever in the Friendly Confines. "The thing is that after a while, as much as I love it here, you start getting tired of playing for lousy Cubs teams every year," said Grace before re-upping for two more years in Chicago, where his production has become very, very ordinary.

Year	Team	Lg.	Pos.	G	AB	R	H	HR	RBI	SB	BA
1993	Chicago	NL	1B	155	594	86	193	14	98	8	.325
1994	Chicago	NL	1B	106	403	55	120	6	44	0	.298
1995	Chicago	NL	1B	143	552	97	180	16	92	6	.326
1996	Chicago	NL	1B	142	547	88	181	9	75	2	.331
Post All-Star				72	272	45	89	6	41	1	.327

WILLIE GREENE
Age 25/L   **$15**

Not given to freely offering praise, Reds batting coach Hal McRae liked what he saw of this late-blooming talent. "Willie Greene has the strength and bat speed to hit 35 home runs someday," said McRae late last summer. "The question is whether he wants it enough and if he's smart enough to do it." There's also the question about where he plays, because he is an absolute butcher at third.

Year	Team	Lg.	Pos.	G	AB	R	H	HR	RBI	SB	BA
1993	Cincinnati	NL	SS	15	50	7	8	2	5	0	.160
1994	Cincinnati	NL	3B	16	37	5	8	0	3	0	.216
1995	Cincinnati	NL	3B	8	19	1	2	0	0	0	.105
1996	Cincinnati	NL	3B	115	287	48	70	19	63	0	.244
Post All-Star				64	165	29	39	11	33	0	.236

DAVE HANSEN
Age 28/L   **$1**

A relic of the Lasorda years who has precious little value. He's been kept around because he's "a Dodger." But his bench role was much better filled by . . .

Year	Team	Lg.	Pos.	G	AB	R	H	HR	RBI	SB	BA
1993	Los Angeles	NL	3B	84	105	13	38	4	30	0	.362
1994	Los Angeles	NL	3B	40	44	3	15	0	5	0	.341
1995	Los Angeles	NL	3B	100	181	19	52	1	14	0	.287
1996	Los Angeles	NL	3B	80	104	7	23	0	6	0	.221
Post All-Star				34	47	3	13	0	4	0	.277

LENNY HARRIS
Age 32/L   **$4**

. . . who the Reds love as a spot starter and clubhouse presence. He's a winning player who can effectively fill out your bench.

Year	Team	Lg.	Pos.	G	AB	R	H	HR	RBI	SB	BA
1993	Los Angeles	NL	2B	107	160	20	38	2	11	3	.237
1994	Cincinnati	NL	3B	66	100	13	31	0	14	7	.310
1995	Cincinnati	NL	3B	101	197	32	41	2	16	10	.208
1996	Cincinnati	NL	OF	125	302	33	86	5	32	14	.285
Post All-Star				71	195	23	56	3	19	9	.287

BUTCH HUSKEY
Age 25/R   **$17**

He took a solid first step toward being a productive major league hitter. We see 20 or so home runs a year in his future if he gets the playing time.

Year	Team	Lg.	Pos.	G	AB	R	H	HR	RBI	SB	BA
1993	New York	NL	3B	13	41	2	6	0	3	0	.146
1995	New York	NL	3B	28	90	8	17	3	11	1	.189
1996	New York	NL	1B	118	414	43	115	15	60	1	.278
Post All-Star				47	170	22	53	9	28	0	.312

GREGG JEFFERIES   Age 28/B $16

We spoke last year of how Rotisserians must occasionally hold their noses
and accept the foibles of their proud warriors to produce numbers despite
their being—in some cases, and certainly this one—a tad selfish and arrogant.
But if the numbers aren't there, no one should be expected to keep rooting
for them. The Phillies will try to move Jefferies; so should you.

Year	Team	Lg.	Pos.	G	AB	R	H	HR	RBI	SB	BA
1993	St. Louis	NL	1B	142	544	89	186	16	83	46	.342
1994	St. Louis	NL	1B	103	397	52	129	12	55	12	.325
1995	Philadelphia	NL	1B	114	480	69	147	11	56	9	.306
1996	Philadelphia	NL	1B	104	404	59	118	7	51	20	.292
Post All-Star				71	280	42	89	5	36	16	.318

MARK JOHNSON   Age 29/L $5

He'll hit you some home runs, but he appears destined to be a part-time
player.

Year	Team	Lg.	Pos.	G	AB	R	H	HR	RBI	SB	BA
1995	Pittsburgh	NL	1B	79	221	32	46	13	28	5	.208
1996	Pittsburgh	NL	1B	127	343	55	94	13	47	6	.274
Post All-Star				67	216	32	55	6	26	5	.255

CHIPPER JONES   Age 24/B $36

Last year, we presented Bobby Cox's glowing assessment of Chipper's rookie
season. Now, we present Chapter Two of the growing legend of Chipper. "Jeff
Blauser's X-rays weren't even dry when Chipper was in my office volunteering
to play short if we needed him," said Cox. "We went a couple of weeks going
in other directions and then we get Pendleton and send Chipper to short. Then
we get Blauser back and Chipper's back in my office arguing that he might be
able to best help the club by being a utility guy who I can move around between
short, third, and the outfield depending on what's best for the club on any given
night. Here's a guy who's an All-Star volunteering to be a utility player. He's
unbelievable." Next year, "Chapter Three—The MVP Seasn."

Year	Team	Lg.	Pos.	G	AB	R	H	HR	RBI	SB	BA
1993	Atlanta	NL	SS	8	3	2	2	0	0	0	.667
1995	Atlanta	NL	3B	140	524	87	139	23	86	8	.265
1996	Atlanta	NL	3B	157	598	114	185	30	110	14	.309
Post All-Star				74	271	51	87	13	44	8	.321

KEVIN JORDAN   Age 27/R $2

If his knee comes back, he can be a useful extra player.

Year	Team	Lg.	Pos.	G	AB	R	H	HR	RBI	SB	BA
1995	Philadelphia	NL	2B	24	54	6	10	2	6	0	.185
1996	Philadelphia	NL	1B	43	131	15	37	3	12	2	.282
Post All-Star				0	0	0	0	0	0	0	.000

Catchers
pp. 27–39

Corners
pp. 40–60

Infield
pp. 60–80

Outfield
pp. 80–111

DH
pp. 112–115

Starters
pp. 115–145

Relievers
pp. 146–178

WALLY JOYNER
Age 34/L   **$11**

He was off to his best start since the Wally World days in Anaheim. Then he broke his thumb sliding into second, and when he returned in July, every hard thrower in the National League took dead aim at that tender thumb. That's why his production slid faster than Bob Dole's poll numbers and why he needs to adjust this year or face the same inside-fastball treatment all over again.

Year	Team	Lg.	Pos.	G	AB	R	H	HR	RBI	SB	BA
1993	Kansas City	AL	1B	141	497	83	145	15	65	5	.292
1994	Kansas City	AL	1B	97	363	52	113	8	57	3	.311
1995	Kansas City	AL	1B	131	465	69	144	12	83	3	.310
1996	San Diego	NL	1B	121	433	59	120	8	65	5	.277
Post All-Star				69	249	25	61	3	32	3	.245

ERIC KARROS
Age 29/R   **$33**

He's become a genuine RBI man. Indeed, he was *Da Man* for the Dodgers down the stretch, though considering how this club otherwise surrendered without a whimper, that's not saying much.

Year	Team	Lg.	Pos.	G	AB	R	H	HR	RBI	SB	BA
1993	Los Angeles	NL	1B	158	619	74	153	23	80	0	.247
1994	Los Angeles	NL	1B	111	406	51	108	14	46	2	.266
1995	Los Angeles	NL	1B	143	551	83	164	32	105	4	.298
1996	Los Angeles	NL	1B	154	608	84	158	34	111	8	.260
Post All-Star				73	294	41	78	14	58	6	.265

JEFF KING
Age 32/R   **$26**

It's fitting that he picked a year when there were more than three dozen 100-RBI men to have his breakthrough year. You see, he doesn't exactly like the limelight. When there were rumors he would be traded to a contender, he said, "Well, I liked going to playoffs those years, but it does cut into the hunting season."

Year	Team	Lg.	Pos.	G	AB	R	H	HR	RBI	SB	BA
1993	Pittsburgh	NL	3B	158	611	82	180	9	98	8	.295
1994	Pittsburgh	NL	3B	94	339	36	89	5	42	3	.263
1995	Pittsburgh	NL	3B	122	445	61	118	18	87	7	.265
1996	Pittsburgh	NL	1B	155	591	91	160	30	111	15	.271
Post All-Star				70	255	40	66	9	47	9	.259

SCOTT LIVINGSTONE
Age 31/L   **$1**

There are few better pinch-hitter, spot-starter types.

Year	Team	Lg.	Pos.	G	AB	R	H	HR	RBI	SB	BA
1993	Detroit	AL	3B	98	304	39	89	2	39	1	.293
1994	Detroit	AL	DH	15	23	0	5	0	1	0	.217
1994	San Diego	NL	3B	57	180	11	49	2	10	2	.272
1995	San Diego	NL	1B	99	196	26	66	5	32	2	.337
1996	San Diego	NL	1B	102	172	20	51	2	20	0	.297
Post All-Star				46	42	3	16	1	8	0	.381

JOHN MABRY
Age 26/L **$16**

He opened the Cardinals' eyes with a lot of big RBI. But he made his biggest impression when, after getting reamed by Tony LaRussa for a less-than-intense late-season at bat, he fired right back at the manager and then got three hits with his next three at bats. His power should improve, and there's also the chance that St. Louis will try him at third to make room for Dmitri Young.

Year	Team	Lg.	Pos.	G	AB	R	H	HR	RBI	SB	BA
1994	St. Louis	NL	OF	6	23	2	7	0	3	0	.304
1995	St. Louis	NL	1B	129	388	35	119	5	41	0	.307
1996	St. Louis	NL	1B	151	543	63	161	13	74	3	.297
Post All-Star				70	244	24	62	6	32	2	.254

DAVE MAGADAN
Age 34/L **$1**

Pass.

Year	Team	Lg.	Pos.	G	AB	R	H	HR	RBI	SB	BA
1993	Florida	NL	3B	66	227	22	65	4	29	0	.286
1993	Seattle	AL	1B	71	228	27	59	1	21	2	.259
1994	Florida	NL	3B	74	211	30	58	1	17	0	.275
1995	Houston	NL	3B	127	348	44	109	2	51	2	.313
1996	Chicago	NL	3B	78	169	23	43	3	17	0	.254
Post All-Star				55	127	16	36	3	15	0	.283

DAVE MCCARTY
Age 27/R **$1**

Ditto.

Year	Team	Lg.	Pos.	G	AB	R	H	HR	RBI	SB	BA
1993	Minnesota	AL	OF	98	350	36	75	2	21	2	.214
1994	Minnesota	AL	1B	44	131	21	34	1	12	2	.260
1995	Minnesota	AL	1B	25	55	10	12	0	4	0	.218
1995	San Francisco	NL	OF	12	20	1	5	0	2	1	.250
1996	San Francisco	NL	1B	91	175	16	38	6	24	2	.217
Post All-Star				58	125	7	27	3	14	1	.216

FRED MCGRIFF
Age 33/L **$29**

The numbers were still there at the end, despite going through some of the ugliest stretches of his career. Not having David Justice hitting behind him was part of the problem. And said McGriff, "I don't know, I fell into the habit of thinking too much. I don't hit and think at the same time very well." We feel his pain. We have trouble thinking and writing at the same time very well.

Year	Team	Lg.	Pos.	G	AB	R	H	HR	RBI	SB	BA
1993	San Diego	NL	1B	83	302	52	83	18	46	4	.275
1993	Atlanta	NL	1B	68	255	59	79	19	55	1	.310
1994	Atlanta	NL	1B	113	424	81	135	34	94	7	.318
1995	Atlanta	NL	1B	144	528	85	148	27	93	3	.280
1996	Atlanta	NL	1B	159	617	81	182	28	107	7	.295
Post All-Star				72	276	30	81	8	39	1	.293

Catchers
pp. 27-39

Corners
pp. 40-60

Infield
pp. 60-80

Outfield
pp. 80-111

DH
pp. 112-115

Starters
pp. 115-145

Relievers
pp. 146-178

HAL MORRIS
Age 31/L $15

In the year of the homer, it shouldn't be a surprise that he had his career-high total for big flies. That it was so few is why we expect the Reds to once and for all look for more thump from first base.

Year	Team	Lg.	Pos.	G	AB	R	H	HR	RBI	SB	BA
1993	Cincinnati	NL	1B	101	379	48	120	7	49	2	.317
1994	Cincinnati	NL	1B	112	436	60	146	10	78	6	.335
1995	Cincinnati	NL	1B	101	359	53	100	11	51	1	.279
1996	Cincinnati	NL	1B	142	528	82	165	16	80	7	.313
Post All-Star				66	254	43	85	9	49	2	.335

BILL MUELLER
Age 26/B $4

Late-season numbers often prove to be illusions. But the Giants are so bad, he'll get every chance to prove they weren't a fluke.

Year	Team	Lg.	Pos.	G	AB	R	H	HR	RBI	SB	BA
1996	San Francisco	NL	3B	55	200	31	66	0	19	0	.330
Post All-Star				53	198	31	65	0	19	0	.328

TERRY PENDLETON
Age 36/B $7

The spirit remains willing, but the bat speed was fading over the season's final months and the defensive range had all but disappeared. He's at an age and weight that make comebacks very difficult. We know.

Year	Team	Lg.	Pos.	G	AB	R	H	HR	RBI	SB	BA
1993	Atlanta	NL	3B	161	633	81	172	17	84	5	.272
1994	Atlanta	NL	3B	77	309	25	78	7	30	2	.252
1995	Florida	NL	3B	133	513	70	149	14	78	1	.290
1996	Florida	NL	3B	111	406	30	102	7	58	0	.251
1996	Atlanta	NL	3B	42	162	21	33	4	17	2	.204
Post All-Star				70	263	28	59	6	35	2	.224

ROBERTO PETAGINE
Age 25/L $1

Might have value in a reserve role. Terrific minor league numbers.

Year	Team	Lg.	Pos.	G	AB	R	H	HR	RBI	SB	BA
1994	Houston	NL	1B	8	7	0	0	0	0	0	0.000
1995	San Diego	NL	1B	89	124	15	29	3	17	0	.234
1996	New York	NL	1B	50	99	10	23	4	17	0	.232
Post All-Star				40	72	9	19	4	14	0	.264

J. R. PHILLIPS
Age 26/L $1

A stiff.

Year	Team	Lg.	Pos.	G	AB	R	H	HR	RBI	SB	BA
1993	San Francisco	NL	1B	11	16	1	5	1	4	0	.313
1994	San Francisco	NL	1B	15	38	1	5	1	3	1	.132
1995	San Francisco	NL	1B	92	231	27	45	9	28	1	.195
1996	San Francisco	NL	1B	15	25	3	5	2	5	0	.200
1996	Philadelphia	NL	OF	35	79	9	12	5	10	0	.152
Post All-Star				7	16	1	1	0	0	0	.063

SCOTT ROLEN   Age 21/R $8

Considered the one legit prospect in the miserable Phillies organization, he of course got hurt shortly after arriving last summer. It must be the Cheez Whiz on the cheese steaks that makes bones brittle and muscles flimsy. He'll get his 550 at bats to prove himself this year. The word is that he might be a couple of years away from developing power.

Year	Team	Lg.	Pos.	G	AB	R	H	HR	RBI	SB	BA
1996	Philadelphia	NL	3B	37	130	10	33	4	18	0	.254
Post All-Star				37	130	10	33	4	18	0	.254

CHRIS SABO   Age 35/R $1

Like Spuds McKenzie, after whom he was once nicknamed, he is not of any use anymore.

Year	Team	Lg.	Pos.	G	AB	R	H	HR	RBI	SB	BA
1993	Cincinnati	NL	3B	148	552	86	143	21	82	6	.259
1994	Baltimore	AL	3B	68	258	41	66	11	42	1	.256
1995	Chicago	AL	DH	20	71	10	18	1	8	2	.254
1995	St. Louis	NL	1B	5	13	0	2	0	3	1	.154
1996	Cincinnati	NL	3B	54	125	15	32	3	16	2	.256
Post All-Star				10	21	0	4	0	0	0	.190

DAVID SEGUI   Age 30/B $12

At least his season was ruined by a unique injury. Innocently holding Marquis Grissom on first base one night, he reached to catch a pickoff thrown by Ugueth Urbina. The problem was that Ugie gets a little excited when he's on the mound, and instead of the normal pickoff throw, Ugie launched a 95 mph cut fastball that dove about six inches and snapped Segui's thumb. Now Segui knows better, which should allow him to continue his quiet progress toward a solid career.

Year	Team	Lg.	Pos.	G	AB	R	H	HR	RBI	SB	BA
1993	Baltimore	AL	1B	146	450	54	123	10	60	2	.273
1994	New York	NL	1B	92	336	46	81	10	43	0	.241
1995	New York	NL	OF	33	73	9	24	2	11	1	.329
1995	Montreal	NL	1B	97	383	59	117	10	57	1	.305
1996	Montreal	NL	1B	115	416	69	119	11	58	4	.286
Post All-Star				43	148	28	44	6	24	3	.297

BILL SPIERS   Age 30/L $3

A decent role player.

Year	Team	Lg.	Pos.	G	AB	R	H	HR	RBI	SB	BA
1993	Milwaukee	AL	2B	113	340	43	81	2	36	9	.238
1994	Milwaukee	AL	3B	73	214	27	54	0	17	7	.252
1995	New York	NL	3B	63	72	5	15	0	11	0	.208
1996	Houston	NL	3B	122	218	27	55	6	26	7	.252
Post All-Star				59	123	12	31	3	16	6	.252

Catchers
pp. 27-39

Corners
pp. 40-60

Infield
pp. 60-80

Outfield
pp. 80-111

DH
pp. 112-115

Starters
pp. 115-145

Relievers
pp. 146-178

TIM WALLACH   Age 39/R   No Price

He decided to retire before the season was over. "I'd see pitches I used to at least drive somewhere, and I'd pop them up," he said. "I'd see groundballs I used to suck up go by me. I'd be excited on the bench and look around and see younger guys looking bored. It was time." Hey, draft him as a coach.

Year	Team	Lg.	Pos.	G	AB	R	H	HR	RBI	SB	BA
1993	Los Angeles	NL	3B	133	477	42	106	12	62	0	.222
1994	Los Angeles	NL	3B	113	414	68	116	23	78	0	.280
1995	Los Angeles	NL	3B	97	327	24	87	9	38	0	.266
1996	California	AL	3B	57	190	23	45	8	20	1	.237
1996	Los Angeles	NL	3B	45	162	14	37	4	22	0	.228
Post All-Star				47	169	15	38	4	22	0	.225

MATT WILLIAMS   Age 31/R $36

Great trade by the Indians. If shoulder acts up, he can DH now and then— a real plus for one of the game's great hitters. As long as he can swing a bat, he can play anywhere he wants on our team.

Year	Team	Lg.	Pos.	G	AB	R	H	HR	RBI	SB	BA
1993	San Francisco	NL	3B	145	579	105	170	38	110	1	.294
1994	San Francisco	NL	3B	112	445	74	119	43	96	1	.267
1995	San Francisco	NL	3B	76	283	53	95	23	65	2	.336
1996	San Francisco	NL	3B	105	404	69	122	22	85	1	.302
Post All-Star				21	83	16	26	5	17	1	.313

AMERICAN LEAGUE

GEORGE ARIAS   Age 25/R $5

Made the team out of spring training and lost the starting job by May. Unless Pie Traynor is still around, you have to think Arias will get another shot. Make-or-break year. We say make.

Year	Team	Lg.	Pos.	G	AB	R	H	HR	RBI	SB	BA
1996	California	AL	3B	84	252	19	60	6	28	2	.238
Post All-Star				58	176	13	46	5	23	2	.261

WADE BOGGS   Age 38/L $10

He's getting old, he sits against tough lefties, and he's still a selfish ballplayer. When the Yankees picked up Charlie Hayes, Boggs said, "I guess I'll get my three thousandth hit somewhere else." He later apologized, but that's Boggsy: me first, me second, and the team third. Nobody needs a singles hitter for $2 million a year. People we know in Boston hope he goes to Cooperstown in a Yankee hat. When he visits, that is.

Year	Team	Lg.	Pos.	G	AB	R	H	HR	RBI	SB	BA
1993	New York	AL	3B	143	560	83	169	2	59	0	.302
1994	New York	AL	3B	97	366	61	125	11	55	2	.342
1995	New York	AL	3B	126	460	76	149	5	63	1	.324
1996	New York	AL	3B	132	501	80	156	2	41	1	.311
Post All-Star				57	208	32	59	0	15	1	.284

SCOTT BROSIUS — Age 30/R — $19

Despite missing 50 games, he had his best season. Pay up.

Year	Team	Lg.	Pos.	G	AB	R	H	HR	RBI	SB	BA
1993	Oakland	AL	OF	70	213	26	53	6	25	6	.249
1994	Oakland	AL	3B	96	324	31	77	14	49	2	.238
1995	Oakland	AL	3B	123	389	69	102	17	46	4	.262
1996	Oakland	AL	3B	114	428	73	130	22	71	7	.304
Post All-Star				74	289	41	84	11	37	5	.291

JEFF CIRILLO — Age 27/R — $18

Another good player forced to toil for the commissioner's team.

Year	Team	Lg.	Pos.	G	AB	R	H	HR	RBI	SB	BA
1994	Milwaukee	AL	3B	39	126	17	30	3	12	0	.238
1995	Milwaukee	AL	3B	125	328	57	91	9	39	7	.277
1996	Milwaukee	AL	3B	158	566	101	184	15	83	4	.325
Post All-Star				75	289	52	91	9	44	1	.315

TONY CLARK — Age 24/B — $19

Good HR but comparatively weak RBI. A nice year, but let's see it again.

Year	Team	Lg.	Pos.	G	AB	R	H	HR	RBI	SB	BA
1995	Detroit	AL	1B	27	101	10	24	3	11	0	.238
1996	Detroit	AL	1B	100	376	56	94	27	72	0	.250
Post All-Star				72	277	42	69	21	54	0	.249

WILL CLARK — Age 33/L — $14

The thrill's not all gone, but it's heading for the door. As his lowest BA since '89 indicates, his bat has really slowed down. The Mariners ate him alive with inside heat during a crucial series at the end of last year, and he never showed up in the playoffs.

Year	Team	Lg.	Pos.	G	AB	R	H	HR	RBI	SB	BA
1993	San Francisco	NL	1B	132	491	82	139	14	73	2	.283
1994	Texas	AL	1B	110	389	73	128	13	80	5	.329
1995	Texas	AL	1B	123	454	85	137	16	92	0	.302
1996	Texas	AL	1B	117	436	69	124	13	72	2	.284
Post All-Star				53	195	29	52	7	29	1	.267

RON COOMER — Age 30/R — $7

Nice guy for your third corner man. He'll back up Stahoviak. That's it.

Year	Team	Lg.	Pos.	G	AB	R	H	HR	RBI	SB	BA
1995	Minnesota	AL	1B	37	101	15	26	5	19	0	.257
1996	Minnesota	AL	1B	95	233	34	69	12	41	3	.296
Post All-Star				41	94	12	28	4	15	3	.298

Catchers
pp. 27-39

Corners
pp. 40-60

Infield
pp. 60-80

Outfield
pp. 80-111

DH
pp. 112-115

Starters
pp. 115-145

Relievers
pp. 146-178

RUSS DAVIS   Age 27/R $3

The Russ Davis saga is an old and boring one. Just when it got interesting, he broke his leg. Take him or leave him, just don't start screaming about all his *potential*.

Year	Team	Lg.	Pos.	G	AB	R	H	HR	RBI	SB	BA
1994	New York	AL	3B	4	14	0	2	0	1	0	.143
1995	New York	AL	3B	40	98	14	27	2	12	0	.276
1996	Seattle	AL	3B	51	167	24	39	5	18	2	.234
Post All-Star				0	0	0	0	0	0	0	.000

CECIL FIELDER   Age 33/R $32

Daddy Baseball's contract will keep him in pinstripes for at least one more year, and a full season in that lineup could produce monster numbers, even in Yankee Stadium. And don't overlook that speed on the bases.

Year	Team	Lg.	Pos.	G	AB	R	H	HR	RBI	SB	BA
1993	Detroit	AL	1B	154	573	80	153	30	117	0	.267
1994	Detroit	AL	1B	109	425	67	110	28	90	0	.259
1995	Detroit	AL	1B	136	494	70	120	31	82	0	.243
1996	Detroit	AL	1B	107	391	55	97	26	80	2	.248
1996	New York	AL	DH	53	200	30	52	13	37	0	.260
Post All-Star				72	273	42	72	20	57	0	.264

JULIO FRANCO   Age 35/R $14

Had a bad hamstring for long stretches but still had good numbers. When he does play, he produces. Suddenly seems old, though. Must have been a long year in Japan.

Year	Team	Lg.	Pos.	G	AB	R	H	HR	RBI	SB	BA
1993	Texas	AL	DH	144	532	85	154	14	84	9	.289
1994	Chicago	AL	DH	112	433	72	138	20	98	8	.319
1996	Cleveland	AL	1B	112	432	72	139	14	76	8	.322
Post All-Star				33	128	19	40	4	21	3	.313

TRAVIS FRYMAN   Age 28/R $19

Last year we guaranteed the numbers. We see the same thing for this year.

Year	Team	Lg.	Pos.	G	AB	R	H	HR	RBI	SB	BA
1993	Detroit	AL	SS	151	607	98	182	22	97	9	.300
1994	Detroit	AL	3B	114	464	66	122	18	85	2	.263
1995	Detroit	AL	3B	144	567	79	156	15	81	4	.275
1996	Detroit	AL	3B	157	616	90	165	22	100	4	.268
Post All-Star				74	288	44	77	9	42	2	.267

JASON GIAMBI   Age 26/L $15

Pumping up with Mark McGwire helped pump up his stats. He can handle first, third, and outfield and hits wherever they play him. But don't go crazy until he does it again.

Year	Team	Lg.	Pos.	G	AB	R	H	HR	RBI	SB	BA
1995	Oakland	AL	3B	54	176	27	45	6	25	2	.256
1996	Oakland	AL	1B	140	536	84	156	20	79	0	.291
Post All-Star				59	220	26	54	4	19	0	.245

RENE GONZALES   Age 25/R $1

Forget it.

Year	Team	Lg.	Pos.	G	AB	R	H	HR	RBI	SB	BA
1993	California	AL	3B	118	335	34	84	2	31	5	.251
1994	Cleveland	AL	3B	22	23	6	8	1	5	2	.348
1995	California	AL	3B	30	18	1	6	1	3	0	.333
1996	Texas	AL	1B	51	92	19	20	2	5	0	.217
Post All-Star				27	40	7	2	0	2	0	.050

CHARLIE HAYES   Age 31/R $13

He'll continue to produce, but for whom?

Year	Team	Lg.	Pos.	G	AB	R	H	HR	RBI	SB	BA
1993	Colorado	NL	3B	157	573	89	175	25	98	11	.305
1994	Colorado	NL	3B	113	423	46	122	10	50	3	.288
1995	Philadelphia	NL	3B	141	529	58	146	11	85	5	.276
1996	Pittsburgh	NL	3B	128	459	51	114	10	62	6	.248
1996	New York	AL	3B	20	67	7	19	2	13	0	.284
Post All-Star				65	227	22	59	3	30	2	.260

DAVE HOLLINS   Age 30/B $12

Showed strong signs of getting back to the form he showed in Philly all those injuries ago. Keep your fingers crossed. At his best he's a tough, gritty producer.

Year	Team	Lg.	Pos.	G	AB	R	H	HR	RBI	SB	BA
1993	Philadelphia	NL	3B	143	543	104	148	18	93	2	.273
1994	Philadelphia	NL	3B	44	162	28	36	4	26	1	.222
1995	Philadelphia	NL	1B	65	205	46	47	7	25	1	.229
1995	Boston	AL	DH	5	13	2	2	0	1	0	.154
1996	Minnesota	AL	3B	121	422	71	102	13	53	6	.242
1996	Seattle	AL	3B	28	94	17	33	3	25	0	.351
Post All-Star				68	235	42	70	6	41	4	.298

JACK HOWELL   Age 35/L $1

If he plays at all, it will be off the bench—sparingly.

Year	Team	Lg.	Pos.	G	AB	R	H	HR	RBI	SB	BA
1996	California	AL	3B	66	126	20	34	8	21	0	.270
Post All-Star				31	54	9	15	3	9	0	.278

BRIAN HUNTER   Age 29/R $2

Good role player. Specializes in giving good return on short dollars.

Year	Team	Lg.	Pos.	G	AB	R	H	HR	RBI	SB	BA
1993	Atlanta	NL	1B	37	80	4	11	0	8	0	.138
1994	Pittsburgh	NL	1B	76	233	28	53	11	47	0	.227
1994	Cincinnati	NL	OF	9	23	6	7	4	10	0	.304
1995	Cincinnati	NL	1B	40	79	9	17	1	9	2	.215
1996	Seattle	AL	1B	75	198	21	53	7	28	0	.268
Post All-Star				44	105	9	20	4	11	0	.190

Catchers
pp. 27-39

Corners
pp. 40-60

Infield
pp. 60-80

Outfield
pp. 80-111

DH
pp. 112-115

Starters
pp. 115-145

Relievers
pp. 146-178

JOHN JAHA

Age 30/R $32

Lost among the stars at first base in the American League. He'll never make an All-Star team, but he could make yours.

Year	Team	Lg.	Pos.	G	AB	R	H	HR	RBI	SB	BA
1993	Milwaukee	AL	1B	153	515	78	136	19	70	13	.264
1994	Milwaukee	AL	1B	84	291	45	70	12	39	3	.241
1995	Milwaukee	AL	1B	88	316	59	99	20	65	2	.313
1996	Milwaukee	AL	1B	148	543	108	163	34	118	3	.300
Post All-Star				70	254	54	78	18	53	2	.307

JEFF KENT

Age 29/R $12

The knock on Kent is that he's a pouter, a whiner, and a me-first player. Plus, he doesn't have enough glove for second base and not enough bat for third. What we're trying to say here is that San Francisco got hosed in the Williams giveaway.

Year	Team	Lg.	Pos.	G	AB	R	H	HR	RBI	SB	BA
1993	New York	NL	2B	140	496	65	134	21	80	4	.270
1994	New York	NL	2B	107	415	53	121	14	68	1	.292
1995	New York	NL	2B	125	472	65	131	20	65	3	.278
1996	New York	NL	3B	89	335	45	97	9	39	4	.290
1996	Cleveland	AL	1B	39	102	16	27	3	16	2	.265
Post All-Star				47	127	19	33	3	18	2	.260

SCOTT LEIUS

Age 31/R $1

Worth-leius.

Year	Team	Lg.	Pos.	G	AB	R	H	HR	RBI	SB	BA
1993	Minnesota	AL	SS	10	18	4	3	0	2	0	.167
1994	Minnesota	AL	3B	97	350	57	86	14	49	2	.246
1995	Minnesota	AL	3B	117	372	51	92	4	45	2	.247
1996	Cleveland	AL	3B	27	43	3	6	1	3	0	.140
Post All-Star				2	1	0	1	0	0	0	1.000

JEFF MANTO

Age 32/R $1

Those 17 HR in 1995 were a mirage. Last year he played in Boston, Seattle, and Boston and managed 3 dingers. He plays about 11 positions, though, and will find a home somewhere. Let's hope it's not in your neighborhood.

Year	Team	Lg.	Pos.	G	AB	R	H	HR	RBI	SB	BA
1993	Philadelphia	NL	3B	8	18	0	1	0	0	0	.056
1995	Baltimore	AL	3B	89	254	31	65	17	38	0	.256
1996	Boston	AL	3B	22	48	8	10	2	6	0	.208
1996	Seattle	AL	3B	21	54	7	10	1	4	0	.185
Post All-Star				38	86	13	17	3	10	0	.198

TINO MARTINEZ

Age 29/L $27

He's not Don Mattingly, but as it turns out, he doesn't need to be. He had a career year with Seattle in 1995, then upped the ante last season in the Bronx. Can't miss with Tino.

Year	Team	Lg.	Pos.	G	AB	R	H	HR	RBI	SB	BA
1993	Seattle	AL	1B	109	408	48	108	17	60	0	.265
1994	Seattle	AL	1B	97	329	42	86	20	61	1	.261
1995	Seattle	AL	1B	141	519	92	152	31	111	0	.293
1996	New York	AL	1B	155	595	82	174	25	117	2	.292
Post All-Star				71	265	38	81	11	54	2	.306

Catchers
pp. 27-39

Corners
pp. 40-60

Infield
pp. 60-80

Outfield
pp. 80-111

DH
pp. 112-115

Starters
pp. 115-145

Relievers
pp. 146-178

MARK MCGWIRE   Age 33/R $44

Most AB since 1992. Most HR of his career. Best batting average of his career by more than 20 points. McGwire gave everyone in baseball a three-week head start and then lapped the field. Forget the juiced-ball theory for this guy. He was helped most by a reconstructed home park that suddenly became hitter-friendly. Once he recovered from that spring-training heel injury, he stayed healthy and now seems to have a handle on the nagging injuries that have plagued him. He'll go for big money, but then you can say you had him the year he finally did it. Hit 62, that is.

Year	Team	Lg.	Pos.	G	AB	R	H	HR	RBI	SB	BA
1993	Oakland	AL	1B	27	84	16	28	9	24	0	.333
1994	Oakland	AL	1B	47	135	26	34	9	25	0	.252
1995	Oakland	AL	1B	104	317	75	87	39	90	1	.274
1996	Oakland	AL	1B	130	423	104	132	52	113	0	.312
Post All-Star				65	212	48	62	24	53	0	.292

TIM NAEHRING   Age 30/R $15

A hamstring problem ended his season early, but Naehring still put in a solid 400 AB year. His future seems cloudy in Boston because of the Nomar Garciaparra/John Valentin situation and his own free agency. An excellent all-around player like Naehring will start wherever he plays, so keep an eye on him. Our advice to Boston: sign Naehring, trade Valentin.

Year	Team	Lg.	Pos.	G	AB	R	H	HR	RBI	SB	BA
1993	Boston	AL	2B	39	127	14	42	1	17	1	.331
1994	Boston	AL	2B	80	297	41	82	7	42	1	.276
1995	Boston	AL	3B	126	433	61	133	10	57	0	.307
1996	Boston	AL	3B	116	430	77	124	17	65	2	.288
Post All-Star				51	189	37	46	5	23	0	.243

JOSE OFFERMAN   Age 28/B $10

Offerman's rebirth occurred at first base, but he'll likely end up at second next year, which is nice rosterwise because he qualifies at middle and corner. Plus, the baseball gods are smiling now that he's no longer sullying the position of shortstop with his presence.

Year	Team	Lg.	Pos.	G	AB	R	H	HR	RBI	SB	BA
1993	Los Angeles	NL	SS	158	590	77	159	1	62	30	.269
1994	Los Angeles	NL	SS	72	243	27	51	1	25	2	.210
1995	Los Angeles	NL	SS	119	429	69	123	4	33	2	.287
1996	Kansas City	AL	1B	151	561	85	170	5	47	24	.303
Post All-Star				70	287	51	89	4	28	16	.310

JOHN OLERUD   Age 28/L $14

A comeback of sorts for a nice guy. Still, when you start out like the next Mattingly, and somebody embarrasses himself by saying you're the next Ted

Williams, it kinda hurts when you turn out to be the next Wally Joyner. The Jays are openly shopping him.

Year	Team	Lg.	Pos.	G	AB	R	H	HR	RBI	SB	BA
1993	Toronto	AL	1B	158	551	109	200	24	107	0	.363
1994	Toronto	AL	1B	108	384	47	114	12	67	1	.297
1995	Toronto	AL	1B	135	492	72	143	8	54	0	.291
1996	Toronto	AL	1B	125	398	59	109	18	61	1	.274
Post All-Star				53	163	18	48	4	21	0	.294

RAFAEL PALMEIRO   Age 32/L $39

Even more so than Jaha, this guy was born at the wrong time. Look at these numbers! Forget the BA (which was low for him). Draft him! Draft him! Draft him!

Year	Team	Lg.	Pos.	G	AB	R	H	HR	RBI	SB	BA
1993	Texas	AL	1B	160	597	124	176	37	105	22	.295
1994	Baltimore	AL	1B	111	436	82	139	23	76	7	.319
1995	Baltimore	AL	1B	143	554	89	172	39	104	3	.310
1996	Baltimore	AL	1B	162	626	110	181	39	142	8	.289
Post All-Star				76	294	46	83	17	65	4	.282

DEAN PALMER   Age 28/R $35

Bounced right back from a nasty bicep injury to have his best year ever, the BA being the most pleasant surprise. Can't blame the juiced ball for that.

Year	Team	Lg.	Pos.	G	AB	R	H	HR	RBI	SB	BA
1993	Texas	AL	3B	148	519	88	127	33	96	11	.245
1994	Texas	AL	3B	93	342	50	84	19	59	3	.246
1995	Texas	AL	3B	36	119	30	40	9	24	1	.336
1996	Texas	AL	3B	154	582	98	163	38	107	2	.280
Post All-Star				72	272	43	73	18	41	0	.268

CRAIG PAQUETTE   Age 28/R $15

Very strong year after coming over from Oakland, where he only hinted at these numbers. Qualifies in the outfield, too.

Year	Team	Lg.	Pos.	G	AB	R	H	HR	RBI	SB	BA
1993	Oakland	AL	3B	105	393	35	86	12	46	4	.219
1994	Oakland	AL	3B	14	49	0	7	0	0	1	.143
1995	Oakland	AL	3B	105	283	42	64	13	49	5	.226
1996	Kansas City	AL	3B	118	429	61	111	22	67	5	.259
Post All-Star				66	248	36	68	12	37	3	.274

JOE RANDA   Age 27/R $7

These are the classic statistics of a useful role-playing, complementary player. The Randa Bear may develop into more, but remember, Paquette's presence really devalues this guy.

Year	Team	Lg.	Pos.	G	AB	R	H	HR	RBI	SB	BA
1995	Kansas City	AL	3B	34	70	6	12	1	5	0	.171
1996	Kansas City	AL	3B	110	337	36	102	6	47	13	.303
Post All-Star				53	180	17	55	4	26	6	.306

KEVIN SEITZER

Age 35/R   **$14**

Seitzer keeps threatening to retire, but the trade to the Indians may change his mind. Mike Hargrove liked the spark he brought to the team, even though Albert Belle yelled at him for not scoring from second on a single. Hargrove defended Seitzer in the paper, but that kind of garbage can make hunting and fishing seem awfully appealing to an old pro like Seitzer. Albert Belle accusing you of not hustling? *Please.*

Year	Team	Lg.	Pos.	G	AB	R	H	HR	RBI	SB	BA
1993	Oakland	AL	3B	73	255	24	65	4	27	4	.255
1993	Milwaukee	AL	3B	47	162	21	47	7	30	3	.290
1994	Milwaukee	AL	3B	80	309	44	97	5	49	2	.314
1995	Milwaukee	AL	3B	132	492	56	153	5	69	2	.311
1996	Milwaukee	AL	1B	132	490	74	155	12	62	6	.316
1996	Cleveland	AL	DH	22	83	11	32	1	16	0	.386
Post All-Star				71	261	36	77	3	34	3	.295

ANDY SHEETS

Age 25/R   **$1**

Somebody call the chambermaid.

Year	Team	Lg.	Pos.	G	AB	R	H	HR	RBI	SB	BA
1996	Seattle	AL	3B	47	110	18	21	0	9	2	.191
Post All-Star				27	57	8	9	0	3	1	.158

CHRIS SNOPEK

Age 26/R   **$5**

He won't be taking over for Robin Ventura anytime soon but may be among the players looking to replace Ozzie Guillen. Another middle/corner guy who can contribute in little ways.

Year	Team	Lg.	Pos.	G	AB	R	H	HR	RBI	SB	BA
1995	Chicago	AL	3B	22	68	12	22	1	7	1	.324
1996	Chicago	AL	3B	46	104	18	27	6	18	0	.260
Post All-Star				18	44	8	15	3	11	0	.341

J. T. SNOW

Age 29/B   **$17**

In a huge year for offense, these numbers are awfully soft. No wonder the Giants wanted him.

Year	Team	Lg.	Pos.	G	AB	R	H	HR	RBI	SB	BA
1993	California	AL	1B	129	419	60	101	16	57	3	.241
1994	California	AL	1B	61	223	22	49	8	30	0	.220
1995	California	AL	1B	143	544	80	157	24	102	2	.289
1996	California	AL	1B	155	575	69	148	17	67	1	.257
Post All-Star				69	257	27	65	6	28	0	.253

PAUL SORRENTO

Age 31/L   **$22**

Tino Who? Sorrento is a big part of Seattle's awesome offense. Unfortunately, he still can't hit lefties (.197), but what the hell—neither can we.

Year	Team	Lg.	Pos.	G	AB	R	H	HR	RBI	SB	BA
1993	Cleveland	AL	1B	148	463	75	119	18	65	3	.257
1994	Cleveland	AL	1B	95	322	43	90	14	62	0	.280
1995	Cleveland	AL	1B	104	323	50	76	25	79	1	.235
1996	Seattle	AL	1B	143	471	67	136	23	93	0	.289
Post All-Star				69	218	29	55	8	39	0	.252

Catchers
pp. 27–39

Corners
pp. 40–60

Infield
pp. 60–80

Outfield
pp. 80–111

DH
pp. 112–115

Starters
pp. 115–145

Relievers
pp. 146–178

ED SPRAGUE Age 29/R $25

One of the few bright spots in the Toronto lineup. Sprague is the real thing and no longer the second-best athlete in his marriage.

Year	Team	Lg.	Pos.	G	AB	R	H	HR	RBI	SB	BA
1993	Toronto	AL	3B	150	546	50	142	12	73	1	.260
1994	Toronto	AL	3B	109	405	38	97	11	44	1	.240
1995	Toronto	AL	3B	144	521	77	127	18	74	0	.244
1996	Toronto	AL	3B	159	591	88	146	36	101	0	.247
Post All-Star				75	283	35	63	13	39	0	.223

SCOTT STAHOVIAK Age 27/L $12

Stahoviak may have finally solved the Twins' problems at first. With all those consonants, he's a worthy successor to Kent Hrbek. Now all he has to do is *eat* and *hit* a bunch of taters.

Year	Team	Lg.	Pos.	G	AB	R	H	HR	RBI	SB	BA
1993	Minnesota	AL	3B	20	57	1	11	0	1	0	.193
1995	Minnesota	AL	1B	94	263	28	70	3	23	5	.266
1996	Minnesota	AL	1B	130	405	72	115	13	61	3	.284
Post All-Star				62	206	30	56	6	29	2	.272

DOUG STRANGE Age 32/B $2

Who could have figured Mike Blowers would be so hard to replace?

Year	Team	Lg.	Pos.	G	AB	R	H	HR	RBI	SB	BA
1993	Texas	AL	2B	145	484	58	124	7	60	6	.256
1994	Texas	AL	2B	73	226	26	48	5	26	1	.212
1995	Seattle	AL	3B	74	155	19	42	2	21	0	.271
1996	Seattle	AL	3B	88	183	19	43	3	23	1	.235
Post All-Star				48	100	9	24	2	12	1	.240

B. J. SURHOFF Age 32/L $18

Just as his speed officially deserted him, he found a power stroke. Should become a fixture at Camden Yards. Qualifies in the outfield, too, which matters in the Rotisserie world a lot more than it does in the other world.

Year	Team	Lg.	Pos.	G	AB	R	H	HR	RBI	SB	BA
1993	Milwaukee	AL	3B	148	552	66	151	7	79	12	.274
1994	Milwaukee	AL	3B	40	134	20	35	5	22	0	.261
1995	Milwaukee	AL	OF	117	415	72	133	13	73	7	.320
1996	Baltimore	AL	3B	143	537	74	157	21	82	0	.292
Post All-Star				71	262	37	79	8	33	0	.302

FRANK THOMAS   Age 28/R $41

Obviously one of the best players in baseball, maybe even in baseball history. But last year he took a page from Albert Belle's playbook in a very public argument with Robin Ventura, who was merely trying keep him from getting bounced from his second game in a row during a pennant race. Thomas's childish reaction was caused by frustration over his slow return from a broken foot, and frustration that the White Sox were slipping out of the wild card picture. The Big Hurt may be hurting, tired of playing for an also-ran.

Year	Team	Lg.	Pos.	G	AB	R	H	HR	RBI	SB	BA
1993	Chicago	AL	1B	153	549	106	174	41	128	4	.317
1994	Chicago	AL	1B	113	399	106	141	38	101	2	.353
1995	Chicago	AL	1B	145	493	102	152	40	111	3	.308
1996	Chicago	AL	1B	141	527	110	184	40	134	1	.349
Post All-Star				54	195	44	68	17	49	0	.349

JIM THOME   Age 26/L $28

Last year we said to look for 30 HR and 90 RBI, which both would have been career highs. We didn't know they were going to juice up the ball, or we would have said 38 and 116.

Year	Team	Lg.	Pos.	G	AB	R	H	HR	RBI	SB	BA
1993	Cleveland	AL	3B	47	154	28	41	7	22	2	.266
1994	Cleveland	AL	3B	98	321	58	86	20	52	3	.268
1995	Cleveland	AL	3B	137	452	92	142	25	73	4	.314
1996	Cleveland	AL	3B	151	505	122	157	38	116	2	.311
Post All-Star				69	247	60	77	22	65	1	.312

MO VAUGHN   Age 29/L $39

Still maturing as a hitter, as shown by a nearly 50 percent increase in walks. Played most of the year with a broken middle finger on his right hand. Late-season surge due in part to a padding contraption for the finger that Big Mo came up with himself. Whatever it takes to win. One of the best there is.

Year	Team	Lg.	Pos.	G	AB	R	H	HR	RBI	SB	BA
1993	Boston	AL	1B	152	539	86	160	29	101	4	.297
1994	Boston	AL	1B	111	394	65	122	26	82	4	.310
1995	Boston	AL	1B	140	550	98	165	39	126	11	.300
1996	Boston	AL	1B	161	635	118	207	44	143	2	.326
Post All-Star				76	294	53	89	18	65	2	.303

ROBIN VENTURA   Age 29/L $34

Starting at third base for the 1997 American League All-Stars. If there's any justice.

Year	Team	Lg.	Pos.	G	AB	R	H	HR	RBI	SB	BA
1993	Chicago	AL	3B	157	554	85	145	22	94	1	.262
1994	Chicago	AL	3B	109	401	57	113	18	78	3	.282
1995	Chicago	AL	3B	135	492	79	145	26	93	4	.295
1996	Chicago	AL	3B	158	586	96	168	34	105	1	.287
Post All-Star				74	274	46	80	15	50	1	.292

KEVIN YOUNG
Age 27/R   **$4**

With Offerman likely to move over to 2B, Young would seem to have the inside track on the full-time 1B job. Talk about a sleeper pick. Grab him cheap and thank us later.

Year	Team	Lg.	Pos.	G	AB	R	H	HR	RBI	SB	BA
1993	Pittsburgh	NL	1B	141	449	38	106	6	47	2	.236
1994	Pittsburgh	NL	1B	59	122	15	25	1	11	0	.205
1995	Pittsburgh	NL	3B	56	181	13	42	6	22	1	.232
1996	Kansas City	AL	1B	55	132	20	32	8	23	3	.242
Post All-Star				37	90	14	20	4	12	1	.222

TODD ZEILE
Age 31/R   **$13**

His arrival coincided with the Orioles' late surge into the wild card spot. A steady producer wherever he's been, but don't count on another 25-HR year.

Year	Team	Lg.	Pos.	G	AB	R	H	HR	RBI	SB	BA
1993	St. Louis	NL	3B	157	571	82	158	17	103	5	.277
1994	St. Louis	NL	3B	113	415	62	111	19	75	1	.267
1995	St. Louis	NL	1B	34	127	16	37	5	22	1	.291
1995	Chicago	NL	3B	79	299	34	68	9	30	0	.227
1996	Philadelphia	NL	3B	134	500	61	134	20	80	1	.268
1996	Baltimore	AL	3B	29	117	17	28	5	19	0	.239
Post All-Star				77	289	38	76	12	50	0	.263

Up the Middle

NATIONAL LEAGUE

KURT ABBOTT
Age 27/R   **$8**

Loaded with ability but lacking confidence to the point where he worried his way into the minors for a period of last season. Jim Leyland is a master at building people up, but the Marlins have so many infielders on the way up that they shipped him to Baltimore. Change of scenery could help.

Year	Team	Lg.	Pos.	G	AB	R	H	HR	RBI	SB	BA
1993	Oakland	AL	OF	20	61	11	15	3	9	2	.246
1994	Florida	NL	SS	101	345	41	86	9	33	3	.249
1995	Florida	NL	SS	120	420	60	107	17	60	4	.255
1996	Florida	NL	SS	109	320	37	81	8	33	3	.253
Post All-Star				59	155	20	40	5	25	2	.258

EDGARDO ALFONZO
Age 23/R   **$2**

The worry is that he may not ever hit enough to be more than a role player.

Year	Team	Lg.	Pos.	G	AB	R	H	HR	RBI	SB	BA
1995	New York	NL	3B	101	335	26	93	4	41	1	.278
1996	New York	NL	2B	123	368	36	96	4	40	2	.261
Post All-Star				67	236	17	62	4	32	1	.263

LUIS ALICEA
Age 31/B   **$4**

St. Louis figures Delino DeShields has more upside and that's probably true. But this guy is a steady performer worth a minor investment.

Year	Team	Lg.	Pos.	G	AB	R	H	HR	RBI	SB	BA
1993	St. Louis	NL	2B	115	362	50	101	3	46	11	.279
1994	St. Louis	NL	2B	88	205	32	57	5	29	4	.278
1995	Boston	AL	2B	132	419	64	113	6	44	13	.270
1996	St. Louis	NL	2B	129	380	54	98	5	42	11	.258
Post All-Star				49	120	22	36	1	13	6	.300

RICH AURILIA
Age 25/R   **$3**

With Shawon Dunston heading back to the friendly confines, Aurilia gets a chance to be the Giants' regular shortstop. Neither the Giants nor you should be excited about the prospect.

Year	Team	Lg.	Pos.	G	AB	R	H	HR	RBI	SB	BA
1995	San Francisco	NL	SS	9	19	4	9	2	4	1	.474
1996	San Francisco	NL	SS	105	318	27	76	3	26	4	.239
Post All-Star				62	210	17	52	0	16	4	.248

CARLOS BAERGA
Age 28/B   **$14**

When the Trade first went down, it seemed like a steal for the Mets. Then we heard all the Indians talk about how Carlos was never serious about conditioning. Then we heard all the stories about how much Carlos loved the nightlife. Then Indians GM John Hart told us, "If we were talking about the Carlos Baerga of three years ago, there's no way we would have thought about trading him. I still love the guy. But he has been going backward since the middle of the 1995 season, and we had the chance to dump a big salary." Then he arrived in New York out of shape, soon got injured, was a nonfactor, and ended the year with Mets whispering about how much his skills have eroded. So, spend on him if you like. We don't think he'll ever approach his former heights.

Year	Team	Lg.	Pos.	G	AB	R	H	HR	RBI	SB	BA
1993	Cleveland	AL	2B	154	624	105	200	21	114	15	.321
1994	Cleveland	AL	2B	103	442	81	139	19	80	8	.314
1995	Cleveland	AL	2B	135	557	87	175	15	90	11	.314
1996	Cleveland	AL	2B	100	424	54	113	10	55	1	.267
1996	New York	NL	1B	26	83	5	16	2	11	0	.193
Post All-Star				41	142	13	35	3	16	1	.246

JASON BATES
Age 26/B   **$1**

We thought he'd be much better. He might hang on as a utility guy, but big-time prospect Neifi Perez will leave him in the dust for everyday playing time.

Year	Team	Lg.	Pos.	G	AB	R	H	HR	RBI	SB	BA
1995	Colorado	NL	2B	116	322	42	86	8	46	3	.267
1996	Colorado	NL	2B	88	160	19	33	1	9	2	.206
Post All-Star				40	64	6	12	0	4	1	.188

Catchers pp. 27–39

Corners pp. 40–60

Infield pp. 60–80

Outfield pp. 80–111

DH pp. 112–115

Starters pp. 115–145

Relievers pp. 146–178

JAY BELL   Age 31/R $11

When Pittsburgh people whine about how they can't compete financially with the big boys, we like to point out that they didn't HAVE to give this slightly above average player a four-year contract worth $16 million. Bell still has some pop, though, so somebody will take his paycheck off the Pirates' hands. Frankly, we're tired of Pittsburgh.

Year	Team	Lg.	Pos.	G	AB	R	H	HR	RBI	SB	BA
1993	Pittsburgh	NL	SS	154	604	102	187	9	51	16	.310
1994	Pittsburgh	NL	SS	110	424	68	117	9	45	2	.276
1995	Pittsburgh	NL	SS	138	530	79	139	13	55	2	.262
1996	Pittsburgh	NL	SS	151	527	65	132	13	71	6	.250
Post All-Star				68	230	31	65	7	33	3	.283

RAFAEL BELLIARD   Age 35/R $1

What would the Braves be without Raffy? "You gotta love him; he'll sit for six months, and then we're in the playoffs and you look up and there he is making a play or actually getting a hit," says teammate Tom Glavine about Raffy. "He's amazing." Just as amazing is anyone spending more than pocket change on him. Never even drafted in most Rotisserie leagues. Shows what we know.

Year	Team	Lg.	Pos.	G	AB	R	H	HR	RBI	SB	BA
1993	Atlanta	NL	SS	91	79	6	18	0	6	0	.228
1994	Atlanta	NL	SS	46	120	9	29	0	9	0	.242
1995	Atlanta	NL	SS	75	180	12	40	0	7	2	.222
1996	Atlanta	NL	SS	87	142	9	24	0	3	3	.169
Post All-Star				39	55	5	10	0	0	1	.182

CRAIG BIGGIO   Age 31/R $33

A great player who had just an okay season. He admitted that he pressed early to justify his big, new contract. Like many of his teammates, he also did not get along with departed manager Terry Collins. We see him bouncing back big-time this year.

Year	Team	Lg.	Pos.	G	AB	R	H	HR	RBI	SB	BA
1993	Houston	NL	2B	155	610	98	175	21	64	15	.287
1994	Houston	NL	2B	114	437	88	139	6	56	39	.318
1995	Houston	NL	2B	141	553	123	167	22	77	33	.302
1996	Houston	NL	2B	162	605	113	174	15	75	25	.288
Post All-Star				73	272	46	74	5	28	9	.272

JEFF BLAUSER   Age 31/R $14

He was hurt all year, which translated into a second straight down season. But Atlanta would prefer not to play Chipper Jones at short, and the Braves' talent factory is at least a year away from producing any reasonable shortstop alternatives. So unless Atlanta goes the free-agent route for a shortstop (highly unlikely), Blauser will have the job, and if he stays healthy, we think he can bounce back with close to 20 homers.

Year	Team	Lg.	Pos.	G	AB	R	H	HR	RBI	SB	BA
1993	Atlanta	NL	SS	161	597	110	182	15	73	16	.305
1994	Atlanta	NL	SS	96	380	56	98	6	45	1	.258
1995	Atlanta	NL	SS	115	431	60	91	12	31	8	.211
1996	Atlanta	NL	SS	83	265	48	65	10	35	6	.245
Post All-Star				15	30	8	7	0	4	2	.233

BRET BOONE — Age 27/R — $12

His numbers looked sour. But he had a good excuse. "He could hardly swing the bat for the first three months because of his back, but he never complained," said manager Ray Knight. "He killed his season, but he wouldn't come out, because he knew how much he helps us defensively." Bet on a rebound. Reds tried to move him all fall, so beware.

Year	Team	Lg.	Pos.	G	AB	R	H	HR	RBI	SB	BA
1993	Seattle	AL	2B	76	271	31	68	12	38	2	.251
1994	Cincinnati	NL	2B	108	381	59	122	12	68	3	.320
1995	Cincinnati	NL	2B	138	513	63	137	15	68	5	.267
1996	Cincinnati	NL	2B	142	520	56	121	12	69	3	.233
Post All-Star				76	283	27	64	4	33	1	.226

JEFF BRANSON — Age 30/L — $5

A nice player to have in your mix.

Year	Team	Lg.	Pos.	G	AB	R	H	HR	RBI	SB	BA
1993	Cincinnati	NL	SS	125	381	40	92	3	22	4	.241
1994	Cincinnati	NL	2B	58	109	18	31	6	16	0	.284
1995	Cincinnati	NL	3B	122	331	43	86	12	45	2	.260
1996	Cincinnati	NL	3B	129	311	34	76	9	37	2	.244
Post All-Star				56	122	13	32	4	15	1	.262

JUAN CASTRO — Age 24/R — $1

He can't hit a lick, but he sure smokes a mean cigar.

Year	Team	Lg.	Pos.	G	AB	R	H	HR	RBI	SB	BA
1995	Los Angeles	NL	3B	11	4	0	1	0	0	0	.250
1996	Los Angeles	NL	SS	70	132	16	26	0	5	1	.197
Post All-Star				27	42	5	7	0	2	1	.167

ANDUJAR CEDENO — Age 27/R — $1

When you can't stick with the Tigers, you know your career is hanging by a thread.

Year	Team	Lg.	Pos.	G	AB	R	H	HR	RBI	SB	BA
1993	Houston	NL	SS	149	505	69	143	11	56	9	.283
1994	Houston	NL	SS	98	342	38	90	9	49	1	.263
1995	San Diego	NL	SS	120	390	42	82	6	31	5	.210
1996	San Diego	NL	SS	49	154	10	36	3	18	3	.234
1996	Detroit	AL	SS	52	179	19	35	7	20	2	.196
1996	Houston	NL	SS	3	2	1	0	0	0	0	0.000
Post All-Star				40	130	15	26	7	17	1	.200

ROYCE CLAYTON — Age 27/R — $13

All in all, he held his own in the Land of Oz. He'll never put up big power numbers, but we like the steals and his overall production will improve when the Cardinals get him out of the leadoff spot, for which he's ill-suited.

Year	Team	Lg.	Pos.	G	AB	R	H	HR	RBI	SB	BA
1993	San Francisco	NL	SS	153	549	54	155	6	70	11	.282
1994	San Francisco	NL	SS	108	385	38	91	3	30	23	.236
1995	San Francisco	NL	SS	138	509	56	124	5	58	24	.244
1996	St. Louis	NL	SS	129	491	64	136	6	35	33	.277
Post All-Star				56	214	28	59	3	16	15	.276

Catchers pp. 27-39

Corners pp. 40-60

Infield pp. 60-80

Outfield pp. 80-111

DH pp. 112-115

Starters pp. 115-145

Relievers pp. 146-178

DELINO DeSHIELDS   Age 28/L $15

New job in St. Louis could revive a strangely fading career. Remember when they used to talk about him as a potential batting champion?

Year	Team	Lg.	Pos.	G	AB	R	H	HR	RBI	SB	BA
1993	Montreal	NL	2B	123	481	75	142	2	29	43	.295
1994	Los Angeles	NL	2B	89	320	51	80	2	33	27	.250
1995	Los Angeles	NL	2B	127	425	66	109	8	37	39	.256
1996	Los Angeles	NL	2B	154	581	75	130	5	41	48	.224
Post All-Star				68	239	33	44	0	12	18	.184

SHAWON DUNSTON   Age 34/R $16

Injuries sliced his season in half, but as he was one of the few major league players left in San Francisco, we figured he'd stay, maybe move to center field. Guess if you've actually played on that "team" you grab any chance you can to get out. Still has a bat, but we wonder whether injuries haven't worn him down too much for him to be an everyday shortstop.

Year	Team	Lg.	Pos.	G	AB	R	H	HR	RBI	SB	BA
1993	Chicago	NL	SS	7	10	3	4	0	2	0	.400
1994	Chicago	NL	SS	88	331	38	92	11	35	3	.278
1995	Chicago	NL	SS	127	477	58	141	14	69	10	.296
1996	San Francisco	NL	SS	82	287	27	86	5	25	8	.300
Post All-Star				22	75	3	20	0	3	3	.267

CHAD FONVILLE   Age 26/B $1

No thanks.

Year	Team	Lg.	Pos.	G	AB	R	H	HR	RBI	SB	BA
1995	Montreal	NL	2B	14	12	2	4	0	0	0	.333
1995	Los Angeles	NL	SS	88	308	41	85	0	16	20	.276
1996	Los Angeles	NL	OF	103	201	34	41	0	13	7	.204
Post All-Star				30	41	5	4	0	3	0	.098

GREG GAGNE   Age 35/R $6

Nice power at times, but NL scouts say his arm and range have significantly gone backward—and if this guy can't field, his bat isn't going to carry him.

Year	Team	Lg.	Pos.	G	AB	R	H	HR	RBI	SB	BA
1993	Kansas City	AL	SS	159	540	66	151	10	57	10	.280
1994	Kansas City	AL	SS	107	375	39	97	7	51	10	.259
1995	Kansas City	AL	SS	120	430	58	110	6	49	3	.256
1996	Los Angeles	NL	SS	128	428	48	109	10	55	4	.255
Post All-Star				73	248	26	60	5	33	2	.242

MIKE GALLEGO   Age 36/R $1

There's not much left in his tank.

Year	Team	Lg.	Pos.	G	AB	R	H	HR	RBI	SB	BA
1993	New York	AL	SS	119	403	63	114	10	54	3	.283
1994	New York	AL	SS	89	306	39	73	6	41	0	.239
1995	Oakland	AL	2B	43	120	11	28	0	8	0	.233
1996	St. Louis	NL	2B	51	143	12	30	0	4	0	.210
Post All-Star				51	143	12	30	0	4	0	.210

CARLOS GARCIA

Age 29/R   **$12**

At various times, he was rumored to be headed to San Diego, the Yankees, Baltimore, Los Angeles, Atlanta, and Texas. So naturally he ended up in Toronto. The Pirates have dropped all pretense of trying to compete, so they accepted Buptus in return, just to shed his salary, he'll probably end up somewhere else. On a good club, and Toronto has become one again, his considerable skills should really blossom.

Year	Team	Lg.	Pos.	G	AB	R	H	HR	RBI	SB	BA
1993	Pittsburgh	NL	2B	141	546	77	147	12	47	18	.269
1994	Pittsburgh	NL	2B	98	412	49	114	6	28	18	.277
1995	Pittsburgh	NL	2B	104	367	41	108	6	50	8	.294
1996	Pittsburgh	NL	2B	101	390	66	111	6	44	16	.285
Post All-Star				39	149	26	41	3	16	2	.275

CHRIS GOMEZ

Age 25/R   **$6**

His power hasn't developed the way many thought it would. But he was a slick pickup for the Padres and is certain to be their regular shortstop.

Year	Team	Lg.	Pos.	G	AB	R	H	HR	RBI	SB	BA
1993	Detroit	AL	SS	46	128	11	32	0	11	2	.250
1994	Detroit	AL	SS	84	296	32	76	8	53	5	.257
1995	Detroit	AL	SS	123	431	49	96	11	50	4	.223
1996	Detroit	AL	SS	48	128	21	31	1	16	1	.242
1996	San Diego	NL	SS	89	328	32	86	3	29	2	.262
Post All-Star				71	269	27	68	2	22	0	.253

MARK GRUDZEILANEK

Age 26/R   **$14**

He wore down a little toward the end of the year (see Mike Lansing). But in the Year of the Young Shortstop, he can hold his own. The Expos think he will add power as he gains experience.

Year	Team	Lg.	Pos.	G	AB	R	H	HR	RBI	SB	BA
1995	Montreal	NL	SS	78	269	27	66	1	20	8	.245
1996	Montreal	NL	SS	153	657	99	201	6	49	33	.306
Post All-Star				73	300	33	84	1	19	16	.280

RICKY GUTIERREZ

Age 26/R   **$1**

Bow-wow.

Year	Team	Lg.	Pos.	G	AB	R	H	HR	RBI	SB	BA
1993	San Diego	NL	SS	133	438	76	110	5	26	4	.251
1994	San Diego	NL	SS	90	275	27	66	1	28	2	.240
1995	Houston	NL	SS	52	156	22	43	0	12	5	.276
1996	Houston	NL	SS	89	218	28	62	1	15	6	.284
Post All-Star				35	79	6	19	1	4	1	.241

JOSE HERNANDEZ

Age 27/R   **$5**

Surprising pop makes him a nice sleeper in a reserve role.

Year	Team	Lg.	Pos.	G	AB	R	H	HR	RBI	SB	BA
1994	Chicago	NL	3B	56	132	18	32	1	9	2	.242
1995	Chicago	NL	SS	93	245	37	60	13	40	1	.245
1996	Chicago	NL	SS	131	331	52	80	10	41	4	.242
Post All-Star				62	146	32	39	7	23	2	.267

Catchers
pp. 27-39

Corners
pp. 40-60

Infield
pp. 60-80

Outfield
pp. 80-111

DH
pp. 112-115

Starters
pp. 115-145

Relievers
pp. 146-178

MIKE LANSING   Age 28/R $15

Expos people think he's among the most underrated players in baseball, and so do we. However, Montreal needs to find some room in their tightwad budget for some reserve help. "We didn't have much in the way of backup infielders, so unfortunately, we had to play Mike to death," said Felipe Alou. "He was dragging by the end of the year, and it showed in his play. But what can I do?" Well, Felipe, you could go manage in another city that can support major league baseball and give yourself a fair chance to win.

Year	Team	Lg.	Pos.	G	AB	R	H	HR	RBI	SB	BA
1993	Montreal	NL	3B	141	491	64	141	3	45	23	.287
1994	Montreal	NL	2B	106	394	44	105	5	35	12	.266
1995	Montreal	NL	2B	127	467	47	119	10	62	27	.255
1996	Montreal	NL	2B	159	641	99	183	11	53	23	.285
Post All-Star				74	297	41	77	6	24	11	.259

BARRY LARKIN   Age 32/R $34

It was shortly after Marge Schott's latest journey into the world of ethnic cleansing and you'd think there would be an aura of discord around the Reds. But Larkin wouldn't let it happen. "He's amazing, he got the whole team together in the clubhouse and made sure we all knew that this crap had nothing to do with us," said Jeff Brantley. "He made sure we kept our dignity as players while all that other stuff was going on." Dignity, schmignity. We like all those home runs.

Year	Team	Lg.	Pos.	G	AB	R	H	HR	RBI	SB	BA
1993	Cincinnati	NL	SS	100	384	57	121	8	51	14	.315
1994	Cincinnati	NL	SS	110	427	78	119	9	52	26	.279
1995	Cincinnati	NL	SS	131	496	98	158	15	66	51	.319
1996	Cincinnati	NL	SS	152	517	117	154	33	89	36	.298
Post All-Star				76	251	67	78	21	55	15	.311

MARK LEMKE   Age 31/B $3

We probably overquote Bobby Cox, but it's hard to resist the novelty of someone being honest. So, we asked the manager of all those Braves stars who his favorite Atlanta player is. Without hesitation, the answer was, "Oh, it has to be Lemke. He's a beauty, a dirtball, the kind of guy that used to play on the sandlots 30 years ago. I love that guy." Alas, a manager's favorite is not always a Rotisserie dream. Could end up in Yankee pinstripes.

Year	Team	Lg.	Pos.	G	AB	R	H	HR	RBI	SB	BA
1993	Atlanta	NL	2B	151	493	52	124	7	49	1	.252
1994	Atlanta	NL	2B	104	350	40	103	3	31	0	.294
1995	Atlanta	NL	2B	116	399	42	101	5	38	2	.253
1996	Atlanta	NL	2B	135	498	64	127	5	37	5	.255
Post All-Star				68	245	27	57	1	16	3	.233

NELSON LIRIANO   Age 32/B $1

Can help a bench.

Year	Team	Lg.	Pos.	G	AB	R	H	HR	RBI	SB	BA
1993	Colorado	NL	SS	48	151	28	46	2	15	6	.305
1994	Colorado	NL	2B	87	255	39	65	3	31	0	.255
1995	Pittsburgh	NL	2B	107	259	29	74	5	38	2	.286
1996	Pittsburgh	NL	2B	112	217	23	58	3	30	2	.267
Post All-Star				52	102	13	31	2	23	2	.304

ORLANDO MILLER   Age 28/R $13

His wild throwing arm still scares the heck out of fans behind first base, which isn't a major problem in Houston since they don't have that many fans sitting behind first (or third) base. But that power shouldn't scare you at all, and he's added 10 pounds of muscle that could make him even better.

Year	Team	Lg.	Pos.	G	AB	R	H	HR	RBI	SB	BA
1994	Houston	NL	SS	16	40	3	13	2	9	1	.325
1995	Houston	NL	SS	92	324	36	85	5	36	3	.262
1996	Houston	NL	SS	139	468	43	120	15	58	3	.256
Post All-Star				67	219	16	53	8	22	2	.242

RALPH MILLIARD   Age 23/R $1

He'll get a shot at being the Marlins' second baseman because he can field the position with anyone. Unfortunately, this Netherlands native hits like the Little Dutch Boy. Stay tuned.

Year	Team	Lg.	Pos.	G	AB	R	H	HR	RBI	SB	BA
1996	Florida	NL	2B	24	62	7	10	0	1	2	.161
Post All-Star				6	21	2	3	0	0	2	.143

MICKEY MORANDINI   Age 30/L $7

One of the few real pros left in Philadelphia, last year's losing affected his performance. That's why it was surprising when he agreed to a new multiyear contract with the Phillies. "Hey, I know I'll play here, and how can it ever get worse than it was here this year?" explained the Mick. Good point.

Year	Team	Lg.	Pos.	G	AB	R	H	HR	RBI	SB	BA
1993	Philadelphia	NL	2B	120	425	57	105	3	33	13	.247
1994	Philadelphia	NL	2B	87	274	40	80	2	26	10	.292
1995	Philadelphia	NL	2B	127	494	65	140	6	49	9	.283
1996	Philadelphia	NL	2B	140	539	64	135	3	32	26	.250
Post All-Star				68	254	27	58	1	16	7	.228

MIKE MORDECAI   Age 29/R $1

Can you break a buck?

Year	Team	Lg.	Pos.	G	AB	R	H	HR	RBI	SB	BA
1994	Atlanta	NL	SS	4	4	1	1	1	3	0	.250
1995	Atlanta	NL	2B	69	75	10	21	3	11	0	.280
1996	Atlanta	NL	2B	66	108	12	26	2	8	1	.241
Post All-Star				38	61	6	14	2	5	0	.230

REY ORDONEZ   Age 24/R $2

Early in the season, he was hitting .350 and the always-restrained New York media was speculating how well he would deliver his induction speech at Cooperstown. But the lamentedly departed Dallas Green was not convinced. "Yeah, he makes plays I've never seen anyone make, and when he grows up emotionally and physically, he'll hit a little," said Green. "But once every team gets a look at him, they'll knock the bat out of his hands. And if he keeps trying to make every play look hard, he might end up with more errors

Catchers
pp. 27–39

Corners
pp. 40–60

Infield
pp. 60–80

Outfield
pp. 80–111

DH
pp. 112–115

Starters
pp. 115–145

Relievers
pp. 146–178

than RBI." Well, Dallas was wrong about that one. Ordonez made 27 errors but drove in 29 runs. Maybe that's why Joe McIlvaine made Green the scapegoat for injuries and a not-ready-for-prime-time roster.

Year	Team	Lg.	Pos.	G	AB	R	H	HR	RBI	SB	BA
1996	New York	NL	SS	151	502	51	129	1	30	1	.257
Post All-Star				70	230	25	58	1	17	1	.252

JODY REED   Age 34/R $1

Still feisty.

Year	Team	Lg.	Pos.	G	AB	R	H	HR	RBI	SB	BA
1993	Los Angeles	NL	2B	132	445	48	123	2	31	1	.276
1994	Milwaukee	AL	2B	108	399	48	108	2	37	5	.271
1995	San Diego	NL	2B	131	445	58	114	4	40	6	.256
1996	San Diego	NL	2B	146	495	45	121	2	49	2	.244
Post All-Star				64	191	17	49	1	20	0	.257

EDGAR RENTERIA   Age 21/R $13

He is a five-category superstar waiting to happen. Grab him before his price goes into orbit.

Year	Team	Lg.	Pos.	G	AB	R	H	HR	RBI	SB	BA
1996	Florida	NL	SS	106	431	68	133	5	31	16	.309
Post All-Star				74	302	54	101	4	24	16	.334

REY SANCHEZ   Age 29/R $1

He was bothered by a bad wrist all season. But even at his best, he's never going to bring much to the dance.

Year	Team	Lg.	Pos.	G	AB	R	H	HR	RBI	SB	BA
1993	Chicago	NL	SS	105	344	35	97	0	28	1	.282
1994	Chicago	NL	2B	96	291	26	83	0	24	2	.285
1995	Chicago	NL	2B	114	428	57	119	3	27	6	.278
1996	Chicago	NL	SS	95	289	28	61	1	12	7	.211
Post All-Star				43	128	14	27	0	5	2	.211

RYNE SANDBERG   Age 37/R $18

Topped 100 strikeouts (113) for only the second time in his illustrious career (he had 101 in 1984—in 82 more AB) and batted 45 points below his career average, so you figure his bat has slowed down some. But when he did make contact—kapow! Some midwinter rumblings out of Chicago that he might be going elsewhere. If he does become an ex-Cub, go bearish—at this stage in his career, he needs Wrigley Field more than Wrigley Field needs him.

Year	Team	Lg.	Pos.	G	AB	R	H	HR	RBI	SB	BA
1993	Chicago	NL	2B	117	456	67	141	9	45	9	.309
1994	Chicago	NL	2B	57	223	36	53	5	24	2	.238
1996	Chicago	NL	2B	150	554	85	135	25	92	12	.244
Post All-Star				72	258	41	62	11	43	6	.240

STEVE SCARSONE
Age 30/R   **$3**

He looks like so many other Giants. And that is not a compliment.

Year	Team	Lg.	Pos.	G	AB	R	H	HR	RBI	SB	BA
1993	San Francisco	NL	2B	44	103	16	26	2	15	0	.252
1994	San Francisco	NL	2B	52	103	21	28	2	13	0	.272
1995	San Francisco	NL	3B	80	233	33	62	11	29	3	.266
1996	San Francisco	NL	2B	105	283	28	62	5	23	2	.219
Post All-Star				44	104	10	19	1	8	2	.183

OZZIE SMITH
Age 42/B   **Priceless**

Count on him turning up on one of the networks this year and in Cooperstown five years from now. Rarely has an opposing player ever had a warmer reception than the Wizard received on his farewell tour to National League cities. He didn't even get booed in Philadelphia.

Year	Team	Lg.	Pos.	G	AB	R	H	HR	RBI	SB	BA
1993	St. Louis	NL	SS	141	545	75	157	1	53	21	.288
1994	St. Louis	NL	SS	98	381	51	100	3	30	6	.262
1995	St. Louis	NL	SS	44	156	16	31	0	11	4	.199
1996	St. Louis	NL	SS	82	227	36	64	2	18	7	.282
Post All-Star				48	126	25	37	2	10	5	.294

KEVIN STOCKER
Age 27/B   **$5**

Here's how much the Phillies thought of him: they tried giving away his job to a parade of immortals starting with Mike Benjamin and continuing through Kevin Sefcik, David Doster, and Desi Relaford. It shouldn't be a surprise that, after all that, Stocker started looking good again. He regained much of his shattered confidence and over the last six weeks swung the bat like he did in 1993. Definitely a sleeper in this year's draft.

Year	Team	Lg.	Pos.	G	AB	R	H	HR	RBI	SB	BA
1993	Philadelphia	NL	SS	70	259	46	84	2	31	5	.324
1994	Philadelphia	NL	SS	82	271	38	74	2	28	2	.273
1995	Philadelphia	NL	SS	125	412	42	90	1	32	6	.218
1996	Philadelphia	NL	SS	119	394	46	100	5	41	6	.254
Post All-Star				66	229	31	67	2	22	1	.293

ROBBY THOMPSON
Age 34/R   **$2**

It looks like the end of the road unless he surfaces in the American League, where he might still have some use.

Year	Team	Lg.	Pos.	G	AB	R	H	HR	RBI	SB	BA
1993	San Francisco	NL	2B	128	494	85	154	19	65	10	.312
1994	San Francisco	NL	2B	35	129	13	27	2	7	3	.209
1995	San Francisco	NL	2B	95	336	51	75	8	23	1	.223
1996	San Francisco	NL	2B	63	227	35	48	5	21	2	.211
Post All-Star				15	42	2	6	0	5	0	.143

QUILVIO VERAS
Age 25/B   **$12**

It takes character to admit mistakes. We branded him a future star. How would we know that he'd hit nearly 80 points lower vs. right-handers, become erratic in the field, and lose his confidence (and with it most of his base-

Catchers
pp. 27-39

Corners
pp. 40-60

Infield
pp. 60-80

Outfield
pp. 80-111

DH
pp. 112-115

Starters
pp. 115-145

Relievers
pp. 146-178

stealing verve)? How would we know he'd disappear from sight after midseason? We do know that, with all that speed and a healed hamstring, he could be the steal of the draft.

Year	Team	Lg.	Pos.	G	AB	R	H	HR	RBI	SB	BA
1995	Florida	NL	2B	124	440	86	115	5	32	56	.261
1996	Florida	NL	2B	73	253	40	64	4	14	8	.253
Post All-Star				23	82	18	21	1	5	2	.256

WALT WEISS   Age 33/B $6

Who says the ball was juiced? He had 3 homers in his 405 National League games prior to last year and then hit 8 last year alone. A pro's pro who lends some seasoned sanity to the Rockies' home-away schizophrenia. However, he could become expendable because of money and Neifi Perez, that is, unless the Rockies decide instead to shop . . .

Year	Team	Lg.	Pos.	G	AB	R	H	HR	RBI	SB	BA
1993	Florida	NL	SS	158	500	50	133	1	39	7	.266
1994	Colorado	NL	SS	110	423	58	106	1	32	12	.251
1995	Colorado	NL	SS	137	427	65	111	1	25	15	.260
1996	Colorado	NL	SS	155	517	89	146	8	48	10	.282
Post All-Star				70	227	33	58	6	23	6	.256

ERIC YOUNG   Age 29/R $22

. . . who had a monster year that was strangely unappreciated by Rockies people, who view him as a selfish player and a self-promoter. Selfish doesn't bother us, not when you put up numbers like this.

Year	Team	Lg.	Pos.	G	AB	R	H	HR	RBI	SB	BA
1993	Colorado	NL	2B	144	490	82	132	3	42	42	.269
1994	Colorado	NL	OF	90	228	37	62	7	30	18	.272
1995	Colorado	NL	2B	120	366	68	116	6	36	35	.317
1996	Colorado	NL	2B	141	568	113	184	8	74	53	.324
Post All-Star				72	293	53	89	4	36	22	.304

AMERICAN LEAGUE

MANNY ALEXANDER   Age 26/R $1

Missed his opportunity to be the Babe Dahlgren of our times. Not that he knows, or cares, who Babe Dahlgren is.

Year	Team	Lg.	Pos.	G	AB	R	H	HR	RBI	SB	BA
1993	Baltimore	AL	DH	3	0	1	0	0	0	0	0.000
1995	Baltimore	AL	2B	94	242	35	57	3	23	11	.236
1996	Baltimore	AL	SS	53	68	6	7	0	4	3	.103
Post All-Star				28	32	3	1	0	0	0	.031

ROBERTO ALOMAR   Age 29/B $33

Guess what folks, the Ponce Peach is still the best darn second baseman in the world, even if he was—temporarily, it will never happen again, really—in league with Satan.

Year	Team	Lg.	Pos.	G	AB	R	H	HR	RBI	SB	BA
1993	Toronto	AL	2B	153	589	109	192	17	93	55	.326
1994	Toronto	AL	2B	107	392	78	120	8	38	19	.306
1995	Toronto	AL	2B	130	517	71	155	13	66	30	.300
1996	Baltimore	AL	2B	153	588	132	193	22	94	17	.328
Post All-Star				69	261	62	78	11	41	6	.299

Catchers
pp. 27-39

Corners
pp. 40-60

Infield
pp. 60-80

Outfield
pp. 80-111

DH
pp. 112-115

Starters
pp. 115-145

Relievers
pp. 146-178

TONY BATISTA   Age 23/R $4

For many years, this space was used to sing the praises of Carlos Baerga and his wonder bat. We can't sing the praises of Tony Batista just yet, but these are nice numbers to warm up with.

Year	Team	Lg.	Pos.	G	AB	R	H	HR	RBI	SB	BA
1996	Oakland	AL	2B	74	238	38	71	6	25	7	.298
Post All-Star				56	198	30	57	5	24	6	.288

MIKE BORDICK   Age 31/R $6

Amazing how different this game is from actual baseball. Tony LaRussa used to say Bordick was the most valuable player in Oakland. Maybe he still is, in their game.

Year	Team	Lg.	Pos.	G	AB	R	H	HR	RBI	SB	BA
1993	Oakland	AL	SS	159	546	60	136	3	48	10	.249
1994	Oakland	AL	SS	114	391	38	99	2	37	7	.253
1995	Oakland	AL	SS	126	428	46	113	8	44	11	.264
1996	Oakland	AL	SS	155	525	46	126	5	54	5	.240
Post All-Star				72	247	23	64	3	24	2	.259

RAFAEL BOURNIGAL   Age 30/R $1

If you had this Bournigal last year, pray he doesn't return.

Year	Team	Lg.	Pos.	G	AB	R	H	HR	RBI	SB	BA
1993	Los Angeles	NL	2B	8	18	0	9	0	3	0	.500
1994	Los Angeles	NL	SS	40	116	2	26	0	11	0	.224
1996	Oakland	AL	2B	88	252	33	61	0	18	4	.242
Post All-Star				45	125	12	23	0	8	0	.184

DOMINGO CEDENO   Age 28/B $2

He used to make a living backing up the Splendid Spitter. Now he's backing up Ray Durham.

Year	Team	Lg.	Pos.	G	AB	R	H	HR	RBI	SB	BA
1993	Toronto	AL	SS	15	46	5	8	0	7	1	.174
1994	Toronto	AL	2B	47	97	14	19	0	10	1	.196
1995	Toronto	AL	SS	51	161	18	38	4	14	0	.236
1996	Toronto	AL	2B	77	282	44	79	2	17	5	.280
1996	Chicago	AL	2B	12	19	2	3	0	3	1	.158
Post All-Star				27	67	11	16	1	4	2	.239

JOEY CORA   Age 31/B $3

The errors came down but so did the stolen bases, which is where his Rotisserie value was. There was a feeling that Arquimedez Pozo would push him aside, but they sent him to Boston, probably because he missed a bunt sign in high school that Piniella got wind of. Anyway, Cora is safe, despite

---

these numbers, because the Mariners need to spend all their money on pitching. You still don't want him.

Year	Team	Lg.	Pos.	G	AB	R	H	HR	RBI	SB	BA
1993	Chicago	AL	2B	153	579	95	155	2	51	20	.268
1994	Chicago	AL	2B	90	312	55	86	2	30	8	.276
1995	Seattle	AL	2B	120	427	64	127	3	39	18	.297
1996	Seattle	AL	2B	144	530	90	154	6	45	5	.291
Post All-Star				68	242	45	73	3	20	0	.302

WIL CORDERO   Age 25/R $14

The Red Sox have themselves a nice left fielder-shortstop-second baseman here. Unfortunately, he really can't field any of those positions. Hey, that's their problem. He can hit for you from wherever he plays. His moving around is good for your roster, anyway. Look for him to get back on track.

Year	Team	Lg.	Pos.	G	AB	R	H	HR	RBI	SB	BA
1993	Montreal	NL	SS	138	475	56	118	10	58	12	.248
1994	Montreal	NL	SS	110	415	65	122	15	63	16	.294
1995	Montreal	NL	SS	131	514	64	147	10	49	9	.286
1996	Boston	AL	2B	59	198	29	57	3	37	2	.288
Post All-Star				21	41	8	12	1	9	0	.293

GARY DISARCINA   Age 29/R $5

He produced a lot more in 1995 when he played 51 fewer games. Last year, he hit .203 and had 3 RBI, no HR, and no SB in September. That tells us that 5 HR, 40-something RBI, and a couple of steals are what you'll get. When he nears those marks, try to trade him to someone who doesn't own this book.

Year	Team	Lg.	Pos.	G	AB	R	H	HR	RBI	SB	BA
1993	California	AL	SS	126	416	44	99	3	45	5	.238
1994	California	AL	SS	112	389	53	101	3	33	3	.260
1995	California	AL	SS	99	362	61	111	5	41	7	.307
1996	California	AL	SS	150	536	62	137	5	48	2	.256
Post All-Star				68	254	29	68	4	19	2	.268

MARIANO DUNCAN   Age 34/R $10

Picking up a guy like this for a song on draft day and having him perform this way is how Rotisserie dreams come true. From third-string to the best hitter in the Bronx, and you had him. Now get rid of him because it's not gonna happen again.

Year	Team	Lg.	Pos.	G	AB	R	H	HR	RBI	SB	BA
1993	Philadelphia	NL	2B	124	496	68	140	11	73	6	.282
1994	Philadelphia	NL	2B	88	347	49	93	8	48	10	.268
1995	Philadelphia	NL	2B	52	196	20	56	3	23	1	.286
1995	Cincinnati	NL	2B	29	69	16	20	3	13	0	.290
1996	New York	AL	2B	109	400	62	136	8	56	4	.340
Post All-Star				56	199	31	73	4	29	2	.367

RAY DURHAM   Age 25/B $25

Other than a ghastly June (no HR, no SB, 5 RBI), this guy had a great year. He is most productive hitting seventh or eighth, so take note in spring training if the White Sox try to make him a number-two guy (where he steals more, but all the other numbers fall way off). Overall, expect more improvement across the board, as Durham is just entering his prime. On a personal note, Red Sox fans love him since he almost clobbered Bill Buckner in September.

Year	Team	Lg.	Pos.	G	AB	R	H	HR	RBI	SB	BA
1995	Chicago	AL	2B	125	471	68	121	7	51	18	.257
1996	Chicago	AL	2B	156	557	79	153	10	65	30	.275
Post All-Star				75	273	42	78	5	34	22	.286

DAMION EASLEY   Age 27/B $3

There is nothing more limiting than being a limited role player on the Detroit Tigers.

Year	Team	Lg.	Pos.	G	AB	R	H	HR	RBI	SB	BA
1993	California	AL	2B	73	230	33	72	2	22	6	.313
1994	California	AL	3B	88	316	41	68	6	30	4	.215
1995	California	AL	2B	114	357	35	77	4	35	5	.216
1996	California	AL	SS	28	45	4	7	2	7	0	.156
1996	Detroit	AL	2B	21	67	10	23	2	10	3	.343
Post All-Star				26	72	10	23	2	10	3	.319

KEVIN ELSTER   Age 32/R $10

If you think Kevin Elster will hit 20 HR and approach 100 RBI this year, you will finish last in your league. It was a mirage, an enigma, a trick. If you still have Elster, trade him *now*, before your co-owners get their hands on this book.

Year	Team	Lg.	Pos.	G	AB	R	H	HR	RBI	SB	BA
1994	New York	AL	SS	7	20	0	0	0	0	0	.000
1995	New York	AL	SS	10	17	1	2	0	0	0	.118
1995	Philadelphia	NL	SS	26	53	10	11	1	9	0	.208
1996	Texas	AL	SS	157	515	79	130	24	99	4	.252
Post All-Star				72	243	35	59	11	41	1	.243

ANDY FOX   Age 26/L $1

We know a dentist in Longmeadow, Massachusetts, named Andy Fox. He has better hands and can probably hit for a better average. Unless you want to experience all the joys of a root canal job, be silent if this Andy Fox's name comes up at your draft.

Year	Team	Lg.	Pos.	G	AB	R	H	HR	RBI	SB	BA
1996	New York	AL	2B	113	189	26	37	3	13	11	.196
Post All-Star				54	72	11	13	1	5	2	.181

JEFF FRYE   Age 30/R $12

Solid year, indicative of more good things to come. Unfortunately, he's in Boston, where they seem to have forgotten how to run a baseball team. He's a good pick, but watch where he ends up.

Year	Team	Lg.	Pos.	G	AB	R	H	HR	RBI	SB	BA
1994	Texas	AL	2B	57	205	37	67	0	18	6	.327
1995	Texas	AL	2B	90	313	38	87	4	29	3	.278
1996	Boston	AL	2B	105	419	74	120	4	41	18	.286
Post All-Star				76	303	52	94	4	33	18	.310

Catchers
pp. 27–39

Corners
pp. 40–60

Infield
pp. 60–80

Outfield
pp. 80–111

DH
pp. 112–115

Starters
pp. 115–145

Relievers
pp. 146–178

BRENT GATES   Age 27/B $4

Not as impressive as we expected him to be.

Year	Team	Lg.	Pos.	G	AB	R	H	HR	RBI	SB	BA
1993	Oakland	AL	2B	139	535	64	155	7	69	7	.290
1994	Oakland	AL	2B	64	233	29	66	2	24	3	.283
1995	Oakland	AL	2B	136	524	60	133	5	56	3	.254
1996	Oakland	AL	2B	64	247	26	65	2	30	1	.263
Post All-Star				0	0	0	0	0	0	0	.000

ALEX GONZALEZ   Age 23/R $12

Decent power and respectable speed, but it all hinges on that batting average. Last year, he had more strikeouts than hits. Still, he's only 23 and shows a lot of natural talent. One of the game's brightest prospects at SS two years ago, and he's not even talked about anymore. Actually, that's good. You might get him cheap.

Year	Team	Lg.	Pos.	G	AB	R	H	HR	RBI	SB	BA
1994	Toronto	AL	SS	15	53	7	8	0	1	3	.151
1995	Toronto	AL	SS	111	367	51	89	10	42	4	.243
1996	Toronto	AL	SS	147	527	64	124	14	64	16	.235
Post All-Star				68	230	30	52	8	29	7	.226

OZZIE GUILLEN   Age 33/L $5

Last year, we predicted a comeback. We couldn't have been more wrong. Not as far gone as the other Ozzie, but he's fading fast.

Year	Team	Lg.	Pos.	G	AB	R	H	HR	RBI	SB	BA
1993	Chicago	AL	SS	134	457	44	128	4	50	5	.280
1994	Chicago	AL	SS	100	365	46	105	1	39	5	.288
1995	Chicago	AL	SS	122	415	50	103	1	41	6	.248
1996	Chicago	AL	SS	150	499	62	131	4	45	6	.263
Post All-Star				67	205	19	50	2	19	1	.244

DAVE HOWARD   Age 30/B $3

Guys that hit .219 in their sixth major league season are long shots for a seventh. He hits .225 vs. righties and .205 vs. lefties. Why bother switch-hitting? Look, ma! I can't do it from either side!

Year	Team	Lg.	Pos.	G	AB	R	H	HR	RBI	SB	BA
1993	Kansas City	AL	2B	15	24	5	8	0	2	1	.333
1994	Kansas City	AL	3B	46	83	9	19	1	13	3	.229
1995	Kansas City	AL	2B	95	255	23	62	0	19	6	.243
1996	Kansas City	AL	SS	143	420	51	92	4	48	5	.219
Post All-Star				58	151	19	28	2	22	0	.185

MATT HOWARD   Age 29/R $1

The unwelcome Matt.

Year	Team	Lg.	Pos.	G	AB	R	H	HR	RBI	SB	BA
1996	New York	AL	2B	35	54	9	11	1	9	1	.204
Post All-Star				12	17	2	5	0	5	0	.294

REX HUDLER
Age 36/R   **$9**

It took him awhile, but he finally had a career year before his career ended. One of the few things that worked out for the Angels last year was the Velarde/Hudler platoon at second base. Don't expect 16 HR, though. They won't juice the ball two years in a row.

Year	Team	Lg.	Pos.	G	AB	R	H	HR	RBI	SB	BA
1994	California	AL	2B	56	124	17	37	8	20	2	.298
1995	California	AL	2B	84	223	30	59	6	27	13	.265
1996	California	AL	2B	92	302	60	94	16	40	14	.311
Post All-Star				38	120	21	36	5	12	4	.300

DEREK JETER
Age 22/R   **$18**

Terrific player who richly deserved AL Rookie of the Year. Showed guts throughout the playoffs and doesn't seem like a sophomore slump–type kid. He knows Alex Rodriguez is penciled in as the All-Star starting shortstop until 2010, which will only make him play that much harder. Draft him young and watch him improve.

Year	Team	Lg.	Pos.	G	AB	R	H	HR	RBI	SB	BA
1995	New York	AL	SS	15	48	5	12	0	7	0	.250
1996	New York	AL	SS	157	582	104	183	10	78	14	.314
Post All-Star				75	297	63	104	6	40	8	.350

CHUCK KNOBLAUCH
Age 28/R   **$31**

The second-best second baseman in baseball, which means he's very, very good.

Year	Team	Lg.	Pos.	G	AB	R	H	HR	RBI	SB	BA
1993	Minnesota	AL	2B	153	602	82	167	2	41	29	.277
1994	Minnesota	AL	2B	109	445	85	139	5	51	35	.312
1995	Minnesota	AL	2B	136	538	107	179	11	63	46	.333
1996	Minnesota	AL	2B	153	578	140	197	13	72	45	.341
Post All-Star				74	270	75	83	5	27	28	.307

MARK LEWIS
Age 27/R   **$12**

Wow! What's this? A promising Detroit Tiger? Believe it. This guy's been around but he's still young, and you can't go wrong with numbers like these. It may be asking too much, but wouldn't it be nice if he played winter ball with SS Norberto Martin. Martin and Lewis. Get it? Never mind.

Year	Team	Lg.	Pos.	G	AB	R	H	HR	RBI	SB	BA
1993	Cleveland	AL	SS	14	52	6	13	1	5	3	.250
1994	Cleveland	AL	SS	20	73	6	15	1	8	1	.205
1995	Cincinnati	NL	3B	81	171	25	58	3	30	0	.339
1996	Detroit	AL	2B	145	545	69	147	11	55	6	.270
Post All-Star				61	220	28	49	3	22	3	.223

Catchers
pp. 27–39

Corners
pp. 40–60

Infield
pp. 60–80

Outfield
pp. 80–111

DH
pp. 112–115

Starters
pp. 115–145

Relievers
pp. 146–178

KEITH LOCKHART   Age 32/L $6

Made the most of Bip Roberts's 19 hamstring pulls and put in a solid year. But it's hard to trust a ballplayer who blossoms in his thirties. It's makes sense for desk jockeys like us, but not for second basemen.

Year	Team	Lg.	Pos.	G	AB	R	H	HR	RBI	SB	BA
1994	San Diego	NL	3B	27	43	4	9	2	6	1	.209
1995	Kansas City	AL	2B	94	274	41	88	6	33	8	.321
1996	Kansas City	AL	2B	138	433	49	118	7	55	11	.273
Post All-Star				60	190	18	42	4	20	2	.221

MARK LORETTA   Age 25/R $2

Maybe in high-heel shoes and a low-neck sweater, he'd be something to sing about. Get back from this, Loretta.

Year	Team	Lg.	Pos.	G	AB	R	H	HR	RBI	SB	BA
1995	Milwaukee	AL	SS	19	50	13	13	1	3	1	.260
1996	Milwaukee	AL	2B	73	154	20	43	1	13	2	.279
Post All-Star				44	94	10	24	1	5	2	.255

NORBERTO MARTIN   Age 30/R $2

Only if he gets traded to the Tigers, so he can form a double-play combo with . . . oh, you've heard that one.

Year	Team	Lg.	Pos.	G	AB	R	H	HR	RBI	SB	BA
1993	Chicago	AL	2B	8	14	3	5	0	2	0	.357
1994	Chicago	AL	2B	45	131	19	36	1	16	4	.275
1995	Chicago	AL	2B	72	160	17	43	2	17	5	.269
1996	Chicago	AL	SS	70	140	30	49	1	14	10	.350
Post All-Star				44	91	19	29	1	12	7	.319

MARK MCLEMORE   Age 32/B $13

Worth a little less than half a Knoblauch.

Year	Team	Lg.	Pos.	G	AB	R	H	HR	RBI	SB	BA
1993	Baltimore	AL	OF	148	581	81	165	4	72	21	.284
1994	Baltimore	AL	2B	104	343	44	88	3	29	20	.257
1995	Texas	AL	OF	129	467	73	122	5	41	21	.261
1996	Texas	AL	2B	147	517	84	150	5	46	27	.290
Post All-Star				69	252	38	69	3	17	13	.274

PAT MEARES   Age 28/R $8

Meares, Meares, on the wall! Who's the best, cheap middle infielder of them all?

Year	Team	Lg.	Pos.	G	AB	R	H	HR	RBI	SB	BA
1993	Minnesota	AL	SS	111	346	33	87	0	33	4	.251
1994	Minnesota	AL	SS	80	229	29	61	2	24	5	.266
1995	Minnesota	AL	SS	116	390	57	105	12	49	10	.269
1996	Minnesota	AL	SS	152	517	66	138	8	67	9	.267
Post All-Star				71	242	33	68	3	28	4	.281

TOMAS PEREZ   Age 23/B $3

The Blue Jays begged him to step up and take second base. An ever-so-slight offensive improvement leaves this job open. Still, we like his chances over Tilson Brito, Felipe Crespo, and Miguel Cairo. Of course, we like *our* chances over that trio.

Year	Team	Lg.	Pos.	G	AB	R	H	HR	RBI	SB	BA
1995	Toronto	AL	SS	41	98	12	24	1	8	0	.245
1996	Toronto	AL	2B	91	295	24	74	1	19	1	.251
Post All-Star				59	190	15	45	0	10	1	.237

JEFF REBOULET   Age 32/R $2

Despite hitting no HR and dropping 70 points off his BA, Reboulet still managed to crank out 23 RBI. We said it last year, we'll say it again, he plugs holes. The only positions he didn't play were center field and catcher.

Year	Team	Lg.	Pos.	G	AB	R	H	HR	RBI	SB	BA
1993	Minnesota	AL	SS	109	240	33	62	1	15	5	.258
1994	Minnesota	AL	SS	74	189	28	49	3	23	0	.259
1995	Minnesota	AL	SS	87	216	39	63	4	23	1	.292
1996	Minnesota	AL	SS	107	234	20	52	0	23	4	.222
Post All-Star				53	105	8	25	0	11	2	.238

BILLY RIPKEN   Age 32/R $1

Pay attention during the draft. You don't want to say "$23" when this guy comes up.

Year	Team	Lg.	Pos.	G	AB	R	H	HR	RBI	SB	BA
1993	Texas	AL	2B	50	132	12	25	0	11	0	.189
1994	Texas	AL	3B	32	81	9	25	0	6	2	.309
1995	Cleveland	AL	2B	8	17	4	7	2	3	0	.412
1996	Baltimore	AL	2B	57	135	19	31	2	12	0	.230
Post All-Star				22	39	6	6	0	3	0	.154

CAL RIPKEN   Age 36/R $23

Yeah, he's a hero, but his dark side began to show this year. Somewhere along the way he became a real prima donna. He'll keep hitting, but only in streaks, and the O's defense didn't go down because Robbie Alomar can't field his position. Plus, the guy hasn't given anybody else a chance in over 2,200 games. Time to sit down a few for the team.

Year	Team	Lg.	Pos.	G	AB	R	H	HR	RBI	SB	BA
1993	Baltimore	AL	SS	162	641	87	165	24	90	1	.257
1994	Baltimore	AL	SS	112	444	71	140	13	75	1	.315
1995	Baltimore	AL	SS	144	550	71	144	17	88	0	.262
1996	Baltimore	AL	SS	163	640	94	178	26	102	1	.278
Post All-Star				77	306	45	82	9	37	1	.268

BIP ROBERTS   Age 33/B $3

When he doesn't steal, he's just another player. Hamstrings don't get better with age, so take him as a last resort.

Year	Team	Lg.	Pos.	G	AB	R	H	HR	RBI	SB	BA
1993	Cincinnati	NL	2B	83	292	46	70	1	18	26	.240
1994	San Diego	NL	2B	105	403	52	129	2	31	21	.320
1995	San Diego	NL	OF	73	296	40	90	2	25	20	.304
1996	Kansas City	AL	2B	90	339	39	96	0	52	12	.283
Post All-Star				34	117	12	29	0	18	5	.248

Catchers
pp. 27-39

Corners
pp. 40-60

Infield
pp. 60-80

Outfield
pp. 80-111

DH
pp. 112-115

Starters
pp. 115-145

Relievers
pp. 146-178

ALEX RODRIGUEZ   Age 21/R $40

Last year we said he would wake everybody up with his sparkling talents.
But even we weren't expecting the finest offensive season in the history of
shortstops. He's only 21, so you have to think he'll improve somewhere,
though it's hard to think of where that might be. If Ripken starts at short
in the All-Star game, they should call the whole thing off. If only they didn't
call him "A-Rod."

Year	Team	Lg.	Pos.	G	AB	R	H	HR	RBI	SB	BA
1994	Seattle	AL	SS	17	54	4	11	0	2	3	.204
1995	Seattle	AL	SS	48	142	15	33	5	19	4	.232
1996	Seattle	AL	SS	146	601	141	215	36	123	15	.358
Post All-Star				76	312	74	118	19	58	10	.378

TONY RODRIGUEZ   Age 26/R $1

The Red Sox have two of their best players at SS. This guy isn't one of them.

Year	Team	Lg.	Pos.	G	AB	R	H	HR	RBI	SB	BA
1996	Boston	AL	SS	27	67	7	16	1	9	0	.239
Post All-Star				26	67	7	16	1	9	0	.239

LUIS SOJO   Age 31/R $1

The pride of Barquisimeto, Venezuela, is winding it down. He looked good
for the Yanks down the stretch but may not be there if all those hurt middle
infielders get healthy. Full disclosure: we follow the game pretty closely and
we didn't even notice when the Bombers picked him up. Of course, that
may say more about us than it does about him.

Year	Team	Lg.	Pos.	G	AB	R	H	HR	RBI	SB	BA
1993	Toronto	AL	2B	19	47	5	8	0	6	0	.170
1994	Seattle	AL	2B	63	213	32	59	6	22	2	.277
1995	Seattle	AL	SS	102	339	50	98	7	39	4	.289
1996	Seattle	AL	3B	77	247	20	52	1	16	2	.211
1996	New York	AL	2B	18	40	3	11	0	5	0	.275
Post All-Star				40	105	6	21	0	10	0	.200

KURT STILLWELL   Age 31/B $1

Based on these numbers, Kurt still bad.

Year	Team	Lg.	Pos.	G	AB	R	H	HR	RBI	SB	BA
1993	San Diego	NL	SS	57	121	9	26	1	11	4	.215
1993	California	AL	2B	22	61	2	16	0	3	2	.262
1996	Texas	AL	2B	46	77	12	21	1	4	0	.273
Post All-Star				23	30	7	7	1	1	0	.233

ALAN TRAMMELL   Age 39/R   No Price

We said good-bye last year, but the old trooper showed up for one last tour.
He got a hit in his last at bat and hangs 'em up the same way he played
the game, with class.

Year	Team	Lg.	Pos.	G	AB	R	H	HR	RBI	SB	BA
1993	Detroit	AL	SS	112	401	72	132	12	60	12	.329
1994	Detroit	AL	SS	76	292	38	78	8	28	3	.267
1995	Detroit	AL	SS	74	223	28	60	2	23	3	.269
1996	Detroit	AL	SS	66	193	16	45	1	16	6	.233
Post All-Star				13	31	1	4	0	2	1	.129

JOHN VALENTIN   Age 30/R $16

There isn't a tougher guy in baseball. He eked out these stats with a shoulder that begged for surgery. If the Red Sox push him to third, he'll just dig in and keep producing. That being said, the guy has never played more than 144 games in a season. You have to be tough when you're always hurt. May go somewhere in a deal for a centerfielder.

Year	Team	Lg.	Pos.	G	AB	R	H	HR	RBI	SB	BA
1993	Boston	AL	SS	144	468	50	130	11	66	3	.278
1994	Boston	AL	SS	84	301	53	95	9	49	3	.316
1995	Boston	AL	SS	135	520	108	155	27	102	20	.298
1996	Boston	AL	SS	131	527	84	156	13	59	9	.296
Post All-Star				47	181	30	55	3	20	3	.304

JOSE VALENTIN   Age 27/B $20

Dramatically improved in two areas last year, upping his average and continuing to hit with power. The race is on: 1997 will determine the best Valentin in the American League.

Year	Team	Lg.	Pos.	G	AB	R	H	HR	RBI	SB	BA
1993	Milwaukee	AL	SS	19	53	10	13	1	7	1	.245
1994	Milwaukee	AL	SS	97	285	47	68	11	46	12	.239
1995	Milwaukee	AL	SS	112	338	62	74	11	49	16	.219
1996	Milwaukee	AL	SS	154	552	90	143	24	95	17	.259
Post All-Star				71	245	40	58	12	38	7	.237

RANDY VELARDE   Age 34/R $14

Got away from the Yanks and showed he could produce every day. The 500 AB agreed with him. No reason he can't continue to improve. Nice to see a player who takes an opportunity and runs with it.

Year	Team	Lg.	Pos.	G	AB	R	H	HR	RBI	SB	BA
1993	New York	AL	OF	85	226	28	68	7	24	2	.301
1994	New York	AL	SS	77	280	47	78	9	34	4	.279
1995	New York	AL	2B	111	367	60	102	7	46	5	.278
1996	California	AL	2B	136	530	82	151	14	54	7	.285
Post All-Star				63	246	37	66	8	24	5	.268

FERNANDO VINA   Age 27/L $10

Known across America as the victim of one of Albert Belle's psychotic episodes. Known in Rotisserie-land as another quietly productive Milwaukee Brewer.

Year	Team	Lg.	Pos.	G	AB	R	H	HR	RBI	SB	BA
1993	Seattle	AL	2B	24	45	5	10	0	2	6	.222
1994	New York	NL	2B	79	124	20	31	0	6	3	.250
1995	Milwaukee	AL	2B	113	288	46	74	3	29	6	.257
1996	Milwaukee	AL	2B	140	554	94	157	7	46	16	.283
Post All-Star				69	275	40	70	3	22	7	.255

JOSE VIZCAINO   Age 29/B $19

The worst thing about the Baerga trade is that nobody gets to hear Mets' announcer Bob Murphy say "Jose Vizcaino" anymore. He really let it rip with

Catchers
pp. 27–39

Corners
pp. 40–60

Infield
pp. 60–80

Outfield
pp. 80–111

DH
pp. 112–115

Starters
pp. 115–145

Relievers
pp. 146–178

gusto. Anyway, this guy's a decent ballplayer, but you have to wonder if Giants fans—are there any?—will forgive him for being part of the Matt Williams deal.

Year	Team	Lg.	Pos.	G	AB	R	H	HR	RBI	SB	BA
1993	Chicago	NL	SS	151	551	74	158	4	54	12	.287
1994	New York	NL	SS	103	410	47	105	3	33	1	.256
1995	New York	NL	SS	135	509	66	146	3	56	8	.287
1996	New York	NL	2B	96	363	47	110	1	32	9	.303
1996	Cleveland	AL	2B	48	179	23	51	0	13	6	.285
Post All-Star				64	249	33	71	0	21	7	.285

OMAR VIZQUEL   Age 29/B $18

No longer Omar the Outmaker. Look at the improvement in exactly the same number of AB. That's encouraging. Omar is the best of Cleveland's Viz Kids.

Year	Team	Lg.	Pos.	G	AB	R	H	HR	RBI	SB	BA
1993	Seattle	AL	SS	158	560	68	143	2	31	12	.255
1994	Cleveland	AL	SS	69	286	39	78	1	33	13	.273
1995	Cleveland	AL	SS	136	542	87	144	6	56	29	.266
1996	Cleveland	AL	SS	151	542	98	161	9	64	35	.297
Post All-Star				65	236	47	70	5	26	15	.297

In the Outfield

NATIONAL LEAGUE

JERMAINE ALLENSWORTH   Age 25/R $8

With good speed and a little power, he's on track to be a legit leadoff hitter. In other words, he's a name to remember.

Year	Team	Lg.	Pos.	G	AB	R	H	HR	RBI	SB	BA
1996	Pittsburgh	NL	OF	61	229	32	60	4	31	11	.262
Post All-Star				61	229	32	60	4	31	11	.262

MOISES ALOU   Age 30/R $24

He's not a kid anymore, and now he's not an Expo anymore, either. Scouts whisper his bat has slowed down and critics like to point out that he's missed parts of each of the last five seasons with injuries. But in that awesome Marlins lineup, the numbers won't be hard to take.

Year	Team	Lg.	Pos.	G	AB	R	H	HR	RBI	SB	BA
1993	Montreal	NL	OF	136	482	70	138	18	85	17	.286
1994	Montreal	NL	OF	107	422	81	143	22	78	7	.339
1995	Montreal	NL	OF	93	344	48	94	14	58	4	.273
1996	Montreal	NL	OF	143	540	87	152	21	96	9	.281
Post All-Star				58	216	37	67	9	42	5	.310

RUBEN AMARO   Age 32/B $1

"Until this season, I always thought I should be an everyday player, but now I see my role is likely to be as a pinch hitter, so I've learned to enjoy that challenge," he said. Funny how everyone else who's ever seen him play knew he'd never be an everyday player. But indeed he did deliver as a pinch hitter.

Year	Team	Lg.	Pos.	G	AB	R	H	HR	RBI	SB	BA
1993	Philadelphia	NL	OF	25	48	7	16	1	6	0	.333
1994	Cleveland	AL	OF	26	23	5	5	2	5	2	.217
1995	Cleveland	AL	OF	28	60	5	12	1	7	1	.200
1996	Philadelphia	NL	OF	61	117	14	37	2	15	0	.316
Post All-Star				55	107	12	34	2	15	0	.318

BILLY ASHLEY   Age 26/R $6

Over 50% of his hits went for extra bases. He averaged an RBI for every 4.5 at bats. The average distance of his home runs was 414 feet. Impressed yet? We didn't think so.

Year	Team	Lg.	Pos.	G	AB	R	H	HR	RBI	SB	BA
1993	Los Angeles	NL	OF	14	37	0	9	0	0	0	.243
1994	Los Angeles	NL	OF	2	6	0	2	0	0	0	.333
1995	Los Angeles	NL	OF	81	215	17	51	8	27	0	.237
1996	Los Angeles	NL	OF	71	110	18	22	9	25	0	.200
Post All-Star				34	38	8	11	5	15	0	.289

DEREK BELL   Age 28/R $21

The word has been that the Astros might shop his services, which should matter not at all to you. He's going to keep hitting no matter where he plays.

Year	Team	Lg.	Pos.	G	AB	R	H	HR	RBI	SB	BA
1993	San Diego	NL	OF	150	542	73	142	21	72	26	.262
1994	San Diego	NL	OF	108	434	54	135	14	54	24	.311
1995	Houston	NL	OF	112	452	63	151	8	86	27	.334
1996	Houston	NL	OF	158	627	84	165	17	113	29	.263
Post All-Star				69	266	27	61	8	47	11	.229

MARVIN BENARD   Age 27/L $8

A better-than-average fringe guy with speed to burn.

Year	Team	Lg.	Pos.	G	AB	R	H	HR	RBI	SB	BA
1995	San Francisco	NL	OF	13	34	5	13	1	4	1	.382
1996	San Francisco	NL	OF	135	488	89	121	5	27	25	.248
Post All-Star				69	256	53	61	5	16	16	.238

DANTE BICHETTE   Age 33/R $37

By the end of another monster season, he could hardly run because of a bum knee and a ballooning waistline. The knee required major surgery, and now the Rockies are holding their breath. Bichette has never been accused of working too hard on conditioning, and given the inactivity he must endure because of the surgery, the worry is that when the Rockies next see Bichette,

Catchers
pp. 27-39

Corners
pp. 40-60

Infield
pp. 60-80

Outfield
pp. 80-111

DH
pp. 112-115

Starters
pp. 115-145

Relievers
pp. 146-178

he'll resemble Nate Newton. We think he will prove his critics wrong and, the knee willing, keep being a prime-time player.

Year	Team	Lg.	Pos.	G	AB	R	H	HR	RBI	SB	BA
1993	Colorado	NL	OF	141	538	93	167	21	89	14	.310
1994	Colorado	NL	OF	116	484	74	147	27	95	21	.304
1995	Colorado	NL	OF	139	579	102	197	40	128	13	.340
1996	Colorado	NL	OF	159	633	114	198	31	141	31	.313
Post All-Star				73	275	43	78	14	61	17	.284

BARRY BONDS   Age 32/L $45

We'd have loved to see him reunited with Jim Leyland in Florida. It's a shame to see this much electricity squandered for arguably the most clueless organization in baseball. He's still the best player in baseball, by the way— and yes, that *includes* Junior.

Year	Team	Lg.	Pos.	G	AB	R	H	HR	RBI	SB	BA
1993	San Francisco	NL	OF	159	539	129	181	46	123	29	.336
1994	San Francisco	NL	OF	112	391	89	122	37	81	29	.312
1995	San Francisco	NL	OF	144	506	109	149	33	104	31	.294
1996	San Francisco	NL	OF	158	517	122	159	42	129	40	.308
Post All-Star				72	198	55	63	19	61	20	.318

ELLIS BURKS   Age 32/R $33

We dismissed him a year ago as a nonentity. Hey, if we were right all the time, life would be boring. This year, we predict that he'll never duplicate those unbelieveable numbers. But he'll come close.

Year	Team	Lg.	Pos.	G	AB	R	H	HR	RBI	SB	BA
1993	Chicago	AL	OF	146	499	75	137	17	74	6	.275
1994	Colorado	NL	OF	42	149	33	48	13	24	3	.322
1995	Colorado	NL	OF	103	278	41	74	14	49	7	.266
1996	Colorado	NL	OF	156	613	142	211	40	128	32	.344
Post All-Star				73	279	65	97	18	56	17	.348

BRETT BUTLER   Age 39/L $2

The most cynical of people couldn't help being moved by his amazing saga. The question is whether he'll muster up the grit to come back. If he does, count on him being a contributor.

Year	Team	Lg.	Pos.	G	AB	R	H	HR	RBI	SB	BA
1993	Los Angeles	NL	OF	156	607	80	181	1	42	39	.298
1994	Los Angeles	NL	OF	111	417	79	131	8	33	27	.314
1995	New York	NL	OF	90	367	54	114	1	25	21	.311
1995	Los Angeles	NL	OF	39	146	24	40	0	13	11	.274
1996	Los Angeles	NL	OF	34	131	22	35	0	8	8	.267
Post All-Star				5	14	4	4	0	1	1	.286

JOHN CANGELOSI   Age 34/B $3

Short and scrappy. A classic $1 ballplayer. The bonus is for the SB.

Year	Team	Lg.	Pos.	G	AB	R	H	HR	RBI	SB	BA
1994	New York	NL	OF	62	111	14	28	0	4	5	.252
1995	Houston	NL	OF	90	201	46	64	2	18	21	.318
1996	Houston	NL	OF	108	262	49	69	1	16	17	.263
Post All-Star				45	117	19	26	0	3	3	.222

ROGER CEDENO Age 22/B $4

He could get a shot at center field, where he has tools that might not equal Cesar's but will likely surpass Andujar's. Still a huge upside.

Year	Team	Lg.	Pos.	G	AB	R	H	HR	RBI	SB	BA
1995	Los Angeles	NL	OF	40	42	4	10	0	3	1	.238
1996	Los Angeles	NL	OF	86	211	26	52	2	18	5	.246
Post All-Star				14	13	1	1	0	0	0	.077

DAVE CLARK Age 34/L $3

Good guy to have around.

Year	Team	Lg.	Pos.	G	AB	R	H	HR	RBI	SB	BA
1993	Pittsburgh	NL	OF	110	277	43	75	11	46	1	.271
1994	Pittsburgh	NL	OF	86	223	37	66	10	46	2	.296
1995	Pittsburgh	NL	OF	77	196	30	55	4	24	3	.281
1996	Pittsburgh	NL	OF	92	211	28	58	8	35	2	.275
1996	Los Angeles	NL	OF	15	15	0	3	0	1	0	.200
Post All-Star				55	116	16	29	5	15	1	.250

JEFF CONINE Age 30/R $26

A Steve Garvey type—always there, usually productive.

Year	Team	Lg.	Pos.	G	AB	R	H	HR	RBI	SB	BA
1993	Florida	NL	OF	162	595	75	174	12	79	2	.292
1994	Florida	NL	OF	115	451	60	144	18	82	1	.319
1995	Florida	NL	OF	133	483	72	146	25	105	2	.302
1996	Florida	NL	OF	157	597	84	175	26	95	1	.293
Post All-Star				72	276	40	79	11	46	0	.286

MIDRE CUMMINGS Age 25/L $1

Stick a fork in him.

Year	Team	Lg.	Pos.	G	AB	R	H	HR	RBI	SB	BA
1993	Pittsburgh	NL	OF	13	36	5	4	0	3	0	.111
1994	Pittsburgh	NL	OF	24	86	11	21	1	12	0	.244
1995	Pittsburgh	NL	OF	59	152	13	37	2	15	1	.243
1996	Pittsburgh	NL	OF	24	85	11	19	3	7	0	.224
Post All-Star				0	0	0	0	0	0	0	.000

CHAD CURTIS Age 28/R $9

Had trouble adjusting to NL. Could be a happy surprise.

Year	Team	Lg.	Pos.	G	AB	R	H	HR	RBI	SB	BA
1993	California	AL	OF	152	583	94	166	6	59	48	.285
1994	California	AL	OF	114	453	67	116	11	50	25	.256
1995	Detroit	AL	OF	144	586	96	157	21	67	27	.268
1996	Detroit	AL	OF	104	400	65	105	10	37	16	.262
1996	Los Angeles	NL	OF	43	104	20	22	2	9	2	.212
Post All-Star				61	174	35	40	6	17	6	.230

ERIC DAVIS Age 34/R $21

The Comeback from two perspectives—Davis: "I never realized how much fun baseball is to play until I didn't play it for a year. I had a great time

Catchers
pp. 27-39

Corners
pp. 40-60

Infield
pp. 60-80

Outfield
pp. 80-111

DH
pp. 112-115

Starters
pp. 115-145

Relievers
pp. 146-178

this year, just playing for fun and staying loose." Reds GM Jim Bowden: "We brought him to camp really out of nostalgia for what he had meant to the club years ago. We expected nothing. We were as surprised as anybody by what happened." Can it happen again? Why not.

Year	Team	Lg.	Pos.	G	AB	R	H	HR	RBI	SB	BA
1993	Los Angeles	NL	OF	108	376	57	88	14	53	33	.234
1993	Detroit	AL	OF	23	75	14	19	6	15	2	.253
1994	Detroit	AL	OF	37	120	19	22	3	13	5	.183
1996	Cincinnati	NL	OF	129	415	81	119	26	83	23	.287
Post All-Star				66	212	35	62	12	33	13	.292

JERMAINE DYE   Age 23/R $13

Says Braves coach Pat Corrales, who rarely hands out compliments, "He's loaded with ability and all that stuff. But the thing about this guy is that he's the nicest kid I've ever seen come to the majors. You gotta root for him." He's in the majors much more quickly than the Braves ever thought he would be, and there's always the chance he'll be one of the guys used in Atlanta's annual big trade. But you're looking at a potential 30-homer player.

Year	Team	Lg.	Pos.	G	AB	R	H	HR	RBI	SB	BA
1996	Atlanta	NL	OF	98	292	32	82	12	37	1	.281
Post All-Star				67	208	21	56	7	23	1	.269

LENNY DYKSTRA   Age 34/L   No Price

The Dude was telling people over the winter that he'd show up for spring training, work out a couple of days to allow the Phillies to qualify for insurance that pays off his ridiculous contract, and then shut himself down because of back pain. If you happened to have drafted him, that's probably not the scouting report you wanted to read.

Year	Team	Lg.	Pos.	G	AB	R	H	HR	RBI	SB	BA
1993	Philadelphia	NL	OF	161	637	143	194	19	66	37	.305
1994	Philadelphia	NL	OF	84	315	68	86	5	24	15	.273
1995	Philadelphia	NL	OF	62	254	37	67	2	18	10	.264
1996	Philadelphia	NL	OF	40	134	21	35	3	13	3	.261
Post All-Star				0	0	0	0	0	0	0	.000

JIM EISENREICH   Age 37/L $6

Here's a little example of how mismanaged the Philadelphia Phillies are. This veteran hitter was sought by several contenders. However, the crack Phillies front office put a huge price of *three* legitimate players on his head, which made him untradeable, since all we're talking about here is a part-time player with no power. The explanation from crack GM Lee Thomas was, "Well he's not only a solid player, he's so popular with our fans that we can't just trade him away for anything." What fans? Phillies attendance dropped a half million, and though Eisenreich is well liked, trading him isn't exactly like the Phillies' trading Mike Schmidt. The fans would have welcomed him back with a nice ovation, and that's it. Finally the hook to all this popularity is that Eisenreich told anyone who'd listen that he'd look elsewhere for work when he became a free agent.

Year	Team	Lg.	Pos.	G	AB	R	H	HR	RBI	SB	BA
1993	Philadelphia	NL	OF	153	362	51	115	7	54	5	.318
1994	Philadelphia	NL	OF	104	290	42	87	4	43	6	.300
1995	Philadelphia	NL	OF	129	377	46	119	10	55	10	.316
1996	Philadelphia	NL	OF	113	338	45	122	3	41	11	.361
Post All-Star				41	138	18	54	1	19	3	.391

CARL EVERETT
Age 25/B   **$1**

"Thud" went his career development.

Year	Team	Lg.	Pos.	G	AB	R	H	HR	RBI	SB	BA
1993	Florida	NL	OF	11	19	0	2	0	0	1	.105
1994	Florida	NL	OF	16	51	7	11	2	6	4	.216
1995	New York	NL	OF	79	289	48	75	12	54	2	.260
1996	New York	NL	OF	101	192	29	46	1	16	6	.240
Post All-Star				59	116	17	32	1	11	3	.276

STEVE FINLEY
Age 32/L   **$24**

All that power might be a reflection of how aberrational so many big years were in '96. But he brings a lot to the table even if the home runs level off.

Year	Team	Lg.	Pos.	G	AB	R	H	HR	RBI	SB	BA
1993	Houston	NL	OF	142	545	69	145	8	44	19	.266
1994	Houston	NL	OF	94	373	64	103	11	33	13	.276
1995	San Diego	NL	OF	139	562	104	167	10	44	36	.297
1996	San Diego	NL	OF	161	655	126	195	30	95	22	.298
Post All-Star				73	289	57	89	13	41	12	.308

CLIFF FLOYD
Age 24/L   **$8**

This might be the year he finally puts his injuries and position switches behind him and blossoms. We like his chances, and so does Felipe Alou. "Clifford Floyd is capable of hitting the ball harder than anyone we've had here," says the Expos' manager.

Year	Team	Lg.	Pos.	G	AB	R	H	HR	RBI	SB	BA
1993	Montreal	NL	1B	10	31	3	7	1	2	0	.226
1994	Montreal	NL	1B	100	334	43	94	4	41	10	.281
1995	Montreal	NL	1B	29	69	6	9	1	8	3	.130
1996	Montreal	NL	OF	117	227	29	55	6	26	7	.242
Post All-Star				64	150	20	33	4	15	4	.220

RON GANT
Age 32/R   **$28**

The Braves made the right business decision a few years ago when they dropped him rather than guarantee him $3 million when he hadn't yet come back from a broken leg. The Reds made the right business decision by not giving him a four-year contract. The Cardinals made the right business decision by making him one of the centerpieces of their revival. And you can make the right business decision by grabbing him and getting a sure 30 home runs.

Year	Team	Lg.	Pos.	G	AB	R	H	HR	RBI	SB	BA
1993	Atlanta	NL	OF	157	606	113	166	36	117	26	.274
1995	Cincinnati	NL	OF	119	410	79	113	29	88	23	.276
1996	St. Louis	NL	OF	122	419	74	103	30	82	13	.246
Post All-Star				67	245	43	62	18	41	7	.253

Catchers
pp. 27–39

Corners
pp. 40–60

Infield
pp. 60–80

Outfield
pp. 80–111

DH
pp. 112–115

Starters
pp. 115–145

Relievers
pp. 146–178

BERNARD GILKEY　　　　　　　　　　　Age 30/R　　$26

The embodiment of how difficult it is truly to assess last season's numbers. Nothing in his otherwise decent career prepared anyone for the monster year he put together. Was it legit? Yes. Can it happen again? No.

Year	Team	Lg.	Pos.	G	AB	R	H	HR	RBI	SB	BA
1993	St. Louis	NL	OF	137	557	99	170	16	70	15	.305
1994	St. Louis	NL	OF	105	380	52	96	6	45	15	.253
1995	St. Louis	NL	OF	121	480	73	143	17	69	12	.298
1996	New York	NL	OF	153	571	108	181	30	117	17	.317
Post All-Star				69	253	53	85	14	55	7	.336

DOUG GLANVILLE　　　　　　　　　　Age 26/R　　$2

Might get a chance in left field for the Cubs. Probably won't do much with the chance.

Year	Team	Lg.	Pos.	G	AB	R	H	HR	RBI	SB	BA
1996	Chicago	NL	OF	49	83	10	20	1	10	2	.241
Post All-Star				32	50	7	13	1	7	1	.260

LUIS GONZALEZ　　　　　　　　　　　Age 29/L　　$14

He didn't take to third base very well and doesn't hit enough home runs to justify being in the Wrigley Field outfield. That makes him too expendable for our tastes.

Year	Team	Lg.	Pos.	G	AB	R	H	HR	RBI	SB	BA
1993	Houston	NL	OF	154	540	82	162	15	72	20	.300
1994	Houston	NL	OF	112	392	57	107	8	67	15	.273
1995	Houston	NL	OF	56	209	35	54	6	35	1	.258
1995	Chicago	NL	OF	77	262	34	76	7	34	5	.290
1996	Chicago	NL	OF	146	483	70	131	15	79	9	.271
Post All-Star				67	223	37	61	9	35	6	.274

CURTIS GOODWIN　　　　　　　　　　Age 24/L　　$11

After being a stiff in spring training, all those smug Orioles people who think they invented the game clucked knowingly about how smart they were to have dealt him away for Belushi-esque left-hander David Wells. But he went to the minors, got his act together, and returned to show flashes of being a decent leadoff hitter. He'll get the shot this spring for Cincinnati unless he turns into a stiff again in spring training.

Year	Team	Lg.	Pos.	G	AB	R	H	HR	RBI	SB	BA
1995	Baltimore	AL	OF	87	289	40	76	1	24	22	.263
1996	Cincinnati	NL	OF	49	136	20	31	0	5	15	.228
Post All-Star				35	96	18	22	0	5	14	.229

MARQUIS GRISSOM　　　　　　　　　Age 29/R　　$29

Perfect. He has his career year, reestablishes his value as one of the game's best center fielders and leadoff men, just in time for the Braves to shop him over the next two years now that the arrival of Andruw Jones and Jermaine Dye makes him expendable. Atlanta gets all the breaks.

Year	Team	Lg.	Pos.	G	AB	R	H	HR	RBI	SB	BA
1993	Montreal	NL	OF	157	630	104	188	19	95	53	.298
1994	Montreal	NL	OF	110	475	96	137	11	45	36	.288
1995	Atlanta	NL	OF	139	551	80	142	12	42	29	.258
1996	Atlanta	NL	OF	158	671	106	207	23	74	28	.308
Post All-Star				71	304	45	99	10	35	14	.326

TONY GWYNN
Age 36/L **$25**

This year's stat we love: .353 vs. left-handers; .352 vs. right-handers.

Year	Team	Lg.	Pos.	G	AB	R	H	HR	RBI	SB	BA
1993	San Diego	NL	OF	122	489	70	175	7	59	14	.358
1994	San Diego	NL	OF	110	419	79	165	12	64	5	.394
1995	San Diego	NL	OF	135	535	82	197	9	90	17	.368
1996	San Diego	NL	OF	116	451	67	159	3	50	11	.353
Post All-Star				46	182	23	68	0	16	2	.374

RICKEY HENDERSON
Age 38/R **$17**

Say what you will about attitude, but he played hard last year, didn't pout when he was made a part-timer after Greg Vaughn arrived, and was a big factor in the Padres' drive for the division title. What about this year? We worry that he'll pout about being a part-timer and for his sake (and ours) hope he gets traded before that happens.

Year	Team	Lg.	Pos.	G	AB	R	H	HR	RBI	SB	BA
1993	Oakland	AL	OF	90	318	77	104	17	47	31	.327
1993	Toronto	AL	OF	44	163	37	35	4	12	22	.215
1994	Oakland	AL	OF	87	296	66	77	6	20	22	.260
1995	Oakland	AL	OF	112	407	67	122	9	54	32	.300
1996	San Diego	NL	OF	148	465	110	112	9	29	37	.241
Post All-Star				69	201	45	50	2	8	14	.249

GLENALLEN HILL
Age 32/R **$18**

Broke his wrist in August, an injury that won't linger but an injury that cost him some big numbers. The Giants say it cost them the pennant. Right, and Bob Dole is going to tour this spring with Kiss.

Year	Team	Lg.	Pos.	G	AB	R	H	HR	RBI	SB	BA
1993	Cleveland	AL	OF	66	174	19	39	5	25	7	.224
1993	Chicago	NL	OF	31	87	14	30	10	22	1	.345
1994	Chicago	NL	OF	89	269	48	80	10	38	19	.297
1995	San Francisco	NL	OF	132	497	71	131	24	86	25	.264
1996	San Francisco	NL	OF	98	379	56	106	19	67	6	.280
Post All-Star				53	209	32	60	9	36	1	.287

TODD HOLLANDSWORTH
Age 23/L **$16**

Another solid, albeit unspectacular, Dodgers rookie who might be as good as he's going to get. How can a team that has the rookie of the year every year never go far in the playoffs? Is it because the ROY award is one of the more meaningless in baseball? Or is it because the Dodgers have a fatal character flaw? Food for thought.

Year	Team	Lg.	Pos.	G	AB	R	H	HR	RBI	SB	BA
1995	Los Angeles	NL	OF	41	103	16	24	5	13	2	.233
1996	Los Angeles	NL	OF	149	478	64	139	12	59	21	.291
Post All-Star				70	255	37	75	7	30	8	.294

Catchers
pp. 27-39

Corners
pp. 40-60

Infield
pp. 60-80

Outfield
pp. 80-111

DH
pp. 112-115

Starters
pp. 115-145

Relievers
pp. 146-178

THOMAS HOWARD
Age 32/L $4

Nice bench player.

Year	Team	Lg.	Pos.	G	AB	R	H	HR	RBI	SB	BA
1993	Cleveland	AL	OF	74	178	26	42	3	23	5	.236
1993	Cincinnati	NL	OF	38	141	22	39	4	13	5	.277
1994	Cincinnati	NL	OF	83	178	24	47	5	24	4	.264
1995	Cincinnati	NL	OF	113	281	42	85	3	26	17	.302
1996	Cincinnati	NL	OF	121	360	50	98	6	42	6	.272
Post All-Star				68	227	36	65	3	25	2	.286

BRIAN L. HUNTER
Age 26/R $19

Intense Terry Collins bruised the kid's confidence by platooning him with John Cangelosi. This year, look for the more laid-back Larry Dierker (*Larry Dierker?*) to let the kid play every day and let his skills mature. In return, the Astros get a bundle of steals and double-figure big flies.

Year	Team	Lg.	Pos.	G	AB	R	H	HR	RBI	SB	BA
1994	Houston	NL	OF	6	24	2	6	0	0	2	.250
1995	Houston	NL	OF	78	321	52	97	2	28	24	.302
1996	Houston	NL	OF	132	526	74	145	5	35	35	.276
Post All-Star				55	212	33	60	3	13	15	.283

STAN JAVIER
Age 33/B   -$2

Nice as a spare part on a good team. Disaster as an everyday player on a bad team.

Year	Team	Lg.	Pos.	G	AB	R	H	HR	RBI	SB	BA
1993	California	AL	OF	92	237	33	69	3	28	12	.291
1994	Oakland	AL	OF	109	419	75	114	10	44	24	.272
1995	Oakland	AL	OF	130	442	81	123	8	56	36	.278
1996	San Francisco	NL	OF	71	274	44	74	2	22	14	.270
Post All-Star				6	23	3	7	0	4	2	.304

LANCE JOHNSON
Age 33/L $26

Purists might cringe at L's habit of swinging at the first pitch nearly 60 percent of the time. Tell the purists to take in a movie with Ken Burns and Bob Costas and Dan Okrent in that ratty red sweater and leave us alone. We are numbers-crunchers and rarely have we ever had the pleasure of crunching numbers like these. Look for more of the same.

Year	Team	Lg.	Pos.	G	AB	R	H	HR	RBI	SB	BA
1993	Chicago	AL	OF	147	540	75	168	0	47	35	.311
1994	Chicago	AL	OF	106	412	56	114	3	54	26	.277
1995	Chicago	AL	OF	142	607	98	186	10	57	40	.306
1996	New York	NL	OF	160	682	117	227	9	69	50	.333
Post All-Star				73	306	52	106	4	29	22	.346

ANDRUW JONES
Age 19/R $16

The Barry Bonds of the next century—at the lowest price he'll be in this century.

Year	Team	Lg.	Pos.	G	AB	R	H	HR	RBI	SB	BA
1996	Atlanta	NL	OF	31	106	11	23	5	13	3	.217
Post All-Star				31	106	11	23	5	13	3	.217

CHRIS JONES — Age 31/R — $2

A pinch hitter.

Year	Team	Lg.	Pos.	G	AB	R	H	HR	RBI	SB	BA
1993	Colorado	NL	OF	86	209	29	57	6	31	9	.273
1994	Colorado	NL	OF	21	40	6	12	0	2	0	.300
1995	New York	NL	OF	79	182	33	51	8	31	2	.280
1996	New York	NL	OF	89	149	22	36	4	18	1	.242
Post All-Star				37	55	8	9	1	5	0	.164

BRIAN JORDAN — Age 30/R — $29

For two months, he and Tony LaRussa were like two pit bulls, sniffing around each other for a sign of weakness. Then they locked themselves in the visiting clubhouse in Atlanta one night, had it out for about an hour, and emerged as tag-team partners. In the process, Jordan emerged as The Man in St. Louis and he will be even better this season.

Year	Team	Lg.	Pos.	G	AB	R	H	HR	RBI	SB	BA
1993	St. Louis	NL	OF	67	223	33	69	10	44	6	.309
1994	St. Louis	NL	OF	53	178	14	46	5	15	4	.258
1995	St. Louis	NL	OF	131	490	83	145	22	81	24	.296
1996	St. Louis	NL	OF	140	513	82	159	17	104	22	.310
Post All-Star				69	249	35	80	8	54	10	.321

DAVE JUSTICE — Age 30/L — $22

A likely trade to somewhere. A likely great investment for someone. A likely great catch for someone not scared away by his nasty divorce from Halle Berry.

Year	Team	Lg.	Pos.	G	AB	R	H	HR	RBI	SB	BA
1993	Atlanta	NL	OF	157	585	90	158	40	120	3	.270
1994	Atlanta	NL	OF	104	352	61	110	19	59	2	.313
1995	Atlanta	NL	OF	120	411	73	104	24	78	4	.253
1996	Atlanta	NL	OF	40	140	23	45	6	25	1	.321
Post All-Star				0	0	0	0	0	0	0	.000

MIKE KINGERY — Age 36/L — $3

The Pirates were disappointed. That's all you need to know.

Year	Team	Lg.	Pos.	G	AB	R	H	HR	RBI	SB	BA
1994	Colorado	NL	OF	105	301	56	105	4	41	5	.349
1995	Colorado	NL	OF	119	350	66	94	8	37	13	.269
1996	Pittsburgh	NL	OF	117	276	32	68	3	27	2	.246
Post All-Star				44	100	10	25	3	14	0	.250

WAYNE KIRBY — Age 33/L — $2

All their wealth of talent, all their money, all their supposed glamor, and this was the Dodgers' everyday center fielder down the stretch. A nice role player, but everyday center fielder? Uh-uh.

Year	Team	Lg.	Pos.	G	AB	R	H	HR	RBI	SB	BA
1993	Cleveland	AL	OF	131	458	71	123	6	60	17	.269
1994	Cleveland	AL	OF	78	191	33	56	5	23	11	.293
1995	Cleveland	AL	OF	101	188	29	39	1	14	10	.207
1996	Cleveland	AL	OF	27	16	3	4	0	1	0	.250
1996	Los Angeles	NL	OF	65	188	23	51	1	11	4	.271
Post All-Star				59	178	23	51	1	11	4	.287

Catchers
pp. 27-39

Corners
pp. 40-60

Infield
pp. 60-80

Outfield
pp. 80-111

DH
pp. 112-115

Starters
pp. 115-145

Relievers
pp. 146-178

RYAN KLESKO · Age 25/L · $30

Needs to avoid the long slumps. Needs to develop better consistency. Needs to handle lefthanders better (only .230 vs. LH). Needs to hit better away from Atlanta (.240 on the road). But if he doesn't change a thing, he's still a great addition to any team.

Year	Team	Lg.	Pos.	G	AB	R	H	HR	RBI	SB	BA
1993	Atlanta	NL	1B	22	17	3	6	2	5	0	.353
1994	Atlanta	NL	OF	92	245	42	68	17	47	1	.278
1995	Atlanta	NL	OF	107	329	48	102	23	70	5	.310
1996	Atlanta	NL	OF	153	528	90	149	34	93	6	.282
Post All-Star				69	229	35	64	12	41	3	.279

RAY LANKFORD · Age 29/L · $27

Possibly expendable if John Mabry goes to outfield. Has always struck out too much to take that next step into superstardom, and it seems too late for him to change now.

Year	Team	Lg.	Pos.	G	AB	R	H	HR	RBI	SB	BA
1993	St. Louis	NL	OF	127	407	64	97	7	45	14	.238
1994	St. Louis	NL	OF	109	416	89	111	19	57	11	.267
1995	St. Louis	NL	OF	132	483	81	134	25	82	24	.277
1996	St. Louis	NL	OF	149	545	100	150	21	86	35	.275
Post All-Star				67	244	44	66	7	37	19	.270

WENDELL MAGEE · Age 24/R · $1

Has some skills but no polish whatsoever and little plate discipline. "He'd swing at the resin bag if they threw it high in the strike zone," says ex–Phillies manager Jim Fregosi.

Year	Team	Lg.	Pos.	G	AB	R	H	HR	RBI	SB	BA
1996	Philadelphia	NL	OF	38	142	9	29	2	14	0	.204
Post All-Star				38	142	9	29	2	14	0	.204

AL MARTIN · Age 29/L · $22

A pretty good player, which is about as good as it's going to get with anyone wearing a Pirates uniform.

Year	Team	Lg.	Pos.	G	AB	R	H	HR	RBI	SB	BA
1993	Pittsburgh	NL	OF	143	480	85	135	18	64	16	.281
1994	Pittsburgh	NL	OF	82	276	48	79	9	33	15	.286
1995	Pittsburgh	NL	OF	124	439	70	124	13	41	20	.282
1996	Pittsburgh	NL	OF	155	630	101	189	18	72	38	.300
Post All-Star				69	277	47	86	7	32	18	.310

DERRICK MAY · Age 28/L · $4

Belongs in AL as platoon DH.

Year	Team	Lg.	Pos.	G	AB	R	H	HR	RBI	SB	BA
1993	Chicago	NL	OF	128	465	62	137	10	77	10	.295
1994	Chicago	NL	OF	100	345	43	98	8	51	3	.284
1995	Milwaukee	AL	OF	32	113	15	28	1	9	0	.248
1995	Houston	NL	OF	78	206	29	62	8	41	5	.301
1996	Houston	NL	OF	109	259	24	65	5	33	2	.251
Post All-Star				52	121	11	28	2	10	1	.231

QUINTON McCRACKEN
Age 27/B   **$4**

Ideally, he's an extra guy. But he can provide decent return in several areas in whatever role he's asked to fill.

Year	Team	Lg.	Pos.	G	AB	R	H	HR	RBI	SB	BA
1995	Colorado	NL	OF	3	1	0	0	0	0	0	.000
1996	Colorado	NL	OF	124	283	50	82	3	40	17	.290
Post All-Star				61	189	35	58	3	30	12	.307

WILLIE McGEE
Age 38/B   **$1**

"I love the guy," said Tony LaRussa. "He's older and obviously can't play every day, but otherwise he's the same player he was when he was an MVP. He still can run the same. He hits the same. He fields the same. He even makes the same mistakes he's always made." Don't make the mistake, however, of paying too much for him anymore.

Year	Team	Lg.	Pos.	G	AB	R	H	HR	RBI	SB	BA
1993	San Francisco	NL	OF	130	475	53	143	4	46	10	.301
1994	San Francisco	NL	OF	45	156	19	44	5	23	3	.282
1995	Boston	AL	OF	67	200	32	57	2	15	5	.285
1996	St. Louis	NL	OF	123	309	52	95	5	41	5	.307
Post All-Star				58	121	18	36	2	12	2	.298

BRIAN McRAE
Age 29/B   **$28**

Some power and a lot of speed—not a bad combination which is why the Cubs kept him and why, if he's yours, you should too.

Year	Team	Lg.	Pos.	G	AB	R	H	HR	RBI	SB	BA
1993	Kansas City	AL	OF	153	627	78	177	12	69	23	.282
1994	Kansas City	AL	OF	114	436	71	119	4	40	28	.273
1995	Chicago	NL	OF	137	580	92	167	12	48	27	.288
1996	Chicago	NL	OF	157	624	111	172	17	66	37	.276
Post All-Star				71	270	57	79	14	39	12	.293

ORLANDO MERCED
Age 30/L   **$24**

A pretty good player, which is about as good as it's going to get with anyone wearing a Pirates uniform, but he makes a market salary, so he's no longer wearing a Pirates uniform.

Year	Team	Lg.	Pos.	G	AB	R	H	HR	RBI	SB	BA
1993	Pittsburgh	NL	OF	137	447	68	140	8	70	3	.313
1994	Pittsburgh	NL	OF	108	386	48	105	9	51	4	.272
1995	Pittsburgh	NL	OF	132	487	75	146	15	83	7	.300
1996	Pittsburgh	NL	OF	120	453	69	130	17	80	8	.287
Post All-Star				50	185	24	53	5	44	2	.286

KEVIN MITCHELL
Age 35/R   **$22**

Large. Take his uniform and use it to cover your infield.

Year	Team	Lg.	Pos.	G	AB	R	H	HR	RBI	SB	BA
1993	Cincinnati	NL	OF	93	323	56	110	19	64	1	.341
1994	Cincinnati	NL	OF	95	310	57	101	30	77	2	.326
1996	Boston	AL	OF	27	92	9	28	2	13	0	.304
1996	Cincinnati	NL	OF	37	114	18	37	6	26	0	.325
Post All-Star				47	148	23	48	7	32	0	.324

Catchers
pp. 27–39

Corners
pp. 40–60

Infield
pp. 60–80

Outfield
pp. 80–111

DH
pp. 112–115

Starters
pp. 115–145

Relievers
pp. 146–178

RAUL MONDESI   Age 26/R $28

Some Dodgers whisper about his attitude. Others whisper about how he
should be much better. But nobody likes anyone else in a clubhouse that
embodies the 25 players, 25 limos mentality. And if the Dodgers don't want
him on their team, we'll be glad to have him on ours.

Year	Team	Lg.	Pos.	G	AB	R	H	HR	RBI	SB	BA
1993	Los Angeles	NL	OF	42	86	13	25	4	10	4	.291
1994	Los Angeles	NL	OF	112	434	63	133	16	56	11	.306
1995	Los Angeles	NL	OF	139	536	91	153	26	88	27	.285
1996	Los Angeles	NL	OF	157	634	98	188	24	88	14	.297
Post All-Star				72	291	47	97	8	38	5	.333

JAMES MOUTON   Age 28/R $6

A spare part with a lot of speed.

Year	Team	Lg.	Pos.	G	AB	R	H	HR	RBI	SB	BA
1994	Houston	NL	OF	99	310	43	76	2	16	24	.245
1995	Houston	NL	OF	104	298	42	78	4	27	25	.262
1996	Houston	NL	OF	122	300	40	79	3	34	21	.263
Post All-Star				59	153	23	42	2	10	11	.275

SHERMAN OBANDO   Age 27/R $3

Originally signed by the Yankees as part of that great Panamanian pipeline
that, for example, brought Mariano Rivera and Ruben Rivera to New York
this year. Alas, this Canal Zone resident has developed into nothing more
than a pinch hitter with power.

Year	Team	Lg.	Pos.	G	AB	R	H	HR	RBI	SB	BA
1993	Baltimore	AL	DH	31	92	8	25	3	15	0	.272
1995	Baltimore	AL	DH	16	38	0	10	0	3	1	.263
1996	Montreal	NL	OF	89	178	30	44	8	22	2	.247
Post All-Star				28	43	11	11	3	6	1	.256

ALEX OCHOA   Age 25/R $4

The always reserved New York sports pages pressed the Mets all year to bring
him to the majors, making it sound like the Mets somehow were keeping Willie
Mays from taking his rightful place in the Hall of Fame. In truth, he has a
chance to be a decent hitter and great defensive outfielder. But he has never
shown big-time power at any point in his professional career, and he's about at
the age where if the power hasn't surfaced yet, it ain't never going to surface.

Year	Team	Lg.	Pos.	G	AB	R	H	HR	RBI	SB	BA
1995	New York	NL	OF	11	37	7	11	0	0	1	.297
1996	New York	NL	OF	82	282	37	83	4	33	4	.294
Post All-Star				67	224	26	64	1	18	2	.286

JOE ORSULAK   Age 34/L $1

One of the good guys, he's now struggling to hang on.

Year	Team	Lg.	Pos.	G	AB	R	H	HR	RBI	SB	BA
1993	New York	NL	OF	134	409	59	116	8	35	5	.284
1994	New York	NL	OF	96	292	39	76	8	42	4	.260
1995	New York	NL	OF	108	290	41	82	1	37	1	.283
1996	Florida	NL	OF	120	217	23	48	2	19	1	.221
Post All-Star				62	134	8	32	1	13	0	.239

RICKY OTERO

Age 24/B   **$2**

He is capable of supplying some occasional life with his speed. Affectionately called "Little Ricky" by the Phillies. That's because Lucy had as much pop in her bat as Little Ricky.

Year	Team	Lg.	Pos.	G	AB	R	H	HR	RBI	SB	BA
1995	New York	NL	OF	35	51	5	7	0	1	2	.137
1996	Philadelphia	NL	OF	104	411	54	112	2	32	16	.273
Post All-Star				66	255	34	71	0	17	7	.278

LUIS POLONIA

Age 32/L   **$1**

No thanks.

Year	Team	Lg.	Pos.	G	AB	R	H	HR	RBI	SB	BA
1993	California	AL	OF	152	576	75	156	1	32	55	.271
1994	New York	AL	OF	95	350	62	109	1	36	20	.311
1995	New York	AL	OF	67	238	37	62	2	15	10	.261
1995	Atlanta	NL	OF	28	53	6	14	0	2	3	.264
1996	Baltimore	AL	OF	58	175	25	42	2	14	8	.240
1996	Atlanta	NL	OF	22	31	3	13	0	2	1	.419
Post All-Star				39	74	11	24	0	3	2	.324

HENRY RODRIGUEZ

Age 29/L   **$22**

We only hope you weren't one of those unfortunate souls who watched those home runs pile up in the first half of the season, gave away a lot to get HR in a trade, and then watched helplessly as those home runs came every two weeks or so over the last three months. As with so many others who had career numbers last year, Rodriguez doesn't warrant a hasty judgment.

Year	Team	Lg.	Pos.	G	AB	R	H	HR	RBI	SB	BA
1993	Los Angeles	NL	OF	76	176	20	39	8	23	1	.222
1994	Los Angeles	NL	OF	104	306	33	82	8	49	0	.268
1995	Los Angeles	NL	OF	21	80	6	21	1	10	0	.262
1995	Montreal	NL	1B	24	58	7	12	1	5	0	.207
1996	Montreal	NL	OF	145	532	81	147	36	103	2	.276
Post All-Star				65	213	29	58	11	33	0	.272

REGGIE SANDERS

Age 29/R   **$32**

Came out of miserable '95 postseason and proceeded to be one of last season's big disappointments. He limped around with so many little aches and pains that Reds people openly began questioning his true grit. So he will be challenged this spring, and we think he will bounce back in a big way.

Year	Team	Lg.	Pos.	G	AB	R	H	HR	RBI	SB	BA
1993	Cincinnati	NL	OF	138	496	90	136	20	83	27	.274
1994	Cincinnati	NL	OF	107	400	66	105	17	62	21	.262
1995	Cincinnati	NL	OF	133	484	91	148	28	99	36	.306
1996	Cincinnati	NL	OF	81	287	49	72	14	33	24	.251
Post All-Star				43	146	20	32	7	16	12	.219

F. P. SANTANGELO

Age 29/B   **$8**

A plucky spare outfielder with surprising RBI punch.

Year	Team	Lg.	Pos.	G	AB	R	H	HR	RBI	SB	BA
1995	Montreal	NL	OF	35	98	11	29	1	9	1	.296
1996	Montreal	NL	OF	152	393	54	109	7	56	5	.277
Post All-Star				68	197	27	56	4	24	3	.284

Catchers
pp. 27-39

Corners
pp. 40-60

Infield
pp. 60-80

Outfield
pp. 80-111

DH
pp. 112-115

Starters
pp. 115-145

Relievers
pp. 146-178

GARY SHEFFIELD　　　　　　　　　　　　　　Age 28/R　　　$42

One of the four or five best hitters in the league, he should reach new heights under the cool hand of Jim Leyland.

Year	Team	Lg.	Pos.	G	AB	R	H	HR	RBI	SB	BA
1993	San Diego	NL	3B	68	258	34	76	10	36	5	.295
1993	Florida	NL	3B	72	236	33	69	10	37	12	.292
1994	Florida	NL	OF	87	322	61	89	27	78	12	.276
1995	Florida	NL	OF	63	213	46	69	16	46	19	.324
1996	Florida	NL	OF	161	519	118	163	42	120	16	.314
Post All-Star				74	229	57	77	17	58	11	.336

DWIGHT SMITH　　　　　　　　　　　　　　Age 33/L　　　$1

Nope.

Year	Team	Lg.	Pos.	G	AB	R	H	HR	RBI	SB	BA
1993	Chicago	NL	OF	111	310	51	93	11	35	8	.300
1994	California	AL	OF	45	122	19	32	5	18	2	.262
1994	Baltimore	AL	OF	28	74	12	23	3	12	0	.311
1995	Atlanta	NL	OF	103	131	16	33	3	21	0	.252
1996	Atlanta	NL	OF	101	153	16	31	3	16	1	.203
Post All-Star				41	50	3	8	0	5	0	.160

SAMMY SOSA　　　　　　　　　　　　　　Age 28/R　　　$39

"I want to be recognized as a great player, but something always happens," said Sammy last year after his injury. Keep pounding out those 40 dingers and we'll call you great at the top of our lungs.

Year	Team	Lg.	Pos.	G	AB	R	H	HR	RBI	SB	BA
1993	Chicago	NL	OF	159	598	92	156	33	93	36	.261
1994	Chicago	NL	OF	105	426	59	128	25	70	22	.300
1995	Chicago	NL	OF	144	564	89	151	36	119	.34	.268
1996	Chicago	NL	OF	124	498	84	136	40	100	18	.273
Post All-Star				37	145	27	45	13	37	0	.310

MARK SWEENEY　　　　　　　　　　　　　Age 27/L　　　$1

Decent role player. Nothing more than that.

Year	Team	Lg.	Pos.	G	AB	R	H	HR	RBI	SB	BA
1995	St. Louis	NL	1B	37	77	5	21	2	13	1	.273
1996	St. Louis	NL	OF	98	170	32	45	3	22	3	.265
Post All-Star				37	50	11	13	0	5	2	.260

MILT THOMPSON　　　　　　　　　　　　Age 38/L　　　$1

Say goodbye, Uncle Miltie.

Year	Team	Lg.	Pos.	G	AB	R	H	HR	RBI	SB	BA
1993	Philadelphia	NL	OF	129	340	42	89	4	44	9	.262
1994	Philadelphia	NL	OF	87	220	29	60	3	30	7	.273
1994	Houston	NL	OF	9	21	5	6	1	3	2	.286
1995	Houston	NL	OF	92	132	14	29	2	19	4	.220
1996	Los Angeles	NL	OF	48	51	2	6	0	1	1	.118
1996	Colorado	NL	OF	14	15	1	1	0	2	0	.067
Post All-Star				7	9	1	1	0	2	0	.111

OZZIE TIMMONS   Age 26/R $3

Loaded with power. Alas, also loaded with holes in his swing.

Year	Team	Lg.	Pos.	G	AB	R	H	HR	RBI	SB	BA
1995	Chicago	NL	OF	77	171	30	45	8	28	3	.263
1996	Chicago	NL	OF	65	140	18	28	7	16	1	.200
Post All-Star				32	82	12	21	6	15	1	.256

JOHN VANDERWAL   Age 30/L $3

When a pinch hitter either slumps or gets to play too much, it can really hurt his value.

Year	Team	Lg.	Pos.	G	AB	R	H	HR	RBI	SB	BA
1993	Montreal	NL	1B	106	215	34	50	5	30	6	.233
1994	Colorado	NL	1B	91	110	12	27	5	15	2	.245
1995	Colorado	NL	1B	105	101	15	35	5	21	1	.347
1996	Colorado	NL	OF	104	151	20	38	5	31	2	.252
Post All-Star				46	49	8	12	1	8	1	.245

GREG VAUGHN   Age 31/R $36

Our concern is not how much he struggled for two months in the National League. We wonder how he'll hold up playing the outfield all the time without having that DH security blanket to fall back on when he's hurting. Otherwise, the power will be there for the Padres, just like it was for the Brewers.

Year	Team	Lg.	Pos.	G	AB	R	H	HR	RBI	SB	BA
1993	Milwaukee	AL	OF	154	569	97	152	30	97	10	.267
1994	Milwaukee	AL	OF	95	370	59	94	19	55	9	.254
1995	Milwaukee	AL	DH	108	392	67	88	17	59	10	.224
1996	Milwaukee	AL	OF	102	375	78	105	31	95	5	.280
1996	San Diego	NL	OF	43	141	20	29	10	22	4	.206
Post All-Star				62	211	33	47	17	42	4	.223

LARRY WALKER   Age 30/L $35

It's one thing to separate your shoulder crashing into an outfield fence. But how on earth did he separate the same shoulder while *fishing*? That injury makes him iffy for the start of the season, but he'll eventually come back and shoulder a big offensive burden.

Year	Team	Lg.	Pos.	G	AB	R	H	HR	RBI	SB	BA
1993	Montreal	NL	OF	138	490	85	130	22	86	29	.265
1994	Montreal	NL	OF	103	395	76	127	19	86	15	.322
1995	Colorado	NL	OF	131	494	96	151	36	101	16	.306
1996	Colorado	NL	OF	83	272	58	75	18	58	18	.276
Post All-Star				30	74	18	19	4	15	6	.257

JEROME WALTON   Age 31/R $3

He hurt his hamstring in May and never returned. Nor should he this year.

Year	Team	Lg.	Pos.	G	AB	R	H	HR	RBI	SB	BA
1993	California	AL	DH	5	2	2	0	0	0	1	0.000
1994	Cincinnati	NL	OF	46	68	10	21	1	9	1	.309
1995	Cincinnati	NL	OF	102	162	32	47	8	22	10	.290
1996	Atlanta	NL	OF	37	47	9	16	1	4	0	.340
Post All-Star				0	0	0	0	0	0	0	.000

Catchers
pp. 27–39

Corners
pp. 40–60

Infield
pp. 60–80

Outfield
pp. 80–111

DH
pp. 112–115

Starters
pp. 115–145

Relievers
pp. 146–178

DEVON WHITE   Age 34/B $21

Considering that he had a bad hamstring for two months, that he never had anyone decent batting behind him, and that it took him half a season to adjust to a new league, he wasn't a bad catch for the Marlins. Look for even better things from him this year.

Year	Team	Lg.	Pos.	G	AB	R	H	HR	RBI	SB	BA
1993	Toronto	AL	OF	146	598	116	163	15	52	34	.273
1994	Toronto	AL	OF	100	403	67	109	13	49	11	.270
1995	Toronto	AL	OF	101	427	61	121	10	53	11	.283
1996	Florida	NL	OF	146	552	77	151	17	84	22	.274
Post All-Star				68	249	42	68	10	51	13	.273

RONDELL WHITE   Age 25/R $24

Give him a healthy season and 550 at bats and you'll have a star. We remain convinced until proven otherwise.

Year	Team	Lg.	Pos.	G	AB	R	H	HR	RBI	SB	BA
1993	Montreal	NL	OF	23	73	9	19	2	15	1	.260
1994	Montreal	NL	OF	40	97	16	27	2	13	1	.278
1995	Montreal	NL	OF	130	474	87	140	13	57	25	.295
1996	Montreal	NL	OF	88	334	35	98	6	41	14	.293
Post All-Star				64	234	23	68	3	22	10	.291

AMERICAN LEAGUE

RICH AMARAL   Age 34/R $14

Buhner, Griffey, Rodriguez, and Martinez can cover him in the RBI department but 29 is still awfully low. The saving grace is that he stole 25 bases, thereby covering Buhner and Martinez in that department. The Amaral/Whiten platoon may be worth investing in.

Year	Team	Lg.	Pos.	G	AB	R	H	HR	RBI	SB	BA
1993	Seattle	AL	2B	110	373	53	108	1	44	19	.290
1994	Seattle	AL	2B	77	228	37	60	4	18	5	.263
1995	Seattle	AL	OF	90	238	45	67	2	19	21	.282
1996	Seattle	AL	OF	118	312	69	91	1	29	25	.292
Post All-Star				58	154	33	46	1	12	15	.299

BRADY ANDERSON   Age 33/L $25

Corked bat? Juiced ball? Whatever. This guy never hit more than 21 in his eight-year career and he comes along and gives Maris a run for his money. Please. If he hit 35, we'd love him, but 50 is just too much to take. Guess what, he'll never do it again. Trade him now and get two good starters and a closer for this year based on what this guy did last year.

Year	Team	Lg.	Pos.	G	AB	R	H	HR	RBI	SB	BA
1993	Baltimore	AL	OF	142	560	87	147	13	66	24	.262
1994	Baltimore	AL	OF	111	453	78	119	12	48	31	.263
1995	Baltimore	AL	OF	143	554	108	145	16	64	26	.262
1996	Baltimore	AL	OF	149	579	117	172	50	110	21	.297
Post All-Star				70	272	52	81	20	48	9	.298

Catchers
pp. 27-39

Corners
pp. 40-60

Infield
pp. 60-80

Outfield
pp. 80-111

DH
pp. 112-115

Starters
pp. 115-145

Relievers
pp. 146-178

GARRET ANDERSON
Age 24/L   **$15**

Did not improve the way one would have hoped and displayed an unbecoming crankiness for such a young player. Then again, things were pretty bleak in Disneyland all season. Look for a big year.

Year	Team	Lg.	Pos.	G	AB	R	H	HR	RBI	SB	BA
1994	California	AL	OF	5	13	0	5	0	1	0	.385
1995	California	AL	OF	106	374	50	120	16	69	6	.321
1996	California	AL	OF	150	607	79	173	12	72	7	.285
Post All-Star				64	252	32	70	3	35	3	.278

KIMERA BARTEE
Age 24/R   **$15**

Nice debut for the new CF in Detroit. Capable defense and the only source of speed in town besides rookie Curtis Pride. Bartee has the job.

Year	Team	Lg.	Pos.	G	AB	R	H	HR	RBI	SB	BA
1996	Detroit	AL	OF	110	217	32	55	1	14	20	.253
Post All-Star				62	156	22	37	1	9	10	.237

RICH BECKER
Age 25/B   **$18**

Finally!

Year	Team	Lg.	Pos.	G	AB	R	H	HR	RBI	SB	BA
1993	Minnesota	AL	OF	3	7	3	2	0	0	1	.286
1994	Minnesota	AL	OF	28	98	12	26	1	8	6	.265
1995	Minnesota	AL	OF	106	392	45	93	2	33	8	.237
1996	Minnesota	AL	OF	148	525	92	153	12	71	19	.291
Post All-Star				73	282	55	91	7	51	10	.323

ALBERT BELLE
Age 30/R   **$45**

You want a role model, draft somebody else. You want the most exciting power hitter in baseball, pay the price.

Year	Team	Lg.	Pos.	G	AB	R	H	HR	RBI	SB	BA
1993	Cleveland	AL	OF	159	594	93	172	38	129	23	.290
1994	Cleveland	AL	OF	106	412	90	147	36	101	9	.357
1995	Cleveland	AL	OF	143	546	121	173	50	126	5	.317
1996	Cleveland	AL	OF	158	602	124	187	48	148	11	.311
Post All-Star				73	281	58	93	21	74	6	.331

BOBBY BONILLA
Age 34/B   **$22**

The classic Bonilla year plus about 20 RBI. Now he's back with Jim Leyland, he doesn't have to DH, and he's happy. We see another classic Bonilla season—minus about 20 RBI.

Year	Team	Lg.	Pos.	G	AB	R	H	HR	RBI	SB	BA
1993	New York	NL	OF	139	502	81	133	34	87	3	.265
1994	New York	NL	3B	108	403	60	117	20	67	1	.290
1995	New York	NL	3B	80	317	49	103	18	53	0	.325
1995	Baltimore	AL	OF	61	237	47	79	10	46	0	.333
1996	Baltimore	AL	OF	159	595	107	171	28	116	1	.287
Post All-Star				77	287	55	84	18	64	0	.293

BRENT BOWERS   Age 25/L $1

He may stick around to save Angelos some money. Don't waste yours.

Year	Team	Lg.	Pos.	G	AB	R	H	HR	RBI	SB	BA
1996	Baltimore	AL	OF	21	39	6	12	0	3	0	.308
Post All-Star				21	39	6	12	0	3	0	.308

DARREN BRAGG   Age 27/L $11

With the help of Jeff Frye, Bragg dragged the Red Sox into the wild card race with great defense and plenty of hustle. He'll start in center or right and should blossom into a Fenway fixture

Year	Team	Lg.	Pos.	G	AB	R	H	HR	RBI	SB	BA
1994	Seattle	AL	DH	8	19	4	3	0	2	0	.158
1995	Seattle	AL	OF	52	145	20	34	3	12	9	.234
1996	Seattle	AL	OF	69	195	36	53	7	25	8	.272
1996	Boston	AL	OF	58	222	38	56	3	22	6	.252
Post All-Star				73	260	44	67	3	28	6	.258

JACOB BRUMFIELD   Age 31/R $12

Worth a few extra bucks simply because he sounds like a guy who did business with Ebenezer Scrooge.

Year	Team	Lg.	Pos.	G	AB	R	H	HR	RBI	SB	BA
1993	Cincinnati	NL	OF	103	272	40	73	6	23	20	.268
1994	Cincinnati	NL	OF	68	122	36	38	4	11	6	.311
1995	Pittsburgh	NL	OF	116	402	64	109	4	26	22	.271
1996	Pittsburgh	NL	OF	29	80	11	20	2	8	3	.250
1996	Toronto	AL	OF	90	308	52	79	12	52	12	.256
Post All-Star				52	175	29	46	5	32	10	.263

DAMON BUFORD   Age 26/R $8

Buford is the ideal fifth OF. Anything cheaper is a bona fide steal. If you can get his platoon partner Newson, you're stylin'.

Year	Team	Lg.	Pos.	G	AB	R	H	HR	RBI	SB	BA
1993	Baltimore	AL	OF	53	79	18	18	2	9	2	.228
1994	Baltimore	AL	DH	4	2	2	1	0	0	0	.500
1995	Baltimore	AL	OF	24	32	6	2	0	2	3	.063
1995	New York	NL	OF	44	136	24	32	4	12	7	.235
1996	Texas	AL	OF	90	145	30	41	6	20	8	.283
Post All-Star				42	59	13	17	2	7	0	.288

JAY BUHNER   Age 32/R $37

George Steinbrenner's biggest Broglio richly deserves the highest accolade players give to each other: a gamer.

Year	Team	Lg.	Pos.	G	AB	R	H	HR	RBI	SB	BA
1993	Seattle	AL	OF	158	563	91	153	27	98	2	.272
1994	Seattle	AL	OF	101	358	74	100	21	68	0	.279
1995	Seattle	AL	OF	126	470	86	123	40	121	0	.262
1996	Seattle	AL	OF	150	564	107	153	44	138	0	.271
Post All-Star				72	273	49	70	21	66	0	.256

JEROMY BURNITZ   Age 27/L $14

He'll start for the Brewers after whining his way out of Cleveland. It seems Jeromy felt the best outfield in the league would have been better with him in it. He'll benefit from the change of scenery, and so could you. Smart pick.

Year	Team	Lg.	Pos.	G	AB	R	H	HR	RBI	SB	BA
1993	New York	NL	OF	86	263	49	64	13	38	3	.243
1994	New York	NL	OF	45	143	26	34	3	15	1	.238
1995	Cleveland	AL	OF	9	7	4	4	0	0	0	.571
1996	Cleveland	AL	OF	71	128	30	36	7	26	2	.281
1996	Milwaukee	AL	OF	23	72	8	17	2	14	2	.236
Post All-Star				58	150	22	39	6	32	3	.260

CHUCK CARR   Age 28/R $3

If you saw the tape of Carr breaking his leg last year, you'll head for the refreshment table when his name comes up. Or you'll call your wife. Or you'll run and hide. But you won't bid big bucks.

Year	Team	Lg.	Pos.	G	AB	R	H	HR	RBI	SB	BA
1993	Florida	NL	OF	142	551	75	147	4	41	58	.267
1994	Florida	NL	OF	106	433	61	114	2	30	32	.263
1995	Florida	NL	OF	105	308	54	70	2	20	25	.227
1996	Milwaukee	AL	OF	27	106	18	29	1	11	5	.274
Post All-Star				0	0	0	0	0	0	0	0.000

JOE CARTER   Age 37/R $24

Back in the 100 RBI club where he belongs. Signed a one-year deal, which always seems to motivate players. Even future Hall of Famers. If Toronto continues to falter, he may be on the blocks again, which means he'll kick butt for you, and somebody other than the Blue Jays.

Year	Team	Lg.	Pos.	G	AB	R	H	HR	RBI	SB	BA
1993	Toronto	AL	OF	155	603	92	153	33	121	8	.254
1994	Toronto	AL	OF	111	435	70	118	27	103	11	.271
1995	Toronto	AL	OF	139	558	70	141	25	76	12	.253
1996	Toronto	AL	OF	157	625	84	158	30	107	7	.253
Post All-Star				70	283	28	61	10	37	3	.216

MARTY CORDOVA   Age 27/R $22

Not a lot of guys can go from 24 to 16 HR and still increase their RBI total by 27. SB also went down but the BA soared, which is where the ribbies came from. This is the way the Rookie of the Year is supposed to play.

Year	Team	Lg.	Pos.	G	AB	R	H	HR	RBI	SB	BA
1995	Minnesota	AL	OF	137	512	81	142	24	84	20	.277
1996	Minnesota	AL	OF	145	569	97	176	16	111	11	.309
Post All-Star				72	278	44	83	9	55	2	.299

JOHNNY DAMON
Age 23/L $15

Damon didn't have the season that most people expected, but it's only a matter of time. Expect a few more HR and a better BA. And KC can't be this bad forever.

Year	Team	Lg.	Pos.	G	AB	R	H	HR	RBI	SB	BA
1995	Kansas City	AL	OF	47	188	32	53	3	23	7	.282
1996	Kansas City	AL	OF	145	517	61	140	6	50	25	.271
Post All-Star				61	213	26	54	2	22	10	.254

MIKE DEVEREAUX
Age 33/R $4

Acceptabeaux stats for a fourth or fifth OF.

Year	Team	Lg.	Pos.	G	AB	R	H	HR	RBI	SB	BA
1993	Baltimore	AL	OF	131	527	72	132	14	75	3	.250
1994	Baltimore	AL	OF	85	301	35	61	9	33	1	.203
1995	Chicago	AL	OF	92	333	48	102	10	55	6	.306
1995	Atlanta	NL	OF	29	55	7	14	1	8	2	.255
1996	Baltimore	AL	OF	127	323	49	74	8	34	8	.229
Post All-Star				61	106	18	20	4	12	2	.189

ALEX DIAZ
Age 28/B $1

Call it the Diaz Declaration. Don't pay more than a buck for a guy who won't get 100 AB. Amaral and Whiten pretty much guarantee that this guy won't play.

Year	Team	Lg.	Pos.	G	AB	R	H	HR	RBI	SB	BA
1993	Milwaukee	AL	OF	32	69	9	22	0	1	5	.319
1994	Milwaukee	AL	OF	79	187	17	47	1	17	5	.251
1995	Seattle	AL	OF	103	270	44	67	3	27	18	.248
1996	Seattle	AL	OF	38	79	11	19	1	5	6	.241
Post All-Star				18	27	2	8	0	2	4	.296

JIM EDMONDS
Age 26/L $29

Give the guy credit for giving his all on defense, but all these injuries are making him look like the next Paul Molitor—at least in that his days in the field appear to be numbered. He's a good hitter, but not Molitor-good.

Year	Team	Lg.	Pos.	G	AB	R	H	HR	RBI	SB	BA
1993	California	AL	OF	18	61	5	15	0	4	0	.246
1994	California	AL	OF	94	289	35	79	5	37	4	.273
1995	California	AL	OF	141	558	120	162	33	107	1	.290
1996	California	AL	OF	114	431	73	131	27	66	4	.304
Post All-Star				66	244	43	74	14	32	3	.303

DARIN ERSTAD
Age 22/L $2

Lots of potential but he sure hasn't taken the job away from Garret Anderson. Somebody will have to get traded for him to become a full-timer.

Year	Team	Lg.	Pos.	G	AB	R	H	HR	RBI	SB	BA
1996	California	AL	OF	57	208	34	59	4	20	3	.284
Post All-Star				34	112	15	29	1	7	2	.259

JUAN GONZALEZ   Age 27/R $44

He slimmed down a bit, and the bat speed came back. Other than some time lost to a hamstring injury, Gonzalez didn't have the physical problems that had hampered him when he tried to play baseball with Lou Ferrigno's body. His performance against the Yankees in the playoffs put an exclamation point on a great year. Welcome back, not-quite-so-big guy.

Year	Team	Lg.	Pos.	G	AB	R	H	HR	RBI	SB	BA
1993	Texas	AL	OF	140	536	105	166	46	118	4	.310
1994	Texas	AL	OF	107	422	57	116	19	85	6	.275
1995	Texas	AL	DH	90	352	57	104	27	82	0	.295
1996	Texas	AL	OF	134	541	89	170	47	144	2	.314
Post All-Star				72	297	44	92	25	74	2	.310

TOM GOODWIN   Age 28/L $40

Speed thrills—always has, always will. One puzzle: he hit .228 at home. We're not going to lose any sleep over it, but that's the sort of thing we worry about over the winter.

Year	Team	Lg.	Pos.	G	AB	R	H	HR	RBI	SB	BA
1993	Los Angeles	NL	OF	30	17	6	5	0	1	1	.294
1994	Kansas City	AL	DH	2	2	0	0	0	0	0	0.000
1995	Kansas City	AL	OF	133	480	72	138	4	28	50	.287
1996	Kansas City	AL	OF	143	524	80	148	1	35	66	.282
Post All-Star				59	207	31	59	0	14	28	.285

SHAWN GREEN   Age 24/L $12

More was expected of this guy, but these numbers are fine. Get Brumfield too and you'll have the stats of a good third OF.

Year	Team	Lg.	Pos.	G	AB	R	H	HR	RBI	SB	BA
1993	Toronto	AL	OF	3	6	0	0	0	0	0	0.000
1994	Toronto	AL	OF	14	33	1	3	0	1	1	.091
1995	Toronto	AL	OF	121	379	52	109	15	54	1	.288
1996	Toronto	AL	OF	132	422	52	118	11	45	5	.280
Post All-Star				61	193	27	65	4	19	5	.337

MIKE GREENWELL   Age 33/L $10

Got 20% of his RBI in one night against Seattle. Made a lot of noise when the BoSox wouldn't promise him a full-time job, a promise you shouldn't make either.

Year	Team	Lg.	Pos.	G	AB	R	H	HR	RBI	SB	BA
1993	Boston	AL	OF	146	540	77	170	13	72	5	.315
1994	Boston	AL	OF	95	327	60	88	11	45	2	.269
1995	Boston	AL	OF	120	481	67	143	15	76	9	.297
1996	Boston	AL	OF	77	295	35	87	7	44	4	.295
Post All-Star				54	205	28	67	6	36	3	.327

RUSTY GREER   Age 28/L $23

On the other hand, promise old Rusty anything he wants.

Year	Team	Lg.	Pos.	G	AB	R	H	HR	RBI	SB	BA
1994	Texas	AL	OF	80	277	36	87	10	46	0	.314
1995	Texas	AL	OF	131	417	58	113	13	61	3	.271
1996	Texas	AL	OF	139	542	96	180	18	100	9	.332
Post All-Star				60	243	44	85	10	46	5	.350

Catchers
pp. 27–39

Corners
pp. 40–60

Infield
pp. 60–80

Outfield
pp. 80–111

DH
pp. 112–115

Starters
pp. 115–145

Relievers
pp. 146–178

KEN GRIFFEY, JR. Age 27/L $45

This kid's got a lot of nerve. He missed 22 games and still hit 49 homers. Too bad he gave up on that Presidency thing so soon. He couldn't have done worse than Dole.

Year	Team	Lg.	Pos.	G	AB	R	H	HR	RBI	SB	BA
1993	Seattle	AL	OF	156	582	113	180	45	109	17	.309
1994	Seattle	AL	OF	111	433	94	140	40	90	11	.323
1995	Seattle	AL	OF	72	260	52	67	17	42	4	.258
1996	Seattle	AL	OF	140	545	125	165	49	140	16	.303
Post All-Star				73	284	63	87	26	80	6	.306

DARRYL HAMILTON Age 32/L $13

Nice pickup by the Rangers. Great comeback by Hamilton. This means nothing to us, but he played over 1,200 innings and didn't commit a single error. He'll keep his job, and continue to improve across the board.

Year	Team	Lg.	Pos.	G	AB	R	H	HR	RBI	SB	BA
1993	Milwaukee	AL	OF	135	520	74	161	9	48	21	.310
1994	Milwaukee	AL	OF	36	141	23	37	1	13	3	.262
1995	Milwaukee	AL	OF	112	398	54	108	5	44	11	.271
1996	Texas	AL	OF	148	627	94	184	6	51	15	.293
Post All-Star				67	286	43	79	4	23	6	.276

JEFFREY HAMMONDS Age 26/R $5

What to do, what to do? Catch "Barney & Friends on Ice" at the abandoned asbestos factory? Draft Jeffrey Hammonds? Man, that purple thing can skate.

Year	Team	Lg.	Pos.	G	AB	R	H	HR	RBI	SB	BA
1993	Baltimore	AL	OF	33	105	10	32	3	19	4	.305
1994	Baltimore	AL	OF	68	250	45	74	8	31	5	.296
1995	Baltimore	AL	OF	57	178	18	43	4	23	4	.242
1996	Baltimore	AL	OF	71	248	38	56	9	27	3	.226
Post All-Star				15	54	11	10	3	8	0	.185

JOSE HERRERA Age 24/L $4

Herrera is a guy who can give you a lot of little things.

Year	Team	Lg.	Pos.	G	AB	R	H	HR	RBI	SB	BA
1995	Oakland	AL	OF	33	70	9	17	0	2	1	.243
1996	Oakland	AL	OF	108	320	44	86	6	30	8	.269
Post All-Star				55	144	16	36	2	9	2	.250

BOB HIGGINSON Age 26/L $26

Higginson is a guy who can give you a lot of big things.

Year	Team	Lg.	Pos.	G	AB	R	H	HR	RBI	SB	BA
1995	Detroit	AL	OF	131	410	61	92	14	43	6	.224
1996	Detroit	AL	OF	130	440	75	141	26	81	6	.320
Post All-Star				70	237	39	79	12	39	1	.333

DENNY HOCKING
Age 26/B   **$1**

Sorry, did you say something?

Year	Team	Lg.	Pos.	G	AB	R	H	HR	RBI	SB	BA
1993	Minnesota	AL	SS	15	36	7	5	0	0	1	.139
1994	Minnesota	AL	SS	11	31	3	10	0	2	2	.323
1995	Minnesota	AL	SS	9	25	4	5	0	3	1	.200
1996	Minnesota	AL	OF	49	127	16	25	1	10	3	.197
Post All-Star				23	52	7	14	0	3	1	.269

DAVID HULSE
Age 29/L   **$1**

Hulse no longer has a pulse. The Brewers have too many other options.

Year	Team	Lg.	Pos.	G	AB	R	H	HR	RBI	SB	BA
1993	Texas	AL	OF	114	407	71	118	1	29	29	.290
1994	Texas	AL	OF	77	310	58	79	1	19	18	.255
1995	Milwaukee	AL	OF	119	339	46	85	3	47	15	.251
1996	Milwaukee	AL	OF	81	117	18	26	0	6	4	.222
Post All-Star				39	49	8	10	0	4	4	.204

PETE INCAVIGLIA
Age 32/R   **$12**

Almost makes you miss Dave Kingman, doesn't he?

Year	Team	Lg.	Pos.	G	AB	R	H	HR	RBI	SB	BA
1993	Philadelphia	NL	OF	116	368	60	101	24	89	1	.274
1994	Philadelphia	NL	OF	80	244	28	56	13	32	1	.230
1996	Philadelphia	NL	OF	99	269	33	63	16	42	2	.234
1996	Baltimore	AL	OF	12	33	4	10	2	8	0	.303
Post All-Star				39	86	11	18	4	13	0	.209

REGGIE JEFFERSON
Age 28/L   **$22**

If by some miracle Canseco is gone, get him. Otherwise, it's another part-time season. He's not much of an outfielder and the Red Sox have first base pretty well covered.

Year	Team	Lg.	Pos.	G	AB	R	H	HR	RBI	SB	BA
1993	Cleveland	AL	DH	113	366	35	91	10	34	1	.249
1994	Seattle	AL	DH	63	162	24	53	8	32	0	.327
1995	Boston	AL	DH	46	121	21	35	5	26	0	.289
1996	Boston	AL	DH	122	386	67	134	19	74	0	.347
Post All-Star				64	213	38	69	10	41	0	.324

ROBERTO KELLY
Age 32/R   **$8**

All that traveling must have caught up with him. Not one of Tom Kelly's favorites, so don't expect a lot more playing time.

Year	Team	Lg.	Pos.	G	AB	R	H	HR	RBI	SB	BA
1993	Cincinnati	NL	OF	78	320	44	102	9	35	21	.319
1994	Cincinnati	NL	OF	47	179	29	54	3	21	9	.302
1994	Atlanta	NL	OF	63	255	44	73	6	24	10	.286
1995	Montreal	NL	OF	24	95	11	26	1	9	4	.274
1995	Los Angeles	NL	OF	112	409	47	114	6	48	15	.279
1996	Minnesota	AL	OF	98	322	41	104	6	47	10	.323
Post All-Star				45	149	20	50	5	25	2	.336

Catchers
pp. 27-39

Corners
pp. 40-60

Infield
pp. 60-80

Outfield
pp. 80-111

DH
pp. 112-115

Starters
pp. 115-145

Relievers
pp. 146-178

KEVIN KOSLOFSKI   Age 30/L $1

Hard to imagine this guy playing much, since the Brewers picked up Jeromy Burnitz and Gerald Williams. Guess they'll have to take down the Koslofski's Korner sign. Pity.

Year	Team	Lg.	Pos.	G	AB	R	H	HR	RBI	SB	BA
1993	Kansas City	AL	OF	15	26	4	7	1	2	0	.269
1994	Kansas City	AL	OF	2	4	2	1	0	0	0	.250
1996	Milwaukee	AL	OF	25	42	5	9	0	6	0	.214
Post All-Star				0	0	0	0	0	0	0	.000

MATT LAWTON   Age 25/L $2

Got a huge opportunity to show his stuff when Kirby went down with his eye trouble. Way to blow that one, Matt.

Year	Team	Lg.	Pos.	G	AB	R	H	HR	RBI	SB	BA
1995	Minnesota	AL	OF	21	60	11	19	1	12	1	.317
1996	Minnesota	AL	OF	79	252	34	65	6	42	4	.258
Post All-Star				41	113	19	33	4	21	1	.292

DARREN LEWIS   Age 29/R $12

Definitely gets a vote for disappointment of the year. He stole 22 bases, but that's about it. Nice move by the White Sox to let Lance Johnson go. Who needs all those triples?

Year	Team	Lg.	Pos.	G	AB	R	H	HR	RBI	SB	BA
1993	San Francisco	NL	OF	136	522	84	132	2	48	46	.253
1994	San Francisco	NL	OF	114	451	70	116	4	29	30	.257
1995	San Francisco	NL	OF	74	309	47	78	1	16	21	.252
1995	Cincinnati	NL	OF	58	163	19	40	0	8	11	.245
1996	Chicago	AL	OF	141	337	55	77	4	53	21	.228
Post All-Star				63	130	19	26	1	18	9	.200

PAT LISTACH   Age 29/B $3

This is *not* the way a Rookie of the Year is supposed to play. We like the way he frosted Steinbrenner's toenails. Listach is pretty much worthless. Houston will love his speed.

Year	Team	Lg.	Pos.	G	AB	R	H	HR	RBI	SB	BA
1993	Milwaukee	AL	SS	98	356	50	87	3	30	18	.244
1994	Milwaukee	AL	SS	16	54	8	16	0	2	2	.296
1995	Milwaukee	AL	2B	101	334	35	73	0	25	13	.219
1996	Milwaukee	AL	OF	87	317	51	76	1	33	25	.240
Post All-Star				34	125	18	24	0	13	8	.192

KENNY LOFTON   Age 29/L $45

If you're going to overpay for one guy in baseball, make it the guy who's worth every penny.

Year	Team	Lg.	Pos.	G	AB	R	H	HR	RBI	SB	BA
1993	Cleveland	AL	OF	148	569	116	185	1	42	70	.325
1994	Cleveland	AL	OF	112	459	105	160	12	57	60	.349
1995	Cleveland	AL	OF	118	481	93	149	7	53	54	.310
1996	Cleveland	AL	OF	154	662	132	210	14	67	75	.317
Post All-Star				68	299	70	96	8	27	33	.321

DAVE MARTINEZ
Age 32/L   **$11**

In what was supposed to be a year spent as a backup, Martinez delivered his best season ever. Could get the departed Tartabull's AB as the full-time right fielder.

Year	Team	Lg.	Pos.	G	AB	R	H	HR	RBI	SB	BA
1993	San Francisco	NL	OF	91	241	28	58	5	27	6	.241
1994	San Francisco	NL	OF	97	235	23	58	4	27	3	.247
1995	Chicago	AL	OF	118	303	49	93	5	37	8	.307
1996	Chicago	AL	OF	146	440	85	140	10	53	15	.318
Post All-Star				70	234	45	76	5	22	9	.325

DAMON MASHORE
Age 27/L   **$1**

Fifty outfielder potential.

Year	Team	Lg.	Pos.	G	AB	R	H	HR	RBI	SB	BA
1996	Oakland	AL	OF	50	105	20	28	3	12	4	.267
Post All-Star				27	56	11	15	2	7	2	.268

MATT MIESKE
Age 29/R   **$12**

Despite the best numbers of his career, Mieske seems destined to be the fourth OF in Milwaukee. All in all, not the worst guy you could take, and if one of Bud's starters should falter, he could be one of the best.

Year	Team	Lg.	Pos.	G	AB	R	H	HR	RBI	SB	BA
1993	Milwaukee	AL	OF	23	58	9	14	3	7	0	.241
1994	Milwaukee	AL	OF	84	259	39	67	10	38	3	.259
1995	Milwaukee	AL	OF	117	267	42	67	12	48	2	.251
1996	Milwaukee	AL	OF	127	374	46	104	14	64	1	.278
Post All-Star				52	154	16	41	5	29	0	.266

LYLE MOUTON
Age 27/R   **$5**

Last year we said he'd be okay. He was okay. Okay?

Year	Team	Lg.	Pos.	G	AB	R	H	HR	RBI	SB	BA
1995	Chicago	AL	OF	58	179	23	54	5	27	1	.302
1996	Chicago	AL	OF	87	214	25	63	7	39	3	.294
Post All-Star				37	106	13	31	3	21	1	.292

MARC NEWFIELD
Age 24/R   **$5**

Mr. Potential finally showed us a little something. Never a good sign. He's a fifth OF and always will be.

Year	Team	Lg.	Pos.	G	AB	R	H	HR	RBI	SB	BA
1993	Seattle	AL	DH	22	66	5	15	1	7	0	.227
1994	Seattle	AL	DH	12	38	3	7	1	4	0	.184
1995	Seattle	AL	OF	24	85	7	16	3	14	0	.188
1995	San Diego	NL	OF	21	55	6	17	1	7	0	.309
1996	San Diego	NL	OF	84	191	27	48	5	26	1	.251
1996	Milwaukee	AL	OF	49	179	21	55	7	31	0	.307
Post All-Star				67	221	26	60	8	35	0	.271

WARREN NEWSON   Age 32/L $5

See Damon Buford.

Year	Team	Lg.	Pos.	G	AB	R	H	HR	RBI	SB	BA
1993	Chicago	AL	DH	26	40	9	12	2	6	0	.300
1994	Chicago	AL	OF	63	102	16	26	2	7	1	.255
1995	Chicago	AL	OF	51	85	19	20	3	9	1	.235
1995	Seattle	AL	OF	33	72	15	21	2	6	1	.292
1996	Texas	AL	OF	91	235	34	60	10	31	3	.255
Post All-Star				34	79	10	17	2	5	1	.215

MELVIN NIEVES   Age 25/B $23

Adjusted nicely to the AL by increasing his power numbers and raising his BA by 40 points. One of four Tigers to hit more than 20 HR. This year, make it 30.

Year	Team	Lg.	Pos.	G	AB	R	H	HR	RBI	SB	BA
1993	San Diego	NL	OF	19	47	4	9	2	3	0	.191
1994	San Diego	NL	OF	10	19	2	5	1	4	0	.263
1995	San Diego	NL	OF	98	234	32	48	14	38	2	.205
1996	Detroit	AL	OF	120	431	71	106	24	60	1	.246
Post All-Star				56	210	39	53	16	35	1	.252

DAVE NILSSON   Age 27/L $20

The Aussie seems to be hitting his stride, and his numbers should earn him more playing time. It helps Nilsson that he plays 1B and OF. Which, in turn, will help you.

Year	Team	Lg.	Pos.	G	AB	R	H	HR	RBI	SB	BA
1993	Milwaukee	AL	C	100	296	35	76	7	40	3	.257
1994	Milwaukee	AL	C	109	397	51	109	12	69	1	.275
1995	Milwaukee	AL	OF	81	263	41	73	12	53	2	.278
1996	Milwaukee	AL	OF	123	453	81	150	17	84	2	.331
Post All-Star				72	272	42	90	8	45	2	.331

OTIS NIXON   Age 38/B $24

Home runs? Nope. RBI? Nope. Stolen bases? Yup.

Year	Team	Lg.	Pos.	G	AB	R	H	HR	RBI	SB	BA
1993	Atlanta	NL	OF	134	461	77	124	1	24	47	.269
1994	Boston	AL	OF	103	398	60	109	0	25	42	.274
1995	Texas	AL	OF	139	589	87	174	0	45	50	.295
1996	Toronto	AL	OF	125	496	87	142	1	29	54	.286
Post All-Star				62	253	38	73	0	17	34	.289

LES NORMAN   Age 28/R $1

The less Norman the better.

Year	Team	Lg.	Pos.	G	AB	R	H	HR	RBI	SB	BA
1995	Kansas City	AL	OF	24	40	6	9	0	4	0	.225
1996	Kansas City	AL	OF	54	49	9	6	0	0	1	.122
Post All-Star				19	18	5	2	0	0	0	.111

JON NUNNALLY
Age 25/L   **$2**

Do not get thee a Nunnally.

Year	Team	Lg.	Pos.	G	AB	R	H	HR	RBI	SB	BA
1995	Kansas City	AL	OF	119	303	51	74	14	42	6	.244
1996	Kansas City	AL	OF	35	90	16	19	5	17	0	.211
Post All-Star				21	66	12	15	4	10	0	.227

TROY O'LEARY
Age 27/L   **$14**

Capable fourth OF who seems to fit in at Fenway.

Year	Team	Lg.	Pos.	G	AB	R	H	HR	RBI	SB	BA
1993	Milwaukee	AL	OF	19	41	3	12	0	3	0	.293
1994	Milwaukee	AL	OF	27	66	9	18	2	7	1	.273
1995	Boston	AL	OF	112	399	60	123	10	49	5	.308
1996	Boston	AL	OF	149	497	68	129	15	81	3	.260
Post All-Star				68	214	30	58	7	39	2	.271

PAUL O'NEILL
Age 34/L   **$20**

The great crybaby toned down the hissy-fits but also toned down the power numbers. In a remarkable year for HR and RBI, O'Neill turned in a relatively soft year. Maybe he needs more fire in his belly. Still, a solid pick for your third or fourth OF.

Year	Team	Lg.	Pos.	G	AB	R	H	HR	RBI	SB	BA
1993	New York	AL	OF	141	498	71	155	20	75	2	.311
1994	New York	AL	OF	103	368	68	132	21	83	5	.359
1995	New York	AL	OF	127	460	82	138	22	96	1	.300
1996	New York	AL	OF	150	546	89	165	19	91	0	.302
Post All-Star				66	240	36	67	11	39	0	.279

ORLANDO PALMEIRO
Age 28/L   **$1**

The wrong Palmeiro.

Year	Team	Lg.	Pos.	G	AB	R	H	HR	RBI	SB	BA
1995	California	AL	OF	15	20	3	7	0	1	0	.350
1996	California	AL	OF	50	87	6	25	0	6	0	.287
Post All-Star				31	43	2	13	0	6	0	.302

ROBERT PEREZ
Age 27/R   **$5**

Perez looks like a solid player, and he may get a chance to be more as the rebuilding continues in Toronto.

Year	Team	Lg.	Pos.	G	AB	R	H	HR	RBI	SB	BA
1994	Toronto	AL	OF	4	8	0	1	0	0	0	.125
1995	Toronto	AL	OF	17	48	2	9	1	3	0	.188
1996	Toronto	AL	OF	86	202	30	66	2	21	3	.327
Post All-Star				40	97	15	31	2	10	1	.320

Catchers
pp. 27-39

Corners
pp. 40-60

Infield
pp. 60-80

Outfield
pp. 80-111

DH
pp. 112-115

Starters
pp. 115-145

Relievers
pp. 146-178

TONY PHILLIPS
Age 37/B   **$15**

Age may be catching up with Phillips, but he still has some stuff left. His first move last year was to retire for a week, so make sure he's playing before you pick him up.

Year	Team	Lg.	Pos.	G	AB	R	H	HR	RBI	SB	BA
1993	Detroit	AL	OF	151	566	113	177	7	57	16	.313
1994	Detroit	AL	OF	114	438	91	123	19	61	13	.281
1995	California	AL	3B	139	525	119	137	27	61	13	.261
1996	Chicago	AL	OF	153	581	119	161	12	63	13	.277
Post All-Star				68	250	48	62	5	18	7	.248

CURTIS PRIDE
Age 28/L   **$10**

Curtis had plenty to be proud of last year and so did the guy who drafted him.

Year	Team	Lg.	Pos.	G	AB	R	H	HR	RBI	SB	BA
1993	Montreal	NL	OF	10	9	3	4	1	5	1	.444
1995	Montreal	NL	OF	48	63	10	11	0	2	3	.175
1996	Detroit	AL	OF	95	267	52	80	10	31	11	.300
Post All-Star				49	141	28	44	7	18	5	.312

TIM RAINES
Age 37/B   **$10**

Rock was injured most of last year and would seem to be out of the Yankees' plans. That doesn't mean he should be out of yours.

Year	Team	Lg.	Pos.	G	AB	R	H	HR	RBI	SB	BA
1993	Chicago	AL	OF	115	415	75	127	16	54	21	.306
1994	Chicago	AL	OF	101	384	80	102	10	52	13	.266
1995	Chicago	AL	OF	133	502	81	143	12	67	13	.285
1996	New York	AL	OF	59	201	45	57	9	33	10	.284
Post All-Star				36	117	25	33	7	23	4	.282

MANNY RAMIREZ
Age 24/R   **$35**

Name a better young outfielder. We're waiting . . .

Year	Team	Lg.	Pos.	G	AB	R	H	HR	RBI	SB	BA
1993	Cleveland	AL	DH	22	53	5	9	2	5	0	.170
1994	Cleveland	AL	OF	91	290	51	78	17	60	4	.269
1995	Cleveland	AL	OF	137	484	85	149	31	107	6	.308
1996	Cleveland	AL	OF	152	550	94	170	33	112	8	.309
Post All-Star				68	258	44	88	13	48	3	.341

RUBEN RIVERA
Age 23/R   **$10**

Loads of potential but he seems to be something of a head case. It's only a matter of time before he starts, and the talent is all there. You can thank us if he plays like Albert Belle. Just don't blame us if he acts like Albert Belle.

Year	Team	Lg.	Pos.	G	AB	R	H	HR	RBI	SB	BA
1995	New York	AL	OF	5	1	0	0	0	0	0	0.000
1996	New York	AL	OF	46	88	17	25	2	16	6	.284
Post All-Star				29	41	10	12	1	6	3	.293

TIM SALMON
Age 28/R   **$32**

A bit of a let-down, especially after 1995. Chalk it up to the general malaise that beset the Angels all season. Look for Salmon to head upstream. (Sorry, we couldn't resist.)

Year	Team	Lg.	Pos.	G	AB	R	H	HR	RBI	SB	BA
1993	California	AL	OF	142	515	93	146	31	95	5	.283
1994	California	AL	OF	100	373	67	107	23	70	1	.287
1995	California	AL	OF	143	537	111	177	34	105	5	.330
1996	California	AL	OF	156	581	90	166	30	98	4	.286
Post All-Star				69	260	36	72	8	40	0	.277

JUAN SAMUEL
Age 36/R   **$6**

We think he can do it juan more time.

Year	Team	Lg.	Pos.	G	AB	R	H	HR	RBI	SB	BA
1993	Cincinnati	NL	2B	103	261	31	60	4	26	9	.230
1994	Detroit	AL	OF	59	136	32	42	5	21	5	.309
1995	Detroit	AL	1B	76	171	28	48	10	34	5	.281
1995	Kansas City	AL	DH	15	34	3	6	2	5	1	.176
1996	Toronto	AL	DH	69	188	34	48	8	26	9	.255
Post All-Star				36	91	18	24	4	14	6	.264

DUANE SINGLETON
Age 24/L   **$1**

Forget it.

Year	Team	Lg.	Pos.	G	AB	R	H	HR	RBI	SB	BA
1994	Milwaukee	AL	OF	2	0	0	0	0	0	0	0.000
1995	Milwaukee	AL	OF	13	31	0	2	0	0	1	.065
1996	Detroit	AL	OF	18	56	5	9	0	3	0	.161
Post All-Star				0	0	0	0	0	0	0	.000

MARK SMITH
Age 26/R   **$2**

Mark Smith down as your last option in the outfield.

Year	Team	Lg.	Pos.	G	AB	R	H	HR	RBI	SB	BA
1994	Baltimore	AL	OF	3	7	0	1	0	2	0	.143
1995	Baltimore	AL	OF	37	104	11	24	3	15	3	.231
1996	Baltimore	AL	OF	27	78	9	19	4	10	0	.244
Post All-Star				7	19	4	7	1	2	0	.368

MATT STAIRS
Age 29/L   **$7**

He's a terrific pinch hitter, but why take the stairs when you can ride the elevator, you know?

Year	Team	Lg.	Pos.	G	AB	R	H	HR	RBI	SB	BA
1993	Montreal	NL	OF	6	8	1	3	0	2	0	.375
1995	Boston	AL	OF	39	88	8	23	1	17	0	.261
1996	Oakland	AL	OF	61	137	21	38	10	23	1	.277
Post All-Star				48	112	16	31	7	12	1	.277

DARRYL STRAWBERRY   Age 35/L $8

Fielder will limit Straw's AB at DH, and Dar-ryl will never be a Gold Glover in the field, so don't get caught in a bidding war for this guy. But if you can get him cheap, he'll be fun to watch.

Year	Team	Lg.	Pos.	G	AB	R	H	HR	RBI	SB	BA
1993	Los Angeles	NL	OF	32	100	12	14	5	12	1	.140
1994	San Francisco	NL	OF	29	92	13	22	4	17	0	.239
1995	New York	AL	DH	32	87	15	24	3	13	0	.276
1996	New York	AL	OF	63	202	35	53	11	36	6	.262
Post All-Star				62	198	35	53	11	36	6	.268

DANNY TARTABULL   Age 34/R $25

Pretty good season from one of our least favorite players. Chicago doesn't want him back, so he could land anywhere.

Year	Team	Lg.	Pos.	G	AB	R	H	HR	RBI	SB	BA
1993	New York	AL	DH	138	513	87	128	31	102	0	.250
1994	New York	AL	DH	104	399	68	102	19	67	1	.256
1995	New York	AL	DH	59	192	25	43	6	28	0	.224
1995	Oakland	AL	DH	24	88	9	23	2	7	0	.261
1996	Chicago	AL	OF	132	472	58	120	27	101	1	.254
Post All-Star				60	214	29	57	16	56	0	.266

LEE TINSLEY   Age 28/B $3

Seems to be bottoming out on a low rung of the old career ladder.

Year	Team	Lg.	Pos.	G	AB	R	H	HR	RBI	SB	BA
1993	Seattle	AL	OF	11	19	2	3	1	2	0	.158
1994	Boston	AL	OF	78	144	27	32	2	14	13	.222
1995	Boston	AL	OF	100	341	61	97	7	41	18	.284
1996	Philadelphia	NL	OF	31	52	1	7	0	2	2	.135
1996	Boston	AL	OF	92	192	28	47	3	14	6	.245
Post All-Star				68	107	21	23	2	6	2	.215

MICHAEL TUCKER   Age 25/L $12

Solid.

Year	Team	Lg.	Pos.	G	AB	R	H	HR	RBI	SB	BA
1995	Kansas City	AL	OF	62	177	23	46	4	17	2	.260
1996	Kansas City	AL	OF	108	339	55	88	12	53	10	.260
Post All-Star				39	128	21	40	4	20	2	.313

TURNER WARD   Age 31/B $1

If you spend more than a buck on this guy, you should be in a mental ward.

Year	Team	Lg.	Pos.	G	AB	R	H	HR	RBI	SB	BA
1993	Toronto	AL	OF	72	167	20	32	4	28	3	.192
1994	Milwaukee	AL	OF	102	367	55	85	9	45	6	.232
1995	Milwaukee	AL	OF	44	129	19	34	4	16	6	.264
1996	Milwaukee	AL	OF	43	67	7	12	2	10	3	.179
Post All-Star				9	13	1	1	0	1	1	.077

MARK WHITEN
Age 30/B   **$7**

We don't know what to make of Whiten's clutch performance for Seattle last year any more than the people in Atlanta, Philadelphia, Boston, St. Louis, Cleveland, or Toronto, who all had him and let him go. We strongly suggest that you not grow too emotionally attached.

Year	Team	Lg.	Pos.	G	AB	R	H	HR	RBI	SB	BA
1993	St. Louis	NL	OF	152	562	81	142	25	99	15	.253
1994	St. Louis	NL	OF	92	334	57	98	14	53	10	.293
1995	Boston	AL	OF	32	108	13	20	1	10	1	.185
1995	Philadelphia	NL	OF	60	212	38	57	11	37	7	.269
1996	Philadelphia	NL	OF	60	182	33	43	7	21	13	.236
1996	Atlanta	NL	OF	36	90	12	23	3	17	2	.256
1996	Seattle	AL	OF	40	140	31	42	12	33	2	.300
Post All-Star				65	201	41	57	15	47	2	.284

BERNIE WILLIAMS
Age 28/B   **$31**

Williams has now done the thing that we demand of all Rotisserie players looking to be Rotisserie stars: he's done it two years in a row. The guy didn't start playing the game until he was a teenager, and the way he's improved over the past few years indicates he ain't through yet. More HR would have been nice, particularly the way the ball was jumping this year, but none of the Bombers excelled in that category. We don't like him quite as much as Peter Gammons seems to, but we're also not nearly as well respected.

Year	Team	Lg.	Pos.	G	AB	R	H	HR	RBI	SB	BA
1993	New York	AL	OF	139	567	67	152	12	68	9	.268
1994	New York	AL	OF	108	408	80	118	12	57	16	.289
1995	New York	AL	OF	144	563	93	173	18	82	8	.307
1996	New York	AL	OF	143	551	108	168	29	102	17	.305
Post All-Star				73	281	56	80	13	46	7	.285

GERALD WILLIAMS
Age 30/R   **$7**

He should finally get the chance to play full-time in Milwaukee that he never got in New York.

Year	Team	Lg.	Pos.	G	AB	R	H	HR	RBI	SB	BA
1993	New York	AL	OF	42	67	11	10	0	6	2	.149
1994	New York	AL	OF	57	86	19	25	4	13	1	.291
1995	New York	AL	OF	100	182	33	45	6	28	4	.247
1996	New York	AL	OF	99	233	37	63	5	30	7	.270
1996	Milwaukee	AL	OF	26	92	6	19	0	4	3	.207
Post All-Star				58	142	12	24	0	8	3	.169

ERNIE YOUNG
Age 27/R   **$13**

The A's have quietly assembled a good young team. Ernie is a prime example of what we're talking about.

Year	Team	Lg.	Pos.	G	AB	R	H	HR	RBI	SB	BA
1994	Oakland	AL	OF	11	30	2	2	0	3	0	.067
1995	Oakland	AL	OF	26	50	9	10	2	5	0	.200
1996	Oakland	AL	OF	141	462	72	112	19	64	7	.242
Post All-Star				65	191	30	47	7	23	4	.246

Designated Hitters

HAROLD BAINES
Age 38/L $18

Most AB in seven years. Most RBIs in ten years. Second best BA of his career. Slowing down? On those knees he can't get any slower. But the man can still hit.

Year	Team	Lg.	Pos.	G	AB	R	H	HR	RBI	SB	BA
1993	Baltimore	AL	DH	118	416	64	130	20	78	0	.313
1994	Baltimore	AL	DH	94	326	44	96	16	54	0	.294
1995	Baltimore	AL	DH	127	385	60	115	24	63	0	.299
1996	Chicago	AL	DH	143	495	80	154	22	95	3	.311
Post All-Star				69	231	36	71	7	33	3	.307

GERONIMO BERROA
Age 32/L $27

Berroa must mean "late-bloomer" in Geronimo's lecicon.

Year	Team	Lg.	Pos.	G	AB	R	H	HR	RBI	SB	BA
1993	Florida	NL	OF	14	34	3	4	0	0	0	.118
1994	Oakland	AL	DH	96	340	55	104	13	65	7	.306
1995	Oakland	AL	DH	141	546	87	152	22	88	7	.278
1996	Oakland	AL	DH	153	586	101	170	36	106	0	.290
Post All-Star				72	267	53	76	17	50	0	.285

JOSE CANSECO
Age 32/R $30

Another year of solid production, another year of fewer than 400 AB. We know it's the end result that counts, but it's annoying to have one of your key guys out for six weeks every year. Just ask the Red Sox. Canseco finally had the back surgery that he said was the smartest thing he's ever done. He returned quickly and should be in great shape this spring. He was squawking about playing the OF again and stealing bases again. A new man or the sold old José? You can't lose either way. Even if he's in a wheelchair for three months, you'll still get 25 HR and 80 RBI.

Year	Team	Lg.	Pos.	G	AB	R	H	HR	RBI	SB	BA
1993	Texas	AL	OF	60	231	30	59	10	46	6	.255
1994	Texas	AL	DH	111	429	88	121	31	90	15	.282
1995	Boston	AL	DH	102	396	64	121	24	81	4	.306
1996	Boston	AL	DH	96	360	68	104	28	82	3	.289
Post All-Star				25	85	15	20	2	19	1	.235

CHILI DAVIS
Age 37/B $24

This is what they had in mind when they came up with the DH rule. Would you really rather see Kevin Appier swing the bat instead of Chili Davis? But we wonder how often he'll clear the fences in K.C.

Year	Team	Lg.	Pos.	G	AB	R	H	HR	RBI	SB	BA
1993	California	AL	DH	153	573	74	139	27	112	4	.243
1994	California	AL	DH	108	392	72	122	26	84	3	.311
1995	California	AL	DH	119	424	81	135	20	86	3	.318
1996	California	AL	DH	145	530	73	155	28	95	5	.292
Post All-Star				68	249	35	71	12	43	4	.285

CARLOS DELGADO Age 24/L $19

This is not what they had in mind when they came up with the DH. A 24-year-old should be able to play *somewhere*. To be fair, Delgado isn't quite Sweeney Todd at first base, but he's no Keith Hernandez either. If the Blue Jays unload Olerud, Delgado may very well become an actual ballplayer.

Year	Team	Lg.	Pos.	G	AB	R	H	HR	RBI	SB	BA
1993	Toronto	AL	DH	2	1	0	0	0	0	0	0.000
1994	Toronto	AL	OF	43	130	17	28	9	24	1	.215
1995	Toronto	AL	OF	37	91	7	15	3	11	0	.165
1996	Toronto	AL	DH	138	488	68	132	25	92	0	.270
Post All-Star				62	203	21	50	10	32	0	.246

BRIAN GILES Age 26/L $4

Giles's development allowed the Indians to trade Jeromy Burnitz for Kevin Seitzer. Seitzer, however, may be the guy who keeps Giles on the bench. Nice sleeper pick.

Year	Team	Lg.	Pos.	G	AB	R	H	HR	RBI	SB	BA
1995	Cleveland	AL	OF	6	9	6	5	1	3	0	.556
1996	Cleveland	AL	DH	51	121	26	43	5	27	3	.355
Post All-Star				51	121	26	43	5	27	3	.355

BOB HAMELIN Age 29/L $5

Grab him cheap and hope he wakes up. The Royals need all the power they can get, so he'll have a chance to play. Old Honey Baked here is a good example of why the buck-a-homer theory doesn't apply at the low end of the food chain. Nine bucks for this guy is crazy. Save up for the big boppers and use what's left on guys like Hamelin.

Year	Team	Lg.	Pos.	G	AB	R	H	HR	RBI	SB	BA
1993	Kansas City	AL	1B	16	49	2	11	2	5	0	.224
1994	Kansas City	AL	DH	101	312	64	88	24	65	4	.282
1995	Kansas City	AL	DH	72	208	20	35	7	25	0	.168
1996	Kansas City	AL	DH	89	239	31	61	9	40	5	.255
Post All-Star				35	102	10	29	4	12	2	.284

EDGAR MARTINEZ Age 34/R $32

During one stretch early in the season, eleven consecutive hits were doubles. There are a ton of Edgar Martinez = Pure Hitter stories, but that's one of our favorites. Badly bruised ribs in late July snuffed out another batting clinic—only four homers the last two months of the season—but he's still the AL's answer to Tony Gwynn.

Year	Team	Lg.	Pos.	G	AB	R	H	HR	RBI	SB	BA
1993	Seattle	AL	DH	42	135	20	32	4	13	0	.237
1994	Seattle	AL	3B	89	326	47	93	13	51	6	.285
1995	Seattle	AL	DH	145	511	121	182	29	113	4	.356
1996	Seattle	AL	DH	139	499	121	163	26	103	3	.327
Post All-Star				54	184	42	54	4	25	0	.293

Catchers
pp. 27–39

Corners
pp. 40–60

Infield
pp. 60–80

Outfield
pp. 80–111

DH
pp. 112–115

Starters
pp. 115–145

Relievers
pp. 146–178

PAUL MOLITOR Age 40/R $23

Hey, maybe *he's* the AL's answer to Tony Gwynn. We told you last year that the strike talks took a lot out of him and that a restful off-season would rev him up. Most RBI and the best BA of his career, plus leading the league in hits with 225—and 18 SB! Has anybody told him how old he is?

Year	Team	Lg.	Pos.	G	AB	R	H	HR	RBI	SB	BA
1993	Toronto	AL	DH	160	636	121	211	22	111	22	.332
1994	Toronto	AL	DH	115	454	86	155	14	75	20	.341
1995	Toronto	AL	DH	130	525	63	142	15	60	12	.270
1996	Minnesota	AL	DH	161	660	99	225	9	113	18	.341
Post All-Star				75	306	44	110	3	59	11	.359

PEDRO MUNOZ Age 28/R $9

A knee injury ruined his season. Worth a look.

Year	Team	Lg.	Pos.	G	AB	R	H	HR	RBI	SB	BA
1993	Minnesota	AL	OF	104	326	34	76	13	38	1	.233
1994	Minnesota	AL	OF	75	244	35	72	11	36	0	.295
1995	Minnesota	AL	DH	104	376	45	113	18	58	0	.301
1996	Oakland	AL	DH	34	121	17	31	6	18	0	.256
Post All-Star				0	0	0	0	0	0	0	.000

EDDIE MURRAY Age 41/B $18

His return to Baltimore sparked the team right into the post-season. One of the best hitters in the game for the last 19 years. Make it 20.

Year	Team	Lg.	Pos.	G	AB	R	H	HR	RBI	SB	BA
1993	New York	NL	1B	154	610	77	174	27	100	2	.285
1994	Cleveland	AL	DH	108	433	57	110	17	76	8	.254
1995	Cleveland	AL	DH	113	436	68	141	21	82	5	.323
1996	Cleveland	AL	DH	88	336	33	88	12	45	3	.262
1996	Baltimore	AL	DH	64	230	36	59	10	34	1	.257
Post All-Star				69	243	38	63	11	40	1	.259

RUBEN SIERRA Age 31/B $19

The worst year ever for a clueless malcontent who just doesn't get it. Sierra is too volatile to invest a lot of money in because he could be traded or benched at any time. He was much more valuable when he toiled anonymously in Texas at the beginning of his career. Those days are gone and there are plenty of better risks out there.

Year	Team	Lg.	Pos.	G	AB	R	H	HR	RBI	SB	BA
1993	Oakland	AL	OF	158	630	77	147	22	101	25	.233
1994	Oakland	AL	OF	110	426	71	114	23	92	8	.268
1995	Oakland	AL	OF	70	264	40	70	12	42	4	.265
1995	New York	AL	DH	56	215	33	56	7	44	1	.260
1996	New York	AL	DH	96	360	39	93	11	52	1	.258
1996	Detroit	AL	OF	46	158	22	35	1	20	3	.222
Post All-Star				63	217	26	51	3	29	4	.235

MICKEY TETTLETON Age 36/B $17

Pick him up and trade him as soon as he gets hot. Rotisserie doesn't hold whiffs against a guy.

Year	Team	Lg.	Pos.	G	AB	R	H	HR	RBI	SB	BA
1993	Detroit	AL	1B	152	522	79	128	32	110	3	.245
1994	Detroit	AL	C	107	339	57	84	17	51	0	.248
1995	Texas	AL	OF	134	429	76	102	32	78	0	.238
1996	Texas	AL	DH	143	491	78	121	24	83	2	.246
Post All-Star				60	205	22	48	9	36	1	.234

Catchers
pp. 27–39

Corners
pp. 40–60

Infield
pp. 60–80

Outfield
pp. 80–111

DH
pp. 112–115

Starters
pp. 115–145

Relievers
pp. 146–178

JOE VITIELLO   Age 26/R $7

Last year we said Vitiello would send Hamelin to the minors for good. We meant this year. Actually, grabbing the two of them for around $12 might not be such a bad idea. Hamelin qualifies at 1B, so you could pull it off.

Year	Team	Lg.	Pos.	G	AB	R	H	HR	RBI	SB	BA
1995	Kansas City	AL	DH	53	130	13	33	7	21	0	.254
1996	Kansas City	AL	DH	85	257	29	62	8	40	2	.241
Post All-Star				15	51	3	13	1	8	0	.255

EDDIE WILLIAMS   Age 32/R $5

Not what the Tigers had in mind. They thought he was a late-bloomer. Turns out he's already bloomed.

Year	Team	Lg.	Pos.	G	AB	R	H	HR	RBI	SB	BA
1994	San Diego	NL	1B	49	175	32	58	11	42	0	.331
1995	San Diego	NL	1B	97	296	35	77	12	47	0	.260
1996	Detroit	AL	DH	77	215	22	43	6	26	0	.200
Post All-Star				21	49	2	5	0	2	0	.102

On the Mound

NATIONAL LEAGUE

ANDY ASHBY   Age 29/R $12

Arm trouble made him largely ineffective for the last few months. However, it was not a serious problem and he should bounce back and give you at least a dozen wins.

Year	Team	Lg.	G	IP	H	BB	SO	W	L	ERA	SV	Ratio
1993	Colorado	NL	20	54.0	89	32	33	0	4	8.50	1	2.241
1993	San Diego	NL	12	69.0	79	24	44	3	6	5.48	0	1.493
1994	San Diego	NL	24	164.1	145	43	121	6	11	3.40	0	1.144
1995	San Diego	NL	31	192.2	180	62	150	12	10	2.94	0	1.256
1996	San Diego	NL	24	150.2	147	34	85	9	5	3.23	0	1.201
Post All-Star			9	49.1	49	12	26	1	3	3.83	0	1.236

PEDRO ASTACIO   Age 27/R $7

A .500 pitcher is not the worst thing in the world.

Year	Team	Lg.	G	IP	H	BB	SO	W	L	ERA	SV	Ratio
1993	Los Angeles	NL	31	186.1	165	68	122	14	9	3.57	0	1.250
1994	Los Angeles	NL	23	149.0	142	47	108	6	8	4.29	0	1.268
1995	Los Angeles	NL	48	104.0	103	29	80	7	8	4.24	0	1.269
1996	Los Angeles	NL	35	211.2	207	67	130	9	8	3.44	0	1.294
Post All-Star			16	105.1	99	28	60	5	1	3.08	0	1.206

STEVE AVERY
                              Age 26/L $6

Atlanta has talked about trying to re-sign him and make him into a reliever. What's more likely is that he departs via free agency and becomes someone else's enigma. There should still be a bunch of wins left in that young left arm. But what you have to hope is that he isn't another Kent Mercker.

Year	Team	Lg.	G	IP	H	BB	SO	W	L	ERA	SV	Ratio
1993	Atlanta	NL	35	223.1	216	43	125	18	6	2.94	0	1.160
1994	Atlanta	NL	24	151.2	127	55	122	8	3	4.04	0	1.200
1995	Atlanta	NL	29	173.1	165	52	141	7	13	4.67	0	1.252
1996	Atlanta	NL	24	131.0	146	40	86	7	10	4.47	0	1.420
Post All-Star			5	13.0	22	8	4	0	3	9.00	0	2.308

ROGER BAILEY
                              Age 26/R $1

Had a couple of decent starts. Had a few that weren't so decent. Like most Rockies pitchers, he is not worth a major investment.

Year	Team	Lg.	G	IP	H	BB	SO	W	L	ERA	SV	Ratio
1995	Colorado	NL	39	81.1	88	39	33	7	6	4.98	0	1.561
1996	Colorado	NL	24	83.2	94	52	45	2	3	6.24	1	1.745
Post All-Star			16	65.2	74	37	31	2	2	5.76	1	1.690

ALAN BENES
                              Age 25/R $10

It couldn't get much better for the Benes family. Rookie Alan wowed such demanding folks as Dave Duncan, who says, "He stopped being a rookie after about six weeks of the season. He's going to win games in the majors for a lot of years to come." Then there was the older brother . . .

Year	Team	Lg.	G	IP	H	BB	SO	W	L	ERA	SV	Ratio
1995	St. Louis	NL	3	16.0	24	4	20	1	2	8.44	0	1.750
1996	St. Louis	NL	34	191.0	192	87	131	13	10	4.90	0	1.461
Post All-Star			16	85.0	86	42	55	5	5	4.66	0	1.506

ANDY BENES
                              Age 29/R $15

. . . who after all these years finally went beyond being a good pitcher with great stuff. Remember, he's not 30 years old yet, he's just hitting his prime, he's never had arm trouble, and Duncan has him pitching with aggressiveness he's never shown before. Meanwhile, their sister Elaine Benes has developed a decent career as a writer for the J. Peterman Catalog when she isn't hanging out with Jerry, George, and Kramer.

Year	Team	Lg.	G	IP	H	BB	SO	W	L	ERA	SV	Ratio
1993	San Diego	NL	34	230.2	200	86	179	15	15	3.78	0	1.240
1994	San Diego	NL	25	172.1	155	51	189	6	14	3.86	0	1.195
1995	San Diego	NL	19	118.2	121	45	126	4	7	4.17	0	1.399
1995	Seattle	AL	12	63.0	72	33	45	7	2	5.86	0	1.667
1996	St. Louis	NL	36	230.1	215	77	160	18	10	3.83	1	1.268
Post All-Star			17	112.0	98	45	77	12	2	3.29	0	1.277

KEVIN BROWN
                              Age 32/R $21

Eye-popping numbers—RH hit .219; LH hit .221; an ERA that was more than two runs lower than the league average; 8 home runs allowed, 33 walks, and 159 strikeouts. "Only" 17 wins because his team didn't score for him, which is fitting for someone never very popular in any of the clubhouses he's inhabited. But the heck with personality, he has hellacious stuff, which makes him very capable of matching last season.

Year	Team	Lg.	G	IP	H	BB	SO	W	L	ERA	SV	Ratio
1993	Texas	AL	34	233.0	228	74	142	15	12	3.59	0	1.296
1994	Texas	AL	26	170.0	218	50	123	7	9	4.82	0	1.576
1995	Baltimore	AL	26	172.1	155	48	117	10	9	3.60	0	1.178
1996	Florida	NL	32	233.0	187	33	159	17	11	1.89	0	0.944
Post All-Star			15	114.0	82	17	80	10	4	1.89	0	0.868

DAVE BURBA   Age 30/R $9

You don't think the Mariners or the Giants wouldn't like to see him wearing their uniform again, do you? Nothing flashy, just a lot of innings and a chance to win 80 percent of the starts he makes.

Year	Team	Lg.	G	IP	H	BB	SO	W	L	ERA	SV	Ratio
1993	San Francisco	NL	54	95.1	95	37	88	10	3	4.25	0	1.385
1994	San Francisco	NL	57	74.0	59	45	84	3	6	4.38	0	1.405
1995	San Francisco	NL	37	43.1	38	25	46	4	2	4.98	0	1.454
1995	Cincinnati	NL	15	63.1	52	26	50	6	2	3.27	0	1.232
1996	Cincinnati	NL	34	195.0	179	97	148	11	13	3.83	0	1.415
Post All-Star			15	90.2	82	41	66	8	4	3.57	0	1.357

TOM CANDIOTTI   Age 39/R $6

It's been six years since he's had a winning record. His ERA gained nearly a run from the year before. Chan Ho Park waits in the wings. This is one knuckler headed for mothballs.

Year	Team	Lg.	G	IP	H	BB	SO	W	L	ERA	SV	Ratio
1993	Los Angeles	NL	33	213.2	192	71	155	8	10	3.12	0	1.231
1994	Los Angeles	NL	23	153.0	149	54	102	7	7	4.12	0	1.327
1995	Los Angeles	NL	30	190.1	187	58	141	7	14	3.50	0	1.287
1996	Los Angeles	NL	28	152.1	172	43	79	9	11	4.49	0	1.411
Post All-Star			10	52.2	59	15	30	3	4	5.30	0	1.405

FRANK CASTILLO   Age 27/R $3

Because he's such a wretched hitter, some of his teammates promised they'd buy him a new Mercedes if he hit a home run, even if it was in batting practice. Now, we'll leave it to deep thinkers like George Will and Molly Ivins to argue the socioeconomic implications of mindless millionaires throwing away $40,000 on a locker room bet. What we wonder is if this quest for the elusive tater could have distratcted Castillo from his pitching, which suggested that 1995 he had might have been a fluke.

Year	Team	Lg.	G	IP	H	BB	SO	W	L	ERA	SV	Ratio
1993	Chicago	NL	29	141.1	162	39	84	5	8	4.84	0	1.422
1994	Chicago	NL	4	23.0	25	5	19	2	1	4.30	0	1.304
1995	Chicago	NL	29	188.0	179	52	135	11	10	3.21	0	1.229
1996	Chicago	NL	33	182.1	209	46	139	7	16	5.28	0	1.399
Post All-Star			15	86.0	98	20	64	5	5	4.19	0	1.372

MARK CLARK   Age 28/R $10

Who would have thunk that the Mets' ace would turn out to be not one of the overhyped wunderkinds but this veteran pitching for his third different

Catchers
pp. 27-39

Corners
pp. 40-60

Infield
pp. 60-80

Outfield
pp. 80-111

DH
pp. 112-115

Starters
pp. 115-145

Relievers
pp. 146-178

organization. No matter what happens with the wunderkinds, he will be a solid part of the rotation.

Year	Team	Lg.	G	IP	H	BB	SO	W	L	ERA	SV	Ratio
1993	Cleveland	AL	26	109.1	119	25	57	7	5	4.28	0	1.317
1994	Cleveland	AL	20	127.1	133	40	60	11	3	3.82	0	1.359
1995	Cleveland	AL	22	124.2	143	42	68	9	7	5.27	0	1.484
1996	New York	NL	32	212.1	217	48	142	14	11	3.43	0	1.248
Post All-Star			15	94.0	104	24	63	6	5	3.93	0	1.362

RHEAL CORMIER   Age 29/L $3

A serviceable type.

Year	Team	Lg.	G	IP	H	BB	SO	W	L	ERA	SV	Ratio
1993	St. Louis	NL	38	145.1	163	27	75	7	6	4.33	0	1.307
1994	St. Louis	NL	7	39.2	40	7	26	3	2	5.45	0	1.185
1995	Boston	AL	48	115.0	131	31	69	7	5	4.07	0	1.409
1996	Montreal	NL	33	159.2	165	41	100	7	10	4.17	0	1.290
Post All-Star			15	49.2	54	11	31	2	5	5.26	0	1.309

DANNY DARWIN   Age 41/R $2

He's come back more times than some of our neckties and can still be useful in the right situation. However, it was a little difficult to comprehend how acquiring him was supposedly going to be such a major pennant-race move for the Astros.

Year	Team	Lg.	G	IP	H	BB	SO	W	L	ERA	SV	Ratio
1993	Boston	AL	34	229.1	196	49	130	15	11	3.26	0	1.068
1994	Boston	AL	13	75.2	101	24	54	7	5	6.30	0	1.652
1995	Toronto	AL	13	65.0	91	24	36	1	8	7.62	0	1.769
1995	Texas	AL	7	34.0	40	7	22	2	2	7.15	0	1.382
1996	Pittsburgh	NL	19	122.1	117	16	69	7	9	3.02	0	1.087
1996	Houston	NL	15	42.1	43	11	27	3	2	5.95	0	1.276
Post All-Star			16	49.1	50	12	30	3	3	5.84	0	1.257

DOUG DRABEK   Age 34/R $3

Has become just a fringe pitcher who will likely be looking for work.

Year	Team	Lg.	G	IP	H	BB	SO	W	L	ERA	SV	Ratio
1993	Houston	NL	34	237.2	242	60	157	9	18	3.79	0	1.271
1994	Houston	NL	23	164.2	132	45	121	12	6	2.84	0	1.075
1995	Houston	NL	31	185.0	205	54	143	10	9	4.77	0	1.400
1996	Houston	NL	30	175.1	208	60	137	7	9	4.57	0	1.529
Post All-Star			13	78.1	86	21	52	3	3	4.25	0	1.366

SHAWN ESTES   Age 24/L $2

Arm trouble killed two developmental seasons for this former big-time prospect given up on by the Seattle organization. For a change, maybe the Giants will get lucky with a pitcher. And for a little added value, he's also a switch-hitter.

Year	Team	Lg.	G	IP	H	BB	SO	W	L	ERA	SV	Ratio
1995	San Francisco	NL	3	17.1	16	5	14	0	3	6.75	0	1.212
1996	San Francisco	NL	11	70.0	63	39	60	3	5	3.60	0	1.457
Post All-Star			11	70.0	63	39	60	3	5	3.60	0	1.457

JEFF FASSERO
Age 34/L   **$14**

From one side of the continent to the other. Pitching in front of that big-hitting lineup should take some of the sting out of pitching in that horrible stadium and having to deal with nine hitters instead of eight. He figures to be the guy that puts the Mariners over the top this year, assuming the Big Unit comes back firing on all cylinders.

Year	Team	Lg.	G	IP	H	BB	SO	W	L	ERA	SV	Ratio
1993	Montreal	NL	56	149.2	119	54	140	12	5	2.29	1	1.156
1994	Montreal	NL	21	138.2	119	40	119	8	6	2.99	0	1.147
1995	Montreal	NL	30	189.0	207	74	164	13	14	4.33	0	1.487
1996	Montreal	NL	34	231.2	217	55	222	15	11	3.30	0	1.174
Post All-Star			16	108.2	112	31	109	7	5	3.48	0	1.316

OSVALDO FERNANDEZ
Age 28/R   **$7**

His best stretch of pitching came after he was able to get relatives out of Cuba, which is a tale of family values much more meaningful than some stupid speech at a political convention.

Year	Team	Lg.	G	IP	H	BB	SO	W	L	ERA	SV	Ratio
1996	San Francisco	NL	30	171.2	193	57	106	7	13	4.61	0	1.456
Post All-Star			12	70.2	73	23	38	3	4	3.18	0	1.358

SID FERNANDEZ
Age 34/L   **$8**

Acerbic Larry Bowa, then a Phillies coach, watched Fernandez amble by with an ice pack attached to his elbow. "You know, Sid would be perfect for a club that had a 12-man starting rotation," said Bowa. "He might hold up for a couple of months if he pitched every two weeks." There's always something wrong with El Sid, but you just know someone will take a chance on him. We hope it's not you.

Year	Team	Lg.	G	IP	H	BB	SO	W	L	ERA	SV	Ratio
1993	New York	NL	18	119.2	82	36	81	5	6	2.93	0	0.986
1994	Baltimore	AL	19	115.1	109	46	95	6	6	5.15	0	1.344
1995	Baltimore	AL	8	28.0	36	17	31	0	4	7.39	0	1.893
1995	Philadelphia	NL	11	64.2	48	21	79	6	1	3.34	0	1.067
1996	Philadelphia	NL	11	63.0	50	26	77	3	6	3.43	0	1.206
Post All-Star			0	0.0	0	0	0	0	0	0.00	0	0.000

KEVIN FOSTER
Age 28/R   **$1**

If you love home runs, you have to love watching this guy pitch. In his last 254 innings, he's served up a whopping 48 Big Flies.

Year	Team	Lg.	G	IP	H	BB	SO	W	L	ERA	SV	Ratio
1993	Philadelphia	NL	2	6.2	13	7	6	0	1	14.85	0	3.000
1994	Chicago	NL	13	81.0	70	35	75	3	4	2.89	0	1.296
1995	Chicago	NL	30	167.2	149	65	146	12	11	4.51	0	1.276
1996	Chicago	NL	17	87.0	98	35	53	7	6	6.21	0	1.529
Post All-Star			9	47.0	47	13	32	4	4	4.98	0	1.277

MARK GARDNER
Age 35/R   **$5**

He sort of fell into the Giants' laps and was their big winner. Being the Giants' big winner is not the most impressive credential to have on your

Catchers
pp. 27-39

Corners
pp. 40-60

Infield
pp. 60-80

Outfield
pp. 80-111

DH
pp. 112-115

Starters
pp. 115-145

Relievers
pp. 146-178

résumé. Nor is it something likely to repeat itself. But if you want credentials, how about the credentials owned by . . .

Year	Team	Lg.	G	IP	H	BB	SO	W	L	ERA	SV	Ratio
1993	Kansas City	AL	17	91.2	92	36	54	4	6	6.19	0	1.396
1994	Florida	NL	20	92.1	97	30	57	4	4	4.87	0	1.375
1995	Florida	NL	39	102.1	109	43	87	5	5	4.49	1	1.485
1996	San Francisco	NL	30	179.1	200	57	145	12	7	4.42	0	1.433
Post All-Star			13	80.1	103	30	57	4	4	5.27	0	1.656

TOM GLAVINE   Age 31/L $21

. . . who since 1991 has won more games (106) than any pitcher in baseball. He should contend for that same title into the next millennium.

Year	Team	Lg.	G	IP	H	BB	SO	W	L	ERA	SV	Ratio
1993	Atlanta	NL	36	239.1	236	90	120	22	6	3.20	0	1.362
1994	Atlanta	NL	25	165.1	173	70	140	13	9	3.97	0	1.470
1995	Atlanta	NL	29	198.2	182	66	127	16	7	3.08	0	1.248
1996	Atlanta	NL	36	235.1	222	85	181	15	10	2.98	0	1.305
Post All-Star			17	110.2	108	45	83	6	5	3.50	0	1.383

MIKE GRACE   Age 26/R $9

En route to a big season, he blew his arm out, as Phillies pitchers have a habit of doing. The prognosis is good that he can come back. But given how so many Phillies decisions are wrong, we shouldn't trust their doctors either.

Year	Team	Lg.	G	IP	H	BB	SO	W	L	ERA	SV	Ratio
1995	Philadelphia	NL	2	11.1	10	4	7	1	1	3.18	0	1.235
1996	Philadelphia	NL	12	80.0	72	16	49	7	2	3.49	0	1.100
Post All-Star			0	0.0	0	0	0	0	0	0.00	0	0.000

JOEY HAMILTON   Age 26/R $16

If not for three 1–0 losses, he would have been pushing for 20 wins. Our scouting experts are right sometimes. They said four years ago that this was a guy with the stuff and toughness to be a big-time pitcher. They said it might take him a few years to get it all together because he was very raw coming out of college. They said that once the rough edges were smoothed, he'd be an ace-caliber pitcher. And that he is.

Year	Team	Lg.	G	IP	H	BB	SO	W	L	ERA	SV	Ratio
1994	San Diego	NL	16	108.2	98	29	61	9	6	2.98	0	1.169
1995	San Diego	NL	31	204.1	189	56	123	6	9	3.08	0	1.199
1996	San Diego	NL	34	211.2	206	83	184	15	9	4.17	0	1.365
Post All-Star			15	95.1	94	41	92	5	5	3.49	0	1.416

MIKE HAMPTON   Age 24/L $11

A very underrated pitcher who needs to add endurance. His teammates say he hits the wall after about 140 innings.

Year	Team	Lg.	G	IP	H	BB	SO	W	L	ERA	SV	Ratio
1993	Seattle	AL	13	17.0	28	17	8	1	3	9.53	1	2.647
1994	Houston	NL	44	41.1	46	16	24	2	1	3.70	0	1.500
1995	Houston	NL	24	150.2	141	49	115	9	8	3.35	0	1.261
1996	Houston	NL	27	160.1	175	49	101	10	10	3.59	0	1.397
Post All-Star			11	62.0	78	18	34	4	5	4.21	0	1.548

PETE HARNISCH
Age 30/R   **$6**

No matter what, he gives you everything he has to give. Unfortunately, there is too much scar tissue attached to whatever he has to give.

Year	Team	Lg.	G	IP	H	BB	SO	W	L	ERA	SV	Ratio
1993	Houston	NL	33	217.2	171	79	185	16	9	2.98	0	1.149
1994	Houston	NL	17	95.0	100	39	62	8	5	5.40	0	1.463
1995	New York	NL	18	110.0	111	24	82	2	8	3.68	0	1.227
1996	New York	NL	31	194.2	195	61	114	8	12	4.21	0	1.315
Post All-Star			15	99.1	94	34	60	4	6	3.71	0	1.289

RICH HUNTER
Age 22/R   **$1**

Desperate for arms, clueless about developing pitching, the Phillies rushed this kid from Double-A. He was bombed back to the minors, resurfaced late but never showed he belonged. All of which is why Philly veterans called him "Catnip Hunter."

Year	Team	Lg.	G	IP	H	BB	SO	W	L	ERA	SV	Ratio
1996	Philadelphia	NL	14	69.1	84	33	32	3	7	6.49	0	1.688
Post All-Star			8	41.0	45	15	13	2	5	6.59	0	1.463

JASON ISRINGHAUSEN
Age 24/R   **$4**

Since Walter Johnson was a mere pup, wise old baseball heads have said it is always risky to rush young pitchers to the majors. As the immortal Paul Richards, one of the wisest who ever lived, used to say, "Until they get humbled a little, until they pitch 500 professional innings, and until they learn to maintain proper pitching mechanics, young pitchers sometimes think they're indestructible. And when that happens, they get hurt." Bill Pulsipher was Case Study Number One and here is Case Study Number Two: He needed operations on both his elbow and his shoulder, and his situation isn't likely to become clear until late spring. Mets player development people have quietly said since last year that this kid was a little cocky and needed to smooth out his delivery. Now he's paying the price, and he might end up losing a year to learn his lessons.

Year	Team	Lg.	G	IP	H	BB	SO	W	L	ERA	SV	Ratio
1995	New York	NL	14	93.0	88	31	55	9	2	2.81	0	1.280
1996	New York	NL	27	171.2	190	73	114	6	14	4.77	0	1.532
Post All-Star			9	58.2	67	18	34	2	4	4.76	0	1.449

KEVIN JARVIS
Age 27/R   **$1**

No thanks.

Year	Team	Lg.	G	IP	H	BB	SO	W	L	ERA	SV	Ratio
1994	Cincinnati	NL	6	17.2	22	5	10	1	1	7.13	0	1.528
1995	Cincinnati	NL	19	79.0	91	32	33	3	4	5.70	0	1.557
1996	Cincinnati	NL	24	120.1	152	43	63	8	9	5.98	0	1.620
Post All-Star			15	79.1	104	27	42	6	8	7.15	0	1.651

BOBBY JONES
Age 27/R   **$7**

No one is dazzled by his stuff. He isn't a flashy guy that the Mets can put on posters. And whenever there's a Mets trade rumor (of which there are many, since the Mets have been dwarfed so much in New York by the

Catchers
pp. 27-39

Corners
pp. 40-60

Infield
pp. 60-80

Outfield
pp. 80-111

DH
pp. 112-115

Starters
pp. 115-145

Relievers
pp. 146-178

Yankees' shadow that they try to float their own trade rumors all the time), his name is certain to be mentioned. But no other Met has won double figures in each of the last three years. Consistency means something.

Year	Team	Lg.	G	IP	H	BB	SO	W	L	ERA	SV	Ratio
1993	New York	NL	9	61.2	61	22	35	2	4	3.65	0	1.346
1994	New York	NL	24	160.0	157	56	80	12	7	3.15	0	1.331
1995	New York	NL	30	195.2	209	53	127	10	10	4.19	0	1.339
1996	New York	NL	31	195.2	219	46	116	12	8	4.42	0	1.354
Post All-Star			14	88.1	95	17	57	4	3	4.28	0	1.268

DARRYL KILE   Age 28/R $8

His stuff is too good to allow 233 hits. His stuff is too good to allow left-handed hitters to rough him up at a .313 clip. But his stuff is also too good for him not to win a dozen or so games a year into the foreseeable future.

Year	Team	Lg.	G	IP	H	BB	SO	W	L	ERA	SV	Ratio
1993	Houston	NL	32	171.2	152	69	141	15	8	3.51	0	1.287
1994	Houston	NL	24	147.2	153	82	105	9	6	4.57	0	1.591
1995	Houston	NL	25	127.0	114	73	113	4	12	4.96	0	1.472
1996	Houston	NL	35	219.0	233	97	219	12	11	4.19	0	1.507
Post All-Star			16	96.0	108	40	91	4	6	4.88	0	1.542

AL LEITER   Age 31/L $17

What a year for the Leiter family. This brother, finally healthy and poised for several more seasons of strong pitching, justified the big free-agent bucks with a breakthrough season that included a no-hitter. And as for older brother . . .

Year	Team	Lg.	G	IP	H	BB	SO	W	L	ERA	SV	Ratio
1993	Toronto	AL	34	105.0	93	56	66	9	6	4.11	2	1.419
1994	Toronto	AL	20	111.2	125	65	100	6	7	5.08	0	1.701
1995	Toronto	AL	28	183.0	162	108	153	11	11	3.64	0	1.475
1996	Florida	NL	33	215.1	153	119	200	16	12	2.93	0	1.263
Post All-Star			15	96.2	68	56	95	7	5	3.54	0	1.283

MARK LEITER   Age 33/R $3

. . . it was also a memorable year. He gave up more home runs than any pitcher in the National League and he summed up the misery of pitching in San Francisco when he actually said upon being traded to that baseball hotbed in Montreal, "I think this move is the best thing that could happen to my career." He's worth a fraction of his brother, but you can fill your fifth starter's spot with a lot worse.

Year	Team	Lg.	G	IP	H	BB	SO	W	L	ERA	SV	Ratio
1993	Detroit	AL	27	106.2	111	44	70	6	6	4.72	0	1.453
1994	California	AL	40	95.1	99	35	71	4	7	4.72	2	1.406
1995	San Francisco	NL	30	195.2	185	55	129	10	12	3.82	0	1.227
1996	San Francisco	NL	23	135.1	151	50	118	4	10	5.19	0	1.485
1996	Montreal	NL	12	69.2	68	19	46	4	2	4.39	0	1.249
Post All-Star			16	88.1	97	27	59	4	5	5.20	0	1.404

JON LIEBER
Age 26/R **$1**

If you have a spare buck and the instant lottery ticket outlet is closed, be our guest.

Year	Team	Lg.	G	IP	H	BB	SO	W	L	ERA	SV	Ratio
1994	Pittsburgh	NL	17	108.2	116	25	71	6	7	3.73	0	1.298
1995	Pittsburgh	NL	21	72.2	103	14	45	4	7	6.32	0	1.610
1996	Pittsburgh	NL	51	142.0	156	28	94	9	5	3.99	1	1.296
Post All-Star			17	95.0	105	21	60	7	3	3.88	0	1.326

GREG MADDUX
Age 30/R **$28**

We asked Tommy Glavine one day about why Mad Dog was so, uh, so human for a stretch of last season. "Well, he's been complaining about how he occasionally has been fractionally deviating from his throwing lanes, which results in him missing his spot by an inch or two, which is just enough to cause a base hit on those occasions when that pitch is put into play," said Glavine. "No, I don't fully understand it all either. You have to understand that Mad Dog plays a game that is somewhat on a different level from the one everyone else plays. We're talking about maybe a half-dozen pitches a game out of the 100 he throws. He's not worried." Neither are we. If 1996 was a bad year, we're happy to live with it.

Year	Team	Lg.	G	IP	H	BB	SO	W	L	ERA	SV	Ratio
1993	Atlanta	NL	36	267.0	228	52	197	20	10	2.36	0	1.049
1994	Atlanta	NL	25	202.0	150	31	156	16	6	1.56	0	0.896
1995	Atlanta	NL	28	209.2	147	23	181	19	2	1.63	0	0.811
1996	Atlanta	NL	35	245.0	225	28	172	15	11	2.72	0	1.033
Post All-Star			15	101.2	87	14	62	6	5	2.48	0	0.993

PEDRO MARTINEZ
Age 25/R **$18**

With each year, he gets a little better. And by putting fear in the back of every hitter's mind, he's made all his other stuff that much more effective.

Year	Team	Lg.	G	IP	H	BB	SO	W	L	ERA	SV	Ratio
1993	Los Angeles	NL	65	107.0	76	57	119	10	5	2.61	2	1.243
1994	Montreal	NL	24	144.2	115	45	142	11	5	3.42	1	1.106
1995	Montreal	NL	30	194.2	158	66	174	14	10	3.51	0	1.151
1996	Montreal	NL	33	216.2	189	70	222	13	10	3.70	0	1.195
Post All-Star			15	96.0	84	32	99	6	7	3.75	0	1.208

RAMON MARTINEZ
Age 29/R **$18**

Only a nasty groin pull suffered in a Wrigley Field blizzard kept him from having his best year yet. We think he's ready to take the next step and make a run at ending Atlanta's exclusive ownership of the Cy Young Award.

Year	Team	Lg.	G	IP	H	BB	SO	W	L	ERA	SV	Ratio
1993	Los Angeles	NL	32	211.2	202	104	127	10	12	3.44	0	1.446
1994	Los Angeles	NL	24	170.0	160	56	119	12	7	3.97	0	1.271
1995	Los Angeles	NL	30	206.1	176	81	138	17	7	3.66	0	1.246
1996	Los Angeles	NL	28	168.2	153	86	134	15	6	3.42	0	1.417
Post All-Star			17	107.1	89	54	89	9	3	3.27	0	1.332

MICHAEL MIMBS

Age 28/L   **$1**

Marginal—on his good days.

Year	Team	Lg.	G	IP	H	BB	SO	W	L	ERA	SV	Ratio
1995	Philadelphia	NL	35	136.2	127	75	93	9	7	4.15	1	1.478
1996	Philadelphia	NL	21	99.1	116	41	56	3	9	5.53	0	1.581
Post All-Star			11	53.2	58	17	28	3	5	5.37	0	1.398

MIKE MORGAN

Age 37/R   **$1**

Is there a club left he hasn't pitched for?

Year	Team	Lg.	G	IP	H	BB	SO	W	L	ERA	SV	Ratio
1993	Chicago	NL	32	207.2	206	74	111	10	15	4.03	0	1.348
1994	Chicago	NL	15	80.2	111	35	57	2	10	6.69	0	1.810
1995	Chicago	NL	4	24.2	19	9	15	2	1	2.19	0	1.135
1995	St. Louis	NL	17	106.2	114	25	46	5	6	3.88	0	1.303
1996	St. Louis	NL	18	103.0	118	40	55	4	8	5.24	0	1.534
1996	Cincinnati	NL	5	27.1	28	7	19	2	3	2.30	0	1.280
Post All-Star			13	69.1	82	20	44	4	8	4.41	0	1.471

JAIME NAVARRO

Age 29/R   **$10**

One of baseball's best innings-eater who told the Cubs to take a hike and went the free-agent route. If he turns up on a club that scores runs and has a good bullpen, he will be a big-time acquisition.

Year	Team	Lg.	G	IP	H	BB	SO	W	L	ERA	SV	Ratio
1993	Milwaukee	AL	35	214.1	254	73	114	11	12	5.33	0	1.526
1994	Milwaukee	AL	29	89.2	115	35	65	4	9	6.62	0	1.673
1995	Chicago	NL	29	200.1	194	56	128	14	6	3.28	0	1.248
1996	Chicago	NL	35	236.2	244	72	158	15	12	3.92	0	1.335
Post All-Star			16	99.0	110	32	66	9	4	4.18	0	1.434

DENNY NEAGLE

Age 28/L   **$16**

Cleveland GM John Hart insists to this day he made a better offer for Neagle than the one Atlanta made that got Neagle away from Pittsburgh. Neagle isn't complaining. "I don't know how to describe how much I learn every day watching these other guys pitch," said Neagle after a few weeks in Atlanta. "I almost didn't feel I belonged for a little while." The adjustment period is over. He should be a lock for 15 or so wins.

Year	Team	Lg.	G	IP	H	BB	SO	W	L	ERA	SV	Ratio
1993	Pittsburgh	NL	50	81.1	82	37	73	3	5	5.31	1	1.463
1994	Pittsburgh	NL	24	137.0	135	49	122	9	10	5.12	0	1.343
1995	Pittsburgh	NL	31	209.2	221	45	150	13	8	3.43	0	1.269
1996	Pittsburgh	NL	27	182.2	186	34	131	14	6	3.05	0	1.204
1996	Atlanta	NL	6	38.2	40	14	18	2	3	5.59	0	1.397
Post All-Star			16	107.2	110	27	59	7	5	4.10	0	1.272

HIDEO NOMO

Age 28/R   **$22**

The Dodgers have provided a personal translator for Nomo-san over the last two years. Though he's an agreeable lad, some in the media have questioned whether the translator supplies the truth, the whole truth, and nothing but the truth. Such uncertainty was fueled one afternoon when an interviewer asked Nomo, through the translator, how irritating were the hordes of Japanese reporters and photographers that followed his every move. The usually expressionless Nomo listened to the question and then responded with a lengthy animated answer in which he made what appeared to be emphatically disdainful gestures and at one point seemed to actually spit in disgust. The translator's answer to the question: "I realize that they have a job to do and they are really no bother." What does *not* get lost in the translation is one of the best pitchers in baseball who is just hitting his prime.

Year	Team	Lg.	G	IP	H	BB	SO	W	L	ERA	SV	Ratio
1995	Los Angeles	NL	28	191.1	124	78	236	13	6	2.54	0	1.056
1996	Los Angeles	NL	33	228.1	180	85	234	16	11	3.19	0	1.161
Post All-Star			15	107.2	73	46	101	7	4	2.84	0	1.105

DONOVAN OSBORNE   Age 27/L $19

We were ahead of the curve when we suggested he would have a breakout year if he recovered from his arm troubles. Expect him to keep getting better.

Year	Team	Lg.	G	IP	H	BB	SO	W	L	ERA	SV	Ratio
1993	St. Louis	NL	26	155.2	153	47	83	10	7	3.76	0	1.285
1995	St. Louis	NL	19	113.1	112	34	82	4	6	3.81	0	1.288
1996	St. Louis	NL	30	198.2	191	57	134	13	9	3.53	0	1.248
Post All-Star			15	95.0	96	38	74	5	5	3.98	0	1.411

ROBERT PERSON   Age 27/R $5

A chance to help the Mets if all the other phenoms remain disabled.

Year	Team	Lg.	G	IP	H	BB	SO	W	L	ERA	SV	Ratio
1995	New York	NL	3	12.0	5	2	10	1	0	0.75	0	0.583
1996	New York	NL	27	89.2	86	35	76	4	5	4.52	0	1.349
Post All-Star			15	55.1	51	26	49	2	2	4.88	0	1.392

MARK PORTUGAL   Age 34/R $9

A battler.

Year	Team	Lg.	G	IP	H	BB	SO	W	L	ERA	SV	Ratio
1993	Houston	NL	33	208.0	194	77	131	18	4	2.77	0	1.303
1994	San Francisco	NL	21	137.1	135	45	87	10	8	3.93	0	1.311
1995	San Francisco	NL	17	104.0	106	34	63	5	5	4.15	0	1.346
1995	Cincinnati	NL	14	77.2	79	22	33	6	5	3.82	0	1.300
1996	Cincinnati	NL	27	156.0	146	42	93	8	9	3.98	0	1.205
Post All-Star			11	56.1	54	8	27	3	4	3.99	0	1.101

PAT RAPP   Age 29/R $1

No thanks.

Year	Team	Lg.	G	IP	H	BB	SO	W	L	ERA	SV	Ratio
1993	Florida	NL	16	94.0	101	39	57	4	6	4.02	0	1.489
1994	Florida	NL	24	133.1	132	69	75	7	8	3.85	0	1.508
1995	Florida	NL	28	167.1	158	76	102	14	7	3.44	0	1.398
1996	Florida	NL	30	162.1	184	91	86	8	16	5.10	0	1.694
Post All-Star			12	61.0	82	37	36	4	5	6.79	0	1.951

Catchers
pp. 27–39

Corners
pp. 40–60

Infield
pp. 60–80

Outfield
pp. 80–111

DH
pp. 112–115

Starters
pp. 115–145

Relievers
pp. 146–178

SHANE REYNOLDS   Age 29/R $20

In those worlds not inhabited by Braves or Kevin Brown, he has become as good as anybody in the league.

Year	Team	Lg.	G	IP	H	BB	SO	W	L	ERA	SV	Ratio
1993	Houston	NL	5	11.0	11	6	10	0	0	0.82	0	1.545
1994	Houston	NL	33	124.0	128	21	110	8	5	3.05	0	1.202
1995	Houston	NL	30	189.1	196	37	175	10	11	3.47	0	1.231
1996	Houston	NL	35	239.0	227	44	204	16	10	3.65	0	1.134
Post All-Star			16	109.2	97	16	85	6	5	3.53	0	1.030

ARMANDO REYNOSO   Age 30/R $14

His pickoff move is generally considered the best by a right-handed pitcher. His fielding skills are generally considered among the best among all pitchers. He's also a good base runner and bunter. Unfortunately, none of these admirable traits means a damned thing to a Rotisserie franchise owner. But his ERA will drop by a run now that he's a Met. That *does* matter.

Year	Team	Lg.	G	IP	H	BB	SO	W	L	ERA	SV	Ratio
1993	Colorado	NL	30	189.0	206	63	117	12	11	4.00	0	1.423
1994	Colorado	NL	9	52.1	54	22	25	3	4	4.82	0	1.452
1995	Colorado	NL	20	93.0	116	36	40	7	7	5.32	0	1.634
1996	Colorado	NL	30	168.2	195	49	88	8	9	4.96	0	1.447
Post All-Star			13	70.2	86	29	33	4	3	5.35	0	1.627

KEVIN RITZ   Age 31/R $6

Other than the inevitable Rocky Mountain ERA, here's the Rockies pitcher to spend a few bucks on acquiring.

Year	Team	Lg.	G	IP	H	BB	SO	W	L	ERA	SV	Ratio
1994	Colorado	NL	15	73.2	88	35	53	5	6	5.62	0	1.670
1995	Colorado	NL	31	173.1	171	65	120	11	11	4.21	2	1.362
1996	Colorado	NL	35	213.0	236	105	105	17	11	5.28	0	1.601
Post All-Star			16	95.2	121	39	49	7	6	6.21	0	1.672

KIRK RUETER   Age 26/L $2

A craft southpaw.

Year	Team	Lg.	G	IP	H	BB	SO	W	L	ERA	SV	Ratio
1993	Montreal	NL	14	85.2	85	18	31	8	0	2.73	0	1.202
1994	Montreal	NL	20	92.1	106	23	50	7	3	5.17	0	1.397
1995	Montreal	NL	9	47.1	38	9	28	5	3	3.23	0	0.993
1996	Montreal	NL	16	78.2	91	22	30	5	6	4.58	0	1.436
1996	San Francisco	NL	4	23.1	18	5	16	1	2	1.93	0	0.986
Post All-Star			5	25.1	25	8	16	1	2	2.84	0	1.303

SCOTT SANDERS   Age 28/R $11

Look for him in the rotation from the start of the season. Look for very good results.

Year	Team	Lg.	G	IP	H	BB	SO	W	L	ERA	SV	Ratio
1993	San Diego	NL	9	52.1	54	23	37	3	3	4.13	0	1.471
1994	San Diego	NL	23	111.0	103	48	109	4	8	4.78	1	1.360
1995	San Diego	NL	17	90.0	79	31	88	5	5	4.30	0	1.222
1996	San Diego	NL	46	144.0	117	48	157	9	5	3.38	0	1.146
Post All-Star			15	95.2	83	30	98	8	3	3.48	0	1.181

CURT SCHILLING
Age 30/R   **$12**

In an otherwise horrendous Philadelphia season, this comeback was a great story. Said then-manager Jim Fregosi, "The amazing thing was not that he came back so quickly from shoulder surgery. The amazing thing was that when he came back, he was throwing better than he's thrown in three years." Over the last two months of the season, no one pitched better, he actually led the league in complete games, and this year, he'll be pitching for a new contract, which will make him very valuable to you.

Year	Team	Lg.	G	IP	H	BB	SO	W	L	ERA	SV	Ratio
1993	Philadelphia	NL	34	235.1	234	57	186	16	7	4.02	0	1.237
1994	Philadelphia	NL	13	82.1	87	28	58	2	8	4.48	0	1.397
1995	Philadelphia	NL	17	116.0	96	26	114	7	5	3.57	0	1.052
1996	Philadelphia	NL	26	183.1	149	50	182	9	10	3.19	0	1.085
Post All-Star			15	115.1	89	23	120	7	7	3.04	0	0.971

JASON SCHMIDT
Age 24/R   **$2**

Just a hunch, but we have a feeling he didn't start dancing at the news he was going from Atlanta to Pittsburgh. He has the stuff to be a winner but he is raw and he won't be getting much support. Thus his value is likely to be negligible into the near future.

Year	Team	Lg.	G	IP	H	BB	SO	W	L	ERA	SV	Ratio
1995	Atlanta	NL	9	25.0	27	18	19	2	2	5.76	0	1.800
1996	Atlanta	NL	13	58.2	69	32	48	3	4	6.75	0	1.722
1996	Pittsburgh	NL	6	37.2	39	21	26	2	2	4.06	0	1.593
Post All-Star			8	42.1	51	23	28	2	2	5.31	0	1.748

PETE SCHOUREK
Age 27/L   **$14**

If you think he's healthy, grab him. If you have any doubt, don't.

Year	Team	Lg.	G	IP	H	BB	SO	W	L	ERA	SV	Ratio
1993	New York	NL	41	128.1	168	45	72	5	12	5.96	0	1.660
1994	Cincinnati	NL	22	81.1	90	29	69	7	2	4.09	0	1.463
1995	Cincinnati	NL	29	190.1	158	45	160	18	7	3.22	0	1.067
1996	Cincinnati	NL	12	67.1	79	24	54	4	5	6.01	0	1.530
Post All-Star			0	0.0	0	0	0	0	0	0.00	0	0.000

JOHN SMILEY
Age 32/L   **$12**

Gives you your money's worth.

Year	Team	Lg.	G	IP	H	BB	SO	W	L	ERA	SV	Ratio
1993	Cincinnati	NL	18	105.2	117	31	60	3	9	5.62	0	1.401
1994	Cincinnati	NL	24	158.2	169	37	112	11	10	3.86	0	1.298
1995	Cincinnati	NL	28	176.2	173	39	124	12	5	3.46	0	1.200
1996	Cincinnati	NL	35	217.1	207	54	171	13	14	3.64	0	1.201
Post All-Star			16	111.2	99	21	94	5	7	2.98	0	1.075

JOHN SMOLTZ
Age 29/R   **$24**

The stuff has always been there. So why this breakthrough into immortality? "Yeah, he's always had the stuff but Johnny sometimes was the only one who didn't know it," said Bobby Cox. "Now, he goes out there thinking he should win every time out and there's no telling how many games he can

Catchers
pp. 27-39

Corners
pp. 40-60

Infield
pp. 60-80

Outfield
pp. 80-111

DH
pp. 112-115

Starters
pp. 115-145

Relievers
pp. 146-178

win in the next five or seven years." Take out a loan and go along for the ride.

Year	Team	Lg.	G	IP	H	BB	SO	W	L	ERA	SV	Ratio
1993	Atlanta	NL	35	243.2	208	100	208	15	11	3.62	0	1.264
1994	Atlanta	NL	21	134.2	120	48	113	6	10	4.14	0	1.248
1995	Atlanta	NL	29	192.2	166	72	193	12	7	3.18	0	1.235
1996	Atlanta	NL	35	253.2	199	55	276	24	8	2.94	0	1.001
Post All-Star			16	119.2	97	26	127	10	4	2.71	0	1.028

TODD STOTTLEMYRE   Age 31/R $13

As long as Dunc and Tony keep him under their wings, he'll be just fine.

Year	Team	Lg.	G	IP	H	BB	SO	W	L	ERA	SV	Ratio
1993	Toronto	AL	30	176.2	204	69	98	11	12	4.84	0	1.545
1994	Toronto	AL	26	140.2	149	48	105	7	7	4.22	1	1.400
1995	Oakland	AL	31	209.2	228	80	205	14	7	4.55	0	1.469
1996	St. Louis	NL	34	223.1	191	93	194	14	11	3.87	0	1.272
Post All-Star			16	103.0	83	40	86	6	5	3.67	0	1.194

AMAURY TELEMARCO   Age 23/R $2

Might have a chance, but he also has had some kind of arm trouble in each of his last three years.

Year	Team	Lg.	G	IP	H	BB	SO	W	L	ERA	SV	Ratio
1996	Chicago	NL	25	97.1	108	31	64	5	7	5.46	0	1.428
Post All-Star			15	41.1	42	15	25	1	3	6.10	0	1.379

BOB TEWKSBURY   Age 36/R $6

Junk, thrown with precision, still can win some games.

Year	Team	Lg.	G	IP	H	BB	SO	W	L	ERA	SV	Ratio
1993	St. Louis	NL	32	213.2	258	20	97	17	10	3.83	0	1.301
1994	St. Louis	NL	24	155.2	190	22	79	12	10	5.32	0	1.362
1995	Texas	AL	21	129.2	169	20	53	8	7	4.58	0	1.458
1996	San Diego	NL	36	206.2	224	43	126	10	10	4.31	0	1.292
Post All-Star			18	89.1	100	19	51	3	5	4.43	0	1.332

MARK THOMPSON   Age 25/R $2

The Rockies like the way he doesn't get timid despite the beatings all Colorado pitchers inevitably will suffer from time to time. With the run support he's likely to get, he can deliver you a dozen or so wins at a nice bargain price.

Year	Team	Lg.	G	IP	H	BB	SO	W	L	ERA	SV	Ratio
1994	Colorado	NL	2	9.0	16	8	5	1	1	9.00	0	2.667
1995	Colorado	NL	21	51.0	73	22	30	2	3	6.53	0	1.863
1996	Colorado	NL	34	169.2	189	74	99	9	11	5.30	0	1.550
Post All-Star			16	82.0	84	35	49	6	4	4.28	0	1.451

STEVE TRACHSEL   Age 26/R $7

Something of a breakthrough year. But he's one of those guys with a very slim margin for error. And the breakthrough year might instead be a career year never to be repeated.

Year	Team	Lg.	G	IP	H	BB	SO	W	L	ERA	SV	Ratio
1993	Chicago	NL	3	19.2	16	3	14	0	2	4.58	0	0.966
1994	Chicago	NL	22	146.0	133	54	108	9	7	3.21	0	1.281
1995	Chicago	NL	30	160.2	174	76	117	7	13	5.15	0	1.556
1996	Chicago	NL	31	205.0	181	62	132	13	9	3.03	0	1.185
Post All-Star			15	95.2	96	31	65	6	4	4.05	0	1.328

ISMAEL VALDES Age 23/R $19

No staff has more outstanding arms than the Dodgers' collection of bullet-throwers. So who has the best pure stuff? "No contest, it's Izzy, hands down," says Dave Wallace, LA's solid pitching coach. "Some of them have higher radar gun readings than he does. Some might have a better split or a better curve or a better change. But none of our guys has a better collection of four outstanding pitches than Izzy." We think he breaks through and becomes a very big winner.

Year	Team	Lg.	G	IP	H	BB	SO	W	L	ERA	SV	Ratio
1994	Los Angeles	NL	21	28.1	21	10	28	3	1	3.18	0	1.094
1995	Los Angeles	NL	33	197.2	168	51	150	13	11	3.05	1	1.108
1996	Los Angeles	NL	33	225.0	219	54	173	15	7	3.32	0	1.213
Post All-Star			15	102.2	101	30	83	6	2	3.33	0	1.276

FERNANDO VALENZUELA Age 36/L $11

"It's beautiful, man, really beautiful watching the old man do his thing," says Tony Gwynn. "He sent more guys back to the dugout shaking their heads. It's beautiful." The old man is liable to win 20 this year.

Year	Team	Lg.	G	IP	H	BB	SO	W	L	ERA	SV	Ratio
1993	Baltimore	AL	32	178.2	179	79	78	8	10	4.94	0	1.444
1994	Philadelphia	NL	8	45.0	42	7	19	1	2	3.00	0	1.089
1995	San Diego	NL	29	90.1	101	34	57	8	3	4.98	0	1.494
1996	San Diego	NL	33	171.2	177	67	95	13	8	3.62	0	1.421
Post All-Star			14	77.0	73	38	38	8	2	3.39	0	1.442

WILLIAM VAN LANDINGHAM Age 26/R $2

Dusty Baker insisted all spring that this big righthander with the big name would be his big pitcher. We like Dusty, but judging pitching is not one of his strong suits.

Year	Team	Lg.	G	IP	H	BB	SO	W	L	ERA	SV	Ratio
1994	San Francisco	NL	16	84.0	70	43	56	8	2	3.54	0	1.345
1995	San Francisco	NL	18	122.2	124	40	95	6	3	3.67	0	1.337
1996	San Francisco	NL	32	181.2	196	78	97	9	14	5.40	0	1.508
Post All-Star			14	80.1	80	34	33	5	5	4.37	0	1.419

PAUL WAGNER Age 29/R $1

We wouldn't spend *your* dollar on him.

Year	Team	Lg.	G	IP	H	BB	SO	W	L	ERA	SV	Ratio
1993	Pittsburgh	NL	44	141.1	143	42	114	8	8	4.27	2	1.309
1994	Pittsburgh	NL	29	119.2	136	50	86	7	8	4.59	0	1.554
1995	Pittsburgh	NL	33	165.0	174	72	120	5	16	4.80	1	1.491
1996	Pittsburgh	NL	16	81.2	86	39	81	4	8	5.40	0	1.531
Post All-Star			2	7.0	10	5	3	0	2	12.86	0	2.143

Catchers
pp. 27-39

Corners
pp. 40-60

Infield
pp. 60-80

Outfield
pp. 80-111

DH
pp. 112-115

Starters
pp. 115-145

Relievers
pp. 146-178

DONNE WALL
Age 29/R   **$5**

Had some early-season success until the league caught up with him. He has a small place in Astros history. In 1995, he was the pitcher the organization's baseball people wanted to recall in August, but the owner wanted to shove it to his veterans and overruled the baseball people to recall replacement player Craig McMurtry. The rest is history. The Astros folded in '95, folded in '96, and will probably fold annually into the foreseeable future.

Year	Team	Lg.	G	IP	H	BB	SO	W	L	ERA	SV	Ratio
1995	Houston	NL	6	24.1	33	5	16	3	1	5.55	0	1.562
1996	Houston	NL	26	150.0	170	34	99	9	8	4.56	0	1.360
Post All-Star			15	80.1	95	18	57	3	7	5.27	0	1.407

ALLEN WATSON
Age 26/L   **$2**

Another Giants pitcher you don't want. Nor did the Giants, for that matter.

Year	Team	Lg.	G	IP	H	BB	SO	W	L	ERA	SV	Ratio
1993	St. Louis	NL	16	86.0	90	28	49	6	7	4.60	0	1.372
1994	St. Louis	NL	22	115.2	130	53	74	6	5	5.52	0	1.582
1995	St. Louis	NL	21	114.1	126	41	49	7	9	4.96	0	1.461
1996	San Francisco	NL	29	185.2	189	69	128	8	12	4.61	0	1.390
Post All-Star			12	69.2	71	34	49	2	4	5.43	0	1.507

MIKE WILLIAMS
Age 28/R   **$1**

Only for the terminally masochistic.

Year	Team	Lg.	G	IP	H	BB	SO	W	L	ERA	SV	Ratio
1993	Philadelphia	NL	17	51.0	50	22	33	1	3	5.29	0	1.412
1994	Philadelphia	NL	12	50.1	61	20	29	2	4	5.01	0	1.609
1995	Philadelphia	NL	33	87.2	78	29	57	3	3	3.29	0	1.221
1996	Philadelphia	NL	32	167.0	188	67	103	6	14	5.44	0	1.527
Post All-Star			14	72.2	77	37	47	3	8	5.94	0	1.569

PAUL WILSON
Age 24/R   **$10**

Forget last year's numbers—he pitched great his last six starts. Do pay attention to his rehab from off-season shoulder surgery. If he's logging solid innings in spring training, get him—he won't be this cheap again until well into the next century.

Year	Team	Lg.	G	IP	H	BB	SO	W	L	ERA	SV	Ratio
1996	New York	NL	26	149.0	157	71	109	5	12	5.38	0	1.530
Post All-Star			14	80.2	88	36	57	2	7	4.80	0	1.537

TIM WORRELL
Age 29/R   **$9**

Had a handful of good starts, but for most of the year, he was a solid set-up man. The thing is that San Diego has so many good young relievers in their system that it's hard to get a crack, but we still think he can end up being a solid member of the rotation.

Year	Team	Lg.	G	IP	H	BB	SO	W	L	ERA	SV	Ratio
1993	San Diego	NL	21	100.2	104	43	52	2	7	4.92	0	1.460
1994	San Diego	NL	3	14.2	9	5	14	0	1	3.68	0	0.955
1995	San Diego	NL	9	13.1	16	6	13	1	0	4.72	0	1.650
1996	San Diego	NL	50	121.0	109	39	99	9	7	3.05	1	1.223
Post All-Star			27	53.2	52	19	46	3	3	3.19	1	1.323

JAMEY WRIGHT   Age 22/R $3

His nickname is "Big Handsome," which sounds like the star of a porn movie. But what he showed off wasn't skin but some big-time stuff that with maturity will give the Rockies their first home-grown pitching stud.

Year	Team	Lg.	G	IP	H	BB	SO	W	L	ERA	SV	Ratio
1996	Colorado	NL	16	91.1	105	41	45	4	4	4.93	0	1.599
Post All-Star			14	85.0	101	38	41	4	4	5.08	0	1.635

AMERICAN LEAGUE

JIM ABBOTT   Age 29/L $1

The charitable thing to say here is that you have to be pretty good to lose 18 games. Unfortunately, it's simply not true. If you lose 18 games and your ERA is over seven, you stink. Plain and simple. Abbott is 20 games under .500 for his career. That about sums him up. Class act, though. Pitched horribly, got sent to the minors, and pitched horribly there. Through it all, he was calm and polite and never threw a tub of Gatorade at anyone.

Year	Team	Lg.	G	IP	H	BB	SO	W	L	ERA	SV	Ratio
1993	New York	AL	32	214.0	221	73	95	11	14	4.37	0	1.374
1994	New York	AL	24	160.1	167	64	90	9	8	4.55	0	1.441
1995	Chicago	AL	17	112.1	116	35	45	6	4	3.36	0	1.344
1995	California	AL	13	84.2	93	29	41	5	4	4.15	0	1.441
1996	California	AL	27	142.0	171	78	58	2	18	7.48	0	1.754
Post All-Star			9	52.0	64	23	23	1	7	7.27	0	1.673

WILLIE ADAMS   Age 24/R $2

Could be part of the expected renaissance in Oakland.

Year	Team	Lg.	G	IP	H	BB	SO	W	L	ERA	SV	Ratio
1996	Oakland	AL	12	76.1	76	23	68	3	4	4.01	0	1.297
Post All-Star			11	70.1	69	21	66	3	4	3.84	0	1.280

RICK AGUILERA   Age 35/R $6

The Anti-Eck. From great reliever to lousy starter. Forget him.

Year	Team	Lg.	G	IP	H	BB	SO	W	L	ERA	SV	Ratio
1993	Minnesota	AL	65	72.1	60	14	59	4	3	3.11	34	1.023
1994	Minnesota	AL	44	44.2	57	10	46	1	4	3.63	23	1.500
1995	Minnesota	AL	22	25.0	20	6	29	1	1	2.52	12	1.040
1995	Boston	AL	30	30.1	26	7	23	2	2	2.67	20	1.088
1996	Minnesota	AL	19	111.1	124	27	83	8	6	5.42	0	1.356
Post All-Star			12	73.2	80	21	56	6	3	5.13	0	1.371

SCOTT ALDRED   Age 28/L $3

Pitched well after leaving Detroit. Worth a look.

Year	Team	Lg.	G	IP	H	BB	SO	W	L	ERA	SV	Ratio
1993	Colorado	NL	5	6.2	10	9	5	0	0	10.80	0	2.850
1993	Montreal	NL	3	5.1	9	1	4	1	0	6.75	0	1.875
1996	Detroit	AL	11	43.1	60	26	36	0	4	9.35	0	1.985
1996	Minnesota	AL	25	122.0	134	42	75	6	5	5.09	0	1.443
Post All-Star			16	82.0	87	21	51	3	2	4.61	0	1.317

Catchers
pp. 27–39

Corners
pp. 40–60

Infield
pp. 60–80

Outfield
pp. 80–111

DH
pp. 112–115

Starters
pp. 115–145

Relievers
pp. 146–178

WILSON ALVAREZ   Age 27/L $11

In his last eleven starts, he was 2–5 with an ERA over 6. Despite his promise, Alvarez has yet to really put together a great, establishing season. We don't see it happening this year either, especially if Alex Fernandez leaves and Alvarez becomes the number one guy. Numbers don't lie. He's an okay pitcher.

Year	Team	Lg.	G	IP	H	BB	SO	W	L	ERA	SV	Ratio
1993	Chicago	AL	31	207.2	168	122	155	15	8	2.95	0	1.396
1994	Chicago	AL	24	161.2	147	62	108	12	8	3.45	0	1.293
1995	Chicago	AL	29	175.0	171	93	118	8	11	4.32	0	1.509
1996	Chicago	AL	35	217.1	216	97	181	15	10	4.22	0	1.440
Post All-Star			16	100.1	115	39	83	5	6	4.84	0	1.535

KEVIN APPIER   Age 29/R $19

Numbers don't lie. He's a great pitcher. On a mediocre team.

Year	Team	Lg.	G	IP	H	BB	SO	W	L	ERA	SV	Ratio
1993	Kansas City	AL	34	238.2	183	81	186	18	8	2.56	0	1.106
1994	Kansas City	AL	23	155.0	137	63	145	7	6	3.83	0	1.290
1995	Kansas City	AL	31	201.1	163	80	185	15	10	3.89	0	1.207
1996	Kansas City	AL	32	211.1	192	75	207	14	11	3.62	0	1.263
Post All-Star			14	97.1	86	33	98	7	4	3.61	0	1.223

JAMES BALDWIN   Age 25/R $14

Baldwin delivered all year for the White Sox. Unfortunately, he was the only starter who did. He seems to have his act together, and should continue to improve.

Year	Team	Lg.	G	IP	H	BB	SO	W	L	ERA	SV	Ratio
1995	Chicago	AL	6	14.2	32	9	10	0	1	12.89	0	2.795
1996	Chicago	AL	28	169.0	168	57	127	11	6	4.42	0	1.331
Post All-Star			15	97.0	90	26	73	4	5	4.92	0	1.196

TIM BELCHER   Age 35/R $10

A surprisingly decent year on a mediocre team. He won't do it again.

Year	Team	Lg.	G	IP	H	BB	SO	W	L	ERA	SV	Ratio
1993	Cincinnati	NL	22	137.0	134	47	101	9	6	4.47	0	1.321
1993	Chicago	AL	12	71.2	64	27	34	3	5	4.40	0	1.270
1994	Detroit	AL	25	162.0	192	78	76	7	15	5.89	0	1.667
1995	Seattle	AL	28	179.1	188	88	96	10	12	4.52	0	1.539
1996	Kansas City	AL	35	238.2	262	68	113	15	11	3.92	0	1.383
Post All-Star			16	118.1	130	26	50	8	7	3.65	0	1.318

RICKY BONES   Age 27/R $1

His stock has fallen so far that the Brewers just *gave* him to the Yankees as compensation in the Listach fiasco. Not much of a bonus.

Year	Team	Lg.	G	IP	H	BB	SO	W	L	ERA	SV	Ratio
1993	Milwaukee	AL	32	203.2	222	63	63	11	11	4.86	0	1.399
1994	Milwaukee	AL	24	170.2	166	45	57	10	9	3.43	0	1.236
1995	Milwaukee	AL	32	200.1	218	83	77	10	12	4.63	0	1.502
1996	Milwaukee	AL	32	145.0	170	62	59	7	14	5.83	0	1.600
1996	New York	AL	4	7.0	14	6	4	0	0	14.14	0	2.857
Post All-Star			17	40.1	52	18	27	1	4	7.36	0	1.736

SHAWN BOSKIE
Age 30/R   **$5**

Last year we said he was redefining what it meant to be lousy. Then he went out and had a tremendous first half, making us a little sheepish to say the least. But alas, he returned to form, going 2–7 down the stretch with an ERA over 6. The check's in the mail, pal.

Year	Team	Lg.	G	IP	H	BB	SO	W	L	ERA	SV	Ratio
1993	Chicago	NL	39	65.2	63	21	39	5	3	3.43	0	1.279
1994	Chicago	NL	2	3.2	3	0	2	0	0	0.00	0	0.818
1994	Philadelphia	NL	18	84.1	85	29	59	4	6	5.23	0	1.352
1994	Seattle	AL	2	2.2	4	1	0	0	1	6.75	0	1.875
1995	California	AL	20	111.2	127	25	51	7	7	5.64	0	1.361
1996	California	AL	37	189.1	226	67	133	12	11	5.32	0	1.548
Post All-Star			14	77.2	107	33	58	3	8	6.84	0	1.803

JOHN BURKETT
Age 32/R   **$9**

Nice pickup by the Rangers. Nice pickup for your fourth starter.

Year	Team	Lg.	G	IP	H	BB	SO	W	L	ERA	SV	Ratio
1993	San Francisco	NL	34	231.2	224	40	145	22	7	3.65	0	1.140
1994	San Francisco	NL	25	159.1	176	36	85	6	8	3.62	0	1.331
1995	Florida	NL	30	188.1	208	57	126	14	14	4.30	0	1.407
1996	Florida	NL	24	154.0	154	42	108	6	10	4.32	0	1.273
1996	Texas	AL	10	68.2	75	16	47	5	2	4.06	0	1.325
Post All-Star			16	102.0	120	30	70	6	4	4.85	0	1.471

ROGER CLEMENS
Age 34/R   **$12**

One thing last year proved is that the Rocket's still got it. He led the league in K's and one night in Detroit reminded us all of why we love him. Amazing. Still, he's 40–39 over the last four years, he went over 100 walks for the first time in his career, and he was going eight or nine pitches to guys like Luis Sojo. We're talking about an extremely solid number two or three guy here. In Canada, that's worth $8.25 million a year.

Year	Team	Lg.	G	IP	H	BB	SO	W	L	ERA	SV	Ratio
1993	Boston	AL	29	191.2	175	67	160	11	14	4.46	0	1.263
1994	Boston	AL	24	170.2	124	71	168	9	7	2.85	0	1.143
1995	Boston	AL	23	140.0	141	60	132	10	5	4.18	0	1.436
1996	Boston	AL	34	242.2	216	106	257	10	13	3.63	0	1.327
Post All-Star			15	111.1	93	45	123	7	5	3.15	0	1.240

DAVID CONE   Age 34/R $16

Remarkable comeback from a potentially devastating medical problem, but the jury's still out. Remember, he didn't just have some cartilage cleaned up. He had an *aneurysm* removed from his pitching arm. In other words, the thing he does for a living caused a problem that could have killed him. The mental recovery is far more important than the physical one. Cone is older, very rich, and already an accomplished pitcher. He might think twice before reaching back for some extra oomph. Then again, this is David Cone. Forget what we just said. Go get him.

Year	Team	Lg.	G	IP	H	BB	SO	W	L	ERA	SV	Ratio
1993	Kansas City	AL	34	254.0	205	114	191	11	14	3.33	0	1.256
1994	Kansas City	AL	23	171.2	130	54	132	16	5	2.94	0	1.072
1995	Toronto	AL	17	130.1	113	41	102	9	6	3.38	0	1.182
1995	New York	AL	13	99.0	82	47	89	9	2	3.82	0	1.303
1996	New York	AL	11	72.0	50	34	71	7	2	2.88	0	1.167
Post All-Star			5	32.0	22	17	34	3	1	3.94	0	1.219

ROCKY COPPINGER   Age 23/R $4

Pretty abysmal ERA considering that he never had to face the Orioles. Even so, the Rock is worth checking out.

Year	Team	Lg.	G	IP	H	BB	SO	W	L	ERA	SV	Ratio
1996	Baltimore	AL	23	125.0	126	60	104	10	6	5.18	0	1.488
Post All-Star			17	94.0	92	45	81	6	6	5.36	0	1.457

JEFF D'AMICO   Age 21/R $7

Nothing wrong with getting 17 major league starts under your belt before your twenty-first birthday. He's been operated on twice but showed no ill effects last year. So far, he's done nothing to remove himself from the list of the AL's most promising young pitchers.

Year	Team	Lg.	G	IP	H	BB	SO	W	L	ERA	SV	Ratio
1996	Milwaukee	AL	17	86.0	88	31	53	6	6	5.44	0	1.384
Post All-Star			15	76.2	80	24	44	5	5	5.52	0	1.357

CAL ELDRED   Age 29/R $8

He's now two seasons removed from his Tommy John surgery, so this could be a key year for Eldred. Career ERA under 4.00 is pretty impressive for a Milwaukee lifer.

Year	Team	Lg.	G	IP	H	BB	SO	W	L	ERA	SV	Ratio
1993	Milwaukee	AL	36	258.0	232	91	180	16	16	4.01	0	1.252
1994	Milwaukee	AL	25	179.0	158	84	98	11	11	4.68	0	1.352
1995	Milwaukee	AL	4	23.2	24	10	18	1	1	3.42	0	1.437
1996	Milwaukee	AL	15	84.2	82	38	50	4	4	4.46	0	1.417
Post All-Star			15	84.2	82	38	50	4	4	4.46	0	1.417

SCOTT ERICKSON   Age 29/R $12

He pretty much earned the $12 we had him down for last year. But if you saw the Yankees clinch the pennant against him, you'd likely stay away. The opposite of a money performance. Strawberry hit a ball that's still going. Stuff like that can do permanent damage to the old confidence level.

Year	Team	Lg.	G	IP	H	BB	SO	W	L	ERA	SV	Ratio
1993	Minnesota	AL	34	218.2	266	71	116	8	19	5.19	0	1.541
1994	Minnesota	AL	23	144.0	173	59	104	8	11	5.44	0	1.611
1995	Minnesota	AL	15	87.2	102	32	45	4	6	5.95	0	1.529
1995	Baltimore	AL	17	108.2	111	35	61	9	4	3.89	0	1.344
1996	Baltimore	AL	34	222.1	262	66	100	13	12	5.02	0	1.475
Post All-Star			17	109.2	135	27	53	8	6	5.33	0	1.477

ALEX FERNANDEZ   Age 27/R $19

Fernandez is a solid number one pitcher who is one 20-win season away from stardom. We say he reaches that benchmark this year pitching the Marlins to the NL pennant.

Year	Team	Lg.	G	IP	H	BB	SO	W	L	ERA	SV	Ratio
1993	Chicago	AL	34	247.1	221	67	169	18	9	3.13	0	1.164
1994	Chicago	AL	24	170.1	163	50	122	11	7	3.86	0	1.250
1995	Chicago	AL	30	203.2	200	65	159	12	8	3.80	0	1.301
1996	Chicago	AL	35	258.0	248	72	200	16	10	3.45	0	1.240
Post All-Star			16	128.1	105	23	84	8	5	2.81	0	0.997

CHUCK FINLEY   Age 34/L $10

Not prime Chuck. He's become a streaky pitcher, so you'll have to live with the good (May 4–0) and the bad (August 1–5).

Year	Team	Lg.	G	IP	H	BB	SO	W	L	ERA	SV	Ratio
1993	California	AL	35	251.1	243	82	187	16	14	3.15	0	1.293
1994	California	AL	25	183.1	178	71	148	10	10	4.32	0	1.358
1995	California	AL	32	203.0	192	93	195	15	12	4.21	0	1.404
1996	California	AL	35	238.0	241	94	215	15	16	4.16	0	1.408
Post All-Star			16	114.1	111	49	97	6	9	3.31	0	1.399

HUCK FLENER   Age 28/L $3

This kid can do more than paint a fence (or was that the other guy?). Anyway, Huck's a decent hurler to round out your staff. Plus he's a switch-hitter. Not that it helps, but we believe in full disclosure.

Year	Team	Lg.	G	IP	H	BB	SO	W	L	ERA	SV	Ratio
1993	Toronto	AL	6	6.2	7	4	2	0	0	4.05	0	1.650
1996	Toronto	AL	15	70.2	68	33	44	3	2	4.58	0	1.429
Post All-Star			15	70.2	68	33	44	3	2	4.58	0	1.429

DWIGHT GOODEN   Age 32/R $12

Gooden's comeback was one of the best stories of last year. Though he ran out of gas down the stretch, and sat out in the playoffs, there was a span of several months when Doc looked prime. Before passing him over, remember he'd been pitching and trying out for teams since the previous November, and with all that time off over the last three years, his arm really isn't 32.

Year	Team	Lg.	G	IP	H	BB	SO	W	L	ERA	SV	Ratio
1993	New York	NL	29	208.2	188	61	149	12	15	3.45	0	1.193
1994	New York	NL	7	41.1	46	15	40	3	4	6.31	0	1.476
1996	New York	AL	29	170.2	169	88	126	11	7	5.01	0	1.506
Post All-Star			14	76.1	87	46	49	3	3	6.01	0	1.742

TOM GORDON
Age 29/R $10

Gordon is consistently inconsistent. Some nights the curve works; some nights it doesn't. Since you can't predict this stuff any better than he can, just cross your fingers and hope it all balances out in the end.

Year	Team	Lg.	G	IP	H	BB	SO	W	L	ERA	SV	Ratio
1993	Kansas City	AL	48	155.2	125	77	143	12	6	3.58	1	1.298
1994	Kansas City	AL	24	155.1	136	87	126	11	7	4.35	0	1.436
1995	Kansas City	AL	31	189.0	204	89	119	12	12	4.43	0	1.550
1996	Boston	AL	34	215.2	249	105	171	12	9	5.59	0	1.641
Post All-Star			16	109.2	121	47	97	6	5	5.01	0	1.532

KEVIN GROSS
Age 35/R $3

Did a decent job as a spot starter last year, but the arrival of John Burkett could keep Gross in the pen for most of the year. Whatever you spend, it will take him all season to earn it.

Year	Team	Lg.	G	IP	H	BB	SO	W	L	ERA	SV	Ratio
1993	Los Angeles	NL	33	202.1	224	74	150	13	13	4.14	0	1.473
1994	Los Angeles	NL	25	157.1	162	43	124	9	7	3.60	1	1.303
1995	Texas	AL	31	183.2	200	89	106	9	15	5.54	0	1.574
1996	Texas	AL	28	129.1	151	50	78	11	8	5.22	0	1.554
Post All-Star			12	32.2	34	15	24	2	2	4.13	0	1.500

JUAN GUZMAN
Age 30/R $14

The guy leads the league in ERA and only wins 11 games? It's a cruel, cruel world.

Year	Team	Lg.	G	IP	H	BB	SO	W	L	ERA	SV	Ratio
1993	Toronto	AL	33	221.0	211	110	194	14	3	3.99	0	1.452
1994	Toronto	AL	25	147.1	165	76	124	12	11	5.68	0	1.636
1995	Toronto	AL	24	135.1	151	73	94	4	14	6.32	0	1.655
1996	Toronto	AL	27	187.2	158	53	165	11	8	2.93	0	1.124
Post All-Star			11	71.1	58	14	60	4	2	2.40	0	1.009

CHRIS HANEY
Age 28/L $5

Given his history, this wasn't a bad year. He pitched over 200 innings and the ERA was average. Take a chance.

Year	Team	Lg.	G	IP	H	BB	SO	W	L	ERA	SV	Ratio
1993	Kansas City	AL	23	124.0	141	53	65	9	9	6.02	0	1.565
1994	Kansas City	AL	6	28.1	36	11	18	2	2	7.31	0	1.659
1995	Kansas City	AL	16	81.1	78	33	31	3	4	3.65	0	1.365
1996	Kansas City	AL	35	228.0	267	51	115	10	14	4.70	0	1.395
Post All-Star			16	103.2	129	22	59	3	8	4.95	0	1.457

ERIK HANSON
Age 31/R $5

This was Hanson's second consecutive year of good health. Unfortunately, his pitching made a lot of his Rotisserie owners sick.

Year	Team	Lg.	G	IP	H	BB	SO	W	L	ERA	SV	Ratio
1993	Seattle	AL	31	215.0	215	60	163	11	12	3.47	0	1.279
1994	Cincinnati	NL	22	122.2	137	23	101	5	5	4.11	0	1.304
1995	Boston	AL	29	186.2	187	59	139	15	5	4.24	0	1.318
1996	Toronto	AL	35	214.2	243	102	156	13	17	5.41	0	1.607
Post All-Star			16	101.1	107	42	72	5	7	4.62	0	1.470

JIMMY HAYNES
Age 24/R   **$3**

Haynes was okay as a spot starter and long reliever, and he may get a shot at the rotation's five spot. After Mussina the Birds don't have much.

Year	Team	Lg.	G	IP	H	BB	SO	W	L	ERA	SV	Ratio
1995	Baltimore	AL	4	24.0	11	12	22	2	1	2.25	0	0.958
1996	Baltimore	AL	26	89.0	122	58	65	3	6	8.29	1	2.022
Post All-Star			9	18.0	35	17	11	1	1	14.50	0	2.889

PAT HENTGEN
Age 28/R   **$20**

Not to take away from Andy Pettitte's performance, but this kid posted 20 wins with a lower ERA and far less run support. Hate to say we told you so. (Actually, we love to say that.)

Year	Team	Lg.	G	IP	H	BB	SO	W	L	ERA	SV	Ratio
1993	Toronto	AL	34	216.1	215	74	122	19	9	3.87	0	1.336
1994	Toronto	AL	24	174.2	158	59	147	13	8	3.40	0	1.242
1995	Toronto	AL	30	200.2	236	90	135	10	14	5.11	0	1.625
1996	Toronto	AL	35	265.2	238	94	177	20	10	3.22	0	1.250
Post All-Star			16	132.2	117	31	96	12	4	2.58	0	1.116

OREL HERSHISER
Age 38/R   **$13**

Orel history is consistent and very productive. Take a course this year.

Year	Team	Lg.	G	IP	H	BB	SO	W	L	ERA	SV	Ratio
1993	Los Angeles	NL	33	215.2	201	72	141	12	14	3.59	0	1.266
1994	Los Angeles	NL	21	135.1	146	42	72	6	6	3.79	0	1.389
1995	Cleveland	AL	26	167.1	151	51	111	16	6	3.87	0	1.207
1996	Cleveland	AL	33	206.0	238	58	125	15	9	4.24	0	1.437
Post All-Star			15	101.2	109	32	64	6	4	4.25	0	1.387

KEN HILL
Age 31/R   **$17**

He finally put up some numbers that resemble his best years in Montreal. With that lineup, expect more of the same this year.

Year	Team	Lg.	G	IP	H	BB	SO	W	L	ERA	SV	Ratio
1993	Montreal	NL	28	183.2	163	74	90	9	7	3.23	0	1.290
1994	Montreal	NL	23	154.2	145	44	85	16	5	3.32	0	1.222
1995	St. Louis	NL	18	110.1	125	45	50	6	7	5.06	0	1.541
1995	Cleveland	AL	12	74.2	77	32	48	4	1	3.98	0	1.460
1996	Texas	AL	35	250.2	250	95	170	16	10	3.63	0	1.376
Post All-Star			16	119.0	121	37	77	7	5	3.18	0	1.328

STERLING HITCHCOCK
Age 25/L   **$12**

Hitchcock's year would have been better had it been a complement to a typical Randy Johnson campaign. The Mariners got what they wanted from Hitchcock, as will you.

Year	Team	Lg.	G	IP	H	BB	SO	W	L	ERA	SV	Ratio
1993	New York	AL	6	31.0	32	14	26	1	2	4.65	0	1.484
1994	New York	AL	23	49.1	48	29	37	4	1	4.20	2	1.561
1995	New York	AL	27	168.1	155	68	121	11	10	4.70	0	1.325
1996	Seattle	AL	35	196.2	245	73	132	13	9	5.35	0	1.617
Post All-Star			16	80.2	113	27	53	5	6	6.14	0	1.736

Catchers pp. 27–39

Corners pp. 40–60

Infield pp. 60–80

Outfield pp. 80–111

DH pp. 112–115

Starters pp. 115–145

Relievers pp. 146–178

MARTY JANZEN   Age 23/R $1

Doesn't he play tennis? If he doesn't, shouldn't he?

Year	Team	Lg.	G	IP	H	BB	SO	W	L	ERA	SV	Ratio
1996	Toronto	AL	15	73.2	95	38	47	4	6	7.33	0	1.805
Post All-Star			6	25.1	34	17	15	0	2	9.24	0	2.013

RANDY JOHNSON   Age 33/L $20

The lanky Johnson has always had to be precise with his mechanics due to his height. The back surgery can't help. But, hey, he's still Randy Johnson. If you scout one guy carefully in spring training, let it be the Big Unit.

Year	Team	Lg.	G	IP	H	BB	SO	W	L	ERA	SV	Ratio
1993	Seattle	AL	35	255.1	185	99	308	19	8	3.24	1	1.112
1994	Seattle	AL	23	172.0	132	72	204	13	6	3.19	0	1.186
1995	Seattle	AL	30	214.1	159	65	294	18	2	2.48	0	1.045
1996	Seattle	AL	14	61.1	48	25	85	5	0	3.67	1	1.190
Post All-Star			6	16.2	14	4	27	0	0	3.24	1	1.080

SCOTT KARL   Age 25/L $12

A solid breakthrough year. And, get this, he's got two first names.

Year	Team	Lg.	G	IP	H	BB	SO	W	L	ERA	SV	Ratio
1995	Milwaukee	AL	25	124.0	141	50	59	6	7	4.14	0	1.540
1996	Milwaukee	AL	32	207.1	220	72	121	13	9	4.86	0	1.408
Post All-Star			15	97.1	108	33	65	5	5	5.27	0	1.449

JIMMY KEY   Age 35/L $9

Took him a while to get going, and he never found his consistent stroke. He's a free agent, so watch where he signs. If he stays with the Yanks, he's worth a shot. If he goes to a lesser team, it's a different story.

Year	Team	Lg.	G	IP	H	BB	SO	W	L	ERA	SV	Ratio
1993	New York	AL	34	236.2	219	43	173	18	6	3.00	0	1.107
1994	New York	AL	25	168.0	177	52	97	17	4	3.27	0	1.363
1995	New York	AL	5	30.1	40	6	14	1	2	5.64	0	1.516
1996	New York	AL	30	169.1	171	58	116	12	11	4.68	0	1.352
Post All-Star			16	92.2	87	34	60	7	5	4.37	0	1.306

MARK LANGSTON   Age 36/L $7

A complete physical breakdown. Lefties die hard, but this one is hurting.

Year	Team	Lg.	G	IP	H	BB	SO	W	L	ERA	SV	Ratio
1993	California	AL	35	256.1	220	85	196	16	11	3.20	0	1.190
1994	California	AL	18	119.1	121	54	109	7	8	4.68	0	1.466
1995	California	AL	31	200.1	212	64	142	15	7	4.63	0	1.378
1996	California	AL	18	123.1	116	45	83	6	5	4.82	0	1.305
Post All-Star			4	27.0	24	10	17	1	1	4.67	0	1.259

FELIPE LIRA   Age 24/R $1

Lira is not worth your lire.

Year	Team	Lg.	G	IP	H	BB	SO	W	L	ERA	SV	Ratio
1995	Detroit	AL	37	146.1	151	56	89	9	13	4.31	1	1.415
1996	Detroit	AL	32	194.2	204	66	113	6	14	5.22	0	1.387
Post All-Star			13	85.2	85	31	53	0	7	4.73	0	1.354

DENNIS MARTINEZ

Age 41/R   No Price

El Presidente is not coming back for another term, but he'll always have our vote as one of the best guys ever to take to the hill.

Year	Team	Lg.	G	IP	H	BB	SO	W	L	ERA	SV	Ratio
1993	Montreal	NL	35	224.2	211	64	138	15	9	3.85	1	1.224
1994	Cleveland	AL	24	176.2	166	44	92	11	6	3.52	0	1.189
1995	Cleveland	AL	28	187.0	174	46	99	12	5	3.08	0	1.176
1996	Cleveland	AL	20	112.0	122	37	48	9	6	4.50	0	1.420
Post All-Star			3	10.2	11	6	5	1	1	3.38	0	1.594

BEN McDONALD

Age 29/R $14

You can't blame Baltimore for letting him go, but considering he would've led the the team in ERA, they sure are sorry they did. We don't care who he does it for. And we bet he does it again.

Year	Team	Lg.	G	IP	H	BB	SO	W	L	ERA	SV	Ratio
1993	Baltimore	AL	34	220.1	185	86	171	13	14	3.39	0	1.230
1994	Baltimore	AL	24	157.1	151	54	94	14	7	4.06	0	1.303
1995	Baltimore	AL	14	80.0	67	38	62	3	6	4.16	0	1.313
1996	Milwaukee	AL	35	221.1	228	67	146	12	10	3.90	0	1.333
Post All-Star			16	104.1	108	32	75	3	7	3.88	0	1.342

JACK McDOWELL

Age 31/R $15

Black Jack spent his first stint on the DL and struggled when he came back. He's one of the grittiest pitchers around and likely won't let it happen again.

Year	Team	Lg.	G	IP	H	BB	SO	W	L	ERA	SV	Ratio
1993	Chicago	AL	34	256.2	261	69	158	22	10	3.37	0	1.286
1994	Chicago	AL	25	181.0	186	42	127	10	9	3.73	0	1.260
1995	New York	AL	30	217.2	211	78	157	15	10	3.93	0	1.328
1996	Cleveland	AL	30	192.0	214	67	141	13	9	5.11	0	1.464
Post All-Star			12	69.0	90	21	55	7	3	6.39	0	1.609

ANGEL MIRANDA

Age 27/L $1

Has an outside chance at the fifth starter spot in Sudsville. Your plans should be roughly the same.

Year	Team	Lg.	G	IP	H	BB	SO	W	L	ERA	SV	Ratio
1993	Milwaukee	AL	22	120.0	100	52	88	4	5	3.30	0	1.267
1994	Milwaukee	AL	8	46.0	39	27	24	2	5	5.28	0	1.435
1995	Milwaukee	AL	30	74.0	83	49	45	4	5	5.23	1	1.784
1996	Milwaukee	AL	46	109.1	116	69	78	7	6	4.94	1	1.692
Post All-Star			26	32.1	41	21	22	4	1	5.29	0	1.918

JAMIE MOYER

Age 34/L $10

Solid season on both coasts. He's been up and down throughout his career so he's due for down. He'll still be good but he won't be starting at the All-Star game.

Year	Team	Lg.	G	IP	H	BB	SO	W	L	ERA	SV	Ratio
1993	Baltimore	AL	25	152.0	154	38	90	12	9	3.43	0	1.263
1994	Baltimore	AL	23	149.0	158	38	87	5	7	4.77	0	1.315
1995	Baltimore	AL	27	115.2	117	30	65	8	6	5.21	0	1.271
1996	Boston	AL	23	90.0	111	27	50	7	1	4.50	0	1.533
1996	Seattle	AL	11	70.2	66	19	29	6	2	3.31	0	1.203
Post All-Star			14	91.1	88	23	41	9	2	2.86	0	1.215

Catchers
pp. 27-39

Corners
pp. 40-60

Infield
pp. 60-80

Outfield
pp. 80-111

DH
pp. 112-115

Starters
pp. 115-145

Relievers
pp. 146-178

TERRY MULHOLLAND

Age 34/L $2

The Mariners can't afford to keep four lefties, so Mullholland will likely take the fall.

Year	Team	Lg.	G	IP	H	BB	SO	W	L	ERA	SV	Ratio
1993	Philadelphia	NL	29	191.0	177	40	116	12	9	3.25	0	1.136
1994	New York	AL	24	120.2	150	37	72	6	7	6.49	0	1.550
1995	San Francisco	NL	29	149.0	190	38	65	5	13	5.80	0	1.530
1996	Philadelphia	NL	21	133.1	157	21	52	8	7	4.66	0	1.335
1996	Seattle	AL	12	69.1	75	28	34	5	4	4.67	0	1.486
Post All-Star			16	101.0	102	31	50	7	5	3.92	0	1.317

MIKE MUSSINA

Age 28/R $19

Mussina was not himself in '96. He was criticized for balking at a four-man rotation. There were whispers (okay, there were shouts) that he couldn't win the big game. He gave up more than 5 runs per outing in May, June, and July, and his second half was no better than average. If anybody has a reason to forget and move on, it's Mussina.

Year	Team	Lg.	G	IP	H	BB	SO	W	L	ERA	SV	Ratio
1993	Baltimore	AL	25	167.2	163	44	117	14	6	4.46	0	1.235
1994	Baltimore	AL	24	176.1	163	42	99	16	5	3.06	0	1.163
1995	Baltimore	AL	32	221.2	187	50	158	19	9	3.29	0	1.069
1996	Baltimore	AL	36	243.1	264	69	204	19	11	4.81	0	1.368
Post All-Star			17	114.0	116	33	94	8	6	4.74	0	1.307

CHARLES NAGY

Age 29/R $18

Pretty good season, but he floundered through the summer (two wins in July and August). Were he consistent, he would have had a shot at the Cy Young. Still, he remains one of the AL's few sure bets.

Year	Team	Lg.	G	IP	H	BB	SO	W	L	ERA	SV	Ratio
1993	Cleveland	AL	9	48.2	66	13	30	2	6	6.29	0	1.623
1994	Cleveland	AL	23	169.1	175	48	108	10	8	3.45	0	1.317
1995	Cleveland	AL	29	178.0	194	61	139	16	6	4.55	0	1.433
1996	Cleveland	AL	32	222.0	217	61	167	17	5	3.41	0	1.252
Post All-Star			14	99.2	95	31	86	6	3	3.25	0	1.264

CHAD OGEA

Age 26/R $9

Ogea will be okay.

Year	Team	Lg.	G	IP	H	BB	SO	W	L	ERA	SV	Ratio
1994	Cleveland	AL	4	16.1	21	10	11	0	1	6.06	0	1.898
1995	Cleveland	AL	20	106.1	95	29	57	8	3	3.05	0	1.166
1996	Cleveland	AL	29	146.2	151	42	101	10	6	4.79	0	1.316
Post All-Star			16	100.0	94	28	67	6	5	4.23	0	1.220

OMAR OLIVARES

Age 29/R $3

Omar won't go far.

Year	Team	Lg.	G	IP	H	BB	SO	W	L	ERA	SV	Ratio
1993	St. Louis	NL	58	118.2	134	54	63	5	3	4.17	1	1.584
1994	St. Louis	NL	14	73.2	84	37	26	3	4	5.74	1	1.643
1995	Colorado	NL	11	31.2	44	21	15	1	3	7.39	0	2.053
1995	Philadelphia	NL	5	10.0	11	2	7	0	1	5.40	0	1.300
1996	Detroit	AL	25	160.0	169	75	81	7	11	4.89	0	1.525
Post All-Star			14	85.2	89	42	45	3	6	5.04	0	1.529

DARREN OLIVER   Age 26/L $14

Despite coming back from surgery last year, Oliver chalked up the most wins of his career. Since he won't be coming back from surgery this year, we predict a letdown. (That's a lie, but it works.)

Year	Team	Lg.	G	IP	H	BB	SO	W	L	ERA	SV	Ratio
1993	Texas	AL	2	3.1	2	1	4	0	0	2.70	0	0.900
1994	Texas	AL	43	50.0	40	35	50	4	0	3.42	2	1.500
1995	Texas	AL	17	49.0	47	32	39	4	2	4.22	0	1.612
1996	Texas	AL	30	173.2	190	76	112	14	6	4.66	0	1.532
Post All-Star			14	79.1	102	31	55	7	4	5.67	0	1.676

ROGER PAVLIK   Age 29/R $14

Continued his remarkable comeback with 200 innings, 34 starts, and 15 wins. But that ERA is horrendous. We think he can bring it down and continue to improve.

Year	Team	Lg.	G	IP	H	BB	SO	W	L	ERA	SV	Ratio
1993	Texas	AL	26	166.1	151	80	131	12	6	3.41	0	1.389
1994	Texas	AL	11	50.1	61	30	31	2	5	7.69	0	1.808
1995	Texas	AL	31	191.2	174	90	149	10	10	4.37	0	1.377
1996	Texas	AL	34	201.0	216	81	127	15	8	5.19	0	1.478
Post All-Star			16	89.0	100	46	56	4	6	5.66	0	1.640

ANDY PETTITTE   Age 24/L $19

The best young starter in the American League. Period.

Year	Team	Lg.	G	IP	H	BB	SO	W	L	ERA	SV	Ratio
1995	New York	AL	31	175.0	183	63	114	12	9	4.17	0	1.406
1996	New York	AL	35	221.0	229	72	162	21	8	3.87	0	1.362
Post All-Star			16	105.1	106	30	87	8	4	3.93	0	1.291

ARIEL PRIETO   Age 27/R $3

Not bad, as Oakland starters go, which is not very good.

Year	Team	Lg.	G	IP	H	BB	SO	W	L	ERA	SV	Ratio
1995	Oakland	AL	14	58.0	57	32	37	2	6	4.97	0	1.534
1996	Oakland	AL	21	125.2	130	54	75	6	7	4.15	0	1.464
Post All-Star			12	84.2	78	30	51	4	4	3.08	0	1.276

BRAD RADKE   Age 24/R $9

Given the ERA and the standards of pitching today, you'd think that he would have won 16 games. If the Twins improve at all, so will Radke's numbers. Big if.

Year	Team	Lg.	G	IP	H	BB	SO	W	L	ERA	SV	Ratio
1995	Minnesota	AL	29	181.0	195	47	75	11	14	5.32	0	1.337
1996	Minnesota	AL	35	232.0	231	57	148	11	16	4.46	0	1.241
Post All-Star			16	108.0	110	25	72	6	6	4.08	0	1.250

Catchers
pp. 27-39

Corners
pp. 40-60

Infield
pp. 60-80

Outfield
pp. 80-111

DH
pp. 112-115

Starters
pp. 115-145

Relievers
pp. 146-178

FREE OPENING DAY *ROTISSERIE HOT LIST*

(See page 252)

RICH ROBERTSON
Age 28/L   **$1**

This unfortunate fellow was 3–11 in the Homerdome. Unless he gets traded, look elsewhere.

Year	Team	Lg.	G	IP	H	BB	SO	W	L	ERA	SV	Ratio
1993	Pittsburgh	NL	9	9.0	15	4	5	0	1	6.00	0	2.111
1994	Pittsburgh	NL	8	15.2	20	10	8	0	0	6.89	0	1.915
1995	Minnesota	AL	25	51.2	48	31	38	2	0	3.83	0	1.529
1996	Minnesota	AL	36	186.1	197	116	114	7	17	5.12	0	1.680
Post All-Star			18	82.1	86	64	43	4	8	5.57	0	1.822

FRANK RODRIGUEZ
Age 24/R   **$9**

Showed reasonable progress in his first full season, though he had a dismal September (0–4). He pitched about a hundred more innings than ever before, so he probably just ran out of gas. If he's going cheap, pick him up.

Year	Team	Lg.	G	IP	H	BB	SO	W	L	ERA	SV	Ratio
1995	Boston	AL	9	15.1	21	10	14	0	2	10.57	0	2.022
1995	Minnesota	AL	16	90.1	93	47	45	5	6	5.38	0	1.550
1996	Minnesota	AL	38	206.2	218	78	110	13	14	5.05	2	1.432
Post All-Star			19	94.1	94	33	54	5	7	4.77	2	1.346

KENNY ROGERS
Age 32/L   **$14**

Twenty million bucks to go 12–8 and do everything in your power to blow it in the playoffs? The Gambler, here, is lucky he wasn't lynched by the Bomber faithful last season, but maybe he deserves a break (big maybe). He struggled with shoulder trouble (that he kept to himself until mid-May) all season, and by September he could hardly lift his arm above his elbow. We think the guy's a head case, but he did once pitch a perfect game. You gotta be good to do that.

Year	Team	Lg.	G	IP	H	BB	SO	W	L	ERA	SV	Ratio
1993	Texas	AL	35	208.1	210	71	140	16	10	4.10	0	1.349
1994	Texas	AL	24	167.1	169	52	120	11	8	4.46	0	1.321
1995	Texas	AL	31	208.0	192	76	140	17	7	3.38	0	1.288
1996	New York	AL	30	179.0	179	83	92	12	8	4.68	0	1.464
Post All-Star			14	81.2	84	34	45	6	4	5.18	0	1.445

JOSE ROSADO
Age 22/L   **$10**

Not bad. Let's see it again.

Year	Team	Lg.	G	IP	H	BB	SO	W	L	ERA	SV	Ratio
1996	Kansas City	AL	16	106.2	101	26	64	8	6	3.21	0	1.191
Post All-Star			15	100.2	97	22	59	8	6	3.22	0	1.182

AARON SELE
Age 26/R   **$6**

Many pitchers take a while to develop, but this kid's taking forever. He's got great stuff, so the problems are clearly mental and there's no timetable for that kind of development. Whoever replaces Kennedy should make this kid a top priority. Pay attention when his name comes up, but remember there is nothing in his past to justify paying more than ten bucks.

Year	Team	Lg.	G	IP	H	BB	SO	W	L	ERA	SV	Ratio
1993	Boston	AL	18	111.2	100	48	93	7	2	2.74	0	1.325
1994	Boston	AL	22	143.1	140	60	105	8	7	3.83	0	1.395
1995	Boston	AL	6	32.1	32	14	21	3	1	3.06	0	1.423
1996	Boston	AL	29	157.1	192	67	137	7	11	5.32	0	1.646
Post All-Star			12	68.2	88	21	65	4	6	4.46	0	1.587

STEVE SPARKS Age 31/R $1

Spend your knuckleball money on Wakefield.

Year	Team	Lg.	G	IP	H	BB	SO	W	L	ERA	SV	Ratio
1995	Milwaukee	AL	33	202.0	210	86	96	9	11	4.63	0	1.465
1996	Milwaukee	AL	20	88.2	103	52	21	4	7	6.60	0	1.748
Post All-Star			7	11.2	14	12	4	0	0	7.71	0	2.229

KEVIN TAPANI Age 33/R $10

A better than average pitcher on an underachieving team. Not the greatest combination. Not the worst one, either.

Year	Team	Lg.	G	IP	H	BB	SO	W	L	ERA	SV	Ratio
1993	Minnesota	AL	36	225.2	243	57	150	12	15	4.43	0	1.329
1994	Minnesota	AL	24	156.0	181	39	91	11	7	4.62	0	1.410
1995	Minnesota	AL	20	133.2	155	34	88	6	11	4.92	0	1.414
1995	Los Angeles	NL	13	57.0	72	14	43	4	2	5.05	0	1.509
1996	Chicago	AL	34	225.1	236	76	150	13	10	4.59	0	1.385
Post All-Star			16	100.1	109	41	67	5	5	5.92	0	1.495

JUSTIN THOMPSON Age 24/L $4

The Tigers have been very careful in handling this talented, though injury-prone, youngster. Last year was simply a trial run under no pressure. This year we think he'll pay the Tigers back for their patience. Hey, things can't get any worse in Detroit.

Year	Team	Lg.	G	IP	H	BB	SO	W	L	ERA	SV	Ratio
1996	Detroit	AL	11	59.0	62	31	44	1	6	4.58	0	1.576
Post All-Star			9	45.2	53	24	31	1	5	5.32	0	1.686

TODD VAN POPPEL Age 25/R $1

Then again, things could get a lot worse in Motown if this stiff takes the mound. Van Poppel must be on every GM's least-wanted list. His claim to fame? While most kids think they'll be the next Greg Maddux, they mostly end up the next Todd Van Poppel.

Year	Team	Lg.	G	IP	H	BB	SO	W	L	ERA	SV	Ratio
1993	Oakland	AL	16	84.0	76	62	47	6	6	5.04	0	1.643
1994	Oakland	AL	23	116.2	108	89	83	7	10	6.09	0	1.689
1995	Oakland	AL	36	138.1	125	56	122	4	8	4.88	0	1.308
1996	Oakland	AL	28	63.0	86	33	37	1	5	7.71	1	1.889
1996	Detroit	AL	9	36.1	53	29	16	2	4	11.39	0	2.257
Post All-Star			13	39.2	61	29	17	2	5	11.57	1	2.269

Catchers
pp. 27–39

Corners
pp. 40–60

Infield
pp. 60–80

Outfield
pp. 80–111

DH
pp. 112–115

Starters
pp. 115–145

Relievers
pp. 146–178

MATT WAGNER
Age 24/R   **$1**

Stick to opera, kiddo.

Year	Team	Lg.	G	IP	H	BB	SO	W	L	ERA	SV	Ratio
1996	Seattle	AL	15	80.0	91	38	41	3	5	6.86	0	1.612
Post All-Star			8	35.2	41	20	19	1	3	7.82	0	1.710

TIM WAKEFIELD
Age 30/R   **$13**

Bottom line, the guy's decent. He gives up a lot, but he takes the ball once a week and somehow manages to get guys out. He's won 30 games over the past two seasons and there's no reason to think he can't keep on going.

Year	Team	Lg.	G	IP	H	BB	SO	W	L	ERA	SV	Ratio
1993	Pittsburgh	NL	24	128.1	145	75	59	6	11	5.61	0	1.714
1995	Boston	AL	27	195.1	163	68	119	16	8	2.95	0	1.183
1996	Boston	AL	32	211.2	238	90	140	14	13	5.14	0	1.550
Post All-Star			15	110.2	103	38	67	9	4	4.15	0	1.274

JOHN WASDIN
Age 24/R   **$1**

He should make the Oakland rotation, and will continue to hover around mediocrity. Every roster can handle exactly one Wasdin.

Year	Team	Lg.	G	IP	H	BB	SO	W	L	ERA	SV	Ratio
1995	Oakland	AL	5	17.1	14	3	6	1	1	4.67	0	0.981
1996	Oakland	AL	25	131.1	145	50	75	8	7	5.96	0	1.485
Post All-Star			16	76.1	87	38	45	2	5	6.84	0	1.638

BOB WELLS
Age 30/R   **$8**

Twelve wins is nice, but not when you're 9–1 at the end of June.

Year	Team	Lg.	G	IP	H	BB	SO	W	L	ERA	SV	Ratio
1994	Philadelphia	NL	6	5.0	4	3	3	1	0	1.80	0	1.400
1994	Seattle	AL	1	4.0	4	1	3	1	0	2.25	0	1.250
1995	Seattle	AL	30	76.2	88	39	38	4	3	5.75	0	1.657
1996	Seattle	AL	36	130.2	141	46	94	12	7	5.30	0	1.431
Post All-Star			13	50.0	68	14	29	3	5	7.74	0	1.640

DAVID WELLS
Age 33/L   **$8**

He pitched well in the playoffs, and though that matters to the O's, it means absolutely nothing to us. These numbers are scary. Could be the Wells run dry.

Year	Team	Lg.	G	IP	H	BB	SO	W	L	ERA	SV	Ratio
1993	Detroit	AL	32	187.0	183	42	139	11	9	4.19	0	1.203
1994	Detroit	AL	16	111.1	113	24	71	5	7	3.96	0	1.231
1995	Detroit	AL	18	130.1	120	37	83	10	3	3.04	0	1.205
1995	Cincinnati	NL	11	72.2	74	16	50	6	5	3.59	0	1.239
1996	Baltimore	AL	34	224.1	247	51	130	11	14	5.14	0	1.328
Post All-Star			17	106.2	118	30	67	6	6	4.98	0	1.388

DON WENGERT
Age 27/R   **$1**

Baseball is in tough shape when guys like Wengert have a place in it. In other sports, if you perform at this level, you're slurping Budweiser back in

---

Bumblefart, drooling on about the almost-decent old days. But hey, it's not his fault, there are three guys just like him on every roster.

Year	Team	Lg.	G	IP	H	BB	SO	W	L	ERA	SV	Ratio
1995	Oakland	AL	19	29.2	30	12	16	1	1	3.34	0	1.416
1996	Oakland	AL	36	161.1	200	60	75	7	11	5.58	0	1.612
Post All-Star			14	72.1	100	27	27	4	5	6.35	0	1.756

BRIAN WILLIAMS   Age 28/R $1

In April, he was a closer. In June he was a starter. In July he should have been slurping Budweiser back in Bumblefart drooling on about the almost decent old days.

Year	Team	Lg.	G	IP	H	BB	SO	W	L	ERA	SV	Ratio
1993	Houston	NL	42	82.0	76	38	56	4	4	4.83	3	1.390
1994	Houston	NL	20	78.1	112	41	49	6	5	5.74	0	1.953
1995	San Diego	NL	44	72.0	79	38	75	3	10	6.00	0	1.625
1996	Detroit	AL	40	121.0	145	85	72	3	10	6.77	2	1.901
Post All-Star			16	48.1	61	36	30	1	5	8.75	0	2.007

BOBBY WITT   Age 32/R $6

Nice guy for your third or fourth spot. He never developed the way he might have. But then, neither have we.

Year	Team	Lg.	G	IP	H	BB	SO	W	L	ERA	SV	Ratio
1993	Oakland	AL	35	220.0	226	91	131	14	13	4.21	0	1.441
1994	Oakland	AL	24	135.2	151	70	111	8	10	5.04	0	1.629
1995	Florida	NL	19	110.2	104	47	95	2	7	3.90	0	1.364
1995	Texas	AL	10	61.1	81	21	46	3	4	4.55	0	1.663
1996	Texas	AL	33	199.2	235	96	157	16	12	5.41	0	1.658
Post All-Star			15	91.0	106	35	69	9	4	4.75	0	1.549

STEVE WOJCIECHOWSKI   Age 26/L $1

His control got better, but we're willing to bet that it was more than just spelling-anxiety that kept Art Howe from writing this guy's name on the lineup card.

Year	Team	Lg.	G	IP	H	BB	SO	W	L	ERA	SV	Ratio
1995	Oakland	AL	14	48.2	51	28	13	2	3	5.18	0	1.623
1996	Oakland	AL	16	79.2	97	28	30	5	5	5.65	0	1.569
Post All-Star			0	0.0	0	0	0	0	0	0.00	0	0.000

BOB WOLCOTT   Age 23/R $1

From playoff star to regular season stiff. He's still young, but last year he was a mess. If he's going cheap he's worth a look, but only if you've just drafted Wengert.

Year	Team	Lg.	G	IP	H	BB	SO	W	L	ERA	SV	Ratio
1995	Seattle	AL	7	36.2	43	14	19	3	2	4.42	0	1.555
1996	Seattle	AL	30	149.1	179	54	78	7	10	5.73	0	1.560
Post All-Star			12	58.0	65	13	39	2	3	5.12	0	1.345

Out of the Bullpen

NATIONAL LEAGUE

TERRY ADAMS   Age 24/R $6

A hard thrower whose control was always a problem, until the second half of last year when it all started to fall into place. He will get his share of save opportunities this year.

Year	Team	Lg.	G	IP	H	BB	SO	W	L	ERA	SV	Ratio
1995	Chicago	NL	18	18.0	22	10	15	1	1	6.50	1	1.778
1996	Chicago	NL	69	101.0	84	49	78	3	6	2.94	4	1.317
Post All-Star			33	45.1	42	17	38	1	4	3.57	3	1.301

CORY BAILEY   Age 26/R $2

Could develop into a useful middle reliever.

Year	Team	Lg.	G	IP	H	BB	SO	W	L	ERA	SV	Ratio
1993	Boston	AL	11	15.2	12	12	11	0	1	3.45	0	1.532
1994	Boston	AL	5	4.1	10	3	4	0	1	12.46	0	3.000
1995	St. Louis	NL	3	3.2	2	2	5	0	0	7.36	0	1.091
1996	St. Louis	NL	51	57.0	57	30	38	5	2	3.00	0	1.526
Post All-Star			25	28.1	22	15	12	2	1	1.27	0	1.306

JOSE BAUTISTA   Age 32/R $3

Look up the definition for a "Giants pitcher." It will read something like "often injured, prone to allowing home runs, cannot be relied upon from year to year." Good description for this guy, who's nonetheless got a lot of stuff. Then there is the San Francisco mystery named . . .

Year	Team	Lg.	G	IP	H	BB	SO	W	L	ERA	SV	Ratio
1993	Chicago	NL	58	111.2	105	27	63	10	3	2.82	2	1.182
1994	Chicago	NL	58	69.1	75	17	45	4	5	3.89	1	1.327
1995	San Francisco	NL	52	100.2	120	26	45	3	8	6.44	0	1.450
1996	San Francisco	NL	37	69.2	66	15	28	3	4	3.36	0	1.163
Post All-Star			21	39.2	37	7	12	2	3	3.40	0	1.109

ROD BECK   Age 28/R $32

. . . who scouts say has lost 5 to 7 miles per hour, the bite on what used to be one of baseball's best sliders, and the aggressiveness that once made him one of the game's fiercest competitors. A lot of saves, but look at the losses. You blow that many, pretty soon they stop asking you to close out wins— because you can't. Someone will likely take a chance on him. You shouldn't.

Year	Team	Lg.	G	IP	H	BB	SO	W	L	ERA	SV	Ratio
1993	San Francisco	NL	76	79.1	57	13	86	3	1	2.16	48	0.882
1994	San Francisco	NL	48	48.2	49	13	39	2	4	2.77	28	1.274
1995	San Francisco	NL	60	58.2	60	21	42	5	6	4.45	33	1.381
1996	San Francisco	NL	63	62.0	56	10	48	0	9	3.34	35	1.065
Post All-Star			29	27.2	30	6	18	0	4	4.23	18	1.301

MIKE BIELECKI   Age 37/R $4

In his third different tour of duty with the Braves, he learned to throw a knuckle curve and became a reliable long reliever. If only Bobby Cox hadn't yanked him in the fourth game of the Series when he was pitching so well. . . .

Year	Team	Lg.	G	IP	H	BB	SO	W	L	ERA	SV	Ratio
1993	Cleveland	AL	13	68.2	90	23	38	4	5	5.90	0	1.646
1994	Atlanta	NL	19	27.0	28	12	18	2	0	4.00	0	1.481
1995	California	AL	22	75.1	80	31	45	4	6	5.97	0	1.473
1996	Atlanta	NL	40	75.1	63	33	71	4	3	2.63	2	1.274
Post All-Star			21	46.1	42	24	47	3	1	2.33	1	1.424

WILLIE BLAIR   Age 31/R $2

Before he left Southern California for beautiful downtown Detroit, Randy Smith made a habit in San Diego of stockpiling good arms. This is one, and though he has his ups and downs, he will suck up innings and with some luck, grab a few garbage wins. Another good arm acquired by Smith belongs to . . .

Year	Team	Lg.	G	IP	H	BB	SO	W	L	ERA	SV	Ratio
1993	Colorado	NL	46	146.0	184	42	84	6	10	4.75	0	1.548
1994	Colorado	NL	47	77.2	98	39	68	0	5	5.79	3	1.764
1995	San Diego	NL	40	114.0	112	45	83	7	5	4.34	0	1.377
1996	San Diego	NL	60	88.0	80	29	67	2	6	4.60	1	1.239
Post All-Star			25	34.2	34	8	28	1	1	5.19	1	1.212

DOUG BOCHTLER   Age 26/R $3

. . . who has outstanding stuff and is coveted by several other clubs as future closer material. So remember the name.

Year	Team	Lg.	G	IP	H	BB	SO	W	L	ERA	SV	Ratio
1995	San Diego	NL	34	45.1	38	19	45	4	4	3.57	1	1.257
1996	San Diego	NL	63	65.2	45	39	68	2	4	3.02	3	1.279
Post All-Star			32	31.0	12	21	34	2	2	2.03	0	1.065

PEDRO BORBON   Age 29/L $1

He had not allowed one inherited runner to score all season and was baseball's best lefty specialist until he got injured. The Braves fear it might be at least another year before he is back.

Year	Team	Lg.	G	IP	H	BB	SO	W	L	ERA	SV	Ratio
1993	Atlanta	NL	3	1.2	3	3	2	0	0	21.60	0	3.600
1995	Atlanta	NL	41	32.0	29	17	33	2	2	3.09	2	1.438
1996	Atlanta	NL	43	36.0	26	7	31	3	0	2.75	1	0.917
Post All-Star			20	15.1	11	3	12	2	0	2.35	0	0.913

TOBY BORLAND   Age 27/R $5

He can pitch almost every day, which is a useful skill for Mets relievers to possess. And he could be a real bargain because people always downgrade middle relievers.

Year	Team	Lg.	G	IP	H	BB	SO	W	L	ERA	SV	Ratio
1994	Philadelphia	NL	24	34.1	31	14	26	1	0	2.36	1	1.311
1995	Philadelphia	NL	50	74.0	81	37	59	1	3	3.77	6	1.595
1996	Philadelphia	NL	69	90.2	83	43	76	7	3	4.07	0	1.390
Post All-Star			34	44.2	48	22	35	2	1	4.03	0	1.567

Catchers
pp. 27–39

Corners
pp. 40–60

Infield
pp. 60–80

Outfield
pp. 80–111

DH
pp. 112–115

Starters
pp. 115–145

Relievers
pp. 146–178

RICKY BOTTALICO
Age 27/R $35

You read it here first—he'd replace Heathcliff Slocumb and be the Phillies' closer. He did it so well that he made the All-Star team, pitched a shutout inning at the sold-out Vet, after which he returned to the dugout, received congratulations, and could only gasp, "I think I'm going to hyperventilate." You gotta like a closer who can hyperventilate, much less say it.

Year	Team	Lg.	G	IP	H	BB	SO	W	L	ERA	SV	Ratio
1994	Philadelphia	NL	3	3.0	3	1	3	0	0	0.00	0	1.333
1995	Philadelphia	NL	62	87.2	50	42	87	5	3	2.46	1	1.049
1996	Philadelphia	NL	61	67.2	47	23	74	4	5	3.19	34	1.034
Post All-Star			24	25.1	18	4	25	2	1	2.49	14	0.868

KENT BOTTENFIELD
Age 28/R $3

Resurfaced to find a niche as a useful middle reliever.

Year	Team	Lg.	G	IP	H	BB	SO	W	L	ERA	SV	Ratio
1993	Montreal	NL	23	83.0	93	33	33	2	5	4.12	0	1.518
1993	Colorado	NL	14	76.2	86	38	30	3	5	6.10	0	1.617
1994	Colorado	NL	15	24.2	28	10	15	3	1	5.84	1	1.541
1994	San Francisco	NL	1	1.2	5	0	0	0	0	10.80	0	3.000
1996	Chicago	NL	48	61.2	59	19	33	3	5	2.63	1	1.265
Post All-Star			37	45.2	44	16	21	3	5	3.15	1	1.314

JEFF BRANTLEY
Age 33/R $38

He took less money to stay in Cincinnati, not because he likes having dog hair rubbed on his chest but because "this team believed I could be a closer when no one else did." Few get more out of their ability.

Year	Team	Lg.	G	IP	H	BB	SO	W	L	ERA	SV	Ratio
1993	San Francisco	NL	53	113.2	112	46	76	5	6	4.28	0	1.390
1994	Cincinnati	NL	50	65.1	46	28	63	6	6	2.48	15	1.133
1995	Cincinnati	NL	56	70.1	53	20	62	3	2	2.82	28	1.038
1996	Cincinnati	NL	66	71.0	54	28	76	1	2	2.41	44	1.155
Post All-Star			31	30.0	21	13	25	0	1	1.50	22	1.133

DOUG BROCAIL
Age 29/R $1

A utility pitcher.

Year	Team	Lg.	G	IP	H	BB	SO	W	L	ERA	SV	Ratio
1993	San Diego	NL	24	128.1	143	42	70	4	13	4.56	0	1.442
1994	San Diego	NL	12	17.0	21	5	11	0	0	5.82	0	1.529
1995	Houston	NL	36	77.1	87	22	39	6	4	4.19	1	1.409
1996	Houston	NL	23	53.0	58	23	34	1	5	4.58	0	1.528
Post All-Star			13	15.2	26	9	6	0	2	5.74	0	2.234

PAUL BYRD
Age 26/R $1

He had the look of being a solid set-up guy when, like so many other young Mets pitchers, his career was sidetracked by injuries. However, the good news was that he had back troubles, not arm troubles. He should be effective again, especially with the Braves.

Year	Team	Lg.	G	IP	H	BB	SO	W	L	ERA	SV	Ratio
1995	New York	NL	17	22.0	18	7	26	2	0	2.05	0	1.136
1996	New York	NL	38	46.2	48	21	31	1	2	4.24	0	1.479
Post All-Star			28	32.1	33	14	18	0	1	3.90	0	1.454

HECTOR CARRASCO   Age 27/R $1

With Brantley around for another couple of years, he'll remain a middle reliever with huge potential and still-frequent bouts of wildness.

Year	Team	Lg.	G	IP	H	BB	SO	W	L	ERA	SV	Ratio
1994	Cincinnati	NL	45	56.1	42	30	41	5	6	2.24	6	1.278
1995	Cincinnati	NL	64	87.1	86	46	64	2	7	4.12	5	1.511
1996	Cincinnati	NL	56	74.1	58	45	59	4	3	3.75	0	1.386
Post All-Star			30	40.1	33	25	29	2	1	3.79	0	1.438

JASON CHRISTIANSEN   Age 27/L $1

A flop.

Year	Team	Lg.	G	IP	H	BB	SO	W	L	ERA	SV	Ratio
1995	Pittsburgh	NL	63	56.1	49	34	53	1	3	4.15	0	1.473
1996	Pittsburgh	NL	33	44.1	56	19	38	3	3	6.70	0	1.692
Post All-Star			3	1.2	0	2	2	0	0	0.00	0	1.200

BRAD CLONTZ   Age 25/R $2

When asked if being pitched a league-high 81 times might have tired him out and contributed to an inflated ERA over the last six weeks, Rockin' Leo Mazzone, the Braves inimitable pitching coach, just laughed: "Tired? Heck, Clontzie doesn't throw hard enough to get hurt by being tired."

Year	Team	Lg.	G	IP	H	BB	SO	W	L	ERA	SV	Ratio
1995	Atlanta	NL	59	69.0	71	22	55	8	1	3.65	4	1.348
1996	Atlanta	NL	81	80.2	78	33	49	6	3	5.69	1	1.376
Post All-Star			36	36.2	35	21	22	1	1	7.36	0	1.527

FRANCISCO CORDOVA   Age 24/R $5

He was discovered pitching barefoot for a factory team in a small, dusty Mexican outpost. He barely speaks. The Pirates aren't even sure his listed age is correct, how old he is. But he buzzes it in the 90s and has a chance to be a genuine closer. It would be a great story if anyone cared about baseball stories in Pittsburgh.

Year	Team	Lg.	G	IP	H	BB	SO	W	L	ERA	SV	Ratio
1996	Pittsburgh	NL	59	99.0	103	20	95	4	7	4.09	12	1.242
Post All-Star			21	53.1	54	8	49	2	2	4.22	2	1.163

DOUG CREEK   Age 28/L $1

You're up the creek if you need him in your bullpen. Which is where the Giants found themselves after running him out there 61 times. It didn't help that the same Giants' bullpen was forced to use . . .

Year	Team	Lg.	G	IP	H	BB	SO	W	L	ERA	SV	Ratio
1995	St. Louis	NL	6	6.2	2	3	10	0	0	0.00	0	0.750
1996	San Francisco	NL	63	48.1	45	32	38	0	2	6.52	0	1.593
Post All-Star			27	20.1	14	9	19	0	1	7.08	0	1.131

Catchers
pp. 27–39

Corners
pp. 40–60

Infield
pp. 60–80

Outfield
pp. 80–111

DH
pp. 112–115

Starters
pp. 115–145

Relievers
pp. 146–178

RICH DELUCIA   Age 32/R $1

. . . 53 times, most of which were so ineffective that by midseason, one of the Giants' bullpen aces turned out to be . . .

Year	Team	Lg.	G	IP	H	BB	SO	W	L	ERA	SV	Ratio
1993	Seattle	AL	30	42.2	46	23	48	3	6	4.64	0	1.617
1994	Cincinnati	NL	8	10.2	9	5	15	0	0	4.22	0	1.313
1995	St. Louis	NL	56	82.1	63	36	76	8	7	3.39	0	1.202
1996	San Francisco	NL	56	61.2	62	31	55	3	6	5.84	0	1.508
Post All-Star			27	28.2	36	10	24	0	4	6.28	0	1.605

MARK DEWEY   Age 32/R $3

. . . who had a career year, which says something about his career.

Year	Team	Lg.	G	IP	H	BB	SO	W	L	ERA	SV	Ratio
1993	Pittsburgh	NL	21	26.2	14	10	14	1	2	2.36	7	0.900
1994	Pittsburgh	NL	45	51.1	61	19	30	2	1	3.68	1	1.558
1995	San Francisco	NL	27	31.2	30	17	32	1	0	3.13	0	1.484
1996	San Francisco	NL	78	83.1	79	41	57	6	3	4.21	0	1.440
Post All-Star			37	38.1	40	18	27	3	1	5.17	0	1.513

JERRY DiPOTO   Age 28/R $1

He piled up an impressive total of garbage wins, which made whoever took our advice last year and made him an eighth or ninth pitcher very happy indeed. Unfortunately, the art of garbage wins is a very inexact science that rarely repeats itself. And now he's in Pitchers Purgatory.

Year	Team	Lg.	G	IP	H	BB	SO	W	L	ERA	SV	Ratio
1993	Cleveland	AL	46	56.1	57	30	41	4	4	2.40	11	1.544
1994	Cleveland	AL	7	15.2	26	10	9	0	0	8.04	0	2.298
1995	New York	NL	58	78.2	77	29	49	4	6	3.78	2	1.347
1996	New York	NL	57	77.1	91	45	52	7	2	4.19	0	1.759
Post All-Star			31	40.2	45	26	30	4	1	3.76	0	1.746

MIKE DYER   Age 30/R $2

He was once seen trying to put on his uniform top while it was still buttoned. He enjoys heavy metal blasting through headphones. When asked how he was able to get so much out of Dyer last year, then-Expos pitching coach Joe Kerrigan replied, "We got an alien from outer space to talk to him. Mike is one of those guys who's sort of on his own planet."

Year	Team	Lg.	G	IP	H	BB	SO	W	L	ERA	SV	Ratio
1994	Pittsburgh	NL	14	15.1	15	12	13	1	1	5.87	4	1.761
1995	Pittsburgh	NL	55	74.2	81	30	53	4	5	4.34	0	1.487
1996	Montreal	NL	70	75.2	79	34	51	5	5	4.40	2	1.493
Post All-Star			31	33.0	32	14	16	1	3	4.91	0	1.394

DENNIS ECKERSLEY   Age 42/R $26

He can't pitch every day anymore, and on some nights, he is going to have nothing. But you can count on the firm of LaRussa and Duncan to get the maximum out of whatever's left. We only wish he hadn't fired up the Braves by going into his Deion Sanders act after saving the fourth game of the NLCS. Atlanta might have won the thing anyway, but they didn't need to get a wake-up call from the Eck.

Catchers	pp. 27-39
Corners	pp. 40-60
Infield	pp. 60-80
Outfield	pp. 80-111
DH	pp. 112-115
Starters	pp. 115-145
Relievers	pp. 146-178

Year	Team	Lg.	G	IP	H	BB	SO	W	L	ERA	SV	Ratio
1993	Oakland	AL	64	67.0	67	13	80	2	4	4.16	36	1.194
1994	Oakland	AL	45	44.1	49	13	47	5	4	4.26	19	1.398
1995	Oakland	AL	52	50.1	53	11	40	4	6	4.83	29	1.272
1996	St. Louis	NL	63	60.0	65	6	49	0	6	3.30	30	1.183
Post All-Star			35	30.2	33	3	23	0	1	2.93	18	1.174

TONY FOSSAS   Age 39/L $1

One of the several reasons why the St. Louis bullpen kept close tabs on the whole Medicare issue throughout the campaign.

Year	Team	Lg.	G	IP	H	BB	SO	W	L	ERA	SV	Ratio
1993	Boston	AL	71	40.0	38	15	39	1	1	5.18	0	1.325
1994	Boston	AL	44	34.0	35	15	31	2	0	4.76	1	1.471
1995	St. Louis	NL	58	36.2	28	10	40	3	0	1.47	0	1.036
1996	St. Louis	NL	65	47.0	43	21	36	0	4	2.68	2	1.362
Post All-Star			28	20.0	16	10	17	0	0	1.80	0	1.300

JOHN FRANCO   Age 36/L $24

If he's not overworked and if you can swallow the occasional blown save, he remains a formidable closer. And wisely realizing they have little in the way of veteran character in their organization, the Mets have brought him back for another two years.

Year	Team	Lg.	G	IP	H	BB	SO	W	L	ERA	SV	Ratio
1993	New York	NL	35	36.1	46	19	29	4	3	5.20	10	1.789
1994	New York	NL	47	50.0	47	19	42	1	4	2.70	30	1.320
1995	New York	NL	48	51.2	48	17	41	5	3	2.44	29	1.258
1996	New York	NL	51	54.0	54	21	48	4	3	1.83	28	1.389
Post All-Star			23	25.1	25	7	20	2	1	1.78	9	1.263

MARK GUTHRIE   Age 31/L $4

What with all the various soap operas going on around the Dodgers all season, few noticed that from Memorial Day on, he was the best left-handed reliever in the league.

Year	Team	Lg.	G	IP	H	BB	SO	W	L	ERA	SV	Ratio
1993	Minnesota	AL	22	21.0	20	16	15	2	1	4.71	0	1.714
1994	Minnesota	AL	50	51.1	65	18	38	4	2	6.14	1	1.617
1995	Minnesota	AL	36	42.1	47	16	48	5	3	4.46	0	1.488
1995	Los Angeles	NL	24	19.2	19	9	19	0	2	3.66	0	1.424
1996	Los Angeles	NL	66	73.0	65	22	56	2	3	2.22	1	1.192
Post All-Star			30	33.1	36	7	25	1	3	3.51	1	1.290

CHRIS HAMMOND   Age 31/L $1

The Marlins upgraded their rotation so much that he became a long reliever. That does not translate into much value.

Year	Team	Lg.	G	IP	H	BB	SO	W	L	ERA	SV	Ratio
1993	Florida	NL	32	191.0	207	66	108	11	12	4.66	0	1.429
1994	Florida	NL	13	73.1	79	23	40	4	4	3.07	0	1.391
1995	Florida	NL	25	161.0	157	47	126	9	6	3.80	0	1.267
1996	Florida	NL	38	81.0	104	27	50	5	8	6.56	0	1.617
Post All-Star			24	42.1	59	10	27	3	3	5.95	0	1.630

DOUG HENRY   Age 33/R $3

We expected much more. So did the Mets. After transforming another close game into another blowout, Dallas Green was heard to thunder, "How many times am I supposed to have to look at that crap?" The answer is "none," not even if Dallas tunes to Channel 9 to listen to Kiner's Korner. Henry is history, at least as a Met.

Year	Team	Lg.	G	IP	H	BB	SO	W	L	ERA	SV	Ratio
1993	Milwaukee	AL	54	55.0	67	25	38	4	4	5.56	17	1.673
1994	Milwaukee	AL	25	31.1	32	23	20	2	3	4.60	0	1.755
1995	New York	NL	51	67.0	48	25	62	3	6	2.96	4	1.090
1996	New York	NL	58	75.0	82	36	58	2	8	4.68	9	1.573
Post All-Star			24	30.0	37	19	24	0	6	6.30	3	1.867

XAVIER HERNANDEZ   Age 31/R $6

Tireless, reasonably reliable, able to accumulate reasonable numbers of saves and wins in any given year. All admirable traits.

Year	Team	Lg.	G	IP	H	BB	SO	W	L	ERA	SV	Ratio
1993	Houston	NL	72	96.2	75	28	101	4	5	2.61	9	1.066
1994	New York	AL	31	40.0	48	21	37	4	4	5.85	6	1.725
1995	Cincinnati	NL	59	90.0	95	31	84	7	2	4.60	3	1.400
1996	Cincinnati	NL	3	3.1	8	2	3	0	0	13.50	0	3.000
1996	Houston	NL	58	74.2	69	26	78	5	5	4.22	6	1.272
Post All-Star			31	42.0	32	16	44	5	1	3.43	5	1.143

TREVOR HOFFMAN   Age 29/R $39

Opposing hitters batted only .161 against him. He averaged 11 strikeouts for every nine innings pitched. He converted his last 18 save opportunities down the stretch. There just ain't any better.

Year	Team	Lg.	G	IP	H	BB	SO	W	L	ERA	SV	Ratio
1993	Florida	NL	28	35.2	24	19	26	2	2	3.28	2	1.206
1993	San Diego	NL	39	54.1	56	20	53	2	4	4.31	3	1.399
1994	San Diego	NL	47	56.0	39	20	68	4	4	2.57	20	1.054
1995	San Diego	NL	55	53.1	48	14	52	7	4	3.88	31	1.163
1996	San Diego	NL	70	88.0	50	31	111	9	5	2.25	42	0.920
Post All-Star			36	43.1	25	17	51	4	3	3.12	24	0.969

DARREN HOLMES   Age 30/R $1

The Rockies trust him less and less in key situations. If the Rockies don't trust him, neither should you.

Year	Team	Lg.	G	IP	H	BB	SO	W	L	ERA	SV	Ratio
1993	Colorado	NL	62	66.2	56	20	60	3	3	4.05	25	1.140
1994	Colorado	NL	29	28.1	35	24	33	0	3	6.35	3	2.082
1995	Colorado	NL	68	66.2	59	28	61	6	1	3.24	14	1.305
1996	Colorado	NL	62	77.0	78	28	73	5	4	3.97	1	1.377
Post All-Star			27	39.1	31	13	36	3	1	2.29	0	1.119

RICK HONEYCUTT   Age 42/L $1

Part of the only bullpen that is endorsed by the AARP, he was nursed along expertly by LaRussa-Duncan and proved to be a still-useful commodity. But doesn't this have to end someday?

Year	Team	Lg.	G	IP	H	BB	SO	W	L	ERA	SV	Ratio
1993	Oakland	AL	52	41.2	30	20	21	1	4	2.81	1	1.200
1994	Texas	AL	42	25.0	37	9	18	1	2	7.20	1	1.840
1995	Oakland	AL	49	44.2	37	9	21	5	1	2.42	2	1.030
1995	New York	AL	3	1.0	2	1	0	0	0	27.00	0	3.000
1996	St. Louis	NL	61	47.1	42	7	30	2	1	2.85	4	1.035
Post All-Star			28	20.1	21	1	8	0	1	2.66	2	1.082

Catchers
pp. 27-39

Corners
pp. 40-60

Infield
pp. 60-80

Outfield
pp. 80-111

DH
pp. 112-115

Starters
pp. 115-145

Relievers
pp. 146-178

MARK HUTTON   Age 27/R $6

Here's another story that illustrates why it's so much fun to work for the Yankees. After Hutton was traded to Florida for David Weathers and Weathers was not instantly successful in the Bronx, The Boss was chatting one day in the Yanks' clubhouse. "I never heard of this guy Weathers, but my baseball people insisted on getting him," rambled George Steinbrenner. "Then they said they could get this guy Weathers for Hutton. I've been hearing for years from my baseball people what a great prospect this big Australian kid Hutton was and now they're going to trade him for some guy named Weathers who I never heard of. But I don't interfere with my baseball people so I let them trade the big Australian kid for this guy named Weathers, who has not shown me a thing yet. If this guy Weathers can't cut it in New York and the Australian kid wins in Florida, then something's wrong with some of my baseball people." Oh, incidentally, Florida thinks Hutton can be a useful fifth starter and long reliever.

Year	Team	Lg.	G	IP	H	BB	SO	W	L	ERA	SV	Ratio
1993	New York	AL	7	22.0	24	17	12	1	1	5.73	0	1.864
1994	New York	AL	2	3.2	4	0	1	0	0	4.91	0	1.091
1996	New York	AL	12	30.1	32	18	25	0	2	5.04	0	1.648
1996	Florida	NL	13	56.1	47	18	31	5	1	3.67	0	1.154
Post All-Star			16	70.0	61	24	40	5	3	3.86	0	1.214

TODD JONES   Age 28/R $3

Ideally, for the Astros, he can fit into a set-up role behind Wagner and Hudek. Of course, that's not exactly ideal for those of you hoping he can be a closer.

Year	Team	Lg.	G	IP	H	BB	SO	W	L	ERA	SV	Ratio
1993	Houston	NL	27	37.1	28	15	25	1	2	3.13	2	1.152
1994	Houston	NL	48	72.2	52	26	63	5	2	2.72	5	1.073
1995	Houston	NL	68	99.2	89	52	96	6	5	3.07	15	1.415
1996	Houston	NL	51	57.1	61	32	44	6	3	4.40	17	1.622
Post All-Star			14	15.1	17	11	7	0	2	7.04	1	1.826

JEFF JUDEN   Age 26/R $1

He has huge potential, packed into a huge body and a personality that has made him unpopular everywhere he's pitched. That's why when the Expos and Astros had one of the most violent bench-clearing brawls of any season last summer, there were players from both teams trying to get a piece of the big guy.

Year	Team	Lg.	G	IP	H	BB	SO	W	L	ERA	SV	Ratio
1993	Houston	NL	2	5.0	4	4	7	0	1	5.40	0	1.600
1994	Philadelphia	NL	6	27.2	29	12	22	1	4	6.18	0	1.482
1995	Philadelphia	NL	13	62.2	53	31	47	2	4	4.02	0	1.340
1996	San Francisco	NL	36	41.2	39	20	35	4	0	4.10	0	1.416
1996	Montreal	NL	22	32.2	22	14	26	1	0	2.20	0	1.102
Post All-Star			22	32.2	22	14	26	1	0	2.20	0	1.102

CURT LESKANIC   Age 28/R $2

There were always questions among Rockies people about his ability to be a long-term closer. Now the same Rockies people think he's become shell-shocked by arm problems and pitching in Denver. All the above does not constitute a ringing endorsement for his services.

Year	Team	Lg.	G	IP	H	BB	SO	W	L	ERA	SV	Ratio
1993	Colorado	NL	18	57.0	59	27	30	1	5	5.37	0	1.509
1994	Colorado	NL	8	22.1	27	10	17	1	1	5.64	0	1.657
1995	Colorado	NL	76	98.0	83	33	107	6	3	3.40	10	1.184
1996	Colorado	NL	70	73.2	82	38	76	7	5	6.23	6	1.629
Post All-Star			38	40.0	38	20	43	2	2	6.30	0	1.450

BARRY MANUEL   Age 31/R $4

For half the season, we thought it was Barry Manilow pitching for the Expos and we wondered how that skinny little singer geek who's made millions out of sappy love songs that make portly women swoon could have come up with such a good split-finger fastball. Then around the All-Star break, we realized it wasn't Barry Manilow and we immediately became fans of this decent middle reliever with the ability to pile up a useful collection of garbage wins.

Year	Team	Lg.	G	IP	H	BB	SO	W	L	ERA	SV	Ratio
1996	Montreal	NL	53	86.0	70	26	62	4	1	3.24	0	1.116
Post All-Star			24	35.1	28	6	22	2	1	2.55	0	0.962

T. J. MATHEWS   Age 27/R $7

"Everything he throws is nasty—a nasty sinking fastball, a nasty cutter, a nasty slider," said Dave Duncan. "He just has to trust how nasty he throws and that can take some time for a young pitcher to understand." There's no one better to learn "nasty" from than Dunc and Eck. And as Eck takes that last turn toward retirement, this is the guy being groomed as his Cardinals closer successor. So jump on his bandwagon early.

Year	Team	Lg.	G	IP	H	BB	SO	W	L	ERA	SV	Ratio
1995	St. Louis	NL	23	29.2	21	11	28	1	1	1.52	2	1.079
1996	St. Louis	NL	67	83.2	62	32	80	2	6	3.01	6	1.124
Post All-Star			32	36.0	32	13	37	1	4	4.00	3	1.250

GREG McMICHAEL   Age 30/R $6

When asked if being pitched 73 times might have tired him out and contributed to a somewhat inflated late-season ERA, Rockin' Leo Mazzone, the Braves' inimitable pitching coach, just laughed. "Tired? Heck, Mac doesn't throw hard enough to get hurt by being tired," said Mazzone. Pause. "Didn't you ask me the same dumb question about Clontzie?"

Year	Team	Lg.	G	IP	H	BB	SO	W	L	ERA	SV	Ratio
1993	Atlanta	NL	74	91.2	68	29	89	2	3	2.06	19	1.058
1994	Atlanta	NL	51	58.2	66	19	47	4	6	3.84	21	1.449
1995	Atlanta	NL	67	80.2	64	32	74	7	2	2.79	2	1.190
1996	Atlanta	NL	73	86.2	84	27	78	5	3	3.22	2	1.281
Post All-Star			32	37.1	37	12	36	2	2	3.38	1	1.313

DAN MICELI
Age 26/R $1

Jim Leyland never thought he would be a closer. Neither did pitching coach Ray Miller. Now, Miceli is neither's responsibility anymore. Neither is he anything more than a fringe pitcher—for the Tigers, God help him.

Year	Team	Lg.	G	IP	H	BB	SO	W	L	ERA	SV	Ratio
1993	Pittsburgh	NL	9	5.1	6	3	4	0	0	5.06	0	1.688
1994	Pittsburgh	NL	28	27.1	28	11	27	2	1	5.93	2	1.427
1995	Pittsburgh	NL	58	58.0	61	28	56	4	4	4.66	21	1.534
1996	Pittsburgh	NL	44	85.2	99	45	66	2	10	5.78	1	1.681
Post All-Star			14	44.2	56	25	33	1	6	6.85	0	1.813

DAVE MLICKI
Age 28/R $3

Though he is likely never destined for the rotation, he is a valuable guy to have around as a spot starter and utility man in the bullpen.

Year	Team	Lg.	G	IP	H	BB	SO	W	L	ERA	SV	Ratio
1993	Cleveland	AL	3	13.1	11	6	7	0	0	3.38	0	1.275
1995	New York	NL	29	160.2	160	54	123	9	7	4.26	0	1.332
1996	New York	NL	51	90.0	95	33	83	6	7	3.30	1	1.422
Post All-Star			26	38.2	38	17	36	2	4	3.49	0	1.422

ALVIN MORMAN
Age 28/L $1

A lefty equally mediocre against left-handed hitters (.260 vs. him) and right-handed hitters (.261 vs. him). There's something to be said for consistency.

Year	Team	Lg.	G	IP	H	BB	SO	W	L	ERA	SV	Ratio
1996	Houston	NL	53	42.0	43	24	31	4	1	4.93	0	1.595
Post All-Star			24	17.2	17	11	19	3	0	4.08	0	1.585

MIKE MUNOZ
Age 31/L $1

There's also something to be said for being a specialist. So this lefty dominated (.200) lefties as he was paid to do while getting hammered (.352) by those few righties he was allowed to face.

Year	Team	Lg.	G	IP	H	BB	SO	W	L	ERA	SV	Ratio
1993	Detroit	AL	8	3.0	4	6	1	0	1	6.00	0	3.333
1993	Colorado	NL	21	18.0	21	9	16	2	1	4.50	0	1.667
1994	Colorado	NL	57	45.2	37	31	32	4	2	3.74	1	1.489
1995	Colorado	NL	64	43.2	54	27	37	2	4	7.42	2	1.855
1996	Colorado	NL	54	44.2	55	16	45	2	2	6.65	0	1.590
Post All-Star			26	20.2	27	6	23	2	1	6.10	0	1.597

RODNEY MYERS
Age 27/R $1

Fringe guy.

Year	Team	Lg.	G	IP	H	BB	SO	W	L	ERA	SV	Ratio
1996	Chicago	NL	45	67.1	61	38	50	2	1	4.68	0	1.470
Post All-Star			18	30.1	29	23	19	1	0	5.64	0	1.714

Catchers
pp. 27–39

Corners
pp. 40–60

Infield
pp. 60–80

Outfield
pp. 80–111

DH
pp. 112–115

Starters
pp. 115–145

Relievers
pp. 146–178

ROBB NEN
Age 27/R $36

They don't come any better, unless they're named Trevor Hoffman.

Year	Team	Lg.	G	IP	H	BB	SO	W	L	ERA	SV	Ratio
1993	Texas	AL	9	22.2	28	26	12	1	1	6.35	0	2.382
1993	Florida	NL	15	33.1	35	20	27	1	0	7.02	0	1.650
1994	Florida	NL	44	58.0	46	17	60	5	5	2.95	15	1.086
1995	Florida	NL	62	65.2	62	23	68	0	7	3.29	23	1.294
1996	Florida	NL	75	83.0	67	21	92	5	1	1.95	35	1.060
Post All-Star			34	37.0	27	8	39	2	0	1.46	18	0.946

GREGG OLSON
Age 30/R $1

The Otter might be extinct.

Year	Team	Lg.	G	IP	H	BB	SO	W	L	ERA	SV	Ratio
1993	Baltimore	AL	50	45.0	37	18	44	0	2	1.60	29	1.222
1994	Atlanta	NL	16	14.2	19	13	10	0	2	9.20	1	2.182
1995	Cleveland	AL	3	2.2	5	2	0	0	0	13.50	0	2.625
1995	Kansas City	AL	20	30.1	23	17	21	3	3	3.26	3	1.319
1996	Detroit	AL	43	43.0	43	28	29	3	0	5.02	8	1.651
1996	Houston	NL	9	9.1	12	7	8	1	0	4.82	0	2.036
Post All-Star			23	20.2	30	12	17	3	0	6.10	4	2.032

ANTONIO OSUNA
Age 23/R $9

Only a handful of pitchers in the game have his big-time stuff. It just comes down to when he can learn how to maintain consistently all that inside baseball stuff like release points, mechanics, throwing lanes, changes of speed, hitters' tendencies, biorhythms, atmospheric conditions, planetary influences, dietary habits, bilingual adaptation, muscle memory, and luck that create stars. At least his luck has started changing with the departure of Tommy Lasorda, who, for all his contributions to the game's modern era, killed young relievers. At risk of sounding redundant, the same could be said for . . .

Year	Team	Lg.	G	IP	H	BB	SO	W	L	ERA	SV	Ratio
1995	Los Angeles	NL	39	44.2	39	20	46	2	4	4.43	0	1.321
1996	Los Angeles	NL	73	84.0	65	32	85	9	6	3.00	4	1.155
Post All-Star			33	33.1	32	12	37	5	3	4.59	2	1.320

CHAN HO PARK
Age 23/R $8

. . . except for one significant caveat—if and when the Dodgers move aside Tom Candiotti from the rotation, Park will move right in and become one of the league's most promising starting pitchers.

Year	Team	Lg.	G	IP	H	BB	SO	W	L	ERA	SV	Ratio
1994	Los Angeles	NL	2	4.0	5	5	6	0	0	11.25	0	2.500
1995	Los Angeles	NL	2	4.0	2	2	7	0	0	4.50	0	1.000
1996	Los Angeles	NL	48	108.2	82	71	119	5	5	3.64	0	1.408
Post All-Star			19	41.0	35	25	43	0	3	4.39	0	1.463

JEFF PARRETT
Age 35/R $1

Have arm, will travel. It doesn't necessarily make for a valuable Rotisserie plum, but in this day of pampered pitchers who know more about MRI than ERA, there's something to be said for someone who is always willing to take the ball.

Year	Team	Lg.	G	IP	H	BB	SO	W	L	ERA	SV	Ratio
1993	Colorado	NL	40	73.2	78	45	66	3	3	5.38	1	1.670
1995	St. Louis	NL	59	76.2	71	28	71	4	7	3.64	0	1.291
1996	St. Louis	NL	33	42.1	40	20	42	2	2	4.25	0	1.417
1996	Philadelphia	NL	18	24.0	24	11	22	1	1	1.88	0	1.458
Post All-Star			21	27.0	28	12	25	1	1	2.67	0	1.481

BOB PATTERSON   Age 37/L $3

Ditto, albeit more valuable because he's a lefty.

Year	Team	Lg.	G	IP	H	BB	SO	W	L	ERA	SV	Ratio
1993	Texas	AL	52	52.2	59	11	46	2	4	4.78	1	1.329
1994	California	AL	47	42.0	35	15	30	2	3	4.07	1	1.190
1995	California	AL	62	53.1	48	13	41	5	2	3.04	0	1.144
1996	Chicago	NL	79	54.2	46	22	53	3	3	3.13	8	1.244
Post All-Star			34	24.1	24	10	18	0	1	4.81	7	1.397

YORKIS PEREZ   Age 29/L $1

A lefty reliever against whom left-handed hitters bat .299 generally does not get many second chances.

Year	Team	Lg.	G	IP	H	BB	SO	W	L	ERA	SV	Ratio
1994	Florida	NL	44	40.2	33	14	41	3	0	3.54	0	1.156
1995	Florida	NL	69	46.2	35	28	47	2	6	5.21	0	1.350
1996	Florida	NL	64	47.2	51	31	47	3	4	5.29	0	1.720
Post All-Star			23	15.2	25	13	18	1	2	8.62	0	2.426

CHRIS PETERS   Age 25/L $1

Tried as a starter. Tried as a reliever. In the words of another NL manager, "He should be trying in Double-A."

Year	Team	Lg.	G	IP	H	BB	SO	W	L	ERA	SV	Ratio
1996	Pittsburgh	NL	16	64.0	72	25	28	2	4	5.63	0	1.516
Post All-Star			16	64.0	72	25	28	2	4	5.63	0	1.516

MARK PETKOVSEK   Age 31/R $3

He could still return to the rotation but LaRussa loves him in that middle-relief niche and you'd love him too if you picked him up cheap and luxuriated in those 11 wins that followed.

Year	Team	Lg.	G	IP	H	BB	SO	W	L	ERA	SV	Ratio
1993	Pittsburgh	NL	26	32.1	43	9	14	3	0	6.96	0	1.608
1995	St. Louis	NL	26	137.1	136	35	71	6	6	4.00	0	1.245
1996	St. Louis	NL	48	88.2	83	35	45	11	2	3.55	0	1.331
Post All-Star			30	45.0	35	19	28	6	2	2.60	0	1.200

DAN PLESAC   Age 35/L $4

Leyland/Miller used him well in any number of different roles. Now it's back to the AL, where he was once an ace closer. The guy can still pitch.

Year	Team	Lg.	G	IP	H	BB	SO	W	L	ERA	SV	Ratio
1993	Chicago	NL	57	62.2	74	21	47	2	1	4.74	0	1.516
1994	Chicago	NL	54	54.2	61	13	53	2	3	4.61	1	1.354
1995	Pittsburgh	NL	58	60.1	53	27	57	4	4	3.58	3	1.326
1996	Pittsburgh	NL	73	70.1	67	24	76	6	5	4.09	11	1.294
Post All-Star			33	29.2	30	13	31	3	4	3.94	6	1.449

JIM POOLE   Age 30/L $3

To the pitching-awful Giants, he looked like Sandy Koufax. But why is it that we tend automatically to devalue any pitcher unfortunate enough to wear that Giants uniform? He's actually pretty good.

Year	Team	Lg.	G	IP	H	BB	SO	W	L	ERA	SV	Ratio
1993	Baltimore	AL	55	50.1	30	21	29	2	1	2.15	2	1.013
1994	Baltimore	AL	38	20.1	32	11	18	1	0	6.64	0	2.115
1995	Cleveland	AL	42	50.1	40	17	41	3	3	3.75	0	1.132
1996	Cleveland	AL	32	26.2	29	14	19	4	0	3.04	0	1.612
1996	San Francisco	NL	35	23.2	15	13	19	2	1	2.66	0	1.183
Post All-Star			35	23.2	15	13	19	2	1	2.66	0	1.183

JAY POWELL   Age 25/R $3

Outstanding arm, outstanding potential, outstanding situation in that he can establish himself further as a set-up man with Robb Nen closing. That the Orioles traded him away for Bret Barberie is another reason why Pat Gillick inherited such a shaky Orioles organization.

Year	Team	Lg.	G	IP	H	BB	SO	W	L	ERA	SV	Ratio
1995	Florida	NL	9	8.1	7	6	4	0	0	1.08	0	1.560
1996	Florida	NL	67	71.1	71	36	52	4	3	4.54	2	1.500
Post All-Star			39	43.2	48	17	35	2	3	5.15	1	1.489

SCOTT RADINSKY   Age 29/L $3

Another reason why the Dodgers' bullpen trots out better stuff from top to bottom than any in baseball.

Year	Team	Lg.	G	IP	H	BB	SO	W	L	ERA	SV	Ratio
1993	Chicago	AL	73	54.2	61	19	44	8	2	4.28	4	1.463
1995	Chicago	AL	46	38.0	46	17	14	2	1	5.45	1	1.658
1996	Los Angeles	NL	58	52.1	52	17	48	5	1	2.41	1	1.318
Post All-Star			30	26.1	25	8	26	5	0	2.39	0	1.253

STEVE REED   Age 31/R $2

When his name came up in a trade rumor, Rockies manager Don Baylor said, "The trouble with trading Steve Reed is that it would be so hard to find someone to fill that Steve Reed role." We're not quite sure what that means. We do know that you don't gain a whole lot from having that Steve Reed role filled on your team.

Year	Team	Lg.	G	IP	H	BB	SO	W	L	ERA	SV	Ratio
1993	Colorado	NL	64	84.1	80	30	51	9	5	4.48	3	1.304
1994	Colorado	NL	61	64.0	79	26	51	3	2	3.94	3	1.641
1995	Colorado	NL	71	84.0	61	21	79	5	2	2.14	3	0.976
1996	Colorado	NL	70	75.0	66	19	51	4	3	3.96	0	1.133
Post All-Star			30	30.0	29	7	23	3	1	3.30	0	1.200

MEL ROJAS   Age 30/R $34

By being so good, he became unsignable by the Expos' owners, who should do the right thing and just sell the damn club to owners who will bring it to a city where it can be supported and appreciated.

Year	Team	Lg.	G	IP	H	BB	SO	W	L	ERA	SV	Ratio
1993	Montreal	NL	66	88.1	80	30	48	5	8	2.95	10	1.245
1994	Montreal	NL	58	84.0	71	21	84	3	2	3.32	16	1.095
1995	Montreal	NL	59	67.2	69	29	61	1	4	4.12	30	1.448
1996	Montreal	NL	74	81.0	56	28	92	7	4	3.22	36	1.037
Post All-Star			35	37.2	16	10	42	2	1	0.96	24	0.690

BRUCE RUFFIN   Age 33/L $19

For better and sometimes worse, he's the Rockies' closer.

Year	Team	Lg.	G	IP	H	BB	SO	W	L	ERA	SV	Ratio
1993	Colorado	NL	59	139.2	145	69	126	6	5	3.87	2	1.532
1994	Colorado	NL	56	55.2	55	30	65	4	5	4.04	16	1.527
1995	Colorado	NL	37	34.0	26	19	23	0	1	2.12	11	1.324
1996	Colorado	NL	71	69.2	55	29	74	7	5	4.00	24	1.206
Post All-Star			31	33.2	23	14	39	4	2	2.94	11	1.099

KEN RYAN   Age 28/R $12

On a terrible Phillies team, he was one of the very few bright spots. The Ryan-Bottalico bullpen tandem was one of most underrated in baseball, and both of them should be able to do it for a few years to come.

Year	Team	Lg.	G	IP	H	BB	SO	W	L	ERA	SV	Ratio
1993	Boston	AL	47	50.0	43	29	49	7	2	3.60	1	1.440
1994	Boston	AL	42	48.0	46	17	32	2	3	2.44	13	1.313
1995	Boston	AL	28	32.2	34	24	34	0	4	4.96	7	1.776
1996	Philadelphia	NL	62	89.0	71	45	71	3	5	2.43	8	1.303
Post All-Star			29	40.2	33	22	26	1	2	1.77	4	1.352

TIM SCOTT   Age 30/R $1

He used to be a solid middle reliever, but then he got traded to San Francisco, where he's become just another suspect like every other Giants pitcher.

Year	Team	Lg.	G	IP	H	BB	SO	W	L	ERA	SV	Ratio
1993	San Diego	NL	24	37.2	38	15	30	2	0	2.39	0	1.407
1993	Montreal	NL	32	34.0	31	19	35	5	2	3.71	1	1.471
1994	Montreal	NL	40	53.1	51	18	37	5	2	2.70	1	1.294
1995	Montreal	NL	62	63.1	52	23	57	2	0	3.98	2	1.184
1996	Montreal	NL	45	46.1	41	21	37	3	5	3.11	1	1.338
1996	San Francisco	NL	20	19.2	24	9	10	2	2	8.24	0	1.678
Post All-Star			26	25.1	31	14	12	3	3	7.11	0	1.776

JEFF SHAW   Age 30/R $12

Had a monster year for the Reds in which he held lefty hitters to a .191 average and pitched more relief innings than anyone in the league. In the process he made obsolete . . .

Year	Team	Lg.	G	IP	H	BB	SO	W	L	ERA	SV	Ratio
1993	Montreal	NL	55	95.2	91	32	50	2	7	4.14	0	1.286
1994	Montreal	NL	46	67.1	67	15	47	5	2	3.88	1	1.218
1995	Montreal	NL	50	62.1	58	26	45	1	6	4.62	3	1.348
1995	Chicago	AL	9	9.2	12	1	6	0	0	6.52	0	1.345
1996	Cincinnati	NL	78	104.2	99	29	69	8	6	2.49	4	1.223
Post All-Star			39	55.0	46	18	31	6	3	1.96	2	1.164

Catchers
pp. 27–39

Corners
pp. 40–60

Infield
pp. 60–80

Outfield
pp. 80–111

DH
pp. 112–115

Starters
pp. 115–145

Relievers
pp. 146–178

LEE SMITH
Age 39/R   **$1**

. . . who's had a long, great run, but for whom time may have finally run out.

Year	Team	Lg.	G	IP	H	BB	SO	W	L	ERA	SV	Ratio
1993	St. Louis	NL	55	50.0	49	9	49	2	4	4.50	43	1.160
1993	New York	AL	8	8.0	4	5	11	0	0	0.00	3	1.125
1994	Baltimore	AL	41	38.1	34	11	42	1	4	3.29	33	1.174
1995	California	AL	52	49.1	42	25	43	0	5	3.47	37	1.358
1996	California	AL	11	11.0	8	3	6	0	0	2.45	0	1.000
1996	Cincinnati	NL	43	44.1	49	23	35	3	4	4.06	2	1.624
Post All-Star			28	28.2	27	16	25	2	2	3.77	0	1.500

RUSS SPRINGER
Age 28/R   **$1**

No thanks.

Year	Team	Lg.	G	IP	H	BB	SO	W	L	ERA	SV	Ratio
1993	California	AL	14	60.0	73	32	31	1	6	7.20	0	1.750
1994	California	AL	18	45.2	53	14	28	2	2	5.52	2	1.467
1995	California	AL	19	51.2	60	25	38	1	2	6.10	1	1.645
1995	Philadelphia	NL	14	26.2	22	10	32	0	0	3.71	0	1.200
1996	Philadelphia	NL	51	96.2	106	38	94	3	10	4.66	0	1.490
Post All-Star			20	48.1	55	16	34	1	4	4.47	0	1.469

UGUETH URBINA
Age 23/R   **$8**

Montreal often would use a plastic, life-sized baseball player as a training aid for some of their young pitchers when they would throw in practice. The plastic guy was deemphasized, however, after Ugie knocked its head sideways with a 96-mile-per-hour bullet. If the Expos dump Mel Rojas's salary, you're looking at the new Montreal closer. And he could be fun to watch.

Year	Team	Lg.	G	IP	H	BB	SO	W	L	ERA	SV	Ratio
1995	Montreal	NL	7	23.1	26	14	15	2	2	6.17	0	1.714
1996	Montreal	NL	33	114.0	102	44	108	10	5	3.71	0	1.281
Post All-Star			24	64.1	51	28	64	6	3	3.08	0	1.228

MARC VALDES
Age 25/R   **$1**

A long shot to be in the Marlins' rotation, a question mark to be worth anything in the bullpen.

Year	Team	Lg.	G	IP	H	BB	SO	W	L	ERA	SV	Ratio
1995	Florida	NL	3	7.0	17	9	2	0	0	14.14	0	3.714
1996	Florida	NL	11	48.2	63	23	13	1	3	4.81	0	1.767
Post All-Star			11	48.2	63	23	13	1	3	4.81	0	1.767

DAVE VERES
Age 30/R   **$7**

A very useful guy who will remain useful wherever he pitches, assuming that he might earn too many francs to fit in the Expos' budget.

Year	Team	Lg.	G	IP	H	BB	SO	W	L	ERA	SV	Ratio
1994	Houston	NL	32	41.0	39	7	28	3	3	2.41	1	1.122
1995	Houston	NL	72	103.1	89	30	94	5	1	2.26	1	1.152
1996	Montreal	NL	68	77.2	85	32	81	6	3	4.17	4	1.506
Post All-Star			31	31.1	29	13	31	2	1	2.30	0	1.340

TERRELL WADE

Age 24/L   **$6**

Right now, he is a hard-throwing lefty out of the bullpen. That's where he likely stays for the foreseeable future. As our friend Rockin' Leon put it, "Who would you want him to replace in the rotation?"

Year	Team	Lg.	G	IP	H	BB	SO	W	L	ERA	SV	Ratio
1995	Atlanta	NL	3	4.0	3	4	3	0	1	4.50	0	1.750
1996	Atlanta	NL	44	69.2	57	47	79	5	0	2.97	1	1.493
Post All-Star			18	42.1	36	32	50	3	0	4.04	0	1.606

BILLY WAGNER

Age 25/L   **$22**

We defer to teammate Craig Biggio. "In spring training, he looked all right but he was nervous, probably overthrowing, and looked like just another skinny rookie," said Biggio. "But then they brought him up early and they bring him in against the Braves one day and he throws about 10 straight bullets right by McGriff and Klesko. And it was like we all looked at each other in the infield as if to say 'Whoa, what do we have here?'" What we have is a star in the making.

Year	Team	Lg.	G	IP	H	BB	SO	W	L	ERA	SV	Ratio
1995	Houston	NL	1	0.1	0	0	0	0	0	0.00	0	0.000
1996	Houston	NL	37	51.2	28	30	67	2	2	2.44	9	1.123
Post All-Star			26	30.1	19	19	39	1	2	2.67	7	1.253

TURK WENDELL

Age 29/R   **$21**

Stopped trying to be a folk hero and concentrated on pitching. The results were very encouraging.

Year	Team	Lg.	G	IP	H	BB	SO	W	L	ERA	SV	Ratio
1993	Chicago	NL	7	22.2	24	8	15	1	2	4.37	0	1.412
1994	Chicago	NL	6	14.1	22	10	9	0	1	11.93	0	2.233
1995	Chicago	NL	43	60.1	71	24	50	3	1	4.92	0	1.575
1996	Chicago	NL	70	79.1	58	44	75	4	5	2.84	18	1.286
Post All-Star			35	36.1	27	15	27	0	3	3.47	11	1.156

MARK WOHLERS

Age 27/R   **$39**

The next time someone claims that players don't get jacked up for the All-Star game, remember this tale. Pirates catcher Jason Kendall arrived from the bullpen after warming up Wohlers, who was entering the game. "I think he broke my hand," said Kendall. "I can't believe how hard he was throwing." Whereupon, Wohlers reached the mound and his first four pitches were clocked at 101, 99, 100, 100. Aside from usually having a dead arm for a few outings somewhere along the way, he's as good as it gets.

Year	Team	Lg.	G	IP	H	BB	SO	W	L	ERA	SV	Ratio
1993	Atlanta	NL	46	48.0	37	22	45	6	2	4.50	0	1.229
1994	Atlanta	NL	51	51.0	51	33	58	7	2	4.59	1	1.647
1995	Atlanta	NL	65	64.2	51	24	90	7	3	2.09	25	1.160
1996	Atlanta	NL	77	77.1	71	21	100	2	4	3.03	39	1.190
Post All-Star			36	35.2	36	5	49	2	3	3.28	21	1.150

TODD WORRELL
Age 37/R $38

All those years he lost to arm trouble are helping him now, because his arm is much younger than his age. He's better than ever.

Year	Team	Lg.	G	IP	H	BB	SO	W	L	ERA	SV	Ratio
1993	Los Angeles	NL	35	38.2	46	11	31	1	1	6.05	5	1.474
1994	Los Angeles	NL	38	42.0	37	12	44	6	5	4.29	11	1.167
1995	Los Angeles	NL	59	62.1	50	19	61	4	1	2.02	32	1.107
1996	Los Angeles	NL	72	65.1	70	15	66	4	6	3.03	44	1.301
Post All-Star			33	29.0	35	10	27	1	2	3.10	21	1.552

AMERICAN LEAGUE

BRIAN ANDERSON
Age 24/L $2

This is a tough call in our world. He pitches a lot of innings and starts here and there, but never seems to get any wins. But hey, he's a lefty on a good team—may be worth a try.

Year	Team	Lg.	G	IP	H	BB	SO	W	L	ERA	SV	Ratio
1993	California	AL	4	11.1	11	2	4	0	0	3.97	0	1.147
1994	California	AL	18	101.2	120	27	47	7	5	5.22	0	1.446
1995	California	AL	18	99.2	110	30	45	6	8	5.87	0	1.405
1996	Cleveland	AL	10	51.1	58	14	21	3	1	4.91	0	1.403
Post All-Star			5	22.1	23	5	7	3	0	3.63	0	1.254

PAUL ASSENMACHER
Age 36/L $5

The classic tenth pitcher. He can still make guys look silly up there, and you won't look silly if you've got him.

Year	Team	Lg.	G	IP	H	BB	SO	W	L	ERA	SV	Ratio
1993	Chicago	NL	46	38.2	44	13	34	2	1	3.49	0	1.474
1993	New York	AL	26	17.1	10	9	11	2	2	3.12	0	1.096
1994	Chicago	AL	44	33.0	26	13	29	1	2	3.55	1	1.182
1995	Cleveland	AL	47	38.1	32	12	40	6	2	2.82	0	1.148
1996	Cleveland	AL	63	46.2	46	14	44	4	2	3.09	1	1.286
Post All-Star			27	21.0	20	4	20	4	1	4.29	0	1.143

BOBBY AYALA
Age 27/R $4

He gives up too many hits to help you, or the Mariners.

Year	Team	Lg.	G	IP	H	BB	SO	W	L	ERA	SV	Ratio
1993	Cincinnati	NL	43	98.0	106	45	65	7	10	5.60	3	1.541
1994	Seattle	AL	46	56.2	42	26	76	4	3	2.86	18	1.200
1995	Seattle	AL	63	71.0	73	30	77	6	5	4.44	19	1.451
1996	Seattle	AL	50	67.1	65	25	61	6	3	5.88	3	1.337
Post All-Star			32	43.2	43	17	38	5	2	5.36	3	1.374

ARMANDO BENITEZ
Age 24/R $9

If the Orioles are smart, they'll use the long-awaited Benitez in a set-up role the way the Yankees used Mariano Rivera. Last year he showed more than a flash of his promise. But that grand slam lollipop he served to Albert Belle showed how young he is.

Year	Team	Lg.	G	IP	H	BB	SO	W	L	ERA	SV	Ratio
1994	Baltimore	AL	3	10.0	8	4	14	0	0	0.90	0	1.200
1995	Baltimore	AL	44	47.2	37	37	56	1	5	5.66	2	1.552
1996	Baltimore	AL	18	14.1	7	6	20	1	0	3.77	4	0.907
Post All-Star			14	10.1	5	3	14	0	0	2.61	4	0.774

BRIAN BOEHRINGER   Age 27/R $2

With all that Yankee pitching, guys like Boehringer are way down the list. Wait and see.

Year	Team	Lg.	G	IP	H	BB	SO	W	L	ERA	SV	Ratio
1995	New York	AL	7	17.2	24	22	10	0	3	13.75	0	2.604
1996	New York	AL	15	46.1	46	21	37	2	4	5.44	0	1.446
Post All-Star			12	32.1	23	12	30	2	2	3.34	0	1.082

MARK BRANDENBURG   Age 26/R $5

Solid pitcher who could do well in a full season at Fenway. Or, not.

Year	Team	Lg.	G	IP	H	BB	SO	W	L	ERA	SV	Ratio
1995	Texas	AL	11	27.1	36	7	21	0	1	5.93	0	1.573
1996	Texas	AL	26	47.2	48	25	37	1	3	3.21	0	1.531
1996	Boston	AL	29	28.1	28	8	29	4	2	3.81	0	1.271
Post All-Star			34	34.0	37	14	33	4	5	5.03	0	1.500

RAFAEL CARMONA   Age 24/R $5

Carmona is showing nice vulture tendencies. In fact, *Vultura Carmona* is a Mexican delicacy. Worth a shot.

Year	Team	Lg.	G	IP	H	BB	SO	W	L	ERA	SV	Ratio
1995	Seattle	AL	15	47.2	55	34	28	2	4	5.66	1	1.867
1996	Seattle	AL	53	90.1	95	55	62	8	3	4.28	1	1.661
Post All-Star			25	45.1	50	24	27	3	3	4.37	0	1.632

TONY CASTILLO   Age 34/L $5

We said it last year and we'll say it again. Nice little pitcher.

Year	Team	Lg.	G	IP	H	BB	SO	W	L	ERA	SV	Ratio
1993	Toronto	AL	51	50.2	44	22	28	3	2	3.38	0	1.303
1994	Toronto	AL	41	68.0	66	28	43	5	2	2.51	1	1.382
1995	Toronto	AL	55	72.2	64	24	38	1	5	3.22	13	1.211
1996	Toronto	AL	40	72.1	72	20	48	2	3	4.23	1	1.272
1996	Chicago	AL	15	22.2	23	4	9	3	1	1.59	1	1.191
Post All-Star			26	41.2	45	6	23	3	3	3.46	2	1.224

NORM CHARLTON   Age 34/L $15

When Roger Clemens stepped in against Charlton at Fenway in June, Norm just hummed it in there. No curves, no change-ups, no trickery. In response, Clemens ripped a single through the box that knocked Charlton on his ass. After the game, Charlton was unrepentant and took it like a man. We already liked the guy, but he added to his legacy that night. No reason he can't keep these numbers coming.

Year	Team	Lg.	G	IP	H	BB	SO	W	L	ERA	SV	Ratio
1993	Seattle	AL	34	34.2	22	17	48	1	3	2.34	18	1.125
1995	Philadelphia	NL	25	22.0	23	15	12	2	5	7.36	0	1.727
1995	Seattle	AL	30	47.2	23	16	58	2	1	1.51	14	0.818
1996	Seattle	AL	70	75.2	68	38	73	4	7	4.04	20	1.401
Post All-Star			36	38.0	36	19	34	2	4	3.79	7	1.447

MIKE CHRISTOPHER

Age 33/R $1

Last year we said he was promising. Whoops!

Year	Team	Lg.	G	IP	H	BB	SO	W	L	ERA	SV	Ratio
1993	Cleveland	AL	9	11.2	14	2	8	0	0	3.86	0	1.371
1995	Detroit	AL	36	61.1	71	14	34	4	0	3.82	1	1.386
1996	Detroit	AL	13	30.0	47	11	19	1	1	9.30	0	1.933
Post All-Star			0	0.0	0	0	0	0	0	0.00	0	0.000

DENNIS COOK

Age 34/L $4

Competent lefty.

Year	Team	Lg.	G	IP	H	BB	SO	W	L	ERA	SV	Ratio
1993	Cleveland	AL	25	54.0	62	16	34	5	5	5.67	0	1.444
1994	Chicago	AL	38	33.0	29	14	26	3	1	3.55	0	1.303
1995	Cleveland	AL	11	12.2	16	10	13	0	0	6.39	0	2.053
1995	Texas	AL	35	45.0	47	16	40	0	2	4.00	2	1.400
1996	Texas	AL	60	70.1	53	35	64	5	2	4.09	0	1.251
Post All-Star			26	25.1	27	15	22	1	1	6.04	0	1.658

JIM CORSI

Age 35/R $8

Should you draft him? Of corsi.

Year	Team	Lg.	G	IP	H	BB	SO	W	L	ERA	SV	Ratio
1993	Florida	NL	15	20.1	28	10	7	0	2	6.64	0	1.869
1995	Oakland	AL	38	45.0	31	26	26	2	4	2.20	2	1.267
1996	Oakland	AL	57	73.2	71	34	43	6	0	4.03	3	1.425
Post All-Star			29	35.2	36	12	21	3	0	4.54	1	1.346

TIM CRABTREE

Age 27/R $4

Competent righty.

Year	Team	Lg.	G	IP	H	BB	SO	W	L	ERA	SV	Ratio
1995	Toronto	AL	31	32.0	30	13	21	0	2	3.09	0	1.344
1996	Toronto	AL	53	67.1	59	22	57	5	3	2.54	1	1.203
Post All-Star			18	23.2	23	12	20	2	1	3.04	0	1.479

JOHN CUMMINGS

Age 27/L $3

Buddy Bell must have really wanted to get rid of Chad Curtis. All the Tigers got in return was John "Not Candy" Cummings and Joey "He's no Albert" Eischen. Two mediocre lefties for a highly effective yet still undeveloped outfielder. Shrewd.

Year	Team	Lg.	G	IP	H	BB	SO	W	L	ERA	SV	Ratio
1993	Seattle	AL	10	46.1	59	16	19	0	6	6.02	0	1.619
1994	Seattle	AL	17	64.0	66	37	33	2	4	5.63	0	1.609
1995	Seattle	AL	4	5.1	8	7	4	0	0	11.81	0	2.813
1995	Los Angeles	NL	35	39.0	38	10	21	3	1	3.00	0	1.231
1996	Los Angeles	NL	4	5.1	12	2	5	0	1	6.75	0	2.625
1996	Detroit	AL	21	31.2	36	20	24	3	3	5.12	0	1.768
Post All-Star			21	31.2	36	20	24	3	3	5.12	0	1.768

TIM DAVIS
Age 26/L   **$2**

Hard to get excited over this guy.

Year	Team	Lg.	G	IP	H	BB	SO	W	L	ERA	SV	Ratio
1994	Seattle	AL	42	49.1	57	25	28	2	2	4.01	2	1.662
1995	Seattle	AL	5	24.0	30	18	19	2	1	6.38	0	2.000
1996	Seattle	AL	40	42.2	43	17	34	2	2	4.01	0	1.406
Post All-Star			20	23.1	28	7	21	2	0	3.47	0	1.500

JOEY EISCHEN
Age 26/L   **$2**

See John Cummings. Eischen won't be worth talking about until he ends up in a bullpen with Dave Eiland and Mark Eichhorn. Then the fun will begin. The phone rings and the crusty old bullpen catcher answers. "Yello." "Get Eischen warm," says the crusty old pitching coach. "Eiland?" "No. Eischen." "God bless you." "What. Just get Eischen warm." "Eichhorn?" "NO! Eischen!" "God bless you." Click.

Year	Team	Lg.	G	IP	H	BB	SO	W	L	ERA	SV	Ratio
1994	Montreal	NL	1	0.2	4	0	1	0	0	54.00	0	6.000
1995	Los Angeles	NL	17	20.1	19	11	15	0	0	3.10	0	1.475
1996	Los Angeles	NL	28	43.1	48	20	36	0	1	4.78	0	1.569
1996	Detroit	AL	24	25.0	27	14	15	1	1	3.24	0	1.640
Post All-Star			29	30.0	31	15	17	1	2	3.30	0	1.533

MIKE FETTERS
Age 32/R   **$32**

Nearly doubled his innings yet his very nice ERA remained exactly the same. Bottom line: ten more saves and three more wins. If the Brew Crew improves like they should, the Fet-Man could flirt with 40.

Year	Team	Lg.	G	IP	H	BB	SO	W	L	ERA	SV	Ratio
1993	Milwaukee	AL	45	59.1	59	22	23	3	3	3.34	0	1.365
1994	Milwaukee	AL	42	46.0	41	27	31	1	4	2.54	17	1.478
1995	Milwaukee	AL	40	34.2	40	20	33	0	3	3.38	22	1.731
1996	Milwaukee	AL	61	61.1	65	26	53	3	3	3.38	32	1.484
Post All-Star			28	30.1	39	7	33	2	2	4.75	16	1.516

RAMON GARCIA
Age 27/R   **$4**

His ERA was, well, bedeviling (6.66).

Year	Team	Lg.	G	IP	H	BB	SO	W	L	ERA	SV	Ratio
1996	Milwaukee	AL	37	75.2	84	21	40	4	4	6.66	4	1.388
Post All-Star			14	34.1	43	8	18	1	2	7.60	1	1.485

BUDDY GROOM
Age 31/L   **$3**

This can't be the guy who used to stink up Tiger Stadium so bad that they're gonna tear it down? Anyway, old Buddy turned in the kind of year that Rotisserie owners pray for when they get stuck with stiffs like old Buddy. Let's see him do it again. Then we'll believe.

Year	Team	Lg.	G	IP	H	BB	SO	W	L	ERA	SV	Ratio
1993	Detroit	AL	19	36.2	48	13	15	0	2	6.14	0	1.664
1994	Detroit	AL	40	32.0	31	13	27	0	1	3.94	1	1.375
1995	Detroit	AL	23	40.2	55	26	23	1	3	7.52	1	1.992
1995	Florida	NL	14	15.0	26	6	12	1	2	7.20	0	2.133
1996	Oakland	AL	72	77.1	85	34	57	5	0	3.84	1	1.539
Post All-Star			32	30.1	34	18	26	2	0	4.45	0	1.714

Catchers
pp. 27–39

Corners
pp. 40–60

Infield
pp. 60–80

Outfield
pp. 80–111

DH
pp. 112–115

Starters
pp. 115–145

Relievers
pp. 146–178

EDDIE GUARDADO   Age 26/L $4

Has all the skills to be a top-flight vulture.

Year	Team	Lg.	G	IP	H	BB	SO	W	L	ERA	SV	Ratio
1993	Minnesota	AL	19	94.2	123	36	46	3	8	6.18	0	1.680
1994	Minnesota	AL	4	17.0	26	4	8	0	2	8.47	0	1.765
1995	Minnesota	AL	51	91.1	99	45	71	4	9	5.12	2	1.577
1996	Minnesota	AL	83	73.2	61	33	74	6	5	5.25	4	1.276
Post All-Star			36	29.0	21	13	35	2	2	5.90	2	1.172

GREG HANSELL   Age 26/R $4

We'd like to say he throws more like Gretel, but we're not sure which one's which. Anyway, the numbers are decent, whoever he throws like.

Year	Team	Lg.	G	IP	H	BB	SO	W	L	ERA	SV	Ratio
1995	Los Angeles	NL	20	19.1	29	6	13	0	1	7.45	0	1.810
1996	Minnesota	AL	50	74.1	83	31	46	3	0	5.69	3	1.534
Post All-Star			21	23.1	29	13	13	0	0	6.94	0	1.800

MIKE HENNEMAN   Age 35/R $20

Let's put it this way: if you have Mike Henneman you still need a closer. The Rangers certainly could have used one. The guy lost seven games, the third most on the team, and his ERA is pretty scary, too. Talk about 30 saves the hard way. Bid him up to the high teens and let him be somebody else's headache.

Year	Team	Lg.	G	IP	H	BB	SO	W	L	ERA	SV	Ratio
1993	Detroit	AL	63	71.2	69	32	58	5	3	2.64	24	1.409
1994	Detroit	AL	30	34.2	43	17	27	1	3	5.19	8	1.731
1995	Detroit	AL	29	29.1	24	9	24	0	1	1.53	18	1.125
1995	Houston	NL	21	21.0	21	4	19	0	1	3.00	8	1.190
1996	Texas	AL	49	42.0	41	17	34	0	7	5.79	31	1.381
Post All-Star			18	14.2	11	4	14	0	0	1.84	10	1.023

GIL HEREDIA   Age 31/R $1

Then again, when Johnny Oates remembers that Heredia is one of his options, he sort of *has* to put the call out for Henneman.

Year	Team	Lg.	G	IP	H	BB	SO	W	L	ERA	SV	Ratio
1993	Montreal	NL	20	57.1	66	14	40	4	2	3.92	2	1.395
1994	Montreal	NL	39	75.1	85	13	62	6	3	3.46	0	1.301
1995	Montreal	NL	40	119.0	137	21	74	5	6	4.31	1	1.328
1996	Texas	AL	44	73.1	91	14	43	2	5	5.89	1	1.432
Post All-Star			15	31.2	34	3	24	1	2	4.26	1	1.168

ROBERTO HERNANDEZ   Age 32/R $38

Study these numbers. *This* is a major league closer.

Year	Team	Lg.	G	IP	H	BB	SO	W	L	ERA	SV	Ratio
1993	Chicago	AL	70	78.2	66	20	71	3	4	2.29	38	1.093
1994	Chicago	AL	45	47.2	44	19	50	4	4	4.91	14	1.322
1995	Chicago	AL	60	59.2	63	28	84	3	7	3.92	32	1.525
1996	Chicago	AL	72	84.2	65	38	85	6	5	1.91	38	1.217
Post All-Star			32	39.2	35	15	42	5	5	2.72	12	1.261

JOE HUDSON
Age 26/R   **$3**

He pitched more like Joe Gowanus Canal. And that stinks.

Year	Team	Lg.	G	IP	H	BB	SO	W	L	ERA	SV	Ratio
1995	Boston	AL	39	46.0	53	23	29	0	1	4.11	1	1.652
1996	Boston	AL	36	45.0	57	32	19	3	5	5.40	1	1.978
Post All-Star			18	21.0	35	12	6	0	2	6.43	1	2.238

EDWIN HURTADO
Age 27/R   **$1**

This man is evil. Those two wins and two saves are the work of Satan, trying to make you believe there is something here. Be strong.

Year	Team	Lg.	G	IP	H	BB	SO	W	L	ERA	SV	Ratio
1995	Toronto	AL	14	77.2	81	40	33	5	2	5.45	0	1.558
1996	Seattle	AL	16	47.2	61	30	36	2	5	7.74	2	1.909
Post All-Star			0	0.0	0	0	0	0	0	0.00	0	0.000

MIKE JACKSON
Age 32/R   **$5**

Respectable, part-time closer who just never quite put it all together.

Year	Team	Lg.	G	IP	H	BB	SO	W	L	ERA	SV	Ratio
1993	San Francisco	NL	81	77.1	58	24	70	6	6	3.03	1	1.060
1994	San Francisco	NL	36	42.1	23	11	51	3	2	1.49	4	0.803
1995	Cincinnati	NL	40	49.0	38	19	41	6	1	2.39	2	1.163
1996	Seattle	AL	73	72.0	61	24	70	1	1	3.63	6	1.181
Post All-Star			34	32.0	20	10	32	0	0	1.97	3	0.938

JASON JACOME
Age 26/L   **$1**

With this Jason, every day is Friday the 13th.

Year	Team	Lg.	G	IP	H	BB	SO	W	L	ERA	SV	Ratio
1994	New York	NL	8	54.0	54	17	30	4	3	2.67	0	1.315
1995	New York	NL	5	21.0	33	15	11	0	4	10.29	0	2.286
1995	Kansas City	AL	15	84.0	101	21	39	4	6	5.36	0	1.452
1996	Kansas City	AL	49	47.2	67	22	32	0	4	4.72	1	1.867
Post All-Star			18	10.1	17	6	7	0	2	6.10	1	2.226

MIKE JAMES
Age 29/R   **$9**

He pitched 26 more innings last year, and only the walks increased, while the hits and ERA stayed the same. It's a good sign; he may be a late bloomer. You might get lucky and pick up a solid middle reliever for chump change.

Year	Team	Lg.	G	IP	H	BB	SO	W	L	ERA	SV	Ratio
1995	California	AL	46	55.2	49	26	36	3	0	3.88	1	1.347
1996	California	AL	69	81.0	62	42	65	5	5	2.67	1	1.284
Post All-Star			29	31.0	25	16	24	0	1	3.19	0	1.323

Catchers
pp. 27-39

Corners
pp. 40-60

Infield
pp. 60-80

Outfield
pp. 80-111

DH
pp. 112-115

Starters
pp. 115-145

Relievers
pp. 146-178

DOUG JONES Age 39/R $4

The age really isn't a problem since he gets by on good control and lots of garbage. Fetters, however, is the closer, which is a problem. Worth a small investment only.

Year	Team	Lg.	G	IP	H	BB	SO	W	L	ERA	SV	Ratio
1993	Houston	NL	71	85.1	102	21	66	4	10	4.54	26	1.441
1994	Philadelphia	NL	47	54.0	55	6	38	2	4	2.17	27	1.130
1995	Baltimore	AL	52	46.2	55	16	42	0	4	5.01	22	1.521
1996	Chicago	NL	28	32.1	41	7	26	2	2	5.01	2	1.485
1996	Milwaukee	AL	24	31.2	31	13	34	5	0	3.41	1	1.389
Post All-Star			24	31.2	31	13	34	5	0	3.41	1	1.389

MATT KARCHNER Age 29/R $5

We told you to pick him up last year. We apologize for the ERA, but seven wins and a save is about all you can expect from a decent middle relief man, which is what Karchner is. We've dropped our expectations, and so should you.

Year	Team	Lg.	G	IP	H	BB	SO	W	L	ERA	SV	Ratio
1995	Chicago	AL	31	32.0	33	12	24	4	2	1.69	0	1.406
1996	Chicago	AL	50	59.1	61	41	46	7	4	5.76	1	1.719
Post All-Star			11	10.1	20	9	9	0	2	11.32	0	2.806

GREG KEAGLE Age 25/R $1

It's hard to imagine that he could have been worse.

Year	Team	Lg.	G	IP	H	BB	SO	W	L	ERA	SV	Ratio
1996	Detroit	AL	26	87.2	104	68	70	3	6	7.39	0	1.962
Post All-Star			7	24.0	17	14	26	0	0	3.00	0	1.292

BRIAN KEYSER Age 30/R $1

Brian will spend most of his time on his keyster.

Year	Team	Lg.	G	IP	H	BB	SO	W	L	ERA	SV	Ratio
1995	Chicago	AL	23	92.1	114	27	48	5	6	4.97	0	1.527
1996	Chicago	AL	28	59.2	78	28	19	1	2	4.98	1	1.777
Post All-Star			7	11.1	16	5	3	0	2	6.35	0	1.853

RICK KRIVDA Age 27/L $1

Meaningless, undistinguished, and utterly forgettable. And he's missing a vowel.

Year	Team	Lg.	G	IP	H	BB	SO	W	L	ERA	SV	Ratio
1995	Baltimore	AL	13	75.1	76	25	53	2	7	4.54	0	1.341
1996	Baltimore	AL	22	81.2	89	39	54	3	5	4.96	0	1.567
Post All-Star			10	37.1	39	18	20	1	1	5.30	0	1.527

RICHIE LEWIS Age 31/R $2

There are one or two guys like this on every team. Good thing. If you had one or two more, you'd really be lousy.

Year	Team	Lg.	G	IP	H	BB	SO	W	L	ERA	SV	Ratio
1993	Florida	NL	57	77.1	68	43	65	6	3	3.26	0	1.435
1994	Florida	NL	45	54.0	62	38	45	1	4	5.67	0	1.852
1995	Florida	NL	21	36.0	30	15	32	0	1	3.75	0	1.250
1996	Detroit	AL	72	90.1	78	65	78	4	6	4.18	2	1.583
Post All-Star			39	45.1	42	28	37	2	1	4.17	0	1.544

JOSE LIMA   Age 24/R $1

You have to look closely, very, very closely, but there seems to be an ever-so-slight trend of improvement. Ignore it.

Year	Team	Lg.	G	IP	H	BB	SO	W	L	ERA	SV	Ratio
1994	Detroit	AL	3	6.2	11	3	7	0	1	13.50	0	2.100
1995	Detroit	AL	15	73.2	85	18	37	3	9	6.11	0	1.398
1996	Detroit	AL	39	72.2	87	22	59	5	6	5.70	3	1.500
Post All-Star			32	46.0	47	11	46	5	2	4.70	3	1.261

GRAEME LLOYD   Age 29/L $2

The guy comes over from Milwaukee and The Boss says, "I'm sorry to hear that your barber died back in Australia." A month later (he gets paid to pitch, not think) the kid gets it, gets a trim, and shuts down everybody in the playoffs.

Year	Team	Lg.	G	IP	H	BB	SO	W	L	ERA	SV	Ratio
1993	Milwaukee	AL	55	63.2	64	13	31	3	4	2.83	0	1.209
1994	Milwaukee	AL	43	47.0	49	15	31	2	3	5.17	3	1.362
1995	Milwaukee	AL	33	32.0	28	8	13	0	5	4.50	4	1.125
1996	Milwaukee	AL	52	51.0	49	17	24	2	4	2.82	0	1.294
1996	New York	AL	13	5.2	12	5	6	0	2	17.47	0	3.000
Post All-Star			29	18.2	27	10	9	0	4	8.68	0	1.982

ALBIE LOPEZ   Age 25/R $2

One more year of this stuff and he's no longer a prospect. One more year of this stuff and he's off to Japan.

Year	Team	Lg.	G	IP	H	BB	SO	W	L	ERA	SV	Ratio
1993	Cleveland	AL	9	49.2	49	32	25	3	1	5.98	0	1.631
1994	Cleveland	AL	4	17.0	20	6	18	1	2	4.24	0	1.529
1995	Cleveland	AL	6	23.0	17	7	22	0	0	3.13	0	1.043
1996	Cleveland	AL	13	62.0	80	22	45	5	4	6.39	0	1.645
Post All-Star			9	44.2	53	16	32	4	2	5.44	0	1.545

MIKE MADDUX   Age 35/R $2

Followed up a good year in Boston with a decidedly mediocre one. Look elsewhere.

Year	Team	Lg.	G	IP	H	BB	SO	W	L	ERA	SV	Ratio
1993	New York	NL	58	75.0	67	27	57	3	8	3.60	5	1.253
1994	New York	NL	27	44.0	45	13	32	2	1	5.11	2	1.318
1995	Pittsburgh	NL	8	9.0	14	3	4	1	0	9.00	0	1.889
1995	Boston	AL	36	89.2	86	15	65	4	1	3.61	1	1.126
1996	Boston	AL	23	64.1	76	27	32	3	2	4.48	0	1.601
Post All-Star			10	45.0	48	16	25	3	1	4.40	0	1.422

JOE MAGRANE   Age 32/L $1

Baseball is a strange sport. This unremarkable stiff has been making a major league living for ten years. He hasn't earned his money is all but two of them. Enough already, Joe. Retire.

Year	Team	Lg.	G	IP	H	BB	SO	W	L	ERA	SV	Ratio
1993	St. Louis	NL	22	116.0	127	37	38	8	10	4.97	0	1.414
1993	California	AL	8	48.0	48	21	24	3	2	3.94	0	1.438
1994	California	AL	20	74.0	89	51	33	2	6	7.30	0	1.892
1996	Chicago	AL	19	53.2	70	25	21	1	5	6.88	0	1.770
Post All-Star			0	0.0	0	0	0	0	0	0.00	0	0.000

Catchers
pp. 27–39

Corners
pp. 40–60

Infield
pp. 60–80

Outfield
pp. 80–111

DH
pp. 112–115

Starters
pp. 115–145

Relievers
pp. 146–178

PAT MAHOMES   Age 26/R $2

Part of Dan Duquette's insidious scheme to have every active member of the Players' Association play at least one inning for the Red Sox. One aside: It's considered a felony in nine southern states to walk up to a stranger and ask, "Pat Mahomes?"

Year	Team	Lg.	G	IP	H	BB	SO	W	L	ERA	SV	Ratio
1993	Minnesota	AL	12	37.1	47	16	23	1	5	7.71	0	1.688
1994	Minnesota	AL	21	120.0	121	62	53	9	5	4.72	0	1.525
1995	Minnesota	AL	47	94.2	100	47	67	4	10	6.37	3	1.553
1996	Minnesota	AL	20	45.0	63	27	30	1	4	7.20	0	2.000
1996	Boston	AL	11	12.1	9	6	6	2	0	5.84	2	1.216
Post All-Star			11	12.1	9	6	6	2	0	5.84	2	1.216

TERRY MATHEWS   Age 32/R $2

Pitched okay for the Orioles after pitching okay for the Marlins. If okay pitching is what you seek, your quest is at an end.

Year	Team	Lg.	G	IP	H	BB	SO	W	L	ERA	SV	Ratio
1994	Florida	NL	24	43.0	45	9	21	2	1	3.35	0	1.256
1995	Florida	NL	57	82.2	70	27	72	4	4	3.38	3	1.173
1996	Florida	NL	57	55.0	59	27	49	2	4	4.91	4	1.564
1996	Baltimore	AL	14	18.2	20	7	13	2	2	3.38	0	1.446
Post All-Star			32	38.1	43	17	26	2	3	4.70	1	1.565

CHUCK McELROY   Age 29/L $7

Came over in June from the Reds and recorded wins in his first three appearances. Added another in June and one more in September. Such are the fortunes of middle relief. If the Disney folks revamp the starting pitching as they should, McElroy could put up some decent numbers. It's tough to get a save when you're losing 8–2.

Year	Team	Lg.	G	IP	H	BB	SO	W	L	ERA	SV	Ratio
1993	Chicago	NL	49	47.1	51	25	31	2	2	4.56	0	1.606
1994	Cincinnati	NL	52	57.2	52	15	38	1	2	2.34	5	1.162
1995	Cincinnati	NL	44	40.1	46	15	27	3	4	6.02	0	1.512
1996	Cincinnati	NL	12	12.1	13	10	13	2	0	6.57	0	1.865
1996	California	AL	40	36.2	32	13	32	5	1	2.95	0	1.227
Post All-Star			18	17.1	11	9	14	1	1	2.60	0	1.154

RAMIRO MENDOZA   Age 24/R $1

See Brian Boehringer.

Year	Team	Lg.	G	IP	H	BB	SO	W	L	ERA	SV	Ratio
1996	New York	AL	12	53.0	80	10	34	4	5	6.79	0	1.698
Post All-Star			4	17.0	23	1	10	1	1	5.82	0	1.412

JOSE MESA   Age 30/R $37

Pretty good year overall, but Mesa was awfully inconsistent. The seven losses are troubling for a top-flight closer. He's still one of the best, but he more than came back to the pack last year.

Year	Team	Lg.	G	IP	H	BB	SO	W	L	ERA	SV	Ratio
1993	Cleveland	AL	34	208.2	232	62	118	10	12	4.92	0	1.409
1994	Cleveland	AL	51	73.0	71	26	63	7	5	3.82	2	1.329
1995	Cleveland	AL	62	64.0	49	17	58	3	0	1.13	46	1.031
1996	Cleveland	AL	69	72.1	69	28	64	2	7	3.73	39	1.341
Post All-Star			31	35.2	31	12	35	2	4	2.52	15	1.206

ALAN MILLS   Age 30/R $3

It seems like the least precious commodity in baseball is a 30-year-old right-hander who will win a few, save a few, and keep his ERA under 5.00. They're everywhere.

Year	Team	Lg.	G	IP	H	BB	SO	W	L	ERA	SV	Ratio
1993	Baltimore	AL	45	100.1	80	51	68	5	4	3.23	4	1.306
1994	Baltimore	AL	47	45.1	43	24	44	3	3	5.16	2	1.478
1995	Baltimore	AL	21	23.0	30	18	16	3	0	7.43	0	2.087
1996	Baltimore	AL	49	54.2	40	35	50	3	2	4.28	3	1.372
Post All-Star			33	35.1	26	20	31	2	2	4.08	2	1.302

BLAS MINOR   Age 31/R $1

Late season pickups like this kept the Mariners out of the playoffs.

Year	Team	Lg.	G	IP	H	BB	SO	W	L	ERA	SV	Ratio
1993	Pittsburgh	NL	65	94.1	94	26	84	8	6	4.10	2	1.272
1994	Pittsburgh	NL	17	19.0	27	9	17	0	1	8.05	1	1.895
1995	New York	NL	35	46.2	44	13	43	4	2	3.66	1	1.221
1996	New York	NL	17	25.2	23	6	20	0	0	3.51	0	1.130
1996	Seattle	AL	11	25.1	27	11	14	0	1	4.97	0	1.500
Post All-Star			5	15.2	15	7	8	0	1	4.60	0	1.404

MIKE MOHLER   Age 28/L $7

This Mohler will put some teeth in your bullpen.

Year	Team	Lg.	G	IP	H	BB	SO	W	L	ERA	SV	Ratio
1993	Oakland	AL	42	64.1	57	44	42	1	6	5.60	0	1.570
1994	Oakland	AL	1	2.1	2	2	4	0	1	7.71	0	1.714
1995	Oakland	AL	28	23.2	16	18	15	1	1	3.04	1	1.437
1996	Oakland	AL	72	81.0	79	41	64	6	3	3.67	7	1.481
Post All-Star			33	32.0	36	11	23	2	3	5.34	1	1.469

JEFF MONTGOMERY   Age 35/R $5

His year ended with shoulder surgery, which, in our experience, is not necessarily a good thing for 35-year-old pitchers. His 242 career saves warrant a look, but don't expect much.

Year	Team	Lg.	G	IP	H	BB	SO	W	L	ERA	SV	Ratio
1993	Kansas City	AL	69	87.1	65	23	66	7	5	2.27	45	1.008
1994	Kansas City	AL	42	44.2	48	15	50	2	3	4.03	27	1.410
1995	Kansas City	AL	54	65.2	60	25	49	2	3	3.43	31	1.294
1996	Kansas City	AL	48	63.1	59	19	45	4	6	4.26	24	1.232
Post All-Star			15	18.1	18	5	11	3	0	4.42	6	1.255

Catchers
pp. 27–39

Corners
pp. 40–60

Infield
pp. 60–80

Outfield
pp. 80–111

DH
pp. 112–115

Starters
pp. 115–145

Relievers
pp. 146–178

MIKE MYERS
Age 27/L $4

He managed six saves, so he may be in contention to close for the Tigers. (Hey, so's Pedro Bourbon *Senior*.) Otherwise, a maddeningly inconsistent year.

Year	Team	Lg.	G	IP	H	BB	SO	W	L	ERA	SV	Ratio
1995	Florida	NL	2	2.0	1	3	0	0	0	0.00	0	2.000
1995	Detroit	AL	11	6.1	10	4	4	1	0	9.95	0	2.211
1996	Detroit	AL	83	64.2	70	34	69	1	5	5.01	6	1.608
Post All-Star			34	25.0	23	10	27	1	1	3.60	3	1.320

RANDY MYERS
Age 34/L $27

A decent year. He was great in September (0.90 ERA, 5 for 5 in save opportunities) but by the playoffs Davey Johnson lost confidence in him. He still has what it takes, though. Wetteland finished lousy in 1995, and he certainly bounced back. Myers can, too. Until Benitez (3 September saves) establishes himself, Myers is the closer.

Year	Team	Lg.	G	IP	H	BB	SO	W	L	ERA	SV	Ratio
1993	Chicago	NL	73	75.1	65	26	86	2	4	3.11	53	1.208
1994	Chicago	NL	38	40.1	40	16	32	1	5	3.79	21	1.388
1995	Chicago	NL	57	55.2	49	28	59	1	2	3.88	38	1.383
1996	Baltimore	AL	62	58.2	60	29	74	4	4	3.53	31	1.517
Post All-Star			30	28.1	30	13	32	4	2	3.81	13	1.518

DAN NAULTY
Age 27/R $5

Small potatoes here. But they sure are tasty.

Year	Team	Lg.	G	IP	H	BB	SO	W	L	ERA	SV	Ratio
1996	Minnesota	AL	49	57.0	43	35	56	3	2	3.79	4	1.368
Post All-Star			12	11.0	8	9	6	0	2	6.55	3	1.545

JEFF NELSON
Age 30/R $7

Sooner or later this guy's going to put together one hell of a year. His pitches have great natural movement and he's a fierce competitor. Nothing like a World Series ring to really focus a guy.

Year	Team	Lg.	G	IP	H	BB	SO	W	L	ERA	SV	Ratio
1993	Seattle	AL	71	60.0	57	34	61	5	3	4.35	1	1.517
1994	Seattle	AL	28	42.1	35	20	44	0	0	2.76	0	1.299
1995	Seattle	AL	62	78.2	58	27	96	7	3	2.17	2	1.081
1996	New York	AL	73	74.1	75	36	91	4	4	4.36	2	1.493
Post All-Star			34	34.0	29	15	49	1	2	3.71	0	1.294

JESSE OROSCO
Age 40/L $2

The Tony Pena of moundsmen.

Year	Team	Lg.	G	IP	H	BB	SO	W	L	ERA	SV	Ratio
1993	Milwaukee	AL	57	56.2	47	17	67	3	5	3.18	8	1.129
1994	Milwaukee	AL	40	39.0	32	26	36	3	1	5.08	0	1.487
1995	Baltimore	AL	65	49.2	28	27	58	2	4	3.26	3	1.107
1996	Baltimore	AL	66	55.2	42	28	52	3	1	3.40	0	1.257
Post All-Star			38	29.1	20	11	31	1	0	1.23	0	1.057

JOSE PARRA   Age 24/R $2

No way, Jose.

Year	Team	Lg.	G	IP	H	BB	SO	W	L	ERA	SV	Ratio
1995	Los Angeles	NL	8	10.1	10	6	7	0	0	4.35	0	1.548
1995	Minnesota	AL	12	61.2	83	22	29	1	5	7.59	0	1.703
1996	Minnesota	AL	27	70.0	88	27	50	5	5	6.04	0	1.643
Post All-Star			21	42.1	47	20	31	4	2	5.53	0	1.583

TROY PERCIVAL   Age 27/R $36

He's great now and there's nowhere to go but up. If he could save 36 games for the 1996 Angels, there's no telling what he could do on an actual *major league* team.

Year	Team	Lg.	G	IP	H	BB	SO	W	L	ERA	SV	Ratio
1995	California	AL	62	74.0	37	26	94	3	2	1.95	3	0.851
1996	California	AL	62	74.0	38	31	100	0	2	2.31	36	0.932
Post All-Star			26	33.0	20	14	47	0	1	3.00	14	1.030

HIPOLITO PICHARDO   Age 27/R $2

A giant step backward for someone who had been progressing. Don't bother.

Year	Team	Lg.	G	IP	H	BB	SO	W	L	ERA	SV	Ratio
1993	Kansas City	AL	30	165.0	183	53	70	7	8	4.04	0	1.430
1994	Kansas City	AL	45	67.2	82	24	36	5	3	4.92	3	1.567
1995	Kansas City	AL	44	64.0	66	30	43	8	4	4.36	1	1.500
1996	Kansas City	AL	57	68.0	74	26	43	3	5	5.43	3	1.471
Post All-Star			25	30.1	32	13	20	0	2	4.45	2	1.484

ERIC PLUNK   Age 33/R $6

It's not that valuable, but it sure is consistent. Strictly a ninth or tenth guy.

Year	Team	Lg.	G	IP	H	BB	SO	W	L	ERA	SV	Ratio
1993	Cleveland	AL	70	71.0	61	30	77	4	5	2.79	15	1.282
1994	Cleveland	AL	41	71.0	61	37	73	7	2	2.54	3	1.380
1995	Cleveland	AL	56	64.0	48	27	71	6	2	2.67	2	1.172
1996	Cleveland	AL	56	77.2	56	34	85	3	2	2.43	2	1.159
Post All-Star			25	34.0	25	10	40	1	2	2.38	1	1.029

ARTHUR RHODES   Age 27/L $4

The 1996 Vulture of the Year Award goes to Arthur Rhodes. Unfortunately, he won't do it again. He's simply not a good pitcher. The O's know it, too. He pitched a total of three innings in August and September, but since this is a family book, we won't print his ERA in those innings.

Year	Team	Lg.	G	IP	H	BB	SO	W	L	ERA	SV	Ratio
1993	Baltimore	AL	17	85.2	91	49	49	5	6	6.51	0	1.634
1994	Baltimore	AL	10	52.2	51	30	47	3	5	5.81	0	1.538
1995	Baltimore	AL	19	75.1	68	48	77	2	5	6.21	0	1.540
1996	Baltimore	AL	28	53.0	48	23	62	9	1	4.08	1	1.340
Post All-Star			5	3.2	7	1	3	0	1	12.27	0	2.182

Catchers
pp. 27-39

Corners
pp. 40-60

Infield
pp. 60-80

Outfield
pp. 80-111

DH
pp. 112-115

Starters
pp. 115-145

Relievers
pp. 146-178

BILL RISLEY
Age 29/R   **$1**

His entire career is equal to an average year for Tom Gordon. You either get that or you don't. Here's more. No wins + No saves = No value.

Year	Team	Lg.	G	IP	H	BB	SO	W	L	ERA	SV	Ratio
1993	Montreal	NL	2	3.0	2	2	2	0	0	6.00	0	1.333
1994	Seattle	AL	37	52.1	31	19	61	9	6	3.44	0	0.955
1995	Seattle	AL	45	60.1	55	18	65	2	1	3.13	1	1.210
1996	Toronto	AL	25	41.2	33	25	29	0	1	3.89	0	1.392
Post All-Star			11	19.1	13	9	11	0	1	2.79	0	1.138

MARIANO RIVERA
Age 27/R   **$15**

Quite simply the most effective pitcher in baseball last year. In a word, unhittable. Wetteland is still the man, though the Yanks will have to pay to keep him. With this kid waiting in the wings, you have to wonder, why would they?

Year	Team	Lg.	G	IP	H	BB	SO	W	L	ERA	SV	Ratio
1995	New York	AL	19	67.0	71	30	51	5	3	5.51	0	1.507
1996	New York	AL	61	107.2	73	34	130	8	3	2.09	5	0.994
Post All-Star			30	47.2	35	15	60	5	2	2.45	3	1.049

JEFF RUSSELL
Age 35/R   **$3**

Everywhere you look in Jeff Russell's stats, you get threes. Which proves that, while good things happen in threes, so do mediocre things. He's a decent set-up guy, and not much more.

Year	Team	Lg.	G	IP	H	BB	SO	W	L	ERA	SV	Ratio
1993	Boston	AL	51	46.2	39	14	45	1	4	2.70	33	1.136
1994	Boston	AL	29	28.0	30	13	18	0	5	5.14	12	1.536
1994	Cleveland	AL	13	12.2	13	3	10	1	1	4.97	5	1.263
1995	Texas	AL	37	32.2	36	9	21	1	0	3.03	20	1.378
1996	Texas	AL	55	56.0	58	22	23	3	3	3.38	3	1.429
Post All-Star			29	26.2	27	16	8	2	2	2.36	2	1.612

PAUL SHUEY
Age 26/R   **$9**

Nice work in a middle-man role, which is what he seems destined to do for his whole career. Cultural note: Shuey is a native of Lima, Ohio, which is the name of one of Lenny Bruce's best routines. *Vive la Comedie!*

Year	Team	Lg.	G	IP	H	BB	SO	W	L	ERA	SV	Ratio
1994	Cleveland	AL	14	11.2	14	12	16	0	1	8.49	5	2.229
1995	Cleveland	AL	7	6.1	5	5	5	0	2	4.26	0	1.579
1996	Cleveland	AL	42	53.2	45	26	44	5	2	2.85	4	1.323
Post All-Star			25	33.1	26	16	30	3	0	1.89	2	1.260

BILL SIMAS
Age 25/R   **$2**

Simas? No mas.

Year	Team	Lg.	G	IP	H	BB	SO	W	L	ERA	SV	Ratio
1995	Chicago	AL	14	14.0	15	10	16	1	1	2.57	0	1.786
1996	Chicago	AL	64	72.2	75	39	65	2	8	4.58	2	1.569
Post All-Star			25	28.2	34	13	21	2	4	5.34	1	1.640

HEATHCLIFF SLOCUMB

Age 30/R　　**$32**

So we were wrong. Slocumb is a closer, albeit the kind who flirts with danger. He's shown he has the temperament to do the job. After an inconsistent start in a brutal baseball town under a manager who didn't want him, he was the best closer in the AL in September (0.47 ERA in 19 innings with seven saves and three wins). The Red Sox have problems, but not with this guy.

Year	Team	Lg.	G	IP	H	BB	SO	W	L	ERA	SV	Ratio
1993	Chicago	NL	10	10.2	7	4	4	1	0	3.38	0	1.031
1993	Cleveland	AL	20	27.1	28	16	18	3	1	4.28	0	1.610
1994	Philadelphia	NL	52	72.1	75	28	58	5	1	2.86	0	1.424
1995	Philadelphia	NL	61	65.1	64	35	63	5	6	2.89	32	1.515
1996	Boston	AL	75	83.1	68	55	88	5	5	3.02	31	1.476
Post All-Star			36	40.1	35	28	39	3	0	2.68	20	1.562

PAUL SPOLJARIC

Age 26/L　　**$2**

The name sounds kinda gross, and 38 innings renders him irrelevant.

Year	Team	Lg.	G	IP	H	BB	SO	W	L	ERA	SV	Ratio
1994	Toronto	AL	2	2.1	5	9	2	0	1	38.57	0	6.000
1996	Toronto	AL	28	38.0	30	19	38	2	2	3.08	1	1.289
Post All-Star			20	24.0	20	13	22	2	2	3.00	1	1.375

MIKE STANTON

Age 29/L　　**$4**

Won't even do enough to be bad, let alone good.

Year	Team	Lg.	G	IP	H	BB	SO	W	L	ERA	SV	Ratio
1993	Atlanta	NL	63	52.0	51	29	43	4	6	4.67	27	1.538
1994	Atlanta	NL	49	45.2	41	26	35	3	1	3.55	3	1.467
1995	Atlanta	NL	26	19.1	31	6	13	1	1	5.59	1	1.914
1995	Boston	AL	22	21.0	17	8	10	1	0	3.00	0	1.190
1996	Boston	AL	59	56.1	58	23	46	4	3	3.83	1	1.438
1996	Texas	AL	22	22.1	20	4	14	0	1	3.22	0	1.075
Post All-Star			31	28.2	28	8	17	0	2	4.08	0	1.256

DAVE STEVENS

Age 27/R　　**$7**

Had nine saves by June 1. Finished with 11. Don't let the door hit you on the ass on your way out, Dave.

Year	Team	Lg.	G	IP	H	BB	SO	W	L	ERA	SV	Ratio
1994	Minnesota	AL	24	45.0	55	23	24	5	2	6.80	0	1.733
1995	Minnesota	AL	56	65.2	74	32	47	5	4	5.07	10	1.614
1996	Minnesota	AL	49	58.0	58	25	29	3	3	4.66	11	1.431
Post All-Star			22	30.2	30	15	8	2	3	5.87	0	1.467

JULIAN TAVAREZ

Age 23/R　　**$3**

Nobody would mind if a door hit this lunkhead. He goes from being a superstar in waiting to assaulting an umpire to toiling in the minor leagues. Forget him. Okay, so that's a little harsh. Put it this way, forget him.

Year	Team	Lg.	G	IP	H	BB	SO	W	L	ERA	SV	Ratio
1993	Cleveland	AL	8	37.0	53	13	19	2	2	6.57	0	1.784
1994	Cleveland	AL	1	1.2	6	1	0	0	1	21.60	0	4.200
1995	Cleveland	AL	57	85.0	76	21	68	10	2	2.44	0	1.141
1996	Cleveland	AL	51	80.2	101	22	46	4	7	5.36	0	1.525
Post All-Star			19	29.1	39	10	13	1	2	6.14	0	1.670

Catchers
pp. 27–39

Corners
pp. 40–60

Infield
pp. 60–80

Outfield
pp. 80–111

DH
pp. 112–115

Starters
pp. 115–145

Relievers
pp. 146–178

BILLY TAYLOR   Age 35/L $13

Not bad, but 35 is the age at which you're supposed to be winding down, not starting up.

Year	Team	Lg.	G	IP	H	BB	SO	W	L	ERA	SV	Ratio
1994	Oakland	AL	41	46.1	38	18	48	1	3	3.50	1	1.209
1996	Oakland	AL	55	60.1	52	25	67	6	3	4.33	17	1.276
Post All-Star			22	26.2	23	16	30	2	2	6.07	10	1.462

MIKE TIMLIN   Age 31/R $30

From 5 to 31 saves. Who'da thunk it? It looks like Timlin will hold down the fort while the Blue Jays rebuild. Too bad he'll be over the hill by the time they're any good.

Year	Team	Lg.	G	IP	H	BB	SO	W	L	ERA	SV	Ratio
1993	Toronto	AL	54	55.2	63	27	49	4	2	4.69	1	1.617
1994	Toronto	AL	34	40.0	41	20	38	0	1	5.18	2	1.525
1995	Toronto	AL	31	42.0	38	17	36	4	3	2.14	5	1.310
1996	Toronto	AL	59	56.2	47	18	52	1	6	3.65	31	1.147
Post All-Star			30	28.2	26	15	27	1	5	4.71	16	1.430

MIKE TROMBLEY   Age 29/R $8

You can't ask for more from a journeyman, mop-up, vulture-type guy like Trombley. Actually, you can ask for more. You just won't get it.

Year	Team	Lg.	G	IP	H	BB	SO	W	L	ERA	SV	Ratio
1993	Minnesota	AL	44	114.1	131	41	85	6	6	4.88	2	1.504
1994	Minnesota	AL	24	48.1	56	18	32	2	0	6.33	0	1.531
1995	Minnesota	AL	20	97.2	107	42	68	4	8	5.62	0	1.526
1996	Minnesota	AL	43	68.2	61	25	57	5	1	3.01	6	1.252
Post All-Star			30	45.1	46	18	36	3	1	3.57	5	1.412

TOM URBANI   Age 29/L $1

Stay away. He's an earned-run machine.

Year	Team	Lg.	G	IP	H	BB	SO	W	L	ERA	SV	Ratio
1993	St. Louis	NL	18	62.0	73	26	33	1	3	4.65	0	1.597
1994	St. Louis	NL	20	80.1	98	21	43	3	7	5.15	0	1.481
1995	St. Louis	NL	24	82.2	99	21	52	3	5	3.70	0	1.452
1996	St. Louis	NL	3	11.2	15	4	1	1	0	7.71	0	1.629
1996	Detroit	AL	16	23.2	31	14	20	2	2	8.37	0	1.901
Post All-Star			9	9.2	11	8	12	1	1	6.52	0	1.966

JULIO VALERA   Age 28/R $1

When me an' Julio were down by the schoolyard, he didn't work on his pitching. He just hung around and tried to pick up girls. He stunk at that, too.

Year	Team	Lg.	G	IP	H	BB	SO	W	L	ERA	SV	Ratio
1993	California	AL	19	53.0	77	15	28	3	6	6.62	4	1.736
1996	Kansas City	AL	31	61.1	75	27	31	3	2	6.46	1	1.663
Post All-Star			4	6.0	11	5	2	0	0	15.00	0	2.667

RANDY VERES   Age 31/R $1

Done.

Year	Team	Lg.	G	IP	H	BB	SO	W	L	ERA	SV	Ratio
1994	Chicago	NL	10	9.2	12	2	5	1	1	5.59	0	1.448
1995	Florida	NL	47	48.2	46	22	31	4	4	3.88	1	1.397
1996	Detroit	AL	25	30.1	38	23	28	0	4	8.31	0	2.011
Post All-Star			0	0.0	0	0	0	0	0	0.00	0	0.000

RON VILLONE   Age 27/L $1

He's toiled unproductively for three organizations so far. Don't make yours the fourth.

Year	Team	Lg.	G	IP	H	BB	SO	W	L	ERA	SV	Ratio
1995	Seattle	AL	19	19.1	20	23	26	0	2	7.91	0	2.224
1995	San Diego	NL	19	25.2	24	11	37	2	1	4.21	1	1.364
1996	San Diego	NL	21	18.1	17	7	19	1	1	2.95	0	1.309
1996	Milwaukee	AL	23	24.2	14	18	19	0	0	3.28	2	1.297
Post All-Star			30	29.2	21	19	25	1	1	4.55	2	1.348

ED VOSBERG   Age 35/L $5

The Rangers will probably close by committee this year and old Vossie here could grab a few. He's had a nice ERA for the last few seasons, so he's worth a shot. Just don't get scalped on the price.

Year	Team	Lg.	G	IP	H	BB	SO	W	L	ERA	SV	Ratio
1994	Oakland	AL	16	13.2	16	5	12	0	2	3.95	0	1.537
1995	Texas	AL	44	36.0	32	16	36	5	5	3.00	4	1.333
1996	Texas	AL	52	44.0	51	21	32	1	1	3.27	8	1.636
Post All-Star			27	22.0	22	10	14	1	1	3.68	3	1.455

JOHN WETTELAND   Age 30/R $39

While that cruddy old hat he wears is getting a little tired, Wetteland is not. His second year in the AL was as good as any of his best in the NL. He set a record with 24 saves in 24 opportunities on his way to 43. Pay up.

Year	Team	Lg.	G	IP	H	BB	SO	W	L	ERA	SV	Ratio
1993	Montreal	NL	70	85.1	58	28	113	9	3	1.37	43	1.008
1994	Montreal	NL	52	63.2	46	21	68	4	6	2.83	25	1.052
1995	New York	AL	60	61.1	40	14	66	1	5	2.93	31	0.880
1996	New York	AL	62	63.2	54	21	69	2	3	2.83	43	1.178
Post All-Star			24	25.0	21	9	27	2	2	2.52	14	1.200

BOB WICKMAN   Age 28/R $9

His departure from the Bronx leaves only Melido Perez among the players involved in the Steve Sax trade. It's sort of funny that Wickman came to and left New York in controversial trades. Moving right along, Wickman won three games for the Brewers as a middle man and could do very nicely in that role again this year.

Year	Team	Lg.	G	IP	H	BB	SO	W	L	ERA	SV	Ratio
1993	New York	AL	41	140.0	156	69	70	14	4	4.63	4	1.607
1994	New York	AL	53	70.0	54	27	56	5	4	3.09	6	1.157
1995	New York	AL	63	80.0	77	33	51	2	4	4.05	1	1.375
1996	New York	AL	58	79.0	94	34	61	4	1	4.67	0	1.620
1996	Milwaukee	AL	12	16.2	12	10	14	3	0	3.24	0	1.320
Post All-Star			32	39.2	40	26	31	4	0	5.22	0	1.664

Catchers
pp. 27–39

Corners
pp. 40–60

Infield
pp. 60–80

Outfield
pp. 80–111

DH
pp. 112–115

Starters
pp. 115–145

Relievers
pp. 146–178

WOODY WILLIAMS   Age 30/R $2

The problem with Williams is that too many batters get good wood on his pitches.

Year	Team	Lg.	G	IP	H	BB	SO	W	L	ERA	SV	Ratio
1993	Toronto	AL	30	37.0	40	22	24	3	1	4.38	0	1.676
1994	Toronto	AL	38	59.1	44	33	56	1	3	3.64	0	1.298
1995	Toronto	AL	23	53.2	44	28	41	1	2	3.69	0	1.342
1996	Toronto	AL	12	59.0	64	21	43	4	5	4.73	0	1.441
Post All-Star			10	56.2	60	19	40	4	5	4.61	0	1.394

3

By the Numbers

1997 Rotisserie Stat-Pak:
Never Leave for the Auction
Draft Without It

A certain kind of Rotisserie owner breezes into the auction draft without so much as pencil or notepad. The night before, he went to the movies. The week before, he went snorkeling in the Caribbean and didn't see a single newspaper for six days. The month before, he re-read all of Raymond Chandler and the new James Lee Burke. Preparation? Well, he rented *Major League* on Super Bowl Sunday and watched it instead of the game. While other owners at the table are frantically rearranging their lists, agonizing over which of seven alternative strategies to pursue, and trying to remember their own names, he leans back, folds his arms over his chest, and, with a dreamy look in his eyes, asks of no one in particular, "I wonder how much Bobby Bonds will go for?" Six months later, *he*'s the one taking the Yoo-Hoo shower.

We hate that guy.

But we have to admit he may be on to something. Maybe you really don't need to show up at the auction draft with the *Baseball Register,* all the spring training box scores from *USA Today,* Bill James, the last six months of *Baseball America* and *Baseball Weekly,* a stack of computer print-outs, all of John Benson's newsletters for the past year, a well-thumbed copy of *Nine Innings,* and your original 1948 Cleveland Indians cap. Maybe all you need is the Rotisserie Stat-Pak.

The Rotisserie Stat-Pak is the nearest thing in this book to a grand-slam homer. Here you get the top performers in all the Rotissecategories (plus Runs Scored for batters and Strikeouts and Net Wins for pitchers). You also get the *worst* performers in ERA, Ratio, and BA so you can find out in an instant who might hurt you. And for batters, you get the top performers in each category by position. Plus, you get Post All-Star stats so you can scope out who finished strong (and otherwise) last season.

So forget all that other stuff. Just tear out this chapter and travel light. You can wear your lucky Indians cap. But remember to take it off just before they pour the Yoo-Hoo.

LEAGUE LEADERS, 1996

NATIONAL LEAGUE PITCHERS

RATIO
(Minimum 100 Innings Pitched)

1. Brown, K.	0.944	15. Valdes, I.	1.213	29. Lieber, J.	1.296
2. Smoltz, J.	1.001	16. Shaw, J.	1.223	30. Glavine, T.	1.305
3. Maddux, G.	1.033	17. Worrell, T.	1.223	31. Harnisch, P.	1.315
4. Schilling, C.	1.085	18. Neagle, D.	1.238	32. Adams, T.	1.317
5. Reynolds, S.	1.134	19. Clark, M.	1.248	33. Rueter, K.	1.333
6. Darwin, D.	1.136	20. Osborne, D.	1.248	34. Mulholland, T.	1.335
7. Sanders, S.	1.146	21. Leiter, A.	1.263	35. Navarro, J.	1.335
8. Nomo, H.	1.161	22. Benes, A.	1.268	36. Bergman, S.	1.341
9. Fassero, J.	1.174	23. Stottlemyre, T.	1.272	37. Jones, B.	1.354
10. Trachsel, S.	1.185	24. Burkett, J.	1.273	38. Wall, D.	1.360
11. Martinez, P.	1.195	25. Urbina, U.	1.281	39. Hamilton, J.	1.365
12. Smiley, J.	1.201	26. Cormier, R.	1.290	40. Watson, A.	1.390
13. Ashby, A.	1.201	27. Tewksbury, B.	1.292		
14. Portugal, M.	1.205	28. Astacio, P.	1.294		

WORST RATIOS
(Minimum 100 Innings Pitched)

1. Rapp, P.	1.694	14. Benes, A.	1.461	28. Watson, A.	1.390
2. Bullinger, J.	1.639	15. Fernandez, O.	1.456	29. Hamilton, J.	1.365
3. Jarvis, K.	1.620	16. Salkeld, R.	1.448	30. Wall, D.	1.360
4. Freeman, M.	1.604	17. Reynoso, A.	1.447	31. Jones, B.	1.354
5. Ritz, K.	1.601	18. Gardner, M.	1.433	32. Bergman, S.	1.341
6. Thompson, M.	1.550	19. Valenzuela, F.	1.421	33. Navarro, J.	1.335
7. Isringhausen, J.	1.532	20. Avery, S.	1.420	34. Mulholland, T.	1.335
8. Wilson, P.	1.530	21. Martinez, R.	1.417	35. Rueter, K.	1.333
9. Drabek, D.	1.529	22. Burba, D.	1.415	36. Adams, T.	1.317
10. Williams, M.	1.527	23. Candiotti, T.	1.411	37. Harnisch, P.	1.315
11. VanLandingham, W.		24. Park, C.	1.408	38. Glavine, T.	1.305
	1.508	25. Leiter, M.	1.405	39. Lieber, J.	1.296
12. Kile, D.	1.507	26. Castillo, F.	1.399	40. Astacio, P.	1.294
13. Morgan, M.	1.481	27. Hampton, M.	1.397		

EARNED RUN AVERAGE
(Minimum 100 Innings Pitched)

1. Brown, K.	1.89	15. Sanders, S.	3.38	29. Benes, A.	3.83
2. Shaw, J.	2.49	16. Martinez, R.	3.42	30. Burba, D.	3.83
3. Maddux, G.	2.72	17. Clark, M.	3.43	31. Stottlemyre, T.	3.87
4. Leiter, A.	2.93	18. Astacio, P.	3.44	32. Navarro, J.	3.92
5. Adams, T.	2.94	19. Neagle, D.	3.50	33. Rueter, K.	3.97
6. Smoltz, J.	2.94	20. Osborne, D.	3.53	34. Portugal, M.	3.98
7. Glavine, T.	2.98	21. Hampton, M.	3.59	35. Lieber, J.	3.99
8. Trachsel, S.	3.03	22. Valenzuela, F.	3.62	36. Hamilton, J.	4.17
9. Worrell, T.	3.05	23. Smiley, J.	3.64	37. Cormier, R.	4.17
10. Schilling, C.	3.19	24. Park, C.	3.64	38. Kile, D.	4.19
11. Nomo, H.	3.19	25. Reynolds, S.	3.65	39. Harnisch, P.	4.21
12. Ashby, A.	3.23	26. Martinez, P.	3.70	40. Tewksbury, B.	4.31
13. Fassero, J.	3.30	27. Urbina, U.	3.71		
14. Valdes, I.	3.32	28. Darwin, D.	3.77		

WORST EARNED RUN AVERAGES
(Minimum 100 Innings Pitched)

1. Bullinger, J.	6.54	15. Isringhausen, J.	4.77	29. Harnisch, P.	4.21
2. Freeman, M.	6.04	16. Mulholland, T.	4.66	30. Kile, D.	4.19
3. Jarvis, K.	5.98	17. Morgan, M.	4.63	31. Cormier, R.	4.17
4. Williams, M.	5.44	18. Fernandez, O.	4.61	32. Hamilton, J.	4.17
5. VanLandingham, W.		19. Watson, A.	4.61	33. Lieber, J.	3.99
	5.40	20. Drabek, D.	4.57	34. Portugal, M.	3.98
6. Wilson, P.	5.38	21. Wall, D.	4.56	35. Rueter, K.	3.97
7. Thompson, M.	5.30	22. Candiotti, T.	4.49	36. Navarro, J.	3.92
8. Ritz, K.	5.28	23. Avery, S.	4.47	37. Stottlemyre, T.	3.87
9. Castillo, F.	5.28	24. Gardner, M.	4.42	38. Burba, D.	3.83
10. Salkeld, R.	5.20	25. Jones, B.	4.42	39. Benes, A.	3.83
11. Rapp, P.	5.10	26. Bergman, S.	4.37	40. Darwin, D.	3.77
12. Reynoso, A.	4.96	27. Burkett, J.	4.32		
13. Leiter, M.	4.92	28. Tewksbury, B.	4.31		
14. Benes, A.	4.90				

WINS

1. Smoltz, J.	24	16. Stottlemyre, T.	14	31. Hampton, M.	10
2. Benes, A.	18	17. Clark, M.	14	32. Urbina, U.	10
3. Brown, K.	17	18. Valenzuela, F.	13	33. Candiotti, T.	9
4. Ritz, K.	17	19. Smiley, J.	13	34. Schilling, C.	9
5. Leiter, A.	16	20. Osborne, D.	13	35. Ashby, A.	9
6. Neagle, D.	16	21. Martinez, P.	13	36. Astacio, P.	9
7. Reynolds, S.	16	22. Trachsel, S.	13	37. Hoffman, T.	9
8. Nomo, H.	16	23. Benes, A.	13	38. Worrell, T.	9
9. Maddux, G.	15	24. Gardner, M.	12	39. Sanders, S.	9
10. Glavine, T.	15	25. Kile, D.	12	40. Lieber, J.	9
11. Martinez, R.	15	26. Jones, B.	12	41. VanLandingham, W.	9
12. Navarro, J.	15	27. Burba, D.	11	42. Thompson, M.	9
13. Fassero, J.	15	28. Petkovsek, M.	11	43. Osuna, A.	9
14. Hamilton, J.	15	29. Darwin, D.	10	44. Wall, D.	9
15. Valdes, I.	15	30. Tewksbury, B.	10		

Catchers
pp. 27-39

Corners
pp. 40-60

Infield
pp. 60-80

Outfield
pp. 80-111

DH
pp. 112-115

Starters
pp. 115-145

Relievers
pp. 146-178

SAVES

1. Worrell, T.	44	15. Plesac, D.	11	29. Adams, T.	4
2. Brantley, J.	44	16. Henry, D.	9	30. Bochtler, D.	3
3. Hoffman, T.	42	17. Wagner, B.	9	31. Wallace, D.	3
4. Wohlers, M.	39	18. Patterson, B.	8	32. Smith, L.	2
5. Rojas, M.	36	19. Ryan, K.	8	33. Bielecki, M.	2
6. Beck, R.	35	20. Ericks, J.	8	34. Swift, B.	2
7. Nen, R.	35	21. Hernandez, X.	6	35. Boever, J.	2
8. Bottalico, R.	34	22. Leskanic, C.	6	36. Jones, D.	2
9. Eckersley, D.	30	23. Mathews, T.	6	37. Fossas, T.	2
10. Franco, J.	28	24. Honeycutt, R.	4	38. Dyer, M.	2
11. Ruffin, B.	24	25. Shaw, J.	4	39. McMichael, G.	2
12. Wendell, T.	18	26. Mathews, T.	4	40. Moore, M.	2
13. Jones, T.	17	27. Veres, D.	4	41. Hudek, J.	2
14. Cordova, F.	12	28. Osuna, A.	4	42. Powell, J.	2

STRIKEOUTS

1. Smoltz, J.	276	15. Leiter, M.	164	29. Benes, A.	131
2. Nomo, H.	234	16. Benes, A.	160	30. Astacio, P.	130
3. Fassero, J.	222	17. Brown, K.	159	31. Watson, A.	128
4. Martinez, P.	222	18. Navarro, J.	158	32. Tewksbury, B.	126
5. Kile, D.	219	19. Sanders, S.	157	33. Park, C.	119
6. Reynolds, S.	204	20. Neagle, D.	149	34. Jones, B.	116
7. Leiter, A.	200	21. Burba, D.	148	35. Harnisch, P.	114
8. Stottlemyre, T.	194	22. Gardner, M.	145	36. Isringhausen, J.	114
9. Hamilton, J.	184	23. Clark, M.	142	37. Hoffman, T.	111
10. Schilling, C.	182	24. Castillo, F.	139	38. Wilson, P.	109
11. Glavine, T.	181	25. Drabek, D.	137	39. Burkett, J.	108
12. Valdes, I.	173	26. Martinez, R.	134	40. Urbina, U.	108
13. Maddux, G.	172	27. Osborne, D.	134		
14. Smiley, J.	171	28. Trachsel, S.	132		

NET WINS

1. Smoltz, J.	16	16. Nomo, H.	5	31. Trachsel, S.	4
2. Martinez, R.	9	17. Urbina, U.	5	32. Lieber, J.	4
3. Petkovsek, M.	9	18. Grace, M.	5	33. Borland, T.	4
4. Benes, A.	8	19. Wade, T.	5	34. Stottlemyre, T.	3
5. Valdes, I.	8	20. Maddux, G.	4	35. Navarro, J.	3
6. Neagle, D.	7	21. Leiter, A.	4	36. Rojas, M.	3
7. Brown, K.	6	22. Radinsky, S.	4	37. Dewey, M.	3
8. Ritz, K.	6	23. Fassero, J.	4	38. Manuel, B.	3
9. Reynolds, S.	6	24. Ashby, A.	4	39. Clark, M.	3
10. Hamilton, J.	6	25. Osborne, D.	4	40. Martinez, P.	3
11. Valenzuela, F.	5	26. Nen, R.	4	41. Borbon, P.	3
12. Glavine, T.	5	27. Hoffman, T.	4	42. Jones, T.	3
13. Gardner, M.	5	28. Hutton, M.	4	43. Bailey, C.	3
14. Juden, J.	5	29. Sanders, S.	4	44. Salkeld, R.	3
15. DiPoto, J.	5	30. Jones, B.	4	45. Veres, D.	3

NATIONAL LEAGUE POSITION PLAYERS

Catchers
pp. 27–39

Corners
pp. 40–60

Infield
pp. 60–80

Outfield
pp. 80–111

DH
pp. 112–115

Starters
pp. 115–145

Relievers
pp. 146–178

HOME RUNS

1. Galarraga, A.	47	15. Bagwell, J.	31	29. Lopez, J.	23
2. Bonds, B.	42	16. Santiago, B.	30	30. Williams, M.	22
3. Sheffield, G.	42	17. Gant, R.	30	31. Alou, M.	21
4. Hundley, T.	41	18. Finley, S.	30	32. Lankford, R.	21
5. Burks, E.	40	19. King, J.	30	33. Zeile, T.	20
6. Caminiti, K.	40	20. Gilkey, B.	30	34. Hill, G.	19
7. Sosa, S.	40	21. Jones, C.	30	35. Greene, W.	19
8. Castilla, V.	40	22. McGriff, F.	28	36. Andrews, S.	19
9. Rodriguez, H.	36	23. Davis, E.	26	37. Walker, L.	18
10. Piazza, M.	36	24. Conine, J.	26	38. Martin, A.	18
11. Karros, E.	34	25. Sandberg, R.	25	39. White, D.	17
12. Klesko, R.	34	26. Mondesi, R.	24	40. Merced, O.	17
13. Larkin, B.	33	27. Gaetti, G.	23		
14. Bichette, D.	31	28. Grissom, M.	23		

RUNS BATTED IN

1. Galarraga, A.	150	15. McGriff, F.	107	29. Santiago, B.	85
2. Bichette, D.	141	16. Piazza, M.	105	30. Williams, M.	85
3. Caminiti, K.	130	17. Jordan, B.	104	31. White, D.	84
4. Bonds, B.	129	18. Rodriguez, H.	103	32. Davis, E.	83
5. Burks, E.	128	19. Sosa, S.	100	33. Gant, R.	82
6. Sheffield, G.	120	20. Alou, M.	96	34. Gaetti, G.	80
7. Bagwell, J.	120	21. Finley, S.	95	35. Morris, H.	80
8. Gilkey, B.	117	22. Conine, J.	95	36. Zeile, T.	80
9. Bell, D.	113	23. Berry, S.	95	37. Merced, O.	80
10. Castilla, V.	113	24. Klesko, R.	93	38. Gonzalez, L.	79
11. Hundley, T.	112	25. Sandberg, R.	92	39. Pendleton, T.	75
12. King, J.	111	26. Larkin, B.	89	40. Grace, M.	75
13. Karros, E.	111	27. Mondesi, R.	88		
14. Jones, C.	110	28. Lankford, R.	86		

STOLEN BASES

1. Young, E.	53	15. Bell, D.	29	29. Jefferies, G.	20
2. Johnson, L.	50	16. Grissom, M.	28	30. Galarraga, A.	18
3. DeShields, D.	48	17. Morandini, M.	26	31. Walker, L.	18
4. Bonds, B.	40	18. Biggio, C.	25	32. Sosa, S.	18
5. Martin, A.	38	19. Benard, M.	25	33. Cangelosi, J.	17
6. Henderson, R.	37	20. Sanders, R.	24	34. Gilkey, B.	17
7. McRae, B.	37	21. Davis, E.	23	35. McCracken, Q.	17
8. Larkin, B.	36	22. Lansing, M.	23	36. Castillo, L.	17
9. Lankford, R.	35	23. White, D.	22	37. Sheffield, G.	16
10. Hunter, B.	35	24. Finley, S.	22	38. Garcia, C.	16
11. Clayton, R.	33	25. Jordan, B.	22	39. Otero, R.	16
12. Grudzielanek, M.	33	26. Bagwell, J.	21	40. Owens, E.	16
13. Burks, E.	32	27. Mouton, J.	21		
14. Bichette, D.	31	28. Hollandsworth, T.	21		

RUNS SCORED

1. Burks, E.	142	15. Caminiti, K.	109	29. Alou, M.	87
2. Finley, S.	126	16. Gilkey, B.	108	30. Piazza, M.	87
3. Bonds, B.	122	17. Grissom, M.	106	31. Sandberg, R.	85
4. Galarraga, A.	119	18. Martin, A.	101	32. Hundley, T.	85
5. Sheffield, G.	118	19. Lankford, R.	100	33. Sosa, S.	84
6. Larkin, B.	117	20. Lansing, M.	99	34. Conine, J.	84
7. Johnson, L.	117	21. Grudzielanek, M.	99	35. Bell, D.	84
8. Bichette, D.	114	22. Mondesi, R.	98	36. Karros, E.	84
9. Jones, C.	114	23. Castilla, V.	97	37. Morris, H.	82
10. Biggio, C.	113	24. King, J.	91	38. Jordan, B.	82
11. Young, E.	113	25. Klesko, R.	90	39. Davis, E.	81
12. McRae, B.	111	26. Weiss, W.	89	40. McGriff, F.	81
13. Bagwell, J.	111	27. Benard, M.	89		
14. Henderson, R.	110	28. Grace, M.	88		

BATTING AVERAGE
(Minimum 300 At Bats)

1. Eisenreich, J.	.361	15. Jones, C.	.309	29. Mondesi, R.	.297
2. Gwynn, T.	.353	16. Renteria, E.	.309	30. Mabry, J.	.297
3. Burks, E.	.344	17. Grissom, M.	.308	31. McGriff, F.	.295
4. Piazza, M.	.336	18. Bonds, B.	.308	32. White, R.	.293
5. Johnson, L.	.333	19. McGee, W.	.307	33. Conine, J.	.293
6. Grace, M.	.331	20. Grudzielanek, M.	.306	34. Jefferies, G.	.292
7. Caminiti, K.	.326	21. Castilla, V.	.304	35. Hollandsworth, T.	.291
8. Young, E.	.324	22. Galarraga, A.	.304	36. Taubensee, E.	.291
9. Gilkey, B.	.317	23. Vizcaino, J.	.303	37. Kent, J.	.290
10. Bagwell, J.	.315	24. Williams, M.	.302	38. Biggio, C.	.288
11. Sheffield, G.	.314	25. Martin, A.	.300	39. Merced, O.	.287
12. Bichette, D.	.313	26. Kendall, J.	.300	40. Davis, E.	.287
13. Morris, H.	.313	27. Larkin, B.	.298		
14. Jordan, B.	.310	28. Finley, S.	.298		

WORST BATTING AVERAGES
(Minimum 300 At Bats)

1. Johnson, C.	.218	15. Benard, M.	.248	29. Gomez, C.	.262
2. DeShields, D.	.224	16. Hayes, C.	.248	30. Bell, D.	.263
3. Andrews, S.	.227	17. Morandini, M.	.250	31. Mouton, J.	.263
4. Boone, B.	.233	18. Bell, J.	.250	32. Santiago, B.	.264
5. Gomez, L.	.238	19. Abbott, K.	.253	33. Blowers, M.	.265
6. Pendleton, T.	.238	20. Stocker, K.	.254	34. Servais, S.	.265
7. Aurilia, R.	.239	21. Gagne, G.	.255	35. Fletcher, D.	.266
8. Henderson, R.	.241	22. Lemke, M.	.255	36. Zeile, T.	.268
9. Hernandez, J.	.242	23. Miller, O.	.256	37. Pagnozzi, T.	.270
10. Wilkins, R.	.243	24. Ordonez, R.	.257	38. King, J.	.271
11. Sandberg, R.	.244	25. Alicea, L.	.258	39. Gonzalez, L.	.271
12. Branson, J.	.244	26. Hundley, T.	.259	40. Howard, T.	.272
13. Reed, J.	.244	27. Karros, E.	.260		
14. Gant, R.	.246	28. Alfonzo, E.	.261		

AMERICAN LEAGUE PITCHERS

RATIO
(Minimum 100 Innings Pitched)

1. Rivera, M.	0.994	15. McDonald, B.	1.333	29. Martinez, D.	1.420		
2. Guzman, J.	1.124	16. Key, J.	1.352	30. Wells, B.	1.431		
3. Rosado, J.	1.191	17. Aguilera, R.	1.356	31. Rodriguez, F.	1.432		
4. Fernandez, A.	1.240	18. Pettitte, A.	1.362	32. Hershiser, O.	1.437		
5. Radke, B.	1.241	19. Mussina, M.	1.368	33. Alvarez, W.	1.440		
6. Hentgen, P.	1.250	20. Hill, K.	1.376	34. McDowell, J.	1.464		
7. Nagy, C.	1.252	21. Belcher, T.	1.383	35. Rogers, K.	1.464		
8. Appier, K.	1.263	22. Tapani, K.	1.385	36. Prieto, A.	1.464		
9. Langston, M.	1.305	23. Lira, F.	1.387	37. Erickson, S.	1.475		
10. Ogea, C.	1.316	24. Moyer, J.	1.388	38. Pavlik, R.	1.478		
11. Linton, D.	1.317	25. Gubicza, M.	1.391	39. Wasdin, J.	1.485		
12. Clemens, R.	1.327	26. Haney, C.	1.395	40. Coppinger, R.	1.488		
13. Wells, D.	1.328	27. Finley, C.	1.408				
14. Baldwin, J.	1.331	28. Karl, S.	1.408				

WORST RATIOS
(Minimum 100 Innings Pitched)

1. Williams, B.	1.901	15. Hanson, E.	1.607	29. Prieto, A.	1.464
2. Gohr, G.	1.790	16. Reyes, C.	1.594	30. Rogers, K.	1.464
3. Abbott, J.	1.754	17. Aldred, S.	1.585	31. McDowell, J.	1.464
4. Grimsley, J.	1.719	18. Wolcott, B.	1.560	32. Alvarez, W.	1.440
5. Miranda, A.	1.692	19. Gross, K.	1.554	33. Hershiser, O.	1.437
6. Robertson, R.	1.680	20. Wakefield, T.	1.550	34. Rodriguez, F.	1.432
7. Quantrill, P.	1.660	21. Boskie, S.	1.548	35. Wells, B.	1.431
8. Bones, R.	1.658	22. Oliver, D.	1.532	36. Martinez, D.	1.420
9. Witt, B.	1.658	23. Olivares, O.	1.525	37. Karl, S.	1.408
10. Sele, A.	1.646	24. Gooden, D.	1.506	38. Finley, C.	1.408
11. Gordon, T.	1.641	25. Coppinger, R.	1.488	39. Haney, C.	1.395
12. Johns, D.	1.620	26. Wasdin, J.	1.485	40. Gubicza, M.	1.391
13. Hitchcock, S.	1.617	27. Pavlik, R.	1.478		
14. Wengert, D.	1.612	28. Erickson, S.	1.475		

EARNED RUN AVERAGE
(Minimum 100 Innings Pitched)

1. Rivera, M.	2.09	15. Finley, C.	4.16	29. Langston, M.	4.82
2. Guzman, J.	2.93	16. Alvarez, W.	4.22	30. Karl, S.	4.86
3. Rosado, J.	3.21	17. Hershiser, O.	4.24	31. Olivares, O.	4.89
4. Hentgen, P.	3.22	18. Baldwin, J.	4.42	32. Miranda, A.	4.94
5. Nagy, C.	3.41	19. Radke, B.	4.46	33. Gooden, D.	5.01
6. Fernandez, A.	3.45	20. Martinez, D.	4.50	34. Linton, D.	5.02
7. Appier, K.	3.62	21. Tapani, K.	4.59	35. Erickson, S.	5.02
8. Hill, K.	3.63	22. Oliver, D.	4.66	36. Rodriguez, F.	5.05
9. Clemens, R.	3.63	23. Rogers, K.	4.68	37. McDowell, J.	5.11
10. Pettitte, A.	3.87	24. Key, J.	4.68	38. Robertson, R.	5.12
11. McDonald, B.	3.90	25. Haney, C.	4.70	39. Gubicza, M.	5.13
12. Belcher, T.	3.92	26. Reyes, C.	4.78	40. Wells, D.	5.14
13. Moyer, J.	3.98	27. Ogea, C.	4.79		
14. Prieto, A.	4.15	28. Mussina, M.	4.81		

Catchers
pp. 27-39

Corners
pp. 40-60

Infield
pp. 60-80

Outfield
pp. 80-111

DH
pp. 112-115

Starters
pp. 115-145

Relievers
pp. 146-178

WORST EARNED RUN AVERAGES
(Minimum 100 Innings Pitched)

1. Abbott, J.	7.48	15. Hanson, E.	5.41	29. Rodriguez, F.	5.05
2. Gohr, G.	7.24	16. Hitchcock, S.	5.35	30. Erickson, S.	5.02
3. Grimsley, J.	6.84	17. Boskie, S.	5.32	31. Linton, D.	5.02
4. Williams, B.	6.77	18. Sele, A.	5.32	32. Gooden, D.	5.01
5. Bones, R.	6.22	19. Wells, B.	5.30	33. Miranda, A.	4.94
6. Aldred, S.	6.21	20. Lira, F.	5.22	34. Olivares, O.	4.89
7. Johns, D.	5.98	21. Gross, K.	5.22	35. Karl, S.	4.86
8. Wasdin, J.	5.96	22. Pavlik, R.	5.19	36. Langston, M.	4.82
9. Wolcott, B.	5.73	23. Coppinger, R.	5.18	37. Mussina, M.	4.81
10. Gordon, T.	5.59	24. Wakefield, T.	5.14	38. Ogea, C.	4.79
11. Wengert, D.	5.58	25. Wells, D.	5.14	39. Reyes, C.	4.78
12. Quantrill, P.	5.43	26. Gubicza, M.	5.13	40. Haney, C.	4.70
13. Aguilera, R.	5.42	27. Robertson, R.	5.12		
14. Witt, B.	5.41	28. McDowell, J.	5.11		

WINS

1. Pettitte, A.	21	15. Oliver, D.	14	29. Wells, B.	12
2. Hentgen, P.	20	16. Moyer, J.	13	30. Gross, K.	11
3. Mussina, M.	19	17. McDowell, J.	13	31. Gooden, D.	11
4. Nagy, C.	17	18. Hanson, E.	13	32. Wells, D.	11
5. Witt, B.	16	19. Tapani, K.	13	33. Guzman, J.	11
6. Hill, K.	16	20. Erickson, S.	13	34. Baldwin, J.	11
7. Fernandez, A.	16	21. Hitchcock, S.	13	35. Radke, B.	11
8. Hershiser, O.	15	22. Rodriguez, F.	13	36. Clemens, R.	10
9. Finley, C.	15	23. Karl, S.	13	37. Haney, C.	10
10. Belcher, T.	15	24. Key, J.	12	38. Ogea, C.	10
11. Alvarez, W.	15	25. Rogers, K.	12	39. Coppinger, R.	10
12. Pavlik, R.	15	26. Gordon, T.	12	40. Martinez, D.	9
13. Appier, K.	14	27. McDonald, B.	12	41. Rhodes, A.	9
14. Wakefield, T.	14	28. Boskie, S.	12		

SAVES

1. Wetteland, J.	43	17. Jackson, M.	6	33. Lima, J.	3
2. Mesa, J.	39	18. Trombley, M.	6	34. Hansell, G.	3
3. Hernandez, R.	38	19. Myers, M.	6	35. Plunk, E.	2
4. Percival, T.	36	20. Rivera, M.	5	36. Castillo, T.	2
5. Fetters, M.	32	21. Bluma, J.	5	37. Belinda, S.	2
6. Myers, R.	31	22. McDowell, R.	4	38. Williams, B.	2
7. Henneman, M.	31	23. Garcia, R.	4	39. Mahomes, P.	2
8. Timlin, M.	31	24. Guardado, E.	4	40. Nelson, J.	2
9. Slocumb, H.	31	25. Shuey, P.	4	41. Groom, B.	2
10. Montgomery, J.	24	26. Benitez, A.	4	42. Lewis, R.	2
11. Charlton, N.	20	27. Naulty, D.	4	43. Acre, M.	2
12. Taylor, B.	17	28. Russell, J.	3	44. Rodriguez, F.	2
13. Stevens, D.	11	29. Corsi, J.	3	45. Villone, R.	2
14. Vosberg, E.	8	30. Mills, A.	3	46. Hurtado, E.	2
15. Olson, G.	8	31. Pichardo, H.	3	47. Simas, B.	2
16. Mohler, M.	7	32. Ayala, B.	3		

STRIKEOUTS

1. Clemens, R.	257	15. Tapani, K.	150	29. Karl, S.	121
2. Finley, C.	215	16. Radke, B.	148	30. Key, J.	116
3. Appier, K.	207	17. McDonald, B.	146	31. Haney, C.	115
4. Mussina, M.	204	18. McDowell, J.	141	32. Robertson, R.	114
5. Fernandez, A.	200	19. Wakefield, T.	140	33. Belcher, T.	113
6. Alvarez, W.	181	20. Sele, A.	137	34. Lira, F.	113
7. Hentgen, P.	177	21. Boskie, S.	133	35. Oliver, D.	112
8. Gordon, T.	171	22. Hitchcock, S.	132	36. Aldred, S.	111
9. Hill, K.	170	23. Wells, D.	130	37. Rodriguez, F.	110
10. Nagy, C.	167	24. Rivera, M.	130	38. Coppinger, R.	104
11. Guzman, J.	165	25. Pavlik, R.	127	39. Ogea, C.	101
12. Pettitte, A.	162	26. Baldwin, J.	127	40. Erickson, S.	100
13. Witt, B.	157	27. Gooden, D.	126		
14. Hanson, E.	156	28. Hershiser, O.	125		

NET WINS

1. Pettitte, A.	13	16. Johnson, R.	5	31. Hitchcock, S.	4
2. Nagy, C.	12	17. Alvarez, W.	5	32. Ogea, C.	4
3. Moyer, J.	10	18. Groom, B.	5	33. Karl, S.	4
4. Hentgen, P.	10	19. Wells, B.	5	34. Coppinger, R.	4
5. Mussina, M.	8	20. Baldwin, J.	5	35. Gross, K.	3
6. Rhodes, A.	8	21. Carmona, R.	5	36. Martinez, D.	3
7. Oliver, D.	8	22. Rivera, M.	5	37. Burkett, J.	3
8. Pavlik, R.	7	23. Gooden, D.	4	38. Olson, G.	3
9. Hershiser, O.	6	24. Witt, B.	4	39. Gordon, T.	3
10. Hill, K.	6	25. Rogers, K.	4	40. Cook, D.	3
11. Corsi, J.	6	26. Belcher, T.	4	41. Appier, K.	3
12. Fernandez, A.	6	27. McDowell, J.	4	42. Tapani, K.	3
13. Wickman, B.	6	28. McElroy, C.	4	43. Guzman, J.	3
14. Cone, D.	5	29. Poole, J.	4	44. Ayala, B.	3
15. Jones, D.	5	30. Trombley, M.	4	45. Mohler, M.	3

Catchers
pp. 27–39

Corners
pp. 40–60

Infield
pp. 60–80

Outfield
pp. 80–111

DH
pp. 112–115

Starters
pp. 115–145

Relievers
pp. 146–178

AMERICAN LEAGUE POSITION PLAYERS

HOME RUNS

1. McGwire, M.	52	15. Rodriguez, A.	36	29. Clark, T.	27
2. Anderson, B.	50	16. Steinbach, T.	35	30. Ripken, C.	26
3. Griffey Jr, K.	49	17. Ventura, R.	34	31. Martinez, E.	26
4. Belle, A.	48	18. Jaha, J.	34	32. Higginson, B.	26
5. Gonzalez, J.	47	19. Ramirez, M.	33	33. Hoiles, C.	25
6. Buhner, J.	44	20. Vaughn, G.	31	34. Martinez, T.	25
7. Vaughn, M.	44	21. Carter, J.	30	35. Delgado, C.	25
8. Thomas, F.	40	22. Salmon, T.	30	36. Tettleton, M.	24
9. Fielder, C.	39	23. Williams, B.	29	37. Elster, K.	24
10. Palmeiro, R.	39	24. Davis, C.	28	38. Stanley, M.	24
11. Palmer, D.	38	25. Canseco, J.	28	39. Nieves, M.	24
12. Thome, J.	38	26. Bonilla, B.	28	40. Valentin, J.	24
13. Berroa, G.	36	27. Tartabull, D.	27		
14. Sprague, E.	36	28. Edmonds, J.	27		

RUNS BATTED IN

1. Belle, A.	148	15. McGwire, M.	113	29. Fryman, T.	100
2. Gonzalez, J.	144	16. Ramirez, M.	112	30. Greer, R.	100
3. Vaughn, M.	143	17. Cordova, M.	111	31. Elster, K.	99
4. Palmeiro, R.	142	18. Anderson, B.	110	32. Salmon, T.	98
5. Griffey Jr, K.	140	19. Carter, J.	107	33. Baines, H.	95
6. Buhner, J.	138	20. Palmer, D.	107	34. Davis, C.	95
7. Thomas, F.	134	21. Berroa, G.	106	35. Vaughn, G.	95
8. Rodriguez, A.	123	22. Ventura, R.	105	36. Valentin, J.	95
9. Jaha, J.	118	23. Martinez, E.	103	37. Alomar, R.	94
10. Fielder, C.	117	24. Ripken, C.	102	38. Sorrento, P.	93
11. Martinez, T.	117	25. Williams, B.	102	39. Delgado, C.	92
12. Bonilla, B.	116	26. Tartabull, D.	101	40. O'Neill, P.	91
13. Thome, J.	116	27. Sprague, E.	101		
14. Molitor, P.	113	28. Steinbach, T.	100		

STOLEN BASES

1. Lofton, K.	75	15. Becker, R.	19	29. Bragg, D.	14
2. Goodwin, T.	66	16. Molitor, P.	18	30. Jeter, D.	14
3. Nixon, O.	54	17. Frye, J.	18	31. Phillips, T.	13
4. Knoblauch, C.	45	18. Alomar, R.	17	32. Girardi, J.	13
5. Vizquel, O.	35	19. Williams, B.	17	33. Randa, J.	13
6. Durham, R.	30	20. Valentin, J.	17	34. Roberts, B.	12
7. McLemore, M.	27	21. Griffey Jr, K.	16	35. Brumfield, J.	12
8. Amaral, R.	25	22. Curtis, C.	16	36. Belle, A.	11
9. Listach, P.	25	23. Vina, F.	16	37. Pride, C.	11
10. Damon, J.	25	24. Gonzalez, A.	16	38. Lockhart, K.	11
11. Offerman, J.	24	25. Martinez, D.	15	39. Cordova, M.	11
12. Anderson, B.	21	26. Hamilton, D.	15	40. Fox, A.	11
13. Lewis, D.	21	27. Rodriguez, A.	15		
14. Bartee, K.	20	28. Hudler, R.	14		

RUNS SCORED

1. Rodriguez, A.	141	15. Williams, B.	108	29. Ripken, C.	94
2. Knoblauch, C.	140	16. Jaha, J.	108	30. Hamilton, D.	94
3. Alomar, R.	132	17. Bonilla, B.	107	31. Vina, F.	94
4. Lofton, K.	132	18. Buhner, J.	107	32. Ramirez, M.	94
5. Griffey Jr, K.	125	19. McGwire, M.	104	33. Becker, R.	92
6. Belle, A.	124	20. Jeter, D.	104	34. Cora, J.	90
7. Thome, J.	122	21. Berroa, G.	101	35. Fryman, T.	90
8. Martinez, E.	121	22. Cirillo, J.	101	36. Salmon, T.	90
9. Phillips, T.	119	23. Molitor, P.	99	37. Valentin, J.	90
10. Vaughn, M.	118	24. Vizquel, O.	98	38. O'Neill, P.	89
11. Anderson, B.	117	25. Palmer, D.	98	39. Gonzalez, J.	89
12. Rodriguez, I.	116	26. Cordova, M.	97	40. Hollins, D.	88
13. Palmeiro, R.	110	27. Ventura, R.	96		
14. Thomas, F.	110	28. Greer, R.	96		

BATTING AVERAGE
(Minimum 300 At Bats)

1. Rodriguez, A.	.358	15. Franco, J.	.322	29. Williams, B.	.305
2. Thomas, F.	.349	16. Higginson, B.	.320	30. Edmonds, J.	.304
3. Jefferson, R.	.347	17. Martinez, D.	.318	31. Brosius, S.	.304
4. Molitor, P.	.341	18. Lofton, K.	.317	32. Offerman, J.	.303
5. Knoblauch, C.	.341	19. Jeter, D.	.314	33. Griffey Jr, K.	.303
6. Duncan, M.	.340	20. Gonzalez, J.	.314	34. Randa, J.	.303
7. Greer, R.	.332	21. McGwire, M.	.312	35. O'Neill, P.	.302
8. Nilsson, D.	.331	22. Boggs, W.	.311	36. Rodriguez, I.	.300
9. Alomar, R.	.328	23. Hudler, R.	.311	37. Jaha, J.	.300
10. Martinez, E.	.327	24. Baines, H.	.311	38. Anderson, B.	.297
11. Seitzer, K.	.326	25. Thome, J.	.311	39. Vizquel, O.	.297
12. Vaughn, M.	.326	26. Belle, A.	.311	40. Valentin, J.	.296
13. Cirillo, J.	.325	27. Cordova, M.	.309		
14. Kelly, R.	.323	28. Ramirez, M.	.309		

WORST BATTING AVERAGES
(Minimum 300 At Bats)

1. Matheny, M.	.204	15. Clark, T.	.250	29. Murray, E.	.260
2. Howard, D.	.219	16. Fielder, C.	.252	30. Bragg, D.	.261
3. Karkovice, R.	.220	17. Williams, G.	.252	31. Hollins, D.	.262
4. Lewis, D.	.228	18. Elster, K.	.252	32. Curtis, C.	.262
5. Devereaux, M.	.229	19. Carter, J.	.253	33. Guillen, O.	.263
6. Gonzalez, A.	.235	20. Tartabull, D.	.254	34. Alomar Jr, S.	.263
7. O'Brien, C.	.238	21. DiSarcina, G.	.256	35. Baerga, C.	.267
8. Listach, P.	.240	22. Brumfield, J.	.256	36. Meares, P.	.267
9. Bordick, M.	.240	23. Snow, J.	.257	37. Fryman, T.	.268
10. Young, E.	.242	24. Hoiles, C.	.258	38. Herrera, J.	.269
11. Nieves, M.	.246	25. Paquette, C.	.259	39. Stanley, M.	.270
12. Tettleton, M.	.246	26. Valentin, J.	.259	40. Lewis, M.	.270
13. Sprague, E.	.247	27. O'Leary, T.	.260		
14. Sierra, R.	.247	28. Tucker, M.	.260		

Catchers
pp. 27–39

Corners
pp. 40–60

Infield
pp. 60–80

Outfield
pp. 80–111

DH
pp. 112–115

Starters
pp. 115–145

Relievers
pp. 146–178

PRESEASON CHECKLIST

✓ 1. Call Roti•Stats for info about stats service: 800-676-7684.

✓ 2. Join the RLBA (see page 258).

✓ 3. Send in for Free Opening Day Update (see page 252).

✓ 4. Outfit entire neighborhood in Rotisserie Caps and T-shirts (see page 251).

✓ 5. Cancel all business and social plans for two weeks prior to auction draft.

TOP POSITION PLAYERS, 1996

NL CATCHERS
(20 Games or More)

HOME RUNS

1. Hundley, T.	41	12. Servais, S.	11	23. Decker, S.	2
2. Piazza, M.	36	13. Reed, J.	8	24. Zaun, G.	2
3. Santiago, B.	30	14. Johnson, B.	8	25. Manwaring, K.	1
4. Lopez, J.	23	15. Lieberthal, M.	7	26. Prince, T.	1
5. Wilkins, R.	14	16. Lampkin, T.	6	27. Mayne, B.	1
6. Pagnozzi, T.	13	17. Owens, J.	4	28. Spehr, T.	1
7. Flaherty, J.	13	18. Perez, E.	4	29. Eusebio, T.	1
8. Johnson, C.	13	19. Houston, T.	3	30. Knorr, R.	1
9. Fletcher, D.	12	20. Kendall, J.	3	31. Osik, K.	1
10. Taubensee, E.	12	21. Sheaffer, D.	2		
11. Oliver, J.	11	22. Webster, L.	2		

BATTING AVERAGE

1. Piazza, M.	.336	11. Pagnozzi, T.	.271	21. Zaun, G.	.245
2. Houston, T.	.317	12. Eusebio, T.	.270	22. Wilkins, R.	.243
3. Kendall, J.	.299	13. Fletcher, D.	.267	23. Oliver, J.	.242
4. Prince, T.	.297	14. Servais, S.	.265	24. Owens, J.	.239
5. Osik, K.	.293	15. Santiago, B.	.264	25. Lampkin, T.	.232
6. Taubensee, E.	.291	16. Mayne, B.	.263	26. Webster, L.	.230
7. Reed, J.	.285	17. Hundley, T.	.259	27. Manwaring, K.	.229
8. Flaherty, J.	.284	18. Perez, E.	.256	28. Sheaffer, D.	.227
9. Lopez, J.	.282	19. Lieberthal, M.	.253	29. Johnson, C.	.218
10. Johnson, B.	.271	20. Decker, S.	.245	30. Knorr, R.	.195

RUNS BATTED IN

1. Hundley, T.	112	11. Oliver, J.	46	21. Eusebio, T.	19
2. Piazza, M.	105	12. Kendall, J.	42	22. Manwaring, K.	18
3. Santiago, B.	85	13. Reed, J.	37	23. Webster, L.	17
4. Lopez, J.	69	14. Johnson, C.	37	24. Owens, J.	17
5. Flaherty, J.	64	15. Johnson, B.	35	25. Perez, E.	17
6. Servais, S.	63	16. Lampkin, T.	29	26. Zaun, G.	15
7. Wilkins, R.	59	17. Houston, T.	27	27. Osik, K.	14
8. Fletcher, D.	57	18. Lieberthal, M.	23	28. Prince, T.	11
9. Pagnozzi, T.	55	19. Sheaffer, D.	20	29. Knorr, R.	7
10. Taubensee, E.	48	20. Decker, S.	20	30. Mayne, B.	6

STOLEN BASES

1. Kendall, J.	5	7. Houston, T.	3	13. Decker, S.	1
2. Pagnozzi, T.	4	8. Reed, J.	2	14. Spehr, T.	1
3. Owens, J.	4	9. Santiago, B.	2	15. Lopez, J.	1
4. Sheaffer, D.	3	10. Oliver, J.	2	16. Johnson, C.	1
5. Taubensee, E.	3	11. Lampkin, T.	1	17. Zaun, G.	1
6. Flaherty, J.	3	12. Hundley, T.	1	18. Osik, K.	1

RUNS SCORED

1. Piazza, M.	87	11. Flaherty, J.	40	21. Perez, E.	19
2. Hundley, T.	85	12. Reed, J.	34	22. Webster, L.	18
3. Santiago, B.	71	13. Johnson, C.	34	23. Johnson, B.	18
4. Lopez, J.	56	14. Oliver, J.	31	24. Osik, K.	18
5. Kendall, J.	54	15. Owens, J.	31	25. Eusebio, T.	15
6. Wilkins, R.	53	16. Lampkin, T.	26	26. Manwaring, K.	14
7. Pagnozzi, T.	48	17. Decker, S.	24	27. Sheaffer, D.	10
8. Taubensee, E.	46	18. Lieberthal, M.	21	28. Mayne, B.	9
9. Servais, S.	42	19. Houston, T.	21	29. Knorr, R.	7
10. Fletcher, D.	41	20. Zaun, G.	20	30. Prince, T.	6

AL CATCHERS
(20 Games or More)

HOME RUNS

1. Steinbach, T.	35	11. Haselman, B.	8	21. Valle, D.	3
2. Hoiles, C.	25	12. Matheny, M.	8	22. Kreuter, C.	3
3. Stanley, M.	24	13. Leyritz, J.	7	23. Martinez, S.	3
4. Macfarlane, M.	19	14. Slaught, D.	6	24. Williams, G.	3
5. Rodriguez, I.	19	15. Myers, G.	6	25. Girardi, J.	2
6. Wilson, D.	18	16. Fasano, S.	6	26. Walbeck, M.	2
7. O'Brien, C.	13	17. Borders, P.	5	27. Fabregas, J.	2
8. Alomar Jr, S.	11	18. Ausmus, B.	5	28. Greene, T.	2
9. Karkovice, R.	10	19. Sweeney, M.	4	29. Pena, T.	1
10. Parent, M.	9	20. Casanova, R.	4	30. Levis, J.	1

BATTING AVERAGE

1. Slaught, D.	.313	11. Haselman, B.	.274	21. Parent, M.	.226
2. Valle, D.	.302	12. Steinbach, T.	.272	22. Walbeck, M.	.223
3. Rodriguez, I.	.300	13. Stanley, M.	.270	23. Ausmus, B.	.221
4. Girardi, J.	.294	14. Leyritz, J.	.264	24. Karkovice, R.	.220
5. Fabregas, J.	.288	15. Alomar Jr, S.	.263	25. Kreuter, C.	.219
6. Myers, G.	.286	16. Hoiles, C.	.258	26. Durant, M.	.210
7. Wilson, D.	.285	17. Marzano, J.	.245	27. Matheny, M.	.205
8. Sweeney, M.	.279	18. O'Brien, C.	.238	28. Fasano, S.	.203
9. Borders, P.	.277	19. Levis, J.	.236	29. Pena, T.	.195
10. Macfarlane, M.	.274	20. Martinez, S.	.227	30. Greene, T.	.190

RUNS BATTED IN

1. Steinbach, T.	100	11. O'Brien, C.	44	21. Parent, M.	23
2. Rodriguez, I.	86	12. Leyritz, J.	40	22. Levis, J.	21
3. Wilson, D.	83	13. Karkovice, R.	38	23. Fasano, S.	19
4. Hoiles, C.	73	14. Slaught, D.	36	24. Borders, P.	18
5. Stanley, M.	69	15. Ausmus, B.	35	25. Kreuter, C.	18
6. Macfarlane, M.	54	16. Haselman, B.	34	26. Martinez, S.	18
7. Alomar Jr, S.	50	17. Pena, T.	27	27. Valle, D.	17
8. Myers, G.	47	18. Fabregas, J.	26	28. Williams, G.	10
9. Matheny, M.	46	19. Walbeck, M.	24	29. Greene, T.	9
10. Girardi, J.	45	20. Sweeney, M.	24	30. Casanova, R.	9

STOLEN BASES

1. Girardi, J.	13	6. Walbeck, M.	3	11. Greene, T.	2
2. Rodriguez, I.	5	7. Matheny, M.	3	12. Alomar Jr, S.	1
3. Haselman, B.	4	8. Durant, M.	3	13. Wilson, D.	1
4. Ausmus, B.	4	9. Stanley, M.	2	14. Sweeney, M.	1
5. Macfarlane, M.	3	10. Leyritz, J.	2	15. Fasano, S.	1

Catchers
pp. 27–39

Corners
pp. 40–60

Infield
pp. 60–80

Outfield
pp. 80–111

DH
pp. 112–115

Starters
pp. 115–145

Relievers
pp. 146–178

RUNS SCORED

1. Rodriguez, I.	116	11. Myers, G.	37	21. Fabregas, J.	18
2. Steinbach, T.	79	12. O'Brien, C.	33	22. Parent, M.	17
3. Stanley, M.	73	13. Haselman, B.	33	23. Martinez, S.	17
4. Hoiles, C.	64	14. Matheny, M.	31	24. Williams, G.	17
5. Macfarlane, M.	58	15. Levis, J.	27	25. Borders, P.	15
6. Girardi, J.	55	16. Slaught, D.	25	26. Durant, M.	15
7. Alomar Jr, S.	53	17. Walbeck, M.	25	27. Pena, T.	14
8. Wilson, D.	51	18. Leyritz, J.	23	28. Valle, D.	14
9. Ausmus, B.	46	19. Sweeney, M.	23	29. Kreuter, C.	14
10. Karkovice, R.	44	20. Fasano, S.	20	30. Greene, T.	9

NL CORNERS
(20 Games or More)

HOME RUNS

1. Galarraga, A.	47	15. Berry, S.	17	29. Branson, J.	9
2. Caminiti, K.	40	16. Gomez, L.	17	30. Espinoza, A.	8
3. Castilla, V.	40	17. Morris, H.	16	31. Joyner, W.	8
4. Rodriguez, H.	36	18. Colbrunn, G.	16	32. Abbott, K.	8
5. Karros, E.	34	19. Huskey, B.	15	33. Jefferies, G.	7
6. Bagwell, J.	31	20. Miller, O.	15	34. Brogna, R.	7
7. King, J.	30	21. Mabry, J.	13	35. Phillips, J.	7
8. Jones, C.	30	22. Johnson, M.	13	36. Santangelo, F.	7
9. McGriff, F.	28	23. Wallach, T.	12	37. Spiers, B.	6
10. Conine, J.	26	24. Baerga, C.	12	38. Blowers, M.	6
11. Gaetti, G.	23	25. Pendleton, T.	11	39. McCarty, D.	6
12. Williams, M.	22	26. Segui, D.	11	40. Harris, L.	5
13. Greene, W.	19	27. Hernandez, J.	10		
14. Andrews, S.	19	28. Grace, M.	9		

BATTING AVERAGE

1. Grace, M.	.331	15. Jefferies, G.	.292	29. Johnson, M.	.274
2. Mueller, B.	.330	16. Segui, D.	.286	30. Wilson, D.	.271
3. Caminiti, K.	.326	17. Colbrunn, G.	.286	31. King, J.	.271
4. Houston, T.	.317	18. Harris, L.	.285	32. Espinoza, A.	.268
5. Bagwell, J.	.315	19. Sefcik, K.	.285	33. Blowers, M.	.265
6. Morris, H.	.313	20. Jordan, K.	.282	34. Alfonzo, E.	.261
7. Jones, C.	.310	21. Cianfrocco, A.	.281	35. Karros, E.	.260
8. Galarraga, A.	.304	22. Berry, S.	.281	36. Wehner, J.	.259
9. Castilla, V.	.304	23. Huskey, B.	.278	37. Miller, O.	.256
10. Williams, M.	.302	24. Joyner, W.	.277	38. Sabo, C.	.256
11. Livingstone, S.	.296	25. Santangelo, F.	.277	39. Brogna, R.	.255
12. Mabry, J.	.296	26. Arias, A.	.277	40. Magadan, D.	.254
13. McGriff, F.	.295	27. Rodriguez, H.	.276	41. Baerga, C.	.254
14. Conine, J.	.293	28. Gaetti, G.	.274	42. Rolen, S.	.254

RUNS BATTED IN

1. Galarraga, A.	150	15. Pendleton, T.	75	29. Johnson, M.	47
2. Caminiti, K.	130	16. Grace, M.	75	30. Wallach, T.	42
3. Bagwell, J.	120	17. Mabry, J.	74	31. Hernandez, J.	41
4. Castilla, V.	113	18. Colbrunn, G.	69	32. Alfonzo, E.	40
5. King, J.	111	19. Baerga, C.	66	33. Blowers, M.	38
6. Karros, E.	111	20. Joyner, W.	65	34. Branson, J.	37
7. Jones, C.	110	21. Andrews, S.	64	35. Abbott, K.	33
8. McGriff, F.	107	22. Greene, W.	63	36. Harris, L.	32
9. Rodriguez, H.	103	23. Huskey, B.	60	37. Cianfrocco, A.	32
10. Conine, J.	95	24. Segui, D.	58	38. Brogna, R.	30
11. Berry, S.	95	25. Miller, O.	58	39. Espinoza, A.	27
12. Williams, M.	85	26. Gomez, L.	56	40. Houston, T.	27
13. Gaetti, G.	80	27. Santangelo, F.	56		
14. Morris, H.	80	28. Jefferies, G.	51		

STOLEN BASES

1. Bagwell, J.	21	18. Hernandez, J.	4	35. Rodriguez, H.	2
2. Jefferies, G.	20	19. Colbrunn, G.	4	36. McCarty, D.	2
3. Galarraga, A.	18	20. Sheaffer, D.	3	37. Alfonzo, E.	2
4. King, J.	15	21. Batiste, K.	3	38. Jordan, K.	2
5. Harris, L.	14	22. Abbott, K.	3	39. Wallach, T.	1
6. Jones, C.	14	23. Mabry, J.	3	40. Espinoza, A.	1
7. Berry, S.	12	24. Miller, O.	3	41. Williams, M.	1
8. Caminiti, K.	11	25. Andrews, S.	3	42. Baerga, C.	1
9. Karros, E.	8	26. Sefcik, K.	3	43. Conine, J.	1
10. McGriff, F.	7	27. Houston, T.	3	44. Gomez, L.	1
11. Morris, H.	7	28. Gaetti, G.	2	45. Wehner, J.	1
12. Spiers, B.	7	29. Pendleton, T.	2	46. Cianfrocco, A.	1
13. Castilla, V.	7	30. Sabo, C.	2	47. Bogar, T.	1
14. Johnson, M.	6	31. Grace, M.	2	48. Huskey, B.	1
15. Joyner, W.	5	32. Branson, J.	2	49. Bell, D.	1
16. Santangelo, F.	5	33. Silvestri, D.	2	50. Castro, J.	1
17. Segui, D.	4	34. Arias, A.	2	51. Zuber, J.	1

RUNS SCORED

1. Galarraga, A.	119	15. Segui, D.	69	29. Miller, O.	43
2. Jones, C.	114	16. Mabry, J.	63	30. Andrews, S.	43
3. Bagwell, J.	111	17. Colbrunn, G.	60	31. Wallach, T.	37
4. Caminiti, K.	109	18. Joyner, W.	59	32. Abbott, K.	37
5. Castilla, V.	97	19. Jefferies, G.	59	33. Alfonzo, E.	36
6. King, J.	91	20. Baerga, C.	59	34. Branson, J.	34
7. Grace, M.	88	21. Berry, S.	55	35. Harris, L.	33
8. Conine, J.	84	22. Johnson, M.	55	36. Espinoza, A.	31
9. Karros, E.	84	23. Santangelo, F.	54	37. Blowers, M.	31
10. Morris, H.	82	24. Hernandez, J.	52	38. Mueller, B.	31
11. McGriff, F.	81	25. Pendleton, T.	51	39. Spiers, B.	27
12. Rodriguez, H.	81	26. Greene, W.	48	40. Arias, A.	27
13. Gaetti, G.	71	27. Gomez, L.	44		
14. Williams, M.	69	28. Huskey, B.	43		

Catchers
pp. 27-39

Corners
pp. 40-60

Infield
pp. 60-80

Outfield
pp. 80-111

DH
pp. 112-115

Starters
pp. 115-145

Relievers
pp. 146-178

HOME RUNS

1. McGwire, M.	52	15. Delgado, C.	25	29. Franco, J.	14
2. Vaughn, M.	44	16. Tettleton, M.	24	30. Velarde, R.	14
3. Thomas, F.	40	17. Sorrento, P.	23	31. Seitzer, K.	13
4. Fielder, C.	39	18. Fryman, T.	22	32. Clark, W.	13
5. Palmeiro, R.	39	19. Brosius, S.	22	33. Stahoviak, S.	13
6. Palmer, D.	38	20. Paquette, C.	22	34. Hayes, C.	12
7. Thome, J.	38	21. Surhoff, B.	21	35. Kent, J.	12
8. Sprague, E.	36	22. Giambi, J.	20	36. Coomer, R.	12
9. Ventura, R.	34	23. Olerud, J.	18	37. Carreon, M.	11
10. Jaha, J.	34	24. Naehring, T.	17	38. Martinez, D.	10
11. Carter, J.	30	25. Nilsson, D.	17	39. Hamelin, B.	9
12. Clark, T.	27	26. Snow, J.	17	40. Howell, J.	8
13. Zeile, T.	25	27. Hollins, D.	16	41. Young, K.	8
14. Martinez, T.	25	28. Cirillo, J.	15	42. Nevin, P.	8

BATTING AVERAGE

1. Thomas, F.	.349	15. Coomer, R.	.296	29. Palmer, D.	.280
2. Nilsson, D.	.331	16. Surhoff, B.	.292	30. Loretta, M.	.279
3. Seitzer, K.	.326	17. Martinez, T.	.292	31. Olerud, J.	.274
4. Vaughn, M.	.326	18. Nevin, P.	.292	32. Lockhart, K.	.272
5. Cirillo, J.	.325	19. Giambi, J.	.291	33. Delgado, C.	.271
6. Franco, J.	.322	20. Palmeiro, R.	.289	34. Howell, J.	.270
7. Martinez, D.	.318	21. Sorrento, P.	.289	35. Fryman, T.	.268
8. McGwire, M.	.312	22. Naehring, T.	.289	36. Hunter, B.	.268
9. Boggs, W.	.312	23. Ventura, R.	.287	37. Zeile, T.	.263
10. Thome, J.	.311	24. Velarde, R.	.285	38. Hollins, D.	.262
11. Brosius, S.	.304	25. Clark, W.	.284	39. Snopek, C.	.260
12. Offerman, J.	.303	26. Stahoviak, S.	.284	40. Paquette, C.	.259
13. Randa, J.	.303	27. Kent, J.	.284		
14. Jaha, J.	.300	28. Carreon, M.	.281		

RUNS BATTED IN

1. Vaughn, M.	143	15. Sorrento, P.	93	29. Snow, J.	67
2. Palmeiro, R.	142	16. Delgado, C.	92	30. Paquette, C.	67
3. Thomas, F.	134	17. Nilsson, D.	84	31. Carreon, M.	65
4. Jaha, J.	118	18. Tettleton, M.	83	32. Naehring, T.	65
5. Fielder, C.	117	19. Cirillo, J.	83	33. Olerud, J.	61
6. Martinez, T.	117	20. Surhoff, B.	82	34. Stahoviak, S.	61
7. Thome, J.	116	21. Giambi, J.	79	35. Kent, J.	55
8. McGwire, M.	113	22. Seitzer, K.	78	36. Lockhart, K.	55
9. Carter, J.	107	23. Hollins, D.	78	37. Velarde, R.	54
10. Palmer, D.	107	24. Franco, J.	76	38. Martinez, D.	53
11. Ventura, R.	105	25. Hayes, C.	75	39. Offerman, J.	47
12. Sprague, E.	101	26. Clark, W.	72	40. Randa, J.	47
13. Fryman, T.	100	27. Clark, T.	72		
14. Zeile, T.	99	28. Brosius, S.	71		

STOLEN BASES

1. Offerman, J.	24	17. Fryman, T.	4	33. Thome, J.	2
2. Martinez, D.	15	18. Reboulet, J.	4	34. Nilsson, D.	2
3. Randa, J.	13	19. Cirillo, J.	4	35. Davis, R.	2
4. Lockhart, K.	11	20. Carreon, M.	3	36. Loretta, M.	2
5. Fox, A.	11	21. Jaha, J.	3	37. Arias, G.	2
6. Franco, J.	8	22. Young, K.	3	38. Sheets, A.	2
7. Palmeiro, R.	8	23. Stahoviak, S.	3	39. Walker, T.	2
8. Carter, J.	7	24. Coomer, R.	3	40. Boggs, W.	1
9. Velarde, R.	7	25. Tettleton, M.	2	41. Lovullo, T.	1
10. Brosius, S.	7	26. Fielder, C.	2	42. Strange, D.	1
11. Seitzer, K.	6	27. Clark, W.	2	43. Zeile, T.	1
12. Hayes, C.	6	28. Palmer, D.	2	44. Olerud, J.	1
13. Hollins, D.	6	29. Sojo, L.	2	45. Ventura, R.	1
14. Kent, J.	6	30. Naehring, T.	2	46. Thomas, F.	1
15. Paquette, C.	5	31. Martinez, T.	2	47. Snow, J.	1
16. Hamelin, B.	5	32. Vaughn, M.	2	48. Nevin, P.	1

RUNS SCORED

1. Thome, J.	122	15. Martinez, D.	85	29. Stahoviak, S.	72
2. Vaughn, M.	118	16. Offerman, J.	85	30. Clark, W.	69
3. Palmeiro, R.	110	17. Carter, J.	84	31. Snow, J.	69
4. Thomas, F.	110	18. Giambi, J.	84	32. Delgado, C.	68
5. Jaha, J.	108	19. Velarde, R.	82	33. Sorrento, P.	67
6. McGwire, M.	104	20. Martinez, T.	82	34. Kent, J.	61
7. Cirillo, J.	101	21. Nilsson, D.	81	35. Paquette, C.	61
8. Palmer, D.	98	22. Boggs, W.	80	36. Olerud, J.	59
9. Ventura, R.	96	23. Tettleton, M.	78	37. Hayes, C.	58
10. Fryman, T.	90	24. Zeile, T.	78	38. Carreon, M.	56
11. Hollins, D.	88	25. Naehring, T.	77	39. Clark, T.	56
12. Sprague, E.	88	26. Surhoff, B.	74	40. Lockhart, K.	49
13. Fielder, C.	85	27. Brosius, S.	73		
14. Seitzer, K.	85	28. Franco, J.	72		

NL MIDDLE INFIELDERS
(20 Games or More)

HOME RUNS

1. Larkin, B.	33	16. Espinoza, A.	8	31. Benjamin, M.	4
2. King, J.	30	17. Weiss, W.	8	32. Gomez, C.	4
3. Jones, C.	30	18. Young, K.	8	33. Veras, Q.	4
4. Sandberg, R.	25	19. Abbott, K.	8	34. Alfonzo, E.	4
5. Biggio, C.	15	20. Garcia, C.	6	35. Liriano, N.	3
6. Miller, O.	15	21. Clayton, R.	6	36. Morandini, M.	3
7. Bell, J.	13	22. Grudzielanek, M.	6	37. Arias, A.	3
8. Baerga, C.	12	23. Dunston, S.	5	38. Aurilia, R.	3
9. Boone, B.	12	24. Thompson, R.	5	39. Smith, O.	2
10. Lansing, M.	11	25. Lemke, M.	5	40. Reed, J.	2
11. Gagne, G.	10	26. Alicea, L.	5	41. Lopez, L.	2
12. Blauser, J.	10	27. DeShields, D.	5	42. Mordecai, M.	2
13. Cedeno, A.	10	28. Scarsone, S.	5	43. Canizaro, J.	2
14. Hernandez, J.	10	29. Stocker, K.	5		
15. Branson, J.	9	30. Renteria, E.	5		

Catchers
pp. 27–39

Corners
pp. 40–60

Infield
pp. 60–80

Outfield
pp. 80–111

DH
pp. 112–115

Starters
pp. 115–145

Relievers
pp. 146–178

BATTING AVERAGE

1. Young, E.	.324	15. Smith, O.	.282	29. Lemke, M.	.255
2. Shipley, C.	.315	16. Clayton, R.	.277	30. Baerga, C.	.254
3. Jones, C.	.310	17. Arias, A.	.277	31. Stocker, K.	.254
4. Renteria, E.	.309	18. King, J.	.271	32. Abbott, K.	.253
5. Grudzielanek, M.	.306	19. Espinoza, A.	.268	33. Veras, Q.	.253
6. Dunston, S.	.300	20. Liriano, N.	.267	34. Bell, J.	.250
7. Larkin, B.	.298	21. Doster, D.	.267	35. Morandini, M.	.250
8. Biggio, C.	.288	22. Castillo, L.	.262	36. Blauser, J.	.245
9. Stankiewicz, A.	.286	23. Alfonzo, E.	.261	37. Reed, J.	.244
10. Lansing, M.	.286	24. Alicea, L.	.258	38. Branson, J.	.244
11. Garcia, C.	.285	25. Ordonez, R.	.257	39. Sandberg, R.	.244
12. Sefcik, K.	.285	26. Gomez, C.	.256	40. Hernandez, J.	.242
13. Gutierrez, R.	.284	27. Miller, O.	.256		
14. Weiss, W.	.282	28. Gagne, G.	.255		

RUNS BATTED IN

1. King, J.	111	15. Weiss, W.	48	29. Morandini, M.	32
2. Jones, C.	110	16. Gomez, C.	45	30. Renteria, E.	31
3. Sandberg, R.	92	17. Garcia, C.	44	31. Liriano, N.	30
4. Larkin, B.	89	18. Alicea, L.	42	32. Ordonez, R.	30
5. Biggio, C.	75	19. DeShields, D.	41	33. Espinoza, A.	27
6. Young, E.	74	20. Hernandez, J.	41	34. Arias, A.	26
7. Bell, J.	71	21. Stocker, K.	41	35. Aurilia, R.	26
8. Boone, B.	69	22. Alfonzo, E.	40	36. Dunston, S.	25
9. Baerga, C.	66	23. Cedeno, A.	38	37. Scarsone, S.	23
10. Miller, O.	58	24. Lemke, M.	37	38. Thompson, R.	21
11. Gagne, G.	55	25. Branson, J.	37	39. Smith, O.	18
12. Lansing, M.	53	26. Blauser, J.	35	40. Gutierrez, R.	15
13. Reed, J.	49	27. Clayton, R.	35		
14. Grudzielanek, M.	49	28. Abbott, K.	33		

STOLEN BASES

1. Young, E.	53	17. Dunston, S.	8	33. Benjamin, M.	3
2. DeShields, D.	48	18. Veras, Q.	8	34. Boone, B.	3
3. Larkin, B.	36	19. Smith, O.	7	35. Gomez, C.	3
4. Clayton, R.	33	20. Shipley, C.	7	36. Abbott, K.	3
5. Grudzielanek, M.	33	21. Sanchez, R.	7	37. Miller, O.	3
6. Morandini, M.	26	22. Fonville, C.	7	38. Sefcik, K.	3
7. Biggio, C.	25	23. Bell, J.	6	39. Thompson, R.	2
8. Lansing, M.	23	24. Blauser, J.	6	40. Liriano, N.	2
9. Castillo, L.	17	25. Gutierrez, R.	6	41. Reed, J.	2
10. Garcia, C.	16	26. Stocker, K.	6	42. Branson, J.	2
11. Renteria, E.	16	27. Lemke, M.	5	43. Arias, A.	2
12. King, J.	15	28. Cedeno, A.	5	44. Scarsone, S.	2
13. Jones, C.	14	29. Gagne, G.	4	45. Bates, J.	2
14. Sandberg, R.	12	30. Hernandez, J.	4	46. Alfonzo, E.	2
15. Alicea, L.	11	31. Aurilia, R.	4	47. Milliard, R.	2
16. Weiss, W.	10	32. Belliard, R.	3		

RUNS SCORED

1. Larkin, B.	117	15. Morandini, M.	64	29. Abbott, K.	37
2. Jones, C.	114	16. Clayton, R.	64	30. Smith, O.	36
3. Biggio, C.	113	17. Baerga, C.	59	31. Alfonzo, E.	36
4. Young, E.	113	18. Boone, B.	56	32. Thompson, R.	35
5. Lansing, M.	99	19. Alicea, L.	54	33. Branson, J.	34
6. Grudzielanek, M.	99	20. Gomez, C.	53	34. Fonville, C.	34
7. King, J.	91	21. Hernandez, J.	52	35. Espinoza, A.	31
8. Weiss, W.	89	22. Ordonez, R.	51	36. Cedeno, A.	30
9. Sandberg, R.	85	23. Gagne, G.	48	37. Sanchez, R.	28
10. DeShields, D.	75	24. Blauser, J.	48	38. Scarsone, S.	28
11. Renteria, E.	68	25. Stocker, K.	46	39. Gutierrez, R.	28
12. Garcia, C.	66	26. Reed, J.	45	40. Dunston, S.	27
13. Bell, J.	65	27. Miller, O.	43	41. Arias, A.	27
14. Lemke, M.	64	28. Veras, Q.	40	42. Aurilia, R.	27

AL MIDDLE INFIELDERS
(20 Games or More)

HOME RUNS

1. Rodriguez, A.	36	16. Duncan, M.	8	31. Cordero, W.	3
2. Ripken, C.	26	17. Meares, P.	8	32. Fox, A.	3
3. Elster, K.	24	18. Vina, F.	7	33. Ripken, B.	2
4. Valentin, J.	24	19. Lockhart, K.	7	34. Gates, B.	2
5. Alomar, R.	22	20. Cora, J.	6	35. Cedeno, D.	2
6. Fryman, T.	22	21. Batista, T.	6	36. Trammell, A.	1
7. Hudler, R.	16	22. McLemore, M.	5	37. Stillwell, K.	1
8. Velarde, R.	14	23. DiSarcina, G.	5	38. Vizcaino, J.	1
9. Gonzalez, A.	14	24. Bordick, M.	5	39. Sojo, L.	1
10. Knoblauch, C.	13	25. Offerman, J.	5	40. Martin, N.	1
11. Valentin, J.	13	26. Guillen, O.	4	41. Perez, T.	1
12. Lewis, M.	11	27. Howard, D.	4	42. Loretta, M.	1
13. Durham, R.	10	28. Frye, J.	4	43. Brito, T.	1
14. Jeter, D.	10	29. Easley, D.	4	44. Howard, M.	1
15. Vizquel, O.	9	30. Garciaparra, N.	4	45. Rodriguez, T.	1

BATTING AVERAGE

1. Rodriguez, A.	.358	15. Cordero, W.	.288	29. Meares, P.	.267
2. Martin, N.	.350	16. Frye, J.	.287	30. Gates, B.	.263
3. Knoblauch, C.	.341	17. Velarde, R.	.285	31. Guillen, O.	.263
4. Duncan, M.	.340	18. Roberts, B.	.283	32. Valentin, J.	.259
5. Alomar, R.	.328	19. Vina, F.	.283	33. DiSarcina, G.	.255
6. Jeter, D.	.314	20. Loretta, M.	.279	34. Elster, K.	.252
7. Hudler, R.	.311	21. Ripken, C.	.278	35. Perez, T.	.251
8. Offerman, J.	.303	22. Durham, R.	.275	36. Bournigal, R.	.242
9. Batista, T.	.298	23. Stillwell, K.	.273	37. Garciaparra, N.	.241
10. Vizquel, O.	.297	24. Cedeno, D.	.272	38. Bordick, M.	.240
11. Vizcaino, J.	.297	25. Lockhart, K.	.272	39. Rodriguez, T.	.239
12. Valentin, J.	.296	26. Lewis, M.	.270	40. Brito, T.	.238
13. Cora, J.	.291	27. Fryman, T.	.268		
14. McLemore, M.	.290	28. Easley, D.	.268		

Catchers
pp. 27–39

Corners
pp. 40–60

Infield
pp. 60–80

Outfield
pp. 80–111

DH
pp. 112–115

Starters
pp. 115–145

Relievers
pp. 146–178

RUNS BATTED IN

1. Rodriguez, A.	123	15. Lewis, M.	55	29. Hudler, R.	40
2. Ripken, C.	102	16. Lockhart, K.	55	30. Cordero, W.	37
3. Fryman, T.	100	17. Velarde, R.	54	31. Gates, B.	30
4. Elster, K.	99	18. Bordick, M.	54	32. Batista, T.	25
5. Valentin, J.	95	19. Roberts, B.	52	33. Reboulet, J.	23
6. Alomar, R.	94	20. DiSarcina, G.	48	34. Sojo, L.	21
7. Jeter, D.	78	21. Howard, D.	48	35. Cedeno, D.	20
8. Knoblauch, C.	72	22. Offerman, J.	47	36. Perez, T.	19
9. Meares, P.	67	23. McLemore, M.	46	37. Bournigal, R.	18
10. Durham, R.	65	24. Vina, F.	46	38. Easley, D.	17
11. Vizquel, O.	64	25. Guillen, O.	45	39. Trammell, A.	16
12. Gonzalez, A.	64	26. Cora, J.	45	40. Garciaparra, N.	16
13. Valentin, J.	59	27. Vizcaino, J.	45		
14. Duncan, M.	56	28. Frye, J.	41		

STOLEN BASES

1. Knoblauch, C.	45	15. Roberts, B.	12	29. Howard, D.	5
2. Vizquel, O.	35	16. Lockhart, K.	11	30. Garciaparra, N.	5
3. Durham, R.	30	17. Fox, A.	11	31. Duncan, M.	4
4. McLemore, M.	27	18. Martin, N.	10	32. Elster, K.	4
5. Offerman, J.	24	19. Valentin, J.	9	33. Fryman, T.	4
6. Frye, J.	18	20. Meares, P.	9	34. Reboulet, J.	4
7. Alomar, R.	17	21. Velarde, R.	7	35. Bournigal, R.	4
8. Valentin, J.	17	22. Batista, T.	7	36. Easley, D.	3
9. Vina, F.	16	23. Trammell, A.	6	37. Alexander, M.	3
10. Gonzalez, A.	16	24. Guillen, O.	6	38. DiSarcina, G.	2
11. Vizcaino, J.	15	25. Lewis, M.	6	39. Sojo, L.	2
12. Rodriguez, A.	15	26. Cedeno, D.	6	40. Cordero, W.	2
13. Hudler, R.	14	27. Cora, J.	5	41. Loretta, M.	2
14. Jeter, D.	14	28. Bordick, M.	5	42. Sheets, A.	2

RUNS SCORED

1. Rodriguez, A.	141	15. Elster, K.	79	29. Cedeno, D.	46
2. Knoblauch, C.	140	16. Durham, R.	79	30. Roberts, B.	39
3. Alomar, R.	132	17. Frye, J.	74	31. Batista, T.	38
4. Jeter, D.	104	18. Vizcaino, J.	70	32. Bournigal, R.	33
5. Vizquel, O.	98	19. Lewis, M.	69	33. Martin, N.	30
6. Ripken, C.	94	20. Meares, P.	66	34. Cordero, W.	29
7. Vina, F.	94	21. Gonzalez, A.	64	35. Gates, B.	26
8. Cora, J.	90	22. Guillen, O.	62	36. Fox, A.	26
9. Fryman, T.	90	23. Duncan, M.	62	37. Perez, T.	24
10. Valentin, J.	90	24. DiSarcina, G.	62	38. Sojo, L.	23
11. Offerman, J.	85	25. Hudler, R.	60	39. Reboulet, J.	20
12. McLemore, M.	84	26. Howard, D.	51	40. Loretta, M.	20
13. Valentin, J.	84	27. Lockhart, K.	49		
14. Velarde, R.	82	28. Bordick, M.	46		

NL OUTFIELDERS
(20 Games or More)

HOME RUNS

1. Bonds, B.	42	24. Bell, D.	17	47. McGee, W.	5
2. Sheffield, G.	42	25. Jordan, B.	17	48. Harris, L.	5
3. Vaughn, G.	41	26. Gonzalez, L.	15	49. May, D.	5
4. Burks, E.	40	27. Huskey, B.	15	50. Vander Wal, J.	5
5. Sosa, S.	40	28. Sanders, R.	14	51. Hunter, B.	5
6. Rodriguez, H.	36	29. Anthony, E.	12	52. Benard, M.	5
7. Klesko, R.	34	30. Curtis, C.	12	53. Jones, A.	5
8. Bichette, D.	31	31. Hollandsworth, T.	12	54. Jones, C.	4
9. Gant, R.	30	32. Dye, J.	12	55. Ochoa, A.	4
10. Finley, S.	30	33. Henderson, R.	9	56. Allensworth, J.	4
11. Gilkey, B.	30	34. Johnson, L.	9	57. Eisenreich, J.	3
12. Davis, E.	26	35. Ashley, B.	9	58. Gwynn, T.	3
13. Conine, J.	26	36. Mitchell, K.	8	59. Dykstra, L.	3
14. Mondesi, R.	24	37. Clark, D.	8	60. Kingery, M.	3
15. Grissom, M.	23	38. Obando, S.	8	61. Smith, D.	3
16. Alou, M.	21	39. Jefferies, G.	7	62. Bullett, S.	3
17. Lankford, R.	21	40. Timmons, O.	7	63. Cummings, M.	3
18. Hill, G.	19	41. Santangelo, F.	7	64. Mouton, J.	3
19. Walker, L.	18	42. Justice, D.	6	65. Sweeney, M.	3
20. Martin, A.	18	43. Howard, T.	6	66. McCracken, Q.	3
21. White, D.	17	44. McCarty, D.	6	67. Mottola, C.	3
22. Merced, O.	17	45. White, R.	6	68. Cruz, J.	3
23. McRae, B.	17	46. Floyd, C.	6		

BATTING AVERAGE

1. Eisenreich, J.	.361	21. Conine, J.	.293	41. Howard, T.	.272
2. Gwynn, T.	.353	22. Jefferies, G.	.292	42. Otero, R.	.272
3. Burks, E.	.344	23. Hollandsworth,T	.291	43. Gonzalez, L.	.271
4. Walton, J.	.340	24. McCracken, Q.	.290	44. Javier, S.	.270
5. Johnson, L.	.333	25. Merced, O.	.287	45. Clark, D.	.270
6. Justice, D.	.321	26. Davis, E.	.287	46. Kirby, W.	.270
7. Gilkey, B.	.317	27. Harris, L.	.285	47. Butler, B.	.267
8. Amaro, R.	.316	28. Klesko, R.	.282	48. Polonia, L.	.267
9. Mitchell, K.	.315	29. Alou, M.	.281	49. Sweeney, M.	.265
10. Sheffield, G.	.314	30. Dye, J.	.281	50. Cangelosi, J.	.263
11. Bichette, D.	.313	31. Hill, G.	.280	51. Bell, D.	.263
12. Jordan, B.	.310	32. Huskey, B.	.278	52. Mouton, J.	.263
13. Grissom, M.	.309	33. Santangelo, F.	.277	53. Allensworth, J.	.262
14. McGee, W.	.308	34. Rodriguez, H.	.276	54. Dykstra, L.	.261
15. Bonds, B.	.308	35. Walker, L.	.276	55. Vaughn, G.	.260
16. Martin, A.	.300	36. McRae, B.	.276	56. Wehner, J.	.259
17. Finley, S.	.298	37. Hunter, B.	.276	57. Curtis, C.	.252
18. Mondesi, R.	.296	38. Lankford, R.	.275	58. Vander Wal, J.	.251
19. Ochoa, A.	.294	39. White, D.	.273	59. May, D.	.251
20. White, R.	.293	40. Sosa, S.	.273	60. Sanders, R.	.251

Catchers
pp. 27–39

Corners
pp. 40–60

Infield
pp. 60–80

Outfield
pp. 80–111

DH
pp. 112–115

Starters
pp. 115–145

Relievers
pp. 146–178

RUNS BATTED IN

1. Bichette, D.	141	22. Grissom, M.	74	43. Mouton, J.	34		
2. Bonds, B.	129	23. Martin, A.	72	44. May, D.	33		
3. Burks, E.	128	24. Johnson, L.	69	45. Sanders, R.	33		
4. Sheffield, G.	120	25. Hill, G.	67	46. Ochoa, A.	33		
5. Vaughn, G.	117	26. McRae, B.	66	47. Harris, L.	32		
6. Gilkey, B.	117	27. Huskey, B.	60	48. Otero, R.	32		
7. Bell, D.	113	28. Hollandsworth, T.	59	49. Vander Wal, J.	31		
8. Jordan, B.	104	29. Walker, L.	58	50. Allensworth, J.	31		
9. Rodriguez, H.	103	30. Santangelo, F.	56	51. Henderson, R.	29		
10. Sosa, S.	100	31. Jefferies, G.	51	52. Kingery, M.	27		
11. Alou, M.	96	32. Gwynn, T.	50	53. Benard, M.	27		
12. Finley, S.	95	33. Curtis, C.	46	54. Floyd, C.	26		
13. Conine, J.	95	34. Howard, T.	42	55. Justice, D.	25		
14. Klesko, R.	93	35. Eisenreich, J.	41	56. Ashley, B.	25		
15. Mondesi, R.	88	36. McGee, W.	41	57. McCarty, D.	24		
16. Lankford, R.	86	37. White, R.	41	58. Javier, S.	22		
17. White, D.	84	38. McCracken, Q.	40	59. Anthony, E.	22		
18. Davis, E.	83	39. Mitchell, K.	39	60. Obando, S.	22		
19. Gant, R.	82	40. Dye, J.	37	61. Sweeney, M.	22		
20. Merced, O.	80	41. Clark, D.	36				
21. Gonzalez, L.	79	42. Hunter, B.	35				

STOLEN BASES

1. Johnson, L.	50	22. Sosa, S.	18	43. Butler, B.	8		
2. Bonds, B.	40	23. Curtis, C.	18	44. Merced, O.	8		
3. Martin, A.	38	24. Cangelosi, J.	17	45. Bullett, S.	7		
4. Henderson, R.	37	25. Gilkey, B.	17	46. Floyd, C.	7		
5. McRae, B.	37	26. McCracken, Q.	17	47. Fonville, C.	7		
6. Lankford, R.	35	27. Sheffield, G.	16	48. Hill, G.	6		
7. Hunter, B.	35	28. Otero, R.	16	49. Howard, T.	6		
8. Burks, E.	32	29. Owens, E.	16	50. Klesko, R.	6		
9. Bichette, D.	31	30. Goodwin, C.	15	51. Everett, C.	6		
10. Bell, D.	29	31. Javier, S.	14	52. McGee, W.	5		
11. Grissom, M.	28	32. Harris, L.	14	53. Tavarez, J.	5		
12. Benard, M.	25	33. Mondesi, R.	14	54. Cedeno, R.	5		
13. Sanders, R.	24	34. White, R.	14	55. Santangelo, F.	5		
14. Davis, E.	23	35. Gant, R.	13	56. Mejia, M.	5		
15. White, D.	22	36. Eisenreich, J.	11	57. Kirby, W.	4		
16. Finley, S.	22	37. Gwynn, T.	11	58. Ochoa, A.	4		
17. Jordan, B.	22	38. Allensworth, J.	11	59. Dykstra, L.	3		
18. Mouton, J.	21	39. Polonia, L.	9	60. Sweeney, M.	3		
19. Hollandsworth, T.	21	40. Vaughn, G.	9	61. Jones, A.	3		
20. Jefferies, G.	20	41. Alou, M.	9				
21. Walker, L.	18	42. Gonzalez, L.	9				

RUNS SCORED

1. Burks, E.	142	21. Bell, D.	84	41. Sanders, R.	49
2. Finley, S.	126	22. Jordan, B.	82	42. Eisenreich, J.	45
3. Bonds, B.	122	23. Davis, E.	81	43. Javier, S.	44
4. Sheffield, G.	118	24. Rodriguez, H.	81	44. Huskey, B.	43
5. Johnson, L.	117	25. White, D.	77	45. Mouton, J.	40
6. Bichette, D.	114	26. Gant, R.	74	46. Ochoa, A.	37
7. McRae, B.	111	27. Hunter, B.	74	47. White, R.	35
8. Henderson, R.	110	28. Gonzalez, L.	70	48. Fonville, C.	34
9. Gilkey, B.	108	29. Merced, O.	69	49. Harris, L.	33
10. Grissom, M.	106	30. Gwynn, T.	67	50. Kingery, M.	32
11. Martin, A.	101	31. Hollandsworth, T.	64	51. Anthony, E.	32
12. Lankford, R.	100	32. Jefferies, G.	59	52. Sweeney, M.	32
13. Vaughn, G.	98	33. Walker, L.	58	53. Dye, J.	32
14. Mondesi, R.	98	34. Hill, G.	56	54. Allensworth, J.	32
15. Klesko, R.	90	35. Otero, R.	54	55. Obando, S.	30
16. Benard, M.	89	36. Santangelo, F.	54	56. Everett, C.	29
17. Alou, M.	87	37. McGee, W.	52	57. Floyd, C.	29
18. Curtis, C.	85	38. Howard, T.	50	58. Clark, D.	28
19. Sosa, S.	84	39. McCracken, Q.	50	59. Polonia, L.	28
20. Conine, J.	84	40. Cangelosi, J.	49	60. Mitchell, K.	27

AL OUTFIELDERS
(20 Games or More)

HOME RUNS

1. Anderson, B.	50	21. Jefferson, R.	19	41. Martinez, D.	10
2. Griffey Jr, K.	49	22. Young, E.	19	42. Newson, W.	10
3. Belle, A.	48	23. Incaviglia, P.	18	43. Stairs, M.	10
4. Gonzalez, J.	47	24. Greer, R.	18	44. Pride, C.	10
5. Buhner, J.	44	25. Nilsson, D.	17	45. Bragg, D.	10
6. Berroa, G.	36	26. Hudler, R.	16	46. Raines, T.	9
7. Ramirez, M.	33	27. Cordova, M.	16	47. Burnitz, J.	9
8. Carter, J.	30	28. O'Leary, T.	15	48. Hammonds, J.	9
9. Salmon, T.	30	29. Lofton, K.	14	49. Samuel, J.	8
10. Williams, B.	29	30. Brumfield, J.	14	50. Devereaux, M.	8
11. Bonilla, B.	28	31. Mieske, M.	14	51. Greenwell, M.	7
12. Tartabull, D.	27	32. Phillips, T.	12	52. Plantier, P.	7
13. Edmonds, J.	27	33. Sierra, R.	12	53. Hunter, B.	7
14. Higginson, B.	26	34. Newfield, M.	12	54. Mouton, L.	7
15. Nieves, M.	24	35. Becker, R.	12	55. Kelly, R.	6
16. Whiten, M.	22	36. Anderson, G.	12	56. Hamilton, D.	6
17. Paquette, C.	22	37. Tucker, M.	12	57. Buford, D.	6
18. Surhoff, B.	21	38. Coomer, R.	12	58. Damon, J.	6
19. Giambi, J.	20	39. Strawberry, D.	11	59. Herrera, J.	6
20. O'Neill, P.	19	40. Green, S.	11	60. Lawton, M.	6

BATTING AVERAGE

1. Jefferson, R.	.347	22. Greenwell, M.	.295	43. Phillips, T.	.277
2. Greer, R.	.332	23. Mouton, L.	.294	44. Stairs, M.	.277
3. Nilsson, D.	.331	24. Hamilton, D.	.293	45. Carr, C.	.273
4. Perez, R.	.327	25. Surhoff, B.	.292	46. Buhner, J.	.271
5. Kelly, R.	.323	26. Amaral, R.	.292	47. Damon, J.	.271
6. Higginson, B.	.320	27. Becker, R.	.292	48. Herrera, J.	.269
7. Martinez, D.	.318	28. Giambi, J.	.291	49. Hunter, B.	.268
8. Lofton, K.	.317	29. Berroa, G.	.290	50. Mashore, D.	.267
9. Gonzalez, J.	.314	30. Bonilla, B.	.288	51. Burnitz, J.	.265
10. Hudler, R.	.311	31. Palmeiro, O.	.288	52. Strawberry, D.	.262
11. Belle, A.	.311	32. Nixon, O.	.286	53. Whiten, M.	.262
12. Ramirez, M.	.309	33. Salmon, T.	.286	54. Bragg, D.	.261
13. Cordova, M.	.309	34. Anderson, G.	.285	55. O'Leary, T.	.260
14. Bowers, B.	.308	35. Rivera, R.	.284	56. Tucker, M.	.260
15. Williams, B.	.305	36. Raines, T.	.284	57. Paquette, C.	.259
16. Edmonds, J.	.304	37. Erstad, D.	.284	58. Lawton, M.	.258
17. Griffey Jr, K.	.303	38. Buford, D.	.283	59. Samuel, J.	.255
18. O'Neill, P.	.302	39. Goodwin, T.	.282	60. Newson, W.	.255
19. Pride, C.	.300	40. Green, S.	.280	61. Brumfield, J.	.255
20. Anderson, B.	.297	41. Newfield, M.	.278		
21. Coomer, R.	.296	42. Mieske, M.	.278		

RUNS BATTED IN

1. Belle, A.	148	22. Sierra, R.	72	43. Green, S.	45
2. Gonzalez, J.	144	23. Anderson, G.	72	44. Greenwell, M.	44
3. Griffey Jr, K.	140	24. Whiten, M.	71	45. Lawton, M.	42
4. Buhner, J.	138	25. Becker, R.	71	46. Coomer, R.	41
5. Bonilla, B.	116	26. Lofton, K.	67	47. Hudler, R.	40
6. Ramirez, M.	112	27. Paquette, C.	67	48. Burnitz, J.	40
7. Cordova, M.	111	28. Edmonds, J.	66	49. Mouton, L.	39
8. Anderson, B.	110	29. Mieske, M.	64	50. Strawberry, D.	36
9. Carter, J.	107	30. Young, E.	64	51. Goodwin, T.	35
10. Berroa, G.	106	31. Phillips, T.	63	52. Devereaux, M.	34
11. Williams, B.	102	32. Brumfield, J.	60	53. Williams, G.	34
12. Tartabull, D.	101	33. Nieves, M.	60	54. Raines, T.	33
13. Greer, R.	100	34. Newfield, M.	57	55. Listach, P.	33
14. Salmon, T.	98	35. Martinez, D.	53	56. Plantier, P.	31
15. O'Neill, P.	91	36. Lewis, D.	53	57. Newson, W.	31
16. Nilsson, D.	84	37. Tucker, M.	53	58. Pride, C.	31
17. Surhoff, B.	82	38. Hamilton, D.	51	59. Herrera, J.	30
18. O'Leary, T.	81	39. Incaviglia, P.	50	60. Nixon, O.	29
19. Higginson, B.	81	40. Damon, J.	50	61. Amaral, R.	29
20. Giambi, J.	79	41. Kelly, R.	47		
21. Jefferson, R.	74	42. Bragg, D.	47		

STOLEN BASES

1. Lofton, K.	75	23. Cordova, M.	11	45. Carr, C.	5
2. Goodwin, T.	66	24. Raines, T.	10	46. Cole, A.	5
3. Nixon, O.	54	25. Kelly, R.	10	47. Tarasco, T.	5
4. Amaral, R.	25	26. Williams, G.	10	48. Paquette, C.	5
5. Listach, P.	25	27. Tucker, M.	10	49. Green, S.	5
6. Damon, J.	25	28. Battle, A.	10	50. Greenwell, M.	4
7. Anderson, B.	21	29. Samuel, J.	9	51. Sierra, R.	4
8. Lewis, D.	21	30. Greer, R.	9	52. Hulse, D.	4
9. Bartee, K.	20	31. Devereaux, M.	8	53. Salmon, T.	4
10. Becker, R.	19	32. Tinsley, L.	8	54. Burnitz, J.	4
11. Whiten, M.	17	33. Buford, D.	8	55. Edmonds, J.	4
12. Williams, B.	17	34. Ramirez, M.	8	56. Lawton, M.	4
13. Griffey Jr, K.	16	35. Herrera, J.	8	57. Mashore, D.	4
14. Martinez, D.	15	36. Carter, J.	7	58. Ward, T.	3
15. Hamilton, D.	15	37. Cuyler, M.	7	59. Newson, W.	3
16. Brumfield, J.	15	38. Young, E.	7	60. O'Leary, T.	3
17. Hudler, R.	14	39. Anderson, G.	7	61. Hammonds, J.	3
18. Bragg, D.	14	40. Strawberry, D.	6	62. Hocking, D.	3
19. Phillips, T.	13	41. Diaz, A.	6	63. Perez, R.	3
20. Coleman, V.	12	42. Hosey, D.	6	64. Coomer, R.	3
21. Belle, A.	11	43. Higginson, B.	6	65. Mouton, L.	3
22. Pride, C.	11	44. Rivera, R.	6	66. Erstad, D.	3

RUNS SCORED

1. Lofton, K.	132	22. Nilsson, D.	81	43. Pride, C.	52
2. Griffey Jr, K.	125	23. Goodwin, T.	80	44. Green, S.	52
3. Belle, A.	124	24. Anderson, G.	79	45. Listach, P.	51
4. Phillips, T.	119	25. Whiten, M.	76	46. Devereaux, M.	49
5. Anderson, B.	117	26. Higginson, B.	75	47. Newfield, M.	48
6. Williams, B.	108	27. Surhoff, B.	74	48. Mieske, M.	46
7. Bonilla, B.	107	28. Bragg, D.	74	49. Raines, T.	45
8. Buhner, J.	107	29. Edmonds, J.	73	50. Herrera, J.	44
9. Berroa, G.	101	30. Young, E.	72	51. Williams, G.	43
10. Cordova, M.	97	31. Nieves, M.	71	52. Kelly, R.	41
11. Greer, R.	96	32. Amaral, R.	69	53. Burnitz, J.	38
12. Hamilton, D.	94	33. O'Leary, T.	68	54. Hammonds, J.	38
13. Ramirez, M.	94	34. Jefferson, R.	67	55. Incaviglia, P.	37
14. Becker, R.	92	35. Brumfield, J.	63	56. Strawberry, D.	35
15. Salmon, T.	90	36. Sierra, R.	61	57. Greenwell, M.	35
16. O'Neill, P.	89	37. Paquette, C.	61	58. Samuel, J.	34
17. Gonzalez, J.	89	38. Damon, J.	61	59. Newson, W.	34
18. Nixon, O.	87	39. Hudler, R.	60	60. Coomer, R.	34
19. Martinez, D.	85	40. Tartabull, D.	58	61. Lawton, M.	34
20. Carter, J.	84	41. Lewis, D.	55	62. Erstad, D.	34
21. Giambi, J.	84	42. Tucker, M.	55		

AL DESIGNATED HITTERS
(20 Games or More)

HOME RUNS

1. Gonzalez, J.	47	8. Martinez, E.	26	15. Seitzer, K.	13
2. Fielder, C.	39	9. Delgado, C.	25	16. Sierra, R.	12
3. Berroa, G.	36	10. Tettleton, M.	24	17. Strawberry, D.	11
4. Jaha, J.	34	11. Murray, E.	22	18. Pride, C.	10
5. Davis, C.	28	12. Baines, H.	22	19. Molitor, P.	9
6. Canseco, J.	28	13. Jefferson, R.	19	20. Hamelin, B.	9
7. Bonilla, B.	28	14. Nilsson, D.	17		

Sidebar:

Catchers
pp. 27–39

Corners
pp. 40–60

Infield
pp. 60–80

Outfield
pp. 80–111

DH
pp. 112–115

Starters
pp. 115–145

Relievers
pp. 146–178

BATTING AVERAGE

1. Giles, B.	.355	8. Baines, H.	.311	15. Bonilla, B.	.288
2. Jefferson, R.	.347	9. Jaha, J.	.300	16. Sweeney, M.	.279
3. Molitor, P.	.341	10. Pride, C.	.300	17. Delgado, C.	.271
4. Nilsson, D.	.331	11. Mouton, L.	.294	18. Strawberry, D.	.262
5. Martinez, E.	.327	12. Davis, C.	.292	19. Murray, E.	.260
6. Seitzer, K.	.326	13. Berroa, G.	.290	20. Samuel, J.	.255
7. Gonzalez, J.	.314	14. Canseco, J.	.289	21. Hamelin, B.	.255

RUNS BATTED IN

1. Gonzalez, J.	144	8. Baines, H.	95	15. Seitzer, K.	78
2. Jaha, J.	118	9. Davis, C.	95	16. Jefferson, R.	74
3. Fielder, C.	117	10. Delgado, C.	92	17. Sierra, R.	72
4. Bonilla, B.	116	11. Nilsson, D.	84	18. Hamelin, B.	40
5. Molitor, P.	113	12. Tettleton, M.	83	19. Vitiello, J.	40
6. Berroa, G.	106	13. Canseco, J.	82	20. Mouton, L.	39
7. Martinez, E.	103	14. Murray, E.	79		

STOLEN BASES

1. Molitor, P.	18	8. Murray, E.	4	15. Giles, B.	3
2. Pride, C.	11	9. Sierra, R.	4	16. Tettleton, M.	2
3. Samuel, J.	9	10. Baines, H.	3	17. Fielder, C.	2
4. Strawberry, D.	6	11. Canseco, J.	3	18. Gonzalez, J.	2
5. Seitzer, K.	6	12. Martinez, E.	3	19. Nilsson, D.	2
6. Davis, C.	5	13. Jaha, J.	3	20. Vitiello, J.	2
7. Hamelin, B.	5	14. Mouton, L.	3		

RUNS SCORED

1. Martinez, E.	121	8. Seitzer, K.	85	15. Delgado, C.	68
2. Jaha, J.	108	9. Nilsson, D.	81	16. Jefferson, R.	67
3. Bonilla, B.	107	10. Baines, H.	80	17. Sierra, R.	61
4. Berroa, G.	101	11. Tettleton, M.	78	18. Pride, C.	52
5. Molitor, P.	99	12. Davis, C.	73	19. Strawberry, D.	35
6. Gonzalez, J.	89	13. Murray, E.	69	20. Samuel, J.	34
7. Fielder, C.	85	14. Canseco, J.	68		

POST All-STAR LEADERS

Catchers
pp. 27–41

Corners
pp. 41–62

Infield
pp. 63–82

Outfield
pp. 83–113

DH
pp. 114–118

Starters
pp. 119–157

Relievers
pp. 157–193

NATIONAL LEAGUE PITCHERS

BEST ERAS—Post All-Star
(Minimum 45 Innings Pitched)

1. Brown, K.	1.895	11. Benes, A.	3.295	21. Estes, S.	3.600
2. Maddux, G.	2.479	12. Valdes, I.	3.331	22. Stottlemyre, T.	3.670
3. Smoltz, J.	2.708	13. Valenzuela, F.	3.390	23. Harnisch, P.	3.715
4. Nomo, H.	2.842	14. Fassero, J.	3.479	24. Martinez, P.	3.750
5. Smiley, J.	2.982	15. Sanders, S.	3.481	25. Ashby, A.	3.831
6. Schilling, C.	3.043	16. Hamilton, J.	3.493	26. Lieber, J.	3.884
7. Astacio, P.	3.076	17. Glavine, T.	3.497	27. Clark, M.	3.926
8. Fernandez, O.	3.184	18. Reynolds, S.	3.529	28. Osborne, D.	3.979
9. Worrell, T.	3.186	19. Leiter, A.	3.538	29. Portugal, M.	3.994
10. Martinez, R.	3.270	20. Burba, D.	3.574	30. Trachsel, S.	4.045

WORST ERAS—Post All-Star
(Minimum 45 Innings Pitched)

1. Bullinger, J.	7.480	12. Candiotti, T.	5.297	23. Benes, A.	4.659
2. Salkeld, R.	7.347	13. Gardner, M.	5.266	24. Tewksbury, B.	4.433
3. Jarvis, K.	7.147	14. Wall, D.	5.266	25. Morgan, M.	4.413
4. Rapp, P.	6.787	15. Cormier, R.	5.255	26. VanLandingham	4.369
5. Ritz, K.	6.209	16. Leiter, M.	5.196	27. Thompson, M.	4.280
6. Williams, M.	5.945	17. Wright, J.	5.082	28. Jones, B.	4.279
7. Darwin, D.	5.838	18. Foster, K.	4.979	29. Drabek, D.	4.251
8. Bailey, R.	5.756	19. Person, R.	4.880	30. Hampton, M.	4.210
9. Watson, A.	5.426	20. Kile, D.	4.875		
10. Mimbs, M.	5.366	21. Wilson, P.	4.798		
11. Reynoso, A.	5.349	22. Isringhausen, J.	4.756		

AMERICAN LEAGUE PITCHERS

BEST ERAS—Post All-Star
(Minimum 45 Innings Pitched)

1. Guzman, J.	2.397	11. Appier, K.	3.606	21. Hershiser, O.	4.249
2. Hentgen, P.	2.578	12. Belcher, T.	3.651	22. Key, J.	4.371
3. Fernandez, A.	2.805	13. Adams, W.	3.839	23. Sele, A.	4.456
4. Moyer, J.	2.858	14. McDonald, B.	3.882	24. Eldred, C.	4.465
5. Prieto, A.	3.083	15. Mulholland, T.	3.921	25. Flener, H.	4.585
6. Clemens, R.	3.153	16. Pettitte, A.	3.930	26. Aldred, S.	4.610
7. Hill, K.	3.176	17. Radke, B.	4.083	27. Hanson, E.	4.618
8. Rosado, J.	3.219	18. Wakefield, T.	4.148	28. Telgheder, D.	4.651
9. Nagy, C.	3.251	19. Quantrill, P.	4.154	29. Lira, F.	4.728
10. Finley, C.	3.306	20. Ogea, C.	4.230	30. Mussina, M.	4.737

WORST ERAS—Post All-Star
(Minimum 45 Innings Pitched)

1. Williams, B.	8.752	11. Tapani, K.	5.920	21. Rogers, K.	5.180
2. Wells, B.	7.740	12. Oliver, D.	5.672	22. Aguilera, R.	5.131
3. Abbott, J.	7.269	13. Pavlik, R.	5.663	23. Linton, D.	5.121
4. Wasdin, J.	6.838	14. Robertson, R.	5.575	24. Wolcott, B.	5.121
5. Boskie, S.	6.837	15. Johns, D.	5.574	25. Olivares, O.	5.043
6. McDowell, J.	6.391	16. D'Amico, J.	5.517	26. Gordon, T.	5.006
7. Wengert, D.	6.346	17. Coppinger, R.	5.362	27. Wells, D.	4.978
8. Eshelman, V.	6.176	18. Erickson, S.	5.334	28. Haney, C.	4.949
9. Hitchcock, S.	6.136	19. Thompson, J.	5.321	29. Baldwin, J.	4.918
10. Gooden, D.	6.013	20. Karl, S.	5.271	30. Springer, D.	4.891

NATIONAL LEAGUE CATCHERS

BATTING AVERAGE—Post All-Star
(Minimum 125 At Bats)

1. Kendall, J.	.306	6. Santiago, B.	.289	11. Hundley, T.	.260
2. Piazza, M.	.304	7. Lopez, J.	.282	12. Oliver, J.	.250
3. Taubensee, E.	.301	8. Fletcher, D.	.268	13. Pagnozzi, T.	.243
4. Flaherty, J.	.299	9. Servais, S.	.264		
5. Reed, J.	.289	10. Wilkins, R.	.263		

NATIONAL LEAGUE CORNERS

BATTING AVERAGE—Post All-Star
(Minimum 125 At Bats)

1. Caminiti, K.	.360	11. Segui, D.	.297	21. Johnson, M.	.255
2. Morris, H.	.335	12. Gaetti, G.	.296	22. Mabry, J.	.254
3. Galarraga, A.	.334	13. McGriff, F.	.293	23. Rolen, S.	.254
4. Mueller, B.	.328	14. Harris, L.	.287	24. Joyner, W.	.245
5. Grace, M.	.327	15. Magadan, D.	.283	25. Greene, W.	.236
6. Jones, C.	.321	16. Espinoza, A.	.281	26. Wallach, T.	.225
7. Bagwell, J.	.319	17. Berry, S.	.272	27. Pendleton, T.	.224
8. Jefferies, G.	.318	18. Colbrunn, G.	.268	28. McCarty, D.	.216
9. Huskey, B.	.312	19. Karros, E.	.265	29. Gomez, L.	.199
10. Castilla, V.	.302	20. King, J.	.259	30. Andrews, S.	.181

NATIONAL LEAGUE MIDDLE INFIELDERS

BATTING AVERAGE—Post All-Star
(Minimum 125 At Bats)

1. Renteria, E.	.334	12. Alfonzo, E.	.263	23. Gagne, G.	.242
2. Larkin, B.	.311	13. Castillo, L.	.262	24. Sandberg, R.	.240
3. Young, E.	.304	14. Lansing, M.	.259	25. Lemke, M.	.233
4. Smith, O.	.294	15. Abbott, K.	.258	26. Morandini, M.	.228
5. Stocker, K.	.293	16. Reed, J.	.257	27. Boone, B.	.226
6. Bell, J.	.283	17. Weiss, W.	.256	28. Sanchez, R.	.211
7. Grudzielanek, M.	.280	18. Gomez, C.	.253	29. Gallego, M.	.210
8. Clayton, R.	.276	19. Ordonez, R.	.252	30. Cedeno, A.	.200
9. Garcia, C.	.275	20. Aurilia, R.	.248	31. DeShields, D.	.184
10. Biggio, C.	.272	21. Baerga, C.	.246		
11. Hernandez, J.	.267	22. Miller, O.	.242		

NATIONAL LEAGUE OUTFIELDERS

BATTING AVERAGE—Post All-Star
(Minimum 125 At Bats)

1. Eisenreich, J.	.391	17. Hollandsworth, T.	.294	33. Gonzalez, L.	.274
2. Gwynn, T.	.374	18. McRae, B.	.293	34. White, D.	.273
3. Burks, E.	.348	19. Davis, E.	.292	35. Rodriguez, H.	.272
4. Johnson, L.	.346	20. White, R.	.291	36. Lankford, R.	.270
5. Sheffield, G.	.336	21. Hill, G.	.287	37. Dye, J.	.269
6. Gilkey, B.	.336	22. Kirby, W.	.287	38. Allensworth, J.	.262
7. Mondesi, R.	.333	23. Merced, O.	.286	39. Gant, R.	.253
8. Grissom, M.	.326	24. Howard, T.	.286	40. Henderson, R.	.249
9. Mitchell, K.	.324	25. Conine, J.	.286	41. Orsulak, J.	.239
10. Jordan, B.	.321	26. Ochoa, A.	.286	42. Benard, M.	.238
11. Bonds, B.	.318	27. Santangelo, F.	.284	43. Curtis, C.	.230
12. Martin, A.	.310	28. Bichette, D.	.284	44. Bell, D.	.229
13. Sosa, S.	.310	29. Hunter, B.	.283	45. Vaughn, G.	.223
14. Alou, M.	.310	30. Klesko, R.	.279	46. Floyd, C.	.220
15. Finley, S.	.308	31. Otero, R.	.278	47. Sanders, R.	.219
16. McCracken, Q.	.307	32. Mouton, J.	.275	48. Magee, W.	.204

AMERICAN LEAGUE CATCHERS

BATTING AVERAGE—Post All-Star
(Minimum 125 At Bats)

1. Fabregas, J.	.309	7. Macfarlane, M.	.274	13. Karkovice, R.	.232
2. Haselman, B.	.298	8. Steinbach, T.	.274	14. Alomar Jr, S.	.232
3. Girardi, J.	.294	9. Stanley, M.	.265	15. O'Brien, C.	.228
4. Hoiles, C.	.294	10. Wilson, D.	.257	16. Walbeck, M.	.222
5. Rodriguez, I.	.286	11. Ausmus, B.	.247		
6. Sweeney, M.	.279	12. Levis, J.	.240		

AMERICAN LEAGUE CORNERS

BATTING AVERAGE—Post All-Star
(Minimum 125 At Bats)

1.	Thomas, F.	.349	13.	Seitzer, K.	.295	25.	Fielder, C.	.264
2.	Carreon, M.	.324	14.	Olerud, J.	.294	26.	Zeile, T.	.263
3.	Cirillo, J.	.315	15.	McGwire, M.	.292	27.	Arias, G.	.261
4.	Franco, J.	.313	16.	Ventura, R.	.292	28.	Hayes, C.	.260
5.	Thome, J.	.312	17.	Brosius, S.	.291	29.	Kent, J.	.260
6.	Offerman, J.	.310	18.	Boggs, W.	.284	30.	Snow, J.	.253
7.	Jaha, J.	.307	19.	Palmeiro, R.	.282	31.	Sorrento, P.	.252
8.	Martinez, T.	.306	20.	Paquette, C.	.274	32.	Clark, T.	.249
9.	Randa, J.	.306	21.	Stahoviak, S.	.272	33.	Giambi, J.	.245
10.	Vaughn, M.	.303	22.	Palmer, D.	.268	34.	Naehring, T.	.243
11.	Surhoff, B.	.302	23.	Fryman, T.	.267	35.	Sprague, E.	.223
12.	Hollins, D.	.298	24.	Clark, W.	.267			

AMERICAN LEAGUE MIDDLE INFIELDERS

BATTING AVERAGE—Post All-Star
(Minimum 125 At Bats)

1.	Rodriguez, A.	.378	11.	Durham, R.	.286	21.	Elster, K.	.243
2.	Duncan, M.	.367	12.	Vizcaino, J.	.285	22.	Perez, T.	.237
3.	Jeter, D.	.350	13.	Meares, P.	.281	23.	Valentin, J.	.237
4.	Frye, J.	.310	14.	McLemore, M.	.274	24.	Gonzalez, A.	.226
5.	Knoblauch, C.	.307	15.	Velarde, R.	.268	25.	Lewis, M.	.223
6.	Valentin, J.	.304	16.	Ripken, C.	.268	26.	Lockhart, K.	.221
7.	Cora, J.	.302	17.	DiSarcina, G.	.268	27.	Howard, D.	.185
8.	Alomar, R.	.299	18.	Bordick, M.	.259	28.	Bournigal, R.	.184
9.	Vizquel, O.	.297	19.	Vina, F.	.255			
10.	Batista, T.	.288	20.	Guillen, O.	.244			

AMERICAN LEAGUE OUTFIELDERS

BATTING AVERAGE—Post All-Star
(Minimum 125 At Bats)

1.	Greer, R.	.350	17.	Edmonds, J.	.303	33.	Tartabull, D.	.266
2.	Ramirez, M.	.341	18.	Amaral, R.	.299	34.	Mieske, M.	.266
3.	Green, S.	.337	19.	Cordova, M.	.299	35.	Brumfield, J.	.263
4.	Kelly, R.	.336	20.	Anderson, B.	.298	36.	Burnitz, J.	.260
5.	Higginson, B.	.333	21.	Bonilla, B.	.293	37.	Bragg, D.	.258
6.	Belle, A.	.331	22.	Nixon, O.	.289	38.	Buhner, J.	.256
7.	Nilsson, D.	.331	23.	Goodwin, T.	.285	39.	Damon, J.	.254
8.	Greenwell, M.	.327	24.	Williams, B.	.285	40.	Nieves, M.	.252
9.	Martinez, D.	.325	25.	Whiten, M.	.284	41.	Herrera, J.	.250
10.	Jefferson, R.	.324	26.	O'Neill, P.	.279	42.	Phillips, T.	.248
11.	Becker, R.	.323	27.	Anderson, G.	.278	43.	Young, E.	.246
12.	Lofton, K.	.321	28.	Salmon, T.	.277	44.	Bartee, K.	.237
13.	Tucker, M.	.313	29.	Hamilton, D.	.276	45.	Carter, J.	.216
14.	Pride, C.	.312	30.	Newfield, M.	.271	46.	Lewis, D.	.200
15.	Gonzalez, J.	.310	31.	O'Leary, T.	.271	47.	Listach, P.	.192
16.	Griffey Jr, K.	.306	32.	Strawberry, D.	.268	48.	Williams, G.	.169

BATTING AVERAGE—Post All-Star
(Minimum 125 At Bats)

1. Molitor, P.	.359	4. Davis, C.	.285	7. Delgado, C.	.246
2. Baines, H.	.307	5. Berroa, G.	.285	8. Sierra, R.	.235
3. Martinez, E.	.293	6. Murray, E.	.259	9. Tettleton, M.	.234

STATS INK

All the stats in the Scouting Report (Chapter 2) plus all the stats in the Rotisserie Stat-Pak (Chapter 3) that you've just finished memorizing come from STATS, Inc., a band of merry number noodlers whose client list reads like a Who's Who of baseball publications: *Sports Illustrated, The Sporting News,* ESPN, *USA Today,* and, yours truly, *Rotisserie League Baseball.*

STATS, Inc. also publishes several books that belong in every Rotisserie owner's library. Among them:

- *Major League Handbook.* The first baseball annual to hit the bookstores every year (November 1), with player stats for the year just ended plus projections by Bill James for the year coming up.
- *Minor League Handbook.* An essential tool for building your farm system. Year-by-year data for AAA and AA players, plus Bill James's "Major League Equivalencies."
- *Player Profiles.* Detailed situational analyses, including month-by-month performance breakdowns.
- *Matchups!* A compendium of batter vs. pitcher matchups that gives you the lowdown on the game within the game.
- *The Scouting Report.* A mix of stats and analysis, this hardy annual includes "Stars, Bums, and Sleepers," a look at who's on the way up and who's on the way down.

And that's only for starters! For a complete catalog of STATS, Inc. publications and fantasy games (including something called "football"), call the STATS inksters at 800-676-7684.

4

Down on the Farm

Back to Business

The New and Improved Farm System for 1997

by John Benson

For three years this chapter has been filled with explanations—okay, call them excuses—about the unusual and nonrecurring events in major league baseball that were making it difficult to predict the exact arrival time and performance level of every rookie. First we had the expansion year. Then we had the year with no September. And then we had the year with no April.

While analysis of all these changes at the major league level may have been extremely useful for understanding who was coming and going—and why—from the major league player population, the focus on the majors tended to distract us from the main purpose of the Farm Report: to tell you what's happening in the minor leagues. One major improvement for our 1997 report is, therefore, a renewed emphasis on the minors in their own right.

Another improvement in this year's report is a determination to tell you what's happening without the traditionally heavy dose of farming metaphors. Every farmer knows that it's good practice to rotate crops and give every field an occasional rest . . . oops, there I go again.

Anyway, while it might be necessary to use an occasional phrase like "bumper crop" or "down on the farm," I have a definite impression that a new set of metaphors would help these pages.

So, for 1997, farming has become agribusiness. This year's minor league report will be delivered with an extensive use of language from business and economics. The agribusiness theme may sound merely cosmetic, but it ties in neatly with the renewed dedication to understanding what's happening in minor league baseball. And soon you will see that business principles were very much at work in shaping the minors in 1996, and that they will continue to exert much influence in 1997 and beyond.

Before delving into all the economic theories that explain which players

---

are advancing fastest (and why), I have to thank Yankee manager Joe Torre for reminding me that all player movement, which we try so hard to understand and predict, can be linked to good old love of the bottom line.

Near the end of the 1996 season, reflecting on the many players who had contributed to the Bronx team's first AL championship flag in 15 years, Torre said, "Players come and go. It happens on every team. Sometimes the fans don't realize that the new guy is better than the one who was let go, or they don't want to admit it. Or sometimes teams just need different things at different times. The pieces have to fit together for the good of the whole. After all, in the end, this is a business."

On that note, welcome to the new and improved Minor League Report for 1997! For years I have been telling you that farming is dirty, backbreaking work (which is true). Now I can tell you why the minor league population can't be understood by looking at the major leagues, and why it can be understood through the careful application of sound business principles.

Last year, this chapter identified six phenomena, each named in honor of a player who played in the majors and personified a trend from the 1995 season:

1. An increased number of bargain-basement free agents (The Jody Reed Phenomenon).

2. In-shape players shifting from the minor league regular season back to spring training, but at the major league level (The Andy Tomberlin Phenomenon).

3. A related rush of healthy rookie pitchers into major league starting rotations weakened by the longest winter layoff in baseball history (The Juan Acevedo Phenomenon).

4. The increased use of Rule Five draftees (The Jon Nunnally Phenomenon).

5. More hard-throwing but unproven young relievers being pushed into prominent short relief roles (The Ron Villone Phenomenon).

6. And a money-saving trend toward youngsters at the expense of veterans (The Johnny Damon Phenomenon).

Except for numbers one and six, which fit into this year's business theme, those trends didn't really carry over into 1996. In fact, none of the phenomenon namesakes had a very good season within the context of their individual careers.

Shifting from the majors to the minors, and looking for business themes, here is what we found in 1996 (and please note: the "we" includes superscout Lary Bump and superanalyst Tony Blengino, whose combined efforts can be found in the preseason annual guidebook devoted to the minors, *Future Stars*, available from Diamond Library as noted in the shameless commercial plug at the end of this essay).

The Triple-A Depletion Allowance

To understand the minors, it is necessary to look below the Triple-A level. It has long been true that Double-A rosters are richer in real prospects, while Triple-A has become an aged extension of the major league bench. That bench was badly depleted by major league needs in 1996.

Triple-A baseball in 1996 was about as bad as professional baseball can get. The International League, in particular, was at its lowest talent level since 1977. That year, you may recall, was an expansion year. And we have been telling you for three years that expansion is the largest single influence disrupting the traditional distribution of talent in each franchise.

Baseball has yet to overcome the effects of the 1993 expansion. And the problem wasn't just the obvious shortage of pitching, as evidenced by huge offensive years from journeymen like Phil Hiatt and Jerry Brooks. The 1996 Triple-A season was characterized by fumbled grounders, missed cutoff men, and inattentive runners getting picked off. There seemed to be an all-time record number of 12–9 games.

Hope was springing eternal, however, at Double-A and lower levels last year. That hope was especially visible in the form of sound pitching, some of which will eventually reach the majors. All three of the Double-A leagues had at least one qualifier for the ERA crown who came in under 3.00—and these pitchers were real prospects, unlike the retreads who pitched well at Triple-A. The Southern League had only eight .300 hitters. The Texas League, long noted for hitting accomplishments, likewise produced only eight .300 hitters in 1996.

The same trend of strong pitching held in the full-season Class-A leagues. In the Florida State League, the ten best ERA were all under 2.90. In the South Atlantic League, the top ten cutoff was 2.74! Only the California and Midwest leagues had as many as ten .300 hitters. Among the short-season leagues, the New York–Penn and Appalachian each had four pitchers with ERAs under 2.00; the Gulf Coast League had seven such pitchers.

Why did this pitching blossom? Did the lower-level leagues throw away their rabbit balls and play with the same dead ones that seem to be in use when Greg Maddux pitches? Don't think so. Instead, we view this trend as free market forces in action.

A New Curve in Pitching:
The Supply/Demand Function

While the major leagues went on a home run binge—and I still want to see an asterisk on the 1996 Orioles' 257 homers passing the 1961 Yankees' total of 240, because the Maris/Mantle team did their work with eight hitters and a pitcher, while Baltimore trotted out nine hitters every time through their DH-boosted order—every team has been sending its scouts out with specific instructions: "Find us pitchers!"

Another notable fact is that amateur players have realized that the quickest way to a big payday can be as a pitcher. Not only are pitchers in demand, but the job's a lot easier than playing catcher or shortstop, yielding four off days for every day worked by a starter, and allowing eight innings of sit-and-watch for one inning of work by a short reliever.

Whatever the motivation, it's a fact that top scholastic athletes are gravitating to pitching instead of hitting. Two-way college stars are becoming less interested in the hitting route recently followed by John Olerud and Todd Helton. And don't forget the successful hitter-to-pitcher conversions of former catcher Troy Percival, former shortstop Jim Bullinger, and, most recently, former catcher/outfielder Nerio Rodriguez.

Trickle-Down Pitching Value

Not wanting to sound too much like supply-siders who guarantee that every major league pitching staff will soon be enriched by the growing population of up-and-coming pitchers, we must emphasize that the influx of pitching talent will be felt minimally in 1997. The pitchers recommended below are more likely to blossom in 1998–99. But we still believe that by 2001 you will be hearing more ideas like tightening the strike zone, a notion that seemed unthinkable after the 1996 season.

The Rotisserie application of this theory has limitations. Pitchers still make riskier picks than obvious future star hitters. But the minor league pitcher population is already under an unfair cloud of suspicion because of the many major league pitching failures of 1996. For Ultra leagues and farm system picks, there will be opportunities in 1997, especially when minor league pitchers can be safely stored until they show major league ability. If your draft doesn't offer any such opportunities, file this 1997 list away, with a note to yourself to take another look at the pitchers in a year or two; many of them will make good investments in 1998–99 and into the twenty-first century.

Even in 1996, there were opportunities among rookie pitchers. If, like us, you had tabbed Alan Benes, Mariano Rivera, Billy Wagner, and Paul Wilson as the best bets, you would have done well. However, some other talented arms cited here a year ago, like Alan Embree, Bryan Rekar, and Bob Wolcott, kept up the grand tradition of rookie pitchers: they tortured their Rotisseowners.

There still isn't, and never will be, any easy formula to identify the top pitchers coming up. The closest thing to a functional mantra is "Get tall, hard-throwing left-handers in good pitchers' parks." That method may work well in the long run, but in 1996 it didn't exactly match our list or the outcomes. Wagner was the only successful hard-throwing lefty in a good park, and he isn't exactly tall. Toiling at Jacobs Field didn't really help Embree, a lefty who's pretty tall. And Rekar, a truly promising talent a year ago, merely added to the growing conventional wisdom regarding Rockies pitchers: "Just Say No!"

Alvin Toffler Value Adjustments

Future Shock Update: our beloved game is indeed changing faster than most people can comprehend. Even among the superior element of the fan population (i.e., Rotisserians) it will take some time for the hitting explosion of 1996 to sink in.

Huge offensive numbers posted by so many major leaguers and Triple-A players will attract bidders' attention way beyond their true merit in 1997.

On the flip side, speedsters who deliver those vanishing stolen bases in large quantities will be undervalued by those who haven't yet realized that a steal is now *much* scarcer than a home run, even in the National League. The obvious implication is that speed, which doesn't slump and which translates well from minor league basepaths to the major league fields, is especially worth noting on this year's prospect list.

Full Fiscal Year Accounting

One reason there seemed to be much more offense in the major leagues in 1996 was the novel concept of playing a full schedule of 162 games. Think about it, a whole year without work stoppages! We hadn't seen the likes of that since 1993. League totals, and individual offensive numbers, increased 11% across the board from the preceding year just from playing a full season in 1996.

Thus we have one more reason to believe that bidders will be over-enamored with the best veteran hitters of 1996, leaving better bargain opportunities among other segments of the player population, e.g., the aforementioned young pitchers and the minor league hitting stars who got no apparent benefit from a lengthened 1996 season and who faced relatively tougher pitching in most of the lower minors.

Ticket Sales 101

Having stated a general reason to like minor league hitters, here is a specific caution that applies to some of them. Many of the minor league stadiums built in recent years have followed the big league trend toward smaller, cozier, fan-friendly, and thus hitter-friendly parks. That's one reason journeymen such as Hiatt and Brooks became power sources. Charlotte's Knights Castle was one such stadium; the new ballparks in Rochester and Syracuse in 1997 were planned to continue the same trend. And in Buffalo, home of the one newer Triple-A stadium that favored pitchers, the fences were moved in.

Year-End Audit

All the above stories may be true and interesting, but what's the bottom line? Taking a look at last year's prospect list, the most obvious evaluation is that we gave you more quantity, perhaps with diluted quality.

The 1996 Minor League Report gave readers an all-time high of 112 "prospects." Meanwhile, the number of job opportunities in the majors remained about the same or even went down a bit from 1995, when so many out-of-shape veterans needed a rest and others needed something longer-lasting, like a release. Simple arithmetic indicates that our hit rate had to go down, and it did. Just over 60% of the players cited last year made it to the majors.

In addition to the numerical constraint on our outcome, we have another excuse, er, explanation, for last year's lower percentage of listed prospects reaching the majors in the year you found them here. We made a big increase, in both number and proportion, of prospects who got a one-star (long-term) rating. That number shot up from 13 in the 1995 book to 36 last year. Even though 9 of those 36 played in the majors during 1996—including Rey Ordonez, who became a regular—that 25% success rate reduced our overall total significantly.

But did we learn anything? One lesson that we *relearned* is that we will always be, to some extent, at the mercy of external forces in making our picks for the best prospects. Our biggest errors in 1996 recommendations were the most forgivable: those due to injuries. Our only three-star (meaning "ready to be a productive regular now") projected rookies who didn't play in the majors last season were Jay Payton and Antone Williamson, both sidelined with physical woes. Others who were injured, among those we liked, were Damon Hollins, Trot Nixon, and Bartolo Colon. Another uncontrollable factor was trades. Even if Payton had been healthy, the Mets' acquisitions of Bernard Gilkey and Lance Johnson would have kept the rookie from playing much. Similarly, Steve Rodriguez didn't move into the Tigers' second base job because Detroit traded for Mark Lewis. Even so, Rodriguez was ready at Toledo, batting .285 and stealing 18 bases, had the Tigers needed him.

One fact worth noting here is that we could have given you a higher hit rate by simply relisting some of our favorite players from previous years' minor league reports. Quoting ourselves from a year ago: "We still like these players: Carlos Delgado, Tony Clark, David Bell, Butch Huskey, Roger Cedeno, Ray McDavid, Michael Tucker, Ernie Young, Brian Barber, Bill Pulsipher, Paul Shuey, Curtis Goodwin, and Todd Hollandsworth."

The only players on that list who didn't contribute in the majors were McDavid, Barber, and Pulsipher—and they were all injured. So this year we include this bit of obvious advice: take another look at last year's list, if you really want to do your homework well.

Here's a problem we know about but decided not to fix: last year we gave you many more pitching prospects than usual—39. Everybody reading these pages knows that pitching is always a crapshoot. Hurlers such as Steve

Falteisek and Rodney Henderson simply didn't follow up encouraging 1995 seasons to advance to the majors in 1996. Others—such as Matt Drews, Jimmy Haynes, Rafael Orellano, and Matt Whisenant—simply couldn't find home plate until they got behind in the count.

Just leaving pitchers out of this chapter would allow us to say that a very high percentage of our recommendations reach the majors every year. But then we would just be giving you less information, not exactly an improvement over this annual list with pitchers galore.

To pat ourselves on the back for work well done, we note the value of digging deep, and the value of taking a second and third look at players whose numbers may not look so good. Where else but in this book did you see Mariano Rivera listed as one of the top rookies for 1996? Outside the Trammell household, where did you see Bubba Trammell included as more than an interesting name? Who else looked beyond Calvin Maduro's 0–6, 5.09 record at Bowie? And we didn't let Scott Rolen's 1995 injury affect our opinion of his future.

Overall, we're proud of our record, but we're never satisfied and always trying to do better. We'll match our prospect list against anybody's. Because the readers of this chapter generally can't spend much time in Auburn or Buffalo or Charleston, we visit those garden spots for you and report what we find. This year we came up with another long list of prospects for your consideration, including more pitchers than ever. Yes, we're gluttons for punishment from the sore arms and maladjusted psyches of these baseball specialists. But heck, farming is dirty, backbreaking work, and somebody has to do it.

THE BENSON FILE

John Benson publishes *The Rotisserie Baseball Annual, The Benson Baseball Monthly,* and the book *Future Stars—The Minor League Abstract.*

For information on these publications, call 203-834-1231, or write to Diamond Library at 15 Cannon Road, Wilton, CT 06897. Information can also be found at the Internet website www.johnbenson.com.

1997 Farm System Prospects

Most of the members of this Class of 1997 will make it to the majors—some sooner, some later. And some will have a greater impact when they do arrive. Consult the Rating Guide below to see which players we think fit into which category. Owners in leagues with large farm systems, owners in Ultra leagues, and anyone building for the long-term future will want to pay special attention to the players with one-star ratings. Player ages are as of April 1, 1997. Profiles do not include 1996 major league stats (if any), which appear in the Appendix (pages 299–324).

RATING GUIDE

* * *   Ready to be a productive regular now.
* *   Fine talent, should make it to the majors in 1997.
*   Good idea for 1998 or 1999.

CATCHERS

KEVIN BROWN RANGERS Age 23/R * *

Brown has a future as a power-hitting catcher—but probably not in Texas, where Pudge Rodriguez is just two years older.

Team	Level		AB	HR	RBI	SB	BA
Tulsa	AA		460	26	86	0	.263

RAMON CASTRO ASTROS Age 21/R *

Castro has the same tools he had a year ago—primarily his strong arm. His power hitting was down in 1996, but he is nonetheless a year closer to the majors.

Team	Level		AB	HR	RBI	SB	BA
Quad City	A		314	7	43	2	.248

PAT CLINE CUBS Age 22/R *

Let's see if Pat can re-Cline on the other side of Florida, in Orlando, this season. We're inclined to say that his career is not on the decline, unlike our humor.

Team	Level		AB	HR	RBI	SB	BA
Daytona Beach	A		434	17	76	10	.279

TODD GREENE ANGELS Age 25/R * * *

Sure, Greene's home run total fell off from the 40 he swatted in 1995. But he was injured or in Anaheim for much of the season, and was playing in a much tougher ballpark than even the Big A. Greene isn't the greatest catcher, but he is improving.

Team	Level		AB	HR	RBI	SB	BA
Vancouver	AAA		223	5	33	0	.305

MARCUS JENSEN   GIANTS   Age 24/B   * *

Every team would love to have a switch-hitting catcher. Jensen should get plenty of playing time, spelling Rick Wilkins against left-handed pitching.

Team	Level		AB	HR	RBI	SB	BA
Phoenix	AAA		405	5	53	1	.264

ELIESER MARRERO   CARDINALS   Age 23/R   * *

Eli's coming to St. Louis. Hide your would-be base-stealers, National League opponents! There may not be a better all-around catching prospect anywhere.

Team	Level		AB	HR	RBI	SB	BA
Arkansas	AA		374	19	65	9	.270

JULIO MOSQUERA   BLUE JAYS   Age 24/R   * *

By far the best defensive catcher in the Toronto organization, Mosquera survived the mosquitoes and the cold shoulder from cliquish veterans in Syracuse last season. The question is whether he can survive major league pitching.

Team	Level		AB	HR	RBI	SB	BA
Knoxville	AA		318	2	31	6	.230
Syracuse	AAA		72	0	5	0	.250

JORGE POSADA   YANKEES   Age 25/B   * *

No one had more to do with Columbus's International League championship than their catcher. He drew 79 walks to rank among the league leaders in on-base percentage, and he treated base-stealers harshly. If the Yanks didn't already have Joe Girardi, Posada would be their everyday catcher in 1997. He should get plenty of starts against right-handers.

Team	Level		AB	HR	RBI	SB	BA
Columbus	AAA		354	11	62	3	.271

DAMIAN SAPP   RED SOX   Age 20/R   *

Sapp hit well in a very difficult setting for hitters, raising his average 124 points in his third pro season.

Team	Level		AB	HR	RBI	SB	BA
Michigan	AA		335	18	52	3	.322

MIKE SWEENEY   ROYALS   Age 23/R   * * *

Actually, Sweeney already has shown he can be a productive major league regular. He hit so well in the hitters' graveyard at Wilmington in 1995, the Royals promoted him all the way to the majors. They brought him back to stay in the majors late last year.

Team	Level		AB	HR	RBI	SB	BA
Omaha	AAA		101	3	16	0	.257

JOSE VALENTIN   TWINS   Age 21/B   *

Valentin's offensive production nose-dived after a big year in the Midwest League in 1995. If he shows he can hit offspeed pitches at Double-A or Triple-A this year, he'll be back on track to the Metrodome. Don't forget, he is a 21-year-old switch-hitting catcher, which puts him a couple a steps ahead of everyone else before he even takes a swing.

Team	Level	AB	HR	RBI	SB	BA
Fort Myers	A	338	7	54	1	.263
Hardware City	AA	165	3	16	0	.236

JASON VARITEK MARINERS Age 24/B ★ ★

Though he hasn't reached the level of Georgia Tech teammates Nomar Garciaparra and Jay Payton, Varitek made huge strides in his second pro year. His offensive statistics were up in every category but strikeouts—down 33 in 151 more at bats.

Team	Level	AB	HR	RBI	SB	BA
Port City	AA	503	12	67	7	.262

CHRIS WIDGER MARINERS Age 25/R ★ ★

If you're looking for one team to make a trade from one position of strength, it's the Mariners with their catchers—Dan Wilson, Widger, and Varitek. Let's see, what could Seattle use? Pitching, perhaps?

Team	Level	AB	HR	RBI	SB	BA
Tacoma	AAA	352	13	48	7	.304

FIRST BASEMEN

STEVE COX ATHLETICS Age 22/L ★ ★

His falloff from 30 homers and 110 RBI in 1995 can be attributed to the difference between hitting at Modesto and hitting at Huntsville. If he starts well at high-altitude Edmonton, Cox should be ready for the newly configured bandbox at Oakland.

Team	Level	AB	HR	RBI	SB	BA
Huntsville	AA	381	12	61	2	.281

TODD HELTON ROCKIES Age 23/L ★ ★

Helton was a pretty good quarterback (ahead of Peyton Manning) at Tennessee. Now Helton is a very good hitting prospect. Look for more power hitting in 1997.

Team	Level	AB	HR	RBI	SB	BA
New Haven	AA	319	7	51	2	.332
Colorado Springs	AAA	71	2	13	0	.352

PAUL KONERKO DODGERS Age 21/R ★ ★

Konerko was a catcher until the LA management looked down on the field at Dodger Stadium and saw Mike Piazza. But the Dodgers do think Konerko is good enough to supplant 100-RBI man Eric Karros eventually.

Team	Level	AB	HR	RBI	SB	BA
San Antonio	AA	470	29	86	1	.300
Albuquerque	AAA	14	1	2	0	.429

DERREK LEE

PADRES   **Age 21/R**   • •

When the Pads were peddling prospects for a possible pennant, one man they declined to give up was Lee. They have brought him slowly through their system so he could be successful. One caution: he fanned 170 times last season.

Team	Level		AB	HR	RBI	SB	BA
Memphis	AA		500	34	104	13	.280

RICHIE SEXSON

INDIANS   **Age 22/R**   •

After a big '95 season in the Carolina League and a fast start last year, Sexson tailed off the second time around the Eastern League. The 6'6", 206-pounder could develop into a Dave Winfield type or devolve into Tate Seefried. If you don't remember Tate Seefried, you get the point anyway.

Team	Level		AB	HR	RBI	SB	BA
Canton-Akron	AA		518	16	76	2	.276

MARIO VALDEZ

WHITE SOX   **Age 22/L**   •

The thing about big kids (Valdez is 6'2", 190) who hit for average is that they can develop into bigger young men who also hit for power. That's the story on Valdez, who has also improved his batting eye. He won't hit a lot of homers at Birmingham this year, but he will when he plays in smaller parks and gets even more experience at higher levels.

Team	Level		AB	HR	RBI	SB	BA
South Bend	A		202	10	43	2	.376
Birmingham	AA		168	3	28	0	.274

RON WRIGHT

PIRATES   **Age 21/R**   • •

The Bucs weren't entirely fleeced in the Denny Neagle trade. So they were left with no pitching? Big deal. They got Wright, who will hit enough homers to put some fannies in the seats.

Team	Level		AB	HR	RBI	SB	BA
Durham	A		240	20	62	1	.275
Greenville	AA		246	16	52	1	.248

DMITRI YOUNG

CARDINALS   **Age 23/B**   • • •

One of last season's top success stories was Young, who went from being an underachieving, overweight player without a position to a hardworking, upbeat performer. And he was the American Association batting leader. He has regained big-time prospect status.

Team	Level		AB	HR	RBI	SB	BA
Louisville	AAA		459	15	64	16	.333

SECOND BASEMEN

MARLON ANDERSON PHILLIES Age 23/L *

Speed and defense are Anderson's strengths. He has been a leadoff batter, but he doesn't walk often. In the Philadelphia organization, there is a lot of upward mobility, so watch for him to move up at least to Triple-A during 1997.

Team	Level	AB	HR	RBI	SB	BA
Clearwater	A	257	2	22	26	.272
Reading	AA	314	3	28	17	.274

TONY BATISTA ATHLETICS Age 23/R * * *

Batista is another prospect who already has made a mark in the majors. He has excellent power for a middle infielder. Batista played shortstop at Edmonton.

Team	Level	AB	HR	RBI	SB	BA
Edmonton	AAA	205	8	40	2	.322

HOMER BUSH PADRES Age 24/R * *

Injuries have kept Bush from reaching the majors, and have taken away much of his base-stealing speed. When he puts the ball in play, he is a dangerous line-drive hitter, but he had an alarming 33 strikeouts and only three walks last season.

Team	Level	AB	HR	RBI	SB	BA
Wichita	AA	238	3	14	17	.290

FRANK CATALANOTTO TIGERS Age 22/L * *

Catalanotto offers an exciting package of hitting for power and average, stealing bases and reaching base (74 walks in '96). His biggest obstacle to becoming a longtime Tigers second baseman right now is 20-year-old speed merchant Richard Almanzar coming up behind him.

Team	Level	AB	HR	RBI	SB	BA
Jacksonville	AA	497	17	67	15	.298

EDWIN DIAZ RANGERS Age 22/R * *

Diaz is one of the top prospects in the Texas organization. Until recently, that wasn't saying much. His assignment for 1997 is to learn the strike zone (25 walks, 122 whiffs in '96).

Team	Level	AB	HR	RBI	SB	BA
Tulsa	AA	500	16	65	8	.264

WILTON GUERRERO DODGERS Age 22/R * * *

Guerrero is one of the best kind of second basemen: a former shortstop. Delino DeShields is hearing the 5'11", 150-pound Guerrero's soft footsteps. If DeShields hangs on to second base, Guerrero could always move back to short.

Team	Level	AB	HR	RBI	SB	BA
Albuquerque	AAA	425	2	38	26	.344

JASON HARDTKE METS Age 25/B • •

Hardtke is the kind of player to be appreciated for his consistent hard work rather than for isolated brilliant performances. He hits line drives, he draws walks, he hangs in on the double play so long that he risks the kind of knee injury that cost him much of last season. How much playing time can he get for the Mets? Here's a little clue for you all: after Alex Ochoa was called up last season, Bobby Valentine had Hardtke batting cleanup at Norfolk.

Team	Level	AB	HR	RBI	SB	BA
Binghamton	AA	137	3	16	0	.263
Norfolk	AAA	257	9	35	4	.300

RYAN LANE TWINS Age 22/R •

Another former shortstop. And Lane is a former shortstop with good pop, good speed, and good strike-zone judgment. He probably needs a full Double-A season—either at second or at short—before reaching the majors.

Team	Level	AB	HR	RBI	SB	BA
Fort Myers	A	404	9	62	21	.272
Hardware City	AA	117	2	12	3	.222

KEITH LUULOA ANGELS Age 22/R • •

If Luuloa's name were on "Wheel of Fortune," you could go broke buying vowels. He isn't likely to go broke playing baseball, however.

Team	Level	AB	HR	RBI	SB	BA
Midland	AA	531	7	44	4	.260

ADAM RIGGS DODGERS Age 24/R • •

This is the year for Riggs to produce, before he becomes too old to remain a prospect. He can hit (.362 at San Bernardino in '95); if he can get his defensive act together, Riggs could even become a double-play partner for Wilton Guerrero one day.

Team	Level	AB	HR	RBI	SB	BA
San Antonio	AA	506	14	66	16	.283

THIRD BASEMEN

GABE ALVAREZ PADRES Age 23/R • •

Shortstops who switch positions don't always move to second base. Sometimes they slide over to third base—right, Cal? It's the better-hitting shortstops who move to their right. One example is Alvarez, whose pro debut in 1995 was comparable to Darin Erstad's.

Team	Level	AB	HR	RBI	SB	BA
Memphis	AA	368	8	40	2	.247

GEORGE ARIAS — ANGELS — Age 25/R — ***

Arias wasn't ready for the leap from Double-A to the majors out of spring training, but by the end of the season, he was ready, and he obviously doesn't need any more time at Triple-A.

Team	Level		AB	HR	RBI	SB	BA
Vancouver	AAA		243	9	55	2	.337

MIKE BELL — RANGERS — Age 22/R — **

If the name sounds familiar, it should. This isn't the light-hitting first base replacement Mike Bell, but a scion from the Bell family tree that has produced three generations of major leaguers. With his gene pool, he should be able to improve further, and soon.

Team	Level		AB	HR	RBI	SB	BA
Tulsa	AA		484	16	59	3	.267

ADRIAN BELTRE — DODGERS — Age 18/R — *

Beltre put on an awesome power surge for a teenaged pro rookie last year. Some Dodger prospects are so good at such young ages that we can't help being curious about their birth certificates.

Team	Level		AB	HR	RBI	SB	BA
Savannah	A		244	16	59	4	.307
San Bernardino	A		238	10	40	3	.261

AARON BOONE — REDS — Age 24/R — **

Holy third generation, Batman! Bret Boone's little brother blossomed in his second shot at the Southern League. Aaron has some serious pop; he totaled 68 extra-base hits in '96.

Team	Level		AB	HR	RBI	SB	BA
Chattanooga	AA		548	17	95	21	.288

WES HELMS — BRAVES — Age 20/R — *

With Andruw Jones in Atlanta and Ron Wright traded to the Pirates, Helms is the best remaining young prospect in the Braves organization. Like so many young players, he must cut his strikeout total to advance further.

Team	Level		AB	HR	RBI	SB	BA
Durham	A		258	13	54	1	.322
Greenville	AA		231	4	22	2	.255

SCOTT McCLAIN — ORIOLES — Age 24/R — **

The best defensive third baseman in the International League, McClain also put together a good second half at the plate. And you know how we love second-half performance.

Team	Level		AB	HR	RBI	SB	BA
Rochester	AAA		463	17	69	8	.281

KEVIN ORIE — CUBS — Age 24/R — **

Injuries slowed the progress of the Cubs' 1993 first-round draft pick. He has shown an excellent bat, and most likely will continue to show it in Triple-A at the start of the '97 season. No relation to the Houston Rockets' Robert Horry.

Team	Level		AB	HR	RBI	SB	BA
Orlando	AA		296	8	58	2	.314
Iowa	AAA		48	2	6	0	.208

SCOTT ROLEN   PHILLIES   Age 21/R   * * *

Rolen, along with all of Philadelphia, knows that batters lose their rookie status at 130 at bats. He would not be the odds-on favorite for the National League Rookie of the Year award except that on his potential 131st AB last season, his arm was broken by a pitch. Injuries are the only factor that can hold Rolen back.

Team	Level		AB	HR	RBI	SB	BA
Reading	AA		230	9	42	8	.361
Scranton	AAA		168	2	19	4	.274

ROBERT SMITH   BRAVES   Age 22/R   * *

Smith is such a good defensive third baseman that he played some shortstop for the Richmond Braves. If he can handle that position, that could take some pressure off him as a hitter and allow Atlanta to move Chipper Jones back to third.

Team	Level		AB	HR	RBI	SB	BA
Richmond	AAA		445	8	58	15	.256

SCOTT SPIEZIO   ATHLETICS   Age 24/B   * *

Like Roberto Alomar, Jason Kendall, and others, Spiezio has a chance to be a much better player than his father (Ed Spiezio). Scott hits for power without striking out a lot. His biggest problem is the logjam at the corner infield positions in Oakland.

Team	Level		AB	HR	RBI	SB	BA
Edmonton	AAA		523	20	91	6	.262

TODD WALKER   TWINS   Age 23/L   * * *

Walker, an All-American second baseman for Louisiana State's national champions, has brought some Cajun spice upriver to Minneapolis. There's very little he can't do on a baseball diamond.

Team	Level		AB	HR	RBI	SB	BA
Salt Lake City	AAA		551	28	111	13	.339

ANTONE WILLIAMSON   BREWERS   Age 23/L   * *

Like Walker, Williamson is a former first-round draft pick. Injuries slowed his development last season, but he's not far from being a major leaguer.

Team	Level		AB	HR	RBI	SB	BA
New Orleans	AAA		199	5	23	1	.261

SHORTSTOPS

HIRAM BOCACHICA   EXPOS   Age 21/R   *

Arm trouble limited Bocachica to DH duty in '96, and (wow!) did he work on his hitting. When was there last a major leaguer named Hiram? Or an outfield, as there can soon be in Montreal, with the names Hiram, Yamil, and Vladimir? Forget the names and watch the numbers.

Team	Level		AB	HR	RBI	SB	BA
West Palm Beach	A		267	2	26	21	.337

NOMAR GARCIAPARRA   RED SOX   Age 23/R   * * *

And then there's the first big leaguer named Nomar (Ramon spelled backward). Last year, Garciaparra added a wicked bat to his defensive magic. The Bosox didn't hesitate to make him their everyday shortstop during the September stretch run.

Team	Level		AB	HR	RBI	SB	BA
Pawtucket	AAA		172	16	46	3	.343

CHAD HERMANSEN   PIRATES   Age 19/R   *

Hermansen is a number one draft pick likely to have an impact in Pittsburgh before long. Jay Bell's days there appeared numbered at the end of '96, and the power-hitting shortstop at the other end of the calendar is Hermansen.

Team	Level		AB	HR	RBI	SB	BA
Augusta	A		226	14	41	11	.252
Lynchburg	A		251	10	46	5	.275

DAMIAN JACKSON   INDIANS   Age 23/R   * *

Jackson appeared to hit the wall in Double-A, where he spent most of two seasons striking out and committing errors. Then in '96, when he was asked to take over as Buffalo's leadoff hitter, he shouldered the responsibility and led the struggling Bisons back on course to a division title.

Team	Level		AB	HR	RBI	SB	BA
Buffalo	AAA		452	12	49	24	.257

JUAN MELO   PADRES   Age 20/B   *

Our annual salute to our favorite minor league city, Rancho Cucamonga. It helps that San Diego stocks the Quakes with good prospects, but even if they didn't, we'd find someone just so we could read the city's name aloud. And here's a young player who can say yes to the question, "Have you never been Melo?"

Team	Level		AB	HR	RBI	SB	BA
Rancho Cucamonga	A		503	8	75	6	.304

JHONNY PEREZ   ASTROS   Age 20/R   *

Houston's entry in the shortstop name game is this youngster with the funny spelling of his first name. There's nothing funny about Perez's play in the field, at the plate, or on the bases.

Team	Level	AB	HR	RBI	SB	BA
Kissimmee	A	322	12	49	16	.270

POKEY REESE   REDS   Age 23/R   * *

If Baltimore's Ripken moves to third base and something happens to Barry Larkin, Reese could become the majors' best shortstop named Calvin. Reese had a poor season in '96, and he has been a blip on our radar screen for so long, some people think he's no longer a prospect. He's been major league caliber in the field for years, however, and he's a better hitter than he showed last year.

Team	Level	AB	HR	RBI	SB	BA
Indianapolis	AAA	280	1	23	5	.232

MIGUEL TEJADA   ATHLETICS   Age 20/R   *

Tejada found the California League to his liking. But the big test for Oakland farmhands is going from Modesto to Double-A Huntsville.

Team	Level	AB	HR	RBI	SB	BA
Modesto	A	458	20	72	27	.279

ENRIQUE WILSON   INDIANS   Age 21/B   * *

As well as Damian Jackson played last season, Cleveland's best shortstop prospect is still young Wilson. The Indians insisted on getting him in a trade from Minnesota a couple of years ago, so you know the front office is watching.

Team	Level	AB	HR	RBI	SB	BA
Canton-Akron	AA	484	5	50	23	.304
Buffalo	AAA	8	0	0	0	.500

OUTFIELDERS

JEFF ABBOTT   WHITE SOX   Age 24/R   * *

Sox fans may be yelling, "Hey, Abbott!" as early as April. He has a line-drive stroke, but hasn't yet generated real power by turning on a pitch and pulling it.

Team	Level	AB	HR	RBI	SB	BA
Nashville	AAA	440	14	60	12	.325

BOB ABREU   ASTROS   Age 23/L   * *

Abreu's production fell off in his second season in the Pacific Coast League, but he is young enough to bounce back in the bigs. He consistently works pitchers deep into counts (83 walks, 111 strikeouts).

Team	Level	AB	HR	RBI	SB	BA
Tucson	AAA	484	13	68	24	.285

BRUCE AVEN   INDIANS   Age 25/R   **

We were in the not-very-crowded vanguard in telling you about Aven a year ago. He actually improved his performance after moving up to Double-A.

Team	Level	AB	HR	RBI	SB	BA
Canton-Akron	AA	481	23	79	22	.297
Buffalo	AAA	9	1	2	0	.667

YAMIL BENITEZ   EXPOS   Age 24/R   **

Hardly anyone noticed the improvement that Benitez made in his second International League season, because his team took a nosedive. But he raised his batting average 19 points, and showed much better instincts and all-around hustle.

Team	Level	AB	HR	RBI	SB	BA
Ottawa	AAA	439	23	81	11	.278

BRENT BREDE   TWINS   Age 25/L   **

Let me tell you the story of a man named Brede, a real good hitter who can keep his family fed . . . ah, never mind. Just remember that Brede exploded offensively in his Triple-A debut, and it wasn't just a result of playing at a higher altitude. He can be an excellent leadoff batter; he drew 87 walks last year.

Team	Level	AB	HR	RBI	SB	BA
Salt Lake City	AAA	483	11	86	14	.348

MIKE CAMERON   WHITE SOX   Age 24/R   **

Before last season, Cameron was known—if at all—mainly for his strong rightfield arm, one of the best anywhere. Then in '96, he began attacking opposing pitchers with a potent bat, all the more impressive in a pitcher's park.

Team	Level	AB	HR	RBI	SB	BA
Birmingham	AA	473	28	77	39	.300

JACOB CRUZ   GIANTS   Age 24/R   **

Cruz seems younger than Cameron, because Jake has played just three pro seasons to Mike's six, but they are the same age within three weeks. While Cruz was getting his experience in college, Cameron was toiling in the minors. Anyway, the college man is now farther along and ready to say goodbye to the minors.

Team	Level	AB	HR	RBI	SB	BA
Phoenix	AAA	435	7	75	5	.285

JOSE CRUZ, JR.   MARINERS   Age 22/B   **

Then again, there are players with so much talent that they seem born to be in the majors. Jose inherited the hitting gene that enabled his dad to play in the majors past age 40. Junior, who played college ball at Rice, has had just two pro seasons. Even if we didn't know whose kid he is, we love the fact that he earned two promotions last year. In an organization less loaded with outfielders and hitters, he would start '97 in the majors.

Team	Level		AB	HR	RBI	SB	BA
Lancaster	A		203	6	43	7	.325
Port City	AA		181	3	31	5	.282
Tacoma	AAA		76	6	15	1	.237

TODD DUNWOODY   MARLINS   Age 21/L   * *

There was a nice symmetry in Dunwoody's home run and stolen base totals in '96. His season was especially impressive because he jumped from the Midwest League to the Eastern League, skipping a stop on Florida's prospect train. Don't confuse this youngster with 26-year-old Texas League batting champ Todd Dunn.

Team	Level		AB	HR	RBI	SB	BA
Portland	AA		552	24	93	24	.277

DARIN ERSTAD   ANGELS   Age 22/L   * * *

If you don't know Erstad, you weren't following the American League last year, certainly not for Rotisserie purposes; he was one of the most-claimed call-ups of 1996. Still, he spent most of the year in the minors, so here he is. The Angels think he's so good they've talked about trading Garret Anderson to make room in their outfield for a superior defensive player.

Team	Level		AB	HR	RBI	SB	BA
Vancouver	AAA		351	6	41	11	.305

ANTON FRENCH   TIGERS   Age 21/B   *

French has been traded twice in the past two seasons, which says more about his desirability than his dispensibility. The Tigers are quietly assembling an exceptional group of prospects. French's stock-in-trade is his speed and defense.

Team	Level		AB	HR	RBI	SB	BA
Durham	A		210	5	22	23	.248
Lakeland	A		253	0	14	24	.277

KARIM GARCIA   DODGERS   Age 21/L   * * *

It worked for Raul Mondesi, so why not for Garcia? The Dodgers' special treatment for top prospects is to send them back down to Double-A if they spend too much time at Triple-A pouting about not being in the majors. Showing them it's a two-way street often gets them oriented.

Team	Level		AB	HR	RBI	SB	BA
Albuquerque	AAA		327	13	58	6	.297
San Antonio	AA		129	5	22	1	.248

DERRICK GIBSON   ROCKIES   Age 22/R   * *

With his 6'2", 238-pound football player's physique, Gibson plays a power game with some rough edges to smooth out. He has trouble making contact, but when he hits the ball, it stays hit.

Team	Level		AB	HR	RBI	SB	BA
New Haven	AA		449	15	62	3	.256

BEN GRIEVE ATHLETICS Age 20/L   *

The son of former Rangers outfielder and general manager Tom Grieve struggled some after his promotion to Double-A. Expect Ben to do much better in his second try this year.

Team	Level	AB	HR	RBI	SB	BA
Modesto	A	281	11	51	8	.356
Huntsville	AA	232	8	32	0	.237

VLADIMIR GUERRERO EXPOS Age 21/R   * * *

Guerrero also was promoted to Double-A after a fast start, and merely earned Eastern League MVP honors. He is the entire package—hitting for power, hitting for average, speed, a strong rightfield arm—all gift-wrapped for delivery to Montreal.

Team	Level	AB	HR	RBI	SB	BA
West Palm Beach	A	80	5	18	2	.363
Harrisburg	AA	417	19	78	17	.360

JOSE GUILLEN PIRATES Age 20/R   *

In the alphabetical order here, as well as in the pecking order of farm systems, Guerrero and Montreal are tough acts to follow. But Guillen, the Carolina League MVP, deserves his place here.

Team	Level	AB	HR	RBI	SB	BA
Lynchburg	A	528	21	94	24	.322

RICHARD HIDALGO ASTROS Age 21/R   * *

Hidalgo's arm and his line-drive power are highly regarded, but the Astros left him in the Texas League for a second year.

Team	Level	AB	HR	RBI	SB	BA
Jackson	AA	513	14	78	11	.294

GEOFF JENKINS BREWERS Age 22/L   *

Jenkins showed a lot in his injury-shortened '96 season. The lost time may delay the 1995 first-round pick (out of USC) from his major league debut, but it's only a question of time.

Team	Level	AB	HR	RBI	SB	BA
Stockton	A	138	3	25	3	.348
El Paso	AA	77	1	11	1	.286

1997 ROOKIE ALL-STAR TEAM—AMERICAN LEAGUE

C	Todd Greene (Angels)	OF	Shannon Stewart (Blue Jays)
1B	Steve Cox (Athletics)	OF	Jeff Abbott (White Sox)
2B	Edwin Diaz (Rangers)	OF	Ruben Rivera (Yankees)
3B	Todd Walker (Twins)	P	Jaime Bluma (Royals)
SS	Nomar Garciaparra (Red Sox)	P	Trever Miller (Tigers)

ROBIN JENNINGS   CUBS   Age 24/L   * * *

The world discovered in the 1995 Arizona Fall League what we already knew: Jennings can play. He can hit long line drives, and he has a good rightfield arm. If he starts pulling the ball more, he can be a power source at Wrigley Field.

Team	Level	AB	HR	RBI	SB	BA
Iowa	AAA	331	18	56	2	.284

ANDRUW JONES   BRAVES   Age 19/R   * * *

Here's proof that time travel is possible. One of our forebears hopped into a time machine and traveled to the early twenty-first century. He saw a game at Atlanta's Olympic Stadium, featuring Chipper and Andruw. Then he coined the phrase "keeping up with the Joneses." Almost any teenaged major leaguer is a special player. Andruw is a superstar in the making.

Team	Level	AB	HR	RBI	SB	BA
Durham	A	243	17	43	16	.313
Greenville	AA	157	12	37	12	.369
Richmond	AAA	45	5	12	2	.378

RICKY LEDEE   YANKEES   Age 23/L   * *

In a world with no left-handed pitchers, Ledee (pronounced Le-DAY) would be king. He has played seven seasons in the minors already at his young age. Last year, he bulked up his 6'2" frame, and after jumping from the Sally League, he outgrew the Eastern League. Ledee then became a mainstay for International League champion Columbus. He has a strong arm but not great range in the outfield.

Team	Level	AB	HR	RBI	SB	BA
Norwich	AA	137	8	37	2	.365
Columbus	AAA	358	21	64	6	.282

BILLY McMILLON   MARLINS   Age 25/L   * * *

McMillon was the king of Knights Castle last season, sticking around long enough to earn the International League batting title before his promotion to the majors. He has a limited throwing arm. But he plays hard, and he sure can hit!

Team	Level	AB	HR	RBI	SB	BA
Charlotte	AAA	347	17	70	5	.352

ROD MYERS   ROYALS   Age 24/L   * *

This isn't the same Rod Myers who went from the Kansas City organization to pitch for the Cubs. This Rod Myers is an enemy of pitchers such as his former teammate. He added some power, much needed by the big club, to the speed that is characteristic of the Royals.

Team	Level	AB	HR	RBI	SB	BA
Omaha	AAA	411	16	54	37	.292

TROT NIXON   RED SOX   Age 22/L   * *

Nixon's wonderful talent has been diluted by back trouble. The result has been greatly reduced power and less mobility for a one-time can't-miss center field prospect. Even slowed to a trot, Nixon can be a productive major leaguer. Check him out this season; if he doesn't hit home runs at Pawtucket, he may never hit them.

Team	Level		AB	HR	RBI	SB	BA
Trenton	AA		438	11	63	7	.251

JAY PAYTON   METS   Age 24/R   * * *

Speaking of injured potential superstars, Payton had elbow surgery twice last year, so he didn't play in the field. At bat and on the bases, however, he was a genuine terror. There is little question he can make it in the majors. The only question is how bad Georgia Tech's pitching staff had to be to keep a team with Payton, Garciaparra, and Varitek from winning the College World Series.

Team	Level		AB	HR	RBI	SB	BA
Port St. Lucie	A		26	0	1	2	.308
Norfolk	AAA		153	6	26	10	.307
Binghamton	AA		10	0	2	0	.200

DANTE POWELL   GIANTS   Age 23/R   * *

Listen carefully and you can hear Texas League pitchers muttering under their breath, "That infernal Dante." To Powell's many talents, last year he added better strike zone judgment, which allowed him to walk 72 times. He has power, speed, and defensive ability.

Team	Level		AB	HR	RBI	SB	BA
Shreveport	AA		508	21	78	43	.280
Phoenix	AAA		8	0	0	0	.250

RUBEN RIVERA   YANKEES   Age 23/R   * *

The second coming of Mickey Mantle has already fallen far short of the first edition. Rivera's 1996 International League season looked a lot like that of teammate Bubba Carpenter. It was Ruben's cousin, Mariano Rivera, who had the big year in New York. Rivera is, however, already good enough in the outfield to be a major league defensive replacement, and his hitting skills improved visibly after his call-up to New York.

Team	Level		AB	HR	RBI	SB	BA
Columbus	AAA		362	10	46	15	.235

T. J. STATON   PIRATES   Age 22/L   * *

Teammate Charles Peterson has received more attention, but it was Staton who made the Southern League All-Star team. He developed much better discipline at the plate, and as a result, his average increased 16 points despite skipping a link in the Pirates' chain.

Team	Level		AB	HR	RBI	SB	BA
Carolina	AA		386	15	57	17	.308

SHANNON STEWART   BLUE JAYS   Age 23/R   ● ● ●

Close your eyes. Picture a major league center fielder/leadoff hitter. Now, a right-handed batter. That's it; now you have a picture of Shannon Stewart in your mind. Also picture this. He had a big second half in '96.

Team	Level	AB	HR	RBI	SB	BA
Syracuse	AAA	420	6	42	35	.298

ERIC STUCKENSCHNEIDER   DODGERS   Age 25/R   ●

Stucken—let's call him Eric—is older than your average prospect, but he also drew 111 walks last year. Besides, we're pulling for him because he would break the record for the longest surname in major league history—by three letters!

Team	Level	AB	HR	RBI	SB	BA
Savannah	A	470	16	63	50	.277

BUBBA TRAMMELL   TIGERS   Age 25/R   ● ●

Here's another guy we turned you on to last year while few other prospectors were paying attention. Trammell's age is a mild concern—isn't it for every player named Trammell?—but Bubba certainly can hit.

Team	Level	AB	HR	RBI	SB	BA
Jacksonville	AA	311	27	75	3	.328
Toledo	AAA	180	6	24	5	.294

EDGARD VELAZQUEZ   ROCKIES   Age 21/R   ● ●

Roberto Clemente's nephew is a far better player than The Great One's son ever thought of being. Velazquez is a multidimensional talent—strong arm, good defense, hitting for power and average—and he is developing better strike zone judgment.

Team	Level	AB	HR	RBI	SB	BA
New Haven	AA	486	19	62	6	.290

PITCHERS

DARIN BLOOD   GIANTS   Age 22/R   ●

Blood was the California League's Pitcher of the Year and Rookie of the Year. His name reminds me of the old Pittsburgh Steelers player and coach Johnny Blood. And have I told you about the book *Rotisserie Baseball: Playing for Blood* available from . . . ?

Team	Level	W	L	ERA	IP	H	BB	K
San Jose	A	17	6	2.65	170	140	71	93

JAIME BLUMA   ROYALS   Age 24/R   ● ● ●

In the second spot in our pitching order for the second consecutive year (after Alan Benes in '96) is Bluma. He's an exception to our rule—a relief specialist. He had 25 saves in Triple-A, and an opportunity in September to

---

send Jeff Montgomery packing, literally. At worst, Bluma will be a top setup man in 1997.

Team	Level	W	L	ERA	IP	H	BB	K
Omaha	AAA	1	2	3.12	58	57	20	40

MATT CLEMENT　　　　　PADRES　　　Age 22/R　　　*

Clement was a strikeout machine last season, even after moving from the Midwest League to the California League. And he pitched at Ranch-o KOOK-a-munga!

Team	Level	W	L	ERA	IP	H	BB	K
Clinton	A	8	3	2.80	96	66	52	109
Rancho Cucamonga	A	4	5	5.59	56	61	26	75

BARTOLO COLON　　　　　INDIANS　　　Age 21/R　　　**

And number three a year ago was Colon. One thing that hasn't changed is that each of the last two seasons ended with Colon being shut down because of a sore arm. As a result, he's looking more like a reliever than a starter in the majors.

Team	Level	W	L	ERA	IP	H	BB	K
Canton-Akron	AA	2	2	1.74	62	44	17	40
Buffalo	AAA	0	0	6.00	15	16	8	19

JEFF D'AMICO　　　　　BREWERS　　　Age 21/R　　　***

D'Amico is another guy who was on this list a year ago. Since then he has jumped all the way from A-ball to make his presence felt in the majors. All the former first-round pick needed was to stay healthy. He's an excellent control pitcher.

Team	Level	W	L	ERA	IP	H	BB	K
El Paso	AA	5	4	3.19	96	89	13	76

SHANE DENNIS　　　　　PADRES　　　Age 25/L　　　**

Dennis could be one of those late-blooming left-handers. In 1995, he struggled in the Midwest League before finding his stride at—where else?—Rancho Cucamonga. In '96, he pitched well for the Quakes, but even better in the Southern League.

Team	Level	W	L	ERA	IP	H	BB	K
Rancho Cucamonga	A	4	2	3.20	59	57	19	54
Memphis	AA	9	1	2.27	115	83	45	131

KRIS DETMERS　　　　　CARDINALS　　　Age 22 /L　　　**

Detmers fits the bill for a successful young pitcher in the majors—a tall left-hander going to a good pitcher's park, falling short of ideal only in the aspect that he doesn't throw very hard. I like his chances just the same.

Team	Level	W	L	ERA	IP	H	BB	K
Arkansas	AA	12	8	3.35	164	154	70	97

JASON DICKSON   ANGELS   Age 24/R   * *

In 1995, Dickson was pitching in the Midwest League. Last year, he pitched some in the American League. He has good control, but his lack of velocity prevents him from being a top prospect. The major leagues are, of course, filled with pitchers who were never top prospects, either.

Team	Level	W	L	ERA	IP	H	BB	K
Midland	AA	5	2	3.58	55	55	10	40
Vancouver	AAA	7	11	3.80	130	134	40	70

MIKE DRUMRIGHT   TIGERS   Age 22/R   * *

The progress of the Tigers' 1995 first-round pick was slowed by weakness in his shoulder, which sidelined him twice last season. When he was able to pitch, he threw well.

Team	Level	W	L	ERA	IP	H	BB	K
Jacksonville	AA	6	4	3.97	100	80	48	109

SCOTT ELARTON   ASTROS   Age 21/R   *

Elarton pitched even better last season in the Florida State League than he had in the Midwest League in '95. He has both the stamina and the selection of pitches he'll need to be successful in the majors.

Team	Level	W	L	ERA	IP	H	BB	K
Kissimmee	A	12	7	2.92	172	154	54	130

NELSON FIGUEROA   METS   Age 22/R   *

The Sally League's Pitcher of the Year and ERA leader dominated hitters in 1996. Check out his K/BB and H/IP ratios. The Brooklyn-born Figueroa will be spreading around plenty of tickets if he makes it to Shea Stadium.

Team	Level	W	L	ERA	IP	H	BB	K
Columbia	A	14	7	2.04	185	119	58	200

KEITH FOULKE   GIANTS   Age 24/R   * *

Foulke is 25–13 over the last two seasons, but his strikeout rate declined when he advanced to Double-A. His long suits are control and stamina.

Team	Level	W	L	ERA	IP	H	BB	K
Shreveport	AA	12	7	2.76	183	149	35	129

CURT LYONS   REDS   Age 22/R   * *

The Reds believe they have a future staff ace in Lyons. So do a number of other people who have seen him pitch. The 6'5", 230-pounder was the Southern League's Pitcher of the Year.

Team	Level	W	L	ERA	IP	H	BB	K
Chattanooga	AA	13	4	2.41	142	113	52	176

CALVIN MADURO   PHILLIES   Age 22/R   * * *

The Phillies traded some of their past (Pete Incaviglia, Todd Zeile) for the future, represented by Maduro, who has classic form and exceptional control.

One question is whether the fly-ball pitcher will give up too many home runs in the majors. The other question: Where does the native of Aruba go on vacation?

Team	Level	W	L	ERA	IP	H	BB	K
Bowie	AA	9	7	3.26	124	116	36	87
Rochester	AAA	3	5	4.74	44	49	18	40

ETHAN McENTIRE METS Age 21/L *

McEntire was part of an overpowering pitching staff in South Carolina's capital as the next wave of live arms for the Mets. He was much more effective in his second stint there because he threw more strikes. As a lefty, McEntire will rank high until he runs through all nine of his lives.

Team	Level	W	L	ERA	IP	H	BB	K
Columbia	A	9	6	2.22	174	123	61	190

RAMIRO MENDOZA YANKEES Age 24/R * *

Mendoza is a tall, slender right-hander in the mold of Mariano Rivera. Mendoza wasn't quite ready when the Yankees brought him up early last season, but he went back to Columbus and threw nothing but strikes. He may end up, like Rivera, in the bullpen. One difference between the two: about six miles per hour on the fastball (Rivera's is superior).

Team	Level	W	L	ERA	IP	H	BB	K
Columbus	AAA	6	2	2.51	97	96	19	61

TRAVIS MILLER TWINS Age 24/L * *

Tall lefty alert! Miller is 6'3". The only problem is that he'd be pitching his major league home games in the Metrodome, not exactly a pitcher's park. For that matter, Salt Lake is no pitching paradise, either.

Team	Level	W	L	ERA	IP	H	BB	K
Salt Lake City	AAA	8	10	4.83	160	187	57	143

TREVER MILLER TIGERS Age 23/L * *

Let's see . . . a 6'3" rookie left-hander whose name could be written in box scores as "TrMiller." So you have the opportunity to get Trever and Travis confused at some point this season. Aside from the won-lost records and hits allowed, they even had similar seasons in '96.

Team	Level	W	L	ERA	IP	H	BB	K
Toledo	AAA	13	6	4.90	165	167	65	115

MATT MORRIS CARDINALS Age 22/R * *

St. Louis's number one draft pick in 1995 throws gas, but his strikeout totals suffered at the higher levels of the minors. Expect him to hit his stride at Louisville, then be with St. Louis by September. It's in the cards.

Team	Level	W	L	ERA	IP	H	BB	K
Arkansas	AA	12	12	3.88	167	178	48	120
Louisville	AAA	0	1	3.38	8	8	1	9

CARL PAVANO   RED SOX   Age 21/R   * *

It's not clear who's luckier: Pavano for being able to pitch in one of the best settings in minor league baseball, or the fans of Trenton for being able to watch him work. The 6'5" Pavano pointed himself toward Fenway Park with a season that earned him the Eastern League Pitcher of the Year award.

Team	Level	W	L	ERA	IP	H	BB	K
Trenton	AA	16	5	2.63	185	154	47	146

JIM PITTSLEY   ROYALS   Age 22/R   * * *

The only question with the 6'7" Pittsley is the condition of his arm. When healthy last year, he was plenty effective.

Team	Level	W	L	ERA	IP	H	BB	K
Wilmington	A	0	1	11.00	9	13	5	10
Wichita	AA	3	0	0.41	22	9	5	7
Omaha	AAA	7	1	3.97	70	74	39	53

BRITT REAMES   CARDINALS   Age 23/R   *

Standing 5'11" Reames may have looked small to scouts, but he's big enough to strike out better than a batter an inning and lead the Midwest League in ERA.

Team	Level	W	L	ERA	IP	H	BB	K
Peoria	A	15	7	1.90	161	97	41	167

DENNIS REYES   DODGERS   Age 19/L   *

The Mexican Reyes is an up-and-coming candidate for the Dodgers' United Nations rotation. And pay attention: Reyes is a 6'3" lefty who would do his big league pitching at Dodger Stadium.

Team	Level	W	L	ERA	IP	H	BB	K
San Bernardino	A	11	12	4.17	166	166	77	176

RAY RICKEN   YANKEES   Age 23/R   * *

Ricken slipped after a meteoric rise through the farm system in '95. But the encouraging sign was that he maintained his strikeout ratio after his promotion to Triple-A.

Team	Level	W	L	ERA	IP	H	BB	K
Norwich	AA	5	2	4.47	46	42	20	42
Columbus	AAA	4	5	4.76	68	62	37	58

NERIO RODRIGUEZ   ORIOLES   Age 24/R   * *

In 1995, Rodriguez was a catcher batting .236. He had a good arm, though, so the Orioles moved him to the battery's other end, and made him a pitcher. He spent last season striking out shortstops from his hometown of San Pedro de Macoris and a whole lot of other batters, all the way up to the major league level.

Team	Level	W	L	ERA	IP	H	BB	K
Frederick	A	8	7	2.26	111	83	40	114
Rochester	AAA	1	0	1.80	15	10	2	6

GLENDON RUSCH   ROYALS   Age 22/L   * * *

Kansas City rushed Glendon past Double-A last season, and he thrived in the American Association. The only downside was his reduced strikeout ratio. He will join Jose Rosado and Jim Pittsley in a battle for spots in the Royals' rotation.

Team	Level	W	L	ERA	IP	H	BB	K
Omaha	AAA	11	9	3.98	170	177	40	117

BRIAN SACKINSKY   ORIOLES   Age 25/R   * *

Elbow trouble has held Sackinsky back the last two seasons. When he returned last year, he tied for Rochester's team lead in victories even though he pitched only 14 times. Sackinsky throws strikes, which results in a lot of home runs. But at least he doesn't walk a lot of guys to clutter up the bases ahead of those long balls.

Team	Level	W	L	ERA	IP	H	BB	K
Rochester	AAA	7	3	3.46	68	75	15	38
Sarasota	R	1	0	5.19	9	11	1	3

DAN SERAFINI   TWINS   Age 23/L   * *

Predictably, Serafini's statistics soared along with the change in altitude from New Britain to Salt Lake City. But he's young enough to bounce back—and the Twins aren't exactly awash in great arms.

Team	Level	W	L	ERA	IP	H	BB	K
Salt Lake City	AAA	7	7	5.58	131	164	58	109

JEFF SUPPAN   RED SOX   Age 22/R   * * *

The Sox brought Suppan to Boston somewhat prematurely in 1995. Last year, when he was about the only pitcher in the International League who could get anybody out at Pawtucket's McCoy Stadium, he proved he was finally ready. If you don't believe that, check out his strikeout/walk ratio.

Team	Level	W	L	ERA	IP	H	BB	K
Pawtucket	AAA	10	6	3.22	145	130	25	142

JAY TESSMER   YANKEES   Age 24/R   *

We're breaking one of our rules here by including a closer from the lower minors. Typically, they have a snowball's chance in Tampa of making it to the majors in a similar role. Tessmer had 35 saves, and was named the Florida State League MVP.

Team	Level	W	L	ERA	IP	H	BB	K
Tampa	A	12	4	1.48	97	68	19	104

JUSTIN THOMPSON   TIGERS   Age 24/L   * * *

While Detroit's pitchers were struggling to get anyone out early last season, the organization was quietly developing some pitchers at Triple-A. Thompson was the best, but the Tigers resisted the temptation to rush him to the majors until after the All-Star break.

Team	Level	W	L	ERA	IP	H	BB	K
Toledo	AAA	6	3	3.42	84	74	26	69

BRETT TOMKO   REDS   Age 23/R   * *

The Reds chose Tomko with their first pick of the 1995 draft (in the second round). He justified his prospect status in his first full pro season. Chattanooga rode him and Curt Lyons to a second-half title in the Southern League.

Team	Level	W	L	ERA	IP	H	BB	K
Chattanooga	AA	11	7	3.88	158	131	54	164

DEREK WALLACE   METS   Age 25/R   * *

When Bobby Valentine was looking for a closer out of his Norfolk bullpen last season, he gave a shot to Wallace, who had come over from the Kansas City organization. Wallace turned into the International League's best reliever, with 26 saves. By the end of the season, Valentine was managing in New York, and Wallace was there with him, sometimes in save situations.

Team	Level	W	L	ERA	IP	H	BB	K
Norfolk	AAA	5	2	1.72	58	37	17	52

JAY WITASICK   ATHLETICS   Age 24/R   * *

The Athletics obtained Witasick in last winter's Todd Stottlemyre trade. They looked at their new starter, evaluated his stamina, and moved him to the bullpen. When he threw the ball over the plate, Witasick was the strikeout pitcher he had been in the Cards' organization. He could get a better chance in Oakland this year, and has a shot at a prominent relief role.

Team	Level	W	L	ERA	IP	H	BB	K
Huntsville	AA	0	3	2.30	67	47	26	63
Edmonton	AAA	0	0	4.15	9	9	6	9

KERRY WOOD   CUBS   Age 19/R   *

The Cubs are another team quietly building up pitching depth in the minors to counteract the offensive explosion in the majors. Speaking of majors, Wood—Chicago's first-round draft pick in 1995—is indeed a major talent. He just needs to refine his control.

Team	Level	W	L	ERA	IP	H	BB	K
Daytona Beach	A	10	2	2.91	114	72	70	136

1997 ROOKIE ALL-STAR TEAM—NATIONAL LEAGUE

C	Marcus Jensen (Giants)	OF	Vladimir Guerrero (Expos)
1B	Dmitri Young (Cardinals)	OF	Andruw Jones (Braves)
2B	Wilton Guerrero (Dodgers)	OF	Robin Jennings (Cubs)
3B	Scott Rolen (Phillies)	P	Calvin Maduro (Phillies)
SS	Pokey Reese (Reds)	P	Matt Morris (Cardinals)

JAMEY WRIGHT   ROCKIES   Age 22/R   * * *

Put yourself in the place of a pitching prospect in the Colorado organization. You're doing well, so you receive a promotion—to the pitching House of Horrors known as Coors Field. Wright handled that promotion much better than, say, Bryan Rekar—who followed a similar fast track to the majors in 1995 and hasn't been the same since. Maybe Rekar doesn't have the Wright stuff.

Team	Level	W	L	ERA	IP	H	BB	K
New Haven	AA	5	1	0.81	45	27	12	54
Colorado Springs	AAA	4	2	2.72	60	53	22	40

BEST LONG-TERM PROSPECTS

C Jason Varitek (Mariners)	OF Jose Cruz, Jr. (Mariners)
1B Dmitri Young (Cardinals)	OF Andruw Jones (Braves)
2B Wilton Guerrero (Dodgers)	OF Vladimir Guerrero (Expos)
3B Scott Rolen (Phillies)	P Jim Pittsley (Royals)
SS Nomar Garciaparra (Red Sox)	P Jaime Bluma (Royals)

5

Front Office

How to Keep Score

Once upon a time, the entire front office complex of Rotisserie League Baseball consisted of Beloved Founder and Former Commissioner-for-Life Daniel Okrent. There is a fading daguerreotype of Marse Dan, one hand clinching an unfiltered Camel, the other slowly stroking his abacus, sitting alone in his Berkshire woodshed, from which post he spewed out—we use the word advisedly—our fledgling league's biweekly standings every third fortnight or so. We were having too much fun to know any better that first season, but eventually we got smart and figured that the BFFCL would never compile and distribute the standings in a timely fashion until his team, the hapless Fenokees, got themselves in a pennant race and gave him something to crow about. Not willing to wait 'til the end of time or hell froze over, whichever came first, we fired him.

That single, surgical act marked the yawning of a new Rotisserie Era.

You can still do your league's stats by hand, of course—if the task required a mathematical genius, we'd still be waiting for our first standings report for the 1980 season. All you need is a calculator and about four hours of free time a week, every week of the season. (You're going to want weekly standings, whether you know it now or not.) But it's tiresome, tedious work, the only thing about Rotisserie League Baseball that isn't a whole gang of fun. We don't recommend it.

You can develop your own computer program for crunching Rotisserie stats and put the family computer to better use than prepping for the SATs, keeping track of the family fortune, or playing "Jeopardy." At least we think you can. When it comes to computers, the Founding Fathers are still trying to figure out why the light in the refrigerator comes on when you open the door. Other people say it can be done, though—something to do with spreading sheets, we think.

The *best* thing you can do, of course, is to have **Roti•Stats** compile and compute your league's stats. **Roti•Stats** is now the exclusive, officially authorized stats service for Rotisserie League Baseball—the *only* stats service sanctioned by the Founding Fathers of the game. Most important, it's the *best* stats service in the business.

We know. A few years back, after a decade of running our own stats service, we decided to hang up our spikes. We went looking for a new stats service. We examined them all, and we liked what we saw in **Roti•Stats**. They've been in business just about as long as Rotisserie League Baseball, and they have an unparalleled record for accuracy and timeliness. We were delighted with their performance. We think you will be, too. Find out for yourself what they can do for your league. Call **Roti•Stats** toll-free at **800-676-7684**—or contact them on the Web at **www.rotistats.com.**

Roti•Stats!
(You Play. Let Roti•Stats Do the Hard Stuff.)

Each week **Roti•Stats** records your transactions, computes your standings, and rushes a report via first-class mail to your league secretary. (Fax, overnight express, modem, e-mail, and Web services are available for the terminally anxious.) Each weekly report contains the standings, up-to-the-minute rosters for all teams, a list of free agents, and a transactions update. Your league can make free, unlimited transactions that may be made retroactively at any time. Player salaries, contract status, and positions are tracked at no additional cost. No hidden charges. Just one flat fee at the beginning of the season.

- *Quick Turnaround of Opening Day Rosters!* Reports are available after the *first* week of play. Most services make you wait two to three weeks for your first standings report. **Roti•Stats** knows how anxious your owners are to find out where they stand from the first crack of the bat.
- *New for 1997—Web & E-mail Reports!* Surf the Web to **www.roti-stats.com** and get your reports on your league's own customized Web pages. View them onscreen or print them out; either way they look great. Sign up for e-mail service, and voilà, your reports are ready and waiting for you.
- *Free Agent List!* Each weekly report includes a list of unowned players in your league, complete with weekly and year-to-date stats for *every* player in the league.
- *Free Custom Comment Page!* You may add an extra page to your weekly report containing important information for your league members. Many leagues use this page to reflect up-to-the-minute waiver information or to conduct general business among league members.
- *How Your Team Stacks Up Nationwide!* Periodically you'll receive special reports such as "Top Teams" in the country, "Tightest Pennant Races," and much more (see pages 254–255). You'll see how well your team and league stack up against other **Roti•Stats** leagues nationwide.

- **Additional Stat Categories!** Want more than the original eight scoring categories? No problem. Their state-of-the art software lets you include any alternative scoring categories you want—at no extra charge.
- **Same Day & Overnight Fax Service!** Reduced fax charges permit your owners to receive their standings reports the fastest and most efficient way possible—the same day they are generated. (Monday for AL and Mixed; Tuesday for NL).
- **Player Value and Position Eligibility Reports!** Player values are generated by **Roti•Stats'** own proven formulas based on stats for the last two years for each player (by position). An invaluable tool on Auction Draft Day. Also free: a Position Eligibility Report that shows all positions for which each player is eligible to be drafted.
- **League-at-a-Glance Report!** Includes all team rosters with position, salary, and contract information. Great when you're pondering trades.
- **Free League Administration Software!** You can use this program to e-mail or modem weekly moves to **Roti•Stats** each week or just use it to track your league fees. The fee reports alone make this a tremendous aid for your secretary.
- **The Roti•Tiller Newsletter!** Dig the latest dirt in Rotisserie baseball with **Roti•Stats'** highly unofficial, semi-irregular, not-always-polite newsletter called **The Roti•Tiller.** Designed to keep the Rotissespirit alive in your league, **The Roti•Tiller** spreads gossip, stirs up rumors, and occasionally even dispenses nuggets of useful information. Don't be surprised to see your name in headlines!
- **Multiple League Discounts!** Play in more than one league? The RLBA will discreetly provide you with a list of counselors in your region who might be able to help. Better still, **Roti•Stats** will provide significant discounts when all your leagues sign up for the best service in the game.
- **Championship Hat & Certificate!** The winning owner(s) in your league will receive the coveted Roti•Stats Championship Hat, as well as a Championship Certificate suitable for framing.
- **800 Number for Transactions!** Call in your transactions toll-free.

For complete information about **Roti•Stats**, the only stats service officially authorized by the Founding Fathers of Rotisserie League Baseball, call toll-free: **800-676-7684.** You'll get a sign-up kit, sample standings and special reports, and a lot more reasons why **Roti•Stats** should be *your* stats service. Did you get that number? It's still **800-676-7684**. Or **www.rotistats.com** if you're out for a spin on the old info-highway.

The RLBA Wants You!

You've collared a roomful of other baseball fanatics, memorized this book, subscribed to *Baseball America*, made *USA Today* a daily habit, found a newsstand that carries *USA Today Baseball Weekly*, bought every baseball mag on the racks, and appointed someone else to bring chow for your first Auction Draft Day. What's next? Membership in the **Rotisserie League Baseball Association**. Join now and beat the Christmas rush. Here's what your league gets with membership in the **RLBA**:

1. ***Commissioner's Services.*** No need for your league to be rent asunder by rules disputes and internecine fighting: one Civil War was quite enough, thank you. For member leagues of the **RLBA,** we adjudicate disputes, interpret rules, issue Solomonic judgments, and otherwise maintain law and order so you can concentrate on playing the game.

2. ***Position Eligibility List.*** Complete and up-to-date.

3. ***Quarterly Updates.*** Information on rules changes, news from other leagues, baseball gossip, and happenings around the Rotisseworld.

4. ***Opening Day Rosters.*** Official 25-man rosters, complete with last-minute disabled list moves and minor league promotions and demotions. Mailed to you Opening Day.

5. ***Championship Certificate.*** Signed by Beloved Founder and Former Commissioner-for-Life Daniel Okrent, this suitable-for-framing certificate is the perfect grace note for your pennant winner's rec room wall.

6. ***Company Store.*** The right to purchase an astonishing range of Rotisserie products at full retail price. (See the following pages.)

7. ***Yoo-Hoo.*** If you live outside the Yoo-Hoo belt, we'll send you a bottle of the precious nectar to pour over your pennant winner's head, in solemn observance of that most sacred of Rotisserituals.

How does your league join? Easy. Just fill out the form on page 258 and send it with your league's check or money order for $50 (only $25 for renewals) to the **Rotisserie League Baseball Association, 82 Wall Street, Suite 1105, New York, NY 10005.**

Rotisserie Baseball—The Video!
"Great!"—Siskel "Terrible!"—Ebert

That's right. We made a video. Go ahead and laugh. But hey—it works for Madonna, why not us?

Hosted by Reggie Jackson (yeah, *that* Reggie Jackson), **Rotisserie Baseball—The Video** is 30 minutes of rollicking, swashbuckling, gut-wrenching excitement, with enough car chases, frontal nudity, and violence to satisfy even Peter "Sudden Pete" Gethers ("Two thumbs!"). It features Glen "Iron Horse" Waggoner ("Two cheeseburgers!"), Harry Stein ("Not since *Gone with the Wind . . .*"), BFFCL Daniel Okrent ("Not since *Deep Throat . . .*"), and all the fun-loving Rotissegang, talking about the game they love so well.

For people new to The Greatest Game etc., **Rotisserie Baseball—The Video** is an informative, vaguely useful overview of the obsession that will soon take over their lives. For veteran Rotisserie players, it's a handy way to explain what the game is all about to people who don't know a baseball from a bass fiddle. (Just invite them over, cook up a tubful of popcorn, and pop The Video into the old VCR. They'll never be able to thank you enough, so they probably won't even try.) It's also a perfect gift idea for weddings, anniversaries, divorces, bar mitzvahs, and M-O-T-H-E-R on *Her* Day!

Just $15 plus postage and handling. See order form on page 253.

Rotisserie Ready-to-Wear!

Even if you draft like a Pollet Burro, there's no reason you can't dress like a pennant winner. Just order a few dozen official **Rotisserie T-shirts**. Available in a variety of designer colors, all of them white, this top-quality 100% cotton shirt has the famous Rotisserie coat-of-arms emblazoned across the chest in four dazzling colors. Perfect for any social occasion, but especially suitable for Auction Draft Day. A trifling $15 (plus postage and handling). Get a couple in case you slop mustard on yourself at the ballpark.

And what's an official Rotisserie T-shirt without an official **Rotisserie Cap**? Only half a uniform, that's what. The Rotisserie Cap is a top-quality number in breathtaking white with the famous four-color Rotisserie logo. Only $18 (plus postage and handling)—and get this: One size fits all! See page 253 for information on how to order.

Free Opening Day *Rotisserie Hot List!*

Get all the lowdown on late spring training cuts, last-minute deals, nagging injuries, rising and falling stars, rookies who are going to make the club, and much, much more—all just in time for your auction draft!

We'll tell you who's going to be in every rotation (plus the guys in line to step in if somebody falters or gets hurt). We'll tell you which middle-innings relievers have the best shot at picking up 8–10 garbage wins. We'll tab the fourth and fifth outfielders who will pick up 10–15 SB. We'll identify the second-string catchers most likely to deliver five homers for your one-buck investment. We'll go through every bullpen and tell you who's going to get the saves. Trade talk! Rumors! Buzz!

What you get is a news-packed, eight-page newsletter filled with all the up-to-the-minute inside stuff you need to put the finishing touches on your auction draft strategy—*free!* All you have to do is send us your name, your address, and $4.95 to cover postage and handling. We'll ship your official *Rotisserie Hot List* by first-class mail on Thursday, March 27. After that, same-day service on all *Rotisserie Hot List* requests.

Order your *Rotisserie Hot List* now. Send your name, address, and $4.95 to cover postage and handling to **Rotisserie Hot List, 82 Wall Street, Suite 1105, New York, NY 10005.**

TEAR OUT THIS PAGE!

YES! Enroll our league immediately in the **Rotisserie League Baseball Association** and send us the official **1997 Position Eligibility List** by return mail! Enclosed is our check or money order for $50 payable to **RLBA.** (Renewal leagues, send $25.)

☐

HOLD ON! We're not sure yet, we haven't had our organizational meeting, and all we want right now is information about **Roti•Stats,** the **RLBA's** officially authorized stats service.

☐

(Please Print)

Name of League _____

c/o Commissioner _____

Address _____

City _____ State _____ Zip _____

Telephone _____ AL/NL _____

ROTISSERIE T-SHIRTS

Size	Quantity	Price
Small	_____	$15 each
Medium	_____	2 for $28
Large	_____	3 for $39
X-Large	_____	4 for $48
XX-Large	_____	5+ $10 each

ROTISSERIE CAPS

Size	Quantity	Price
One size fits all	_____	$18 each

ROTISSERIE VIDEOS

	Quantity	Price
	_____	$15 each

Guarantee
If not completely satisfied with any Official Rotisserie product, send it back. We'll replace it or refund your money.

Shirts	$_____
Caps	$_____
Videos	$_____
Postage/Hdlg.	$ 3.50
Total	$_____ *

($US only; Check or M/O)
*NY residents add sales tax.

Name _____

Address _____

City _____ State _____ Zip _____

Mail to:
Rotisserie League Baseball Association
82 Wall Street, Suite 1105
New York, NY 10005

ROTI·STATS TOP TEAMS OF 1996

Here are some of the top 1996 Rotisserie teams around the country as tracked by Roti·Stats. These teams managed to capture the highest percentage of their leagues' possible points. Is your team here? It could be next year!

NATIONAL LEAGUES

#	%	TEAM	LEAGUE	TEAMS	CAT	HR	RBI	SB	AVG	W	SV	ERA	RTO
1.	96.9	Fighting Irish	South County Rotisserie	12	8	252	934	211	.286	88	97	3.38	1.246
2.	96.6	Impossible Deuce	Gibbosity	11	8	273	984	255	.278	85	76	3.34	1.231
3.	95.8	Donald's Ducks	Bowling League of Rotisserie	12	8	199	872	199	.286	87	84	3.37	1.208
4.	95.5	Jewmanji	Hebrew National League	11	8	240	1005	236	.281	89	89	3.75	1.232
5.	95.0	Triple Crown	Bay Area Rotisserie Fiends	10	8	348	1239	230	.293	97	60	3.30	1.173
6.	94.3	Black Magic	Pinky's Dead	11	8	211	907	215	.282	86	83	3.69	1.291
7.	94.2	Murder City Mayhem	Waveland and Sheffield Ivy League	12	10	222	964	180	.289	87	88	3.81	1.299
8.	94.0	Long Beach Phillies	Our Little League	5	10	167	765	165	.283	90	51	3.72	1.242
9.	93.8	Billicone ImPlantes	Amber Sky Dome	8	10	249	1078	225	.277	97	74	3.44	1.236
10.	93.8	Karlin Black Labels	Knickerbocker Pioneer	12	8	215	920	172	.284	78	61	3.36	1.196

AMERICAN LEAGUES

#	%	TEAM	LEAGUE	TEAMS	CAT	HR	RBI	SB	AVG	W	SV	ERA	RTO
1.	92.7	Joe Mamas	North Coast American League	12	8	306	1123	154	.285	81	57	4.08	1.361
2.	90.6	Ross Star Fill-ins	Burbank League	4	8	295	1216	203	.294	109	86	4.16	1.341
3.	90.1	Sultans of Space	Say Know to Drugs	12	8	253	983	171	.283	73	69	3.99	1.377
4.	89.2	Watson's Wieners	Blue Springs Bar-B-Que	12	10	246	1092	122	.297	83	69	4.18	1.427
5.	89.1	EZ'S	The Wanderers	8	8	283	1148	164	.292	103	75	3.70	1.301
6.	88.9	Glendale Rajes	R&P Refugees	9	8	358	1294	145	.293	86	35	4.13	1.371
7.	88.1	Springfield of Dreams	C.O.B.R.A.	10	8	264	1061	165	.293	81	78	4.37	1.391
8.	87.5	Rot-Sox	RX Rotisserie A.L.	9	8	327	1284	167	.295	74	97	4.48	1.395
9.	87.5	Youngstown	Branch Rickey League	10	8	250	1136	179	.291	86	72	4.29	1.384
10.	87.3	Lee Der Hose	Barristers' Trust Roto League	11	10	248	1027	142	.284	87	40	4.30	1.440

MIXED LEAGUES

#	%	TEAM	LEAGUE	TEAMS	CAT	HR	RBI	SB	AVG	W	SV	ERA	RTO
1.	93.8	Daph's Diamond Dream	La Samanna	8	10	401	1461	214	.305	112	140	3.36	1.230
2.	92.1	Devastation Inc.	Coast to Coast	12	10	335	1285	242	.293	100	88	3.39	1.206
3.	91.7	New London Sharks	Coast to Coast	12	10	348	1381	218	.298	97	93	3.58	1.259
4.	91.7	Three Musketeers	Narbo	15	8	292	1221	255	.296	92	93	3.75	1.248
5.	91.3	Morrison Hotel	GECC CTO League	8	10	408	1529	228	.288	126	114	3.57	1.258
6.	90.0	Spota's	Tampa Bay EXE League	5	10	386	1406	257	.302	99	139	3.65	1.221
7.	89.2	J.R.'s Reid	North Eastern Rotisserie League	12	10	333	1342	252	.296	105	73	3.80	1.288
8.	88.8	No Pepper Mintz	Lost Wages	10	8	302	1084	179	.287	90	55	3.69	1.249
9.	88.6	Sudden Impact	Roberto Clemente Rotisserie	7	10	353	1323	117	.292	96	96	4.00	1.338
10.	88.6	Out For Justice	Lou Gehrig Rotisserie League	7	10	299	1109	225	.292	95	91	3.72	1.232

ROTI·STATS TIGHTEST PENNANT RACES OF 1996

Talk about close pennant races! Here are some of the most competitive leagues around the country as tracked by Roti·Stats. The "RATING" figure refers to the average point difference among the top five teams in a league.

NATIONAL LEAGUES

#	RATING	LEAGUE	WINNER	TEAMS	CAT	1ST	2ND	3RD	4TH	5TH
1.	.50	Jon Long Memorial League	The Light Brigade	12	8	64.5	64.0	63.5	63.0	62.5
2.	1.50	The Caught Looking League	Suber's Rats	10	8	63.5	59.5	59.5	57.5	57.5
3.	1.50	L.A. / Chicago / N.Y. Syndication League	The Dingers	7	10	48.0	48.0	46.0	45.0	42.0
4.	1.75	Left Coast Athletic League	Dem Bums	11	10	78.0	72.5	71.0	71.0	71.0
5.	1.75	249 rotisserie league	Winning Entry	10	8	57.0	57.0	54.5	53.0	50.0
6.	1.75	Bucks Score Rotisserie League	Shoreshots	9	10	64.5	62.0	62.0	58.0	57.5
7.	1.88	TBN	Dirty Daddies	11	8	56.5	56.0	55.0	52.5	49.0
8.	1.88	Mallorquine League Baseball (MLB)	Ridiculos	8	8	46.0	43.5	42.0	40.5	38.5
9.	1.88	Miller & Martin Rotisserie Baseball Lge.	Gas-House Gorillas	9	8	49.5	48.0	47.0	45.0	42.0
10.	1.88	Pacific Boast League	Marge Shots	12	8	63.5	61.0	60.5	60.5	56.0

AMERICAN LEAGUES

#	RATING	LEAGUE	WINNER	TEAMS	CAT	1ST	2ND	3RD	4TH	5TH
1.	1.50	James River League	Bombers	8	12	71.0	69.0	67.0	66.0	65.0
2.	1.63	Big Jim's	Flying Denim Frogs	10	8	59.5	59.0	58.0	56.5	53.0
3.	1.63	Great American Rotissileague	Corndogs	9	8	52.0	51.0	48.5	45.5	45.5
4.	1.75	Silver Spring American League	Tamarack Terror	8	8	43.0	42.5	42.0	41.0	36.0
5.	2.00	Bay Area Rotisserie (BAR)	Dolomites	12	8	69.0	67.0	62.0	61.0	61.0
6.	2.00	The Tarney League	Mayberry Bears	10	12	78.5	76.0	73.5	72.0	70.5
7.	2.00	North Coast Penal League	M.J.K.	6	8	33.0	31.5	28.5	28.0	25.0
8.	2.25	Cahners Rotisserie Baseball League	First Blood	12	8	74.0	69.5	69.0	66.0	65.0
9.	2.50	Over the Hill Dreamers	Beaker's Hebrew Ntls.	7	10	48.0	45.0	43.0	39.0	38.0
10.	2.50	Beltway Bush League	Bill's Budds	12	8	69.0	67.5	62.5	59.0	59.0

MIXED LEAGUES

#	RATING	LEAGUE	WINNER	TEAMS	CAT	1ST	2ND	3RD	4TH	5TH
1.	1.25	Howie's My Man!	The Home Boys	14	10	91.0	89.0	88.0	86.5	86.0
2.	1.25	Surf City League	"Burnt, Bitter & Blue"	10	10	64.0	63.5	63.0	60.0	59.0
3.	1.50	Little East Rotisserie League	Candyman	12	8	68.0	67.0	67.0	64.0	62.0
4.	1.88	L & R Rotissterie	Treasury III	14	8	83.5	82.0	79.5	78.5	76.0
5.	1.88	Minor Lawyers League	Mud Hens	8	8	44.0	43.0	39.0	37.5	36.5
6.	2.25	BIG 10	Rick's Picks	10	10	65.0	63.5	59.5	57.0	56.0
7.	2.50	The Gellert Baseball Card League	The Davis Minors	8	8	46.0	43.5	39.0	36.5	36.0
8.	2.50	Smog League	Crushers	13	12	108.0	106.5	104.5	101.5	98.0
9.	2.63	The Desk League	Obstructed Views	15	10	100.8	100.3	98.8	94.5	90.3
10.	2.63	Post Office Mixed	NOMO	11	10	72.0	71.5	68.5	64.5	61.5

ROTISSERIE LEAGUE, 1996

FINAL STANDINGS

1. Glenwag Goners	66.0	6. Abel Bakers	47.0
2. Fleder Mice	59.0	7. Okrent Fenokees	35.0
3. Lovinger Spoonfuls	53.0	8. Wulf Gang	32.0
4. Cary Nations	50.0	9. Sklar Gazers	26.0
5. Smoked Fish	47.0	10. Eisenburg Furriers	25.0

PITCHING RECORDS

EARNED RUN AVERAGE			RATIO		
Glenwag Goners	3.45	10.0	Cary Nations	1.220	10.0
Lovinger Spoonfuls	3.50	9.0	Glenwag Goners	1.227	9.0
Cary Nations	3.62	8.0	Lovinger Spoonfuls	1.228	8.0
Smoked Fish	3.73	7.0	Smoked Fish	1.296	7.0
Fleder Mice	4.16	6.0	Fleder Mice	1.372	6.0
Eisenburg Furriers	4.30	5.0	Sklar Gazers	1.378	5.0
Sklar Gazers	4.46	4.0	Eisenburg Furriers	1.391	4.0
Wulf Gang	4.51	3.0	Abel Bakers	1.437	3.0
Abel Bakers	4.58	2.0	Wulf Gang	1.438	2.0
Okrent Fenokees	4.69	1.0	Okrent Fenokees	1.469	1.0

SAVES			WINS		
Abel Bakers	96	10.0	Glenwag Goners	97	10.0
Glenwag Goners	67	9.0	Lovinger Spoonfuls	94	9.0
Lovinger Spoonfuls	64	8.0	Cary Nations	93	8.0
Smoked Fish	55	7.0	Smoked Fish	87	7.0
Eisenburg Furriers	54	6.0	Okrent Fenokees	77	6.0
Wulf Gang	50	5.0	Fleder Mice	75	5.0
Fleder Mice	45	4.0	Eisenburg Furriers	67	4.0
Cary Nations	44	3.0	Wulf Gang	59	3.0
Sklar Gazers	35	2.0	Abel Bakers	55	2.0
Okrent Fenokees	9	1.0	Sklar Gazers	46	1.0

(Continued)

BATTING RECORDS

RUNS BATTED IN			STOLEN BASES		
Fleder Mice	1054	10.0	Fleder Mice	204	10.0
Glenwag Goners	1003	9.0	Cary Nations	194	9.0
Okrent Fenokees	943	8.0	Abel Bakers	187	8.0
Abel Bakers	870	7.0	Lovinger Spoonfuls	184	7.0
Smoked Fish	856	6.0	Smoked Fish	163	6.0
Cary Nations	814	5.0	Okrent Fenokees	151	5.0
Wulf Gang	715	4.0	Wulf Gang	146	4.0
Sklar Gazers	708	3.0	Glenwag Goners	133	3.0
Eisenburg Furriers	700	2.0	Sklar Gazers	114	2.0
Lovinger Spoonfuls	597	1.0	Eisenburg Furriers	94	1.0

HOME RUNS			BATTING AVERAGE		
Glenwag Goners	273	10.0	Lovinger Spoonfuls	.276	10.0
Fleder Mice	262	9.0	Fleder Mice	.276	9.0
Okrent Fenokees	249	8.0	Abel Bakers	.274	8.0
Abel Bakers	202	7.0	Wulf Gang	.273	7.0
Sklar Gazers	178	6.0	Glenwag Goners	.272	6.0
Smoked Fish	177	5.0	Okrent Fenokees	.272	5.0
Wulf Gang	165	4.0	Cary Nations	.270	4.0
Cary Nations	161	3.0	Sklar Gazers	.269	3.0
Eisenburg Furriers	152	2.0	Smoked Fish	.268	2.0
Lovinger Spoonfuls	124	1.0	Eisenburg Furriers	.268	1.0

ROTISSERIE HOOPS!

ROTISSERIE LEAGUE

BASKETBALL

- Compete in eight offensive and defensive categories based on the Official Rule Book.
- Categories include Total Points, Field Goal Percentage, 3-pointers, Free Throws Made, Assists, Rebounds, Steals, and Blocked Shots.
- Designate weekly lineups.
- Make trades. Shaq for the Admiral, anyone?
- Form your own league and we'll track it for you.
- Weekly standings reports and transactions.

- -

Yes, send me information about the Greatest Game for Basketball Fans Since Basketball!

Name _____

Address _____

City _____ State _____ Zip _____

Telephone _____

Mail to:
Rotisserie League Basketball Association
82 Wall Street, Suite 1105,
New York, NY 10005

6

Ground Rules

OFFICIAL CONSTITUTION OF ROTISSERIE LEAGUE BASEBALL

Preamble

We,
the People of the Rotisserie League, in order
to spin a more perfect Game, drive Justice
home, kiss
domestic Tranquility good-bye, promote the
general Welfare in Tidewater—where it's been
tearing up
the International League—and secure the
Blessings of Puberty to ourselves and those
we've left on Base,
do ordain and establish this
Constitution for Rotisserie League Baseball,
and also finish this run-on sentence.

ARTICLE I. OBJECT

To assemble a lineup of 23 National League or American League baseball players whose cumulative statistics during the regular season, compiled and measured by the methods described in these rules, exceed those of all other teams in the League.

ARTICLE II. TEAMS

There are 12 teams in a duly constituted Rotisserie League composed of either National League or American League players.

> **NOTE:** If you choose to play with fewer teams, be sure to make necessary adjustments so that you acquire approximately 80% of all available players at your auction draft. You could have a six-team league using American League players, for example, and draft only from among your seven favorite AL teams. Unless you reduce the available player pool proportionately to reflect a reduced number of teams, you'll never learn to appreciate the value of a good bench.

> **NOTE:** Do *not* mix the two leagues. It's unrealistic and silly, it's not the way the big leagues do it, it means you end up using only All-Stars and established regulars, and it's fattening. (On the other hand, if you *do* mix leagues, we're not going to call out the Rotisserie National Guard or anything.)

ARTICLE III. ROSTER

A team's active roster consists of the following players:

1. **NATIONAL LEAGUE PLAYERS**
   Five outfielders, two catchers, one second baseman, one shortstop, one middle infielder (either second baseman or shortstop), one first baseman, one third baseman, one corner man (either first baseman or third baseman), one utility player (who may play any nonpitching position), and nine pitchers.

2. **AMERICAN LEAGUE PLAYERS**
   The same, except that the utility player is called a designated hitter, consistent with the AL's insistence on perpetuating that perversion of the game.

ARTICLE IV. AUCTION DRAFT DAY

A **Major League Player Auction** is conducted on the first weekend after Opening Day of the baseball season. Each team must acquire 23 players at a total cost not to exceed $260. A team need not spend the maximum. The League by general agreement determines the order in which teams may nominate players for acquisition. The team bidding first opens with a minimum salary bid of $1 for any eligible player, and the bidding proceeds around the room at minimum increments of $1 until only one bidder is left. That team acquires the player for that amount and announces the roster position the player will fill. The process is repeated, with successive team owners introducing players to be bid on, until every team has a squad of 23 players, by requisite position.

- Don't get hung up on the bidding order; it's irrelevant. Do allow plenty of time; your first draft will take all day.
- Players eligible at more than one position may be shifted during the course of the draft.
- No team may make a bid for a player it cannot afford. For example, a team with $3 left and two openings on its roster is limited to a maximum bid of $2 for one player.
- No team may bid for a player who qualifies only at a position that the team has already filled. For example, a team that has acquired two catchers, and whose utility or DH slot is occupied, may not enter the bidding for any player who qualifies *only* at catcher.
- Players who commence the season on a major league team's disabled list *are* eligible to be drafted. If selected, they may be reserved and replaced upon completion of the auction draft. (See **Article XII**, page 269.)

NOTE: Final Opening Day rosters for all National League or American League teams will be needed on Auction Draft Day. Because some teams don't make their final roster moves until the last minute, even *USA Today*'s rosters, published on Opening Day, have holes. The best way to get the most complete, updated rosters is with membership in the **Rotisserie League Baseball Association**. (See page 250 for information on how to join.)

A **Minor League Player Draft** is conducted immediately following the major league auction, in which each Rotisserie League team may acquire players (a) who are not on any National/American League team's active roster; and (b) who still have official rookie status, as defined by major league baseball.

NOTE: The major league rule reads: "A player shall be considered a rookie unless, during a previous season or seasons, he has (a) exceeded 130 at-bats or 50 innings pitched in the major leagues; or (b) accumulated more than 45 days on the active roster of a major league club or clubs during the period of a 25-player limit (excluding time in the military service)."

- Selection takes place in two rounds of a simple draft, not an auction.
- In the first season, the selection order shall be determined by drawing paired numbers from a hat (that is, positions 1 and 24, 2 and 23, and so on in a 12-team league).
- In subsequent years, the selection order in each of the two rounds is determined by the order in which the teams finished in the previous

season. In leagues with 12 teams, the 6th place team selects first, proceeding in descending order to the 12th place team, which is in turn followed by the 5th, 4th, 3rd, 2nd, and 1st place teams.

- The price and subsequent salary upon activation of each farm system player drafted is $10.
- See **Article XIII**, page 271, for rules governing farm systems.

NOTE: The order of selection stated above represents a change from early years of Rotisserie baseball, when teams selected in reverse order of the final standings of the preceding season's pennant race. By awarding the first selection to the highest finisher among second-division teams instead of the last-place team, we seek to offer an incentive to teams to keep plugging and a disincentive to finish last (i.e., in the past, a last place finish would be "rewarded" with the first farm system draft pick).

ARTICLE V. POSITION ELIGIBILITY

A player may be assigned to any position at which he appeared in 20 or more games in the preceding season. If a player did not appear in 20 games at a single position, he may be drafted only at the position at which he appeared most frequently. The 20 games/most games measure is used only to determine the position(s) at which a player may be drafted. Once the season is under way (but after Auction Draft Day), a player becomes eligible for assignment to any position at which he has appeared at least once. In American League versions, players selected as DHs may qualify at any position (i.e., they need not have appeared in 20 games as DH the preceding season). In National League versions, players selected for the utility slot may qualify at any position.

NOTE: Two official major league sources for determining player eligibility are the National League's *Green Book* and the American League's *Red Book*. Both list appearances by position under fielding averages. The *Red Book* lists all players who appeared as designated hitters the preceding season. Circulating an eligibility list by position before Auction Draft Day saves a lot of time. Prepare one yourself in March, when the *Green Book* and *Red Book* are published. Or obtain it with membership in the **Rotisserie League Baseball Association**—our list is available at least five months earlier, so you'll be able to spend the winter doing something worthwhile. Spend a few minutes before your auction to settle eligibility questions and assign eligibility to rookies. When in doubt, use common sense (instead of knives) to resolve disputes.

ARTICLE VI. FEES

The Rotisserie League has a schedule of fees covering all player personnel moves. No money passes directly from team to team. No bets are made on the outcome of any game. All fees are payable into the prize pool and are subsequently distributed to the top four teams in the final standings. (See **Articles VIII** and **IX**, page 266.)

1. **BASIC:** The cumulative total of salaries paid for acquisition of a 23-man roster on Auction Draft Day may not exceed $260.

2. **TRANSACTIONS:** $10 per trade (no matter how many players are involved) or player activation (from reserve list or farm system). In a trade, the team that pays the fee is subject to negotiation.

3. **CALL-UP FROM FREE AGENT POOL:** $25 for each player called up from the free agent pool.

4. **RESERVE:** $10 for each player placed on a team's reserve list (see **Article XII**, page 269).

5. **FARM SYSTEM:** $10 for each player in a team's farm system (see **Article XIII**, page 271).

6. **ACTIVATION:** $10 for each player activated from the reserve list or farm system.

7. **WAIVERS:** $10 for each player claimed on waivers (see **Article XV**, page 274).

8. **SEPTEMBER ROSTER EXPANSION:** $50 (see **Article XVI**, page 275).

ARTICLE VII. PLAYER SALARIES

The salary of a player is determined by the time and means of his acquisition and does not change unless the player becomes a free agent or is signed to a guaranteed long-term contract. (See **Article XVII**, page 275.)

- The salary of a player acquired in the major league draft is his auction price.
- The salary of a player called up from the free agent pool during the season is $10.
- The salary of a player activated from a team's farm system during the season is $10.
- The salary of a player claimed on waivers is $10.
- The salary of a player called up during September Roster Expansion to supplement the 23-man roster is $25 if he is drawn from the free agent pool. (See **Article XVI**, page 275.)

NOTE: Because you can commit only $260 for salaries on Auction Draft Day, and because you will keep some of your players from one season to the next, salaries are *extremely* important, particularly after the first season ends and winter trading begins. Would you trade Albert Belle for Paul O'Neill? The Indians wouldn't, not even if Blowhard George threw in Yankee Stadium (which he would be only too happy to do, outfield monuments and all). But a smart Rotisserie League owner just might make such a deal *in the off-season*, because the $15-plus difference between Belle's and O'Neill's auction price is enough to buy a front-line starter.

Maintaining accurate, centralized player-personnel records of salary and contract status is *the most important* task of the League Secretary, who deserves hosannas from the other owners for all the work he does.

NOTE: The $260 salary limit pertains to Auction Draft Day *only*. After Auction Draft Day, free agent signings and acquisition of high-priced players in trades may well drive a team's payroll above $260.

ARTICLE VIII. PRIZE MONEY

All fees shall be promptly collected by the League Treasurer, who is empowered to subject owners to public humiliation and assess fines as needed to ensure that payments are made to the League in a timely fashion. The interest income from this investment can be used to defray the cost of a gala postseason awards ceremony and banquet. The principal shall be divided among the first four teams in the final standings as follows:

- 1st place—50%
- 2nd place—20%
- 3rd place—15%
- 4th place—10%
- 5th place—5%

ARTICLE IX. STANDINGS

The following criteria are used to determine team performance:

- Composite batting average (BA)
- Total home runs (HR)
- Total runs batted in (RBI)
- Total stolen bases (SB)
- Composite earned run average (ERA)
- Total wins (W)
- Total saves (S)
- Composite ratio: walks (BB) + hits (H) ÷ innings pitched (IP)

Teams are ranked from first to last in each of the eight categories and given points for each place. For example, in a 12-team league, the first-place team in a category receives 12 points, the second-place team 11, and so on down to 1 point for last place. The team with the most total points wins the pennant.

THE FENOKEE IP REQUIREMENT. A team must pitch a total of 900 innings to receive points in ERA and ratio. A team that does not pitch 900 innings maintains its place in ERA and ratio ranking but receives zero points in both of these categories. (Thus, a team that finished third in ERA but did not have 900 IP would receive no points in that category. The fourth-place team in ERA would still receive 9 points.) This rule was passed in 1988 in response to an "all-relief" strategy attempted by the Okrent Fenokees in the 1987 season. The strategy was not successful because Swampmaster Dan Okrent abandoned it after six weeks or so. But it might have worked, in more disciplined hands. Hence the new rule.

THE FENOKEE AB REQUIREMENT. A team must have 4250 at bats in the season. A team that does not have 4250 at bats maintains its place in the batting average ranking but receives zero points in that category. This rule was passed in 1991 in response to an "all-pitching" strategy attempted by the Okrent Fenokees in 1990. This time, the Beloved Founder and Former Commissioner-for-Life assembled an all-star pitching staff, Tony Gwynn, and 13 Ken Oberkfells (i.e., guys who didn't play enough to bring down Gwynn's "team" BA). The BFFCL hoped to amass 40 pitching points, 10 BA points, and 3 points in the other offensive categories to squeeze into the first division. The strategy was not successful because the Swampmaster abandoned it after six weeks or so. But it might have worked, in more disciplined hands. Hence the new rule.

- Pitchers' offensive stats are *not* counted, mainly because they don't appear weekly in *USA Today*. Nor are the pitching stats of the occasional position player called in to pitch when the score is 16–1 after five innings and the relief corps is hiding under the stands.
- In cases of ties in an individual category, the tied teams are assigned points by totaling points for the rankings at issue and dividing the total by the number of teams tied.
- In cases of ties in total points, final places in the standings are determined by comparing placement of teams in individual categories. Respective performances are calculated and a point given to each team for bettering the other. Should one team total more points than the other, that team is declared the winner.
- Should the point totals still be equal, the tie is broken by adding each team's *total at bats* at season's end, plus *triple the number of its innings pitched*. The team that scores a higher total by this measure wins the pennant.

ARTICLE X. STATS

The weekly player-performance summaries published in *USA Today* beginning in late April constitute the official data base for the computation of standings in Rotisserie League Baseball.

NOTE: When we first started out, we used *The Sporting News*. That was when *TSN* cared more about baseball than about all the Stanley

Cup skate-offs, NBA playoffs, and NFL summer camping rolled into one (which, by the way, is what the Rotisserie League's Founding Fathers believe should be done with them). Not for nothing was the Holy Bible known to baseball people as *The Sporting News* of religion. But that was then, and this is now. *The Sporting News* has passed from the last Spink to new owners who seem intent on taking the "Sporting" part seriously—that is, covering other sports at the expense of baseball.

- The effective date of any transaction for purposes of statistical calculation is the Monday (AL) or Tuesday (NL) *before* the commencement of play on those days. This is because weekly stats appear in *USA Today* on Tuesday for AL games through the preceding Sunday and on Wednesday for NL games through the preceding Monday.
- Reporting deadlines should be established as close to these breaks as possible but not later than the start of any game at the beginning of a new reporting period. Noon on Monday (AL) or Tuesday (NL) makes sense.
- Transactions recorded *on* Auction Draft Day, including trades and call-ups to replace disabled players, are effective retroactive to Opening Day. Transactions occurring *after* Auction Draft Day but *before* the closing date of the first cumulative summaries to appear in *USA Today* in April are effective the Monday (AL) or Tuesday (NL) immediately after the first closing date.
- Performance stats of a player shall be assigned to a Rotisserie League team *only* when he is on the active 23-man roster of that team. It is common for a player to appear on the roster of more than one Rotisserie League team during the season because of trades and waiver-list moves. Even a player who is not traded may spend time on a team's reserve list, during which period any numbers he might compile for his major league team do not count for his Rotisserie League team.
- Standings shall be tabulated and issued in a regular and timely fashion, as determined by the League owners.

NOTE: Keeping score (see pages 247–248) is the only part of Rotisserie League Baseball that isn't any fun. Unless you're computerized, it's tedious and time-consuming. And even if your league does have a computer wonk on board, it still means he or she can't take a vacation between Opening Day and early October. (God forbid your league should go a week without standings!) The best solution: Let the official stat service authorized by the Founding Fathers do all the heavy lifting for you (see page 248).

ARTICLE XI. TRADES

From the completion of the auction draft until August 31, Rotisserie League teams are free to make trades of any kind without limit, except as stipulated below, *so long as the active rosters of both teams involved in a trade reflect the required position distribution upon completion of the transaction.* No trades are permitted from September 1 through the end of the season. Trades made from the day after the season ends until rosters are frozen on

April 2 prior to Auction Draft Day are *not* bound by the position distribution requirement.

> **NOTE:** This means that if Team A wants to swap Marquis Grissom to Team B for Kevin Brown anytime between Auction Draft Day and the trade deadline, Team A will have to throw in a bum pitcher and Team B a duff outfielder to make the deal. During the off-season, the two could be dealt even-up.

- Trades do not affect the salaries or contract status of players.
- Each trade is subject to the $10 transaction fee. The fee is not affected by the number of players involved in the trade.
- Unless you want knife fights to break out among owners, prohibit all trades involving cash, "players to be named later," or "future considerations." Trust us.

NOTE ON DUMPING: "Dumping" is the inelegant but scientifically precise term used to describe what happens when a team out of contention gives up on the season and trades to a contending team its most expensive talent and its players who will be lost to free agency at the end of the year, typically for inexpensive players who can be kept the following season. A "dumping" trade is always unbalanced, sometimes egregiously so, with the contending team giving up far less than it gets, and the noncontending team giving up much more in order to acquire a nucleus for the following season. While this strategy makes sense for both clubs, extreme cases can potentially undermine the results of the auction draft, which should always be the primary indicator of an owner's ability to put together a successful team.

To guard against this, we have in the past employed rigid and restrictive Anti-Dumping measures to control trades between contenders and noncontenders. But in light of major shifts in international politics and economics in recent years, we decided in 1993 that these restrictive measures tended to inhibit rather than enhance the playing of the game.

Accordingly, we swept away all Anti-Dumping legislation in 1993. We did so with some trepidation, but we felt the benefits of a free market would outweigh the potential for abuses. We were right. Let freedom ring.

ARTICLE XII. THE RESERVE LIST

A team may replace any player on its 23-man roster who is:

- placed on the **disabled list**
- **released**
- **traded** to the other league or
- **sent down** to the minors by his major league team

To replace such a player, a Rotisserie League team must first release him outright or place him on its reserve list. A team reserves a player by notifying

---

GROUND RULES •   **269**

the League Secretary and paying the $10 transaction fee. A reserved player is removed from a team's active roster at the end of the stat week (on Monday or Tuesday)—when formal notification is given—and placed on the team's reserve list. There is no limit to the number of players a team may have on its reserve list. Reserving a player protects a team's rights to that player.

A team has two weeks to take action once a player is placed on the disabled list, released, traded to the other league, or sent to the minors by his major league team. If no action is taken, the position is frozen open until the original player's return, and no replacement may be made.

• *A suspended player may not be reserved, released, or replaced.*

NOTE: When we first wrote that, we were thinking about the old-fashioned things players might do to get themselves suspended—Bill Madlock hitting an umpire (1980), say, or Gaylord Perry throwing a spitter (1962 to 1983), although he was suspended for doing it only once (1982). Then came the drug suspensions of 1984 and afterward. We have decided to consider players suspended for substance abuse as if they were on the disabled list, and allow teams to replace them.

• Once a specific action has been taken to remove a player from its 23-man roster (via release or placing him on the reserve list), a team is then free to select any eligible player from the free agent pool of players not already owned by another Rotisserie League team. The salary assigned to a player so selected from the free agent pool is $10; the call-up fee is $25 (see **Article VI**, page 265).
• If the same player is claimed by more than one team in a given week, he goes to the team ranking lowest in the most recent standings.
• Every reserve move must be accompanied by a concomitant replacement move (i.e., a team may not reserve a player without replacing him).
• Placing a player *on* the reserve list and activating a player *from* the reserve list are *each* subject to a $10 transaction fee.
• The call-up takes effect as soon as it is recorded by the League Secretary, although the player's stats do not begin to accrue to his new team until Monday (AL) or Tuesday (NL) of the week the League Secretary records the call-up.
• Player moves are to be made in accordance with the player's status as of the transaction reporting deadline. For instance, if a player is active on his major league roster on the transaction reporting deadline, he cannot be reserved even though he was on the DL earlier in the reporting period.
• A player on a Rotisserie League reserve list may not be traded *unless* the replacement player linked to him is also traded.
• A replacement player may be traded or otherwise replaced (e.g., in case of injury, he could be reserved and a free agent called up to fill his slot). In such a case, the newly acquired player becomes linked to the original reserved player. To avoid even the appearance of collusion, a replacement player traded from one team to another may not be traded back to his original team for three reporting periods.

- When a player on a reserve list returns to active major league duty, he must be **reinstated** to the active 23-man roster of his Rotisserie League team *two weeks* after his activation or be **waived**. Failure to notify the League Secretary shall be considered a waiver of the player on the reserve list. A player may not be **reinstated** or **waived** until he has been activated by his major league team.

NOTE: Intended to prevent stockpiling of players, this rule is tricky to monitor. Daily newspaper transaction columns and telephone sports-information lines don't always catch every single major league roster move. The clock starts ticking when the League Secretary *is made aware of* a player being reactivated. By the way, "two weeks" means two full reporting periods and may actually be as much as two weeks plus six days (as in the case of a player being reactivated the day after a reporting deadline). In fairness, and because this is not full-contact karate but a game played among friends, an owner should be given warning by the League Secretary that time is up and he will lose a player if he doesn't make a move. Especially if there are extenuating circumstances (i.e., anything from retracing Livingston's steps in Africa to just plain laziness).

- When a player is reinstated to the active 23-man Rotisserie League roster from a team's reserve list, the player originally called up to replace him must be waived, unless the replacement player *or* the original player can be shifted to another natural opening on the roster for which he qualifies.
- If the replacement player is replaced (e.g., he is injured, put on reserve, and a free agent is called up), then *his* replacement becomes linked to the original player on the reserve list.
- A player reinstated from the reserve list may not displace any active player on the Rotisserie League team's 23-man roster *other than* his original replacement (or his successor).

NOTE: The intent of all this is to minimize the benefit a team might derive from an injury. Say Jeff Bagwell breaks his wrist (nah, could never happen again) and you call up the inevitable Dave Magaden to replace him. Bagwell comes back. What you'd like to do is activate Bagwell, keep Magadan, and waive your other corner man, Phil Clark, who hasn't had more than 10 at-bats a week since the season began. Our rules say you can't, on the premise that *a team is not ordinarily helped by an injury to a key player.* We know the big leagues don't handle it this way, but art doesn't always imitate life. Without some restriction, an owner might never have to pay the price for his bad judgment in drafting Phil Clark in the first place.

ARTICLE XIII. FARM SYSTEM

If a farm system player is promoted to the active roster of a major league team at any time during the regular season *prior to* September 1 (when major league rosters may expand to 40), his Rotisserie League team has *two weeks* after his promotion to **activate** him (at any position for which he qualifies) or **waive** him.

- The fee for activating a player from a team's farm system is $10.
- If a farm system player is activated, the player displaced from the 23-man roster to make room for him must be placed on waivers, *unless* the farm system player can be activated into a natural opening, in which case no waiver is required. **Example:** One of your pitchers is placed on a major league disabled list; you reserve him and activate a pitcher from your farm system who has been called up by his major league team.
- Once brought up from its farm system by a Rotisserie League team, a player may not be returned to it, although he may be placed on a team's reserve list in the event he is returned to the minor leagues by his major league club.
- A farm system player not brought up to a team's 23-man roster during the season of his initial selection may be kept within the farm system in subsequent seasons upon payment of an additional $10 per year, so long as he retains official rookie status and the League Secretary is duly notified on April 1 each year, when rosters are frozen. (See also **Article XVIII**, page 276.)
- A team may have no more than three players in its farm system.
- A farm system player may be traded during authorized trading periods, subject to prevailing rules governing transactions, as may a team's selection rights in the minor league draft.

NOTE: This means that a team could acquire and exercise as many as three farm system draft picks, providing that it does not exceed the maximum of three players in its farm system at a given time.

ARTICLE XIV. SIGNING FREE AGENTS

Active major league players not on any Rotisserie League team's roster at the conclusion of the auction draft become free agents. During the course of the season the pool of free agents may also include minor league players not in any Rotisserie League's farm system (see **Article XIII**, page 271) who are promoted to an active major league roster; waived players who are not claimed; and players traded from the "other" major league. Such players may be signed in the following manner.

From Opening Day Until the All-Star Game. Free agents may be called up to replace players placed on a Rotisserie League team's reserve list as outlined in **Article XII** (see page 269). The only exception to **Article XII**'s provisions for signing free agents during this period is that a player traded into the league from the "other" major league or signed by a team within the league as a free agent may be signed by a Rotisserie League team with its **Free Agent Acquisition Budget (FAAB)**, as described below.

After the All-Star Game. From the All-Star Game until the last weekly transaction deadline before September 1, free agents may be signed, without limit in number, but within the limitations of a Rotisserie League team's **Free Agent Acquisition Budget:**

- Each team shall have, for the purpose of acquiring free agents during the course of the season, a supplementary budget of $100.
- At the deadline established by each league for recording weekly transactions, a team may submit a *sealed* bid for one or more free agents.
- The minimum bid shall be $5; the maximum shall be the amount remaining in a team's **FAAB**.
- A free agent so selected goes to the highest bidder. If more than one team bids the same amount on a player, and if that amount is the highest bid, the player goes to the team that is lowest in the most recently compiled standings.
- The salary of a free agent signed in this manner is his acquisition price. His contract status is that of a first-year player.
- In addition to the player's acquisition price, a team signing a free agent must pay the $25 transaction fee for calling up free agents as set forth in **Article VI** (page 265).
- For each free agent that it signs, a team *must* at the same time waive or release a player at the same position from its *active* roster. If on a major league team's *active* roster, such a player is *waived*. If he has been placed on a major league team's disabled list, released, traded to the "other" league, or demoted to the minors, such a player is *released* and may not be acquired by a Rotisserie League team until he is once again on a major league roster.
- A free agent signed for a salary in excess of $10 (i.e., more than the customary call-up fee for replacement players) is deemed to have a guaranteed two-year contract. If such a player is not protected the following season (i.e., if he is released into the free agent pool at the time rosters are frozen on April 1), then a contract buyout fee in the amount of twice his salary or $100, whichever is greater, shall be paid by the team owning his contract at the time.
- If a Rotisserie League team loses a player to the "other" league in an interleague trade, then the team's available **FAAB** dollars are increased by an amount equal to the lost player's salary.

NOTE: If a team wishes to replace an injured player and reserve him, it must use the mechanism described in **Article XII** (page 269); it may *not* use the FAAB process without releasing an active player.

NOTE: The provision regarding players acquired for a sum in excess of the customary $10 call-up fee is intended to discourage frivolous bidding for free agents. It is also intended to make teams who are most likely to benefit from signing costly free agents—that is, teams still in the race for the first division—pay for it dearly, by making such players expensive to dump the following spring.

NOTE: Set up a simple, common-sense mechanism for handling the "sealed bid" part of the **FAAB** process. Nothing elaborate is needed. Price, Waterhouse need not be called in. Don't permit bidders to make contingency bids (e.g., "If I don't get Ruth at $29, then I'll bid $25 for Gehrig, and if I don't get Gehrig...") unless your League Secretary doesn't have a day job.

ARTICLE XV. WAIVERS

Under certain conditions, a Rotisserie League player may be waived.

- When a player on a Rotisserie League team's reserve list is activated by his major league team, either he or the player called up earlier to replace him *must* be placed on waivers (see **Article XII**, page 269).
- When a team activates a player from its farm system, except into a natural opening (see **Article XIII**, page 271), the player dropped from the 23-man roster to make room for him *must* be placed on waivers.
- A player no longer on the active roster of his major league team and whose Rotisserie League position is taken by a player activated from the reserve list or farm system may not be placed on waivers but *must* be released outright.
- A player placed on waivers is no longer eligible to be claimed if he is sent down to the minors, traded to the other league, or is placed on the DL by his major league team.

NOTE: This is to prevent a team from picking up a disabled list player on waivers merely for the purpose of releasing him and replacing him with a player of higher quality from the free agent pool.

- The waiver period begins at noon on the Monday (AL) or Tuesday (NL) after the League Secretary has been notified that a player has been waived and lasts one week, at the end of which time the player shall become the property of the lowest-ranked team to have claimed him. To make room on its roster, the team acquiring a player on waivers must assign the player to a natural opening or waive a player at the same position played by the newly acquired player.
- Waiver claims take precedence over the replacement of an injured, released, or demoted player who has been put on reserve. That is, a player on waivers may be signed by a team with a roster opening at his position only if no other team lower in the standings claims the player on waivers.
- A team may acquire on waivers *no more* than one player in a given week, but there is no limit to the number of players a team may acquire on waivers during the season.
- A player who clears waivers—that is, is not claimed by any team—returns to the free agent pool.
- The fee for acquiring a player on waivers is $10. The salary of a player acquired on waivers shall be $10 or his current salary, whichever is greater. His contract status shall remain the same.
- A player with a guaranteed long-term contract may *not* be waived during the season. He may, however, be released and replaced if he is traded to the "other" league.
- A player may be given his outright release *only* if he is
    - (a) unconditionally released,
    - (b) placed on the "designated for assignment" list,
    - (c) sent to the minors,

(d) placed on the "disqualified" list,

(e) traded to the "other" major league, or

(f) placed on the disabled list.

ARTICLE XVI. SEPTEMBER ROSTER EXPANSION

If it chooses, a team may expand its roster for the pennant drive by calling up additional players after September 1 from the free agent pool, its own reserve list, or its own farm system. A team may call up as many players as it wishes, subject to payment of appropriate fees as outlined below, except that at no time may the number of active players on its roster exceed 40.

- The order of selection for September Roster Expansion is determined by the most recent standings, with the last-place team having first selection, and so on. During this 24-hour period, September Roster Expansion claims take precedence over waiver claims and routine call-ups to replace players who are disabled, released, or traded to the other league by their major league teams. This selection order pertains until midnight, September 2, *only,* after which time a team forfeits its order in the selection process, though *not* its right to make a selection. Selection after midnight, September 2, is on a first-come, first-served basis. Also, after midnight, September 2, waiver claims and routine call-ups to fill natural openings take precedence over September Roster Expansion claims.
- Players are selected in a round by round draft format. If, after a selection, no other team wishes to claim a player, a team may then claim as many players consecutively as it wishes up to the 40-man roster limit.
- The performance stats of players called up during September Roster Expansion start to accrue on the Monday (AL) or Tuesday (NL) after the League Secretary has been notified of the player's selection.
- The fee for expanding the roster in September is $50 per player.
- The salary assigned to a September call-up from the free agent pool is $25. The salary of a September call-up from a team's reserve list or farm system is the salary established at the time he was previously acquired (on Auction Draft Day, or subsequently from the free agent pool, or via waivers).

NOTE: A device for heightening the excitement for contending teams and for sweetening the kitty at their expense, September Roster Expansion will generally not appeal to second-division clubs (who should, however, continue to watch the waiver wire in the hope of acquiring "keepers" for next season at a $10 salary).

ARTICLE XVII. THE OPTION YEAR AND
GUARANTEED LONG-TERM CONTRACTS

A player who has been under contract at the same salary during two consecutive seasons and whose service has been uninterrupted (that is, he has not been waived or released, although he may have been traded) must, prior to the freezing of rosters in his third season, be released; signed at the same salary for his option year; or signed to a guaranteed long-term contract.

If **released**, the player returns to the free agent pool and becomes available to the highest bidder at the next auction draft. If signed at the same salary for an **option year**, the player must be released back into the free agent pool at the end of that season. If signed to a **guaranteed long-term contract**, the player's salary in each year covered by the new contract (which commences with the option year) shall be the sum of his current salary plus $5 for each additional year beyond the option year. In addition, a signing bonus, equal to one half the total value of the long-term contract, but not less than $5, shall also be paid.

> **NOTE:** This rule is intended to prevent blue-chippers, low-priced rookies who blossom into superstars, and undervalued players from being tied up for the duration of their careers by the teams who originally drafted them. It guarantees periodic transfusions of top-flight talent for Auction Draft Day and provides rebuilding teams something to rebuild with. And it makes for some interesting decisions at roster-freeze time two years down the pike.

- In determining a player's status, "season" is understood to be a full season or any fraction thereof. Thus, a player called up from the free agent pool in the middle of the 1995 season and subsequently retained at the same salary without being released in 1996 (even though he may have been traded) enters his option year in 1997 and must be released, signed at the same salary for an option year, or signed to a long-term contract.
- A team may sign a player to only one long-term contract, at the end of which he becomes a free agent.
- Option-year and long-term contracts are entirely transferable, both in rights and obligations; the trade of a player in no way affects his contract status.
- If, during the course of a long-term contract, a player is traded from the National League to the American League (or vice versa), the contract is rendered null and void. The team that loses the player's services shall be under no further financial obligations.
- In all other cases—specifically *including* sudden loss of effectiveness—a team must honor the terms of a long-term contract, as follows: A player with such a contract *may* be released back into the free agent pool (that is, not protected on a team's roster prior to Auction Draft Day), but a team that chooses to do so must pay into the prize pool, above the $260 Auction Draft Day limit, a sum equal to *twice* the remaining value of the player's contract or $100, whichever is greater.

ARTICLE XVIII. ROSTER PROTECTION

For the first three seasons of the League's existence, each team must retain, from one season to the next, *no fewer than* **7** but *no more than* **15** of the players on its 23-man roster. After three seasons, this minimum requirement is eliminated, the maximum retained. The minimum is removed because, after three seasons, a team might find it impossible to retain a specific minimum because too many players have played out their option.

- The names of players being retained must be recorded with the League Secretary by midnight, April 1. Specific notice must also be made at that time of any guaranteed long-term contract signings and farm system renewals.
- The cumulative salaries of players protected prior to Auction Draft Day are deducted from a team's $260 expenditure limit, and the balance is available for acquisition of the remaining players needed to complete the team's 23-man roster.
- The League Secretary should promptly notify all teams in the League of each team's protected roster, including player salaries, contract status, and amount available to spend on Auction Draft Day.
- Failure to give notice of a guaranteed long-term contract for a player in his option year will result in his being continued for one season at his prior year's salary and then released into the free agent pool. Failure to renew a farm system player's minor league contract will result in his becoming available to all other teams in the subsequent minor league draft.
- A farm system player whose minor league contract is renewed on April 1 and who subsequently makes his major league team's active roster may, at his Rotisserie League owner's option, be added to the protected list of players on Auction Draft Day (and another player dropped, if necessary, to meet the 15-player limit), or he may be dropped and made available in the auction draft. He may not be retained in his Rotisserie League team's farm system.

NOTE: The April 1 roster-protection deadline was originally set to correspond with the end of the major leagues' spring interleague trading period, a rite of spring that no longer exists. We've stuck to April 1 anyway, because it gives us a week or so to fine-tune draft strategies. Until you know who the other teams are going to keep, you won't know for sure who's going to be available. And until you know how much they will have to spend on Auction Draft Day, you won't be able to complete your own pre-draft budget. So April 1 it is; don't fool with it.

ARTICLE XIX. GOVERNANCE

The Rotisserie League is governed by a Committee of the Whole consisting of all team owners. The Committee of the Whole may designate as many League officials as from time to time it deems appropriate, although only two—the League Secretary and the League Treasurer—ever do any work. The Committee of the Whole also designates annually an Executive Committee composed of three team owners in good standing. The Executive Committee has the authority to interpret playing rules and to handle all necessary and routine League business. All decisions, rulings, and interpretations by the Executive Committee are subject to veto by the Committee of the Whole.

Rule changes, pronouncements, and acts of whimsy are determined by majority vote of the Committee of the Whole. Member leagues of the **Rotisserie League Baseball Association** (see page 250) may appeal to the RLBA for adjudication of disputes and interpretation of rules. The Rotisserie League has three official meetings each year: Auction Draft Day (the first weekend after Opening Day), the Midsummer Trade Meeting (at the All-Star break), and the Gala Postseason Banquet and Awards Ceremony. Failure to attend at least two official meetings is punishable by trade to the Minnesota Twins.

ARTICLE XX. YOO-HOO

To consecrate the bond of friendship that unites all Rotisserie League owners in their pursuit of the pennant, to symbolize the eternal verities and values of the Greatest Game for Baseball Fans Since Baseball, and to soak the head of the League champion with a sticky brown substance before colleagues and friends duly assembled, the **Yoo-Hoo Ceremony** is hereby ordained as the culminating event of the baseball season. Each year, at the awards ceremony and banquet, the owner of the championship team shall have a bottle of Yoo-Hoo poured over his or her head by the preceding year's pennant winner. The Yoo-Hoo Ceremony shall be performed with the dignity and solemnity appropriate to the occasion.

> **NOTE:** If Yoo-Hoo, the chocolate-flavored beverage once endorsed by soft-drink connoisseur Yogi Berra, is not available in your part of the country, you have two options: (a) send up an alternative beverage, one chosen in the Yoo-Hoo spirit, as a pinch-hitter, or (b) move.

ROTISSERIE ULTRA
The Rules of Play

Turn Up the Volume

Rotisserie Ultra requires more scouting, more planning, more wheeling, and more dealing. You move players off and onto your active roster as often as you want to. You ride guys on hot streaks, then ditch them when they go cold. You buy free agents. You bring along youngsters all the way from the low minors. You swing complicated, multiplayer deals. You build a strong bench with waiver moves to carry you through injuries and slumps.

Does playing Rotisserie Ultra mean giving up all pretense of having a normal life? No, you should keep up that pretense as long as you can. It does mean that you're not going to have a lot of time for scuba diving the Great Barrier Reef, reading Joyce, learning to play the saxophone, paneling the rec room, or having a catch with your kid this summer. You're going to be busy, Bucky—or you're going to be in the second division.

Remember that the Sturgeon General himself—Peter Gethers, owner of Peter's Famous Smoked Fish—has warned that playing Rotisserie Ultra *before you're ready* can lead to "sensory overload, stress-related insomnia, pattern baldness, hot flashes, and premature ejaculation."

We recommend that fledgling leagues play the regular version of the game, become acclimated to its demands and pressures, and shake out owners who can't stand the heat of a pennant race before moving on to Ultra. Stay within yourselves, walk before you run, take it one game at a time, and floss regularly. Only then should you consider Ultra. After all, we can't have everybody in America having too much fun all at once.

Editor's Note: *Many of the rules in the Official Constitution of Rotisserie League Baseball also apply to Rotisserie Ultra, so we decided not to repeat every line of fine print that applies to both, except as needed for clarity. That means that the "Rules of Play" that follow for Rotisserie Ultra should be read together with the original Constitution. If you can't handle that assignment, you're going to have* real *trouble with Rotisserie Ultra.*

ULTRA I. THE ROTATION DRAFT

After the conclusion of the auction draft, in which teams acquire their 23-man active rosters for a sum not to exceed $260, owners successively draft up to 17 additional players in 17 separate rounds of selection. Initially, players acquired in this fashion comprise a team's reserve roster.

• Any baseball player is eligible for this draft. *Exception:* In National

League versions, no player on the roster or in the minor league organization of an American League team may be selected; and, in American League versions, the opposite is true. Eligible players include (in the NL version, by way of example) previously undrafted NL players, NL-owned minor leaguers, unsigned players, Japanese players, high-school or college players, and the kid down the block with the great arm.

- In the rotation draft, owners are not required to select players by position. They may select all pitchers, all position players, or a mix.
- The order of selection for each of the 17 rounds is determined by the order of finish in the previous season. In leagues with 12 teams, the 6th place team selects first, proceeding in descending order to the 12th place team, followed by the 5th, 4th, 3rd, 2nd, and 1st place teams.

NOTE: For leagues switching over from Rotisserie League rules to Rotisserie League Ultra rules, the first two rounds of the rotation draft follow the order of the former farm system draft. Only players who have rookie status and are not on a major league 25-man roster or disabled list may be selected in these two rounds. This protects the property rights of teams that may have acquired additional farm system draft picks or improved their draft position via trades prior to the shift to Rotisserie League Ultra.

ULTRA II. THE RESERVE ROSTER

A team's reserve roster consists of those players acquired through the rotation draft, through trades, through demotions from the active roster, or through waiver claims. Any transaction (e.g., trade, demotion, waiver claim) that increases the size of the reserve roster beyond 17 players must be accompanied by a concomitant transaction (e.g., trade, promotion, waiver) that simultaneously returns the reserve roster to its maximum 17.

ULTRA III. FEES

1. **Basic:** The cumulative total of salaries paid for acquisition of a 23-man active roster on Auction Draft Day may not exceed $260.
2. **Reserve Roster:** There are no fees payable for the acquisition of players for the 17-man reserve roster.
3. **Transactions:** $10 per trade (no matter how many players are involved), $10 per player activation or demotion.
4. **Waivers:** $10 for each player claimed on waivers.
5. **September Roster Expansion:** $50 for each player added to a team's active roster after September 1.

ULTRA IV. PLAYER SALARIES

The salary of a player is determined by the time and means of his acquisition and does not change unless the player becomes a free agent by means of release or is signed to a guaranteed long-term contract.

THE TENTH PITCHER OPTION

As everybody in the baseball world knows, a Rotisserie team is composed of 9 pitchers and 14 position players (see **Article III,** page 262). Except, of course, when it's not.

A couple of years back we experimented with a slight variation on the traditional roster configuration and permitted a team to carry 10 pitchers and 13 position players.

Most major league teams carry 10 pitchers and 15 position players. But some (e.g., the Detroit Tigers in April and May in recent years) carry only 9 pitchers, while others (e.g., the Oakland A's) carry 11. It comes down to a GM's assessment of the team's needs, its personnel, and the schedule.

If this flexibility is good for the American and National leagues, why not for the third major league—the Rotisserie League? So a couple of years back we decided to let teams fill the utility slot with a position player *or* a pitcher. The result? An unqualified success.

The Tenth Pitcher Option allows a GM to realize the full potential of Ultra. Let's say you have the usual 9 pitchers and 14 position players on your active roster, and your team starts slipping in wins. Presto! You send down the outfielder hitting .227 in your utility slot and promote a good middle innings guy from your reserve roster. In AL leagues, you must still have a DH, two catchers, and three middle infielders, so the 10th pitcher must come at the expense of a corner or an outfielder.

The Tenth Pitcher Option provides more action, sweetens the pot through additional transaction fees, and is simple to administer and monitor. You can change the mix back and forth as frequently as you wish, provided only that the total number of active players does not exceed 23, and that at no time do you have more than 14 active position players or more than 10 active pitchers.

After hearing from leagues around the country regarding their experience with the Tenth Pitcher Option, we decided to leave it as just that—an option. Some leagues, particularly those using AL players, found it awkward to implement because of the DH. Others thought it was okay for Ultra but not regular Rotisserie. Still others simply didn't like it. Many made the transition smoothly.

Hey, that's why we call it an *Option*.

- The salary of a player acquired in the auction draft is his auction price.
- The salary of a player acquired in the rotation draft is determined as follows: If the player was selected in the first round, $15; rounds 2–6, $10; rounds 7–12, $5; rounds 13–17, $2.
- The salary of a player claimed on waivers is $10 or his previous salary, whichever is greater. His contract status remains the same.

ULTRA V. TRADES

From the completion of the rotation draft until noon on the Monday (AL) or Tuesday (NL) on or following August 31, teams are free to make trades of any kind without limit (except as indicated in **Ultra VI**, below). However, at no time can any team have on its active roster more players at a particular position than allowed under the rules of the auction draft (see **Article III**, page 262 of the Official Constitution of Rotisserie League Baseball). A team may, however, be underrepresented at a position. So long as these strictures are adhered to in the immediate wake of a trade, teams may trade any number of players, at any position, irrespective of the number or position of players being received in such trade (except, again, as indicated below in **Ultra VI**).

- At no point may a team have more than 17 players on its reserve roster or more than 40 players on its active and reserve rosters combined.
- At no point may a team have more than 23 players on its active roster, except during the September Roster Expansion period (see **Ultra X**, page 284).
- No trades of any kind may be made between September 1 and October 15, nor between April 2 (Roster Freeze Day) and the conclusion of the rotation draft on Auction Draft Day.

ULTRA VI. ANTI-DUMPING

Players in the last year of a guaranteed contract or playing out their option year and players with a salary of $25 or more are considered "asterisk" players. Such players may be traded only under the following conditions:

- One team may trade asterisk players to another team provided that for each asterisk player traded, one is received in the same deal.
- The above notwithstanding, a team may trade *one* asterisk player to another team without an asterisk player coming in return or receive *one* asterisk player without giving one up, but may make only *one* such unbalanced trade in the course of the season.
- Between October 15 and Roster Freeze Day, asterisk players on winter rosters may be traded without restrictions whatsoever.

ULTRA VI-A. ANTI-DUMPING REPEALED

Effective Opening Day, 1993, Article **Ultra VI** (above) was repealed. The text of **Ultra VI** is left in place so that newcomers to **Ultra** will know just what is being done away with.

ULTRA VII. MOVEMENT BETWEEN ACTIVE ROSTER AND RESERVE ROSTER

An owner may demote a player from the active roster to the reserve roster, or promote a player in the reverse direction, at any time and for any reason, such promotions to take effect with the subsequent stat deadline (Monday noon for AL leagues, Tuesday noon for NL leagues). However, no player may be demoted without being replaced on the active roster by an eligible player—that is, a player who fulfills position eligibility requirements (which may include shifting another active player into the demoted player's position and the promoted player into the shifted player's position) *and* who is currently on a major league roster and not on a major league disabled list.

- **Exception:** If the acquisition of an active player in a trade places the acquiring team's active roster above the positional limit (e.g., more than two catchers), a player at that position may be sent down without the need for the recall of another player.
- A player acquired by trade from another team's active roster is considered active with the acquiring team on the effective date of the trade, unless the acquiring team chooses (or is compelled by roster restrictions) to demote him. Similarly, a player acquired in a trade from another team's reserve roster is considered to be reserved with the acquiring team, unless the acquiring team promotes him.

ULTRA VIII. SIGNING FREE AGENTS

Active major league players not on any Rotisserie League team's active roster or reserve roster at the conclusion of the auction draft become free agents. During the course of the season the pool of free agents may also include minor league players not on any Rotisserie League team's reserve roster who are promoted to an active major league roster; players traded from the "other" major league; and waived players who are not claimed. Beginning one week after the first standings report, and continuing through the season until the last weekly transaction deadline before September 1, such free agents may be signed, without limit, in the following manner:

- Each team shall have, for the purpose of acquiring free agents during the course of the season, a supplementary budget of $100, known as its **Free Agent Acquisition Budget (FAAB).**
- At the deadline established by each Rotisserie League for recording weekly transactions, a Rotisserie League team may submit a *sealed* bid for one or more free agents.
- The minimum bid shall be $5; the maximum shall be the amount remaining in a team's **FAAB.**
- A free agent so selected goes to the highest bidder. If more than one team bids the same amount on a player, and if that amount is the highest bid, the player goes to the team that is lowest in the most recently compiled standings.
- The salary of a free agent signed in this manner is his acquisition price. His contract status is that of a first-year player.
- For each free agent that it signs, a team *must* at the same time waive or release a player from its *active* roster.
- If a free agent signed for a salary of $25 or more is not protected on the subsequent April 1 Roster Freeze, then the owner of his contract at the time must pay into the prize pool a buyout fee of twice his salary or $100, whichever is greater.

NOTE: The reason for the pre–September 1 deadline is to prevent a Rotisserie League team from completely restocking with $5 players when the major leagues expand their rosters to 40 in September.

NOTE: The mechanics of the "sealed bid" process will vary from league to league. Where practicable, as in leagues that have weekly meetings, the sealed bid should be just that—a bid sealed in an envelope that is opened at the meeting. In other cases, it may be more efficient to recruit a disinterested party to record all bids and report them to the League Secretary for action. Whatever mechanism you devise, keep matters in perspective. These aren't the secrets to nuclear fusion, for Einstein's sake! So try to balance the gee of security with the haw of mutual trust.

ULTRA IX. WAIVERS

Players are placed on waivers (a) when they cannot be accommodated on a team's active or reserve roster, because of space and/or positional limitations; and (b) under the rules governing the winter roster (see **Ultra XI**, page 285).

- The waiver period commences at noon on the Monday (AL) or Tuesday (NL) immediately following the team's notification of waiver to the League Secretary and extends for one full reporting period (i.e., one week). At the conclusion of that week, if the player is unclaimed, he goes into the free agent pool, and may be acquired by a team only as outlined in **Ultra VIII**, above.
- Waiver claims are honored according to the inverse order of the standings effective the week before the close of the waiver period.
- A team may reclaim a player it has waived only if all other teams in the league decline to claim him.
- The fee for acquiring a player on waivers is $10. The salary of a player acquired on waivers shall be $10 or his current salary, whichever is greater; and his contract status shall remain the same.
- Only a player currently on a 25-man major league roster (i.e., not on a disabled list) may be claimed on waivers.
- A player traded to the "other" league may not be placed on waivers.
- A player on a guaranteed long-term contract may not be placed on waivers, even in the final year of his contract.

ULTRA X. SEPTEMBER ROSTER EXPANSION

If it chooses, a team may expand its roster for the pennant drive by promoting from its reserve roster an *unlimited* number of players, as the post–September 1 active-roster size expands to a maximum of 40 players. Such players may play any position.

- September expansions can be effective no earlier than noon on the Monday (AL) or Tuesday (NL) immediately following August 31.

Expansions made later in September become effective the subsequent Monday or Tuesday at noon.

- A fee of $50 must be paid for every promotion that increases the active-roster size beyond 23. Player salaries are not affected by such promotions.

ULTRA XI. WINTER ROSTER

Effective October 15, each owner is required to submit to the League Secretary a list of 23 players, irrespective of position, taken from its combined active and reserve rosters, but one not including any players who have concluded their option year or the last year of a guaranteed long-term contract. This group of players becomes the winter roster.

- Immediately after the submission of winter rosters, a waiver period concluding at noon, November 1, begins. By inverse order of the final standings in the season just ended, teams may select no more than one player from that group of players not protected on a winter roster, again with the exception of players who have concluded their option year or the final year of a guaranteed long-term contract. On claiming such a player, the claiming team must, in turn, waive a player from its own winter roster. Players thus waived become eligible for a second round of waiver claims, for a period of one week, that are conducted in the same fashion. (Unclaimed players from the first waiver period are no longer eligible.) The process continues until there is a week in which no one is claimed.
- All winter-waiver claims cost the claiming team $10, to be paid into the league treasury for the coming season.
- The salary of a player claimed on winter waivers is $10 (or his current salary, whichever is greater), and he shall be deemed to be commencing the first year of a new contract with the coming season.
- After October 23, winter rosters may exceed or fall below 23 players through trading action. Whatever size the roster, however, any successful claim of a player on waivers must be accompanied by the placing of another player from the claiming team on waivers.

ULTRA XII. ROSTER PROTECTION

Roster protection in Rotisserie League and Rotisserie League Ultra is identical (see **Article XVIII**, page 276), except as follows:

- The cumulative salaries of frozen players are deducted from a team's $260 expenditure limit in the auction draft, and the balance is available for the acquisition of the remainder of a team's active roster. However, salaries of players frozen on April 1 who are not on 25-man major league rosters on Auction Draft Day do not count against the $260 limit.
- Frozen players not on 25-man major league rosters count against the limit of 17 players on draft day reserve rosters, and the salaries they carry must be paid into the league treasury on draft day.

- In addition to the 15 players that a team may protect from its winter roster of active and reserve roster players, a team may also protect an additional 3 players on its reserve roster, provided that such players have rookie status and have never been active on a Rotisserie League team.
- Players frozen may include players who have spent the entire previous season on a reserve roster—typically because they played only in the minor leagues. Even so, such players who are subsequently frozen are deemed to be in the *second* year of their contract with their Rotisserie League Ultra team.
- Assignment of frozen players to a reserve roster position is at the owner's discretion. That is, an owner with a $10 minor leaguer carried over from the preceding year might, for strategic reasons, assign that player to the 17th position in the rotation draft, thus forgoing a $2 pick. Or the owner might assign the player to the first round and forgo a $15 pick. The assignment of frozen players by all teams will be made before the rotation draft commences.

NOTE: Some Ultra Leagues believe that the clock on minor leaguers should not start ticking until they are promoted to the majors, as in Rotisserie Regular. We feel this would tie up too many players and eventually undermine the auction draft. Effective in 1991, we increased the number of $2 and $5 players in the rotation draft (see **Ultra IV**, page 280). That should facilitate building a farm system and encourage protection of key players without providing the blanket protection of freezing the clock. This is called a compromise.

Let There Be Lite!

Great ideas often have implausibly pedestrian beginnings.

Isaac Newton was sitting under an apple tree, thinking he would like something sweet but tart and loaded with vitamin A, when the principle of gravity fell into his lap. A man who loved martinis a bit too well, Eli Whitney got his big inspiration when his wife yelled from the kitchen, "Keep your cotton-picking hands off that gin!" And because somebody else was picking up the tab, Daniel Okrent, down from his rustic estate in western Massachusetts to join Manhattan friends for lunch, found himself eating snails and making history over a decade ago in the then-fashionable East Side bistro La Rôtisserie Française, instead of wolfing down a grease-on-white-with-mayo at his favorite New York restaurant—and thus the world was deprived of Blimpie League Baseball.

Maybe there's something in the water up there in the Berkshire Mountains, or maybe there's just nothing else to do, but a few years back yet another bucolic Edison stumbled out of the backwoods with a new widget. Fortunately, BFFCL Okrent recognized his nearby neighbor's creation as an inspired variation on a great theme, an ingenious mechanism for filling an important sociocultural need, a cleverly constructed design with possible commercial potential.

So we stole it.

That's how we are able to bring you the newest version of The Greatest Game for Baseball Fans Since Youknowwhat, Rotisserie Lite! But before we do, common courtesy requires us to say a few words about the country bumpk . . . ah, *squire* whom we city-slickered into giving away his invention for a handful of T-shirts and the promise to spell his name right.

Tony Lake (that's L-A-K-E) is a man for all seasons, though he definitely prefers summer. A hardscrabble farmer then biding his time between crops as a circuit-riding professor of international politics at several pricey New England colleges, Farmer-Professor Lake is currently President Clinton's National Security Adviser and the highest-ranking Rotisserian in the world. He is a terminal Boston Red Sox fan who started playing Rotisserie League Baseball almost a decade ago, when BFFCL Okrent sold him a copy of the rules for 40 acres and a mule. Farmer-Professor Lake says the idea for Rotisserie Lite came to him one day near the end of the 1989 season when he was sitting on his tractor thinking about the Middle East situation.

"Late that season I suddenly found myself going sane," the tiller-scholar recalls. "I caught myself reading boxscores to find out who won, not just to see how my players had done. Some days I even read the front page first. Clearly, I was in trouble."

The academic-agrarian attacked the problem by identifying what he liked best and least about Rotisserie Ultra play in the League of Nations, where his team—the Smuts Peddlers—had always been a strong contender. "I like boxscores, and I like listening to games on the radio," he says. "I don't like the lure of trading, because it appeals to extreme type-A personalities like Okrent. I was spending too much time thinking about trades instead of about foreign policy or that funny sound my tractor was making."

While unwilling to go cold turkey (he still plays in the League of Nations), Farmer-Professor Lake did go looking for a halfway house. He found it when he founded the Washington Slo-Pitch League, a six-team outfit whose owners hail mostly from the nation's capital. (The mayor of the founder's hometown was awarded a one-third ownership in a franchise as a hedge against local tax increases. So far it's worked.)

"I see the game we play in Slo-Pitch as a halfway house in either direction," Farmer-Professor Lake says. "If you've never played Rotisserie before, it's a great way to learn what it's all about. And if you've been playing it too hard or too long, it helps you recapture the whimsy, and whimsy is the whole point of Rotisserie in the first place."

Thanks, Tony. We needed that.

ROTISSERIE LITE
The Rules of Play

Same Auction Draft!　**No Farm System!**
Same Stat Categories!　**No Reserve List!**
Same Yoo-Hoo!　**No Money!**

Editor's Note: *The following rules were lifted from the unwritten constitution of the Washington Slo-Pitch League, with several embellishments and alterations of our own to give them a bogus air of originality. Please note that we were too lazy to repeat all the pertinent rules of Rotisserie Regular that also apply in Rotisserie Lite. That means you'll have to go back and read the* **Official Constitution of Rotisserie League Baseball** *(pages 262–278) to figure out what we're talking about.*

LITE I. FEWER TEAMS

A Rotisserie Lite League using National League or American League players is composed of six teams.

- With only six teams, Rotisserie Lite Leagues have shorter (and probably more orderly) auction drafts, fewer friendships to wreck, and less trouble squeezing into a telephone booth.

LITE II. ONE DIVISION ONLY

A Rotisserie Lite League uses players from only *one* NL or AL division.

- Resist the temptation to draw players from an entire league or—worse still—to mix the two leagues. "Lite" doesn't mean "soft." By restricting the talent pool to players of one division, Lite owners will need to scout as diligently as do Rotisserie Regular and Rotisserie Ultra owners. You'll have to learn which middle innings relievers can be counted on for the greatest number of quality innings, which non-regular corner men will get the most at-bats, and which fourth outfielders will deliver 40 or more RBI. In other words, you'll have to become a better, more knowledgeable fan. And isn't that the Rotisserie Way?
- Using players from only one division helps an owner new to the world of Rotisserie to draw on his or her strength. After all, we all start out as fans of a particular team, which means that we enter the Rotisserie

world knowing and liking one team—and one division—better than others. What better place to start?

LITE III. NO MONEY

Each team has 23 Lite Dollars (L$) to spend at the auction draft to acquire a full roster of 23 active major league players, with a minimum salary and minimum bidding increments of 10 cents. But real money is not used.

- "The intensity of feeling in Rotisserie is unrelated to money anyhow," sez Farmer-Professor Lake. "If you play for traditional Rotissestakes— 260 real dollars for 23 real players—it's enough to be irritating if you lose, but not enough to buy a new car if you win. So what's the point?"
- Using L$ still requires an owner to manage the team budget and cope with the exigencies of free market competition for the services of Matt Williams, Mo Vaughn, and other superstars at the auction draft. Farmer-Professor Lake promises that your throat goes dry and your heart palpitates when the bidding hits L$2.70 for Greg Maddux, the same as when it crosses $30 for baseball's best pitcher in regular Rotisserie. This means that a kid owner can have just as much Rotissefun as a parent owner without having to beg for an advance against the next six months of allowances.
- Playing for L$ also makes a team owner feel a little less hysterical when the *Baseball America* and *Baseball Weekly* subs come due.

LITE IV. MONTHLY TRANSACTIONS

Transaction Day occurs once a month, on the Monday (AL) or Tuesday (NL) before stats appear in *USA Today*. The first Transaction Day falls on the first Monday or Tuesday in May. Except for the All-Star Break Trading Period described below, all Rotisserie Lite roster moves are restricted to Transaction Day.

- On Transaction Day, a Rotisserie Lite team may release players (a) placed on a major league disabled list; (b) demoted to the minor leagues; (c) traded to the other division or to the other major league; or (d) released by their major league team, *without limit* from its current roster and replace them with players from the free agent pool who qualify at the same position. Players may not be reserved. Even players on major league disabled lists must be released if their Rotisserie Lite owner chooses to replace them. Released players go into the free agent pool and may be claimed on the *next* Transaction Day.
- Player moves on Transaction Day shall take place in reverse order of the most recent standings, with the lowest team in the standings having the right of first claim on a player from the free agent pool. While there is no limit on the number of players a team may release and replace, a team may make only one transaction at a time. That is, the last-place team in a six-team league may not make a second

transaction until all other teams in the league have had an opportunity to make a transaction.

- As there is no reserve list in Rotisserie Lite, an owner whose star player is on his major league team's disabled list and isn't scheduled to come off for another two weeks will have to make a strategic call: Ride out the injury and retain the player under contract; or release him into the free agent pool and call up a replacement immediately.
- The salary of a player claimed from the free agent pool on Transaction Day is L$1.

LITE V. TRADE RESTRICTIONS

Except for a two-week trading period ending with the last out of the All-Star Game, no trades are permitted in Rotisserie Lite.

- All trades during the trading period take effect on the first pitch of the first regular season game after the All-Star Game.
- A Rotisserie Lite team may trade only one player with a salary of L$2 or more to any one team.

LITE VI. SAME SCORING CATEGORIES

Standings shall be determined on the same basis as in Rotisserie Regular and Rotisserie Ultra—that is, according to each team's cumulative performance over the course of a full season in eight statistical categories: home runs, RBI, stolen bases, and batting average for batters; wins, saves, ERA, and ratio (hits plus walks divided by innings pitched) for pitchers.

- A team receives points in each category according to its relative position. In a six-team league, the leader in home runs would receive six points, the second-place team five points, and so on. The team with the highest point total wins the Rotisserie Lite pennant.
- Standings should be compiled and distributed weekly. As keeping score is no more fun in Lite than in Regular or Ultra, new Lite leagues should consider the special deal offered by **Roti·Stats**. As transactions only take place monthly, **Roti·Stats** is able to provide timely, accurate weekly stat reports for Rotisserie Lite Leagues at a discount from its regular low rates. (See pages 248–249 for details.)

LITE VII. LONG-TERM CONTRACTS

The same rules governing the option year and long-term contracts that complicate an owner's life in Rotisserie Regular and Rotisserie Ultra shall also pertain in Rotisserie Lite. (See **Article XVII** of the Official Constitution, page 275.)

- **Exception:** A player under a long-term contract in Rotisserie Lite may be released and replaced at any time without penalty, subject only to the restrictions regarding player transactions.

LITE VIII. ROSTER PROTECTION

On April 1, each team may protect a certain number of players according to the following schedule: The team that finished first the preceding year may protect a maximum of 7 players; all other teams, a maximum of 10 players. There is no minimum requirement.

- Yes, this makes it a lot harder to build a dynasty. But trust us: One Harry Stein loose on the land is more than enough.
- Trading is not permitted over the winter on the grounds that Rotisserie Lite owners have better things to do with their time. Particularly those who also play Rotisserie Regular or Rotisserie Ultra.

LITE IX. YOO-HOO

As there is no prize pool to divvy up in Rotisserie Lite, the Yoo-Hoo running down a Rotisserie Lite pennant winner's face and trickling into the corners of his or her mouth will taste all the sweeter, if you can imagine such a thing.

Editor's Postscript: As you play Rotisserie Lite, let us know what you think. It takes a long time to turn a piece of coal into a diamond, and it may take us a couple of seasons to get Lite exactly rite. We particularly want to hear from you about new wrinkles, adaptations, and changes that we might scarf up for next year's book. Just remember: Keep it Lite!

7

Postgame Shower

A Yoo-Hoo to Arms

Editor's Note: *We ended our first book ten years ago with the following dispatch from Maestro Steve Wulf of the Wulfgang. We ended all our other books the same way. It's how we're ending this book. And it's the way we'll end our next book. That's because tradition is everything in Rotisserie League Baseball . . . unless you have to throw it into a deal for a stud power hitter.*

Unseen hands hold you, force your head down, and pour water, dairy whey, corn sweetener, nonfat milk, sugar, coconut oil, cocoa, sodium caseinate, salt, sodium bicarbonate, dipotassium phosphates, calcium phosphates, guar gum, natural flavors, xanthan gum, vanillin (an artificial flavor), sodium ascorbate, ferric orthophosphate, palmitate, niacinamide, vitamin D, and, yes, *riboflavin* all over your hair. The bizarre ritual is a Yoo-Hoo shampoo, and it is what you get for winning the Rotisserie League pennant.

The chocolate-flavored rinse will not leave your locks radiant and soft to the touch, and squirrels will probably follow you around for a day or two. All in all, the ritual is pretty distasteful. But there's not a member of the Rotisserie League who wouldn't gladly suffer the rite so long as it came at the end of a championship season.

Since we traditionally end each Rotisseseason with an outpouring of the chocolate drink of our youth, we figured we may as well end the book the same way. Besides, as the beverage company's former executive vice president for promotions, Lawrence Peter Berra, once noted, or at least we think he noted, "Yoo-Hoo tastes good. And it's good for you, too."

Yoo-Hoo does taste good if your taste buds also happen to be impressed with the nose on strawberry fizzies. To sophisticated palates, Yoo-Hoo tastes a little like the runoff in the gutter outside a Carvel store.

As for Yoo-Hoo being good for you, well, Yogi says he let his kids drink it, and one of them grew up to be the .255-hitting shortstop for the Pittsburgh Pirates. But then, maybe if Dale *hadn't* touched the stuff, he might actually be worth more than the $7 the Fleder Mice paid for him in 1983.

Yoo-Hoo is not unlike the Rotisserie League. Both of them taste good, and both of them are good for you. Just don't tell anybody that. Whenever one of us tries to explain just what the Rotisserie League is, we all get the same kind of look. It's the look one might get from a bartender if one ordered, say, a Kahlua and Yoo-Hoo. The look says, "Aren't you a little too old to be partaking of that stuff?" Our look invariably replies, "But it tastes good, and it's good for you."

Yoo-Hoo's current slogan is "Yoo-Hoo's Got Life." Catchy, isn't it? But then, Yogi Berra used to be a catchy. The Rotisserie League's got life, too. It enlivens not only boxscores, but "Kiner's Korner," as well. Why, the game adds color to every fiber of your being, it gives you a sense of purpose in this crazy, cockeyed world, it puts a spring in your step and a song in your heart, and it makes you care, deeply care, for your fellow man, especially if your fellow man's name is Biff Pocoroba. So the Rotisserie League is childish, is it? Yoo-Hoo and a bottle of rum, barkeep.

In case you're wondering where Yoo-Hoo comes from, we thought we'd tell you. It comes from Carlstadt, N.J. Yoo-Hoo also goes back to the days of Ruth and Gehrig. It first arrived on the American scene as a fruit drink named after a popular greeting of that day. Founder Natale Olivieri was obsessed with making a stable chocolate drink, and after years of experimentation, he hit upon the idea of heating the chocolate. The rest is soft-drink history.

In the '50s, Yoo-Hoo's Golden Age, the product came to be associated with Yogi. A billboard of Yogi and a bottle of Yoo-Hoo greeted fans in Yankee Stadium. And Yogi wasn't the only Yankee who endorsed Yoo-Hoo— Whitey, Mickey, and the Moose could all be seen on the insides of Yoo-Hoo bottle caps. Nowadays, nobody inhabits the inside of the bottle cap. However, if you turn the cap upside down, it reads, "ooh-ooy," which is Yiddish for Rod Scurry's ERA.

Yoo-Hoo is also like baseball: You don't want to know too much about it. In the interests of this chapter, we sent an envoy out to Yankee Stadium to talk to Yogi. Yes, you've read all those funny Berra quotes over the years, about how it's not over until it's over, and about how nobody goes to that restaurant anymore because it's too crowded. To tell you the truth, Yogi is not the man that people suppose him to be. He is actually two different people, depending on his mood. When he is on guard, he is full of monosyllables, and when he is relaxed, he can be genuinely engaging. But the star of "The Hathaways"* he is not.

We—actually, it was only one of us, who shall remain nameless, and if the *New Yorker* can do it, why can't we—asked Yogi if he would mind talking about Yoo-Hoo. He said, "Sorry, I can't." This caught us by surprise, but being quick on our tongue, we asked, "You can't?" Yogi said, "Nope. Ask Cerone."

At which point, we approached Rick Cerone, the catcher who took Yogi's place as executive vice president for promotions. For all their sterling qualities, Berra and Cerone do not strike us as being pillars of the corporate structure, but Yoo-Hoo obviously saw through to their executive talents. We asked Cerone if he would mind talking about Yoo-Hoo. He said, "I can't." This time, we asked, "Why?" and Cerone said, "Because I'm suing them, that's why."

*Does anybody remember who "The Hathaways" were? We've forgotten.

As it turns out, the company has changed hands, and Cerone claims that Yoo-Hoo never paid him for certain appearances. Yogi ran into similar problems, but he settled out of court. So that's why Yoo-Hoo is just like baseball: if you look too closely, it can get ugly on you.

We went back to Yogi and pleaded with him. All we cared about, we said, were the old days of Yoo-Hoo. He warmed to the subject in much the same way Natale Olivieri warmed Yoo-Hoo—slowly. Through his grunts and moans, we determined that Yogi thought Yoo-Hoo tasted good, that his kids drank it, that he wishes he had some money invested in it, and that people still link him with Yoo-Hoo, and vice versa. Then he said, "What's this for, anyway?"

We explained to him about the Rotisserie League and the book. When we said, "Then, at the end of the year, we pour Yoo-Hoo over the head of the winner," Yogi—dripping tobacco juice out of the left side of his mouth— gave us a look of partial disgust and said something like "ooh-ooy."

So, if you decide to take up baseball as played by the Rotisserie League, be warned. People will look at you funny. Pay them no mind. Just pay the Treasurer.

We hate long good-byes. When we meet again, perhaps at a theater near you showing *The Rotisserie League Goes to Japan,* let's just say, "Yoo-Hoo."

APPENDIX

Final 1996 Averages

Editor's Note: These stats have been selected and arranged to reflect the variety of stat categories used in different Rotisserie leagues. Traditional Rotisserie stat category order can be found in Chapter 2, Scouting Report.

NATIONAL LEAGUE: BATTERS

NL Batter	Team	BA	HR	RBI	SB	CS	G	AB	R	BB	OBP
Abbott, K.	Fla	.253	8	33	3	3	109	320	37	22	.307
Abreu, B.	Hou	.227	0	1	0	0	15	22	1	2	.292
Alfonzo, E.	NYN	.261	4	40	2	0	123	368	36	25	.304
Alicea, L.	StL	.258	5	42	11	3	129	380	54	52	.350
Allensworth, J.	Pit	.262	4	31	11	6	61	229	32	23	.337
Alou, M.	Mon	.281	21	96	9	4	143	540	87	49	.339
Amaro, R.	Phi	.316	2	15	0	0	61	117	14	9	.380
Andrews, S.	Mon	.227	19	64	3	1	127	375	43	35	.295
Anthony, E.	Cin	.244	8	13	0	1	47	123	22	22	.359
Anthony, E.	Col	.242	4	9	0	1	32	62	10	10	.342
Arias, A.	Fla	.277	3	26	2	0	100	224	27	17	.335
Ashley, B.	LA	.200	9	25	0	0	71	110	18	21	.331
Aude, R.	Pit	.250	0	1	0	0	7	16	0	0	.250
Aurilia, R.	SF	.239	3	26	4	1	105	318	27	25	.295
Ausmus, B.	SD	.181	1	13	1	4	50	149	16	13	.261
Ayrault, J.	Atl	.200	0	0	0	0	7	5	0	0	.333
Baerga, C.	NYN	.193	2	11	0	0	26	83	5	5	.253
Bagwell, J.	Hou	.315	31	120	21	7	162	568	111	135	.451
Barberie, B.	ChN	.034	1	2	0	1	15	29	4	5	.176
Barron, T.	Mon	.000	0	0	0	0	1	1	0	0	.000
Bates, J.	Col	.206	1	9	2	1	88	160	19	23	.312
Batiste, K.	SF	.208	3	11	3	3	54	130	17	5	.235
Battle, H.	Phi	.000	0	0	0	0	5	5	0	0	.000
Bautista, D.	Atl	.150	0	1	0	0	17	20	1	2	.261
Beamon, T.	Pit	.216	0	6	1	1	24	51	7	4	.273
Belk, T.	Cin	.200	0	0	0	0	7	15	2	1	.250
Bell, D.	StL	.214	1	9	1	1	62	145	12	10	.268
Bell, D.	Hou	.263	17	113	29	3	158	627	84	40	.311
Bell, J.	Pit	.250	13	71	6	4	151	527	65	54	.323
Belliard, R.	Atl	.169	0	3	3	1	87	142	9	2	.179
Benard, M.	SF	.248	5	27	25	11	135	488	89	59	.333
Benitez, Y.	Mon	.167	0	2	0	0	11	12	0	0	.167
Benjamin, M.	Phi	.223	4	13	3	1	35	103	13	12	.316
Bennett, G.	Phi	.250	0	1	0	0	6	16	0	2	.333
Berry, S.	Hou	.281	17	95	12	6	132	431	55	23	.328
Bichette, D.	Col	.313	31	141	31	12	159	633	114	45	.359
Biggio, C.	Hou	.288	15	75	25	7	162	605	113	75	.386
Blauser, J.	Atl	.245	10	35	6	0	83	265	48	40	.356
Blowers, M.	LA	.265	6	38	0	0	92	317	31	37	.341
Bogar, T.	NYN	.213	0	6	1	3	91	89	17	8	.287
Bonds, B.	SF	.308	42	129	40	7	158	517	122	151	.461
Boone, B.	Cin	.233	12	69	3	2	142	520	56	31	.275
Booty, J.	Fla	.500	0	0	0	0	2	2	1	0	.500
Borders, P.	StL	.319	0	4	0	1	26	69	3	1	.329
Bradshaw, T.	StL	.333	0	3	1	1	15	21	4	3	.417
Branson, J.	Cin	.244	9	37	2	0	129	311	34	31	.312
Brito, J.	Col	.071	0	0	0	0	8	14	1	1	.235
Brogna, R.	NYN	.255	7	30	0	0	55	188	18	19	.318
Brooks, J.	Fla	.400	0	3	0	0	8	5	2	1	.571

NL Batter	Team	BA	HR	RBI	SB	CS	G	AB	R	BB	OBP
Brown, B.	ChN	.304	5	9	3	3	29	69	11	2	.329
Brumfield, J.	Pit	.250	2	8	3	1	29	80	11	5	.291
Bullett, S.	ChN	.212	3	16	7	3	109	165	26	10	.256
Burks, E.	Col	.344	40	128	32	6	156	613	142	61	.408
Busch, M.	LA	.217	4	17	0	0	38	83	8	5	.261
Butler, B.	LA	.267	0	8	8	3	34	131	22	9	.313
Caminiti, K.	SD	.326	40	130	11	5	146	546	109	78	.408
Cangelosi, J.	Hou	.263	1	16	17	9	108	262	49	44	.378
Canizaro, J.	SF	.200	2	8	0	2	43	120	11	9	.260
Carreon, M.	SF	.260	9	51	2	3	81	292	40	22	.317
Castellano, P.	Col	.118	0	2	0	0	13	17	1	3	.286
Castilla, V.	Col	.304	40	113	7	2	160	629	97	35	.343
Castillo, A.	NYN	.364	0	0	0	0	6	11	1	0	.364
Castillo, L.	Fla	.262	1	8	17	4	41	164	26	14	.320
Castro, J.	LA	.197	0	5	1	0	70	132	16	10	.254
Cedeno, A.	Hou	.000	0	0	0	0	3	2	1	2	.000
Cedeno, A.	SD	.234	3	18	3	2	49	154	10	9	.279
Cedeno, R.	LA	.246	2	18	5	1	86	211	26	24	.326
Chavez, R.	Mon	.200	0	0	1	0	3	5	1	1	.333
Cianfrocco, A.	SD	.281	2	32	1	0	79	192	21	8	.315
Clark, D.	LA	.200	0	1	0	0	15	15	0	3	.333
Clark, D.	Pit	.275	8	35	2	1	92	211	28	31	.366
Clayton, R.	StL	.277	6	35	33	15	129	491	64	33	.321
Cockrell, A.	Col	.250	0	2	0	0	9	8	0	0	.222
Colbrunn, G.	Fla	.286	16	69	4	5	141	511	60	25	.333
Coleman, V.	Cin	.155	1	4	12	2	33	84	10	9	.237
Conine, J.	Fla	.293	26	95	1	4	157	597	84	62	.360
Cruz, J.	SF	.234	3	10	1	0	33	77	10	12	.352
Cummings, M.	Pit	.224	3	7	0	0	24	85	11	0	.221
Curtis, C.	LA	.212	2	9	2	1	43	104	20	17	.322
Dascenzo, D.	SD	.111	0	0	0	1	21	9	3	1	.200
Daulton, D.	Phi	.167	0	0	0	0	5	12	3	7	.500
Davis, E.	Cin	.287	26	83	23	9	129	415	81	70	.394
Dawson, A.	Fla	.276	2	14	0	0	42	58	6	2	.311
Decker, S.	SF	.230	1	12	0	0	57	122	16	15	.309
Decker, S.	Col	.320	1	8	1	0	10	25	8	3	.393
Deer, R.	SD	.180	4	9	0	0	25	50	9	14	.359
Delgado, W.	SF	.364	0	2	1	0	6	22	3	1	.440
DeShields, D.	LA	.224	5	41	48	11	154	581	75	53	.287
Difelice, M.	StL	.286	0	2	0	0	4	7	0	0	.286
Dorsett, B.	ChN	.122	1	3	0	0	17	41	3	4	.196
Doster, D.	Phi	.267	1	8	0	0	39	105	14	7	.313
Dunston, S.	SF	.300	5	25	8	0	82	287	27	13	.331
Dye, J.	Atl	.281	12	37	1	4	98	292	32	8	.304
Dykstra, L.	Phi	.261	3	13	3	1	40	134	21	26	.387
Echevarria, A.	Col	.286	0	6	0	0	26	21	2	2	.346
Eisenreich, J.	Phi	.361	3	41	11	1	113	338	45	31	.413
Encarnacion, A.	Pit	.318	0	1	0	0	7	22	3	0	.318
Espinoza, A.	NYN	.306	4	16	0	2	48	134	19	4	.324
Estalella, B.	Phi	.353	2	4	1	0	7	17	5	1	.389
Eusebio, T.	Hou	.270	1	19	0	1	58	152	15	18	.343
Everett, C.	NYN	.240	1	16	6	0	101	192	29	21	.326
Fermin, F.	ChN	.125	0	1	0	0	11	16	4	2	.222
Finley, S.	SD	.298	30	95	22	8	161	655	126	56	.354

NL Batter	Team	BA	HR	RBI	SB	CS	G	AB	R	BB	OBP
Flaherty, J.	SD	.303	9	41	2	3	72	264	22	9	.327
Fletcher, D.	Mon	.266	12	57	0	0	127	394	41	27	.321
Floyd, C.	Mon	.242	6	26	7	1	117	227	29	29	.337
Fonville, C.	LA	.204	0	13	7	2	103	201	34	17	.266
Fordyce, B.	Cin	.286	0	1	0	0	4	7	0	3	.500
Franco, M.	NYN	.194	1	2	0	0	14	31	3	1	.235
Gaetti, G.	StL	.274	23	80	2	2	141	522	71	35	.326
Gagne, G.	LA	.255	10	55	4	2	128	428	48	50	.333
Galarraga, A.	Col	.304	47	150	18	8	159	626	119	40	.357
Gallego, M.	StL	.210	0	4	0	0	51	143	12	12	.276
Gant, R.	StL	.246	30	82	13	4	122	419	74	73	.359
Garcia, C.	Pit	.285	6	44	16	6	101	390	66	23	.329
Garcia, K.	LA	.000	0	0	0	0	1	1	0	0	.000
Gibralter, S.	Cin	.000	0	0	0	0	2	2	0	0	.000
Gilkey, B.	NYN	.317	30	117	17	9	153	571	108	73	.393
Giovanola, E.	Atl	.232	0	7	1	0	43	82	10	8	.304
Glanville, D.	ChN	.241	1	10	2	0	49	83	10	3	.264
Goff, J.	Hou	.500	1	2	0	0	1	4	1	0	.500
Gomez, C.	SD	.262	3	29	2	2	89	328	32	39	.349
Gomez, L.	ChN	.238	17	56	1	4	136	362	44	53	.344
Gonzalez, L.	ChN	.271	15	79	9	6	146	483	70	61	.354
Goodwin, C.	Cin	.228	0	5	15	6	49	136	20	19	.323
Grace, M.	ChN	.331	9	75	2	3	142	547	88	62	.396
Graffanino, T.	Atl	.174	0	2	0	0	22	46	7	4	.250
Grebeck, C.	Fla	.211	1	9	0	0	50	95	8	4	.245
Greene, C.	NYN	.000	0	0	0	0	2	1	0	0	.000
Greene, W.	Cin	.244	19	63	0	1	115	287	48	36	.327
Grissom, M.	Atl	.308	23	74	28	11	158	671	106	41	.349
Grudzielanek, M.	Mon	.306	6	49	33	7	153	657	99	26	.340
Guerrero, V.	Mon	.185	1	1	0	0	9	27	2	0	.185
Guerrero, W.	LA	.000	0	0	0	0	5	2	1	0	.000
Gutierrez, R.	Hou	.284	1	15	6	1	89	218	28	23	.359
Gwynn, C.	SD	.178	1	10	0	0	81	90	8	10	.260
Gwynn, T.	SD	.353	3	50	11	4	116	451	67	39	.400
Hajek, D.	Hou	.300	0	0	0	0	8	10	3	2	.417
Hall, M.	SF	.120	0	5	0	0	25	25	3	1	.148
Haney, T.	ChN	.134	0	3	1	0	49	82	11	7	.200
Hansen, D.	LA	.221	0	6	0	0	80	104	7	11	.293
Hardtke, J.	NYN	.193	0	6	0	0	19	57	3	2	.233
Harris, L.	Cin	.285	5	32	14	6	125	302	33	21	.330
Hayes, C.	Pit	.248	10	62	6	0	128	459	51	36	.301
Henderson, R.	SD	.241	9	29	37	15	148	465	110	125	.410
Hernandez, C.	LA	.286	0	0	0	0	13	14	1	2	.375
Hernandez, J.	ChN	.242	10	41	4	0	131	331	52	24	.293
Hill, G.	SF	.280	19	67	6	3	98	379	56	33	.344
Holbert, A.	StL	.000	0	0	0	0	1	3	0	0	.000
Hollandsworth, T.	LA	.291	12	59	21	6	149	478	64	41	.348
Houston, T.	Atl	.222	1	8	0	0	33	27	3	1	.250
Houston, T.	ChN	.339	2	19	3	2	46	115	18	8	.382
Howard, T.	Cin	.272	6	42	6	5	121	360	50	17	.307
Hubbard, M.	ChN	.105	1	4	0	0	21	38	1	0	.103
Hubbard, T.	SF	.207	1	2	0	0	10	29	3	2	.258
Hubbard, T.	Col	.217	1	12	2	0	45	60	12	9	.329
Hundley, T.	NYN	.259	41	112	1	3	153	540	85	79	.356
Hunter, B.	Hou	.276	5	35	35	9	132	526	74	17	.297
Huskey, B.	NYN	.278	15	60	1	2	118	414	43	27	.319

NL Batter	Team	BA	HR	RBI	SB	CS	G	AB	R	BB	OBP
Incaviglia, P.	Phi	.234	16	42	2	0	99	269	33	30	.318
Javier, S.	SF	.270	2	22	14	2	71	274	44	25	.336
Jefferies, G.	Phi	.292	7	51	20	6	104	404	59	36	.348
Jennings, R.	ChN	.224	0	4	1	0	31	58	7	3	.274
Jensen, M.	SF	.211	0	4	0	0	9	19	4	8	.444
Johnson, B.	SD	.272	8	35	0	0	82	243	18	4	.290
Johnson, C.	Fla	.218	13	37	1	0	120	386	34	40	.292
Johnson, L.	NYN	.333	9	69	50	12	160	682	117	33	.362
Johnson, M.	Pit	.274	13	47	6	4	127	343	55	44	.361
Jones, A.	Atl	.217	5	13	3	0	31	106	11	7	.265
Jones, C.	Atl	.309	30	110	14	1	157	598	114	87	.393
Jones, C.	NYN	.242	4	18	1	0	89	149	22	12	.307
Jones, D.	SF	.172	1	7	2	2	34	58	7	8	.269
Jones, T.	Col	.300	0	1	0	0	12	10	6	0	.273
Jordan, B.	StL	.310	17	104	22	5	140	513	82	29	.349
Jordan, K.	Phi	.282	3	12	2	1	43	131	15	5	.309
Joyner, W.	SD	.277	8	65	5	3	121	433	59	69	.377
Justice, D.	Atl	.321	6	25	1	1	40	140	23	21	.409
Karros, E.	LA	.260	34	111	8	0	154	608	84	53	.316
Kelly, M.	Cin	.184	1	7	4	0	19	49	5	9	.333
Kendall, J.	Pit	.300	3	42	5	2	130	414	54	35	.372
Kent, J.	NYN	.290	9	39	4	3	89	335	45	21	.331
Kieschnick, B.	ChN	.345	1	6	0	0	25	29	6	3	.406
King, J.	Pit	.271	30	111	15	1	155	591	91	70	.346
Kingery, M.	Pit	.246	3	27	2	1	117	276	32	23	.304
Kirby, W.	LA	.271	1	11	4	2	65	188	23	17	.333
Klesko, R.	Atl	.282	34	93	6	3	153	528	90	68	.364
Knorr, R.	Hou	.195	1	7	0	1	37	87	7	5	.245
Lampkin, T.	SF	.232	6	29	1	5	66	177	26	20	.324
Lankford, R.	StL	.275	21	86	35	7	149	545	100	79	.366
Lansing, M.	Mon	.285	11	53	23	8	159	641	99	44	.341
Larkin, B.	Cin	.298	33	89	36	10	152	517	117	96	.410
Lemke, M.	Atl	.255	5	37	5	2	135	498	64	53	.323
Lieberthal, M.	Phi	.253	7	23	0	0	50	166	21	10	.297
Liriano, N.	Pit	.267	3	30	2	0	112	217	23	14	.308
Livingstone, S.	SD	.297	2	20	0	1	102	172	20	9	.331
Lopez, J.	Atl	.282	23	69	1	6	138	489	56	28	.322
Lopez, L.	SD	.180	2	11	0	0	63	139	10	9	.233
Lukachyk, R.	Mon	.000	0	0	0	0	2	2	0	0	.000
Mabry, J.	StL	.297	13	74	3	2	151	543	63	37	.342
Magadan, D.	ChN	.254	3	17	0	2	78	169	23	29	.360
Magee, W.	Phi	.204	2	14	0	0	38	142	9	9	.252
Manwaring, K.	Hou	.220	0	4	0	0	37	82	5	3	.264
Manwaring, K.	SF	.234	1	14	0	1	49	145	9	16	.319
Marrero, O.	LA	.375	0	1	0	0	10	8	2	1	.444
Martin, A.	Pit	.300	18	72	38	12	155	630	101	54	.354
Martinez, M.	Phi	.222	0	0	2	1	13	36	2	1	.263
Martinez, P.	Atl	.500	0	0	0	1	4	2	1	0	.500
May, D.	Hou	.251	5	33	2	2	109	259	24	30	.330
Mayne, B.	NYN	.263	1	6	0	1	70	99	9	12	.342
McCarty, D.	SF	.217	6	24	2	1	91	175	16	18	.294
Mccracken, Q.	Col	.290	3	40	17	6	124	283	50	32	.363
McGee, W.	StL	.307	5	41	5	2	123	309	52	18	.348
McGriff, F.	Atl	.295	28	107	7	3	159	617	81	68	.365

• FINAL 1996 AVERAGES

NL Batter	Team	BA	HR	RBI	SB	CS	G	AB	R	BB	OBP
Mcmillon, B.	Fla	.216	0	4	0	0	28	51	4	5	.286
McRae, B.	ChN	.276	17	66	37	9	157	624	111	73	.360
Mejia, M.	StL	.087	0	0	5	3	45	23	10	0	.087
Merced, O.	Pit	.287	17	80	8	4	120	453	69	51	.357
Miller, O.	Hou	.256	15	58	3	7	139	468	43	14	.291
Milliard, R.	Fla	.161	0	1	2	0	24	62	7	14	.312
Mirabelli, D.	SF	.222	0	1	0	0	9	18	2	3	.333
Mitchell, K.	Cin	.267	1	3	0	0	11	15	2	1	.313
Mitchell, K.	Cin	.325	6	26	0	0	37	114	18	26	.447
Mondesi, R.	LA	.297	24	88	14	7	157	634	98	32	.334
Montgomery, R.	Hou	.214	1	4	0	0	12	14	4	1	.267
Morandini, M.	Phi	.250	3	32	26	5	140	539	64	49	.321
Mordecai, M.	Atl	.241	2	8	1	0	66	108	12	9	.297
Morman, R.	Fla	.167	0	0	0	0	6	6	0	1	.286
Morris, H.	Cin	.313	16	80	7	5	142	528	82	50	.374
Mottola, C.	Cin	.215	3	6	2	2	35	79	10	6	.271
Mouton, J.	Hou	.263	3	34	21	9	122	300	40	38	.343
Mueller, B.	SF	.330	0	19	0	0	55	200	31	24	.401
Mulligan, S.	SD	.000	0	0	0	0	2	1	0	0	.000
Murray, G.	Phi	.196	2	6	1	1	38	97	8	7	.250
Natal, B.	Fla	.133	0	2	0	1	44	90	4	15	.257
Newfield, M.	SD	.251	5	26	1	1	84	191	27	16	.311
Obando, S.	Mon	.247	8	22	2	0	89	178	30	22	.332
Ochoa, A.	NYN	.294	4	33	4	3	82	282	37	17	.336
Oliver, J.	Cin	.242	11	46	2	0	106	289	31	28	.311
Ordonez, R.	NYN	.257	1	30	1	3	151	502	51	22	.289
Orsulak, J.	Fla	.221	2	19	1	1	120	217	23	16	.274
Osik, K.	Pit	.293	1	14	1	0	48	140	18	14	.361
Otero, R.	Phi	.273	2	32	16	10	104	411	54	34	.330
Owens, E.	Cin	.200	0	9	16	2	88	205	26	23	.281
Owens, J.	Col	.239	4	17	4	1	73	180	31	27	.338
Pagnozzi, T.	StL	.270	13	55	4	1	119	407	48	24	.311
Parker, R.	LA	.286	0	1	1	0	16	14	2	0	.333
Peltier, D.	SF	.254	0	9	0	0	31	59	3	7	.328
Pendleton, T.	Atl	.204	4	17	2	1	42	162	21	15	.271
Pendleton, T.	Fla	.251	7	58	0	2	111	406	30	26	.298
Perez, E.	Atl	.256	4	17	0	0	68	156	19	8	.293
Perez, E.	Cin	.222	3	5	0	0	18	36	8	5	.317
Perez, N.	Col	.156	0	3	2	2	17	45	4	0	.156
Petagine, R.	NYN	.232	4	17	0	2	50	99	10	9	.313
Phillips, J.	Phi	.152	5	10	0	0	35	79	9	10	.256
Phillips, J.	SF	.200	2	5	0	0	15	25	3	1	.231
Piazza, M.	LA	.336	36	105	0	3	148	547	87	81	.422
Polonia, L.	Atl	.419	0	2	1	1	22	31	3	1	.424
Prince, T.	LA	.297	1	11	0	0	40	64	6	6	.365
Pulliam, H.	Col	.133	0	0	0	0	10	15	2	2	.235
Reed, J.	Col	.284	8	37	2	2	116	341	34	43	.365
Reed, J.	SD	.244	2	49	2	5	146	495	45	59	.325
Relaford, D.	Phi	.175	0	1	1	0	15	40	2	3	.233
Renteria, E.	Fla	.309	5	31	16	2	106	431	68	33	.358
Roberson, K.	NYN	.222	3	9	0	0	27	36	8	7	.348
Rodriguez, H.	Mon	.276	36	103	2	0	145	532	81	37	.325
Rolen, S.	Phi	.254	4	18	0	2	37	130	10	13	.322

NL Batter	Team	BA	HR	RBI	SB	CS	G	AB	R	BB	OBP
Sabo, C.	Cin	.256	3	16	2	0	54	125	15	18	.354
Sanchez, R.	ChN	.211	1	12	7	1	95	289	28	22	.272
Sandberg, R.	ChN	.244	25	92	12	8	150	554	85	54	.316
Sanders, R.	Cin	.251	14	33	24	8	81	287	49	44	.353
Santangelo, F.	Mon	.277	7	56	5	2	152	393	54	49	.369
Santiago, B.	Phi	.264	30	85	2	0	136	481	71	49	.332
Scarsone, S.	SF	.219	5	23	2	3	105	283	28	25	.286
Schall, G.	Phi	.273	2	10	0	0	28	66	7	12	.392
Schu, R.	Mon	.000	0	0	0	0	1	4	0	0	.000
Sefcik, K.	Phi	.284	0	9	3	0	44	116	10	9	.341
Segui, D.	Mon	.286	11	58	4	4	115	416	69	60	.375
Servais, S.	ChN	.265	11	63	0	2	129	445	42	30	.327
Sheaffer, D.	StL	.227	2	20	3	3	79	198	10	9	.271
Sheffield, G.	Fla	.314	42	120	16	9	161	519	118	142	.465
Shipley, C.	SD	.315	1	7	7	0	33	92	13	2	.337
Shumpert, T.	ChN	.226	2	6	0	1	27	31	5	2	.286
Siddall, J.	Fla	.149	0	3	0	0	18	47	0	2	.184
Silvestri, D.	Mon	.204	1	17	2	1	86	162	16	34	.340
Simms, M.	Hou	.176	1	8	1	0	49	68	6	4	.233
Smith, D.	Atl	.203	3	16	1	3	101	153	16	17	.285
Smith, O.	StL	.282	2	18	7	5	82	227	36	25	.358
Sosa, S.	ChN	.273	40	100	18	5	124	498	84	34	.323
Spehr, T.	Mon	.091	1	3	1	0	63	44	4	3	.167
Spiers, B.	Hou	.252	6	26	7	0	122	218	27	20	.320
Stankiewicz, A.	Mon	.286	0	9	1	0	64	77	12	6	.356
Steverson, T.	SD	.000	0	0	0	0	1	1	0	0	.000
Stocker, K.	Phi	.254	5	41	6	4	119	394	46	43	.336
Sveum, D.	Pit	.353	1	5	0	0	12	34	9	6	.450
Sweeney, M.	StL	.265	3	22	3	0	98	170	32	33	.387
Tatum, J.	SD	.000	0	0	0	0	5	3	0	0	.000
Taubensee, E.	Cin	.291	12	48	3	4	108	327	46	26	.338
Tavarez, J.	Fla	.219	0	6	5	1	98	114	14	7	.264
Thompson, J.	SD	.224	2	6	0	0	13	49	4	1	.235
Thompson, M.	LA	.118	0	1	1	1	48	51	2	6	.211
Thompson, M.	Col	.067	0	2	0	0	14	15	1	1	.125
Thompson, R.	SF	.211	5	21	2	2	63	227	35	24	.301
Timmons, O.	ChN	.200	7	16	1	0	65	140	18	15	.282
Tinsley, L.	Phi	.135	0	2	2	4	31	52	1	4	.196
Tomberlin, A.	NYN	.258	3	10	0	0	63	66	12	9	.355
Valdes, P.	ChN	.125	0	1	0	0	9	8	2	1	.222
Vander Wal, J.	Col	.252	5	31	2	2	104	151	20	19	.335
Vaughn, G.	SD	.206	10	22	4	1	43	141	20	24	.329
Veras, Q.	Fla	.253	4	14	8	8	73	253	40	51	.381
Vizcaino, J.	NYN	.303	1	32	9	5	96	363	47	28	.356
Walker, L.	Col	.276	18	58	18	2	83	272	58	20	.342
Wallach, T.	LA	.228	4	22	0	1	45	162	14	12	.286
Walton, J.	Atl	.340	1	4	0	0	37	47	9	5	.389
Webster, L.	Mon	.230	2	17	0	0	78	174	18	25	.332
Wehner, J.	Pit	.259	2	13	1	5	86	139	19	8	.299
Weiss, W.	Col	.282	8	48	10	2	155	517	89	80	.381
White, D.	Fla	.274	17	84	22	6	146	552	77	38	.325
White, R.	Mon	.293	6	41	14	6	88	334	35	22	.340
Whiten, M.	Atl	.256	3	17	2	5	36	90	12	16	.364
Whiten, M.	Phi	.236	7	21	13	3	60	182	33	33	.356
Wilkins, R.	Hou	.213	6	23	0	1	84	254	34	46	.330

NL Batter	Team	BA	HR	RBI	SB	CS	G	AB	R	BB	OBP
Wilkins, R.	SF	.293	8	36	0	2	52	157	19	21	.366
Williams, K.	SF	.250	0	0	0	0	9	20	0	0	.250
Williams, M.	SF	.302	22	85	1	2	105	404	69	39	.367
Wilson, D.	SF	.271	2	12	0	2	41	118	10	12	.338
Womack, T.	Pit	.333	0	7	2	0	17	30	11	6	.459
Young, D.	StL	.241	0	2	0	1	16	29	3	4	.353
Young, E.	Col	.324	8	74	53	19	141	568	113	47	.393
Zaun, G.	Fla	.290	1	2	1	0	10	31	4	3	.353
Zeile, T.	Phi	.268	20	80	1	1	134	500	61	67	.353
Zuber, J.	Phi	.253	1	10	1	0	30	91	7	6	.296

NATIONAL LEAGUE: PITCHERS

NL Pitcher	Team	W	L	SV	ERA	Ratio	GS	IP	H	BB	K
Adams, T.	ChN	3	6	4	2.94	1.317	0	101.0	84	49	78
Adamson, J.	Fla	0	0	0	7.36	2.273	0	11.0	18	7	7
Alston, G.	Col	1	0	0	9.00	2.000	0	6.0	9	3	5
Alvarez, T.	Mon	2	1	0	3.00	1.476	5	21.0	19	12	9
Ashby, A.	SD	9	5	0	3.23	1.201	24	150.2	147	34	85
Astacio, P.	LA	9	8	0	3.44	1.294	32	211.2	207	67	130
Aucoin, D.	Mon	0	1	0	3.38	1.500	0	2.2	3	1	1
Avery, S.	Atl	7	10	0	4.47	1.420	23	131.0	146	40	86
Bailey, C.	StL	5	2	0	3.00	1.526	0	57.0	57	30	38
Bailey, R.	Col	2	3	1	6.24	1.745	11	83.2	94	52	45
Barber, B.	StL	0	0	0	15.00	3.333	1	3.0	4	6	1
Barton, S.	SF	0	0	0	9.72	2.400	0	8.1	19	1	3
Batchelor, R.	StL	2	0	0	1.20	0.667	0	15.0	9	1	11
Batista, M.	Fla	0	0	0	5.56	1.412	0	11.1	9	7	6
Bautista, J.	SF	3	4	0	3.36	1.163	1	69.2	66	15	28
Beck, R.	SF	0	9	35	3.34	1.065	0	62.0	56	10	48
Beckett, R.	Col	0	0	0	13.50	2.813	0	5.1	6	9	6
Beech, M.	Phi	1	4	0	6.97	1.452	8	41.1	49	11	33
Benes, A.	StL	13	10	0	4.90	1.461	32	191.0	192	87	131
Benes, A.	StL	18	10	1	3.83	1.268	34	230.1	215	77	160
Bergman, S.	SD	6	8	0	4.37	1.341	14	113.1	119	33	85
Berumen, A.	SD	0	0	0	5.40	1.500	0	3.1	3	2	4
Bielecki, M.	Atl	4	3	2	2.63	1.274	5	75.1	63	33	71
Blair, W.	SD	2	6	1	4.60	1.239	0	88.0	80	29	67
Blazier, R.	Phi	3	1	0	5.87	1.539	0	38.1	49	10	25
Bochtler, D.	SD	2	4	3	3.02	1.279	0	65.2	45	39	68
Boever, J.	Pit	0	2	2	5.40	1.533	0	15.0	17	6	6
Borbon, P.	Atl	3	0	1	2.75	0.917	0	36.0	26	7	31
Borland, T.	Phi	7	3	0	4.07	1.390	0	90.2	83	43	76
Borowski, J.	Atl	2	4	0	4.85	1.769	0	26.0	33	13	15
Bottalico, R.	Phi	4	5	34	3.19	1.034	0	67.2	47	23	74
Bottenfield, K.	ChN	3	5	1	2.63	1.265	0	61.2	59	19	33
Bourgeois, S.	SF	1	3	0	6.30	2.025	5	40.0	60	21	17
Brantley, J.	Cin	1	2	44	2.41	1.155	0	71.0	54	28	76
Brocail, D.	Hou	1	5	0	4.58	1.528	4	53.0	58	23	34
Brown, K.	Fla	17	11	0	1.89	0.944	32	233.0	187	33	159
Bruske, J.	LA	0	0	0	5.68	1.579	0	12.2	17	3	12
Bullinger, J.	ChN	6	10	1	6.54	1.639	20	129.1	144	68	90
Burba, D.	Cin	11	13	0	3.83	1.415	33	195.0	179	97	148
Burke, J.	Col	2	1	0	7.47	1.787	0	15.2	21	7	19

NL Pitcher	Team	W	L	SV	ERA	Ratio	GS	IP	H	BB	K
Burkett, J.	Fla	6	10	0	4.32	1.273	24	154.0	154	42	108
Busby, M.	StL	0	1	0	18.00	3.250	1	4.0	9	4	4
Byrd, P.	NYN	1	2	0	4.24	1.479	0	46.2	48	21	31
Campbell, M.	ChN	3	1	0	4.46	1.073	5	36.1	29	10	19
Candiotti, T.	LA	9	11	0	4.49	1.411	27	152.1	172	43	79
Carlson, D.	SF	1	0	0	2.70	1.500	0	10.0	13	2	4
Carrara, G.	Cin	1	0	0	5.87	1.913	5	23.0	31	13	13
Carrasco, H.	Cin	4	3	0	3.75	1.386	0	74.1	58	45	59
Casian, L.	ChN	1	1	0	1.88	1.042	0	24.0	14	11	15
Castillo, F.	ChN	7	16	0	5.28	1.399	33	182.1	209	46	139
Christiansen, J.	Pit	3	3	0	6.70	1.692	0	44.1	56	19	38
Clark, M.	NYN	14	11	0	3.43	1.248	32	212.1	217	48	142
Clark, T.	Hou	0	2	0	11.37	2.842	0	6.1	16	2	5
Clontz, B.	Atl	6	3	1	5.69	1.376	0	80.2	78	33	49
Cooke, S.	Pit	0	0	0	7.56	1.920	0	8.1	11	5	7
Cordova, F.	Pit	4	7	12	4.09	1.242	6	99.0	103	20	95
Cormier, R.	Mon	7	10	0	4.17	1.290	27	159.2	165	41	100
Crawford, C.	Phi	0	1	0	4.91	2.455	1	3.2	7	2	4
Creek, D.	SF	0	2	0	6.52	1.593	0	48.1	45	32	38
Cummings, J.	LA	0	1	0	6.75	2.625	0	5.1	12	2	5
Daal, O.	Mon	4	5	0	4.02	1.271	6	87.1	74	37	82
Darwin, D.	Hou	3	2	0	5.95	1.276	6	42.1	43	11	27
Darwin, D.	Pit	7	9	0	3.02	1.087	19	122.1	117	16	69
DeLucia, R.	SF	3	6	0	5.84	1.508	0	61.2	62	31	55
Dessens, E.	Pit	0	2	0	8.28	1.760	3	25.0	40	4	13
Dewey, M.	SF	6	3	0	4.21	1.440	0	83.1	79	41	57
DiPoto, J.	NYN	7	2	0	4.19	1.759	0	77.1	91	45	52
Dishman, G.	Phi	0	0	0	7.71	1.571	1	7.0	9	2	3
Dishman, G.	SD	0	0	0	7.71	1.714	0	2.1	3	1	0
Dougherty, J.	Hou	0	2	0	9.00	1.923	0	13.0	14	11	6
Drabek, D.	Hou	7	9	0	4.57	1.529	30	175.1	208	60	137
Dreifort, D.	LA	1	4	0	4.94	1.479	0	23.2	23	12	24
Dyer, M.	Mon	5	5	2	4.40	1.493	1	75.2	79	34	51
Eckersley, D.	StL	0	6	30	3.30	1.183	0	60.0	65	6	49
Eischen, J.	LA	0	1	0	4.78	1.569	0	43.1	48	20	36
Ericks, J.	Pit	4	5	8	5.79	1.607	4	46.2	56	19	46
Estes, S.	SF	3	5	0	3.60	1.457	11	70.0	63	39	60
Farmer, M.	Col	0	1	0	7.71	1.607	4	28.0	32	13	16
Fassero, J.	Mon	15	11	0	3.30	1.174	34	231.2	217	55	222
Fernandez, O.	SF	7	13	0	4.61	1.456	28	171.2	193	57	106
Fernandez, S.	Phi	3	6	0	3.43	1.206	11	63.0	50	26	77
Florie, B.	SD	2	2	0	4.01	1.459	0	49.1	45	27	51
Fossas, T.	StL	0	4	2	2.68	1.362	0	47.0	43	21	36
Foster, K.	ChN	7	6	0	6.21	1.529	16	87.0	98	35	53
Franco, J.	NYN	4	3	28	1.83	1.389	0	54.0	54	21	48
Freeman, M.	Col	7	9	0	6.04	1.604	23	129.2	151	57	71
Frey, S.	Phi	0	1	0	4.72	1.631	0	34.1	38	18	12
Fyhrie, M.	NYN	0	1	0	15.43	3.000	0	2.1	4	3	0
Gardner, M.	SF	12	7	0	4.42	1.433	28	179.1	200	57	145
Glavine, T.	Atl	15	10	0	2.98	1.305	36	235.1	222	85	181
Grace, M.	Phi	7	2	0	3.49	1.100	12	80.0	72	16	49
Guthrie, M.	LA	2	3	1	2.22	1.192	0	73.0	65	22	56

NL Pitcher	Team	W	L	SV	ERA	Ratio	GS	IP	H	BB	K
Habyan, J.	Col	1	1	0	7.13	2.000	0	24.0	34	14	25
Hall, D.	LA	0	2	0	6.00	1.500	0	12.0	13	5	12
Hamilton, J.	SD	15	9	0	4.17	1.365	33	211.2	206	83	184
Hammond, C.	Fla	5	8	0	6.56	1.617	9	81.0	104	27	50
Hampton, M.	Hou	10	10	0	3.59	1.397	27	160.1	175	49	101
Hancock, L.	Pit	0	0	0	6.38	1.691	0	18.1	21	10	13
Harnisch, P.	NYN	8	12	0	4.21	1.315	31	194.2	195	61	114
Hartgraves, D.	Atl	1	0	0	4.34	1.232	0	18.2	16	7	14
Hartgraves, D.	Hou	0	0	0	5.21	1.789	0	19.0	18	16	16
Hawblitzel, R.	Col	0	1	0	6.00	1.600	0	15.0	18	6	7
Heflin, B.	Phi	0	0	0	6.75	2.100	0	6.2	11	3	4
Helling, R.	Fla	2	1	0	1.95	0.759	4	27.2	14	7	26
Henry, D.	NYN	2	8	9	4.68	1.573	0	75.0	82	36	58
Heredia, F.	Fla	1	1	0	4.32	1.860	0	16.2	21	10	10
Hermanson, D.	SD	1	0	0	8.56	1.610	0	13.2	18	4	11
Hernandez, L.	Fla	0	0	0	0.00	1.667	0	3.0	3	2	2
Hernandez, X.	Cin	0	0	0	13.50	3.000	0	3.1	8	2	3
Hernandez, X.	Hou	5	5	6	4.22	1.272	0	74.2	69	26	78
Hoffman, T.	SD	9	5	42	2.25	0.920	0	88.0	50	31	111
Holmes, D.	Col	5	4	1	3.97	1.377	0	77.0	78	28	73
Holt, C.	Hou	0	1	0	5.79	1.714	0	4.2	5	3	0
Honeycutt, R.	StL	2	1	4	2.85	1.035	0	47.1	42	7	30
Hook, C.	SF	0	1	0	7.43	2.250	0	13.1	16	14	4
Hope, J.	Pit	1	3	0	6.98	1.448	4	19.1	17	11	13
Hudek, J.	Hou	2	0	2	2.81	1.063	0	16.0	12	5	14
Hunter, R.	Phi	3	7	0	6.49	1.688	14	69.1	84	33	32
Hurst, B.	Fla	0	0	0	0.00	2.000	0	2.0	3	1	1
Hutton, M.	Fla	5	1	0	3.67	1.154	9	56.1	47	18	31
Isringhausen, J.	NYN	6	14	0	4.77	1.532	27	171.2	190	73	114
Jackson, D.	StL	1	1	0	4.46	1.349	4	36.1	33	16	27
Jarvis, K.	Cin	8	9	0	5.98	1.620	20	120.1	152	43	63
Johnstone, J.	Hou	1	0	0	5.54	1.692	0	13.0	17	5	5
Jones, B.	NYN	12	8	0	4.42	1.354	31	195.2	219	46	116
Jones, D.	ChN	2	2	2	5.01	1.485	0	32.1	41	7	26
Jones, T.	Hou	6	3	17	4.40	1.622	0	57.1	61	32	44
Jordan, R.	Phi	2	2	0	1.80	1.200	0	25.0	18	12	17
Juden, J.	Mon	1	0	0	2.20	1.102	0	32.2	22	14	26
Juden, J.	SF	4	0	0	4.10	1.416	0	41.2	39	20	35
Kile, D.	Hou	12	11	0	4.19	1.507	33	219.0	233	97	219
Larkin, A.	Fla	0	0	0	1.80	1.400	1	5.0	3	4	2
Leiper, D.	Mon	0	1	0	11.25	2.750	0	4.0	9	2	3
Leiper, D.	Phi	2	0	0	6.43	1.810	0	21.0	31	7	10
Leiter, A.	Fla	16	12	0	2.93	1.263	33	215.1	153	119	200
Leiter, M.	Mon	4	2	0	4.39	1.249	12	69.2	68	19	46
Leiter, M.	SF	4	10	0	5.19	1.485	22	135.1	151	50	118
Leskanic, C.	Col	7	5	6	6.23	1.629	0	73.2	82	38	76
Lieber, J.	Pit	9	5	1	3.99	1.296	15	142.0	156	28	94
Lilliquist, D.	Cin	0	0	0	7.36	1.364	0	3.2	5	0	1
Loaiza, E.	Pit	2	3	0	4.96	1.595	10	52.2	65	19	32
Loiselle, R.	Pit	1	0	0	3.05	1.452	3	20.2	22	8	9
Lomon, K.	Atl	0	0	0	4.91	1.364	0	7.1	7	3	1
Ludwick, E.	StL	0	1	0	9.00	1.400	1	10.0	11	3	12
Lyons, C.	Cin	2	0	0	4.50	1.500	3	16.0	17	7	14

NL Pitcher	Team	W	L	SV	ERA	Ratio	GS	IP	H	BB	K
MacDonald, B.	NYN	0	2	0	4.26	1.316	0	19.0	16	9	12
Maddux, G.	Atl	15	11	0	2.72	1.033	35	245.0	225	28	172
Maduro, C.	Phi	0	1	0	3.52	1.043	2	15.1	13	3	11
Mantei, M.	Fla	1	0	0	6.38	1.855	0	18.1	13	21	25
Manuel, B.	Mon	4	1	0	3.24	1.116	0	86.0	70	26	62
Martinez, P.	Mon	13	10	0	3.70	1.195	33	216.2	189	70	222
Martinez, P.	Cin	0	0	0	6.00	2.000	0	3.0	5	1	3
Martinez, P.	NYN	0	0	0	6.43	2.143	0	7.0	8	7	6
Martinez, R.	LA	15	6	0	3.42	1.417	27	168.2	153	86	134
Mathews, T.	StL	2	6	6	3.01	1.124	0	83.2	62	32	80
Mathews, T.	Fla	2	4	4	4.91	1.564	0	55.0	59	27	49
May, D.	Pit	0	1	0	9.35	2.192	2	8.2	15	4	5
McElroy, C.	Cin	2	0	0	6.57	1.865	0	12.1	13	10	13
McMichael, G.	Atl	5	3	2	3.22	1.281	0	86.2	84	27	78
Miceli, D.	Pit	2	10	1	5.78	1.681	9	85.2	99	45	66
Miller, K.	Fla	1	3	0	6.80	1.942	5	46.1	57	33	30
Mimbs, M.	Phi	3	9	0	5.53	1.581	17	99.1	116	41	56
Minor, B.	NYN	0	0	0	3.51	1.130	0	25.2	23	6	20
Mitchell, L.	Phi	0	0	0	4.50	1.583	0	12.0	14	5	7
Mlicki, D.	NYN	6	7	1	3.30	1.422	2	90.0	95	33	83
Moore, M.	Cin	3	3	2	5.81	1.823	0	26.1	26	22	27
Morel, R.	Pit	2	1	0	5.36	1.810	0	42.0	57	19	22
Morgan, M.	Cin	2	3	0	2.30	1.280	5	27.1	28	7	19
Morgan, M.	StL	4	8	0	5.24	1.534	18	103.0	118	40	55
Morman, A.	Hou	4	1	0	4.93	1.595	0	42.0	43	24	31
Mulholland, T.	Phi	8	7	0	4.66	1.335	21	133.1	157	21	52
Munoz, B.	Phi	0	3	0	7.82	1.934	6	25.1	42	7	8
Munoz, M.	Col	2	2	0	6.65	1.590	0	44.2	55	16	45
Myers, R.	ChN	2	1	0	4.68	1.470	0	67.1	61	38	50
Navarro, J.	ChN	15	12	0	3.92	1.335	35	236.2	244	72	158
Neagle, D.	Atl	2	3	0	5.59	1.397	6	38.2	40	14	18
Neagle, D.	Pit	14	6	0	3.05	1.204	27	182.2	186	34	131
Nen, R.	Fla	5	1	35	1.95	1.060	0	83.0	67	21	92
Nied, D.	Col	0	2	0	13.50	2.438	1	5.1	5	8	4
Nomo, H.	LA	16	11	0	3.19	1.161	33	228.1	180	85	234
Olson, G.	Hou	1	0	0	4.82	2.036	0	9.1	12	7	8
Oquist, M.	SD	0	0	0	2.35	1.304	0	7.2	6	4	4
Osborne, D.	StL	13	9	0	3.53	1.248	30	198.2	191	57	134
Osuna, A.	SD	0	0	0	2.25	1.750	0	4.0	5	2	4
Osuna, A.	LA	9	6	4	3.00	1.155	0	84.0	65	32	85
Pacheco, A.	Mon	0	0	0	11.12	1.588	0	5.2	8	1	7
Painter, L.	Col	4	2	0	5.86	1.599	1	50.2	56	25	48
Pall, D.	Fla	1	1	0	5.79	1.339	0	18.2	16	9	9
Paniagua, J.	Mon	2	4	0	3.53	1.529	11	51.0	55	23	27
Park, C.	LA	5	5	0	3.64	1.408	10	108.2	82	71	119
Parrett, J.	Phi	1	1	0	1.88	1.458	0	24.0	24	11	22
Parrett, J.	StL	2	2	0	4.25	1.417	0	42.1	40	20	42
Parris, S.	Pit	0	3	0	7.18	1.747	4	26.1	35	11	27
Patterson, B.	ChN	3	3	8	3.13	1.244	0	54.2	46	22	53
Pena, A.	Fla	0	1	0	4.50	1.250	0	4.0	4	1	5
Perez, M.	ChN	1	0	0	4.67	1.556	0	27.0	29	13	22
Perez, Y.	Fla	3	4	0	5.29	1.720	0	47.2	51	31	47
Person, R.	NYN	4	5	0	4.52	1.349	13	89.2	86	35	76
Peters, C.	Pit	2	4	0	5.63	1.516	10	64.0	72	25	28
Petkovsek, M.	StL	11	2	0	3.55	1.331	6	88.2	83	35	45

NL Pitcher	Team	W	L	SV	ERA	Ratio	GS	IP	H	BB	K
Plesac, D.	Pit	6	5	11	4.09	1.294	0	70.1	67	24	76
Poole, J.	SF	2	1	0	2.66	1.183	0	23.2	15	13	19
Portugal, M.	Cin	8	9	0	3.98	1.205	26	156.0	146	42	93
Powell, J.	Fla	4	3	2	4.54	1.500	0	71.1	71	36	52
Pugh, T.	Cin	1	1	0	11.49	2.234	0	15.2	24	11	9
Quirico, R.	Phi	0	1	0	37.80	5.400	1	1.2	4	5	1
Radinsky, S.	LA	5	1	1	2.41	1.318	0	52.1	52	17	48
Rapp, P.	Fla	8	16	0	5.10	1.694	29	162.1	184	91	86
Reed, S.	Col	4	3	0	3.96	1.133	0	75.0	66	19	51
Rekar, B.	Col	2	4	0	8.95	1.937	11	58.1	87	26	25
Remlinger, M.	Cin	0	1	0	5.60	1.573	4	27.1	24	19	19
Reynolds, S.	Hou	16	10	0	3.65	1.134	35	239.0	227	44	204
Reynoso, A.	Col	8	9	0	4.96	1.447	30	168.2	195	49	88
Ritz, K.	Col	17	11	0	5.28	1.601	35	213.0	236	105	105
Rojas, M.	Mon	7	4	36	3.22	1.037	0	81.0	56	28	92
Ruebel, M.	Pit	1	1	1	4.60	1.517	7	58.2	64	25	22
Rueter, K.	Mon	5	6	0	4.58	1.436	16	78.2	91	22	30
Rueter, K.	SF	1	2	0	1.93	0.986	3	23.1	18	5	16
Ruffin, B.	Col	7	5	24	4.00	1.206	0	69.2	55	29	74
Ruffin, J.	Cin	1	3	0	5.49	1.733	0	62.1	71	37	69
Ryan, K.	Phi	3	5	8	2.43	1.303	0	89.0	71	45	71
Salkeld, R.	Cin	8	5	0	5.20	1.448	19	116.0	114	54	82
Sanders, S.	SD	9	5	0	3.38	1.146	16	144.0	117	48	157
Schilling, C.	Phi	9	10	0	3.19	1.085	26	183.1	149	50	182
Schmidt, J.	Atl	3	4	0	6.75	1.722	11	58.2	69	32	48
Schmidt, J.	Pit	2	2	0	4.06	1.593	6	37.2	39	21	26
Schourek, P.	Cin	4	5	0	6.01	1.530	12	67.1	79	24	54
Schutz, C.	Atl	0	0	0	2.70	1.500	0	3.1	3	2	5
Scott, T.	Mon	3	5	1	3.11	1.338	0	46.1	41	21	37
Scott, T.	SF	2	2	0	8.24	1.678	0	19.2	24	9	10
Service, S.	Cin	1	0	0	3.94	1.438	1	48.0	51	18	46
Shaw, J.	Cin	8	6	4	2.49	1.223	0	104.2	99	29	69
Small, M.	Hou	0	1	0	5.92	1.890	0	24.1	33	13	16
Smiley, J.	Cin	13	14	0	3.64	1.201	34	217.1	207	54	171
Smith, L.	Cin	3	4	0	4.06	1.624	0	44.1	49	23	35
Smith, Z.	Pit	4	6	0	5.08	1.500	16	83.1	104	21	47
Smoltz, J.	Atl	24	8	0	2.94	1.001	35	253.2	199	55	276
Soderstrom, S.	SF	2	0	0	5.27	1.610	3	13.2	16	6	9
Spradlin, J.	Cin	0	0	0	0.00	0.000	0	0.1	0	0	0
Springer, R.	Phi	3	10	0	4.66	1.490	7	96.2	106	38	94
Stottlemyre, T.	StL	14	11	0	3.87	1.272	33	223.1	191	93	194
Sturtze, T.	ChN	1	0	0	9.00	1.909	0	11.0	16	5	7
Sullivan, S.	Cin	0	0	0	2.25	1.500	0	8.0	7	5	3
Swartzbaugh, D.	ChN	0	2	0	6.38	1.667	5	24.0	26	14	13
Swift, B.	Col	1	1	2	5.40	1.527	3	18.1	23	5	5
Swindell, G.	Hou	0	3	0	7.83	2.000	4	23.0	35	11	15
Tabaka, J.	Hou	0	2	1	6.64	2.066	0	20.1	28	14	18
Telemaco, A.	ChN	5	7	0	5.46	1.428	17	97.1	108	31	64
Tewksbury, B.	SD	10	10	0	4.31	1.292	33	206.2	224	43	126
Thobe, T.	Atl	0	1	0	1.50	0.833	0	6.0	5	0	1
Thompson, M.	Col	9	11	0	5.30	1.550	28	169.2	189	74	99
Trachsel, S.	ChN	13	9	0	3.03	1.185	31	205.0	181	62	132
Trlicek, R.	NYN	0	1	0	3.38	1.125	0	5.1	3	3	3

NL Pitcher	Team	W	L	SV	ERA	Ratio	GS	IP	H	BB	K
Urbani, T.	StL	1	0	0	7.71	1.629	2	11.2	15	4	1
Urbina, U.	Mon	10	5	0	3.71	1.281	17	114.0	102	44	108
Valdes, I.	LA	15	7	0	3.32	1.213	33	225.0	219	54	173
Valdes, M.	Fla	1	3	0	4.81	1.767	8	48.2	63	23	13
Valenzuela, F.	SD	13	8	0	3.62	1.421	31	171.2	177	67	95
VanLandingham,	SF	9	14	0	5.40	1.508	32	181.2	196	78	97
Veras, D.	SD	3	1	0	2.79	1.172	0	29.0	24	10	23
Veres, D.	Mon	6	3	4	4.17	1.506	0	77.2	85	32	81
Villone, R.	SD	1	1	0	2.95	1.309	0	18.1	17	7	19
Wade, T.	Atl	5	0	1	2.97	1.493	8	69.2	57	47	79
Wagner, B.	Hou	2	2	9	2.44	1.123	0	51.2	28	30	67
Wagner, P.	Pit	4	8	0	5.40	1.531	15	81.2	86	39	81
Wainhouse, D.	Pit	1	0	0	5.70	1.352	0	23.2	22	10	16
Walker, P.	SD	0	0	0	0.00	4.500	0	0.2	0	3	1
Wall, D.	Hou	9	8	0	4.56	1.360	23	150.0	170	34	99
Wallace, D.	NYN	2	3	3	4.01	1.743	0	24.2	29	14	15
Watson, A.	SF	8	12	0	4.61	1.390	29	185.2	189	69	128
Weathers, D.	Fla	2	2	0	4.54	1.584	8	71.1	85	28	40
Wendell, T.	ChN	4	5	18	2.84	1.286	0	79.1	58	44	75
West, D.	Phi	2	2	0	4.76	1.482	6	28.1	31	11	22
Wilkins, M.	Pit	4	3	1	3.84	1.480	2	75.0	75	36	62
Williams, M.	Phi	6	14	0	5.44	1.527	29	167.0	188	67	103
Wilson, P.	NYN	5	12	0	5.38	1.530	26	149.0	157	71	109
Wohlers, M.	Atl	2	4	39	3.03	1.190	0	77.1	71	21	100
Woodall, B.	Atl	2	2	0	7.32	1.627	3	19.2	28	4	20
Worrell, T.	SD	9	7	1	3.05	1.223	11	121.0	109	39	99
Worrell, T.	LA	4	6	44	3.03	1.301	0	65.1	70	15	66
Wright, J.	Col	4	4	0	4.93	1.599	15	91.1	105	41	45
Young, A.	Hou	3	3	0	4.59	1.740	0	33.1	36	22	19

AMERICAN LEAGUE: BATTERS

AL Batter	Team	BA	HR	RBI	SB	CS	G	AB	R	BB	OBP
Aldrete, M.	Cal	.150	3	8	0	0	31	40	5	5	.239
Aldrete, M.	NYA	.250	3	12	0	1	32	68	11	9	.338
Alexander, M.	Bal	.103	0	4	3	3	53	68	6	3	.141
Alomar, R.	Bal	.328	22	94	17	6	153	588	132	90	.411
Alomar Jr, S.	Cle	.263	11	50	1	0	127	418	53	19	.299
Amaral, R.	Sea	.292	1	29	25	6	118	312	69	47	.392
Anderson, B.	Bal	.297	50	110	21	8	149	579	117	76	.396
Anderson, G.	Cal	.285	12	72	7	9	150	607	79	27	.314
Arias, G.	Cal	.238	6	28	2	0	84	252	19	16	.284
Ausmus, B.	Det	.248	4	22	3	4	75	226	30	26	.328
Baerga, C.	Cle	.267	10	55	1	1	100	424	54	16	.302
Baines, H.	ChA	.311	22	95	3	1	143	495	80	73	.399
Banks, B.	Mil	.571	1	2	0	0	4	7	2	1	.625
Bartee, K.	Det	.253	1	14	20	10	110	217	32	17	.308
Batista, T.	Oak	.298	6	25	7	3	74	238	38	19	.350
Battle, A.	Oak	.192	1	5	10	2	47	130	20	17	.293
Bautista, D.	Det	.250	2	8	1	2	25	64	12	9	.342
Becker, R.	Min	.291	12	71	19	5	148	525	92	68	.372
Belle, A.	Cle	.311	48	148	11	0	158	602	124	99	.410

AL Batter	Team	BA	HR	RBI	SB	CS	G	AB	R	BB	OBP
Beltre, E.	Bos	.258	0	6	1	0	27	62	6	4	.299
Berroa, G.	Oak	.290	36	106	0	3	153	586	101	47	.344
Boggs, W.	NYA	.311	2	41	1	2	132	501	80	67	.389
Bonilla, B.	Bal	.287	28	116	1	3	159	595	107	75	.363
Borders, P.	Cal	.228	2	8	0	1	19	57	6	3	.267
Borders, P.	ChA	.277	3	6	0	0	31	94	6	5	.313
Bordick, M.	Oak	.240	5	54	5	6	155	525	46	52	.307
Bournigal, R.	Oak	.242	0	18	4	3	88	252	33	16	.290
Bowers, B.	Bal	.308	0	3	0	0	21	39	6	0	.308
Bragg, D.	Bos	.252	3	22	6	4	58	222	38	36	.357
Bragg, D.	Sea	.272	7	25	8	5	69	195	36	33	.376
Brede, B.	Min	.300	0	2	0	0	10	20	2	1	.333
Brito, T.	Tor	.237	1	7	1	1	26	80	10	10	.344
Brosius, S.	Oak	.304	22	71	7	2	114	428	73	59	.393
Brown, K.	Tex	.000	0	1	0	0	3	4	1	2	.000
Brumfield, J.	Tor	.256	12	52	12	3	90	308	52	24	.316
Buford, D.	Tex	.283	6	20	8	5	90	145	30	15	.348
Buhner, J.	Sea	.271	44	138	0	1	150	564	107	84	.369
Burnitz, J.	Cle	.281	7	26	2	1	71	128	30	25	.406
Burnitz, J.	Mil	.236	2	14	2	0	23	72	8	8	.321
Cairo, M.	Tor	.222	0	1	0	0	9	27	5	2	.300
Cameron, M.	ChA	.091	0	0	0	1	11	11	1	1	.167
Candaele, C.	Cle	.250	1	4	0	0	24	44	8	1	.267
Canseco, J.	Bos	.289	28	82	3	1	96	360	68	63	.400
Carr, C.	Mil	.274	1	11	5	4	27	106	18	6	.310
Carreon, M.	Cle	.324	2	14	1	1	38	142	16	11	.385
Carter, J.	Tor	.253	30	107	7	6	157	625	84	44	.306
Casanova, R.	Det	.188	4	9	0	0	25	85	6	6	.242
Cedeno, A.	Det	.196	7	20	2	1	52	179	19	4	.213
Cedeno, D.	ChA	.158	0	3	1	0	12	19	2	0	.143
Cedeno, D.	Tor	.280	2	17	5	3	77	282	44	15	.320
Cirillo, J.	Mil	.325	15	83	4	9	158	566	101	58	.391
Clark, P.	Bos	.000	0	0	0	0	3	3	0	0	.000
Clark, T.	Det	.250	27	72	0	1	100	376	56	29	.299
Clark, W.	Tex	.284	13	72	2	1	117	436	69	64	.377
Cole, A.	Bos	.222	0	7	5	3	24	72	13	8	.296
Coomer, R.	Min	.296	12	41	3	0	95	233	34	17	.340
Cora, J.	Sea	.291	6	45	5	5	144	530	90	35	.340
Cordero, W.	Bos	.288	3	37	2	1	59	198	29	11	.330
Cordova, M.	Min	.309	16	111	11	5	145	569	97	53	.371
Crespo, F.	Tor	.184	0	4	1	0	22	49	6	12	.375
Cruz, F.	Det	.237	0	0	0	0	14	38	5	1	.256
Curtis, C.	Det	.262	10	37	16	10	104	400	65	53	.346
Cuyler, M.	Bos	.200	2	12	7	3	50	110	19	13	.299
Damon, J.	KC	.271	6	50	25	5	145	517	61	31	.313
Davis, C.	Cal	.292	28	95	5	2	145	530	73	86	.387
Davis, R.	Sea	.234	5	18	2	0	51	167	24	17	.312
Delgado, A.	Bos	.250	0	1	0	0	26	20	5	3	.348
Delgado, C.	Tor	.270	25	92	0	0	138	488	68	58	.353
Devarez, C.	Bal	.111	0	0	0	0	10	18	3	1	.158
Devereaux, M.	Bal	.229	8	34	8	2	127	323	49	34	.305
Diaz, A.	Sea	.241	1	5	6	3	38	79	11	2	.274
Diaz, E.	Cle	.000	0	0	0	0	4	1	0	0	.000
DiSarcina, G.	Cal	.256	5	48	2	1	150	536	62	21	.286
Duncan, M.	NYA	.340	8	56	4	3	109	400	62	9	.352
Dunn, T.	Mil	.300	0	1	0	0	6	10	2	0	.300

AL Batter	Team	BA	HR	RBI	SB	CS	G	AB	R	BB	OBP
Durant, M.	Min	.210	0	5	3	0	40	81	15	10	.293
Durham, R.	ChA	.275	10	65	30	4	156	557	79	58	.350
Easley, D.	Cal	.156	2	7	0	0	28	45	4	6	.255
Easley, D.	Det	.343	2	10	3	1	21	67	10	4	.384
Edmonds, J.	Cal	.304	27	66	4	0	114	431	73	46	.375
Eenhoorn, R.	Cal	.267	0	0	0	0	6	15	1	0	.267
Eenhoorn, R.	NYA	.071	0	2	0	0	12	14	2	2	.167
Elster, K.	Tex	.252	24	99	4	1	157	515	79	52	.317
Erstad, D.	Cal	.284	4	20	3	3	57	208	34	17	.333
Espinoza, A.	Cle	.223	4	11	1	1	59	112	12	6	.279
Fabregas, J.	Cal	.287	2	26	0	1	90	254	18	17	.326
Faneyte, R.	Tex	.200	0	1	0	0	8	5	0	0	.200
Fasano, S.	KC	.203	6	19	1	1	51	143	20	14	.283
Fielder, C.	Det	.248	26	80	2	0	107	391	55	63	.354
Fielder, C.	NYA	.260	13	37	0	0	53	200	30	24	.342
Flaherty, J.	Det	.250	4	23	1	0	47	152	18	8	.290
Fox, A.	NYA	.196	3	13	11	3	113	189	26	20	.276
Franco, J.	Cle	.322	14	76	8	8	112	432	72	61	.407
Frazier, L.	Tex	.260	0	5	4	2	30	50	5	8	.373
Frye, J.	Bos	.286	4	41	18	4	105	419	74	54	.372
Fryman, T.	Det	.268	22	100	4	3	157	616	90	57	.329
Garciaparra, N.	Bos	.241	4	16	5	0	24	87	11	4	.272
Garrison, W.	Oak	.000	0	0	0	0	5	9	0	1	.000
Gates, B.	Oak	.263	2	30	1	1	64	247	26	18	.316
Giambi, J.	Oak	.291	20	79	0	1	140	536	84	51	.355
Gil, B.	Tex	.400	0	1	0	1	5	5	0	1	.500
Giles, B.	Cle	.355	5	27	3	0	51	121	26	19	.434
Girardi, J.	NYA	.294	2	45	13	4	124	422	55	30	.346
Gomez, C.	Det	.242	1	16	1	1	48	128	21	18	.340
Gonzales, R.	Tex	.217	2	5	0	0	51	92	19	10	.288
Gonzalez, A.	Tor	.235	14	64	16	6	147	527	64	45	.300
Gonzalez, J.	Tex	.314	47	144	2	0	134	541	89	45	.368
Goodwin, T.	KC	.282	1	35	66	22	143	524	80	39	.334
Green, S.	Tor	.280	11	45	5	1	132	422	52	33	.342
Greene, T.	Cal	.190	2	9	2	0	29	79	9	4	.238
Greenwell, M.	Bos	.295	7	44	4	0	77	295	35	18	.336
Greer, R.	Tex	.332	18	100	9	0	139	542	96	62	.397
Griffey Jr, K.	Sea	.303	49	140	16	1	140	545	125	78	.392
Guillen, O.	ChA	.263	4	45	6	5	150	499	62	10	.273
Hale, C.	Min	.276	1	16	0	0	85	87	8	10	.347
Hamelin, B.	KC	.255	9	40	5	2	89	239	31	54	.391
Hamilton, D.	Tex	.293	6	51	15	5	148	627	94	54	.348
Hammonds, J.	Bal	.226	9	27	3	3	71	248	38	23	.301
Haselman, B.	Bos	.274	8	34	4	2	77	237	33	19	.331
Hatteberg, S.	Bos	.182	0	0	0	0	10	11	3	3	.357
Hayes, C.	NYA	.284	2	13	0	0	20	67	7	1	.294
Herrera, J.	Oak	.269	6	30	8	2	108	320	44	20	.318
Hiatt, P.	Det	.190	0	1	0	0	7	21	3	2	.261
Higginson, B.	Det	.320	26	81	6	3	130	440	75	65	.404
Hocking, D.	Min	.197	1	10	3	3	49	127	16	8	.243
Hoiles, C.	Bal	.258	25	73	0	1	127	407	64	57	.356
Hollins, D.	Min	.242	13	53	6	4	121	422	71	71	.364
Hollins, D.	Sea	.351	3	25	0	2	28	94	17	13	.438
Hosey, D.	Bos	.218	1	3	6	3	28	78	13	7	.282

AL Batter	Team	BA	HR	RBI	SB	CS	G	AB	R	BB	OBP
Howard, D.	KC	.219	4	48	5	6	143	420	51	40	.291
Howard, M.	NYA	.204	1	9	1	0	35	54	9	2	.228
Howell, J.	Cal	.270	8	21	0	1	66	126	20	10	.324
Hudler, R.	Cal	.311	16	40	14	5	92	302	60	9	.337
Huff, M.	Tor	.172	0	0	0	0	11	29	5	1	.200
Hulse, D.	Mil	.222	0	6	4	1	81	117	18	8	.272
Hunter, B.	Sea	.268	7	28	0	1	75	198	21	15	.327
Huson, J.	Bal	.321	0	2	0	0	17	28	5	1	.333
Hyers, T.	Det	.077	0	0	0	0	17	26	1	4	.200
Ibanez, R.	Sea	.000	0	0	0	0	4	5	0	0	.000
Incaviglia, P.	Bal	.303	2	8	0	0	12	33	4	0	.314
Jackson, D.	Cle	.300	0	1	0	0	5	10	2	1	.364
Jaha, J.	Mil	.300	34	118	3	1	148	543	108	85	.398
James, D.	NYA	.167	0	0	1	0	6	12	1	1	.231
Jefferson, R.	Bos	.347	19	74	0	0	122	386	67	25	.388
Jeter, D.	NYA	.314	10	78	14	7	157	582	104	48	.370
Jordan, R.	Sea	.250	1	4	0	0	15	28	4	1	.290
Karkovice, R.	ChA	.220	10	38	0	0	111	355	44	24	.270
Kelly, P.	NYA	.143	0	2	0	1	13	21	4	2	.217
Kelly, R.	Min	.323	6	47	10	2	98	322	41	23	.375
Kent, J.	Cle	.265	3	16	2	1	39	102	16	10	.328
Kingsale, G.	Bal	.000	0	0	0	0	3	0	0	0	.000
Kirby, W.	Cle	.250	0	1	0	1	27	16	3	2	.333
Knoblauch, C.	Min	.341	13	72	45	14	153	578	140	98	.448
Koslofski, K.	Mil	.214	0	6	0	0	25	42	5	4	.298
Kreuter, C.	ChA	.219	3	18	0	0	46	114	14	13	.308
Lawton, M.	Min	.258	6	42	4	4	79	252	34	28	.339
Leius, S.	Cle	.140	1	3	0	0	27	43	3	2	.178
Lennon, P.	KC	.233	0	1	0	0	14	30	5	7	.378
Lesher, B.	Oak	.232	5	16	0	0	26	82	11	5	.281
Levis, J.	Mil	.236	1	21	0	0	104	233	27	38	.348
Lewis, D.	ChA	.228	4	53	21	5	141	337	55	45	.321
Lewis, M.	Det	.270	11	55	6	1	145	545	69	42	.326
Leyritz, J.	NYA	.264	7	40	2	0	88	265	23	30	.355
Listach, P.	Mil	.240	1	33	25	5	87	317	51	36	.317
Lockhart, K.	KC	.273	7	55	11	6	138	433	49	30	.319
Lofton, K.	Cle	.317	14	67	75	17	154	662	132	61	.372
Loretta, M.	Mil	.279	1	13	2	1	73	154	20	14	.339
Lovullo, T.	Oak	.220	3	9	1	2	65	82	15	11	.323
Luke, M.	NYA	.000	0	0	0	0	1	0	1	0	.000
Macfarlane, M.	KC	.274	19	54	3	3	112	379	58	31	.339
Machado, R.	ChA	.667	0	2	0	0	4	6	1	0	.667
Malave, J.	Bos	.235	4	17	0	0	41	102	12	2	.257
Manto, J.	Bos	.208	2	6	0	0	22	48	8	8	.333
Manto, J.	Sea	.185	1	4	0	1	21	54	7	9	.302
Martin, N.	ChA	.350	1	14	10	2	70	140	30	6	.374
Martinez, D.	ChA	.318	10	53	15	7	146	440	85	52	.393
Martinez, E.	Sea	.327	26	103	3	3	139	499	121	123	.464
Martinez, M.	Sea	.235	0	3	2	0	9	17	3	3	.350
Martinez, S.	Tor	.227	3	18	0	0	76	229	17	16	.288
Martinez, T.	NYA	.292	25	117	2	1	155	595	82	68	.364
Marzano, J.	Sea	.245	0	6	0	0	41	106	8	7	.316
Mashore, D.	Oak	.267	3	12	4	0	50	105	20	16	.366

AL Batter	Team	BA	HR	RBI	SB	CS	G	AB	R	BB	OBP
Matheny, M.	Mil	.204	8	46	3	2	106	313	31	14	.243
McGwire, M.	Oak	.312	52	113	0	0	130	423	104	116	.467
McIntosh, T.	NYA	.000	0	0	0	0	3	3	0	0	.000
Mckeel, W.	Bos	.000	0	0	0	0	1	0	0	0	.000
McLemore, M.	Tex	.290	5	46	27	10	147	517	84	87	.389
Meares, P.	Min	.267	8	67	9	4	152	517	66	17	.298
Mercedes, H.	KC	.250	0	0	0	0	4	4	1	0	.250
Mieske, M.	Mil	.278	14	64	1	5	127	374	46	26	.324
Mitchell, K.	Bos	.304	2	13	0	0	27	92	9	11	.385
Molina, I.	Oak	.200	0	1	0	0	14	25	0	1	.231
Molitor, P.	Min	.341	9	113	18	6	161	660	99	56	.390
Moore, K.	Oak	.063	0	0	1	0	22	16	4	2	.167
Mosquera, J.	Tor	.227	0	2	0	1	8	22	2	0	.261
Mouton, L.	ChA	.294	7	39	3	0	87	214	25	22	.361
Munoz, J.	ChA	.259	0	1	0	0	17	27	7	4	.355
Munoz, P.	Oak	.256	6	18	0	0	34	121	17	9	.308
Murray, E.	Bal	.257	10	34	1	0	64	230	36	27	.327
Murray, E.	Cle	.262	12	45	3	0	88	336	33	34	.326
Myers, G.	Min	.286	6	47	0	0	97	329	37	19	.320
Myers, R.	KC	.286	1	11	3	2	22	63	9	7	.357
Naehring, T.	Bos	.288	17	65	2	1	116	430	77	49	.363
Nevin, P.	Det	.292	8	19	1	0	38	120	15	8	.338
Newfield, M.	Mil	.307	7	31	0	1	49	179	21	11	.354
Newson, W.	Tex	.255	10	31	3	0	91	235	34	37	.355
Nieves, M.	Det	.246	24	60	1	2	120	431	71	44	.322
Nilsson, D.	Mil	.331	17	84	2	3	123	453	81	57	.407
Nixon, O.	Tor	.286	1	29	54	13	125	496	87	71	.377
Nixon, T.	Bos	.500	0	0	1	0	2	4	2	0	.500
Norman, L.	KC	.122	0	0	1	1	54	49	9	6	.232
Norton, G.	ChA	.217	2	3	0	1	11	23	4	4	.333
Nunnally, J.	KC	.211	5	17	0	0	35	90	16	13	.308
O'Brien, C.	Tor	.238	13	44	0	1	109	324	33	29	.331
O'Leary, T.	Bos	.260	15	81	3	2	149	497	68	47	.327
O'Neill, P.	NYA	.302	19	91	0	1	150	546	89	102	.411
Offerman, J.	KC	.303	5	47	24	10	151	561	85	74	.384
Olerud, J.	Tor	.274	18	61	1	0	125	398	59	60	.382
Ortiz, L.	Tex	.286	1	1	0	0	3	7	1	0	.286
Palmeiro, O.	Cal	.287	0	6	0	1	50	87	6	8	.361
Palmeiro, R.	Bal	.289	39	142	8	0	162	626	110	95	.381
Palmer, D.	Tex	.280	38	107	2	0	154	582	98	59	.348
Paquette, C.	KC	.259	22	67	5	3	118	429	61	23	.296
Parent, M.	Bal	.182	2	6	0	0	18	33	4	2	.229
Parent, M.	Det	.240	7	17	0	0	38	104	13	3	.259
Pemberton, R.	Bos	.512	1	10	3	1	13	41	11	2	.556
Pena, G.	Cle	.111	1	2	0	0	5	9	1	1	.200
Pena, T.	Cle	.195	1	27	0	1	67	174	14	15	.255
Penn, S.	Det	.071	0	1	0	0	6	14	0	0	.071
Perez, D.	Mil	.000	0	0	0	0	4	4	0	0	.000
Perez, R.	Tor	.327	2	21	3	0	86	202	30	8	.354
Perez, T.	Tor	.251	1	19	1	2	91	295	24	25	.311
Perry, H.	Cle	.083	0	0	1	0	7	12	1	1	.154
Phillips, T.	ChA	.277	12	63	13	8	153	581	119	125	.404
Pirkl, G.	Bos	.000	0	0	0	0	2	2	0	0	.000
Pirkl, G.	Sea	.190	1	1	0	0	7	21	2	0	.190
Plantier, P.	Oak	.212	7	31	2	2	73	231	29	28	.304

AL Batter	Team	BA	HR	RBI	SB	CS	G	AB	R	BB	OBP
Polonia, L.	Bal	.240	2	14	8	6	58	175	25	10	.285
Posada, J.	NYA	.071	0	0	0	0	8	14	1	1	.133
Pozo, A.	Bos	.172	1	11	1	0	21	58	4	2	.210
Pride, C.	Det	.300	10	31	11	6	95	267	52	31	.372
Pritchett, C.	Cal	.154	0	1	0	0	5	13	1	0	.154
Quinlan, T.	Min	.000	0	0	0	0	4	6	0	0	.000
Raabe, B.	Min	.222	0	1	0	0	7	9	0	0	.200
Raines, T.	NYA	.284	9	33	10	1	59	201	45	34	.383
Ramirez, M.	Cle	.309	33	112	8	5	152	550	94	85	.399
Randa, J.	KC	.303	6	47	13	4	110	337	36	26	.351
Reboulet, J.	Min	.222	0	23	4	2	107	234	20	25	.298
Ripken, B.	Bal	.230	2	12	0	0	57	135	19	9	.281
Ripken, C.	Bal	.278	26	102	1	2	163	640	94	59	.341
Rivera, R.	NYA	.284	2	16	6	2	46	88	17	13	.381
Roberts, B.	KC	.283	0	52	12	9	90	339	39	25	.331
Robertson, M.	ChA	.143	0	0	0	0	6	7	0	0	.143
Rodriguez, A.	Sea	.358	36	123	15	4	146	601	141	59	.414
Rodriguez, I.	Tex	.300	19	86	5	0	153	639	116	38	.342
Rodriguez, T.	Bos	.239	1	9	0	0	27	67	7	4	.292
Salmon, T.	Cal	.286	30	98	4	2	156	581	90	93	.386
Samuel, J.	Tor	.255	8	26	9	1	69	188	34	15	.319
Schofield, D.	Cal	.250	0	0	1	0	13	16	3	1	.294
Seitzer, K.	Cle	.386	1	16	0	0	22	83	11	14	.480
Seitzer, K.	Mil	.316	12	62	6	1	132	490	74	73	.406
Selby, B.	Bos	.274	3	6	1	1	40	95	12	9	.337
Sheets, A.	Sea	.191	0	9	2	0	47	110	18	10	.262
Sierra, R.	Det	.222	1	20	3	1	46	158	22	20	.306
Sierra, R.	NYA	.258	11	52	1	3	96	360	39	40	.327
Singleton, D.	Det	.161	0	3	0	2	18	56	5	4	.230
Slaught, D.	Cal	.324	6	32	0	0	62	207	23	13	.366
Slaught, D.	ChA	.250	0	4	0	0	14	36	2	2	.289
Smith, M.	Bal	.244	4	10	0	2	27	78	9	3	.298
Snopek, C.	ChA	.260	6	18	0	1	46	104	18	6	.304
Snow, J.	Cal	.257	17	67	1	6	155	575	69	56	.327
Sojo, L.	NYA	.275	0	5	0	0	18	40	3	1	.286
Sojo, L.	Sea	.211	1	16	2	2	77	247	20	10	.244
Sorrento, P.	Sea	.289	23	93	0	2	143	471	67	57	.370
Spiezio, S.	Oak	.310	2	8	0	1	9	29	6	4	.394
Sprague, E.	Tor	.247	36	101	0	0	159	591	88	60	.325
Stahoviak, S.	Min	.284	13	61	3	3	130	405	72	59	.376
Stairs, M.	Oak	.277	10	23	1	1	61	137	21	19	.367
Stanley, M.	Bos	.270	24	69	2	0	121	397	73	69	.383
Steinbach, T.	Oak	.272	35	100	0	1	145	514	79	49	.342
Stevens, L.	Tex	.231	3	12	0	0	27	78	6	6	.291
Stewart, S.	Tor	.176	0	2	1	0	7	17	2	1	.222
Stillwell, K.	Tex	.273	1	4	0	0	46	77	12	10	.364
Stinnett, K.	Mil	.077	0	0	0	0	14	26	1	2	.172
Strange, D.	Sea	.235	3	23	1	0	88	183	19	14	.290
Strawberry, D.	NYA	.262	11	36	6	5	63	202	35	31	.359
Stynes, C.	KC	.293	0	6	5	2	36	92	8	2	.309
Surhoff, B.	Bal	.292	21	82	0	1	143	537	74	47	.352
Sweeney, M.	KC	.279	4	24	1	2	50	165	23	18	.358
Tarasco, T.	Bal	.238	1	9	5	3	31	84	14	7	.297
Tartabull, D.	ChA	.254	27	101	1	2	132	472	58	64	.340

AL Batter	Team	BA	HR	RBI	SB	CS	G	AB	R	BB	OBP
Tatum, J.	Bos	.125	0	0	0	0	2	8	1	0	.125
Tettleton, M.	Tex	.246	24	83	2	1	143	491	78	95	.366
Thomas, F.	ChA	.349	40	134	1	1	141	527	110	109	.459
Thome, J.	Cle	.311	38	116	2	2	151	505	122	123	.450
Thompson, R.	Cle	.318	1	5	0	0	8	22	2	1	.348
Tinsley, L.	Bos	.245	3	14	6	8	92	192	28	13	.298
Trammell, A.	Det	.233	1	16	6	0	66	193	16	10	.267
Tucker, M.	KC	.260	12	53	10	4	108	339	55	40	.346
Turner, C.	Cal	.333	0	1	0	0	4	3	1	1	.400
Unroe, T.	Mil	.188	0	0	0	1	14	16	5	4	.350
Valentin, J.	Bos	.296	13	59	9	10	131	527	84	63	.374
Valentin, J.	Mil	.259	24	95	17	4	154	552	90	66	.336
Valle, D.	Tex	.302	3	17	0	0	42	86	14	9	.368
Vaughn, G.	Mil	.280	31	95	5	2	102	375	78	58	.378
Vaughn, M.	Bos	.326	44	143	2	0	161	635	118	95	.420
Velarde, R.	Cal	.285	14	54	7	7	136	530	82	70	.372
Ventura, R.	ChA	.287	34	105	1	3	158	586	96	78	.368
Vina, F.	Mil	.283	7	46	16	7	140	554	94	38	.342
Vitiello, J.	KC	.241	8	40	2	0	85	257	29	38	.342
Vizcaino, J.	Cle	.285	0	13	6	2	48	179	23	7	.310
Vizquel, O.	Cle	.297	9	64	35	9	151	542	98	56	.362
Voigt, J.	Tex	.111	0	0	0	0	5	9	1	0	.111
Walbeck, M.	Min	.223	2	24	3	1	63	215	25	9	.252
Walker, T.	Min	.256	0	6	2	0	25	82	8	4	.281
Wallach, T.	Cal	.237	8	20	1	0	57	190	23	18	.306
Ward, T.	Mil	.179	2	10	3	0	43	67	7	13	.309
Whiten, M.	Sea	.300	12	33	2	1	40	140	31	21	.399
Widger, C.	Sea	.182	0	0	0	0	8	11	1	0	.250
Williams, B.	NYA	.305	29	102	17	4	143	551	108	82	.391
Williams, E.	Det	.200	6	26	0	2	77	215	22	18	.267
Williams, G.	Oak	.152	3	10	0	0	56	132	17	28	.311
Williams, G.	Mil	.207	0	4	3	1	26	92	6	4	.247
Williams, G.	NYA	.270	5	30	7	8	99	233	37	15	.319
Wilson, D.	Sea	.285	18	83	1	2	138	491	51	32	.330
Wilson, N.	Cle	.250	2	5	0	0	10	12	2	1	.308
Worthington, C.	Tex	.158	1	4	0	0	13	19	2	6	.333
Young, E.	Oak	.242	19	64	7	5	141	462	72	52	.326
Young, K.	KC	.242	8	23	3	3	55	132	20	11	.301
Zaun, G.	Bal	.231	1	13	0	0	50	108	16	11	.309
Zeile, T.	Bal	.239	5	19	0	0	29	117	17	15	.326

AMERICAN LEAGUE: PITCHERS

AL Pitcher	Team	W	L	SV	ERA	Ratio	GS	IP	H	BB	K
Abbott, J.	Cal	2	18	0	7.48	1.754	23	142.0	171	78	58
Abbott, K.	Cal	0	1	0	20.25	3.750	0	4.0	10	5	3
Acre, M.	Oak	1	3	2	6.12	1.880	0	25.0	38	9	18
Adams, W.	Oak	3	4	0	4.01	1.297	12	76.1	76	23	68
Aguilera, R.	Min	8	6	0	5.42	1.356	19	111.1	124	27	83
Alberro, J.	Tex	0	1	0	5.79	2.250	1	9.1	14	7	2
Aldred, S.	Det	0	4	0	9.35	1.985	8	43.1	60	26	36
Aldred, S.	Min	6	5	0	5.09	1.443	17	122.0	134	42	75

AL Pitcher	Team	W	L	SV	ERA	Ratio	GS	IP	H	BB	K
Alvarez, W.	ChA	15	10	0	4.22	1.440	35	217.1	216	97	181
Anderson, B.	Cle	3	1	0	4.91	1.403	9	51.1	58	14	21
Andujar, L.	ChA	0	2	0	8.22	2.043	5	23.0	32	15	6
Andujar, L.	Tor	1	1	0	5.02	1.047	2	14.1	14	1	5
Appier, K.	KC	14	11	0	3.62	1.263	32	211.1	192	75	207
Assenmacher, P.	Cle	4	2	1	3.09	1.286	0	46.2	46	14	44
Ayala, B.	Sea	6	3	3	5.88	1.337	0	67.1	65	25	61
Baldwin, J.	ChA	11	6	0	4.42	1.331	28	169.0	168	57	127
Belcher, T.	KC	15	11	0	3.92	1.383	35	238.2	262	68	113
Belinda, S.	Bos	2	1	2	6.59	1.779	0	28.2	31	20	18
Benitez, A.	Bal	1	0	4	3.77	0.907	0	14.1	7	6	20
Bennett, E.	Min	2	0	1	7.90	1.793	0	27.1	33	16	13
Bere, J.	ChA	0	1	0	10.26	2.640	5	16.2	26	18	19
Bertotti, M.	ChA	2	0	0	5.14	1.714	2	28.0	28	20	19
Bevil, B.	KC	1	0	0	5.73	1.273	1	11.0	9	5	7
Bluma, J.	KC	0	0	5	3.60	1.100	0	20.0	18	4	14
Boehringer, B.	NYA	2	4	0	5.44	1.446	3	46.1	46	21	37
Bohanon, B.	Tor	0	1	1	7.77	2.091	0	22.0	27	19	17
Bones, R.	Mil	7	14	0	5.83	1.600	23	145.0	170	62	59
Bones, R.	NYA	0	0	0	14.14	2.857	1	7.0	14	6	4
Bosio, C.	Sea	4	4	0	5.93	1.582	9	60.2	72	24	39
Boskie, S.	Cal	12	11	0	5.32	1.548	28	189.1	226	67	133
Boze, M.	Mil	0	2	1	7.79	2.227	0	32.1	47	25	19
Brandenburg, M.	Bos	4	2	0	3.81	1.271	0	28.1	28	8	29
Brandenburg, M.	Tex	1	3	0	3.21	1.531	0	47.2	48	25	37
Brewer, B.	NYA	1	0	0	9.53	2.647	0	5.2	7	8	8
Briscoe, J.	Oak	0	1	1	3.76	1.595	0	26.1	18	24	14
Brow, S.	Tor	1	0	0	5.59	1.810	1	38.2	45	25	23
Burkett, J.	Tex	5	2	0	4.06	1.325	10	68.2	75	16	47
Burrows, T.	Mil	2	0	0	2.84	1.737	0	12.2	12	10	5
Carmona, R.	Sea	8	3	1	4.28	1.661	1	90.1	95	55	62
Carpenter, C.	Mil	0	0	0	7.56	1.680	0	8.1	12	2	2
Carrara, G.	Tor	0	1	0	11.40	2.333	0	15.0	23	12	10
Castillo, T.	ChA	3	1	1	1.59	1.191	0	22.2	23	4	9
Castillo, T.	Tor	2	3	1	4.23	1.272	0	72.1	72	20	48
Charlton, N.	Sea	4	7	20	4.04	1.401	0	75.2	68	38	73
Chouinard, B.	Oak	4	2	0	6.10	1.814	11	59.0	75	32	32
Christopher, M.	Det	1	1	0	9.30	1.933	0	30.0	47	11	19
Clark, T.	KC	1	1	0	7.79	2.019	0	17.1	28	7	12
Clemens, R.	Bos	10	13	0	3.63	1.327	34	242.2	216	106	257
Cone, D.	NYA	7	2	0	2.88	1.167	11	72.0	50	34	71
Cook, D.	Tex	5	2	0	4.09	1.251	0	70.1	53	35	64
Coppinger, R.	Bal	10	6	0	5.18	1.488	22	125.0	126	60	104
Corbin, A.	Bal	2	0	0	2.30	1.610	0	27.1	22	22	20
Corsi, J.	Oak	6	0	3	4.03	1.425	0	73.2	71	34	43
Crabtree, T.	Tor	5	3	1	2.54	1.203	0	67.1	59	22	57
Cummings, J.	Det	3	3	0	5.12	1.768	0	31.2	36	20	24
D'Amico, J.	Mil	6	6	0	5.44	1.384	17	86.0	88	31	53
Darwin, J.	ChA	0	1	0	2.93	1.141	0	30.2	26	9	15
Davis, T.	Sea	2	2	0	4.01	1.406	0	42.2	43	17	34
Davison, S.	Sea	0	0	0	9.00	1.556	0	9.0	11	3	9
Dickson, J.	Cal	1	4	0	4.57	1.615	7	43.1	52	18	20
Doherty, J.	Bos	0	0	0	5.68	1.895	0	6.1	8	4	3
Edenfield, K.	Cal	0	0	0	10.38	2.769	0	4.1	10	2	4
Eichhorn, M.	Cal	1	2	0	5.04	1.549	0	30.1	36	11	24

AL Pitcher	Team	W	L	SV	ERA	Ratio	GS	IP	H	BB	K
Eischen, J.	Det	1	1	0	3.24	1.640	0	25.0	27	14	15
Eldred, C.	Mil	4	4	0	4.46	1.417	15	84.2	82	38	50
Ellis, R.	Cal	0	0	0	0.00	0.800	0	5.0	0	4	5
Embree, A.	Cle	1	1	0	6.39	1.645	0	31.0	30	21	33
Erickson, S.	Bal	13	12	0	5.02	1.475	34	222.1	262	66	100
Eshelman, V.	Bos	6	3	0	7.08	1.939	10	87.2	112	58	59
Farrell, J.	Det	0	2	0	14.21	2.526	2	6.1	11	5	0
Fernandez, A.	ChA	16	10	0	3.45	1.240	35	258.0	248	72	200
Fetters, M.	Mil	3	3	32	3.38	1.484	0	61.1	65	26	53
Finley, C.	Cal	15	16	0	4.16	1.408	35	238.0	241	94	215
Flener, H.	Tor	3	2	0	4.58	1.429	11	70.2	68	33	44
Fletcher, P.	Oak	0	0	0	20.25	5.250	0	1.1	6	1	0
Florie, B.	Mil	0	1	0	6.63	1.737	0	19.0	20	13	12
Freeman, M.	ChA	0	0	0	13.50	2.500	1	2.0	4	1	1
Frohwirth, T.	Cal	0	0	0	11.12	2.471	0	5.2	10	4	1
Garces, R.	Bos	3	2	0	4.91	1.705	0	44.0	42	33	55
Garcia, R.	Mil	4	4	4	6.66	1.388	2	75.2	84	21	40
Gibson, P.	NYA	0	0	0	6.23	1.385	0	4.1	6	0	3
Givens, B.	Mil	1	3	0	12.86	2.786	4	14.0	32	7	10
Gohr, G.	Cal	1	1	1	7.50	1.833	0	24.0	34	10	15
Gohr, G.	Det	4	8	0	7.17	1.778	16	91.2	129	34	60
Gooden, D.	NYA	11	7	0	5.01	1.506	29	170.2	169	88	126
Gordon, T.	Bos	12	9	0	5.59	1.641	34	215.2	249	105	171
Granger, J.	KC	0	0	0	6.61	1.898	0	16.1	21	10	11
Graves, D.	Cle	2	0	0	4.55	1.315	0	29.2	29	10	22
Grimsley, J.	Cal	5	7	0	6.84	1.719	20	130.1	150	74	82
Groom, B.	Oak	5	0	2	3.84	1.539	1	77.1	85	34	57
Gross, K.	Tex	11	8	0	5.22	1.554	19	129.1	151	50	78
Grundt, K.	Bos	0	0	0	27.00	3.000	0	0.1	1	0	0
Guardado, E.	Min	6	5	4	5.25	1.276	0	73.2	61	33	74
Gubicza, M.	KC	4	12	0	5.13	1.391	19	119.1	132	34	55
Guetterman, L.	Sea	0	2	0	4.09	1.909	0	11.0	11	10	6
Gunderson, E.	Bos	0	1	0	8.31	1.673	0	17.1	21	8	7
Guzman, J.	Tor	11	8	0	2.93	1.124	27	187.2	158	53	165
Hancock, R.	Cal	4	1	0	7.48	1.843	4	27.2	34	17	19
Haney, C.	KC	10	14	0	4.70	1.395	35	228.0	267	51	115
Hansell, G.	Min	3	0	3	5.69	1.534	0	74.1	83	31	46
Hanson, E.	Tor	13	17	0	5.41	1.607	35	214.2	243	102	156
Harikkala, T.	Sea	0	1	0	12.46	1.385	1	4.1	4	2	1
Harris, P.	Cal	2	0	0	3.90	1.485	3	32.1	31	17	20
Harris, R.	Bos	0	0	0	12.46	2.769	0	4.1	7	5	4
Hawkins, L.	Min	1	1	0	8.20	1.937	6	26.1	42	9	24
Haynes, J.	Bal	3	6	1	8.29	2.022	11	89.0	122	58	65
Helling, R.	Tex	1	2	0	7.52	1.574	2	20.1	23	9	16
Henneman, M.	Tex	0	7	31	5.79	1.381	0	42.0	41	17	34
Hentgen, P.	Tor	20	10	0	3.22	1.250	35	265.2	238	94	177
Heredia, G.	Tex	2	5	1	5.89	1.432	0	73.1	91	14	43
Hernandez, R.	ChA	6	5	38	1.91	1.217	0	84.2	65	38	85
Hershiser, O.	Cle	15	9	0	4.24	1.437	33	206.0	238	58	125
Hill, K.	Tex	16	10	0	3.63	1.376	35	250.2	250	95	170
Hitchcock, S.	Sea	13	9	0	5.35	1.617	35	196.2	245	73	132
Holtz, M.	Cal	3	3	0	2.45	1.364	0	29.1	21	19	31
Holzemer, M.	Cal	1	0	0	8.76	1.743	0	24.2	35	8	20
Howe, S.	NYA	0	1	1	6.35	1.471	0	17.0	19	6	5
Hudson, J.	Bos	3	5	1	5.40	1.978	0	45.0	57	32	19

AL Pitcher	Team	W	L	SV	ERA	Ratio	GS	IP	H	BB	K
Huisman, R.	KC	2	1	1	4.60	1.466	0	29.1	25	18	23
Hurtado, E.	Sea	2	5	2	7.74	1.909	4	47.2	61	30	36
Hutton, M.	NYA	0	2	0	5.04	1.648	2	30.1	32	18	25
Jackson, M.	Sea	1	1	6	3.63	1.181	0	72.0	61	24	70
Jacome, J.	KC	0	4	1	4.72	1.867	2	47.2	67	22	32
James, M.	Cal	5	5	1	2.67	1.284	0	81.0	62	42	65
Janzen, M.	Tor	4	6	0	7.33	1.805	11	73.2	95	38	47
Johns, D.	Oak	6	12	1	5.98	1.620	23	158.0	187	69	71
Johnson, D.	Tor	0	0	0	3.00	1.111	0	9.0	5	5	7
Johnson, R.	Sea	5	0	1	3.67	1.190	8	61.1	48	25	85
Jones, D.	Mil	5	0	1	3.41	1.389	0	31.2	31	13	34
Jones, S.	ChA	0	0	0	0.00	0.500	0	2.0	0	1	1
Kamieniecki, S.	NYA	1	2	0	11.12	2.426	5	22.2	36	19	15
Karchner, M.	ChA	7	4	1	5.76	1.719	0	59.1	61	41	46
Karl, S.	Mil	13	9	0	4.86	1.408	32	207.1	220	72	121
Keagle, G.	Det	3	6	0	7.39	1.962	6	87.2	104	68	70
Key, J.	NYA	12	11	0	4.68	1.352	30	169.1	171	58	116
Keyser, B.	ChA	1	2	1	4.98	1.777	0	59.2	78	28	19
Kiefer, M.	Mil	0	0	0	8.10	2.000	0	10.0	15	5	5
Klingenbeck, S.	Min	1	1	0	7.85	1.814	3	28.2	42	10	15
Klink, J.	Sea	0	0	0	3.86	1.714	0	2.1	3	1	2
Knackert, B.	Bos	0	1	0	9.00	2.300	0	10.0	16	7	5
Krivda, R.	Bal	3	5	0	4.96	1.567	11	81.2	89	39	54
Lacy, K.	Bos	2	0	0	3.38	2.156	0	10.2	15	8	9
Langston, M.	Cal	6	5	0	4.82	1.305	18	123.1	116	45	83
Leftwich, P.	Cal	0	1	0	7.36	2.045	2	7.1	12	3	4
Levine, A.	ChA	0	1	0	5.40	1.582	0	18.1	22	7	12
Lewis, R.	Det	4	6	2	4.18	1.583	0	90.1	78	65	78
Lima, J.	Det	5	6	3	5.70	1.500	4	72.2	87	22	59
Linton, D.	KC	7	9	0	5.02	1.317	18	104.0	111	26	87
Lira, F.	Det	6	14	0	5.22	1.387	32	194.2	204	66	113
Lloyd, G.	Mil	2	4	0	2.82	1.294	0	51.0	49	17	24
Lloyd, G.	NYA	0	2	0	17.47	3.000	0	5.2	12	5	6
Lopez, A.	Cle	5	4	0	6.39	1.645	10	62.0	80	22	45
Maddux, M.	Bos	3	2	0	4.48	1.601	7	64.1	76	27	32
Magnante, M.	KC	2	2	0	5.67	1.519	0	54.0	58	24	32
Magrane, J.	ChA	1	5	0	6.88	1.770	8	53.2	70	25	21
Mahomes, P.	Bos	2	0	2	5.84	1.216	0	12.1	9	6	6
Mahomes, P.	Min	1	4	0	7.20	2.000	5	45.0	63	27	30
Martinez, D.	Cle	9	6	0	4.50	1.420	20	112.0	122	37	48
Mathews, T.	Bal	2	2	0	3.38	1.446	0	18.2	20	7	13
Maxcy, B.	Det	0	0	0	13.50	3.000	0	3.1	8	2	1
May, D.	Cal	0	0	0	10.13	1.875	0	2.2	3	2	1
Mccarthy, G.	Sea	0	0	0	1.86	1.241	0	9.2	8	4	7
McCaskill, K.	ChA	5	5	0	6.97	1.994	4	51.2	72	31	28
Mccurry, J.	Det	0	0	0	24.30	3.300	0	3.1	9	2	0
McDonald, B.	Mil	12	10	0	3.90	1.333	35	221.1	228	67	146
McDowell, J.	Cle	13	9	0	5.11	1.464	30	192.0	214	67	141
McDowell, R.	Bal	1	1	4	4.25	1.551	0	59.1	69	23	20
McElroy, C.	Cal	5	1	0	2.95	1.227	0	36.2	32	13	32
Meacham, R.	Sea	1	1	1	5.74	1.654	5	42.1	57	13	25
Mecir, J.	NYA	1	1	0	5.13	1.612	0	40.1	42	23	38
Mendoza, R.	NYA	4	5	0	6.79	1.698	11	53.0	80	10	34
Menhart, P.	Sea	2	2	0	7.29	1.905	6	42.0	55	25	18

AL Pitcher	Team	W	L	SV	ERA	Ratio	GS	IP	H	BB	K
Mercedes, J.	Mil	0	2	0	9.18	1.500	0	16.2	20	5	6
Mercker, K.	Bal	3	6	0	7.76	1.862	12	58.0	73	35	22
Mercker, K.	Cle	1	0	0	3.09	1.114	0	11.2	10	3	7
Mesa, J.	Cle	2	7	39	3.73	1.341	0	72.1	69	28	64
Milacki, B.	Sea	1	4	0	6.86	2:143	4	21.0	30	15	13
Milchin, M.	Bal	1	0	0	5.73	1.636	0	11.0	13	5	10
Milchin, M.	Min	2	1	0	8.31	1.985	0	21.2	31	12	19
Miller, T.	Min	1	2	0	9.23	2.051	7	26.1	45	9	15
Miller, T.	Det	0	4	0	9.18	2.220	4	16.2	28	9	8
Mills, A.	Bal	3	2	3	4.28	1.372	0	54.2	40	35	50
Minchey, N.	Bos	0	2	0	15.00	3.500	2	6.0	16	5	4
Minor, B.	Sea	0	1	0	4.97	1.500	0	25.1	27	11	14
Miranda, A.	Mil	7	6	1	4.94	1.692	12	109.1	116	69	78
Moehler, B.	Det	0	1	0	4.35	1.839	2	10.1	11	8	2
Mohler, M.	Oak	6	3	7	3.67	1.481	0	81.0	79	41	64
Monteleone, R.	Cal	0	3	0	5.87	1.630	0	15.1	23	2	5
Montgomery, J.	KC	4	6	24	4.26	1.232	0	63.1	59	19	45
Montgomery, S.	Oak	1	0	0	9.22	2.268	0	13.2	18	13	8
Moyer, J.	Bos	7	1	0	4.50	1.533	10	90.0	111	27	50
Moyer, J.	Sea	6	2	0	3.31	1.203	11	70.2	66	19	29
Mulholland, T.	Sea	5	4	0	4.67	1.486	12	69.1	75	28	34
Mussina, M.	Bal	19	11	0	4.81	1.368	36	243.1	264	69	204
Myers, J.	Bal	0	0	0	7.07	1.500	0	14.0	18	3	6
Myers, M.	Det	1	5	6	5.01	1.608	0	64.2	70	34	69
Myers, R.	Bal	4	4	31	3.53	1.517	0	58.2	60	29	74
Nagy, C.	Cle	17	5	0	3.41	1.252	32	222.0	217	61	167
Naulty, D.	Min	3	2	4	3.79	1.368	0	57.0	43	35	56
Nelson, J.	NYA	4	4	2	4.36	1.493	0	74.1	75	36	91
Nitkowski, C.	Det	2	3	0	8.08	2.190	8	45.2	62	38	36
Ogea, C.	Cle	10	6	0	4.79	1.316	21	146.2	151	42	101
Olivares, O.	Det	7	11	0	4.89	1.525	25	160.0	169	75	81
Oliver, D.	Tex	14	6	0	4.66	1.532	30	173.2	190	76	112
Olson, G.	Det	3	0	8	5.02	1.651	0	43.0	43	28	29
Orosco, J.	Bal	3	1	0	3.40	1.257	0	55.2	42	28	52
Parra, J.	Min	5	5	0	6.04	1.643	5	70.0	88	27	50
Patterson, D.	Tex	0	0	0	0.00	1.500	0	8.2	10	3	5
Pavlas, D.	NYA	0	0	1	2.35	1.304	0	23.0	23	7	18
Pavlik, R.	Tex	15	8	0	5.19	1.478	34	201.0	216	81	127
Pennington, B.	Bos	0	2	0	2.77	1.615	0	13.0	6	15	13
Pennington, B.	Cal	0	0	0	12.27	2.864	0	7.1	5	16	7
Percival, T.	Cal	0	2	36	2.31	0.932	0	74.0	38	31	100
Pettitte, A.	NYA	21	8	0	3.87	1.362	34	221.0	229	72	162
Pichardo, H.	KC	3	5	3	5.43	1.471	0	68.0	74	26	43
Plunk, E.	Cle	3	2	2	2.43	1.159	0	77.2	56	34	85
Polley, D.	NYA	1	3	0	7.89	1.569	0	21.2	23	11	14
Poole, J.	Cle	4	0	0	3.04	1.612	0	26.2	29	14	19
Potts, M.	Mil	1	2	1	7.15	1.941	0	45.1	58	30	21
Prieto, A.	Oak	6	7	0	4.15	1.464	21	125.2	130	54	75
Pugh, T.	KC	0	1	0	5.45	1.486	1	36.1	42	12	27
Quantrill, P.	Tor	5	14	0	5.43	1.660	20	134.1	172	51	86
Radke, B.	Min	11	16	0	4.46	1.241	35	232.0	231	57	148
Reyes, A.	Mil	1	0	0	7.94	1.765	0	5.2	8	2	2
Reyes, C.	Oak	7	10	0	4.78	1.594	10	122.1	134	61	78

AL Pitcher	Team	W	L	SV	ERA	Ratio	GS	IP	H	BB	K
Rhodes, A.	Bal	9	1	1	4.08	1.340	2	53.0	48	23	62
Risley, B.	Tor	0	1	0	3.89	1.392	0	41.2	33	25	29
Rivera, M.	NYA	8	3	5	2.09	0.994	0	107.2	73	34	130
Roa, J.	Cle	0	0	0	10.80	4.200	0	1.2	4	3	0
Robertson, R.	Min	7	17	0	5.12	1.680	31	186.1	197	116	114
Robinson, K.	KC	1	0	0	6.00	2.000	0	6.0	9	3	5
Rodriguez, F.	Min	13	14	2	5.05	1.432	33	206.2	218	78	110
Rodriguez, N.	Bal	0	1	0	4.32	1.500	1	16.2	18	7	12
Rogers, K.	NYA	12	8	0	4.68	1.464	30	179.0	179	83	92
Rosado, J.	KC	8	6	0	3.21	1.191	16	106.2	101	26	64
Ruffcorn, S.	ChA	0	1	0	11.37	2.526	1	6.1	10	6	3
Russell, J.	Tex	3	3	3	3.38	1.429	0	56.0	58	22	23
Sackinsky, B.	Bal	0	0	0	3.86	1.929	0	4.2	6	3	2
Sager, A.	Det	4	5	0	5.01	1.519	9	79.0	91	29	52
Sanderson, S.	Cal	0	2	0	7.50	2.389	4	18.0	39	4	7
Sauveur, R.	ChA	0	0	0	15.00	2.667	0	3.0	3	5	1
Scanlan, B.	Det	0	0	0	10.64	2.273	0	11.0	16	9	3
Scanlan, B.	KC	0	1	0	3.18	1.412	0	11.1	13	3	3
Schmidt, J.	Cal	2	0	0	7.88	2.625	0	8.0	13	8	2
Sele, A.	Bos	7	11	0	5.32	1.646	29	157.1	192	67	137
Serafini, D.	Min	0	1	0	10.38	2.077	1	4.1	7	2	1
Shepherd, K.	Bal	0	1	0	8.71	2.371	0	20.2	31	18	17
Shuey, P.	Cle	5	2	4	2.85	1.323	0	53.2	45	26	44
Silva, J.	Tor	0	0	0	13.50	2.500	0	2.0	5	0	0
Simas, B.	ChA	2	8	2	4.58	1.569	0	72.2	75	39	65
Sirotka, M.	ChA	1	2	0	7.18	1.747	4	26.1	34	12	11
Slocumb, H.	Bos	5	5	31	3.02	1.476	0	83.1	68	55	88
Small, A.	Oak	1	3	0	8.16	2.058	3	28.2	37	22	17
Smith, L.	Cal	0	0	0	2.45	1.000	0	11.0	8	3	6
Sodowsky, C.	Det	1	3	0	11.84	2.466	7	24.1	40	20	9
Sparks, S.	Mil	4	7	0	6.60	1.748	13	88.2	103	52	21
Spoljaric, P.	Tor	2	2	1	3.08	1.289	0	38.0	30	19	38
Springer, D.	Cal	5	6	0	5.51	1.415	15	94.2	91	43	64
Stanton, M.	Bos	4	3	1	3.83	1.438	0	56.1	58	23	46
Stanton, M.	Tex	0	1	0	3.22	1.075	0	22.1	20	4	14
Stephenson, G.	Bal	0	1	0	12.79	2.526	0	6.1	13	3	3
Stevens, D.	Min	3	3	11	4.66	1.431	0	58.0	58	25	29
Suppan, J.	Bos	1	1	0	7.54	1.853	4	22.2	29	13	13
Suzuki, M.	Sea	0	0	0	20.25	3.000	0	1.1	2	2	1
Swindell, G.	Cle	1	1	0	6.59	1.360	2	28.2	31	8	21
Tapani, K.	ChA	13	10	0	4.59	1.385	34	225.1	236	76	150
Tavarez, J.	Cle	4	7	0	5.36	1.525	4	80.2	101	22	46
Taylor, B.	Oak	6	3	17	4.33	1.276	0	60.1	52	25	67
Telgheder, D.	Oak	4	7	0	4.65	1.487	14	79.1	92	26	43
Thomas, L.	ChA	2	3	0	3.23	1.500	0	30.2	32	14	20
Thompson, J.	Det	1	6	0	4.58	1.576	11	59.0	62	31	44
Timlin, M.	Tor	1	6	31	3.65	1.147	0	56.2	47	18	52
Torres, S.	Sea	3	3	0	4.59	1.367	7	49.0	44	23	36
Trombley, M.	Min	5	1	6	3.01	1.252	0	68.2	61	25	57
Urbani, T.	Det	2	2	0	8.37	1.901	2	23.2	31	14	20
Valera, J.	KC	3	2	1	6.46	1.663	2	61.1	75	27	31
Van Poppel, T.	Det	2	4	0	11.39	2.257	9	36.1	53	29	16
Van Poppel, T.	Oak	1	5	1	7.71	1.889	6	63.0	86	33	37
Vanegmond, T.	Mil	3	5	0	5.27	1.482	9	54.2	58	23	33

AL Pitcher	Team	W	L	SV	ERA	Ratio	GS	IP	H	BB	K
Vanryn, B.	Cal	0	0	0	0.00	2.000	0	1.0	1	1	0
Veres, R.	Det	0	4	0	8.31	2.011	0	30.1	38	23	28
Villone, R.	Mil	0	0	2	3.28	1.297	0	24.2	14	18	19
Viola, F.	Tor	1	3	0	7.71	2.110	6	30.1	43	21	18
Vosberg, E.	Tex	1	1	8	3.27	1.636	0	44.0	51	21	32
Wagner, M.	Sea	3	5	0	6.86	1.612	14	80.0	91	38	41
Wakefield, T.	Bos	14	13	0	5.14	1.550	32	211.2	238	90	140
Walker, M.	Det	0	0	1	8.46	2.060	0	27.2	40	17	13
Ware, J.	Tor	1	5	0	9.09	2.020	4	32.2	35	31	11
Wasdin, J.	Oak	8	7	0	5.96	1.485	21	131.1	145	50	75
Weathers, D.	NYA	0	2	0	9.35	2.135	4	17.1	23	14	13
Wells, B.	Sea	12	7	0	5.30	1.431	16	130.2	141	46	94
Wells, D.	Bal	11	14	0	5.14	1.328	34	224.1	247	51	130
Wengert, D.	Oak	7	11	0	5.58	1.612	25	161.1	200	60	75
Wetteland, J.	NYA	2	3	43	2.83	1.178	0	63.2	54	21	69
Whitehurst, W.	NYA	1	1	0	6.75	1.625	2	8.0	11	2	1
Whiteside, M.	Tex	0	1	0	6.68	1.670	0	32.1	43	11	15
Wickander, K.	Mil	2	0	0	4.97	1.697	0	25.1	26	17	19
Wickman, B.	Mil	3	0	0	3.24	1.320	0	16.2	12	10	14
Wickman, B.	NYA	4	1	0	4.67	1.620	0	79.0	94	34	61
Williams, B.	Det	3	10	2	6.77	1.901	17	121.0	145	85	72
Williams, S.	Cal	0	2	0	8.89	2.224	2	28.1	42	21	26
Williams, W.	Tor	4	5	0	4.73	1.441	10	59.0	64	21	43
Witasick, J.	Oak	1	1	0	6.23	1.308	0	13.0	12	5	12
Witt, B.	Tex	16	12	0	5.41	1.658	32	199.2	235	96	157
Wojciechowski, S.	Oak	5	5	0	5.65	1.569	15	79.2	97	28	30
Wolcott, B.	Sea	7	10	0	5.73	1.560	28	149.1	179	54	78
Yan, E.	Bal	0	0	0	5.79	1.714	0	9.1	13	3	7